12 Vol
27 50

W9-DAY-199

THE GOLDEN BOUGH

A STUDY IN MAGIC AND RELIGION

THIRD EDITION

PART I

THE MAGIC ART

AND THE EVOLUTION OF KINGS

VOL. I

MACMILLAN AND CO., Limited
LONDON · BOMBAY · CALCUTTA · MADRAS
MELBOURNE

THE MACMILLAN COMPANY
NEW YORK · BOSTON · CHICAGO
DALLAS · SAN FRANCISCO

THE MACMILLAN CO. OF CANADA, Ltd.
TORONTO

J. M. W. TURNER, Pinxit.

The Golden Bough.

THE MAGIC ART

AND THE EVOLUTION OF KINGS

BY

Sir JAMES GEORGE FRAZER

D.C.L., LL.D., Litt.D.

FELLOW OF TRINITY COLLEGE, CAMBRIDGE
PROFESSOR OF SOCIAL ANTHROPOLOGY IN THE UNIVERSITY OF LIVERPOOL

IN TWO VOLUMES

VOL. I

MACMILLAN AND CO., LIMITED
ST. MARTIN'S STREET, LONDON

1917

CC

"*Nec indigeste tamquam in acervum congessimus digna memoratu: sed variarum rerum disparilitas, auctoribus diversa confusa temporibus, ita in quoddam digesta corpus est, ut quae indistincte atque promiscue ad subsidium memoriae annotaveramus in ordinem instar membrorum cohaerentia convenirent. Nec mihi vitio vertas, si res quas ex lectione varia mutuabor ipsis saepe verbis quibus ab ipsis auctoribus enarratae sunt explicabo, quia praesens opus non eloquentiae ostentationem sed noscendorum congeriem pollicetur: et boni consulas oportet, si notitiam vetustatis modo nostris non obscure modo ipsis antiquorum fideliter verbis recognoscas, prout quaeque se vel enarranda vel transferenda suggesserint. Apes enim quodammodo debemus imitari, quae vaguntur et flores carpunt, deinde quicquid attulere disponunt ac per favos dividunt et sucum varium in unum saporem mixtura quadam et proprietate spiritus sui mutant.*"

MACROBIUS, *Saturnalia, Praefatio.*

857
Fr YB
1
6754

COPYRIGHT

Third Edition March 1911
Reprinted July 1911, 1913, 1917

TO

MY FRIEND

WILLIAM ROBERTSON SMITH

IN

GRATITUDE AND ADMIRATION

PREFACE

WHEN I originally conceived the idea of the work, of which the first part is now laid before the public in a third and enlarged edition, my intention merely was to explain the strange rule of the priesthood or sacred kingship of Nemi and with it the legend of the Golden Bough, immortalised by Virgil, which the voice of antiquity associated with the priesthood. The explanation was suggested to me by some similar rules formerly imposed on kings in Southern India, and at first I thought that it might be adequately set forth within the compass of a small volume. But I soon found that in attempting to settle one question I had raised many more : wider and wider prospects opened out before me ; and thus step by step I was lured on into far-spreading fields of primitive thought which had been but little explored by my predecessors. Thus the book grew on my hands, and soon the projected essay became in fact a ponderous treatise, or rather a series of separate dissertations loosely linked together by a slender thread of connexion with my original subject. With each successive edition these dissertations have grown in number and swollen in bulk by the accretion of fresh materials, till the thread on which they are strung at last threatened to snap under their weight. Accordingly, following the hint of a friendly critic, I decided to resolve my overgrown book into its elements, and to publish separately the various disquisitions of which it is composed. The present volumes, forming the first part of the whole, contain a preliminary enquiry into the principles of Magic and the evolution of the Sacred Kingship in general. They will be followed shortly by a volume which discusses the principles of Taboo in their special application to sacred or priestly kings. The remainder of the work will be mainly devoted to the myth and ritual of the Dying God, and as the subject is large and fruitful, my discussion of it will, for the sake of convenience, be divided into several parts, of which one, dealing with some dying gods of antiquity in Egypt and Western Asia, has already been published under the title of *Adonis, Attis, Osiris*.

But while I have thus sought to dispose my book in its proper form as a collection of essays on a variety of distinct, though related, topics, I have at the same time preserved its unity, as far as possible, by retaining the original title for the whole series of volumes, and by pointing out from time to time the bearing of my general conclusions on the particular problem which furnished the starting-point of the enquiry. It seemed to me that this mode of presenting the subject offered some advantages which outweighed certain obvious drawbacks. By discarding the austere form, without, I hope, sacrificing the solid substance, of a scientific treatise, I thought to cast my materials into a more artistic mould and so perhaps to attract readers, who might have been repelled by a more strictly logical and systematic arrangement of the facts. Thus I put the mysterious priest of Nemi, so to say, in the forefront of the picture, grouping the other sombre figures of the same sort behind him in the background, not certainly because I deemed them of less moment but because the picturesque natural surroundings of the priest of Nemi among the wooded hills of Italy, the very mystery which enshrouds him, and not least the haunting magic of Virgil's verse, all combine to shed a glamour on the tragic figure with the Golden Bough, which fits him to stand as the centre of a gloomy canvas. But I trust that the high relief into which he has thus been thrown in my pages will not lead my readers either to overrate his historical importance by comparison with that of some other figures which stand behind him in the shadow, or to attribute to my theory of the part he played a greater degree of probability than it deserves. Even if it should appear that this ancient Italian priest must after all be struck out from the long roll of men who have masqueraded as gods, the single omission would not sensibly invalidate the demonstration, which I believe I have given, that human pretenders to divinity have been far commoner and their credulous worshippers far more numerous than had been hitherto suspected. Similarly, should my whole theory of this particular priesthood collapse —and I fully acknowledge the slenderness of the foundations on which it rests—its fall would hardly shake my general conclusions as to the evolution of primitive religion and society, which are founded on large collections of entirely independent and well-authenticated facts.

Friends versed in German philosophy have pointed out to me that my views of magic and religion and their relations to each other in history agree to some extent with those of Hegel. The agreement is quite independent and to me unexpected, for I have never studied the philosopher's writings nor attended to his speculations. As, however, we have arrived at similar results by very different roads, the partial coincidence of our conclusions may perhaps be taken to furnish a certain presumption in favour of their truth. To enable my readers to judge of the extent of the coincidence, I have given in an appendix some extracts from Hegel's lectures on the philosophy of religion. The curious may compare them with my chapter on Magic and Religion, which was written in ignorance of the views of my illustrious predecessor.

With regard to the history of the sacred kingship which

I have outlined in these volumes, I desire to repeat a warning which I have given in the text. While I have shewn reason to think that in many communities sacred kings have been developed out of magicians, I am far from supposing that this has been universally true. The causes which have determined the establishment of monarchy have no doubt varied greatly in different countries and at different times: I make no pretence to discuss or even enumerate them all: I have merely selected one particular cause because it bore directly on my special enquiry; and I have laid emphasis on it because it seems to have been overlooked by writers on the origin of political institutions, who, themselves sober and rational according to modern standards, have not reckoned sufficiently with the enormous influence which superstition has exerted in shaping the human past. But I have no wish to exaggerate the importance of this particular cause at the expense of others which may have been equally or even more influential. No one can be more sensible than I am of the risk of stretching an hypothesis too far, of crowding a multitude of incongruous particulars under one narrow formula, of reducing the vast, nay inconceivable complexity of nature and history to a delusive appearance of theoretical simplicity. It may well be that I have erred in this direction again and again; but at least I have been well aware of the danger of error and have striven to guard myself and my readers against it. How far I have succeeded in that and the other objects I have set before me in writing this work, I must leave to the candour of the public to determine.

J. G. FRAZER.

CAMBRIDGE,
5th December 1910.

PREFACE TO THE FIRST EDITION
OF *THE GOLDEN BOUGH*

FOR some time I have been preparing a general work on
primitive superstition and religion. Among the problems
which had attracted my attention was the hitherto unex-
plained rule of the Arician priesthood ; and last spring it
happened that in the course of my reading I came across
some facts which, combined with others I had noted before,
suggested an explanation of the rule in question. As the
explanation, if correct, promised to throw light on some
obscure features of primitive religion, I resolved to develop
it fully, and, detaching it from my general work, to issue it
as a separate study. This book is the result.

Now that the theory, which necessarily presented itself
to me at first in outline, has been worked out in detail, I
cannot but feel that in some places I may have pushed it
too far. If this should prove to have been the case, I will
readily acknowledge and retract my error as soon as it is
brought home to me. Meantime my essay may serve its
purpose as a first attempt to solve a difficult problem, and
to bring a variety of scattered facts into some sort of order
and system.

A justification is perhaps needed of the length at which I
have dwelt upon the popular festivals observed by European
peasants in spring, at midsummer, and at harvest. It can
hardly be too often repeated, since it is not yet generally
recognised, that in spite of their fragmentary character the

popular superstitions and customs of the peasantry are by far the fullest and most trustworthy evidence we possess as to the primitive religion of the Aryans. Indeed the primitive Aryan, in all that regards his mental fibre and texture, is not extinct. He is amongst us to this day. The great intellectual and moral forces which have revolutionised the educated world have scarcely affected the peasant. In his inmost beliefs he is what his forefathers were in the days when forest trees still grew and squirrels played on the ground where Rome and London now stand.

Hence every enquiry into the primitive religion of the Aryans should either start from the superstitious beliefs and observances of the peasantry, or should at least be constantly checked and controlled by reference to them. Compared with the evidence afforded by living tradition, the testimony of ancient books on the subject of early religion is worth very little. For literature accelerates the advance of thought at a rate which leaves the slow progress of opinion by word of mouth at an immeasurable distance behind. Two or three generations of literature may do more to change thought than two or three thousand years of traditional life. But the mass of the people who do not read books remain unaffected by the mental revolution wrought by literature ; and so it has come about that in Europe at the present day the superstitious beliefs and practices which have been handed down by word of mouth are generally of a far more archaic type than the religion depicted in the most ancient literature of the Aryan race.

It is on these grounds that, in discussing the meaning and origin of an ancient Italian priesthood, I have devoted so much attention to the popular customs and superstitions of modern Europe. In this part of my subject I have made great use of the works of the late W. Mannhardt, without which, indeed, my book could scarcely have been written. Fully recognising the truth of the principles which I have imperfectly stated, Mannhardt set himself systematically to collect, compare, and explain the living superstitions of the peasantry. Of this wide field the special department which he marked out for himself was the religion of the woodman and the farmer, in other words, the superstitious beliefs and rites connected with trees and cultivated plants By oral enquiry, and by printed questions scattered broad-cast over Europe, as well as by ransacking the literature of folk-lore, he collected a mass of evidence, part of which he published in a series of admirable works. But his health, always feeble, broke down before he could complete the comprehensive and really vast scheme which he had planned, and at his too early death much of his precious materials remained unpublished. His manuscripts are now deposited in the University Library at Berlin, and in the interest of the study to which he devoted his life it is greatly to be desired that they should be examined, and that such por-tions of them as he has not utilised in his books should be given to the world.

Of his published works the most important are, first, two tracts, *Roggenwolf und Roggenhund*, Danzig, 1865 (second edition, Danzig, 1866), and *Die Korndämonen*, Berlin, 1868. These little works were put forward by him tentatively, in the hope of exciting interest in his enquiries and thereby securing the help of others in pursuing them. But, except from a few learned societies, they met with very little atten-tion. Undeterred by the cold reception accorded to his efforts he worked steadily on, and in 1875 published his chief work, *Der Baumkultus der Germanen und ihrer Nach-barstämme.* This was followed in 1877 by *Antike Wald-und Feldkulte.* His *Mythologische Forschungen,* a posthumous work, appeared in 1884.

Much as I owe to Mannhardt, I owe still more to my friend Professor W. Robertson Smith. My interest in the early history of society was first excited by the works of

Dr. E. B. Tylor, which opened up a mental vista undreamed of by me before. But it is a long step from a lively interest in a subject to a systematic study of it; and that I took this step is due to the influence of my friend W. Robertson Smith. The debt which I owe to the vast stores of his knowledge, the abundance and fertility of his ideas, and his unwearied kindness, can scarcely be overestimated. Those who know his writings may form some, though a very inadequate, conception of the extent to which I have been influenced by him. The views of sacrifice set forth in his article "Sacrifice" in the *Encyclopædia Britannica,* and further developed in his recent work, *The Religion of the Semites,* mark a new departure in the historical study of religion, and ample traces of them will be found in this book. Indeed the central idea of my essay—the conception of the slain god—is derived directly, I believe, from my friend. But it is due to him to add that he is in no way responsible for the general explanation which I have offered of the custom of slaying the god. He has read the greater part of the proofs in circumstances which enhanced the kindness, and has made many valuable suggestions which I have usually adopted; but except where he is cited by name, or where the views expressed coincide with those of his published works, he is not to be regarded as necessarily assenting to any of the theories propounded in this book.

The works of Professor G. A. Wilken of Leyden have been of great service in directing me to the best original authorities on the Dutch East Indies, a very important field to the ethnologist. To the courtesy of the Rev. Walter Gregor, M.A., of Pitsligo, I am indebted for some interesting communications which will be found acknowledged in their proper places. Mr. Francis Darwin has kindly allowed me to consult him on some botanical questions. The manuscript authorities to which I occasionally refer are answers to a list of ethnological questions which I am circulating. Most of them will, I hope, be published in the *Journal of the Anthropological Institute.*

The drawing of the Golden Bough which adorns the cover is from the pencil of my friend Professor J. H. Middleton. The constant interest and sympathy which he has shewn in the progress of the book have been a great help and encouragement to me in writing it.

The Index has been compiled by Mr. A. Rogers, of the University Library, Cambridge.

J. G. FRAZER.

TRINITY COLLEGE, CAMBRIDGE,
    8th March 1890.

PREFACE TO THE SECOND EDITION
OF *THE GOLDEN BOUGH*

THE kind reception accorded by critics and the public to
the first edition of *The Golden Bough* has encouraged me to
spare no pains to render the new one more worthy of their
approbation. While the original book remains almost entire,
it has been greatly expanded by the insertion of much fresh
illustrative matter, drawn chiefly from further reading, but
in part also from previous collections which I had made,
and still hope to use, for another work. Friends and corre-
spondents, some of them personally unknown to me, have
kindly aided me in various ways, especially by indicating
facts or sources which I had overlooked and by correcting
mistakes into which I had fallen. I thank them all for
their help, of which I have often availed myself. Their
contributions will be found acknowledged in their proper
places. But I owe a special acknowledgment to my friends
the Rev. Lorimer Fison and the Rev. John Roscoe, who
have sent me valuable notes on the Fijian and Waganda
customs respectively. Most of Mr. Fison's notes, I believe,
are incorporated in my book. Of Mr. Roscoe's only a small
selection has been given ; the whole series, embracing a
general account of the customs and beliefs of the Waganda,
will be published, I hope, in the *Journal of the Anthropological Institute*. Further, I ought to add that Miss Mary
E. B. Howitt has kindly allowed me to make some extracts

from a work by her on Australian folklore and legends which I was privileged to read in manuscript.

I have seen no reason to withdraw the explanation of the priesthood of Aricia which forms the central theme of my book. On the contrary, the probability of that explanation appears to me to be greatly strengthened by some important evidence which has come to light since my theory was put forward. Readers of the first edition may remember that I explained the priest of Aricia—the King of the Wood—as an embodiment of a tree-spirit, and inferred from a variety of considerations that at an earlier period one of these priests had probably been slain every year in his character of an incarnate deity. But for an undoubted parallel to such a custom of killing a human god annually I had to go as far as ancient Mexico. Now from the *Martyrdom of St. Dasius*, unearthed and published a few years ago by Professor Franz Cumont of Ghent (*Analecta Bollandiana*, xvi. 1897), it is practically certain that in ancient Italy itself a human representative of Saturn—the old god of the seed—was put to death every year at his festival of the Saturnalia, and that though in Rome itself the custom had probably fallen into disuse before the classical era, it still lingered on in remote places down at least to the fourth century after Christ. I cannot but regard this discovery as a confirmation, as welcome as it was unlooked for, of the theory of the Arician priesthood which I had been led independently to propound.

Further, the general interpretation which, following W. Mannhardt, I had given of the ceremonies observed by our European peasantry in spring, at midsummer, and at harvest, has also been corroborated by fresh and striking analogies. If we are right, these ceremonies were originally magical rites designed to cause plants to grow, cattle to thrive, rain to fall, and the sun to shine. Now the remarkable researches of Professor Baldwin Spencer and Mr. F. J. Gillen

among the native tribes of Central Australia have proved that
these savages regularly perform magical ceremonies for the
express purpose of bringing down rain and multiplying the
plants and animals on which they subsist, and further that
these ceremonies are most commonly observed at the approach
of the rainy season, which in Central Australia answers to
our spring.   Here then, at the other side of the world, we find
an exact counterpart of those spring and midsummer rites
which our rude forefathers in Europe probably performed
with a full consciousness of their meaning, and which many
of their descendants still keep up, though the original intention of the rites has been to a great extent, but by no
means altogether, forgotten.   The harvest customs of our
European peasantry have naturally no close analogy among
the practices of the Australian aborigines, since these savages
do not till the ground.   But what we should look for in
vain among the Australians we find to hand among the
Malays.   For recent enquiries, notably those of Mr. J. L.
van der Toorn in Sumatra and of Mr. W. W. Skeat in the
Malay Peninsula, have supplied us with close parallels to the
harvest customs of Europe, as these latter were interpreted
by the genius of Mannhardt.   Occupying a lower plane of
culture than ourselves, the Malays have retained a keen
sense of the significance of rites which in Europe have sunk
to the level of more or less meaningless survivals.

Thus on the whole I cannot but think that the course of
subsequent investigation has tended to confirm the general
principles followed and the particular conclusions reached in
this book.   At the same time I am as sensible as ever of the
hypothetical nature of much that is advanced in it.   It has
been my wish and intention to draw as sharply as possible
the line of demarcation between my facts and the hypotheses
by which I have attempted to colligate them.   Hypotheses
are necessary but often temporary bridges built to connect
isolated facts.   If my light bridges should sooner or later

break down or be superseded by more solid structures, I hope that my book may still have its utility and its interest as a repertory of facts.

But while my views, tentative and provisional as they probably are, thus remain much what they were, there is one subject on which they have undergone a certain amount of change, unless indeed it might be more exact to say that I seem to see clearly now what before was hazy. I mean the relation of magic to religion. When I first wrote this book I failed, perhaps inexcusably, to define even to myself my notion of religion, and hence was disposed to class magic loosely under it as one of its lower forms. I have now sought to remedy this defect by framing as clear a definition of religion as the difficult nature of the subject and my apprehension of it allowed. Hence I have come to agree with Sir A. C. Lyall and Mr. F. B. Jevons in recognising a fundamental distinction and even opposition of principle between magic and religion. More than that, I believe that in the evolution of thought, magic, as representing a lower intellectual stratum, has probably everywhere preceded religion. I do not claim any originality for this latter view. It has been already plainly suggested, if not definitely formulated, by Professor H. Oldenberg in his able book *Die Religion des Veda*, and for aught I know it may have been explicitly stated by many others before and since him. I have not collected the opinions of the learned on the subject, but have striven to form my own directly from the facts. And the facts which bespeak the priority of magic over religion are many and weighty. Some of them the reader will find stated in the following pages ; but the full force of the evidence can only be appreciated by those who have made a long and patient study of primitive superstition. I venture to think that those who submit to this drudgery will come more and more to the opinion I have indicated. That all my readers should agree either with my definition of religion or with the inferences I have drawn from it is not to be expected. But I would ask those who dissent from my conclusions to make sure that they mean the same thing by religion that I do ; for otherwise the difference between us may be more apparent than real.

As the scope and purpose of my book have been seriously misconceived by some courteous critics, I desire to repeat in more explicit language, what I vainly thought I had made quite clear in my original preface, that this is not a general treatise on primitive superstition, but merely the investigation of one particular and narrowly limited problem, to wit, the rule of the Arician priesthood, and that accordingly only such general principles are explained and illustrated in the course of it as seemed to me to throw light on that special problem. If I have said little or nothing of other principles of equal or even greater importance, it is assuredly not because I undervalue them in comparison with those which I have expounded at some length, but simply because it appeared to me that they did not directly bear on the question I had set myself to answer. No one can well be more sensible than I am of the immense variety and complexity of the forces which have gone towards the building up of religion ; no one can recognise more frankly the futility and inherent absurdity of any attempt to explain the whole vast organism as the product of any one simple factor. If I have hitherto touched, as I am quite aware, only the fringe of a great subject——fingered only a few of the countless threads that compose the mighty web,——it is merely because neither my time nor my knowledge has hitherto allowed me to do more. Should I live to complete the works for which I have collected and am collecting materials, I dare to think that they will clear me of any suspicion of treating the early history of religion from a single narrow point of view. But the future is necessarily uncertain, and at the best many years must elapse before I can execute in full the plan which I have traced out for myself. Meanwhile I am unwilling by keeping silence to leave some of my readers under the impression that my outlook on so large a subject does not reach beyond the bounds of the present enquiry. This is my reason for noticing the misconceptions to which I have referred. I take leave to add that some part of my larger plan would probably have been completed before now, were it not that out of the ten years which have passed since this book was first published nearly eight have been spent by me in work of a different kind.

There is a misunderstanding of another sort which I feel constrained to set right. But I do so with great reluctance, because it compels me to express a measure of dissent from the revered friend and master to whom I am under the deepest obligations, and who has passed beyond the reach of controversy. In an elaborate and learned essay on sacrifice (*L'Année Sociologique*, Deuxième Année, 1897-1898), Messrs. H. Hubert and M. Mauss have represented my theory of the slain god as intended to supplement and complete Robertson Smith's theory of the derivation of animal sacrifice in general from a totem sacrament. On this I have to say that the two theories are quite independent of each other. I never assented to my friend's theory, and so far as I can remember he never gave me a hint that he assented to mine. My reason for suspending my judgment in regard to his theory was a simple one. At the time when the theory was propounded, and for many years afterwards, I knew of no single indubitable case of a totem sacrament, that is, of a custom of killing and eating the totem animal as a solemn rite. It is true that in my *Totemism*, and again in the present work, I noted a few cases (four in all) of solemnly killing a sacred animal which, following Robertson Smith, I regarded as probably a totem. But none even of these four cases included the eating of the sacred animal by the worshippers, which was an essential part of my friend's theory, and in regard to all of them it was not positively known that the slain animal was a totem. Hence as time went on and still no certain case of a totem sacrament was reported, I became more and more doubtful of the existence of such a practice at all, and my doubts had almost hardened into incredulity when the long-looked-for rite was discovered by Messrs. Spencer and Gillen in full force among the aborigines of Central Australia, whom I for one must consider to be the most primitive totem tribes as yet known to us. This discovery I welcomed as a very striking proof of the sagacity of my brilliant friend, whose rapid genius had outstripped our slower methods and anticipated what it was reserved for subsequent research positively to ascertain. Thus from being little more than an ingenious hypothesis the totem sacrament has become, at least in my opinion, a well-authenticated fact. But from the practice of the rite by a single set of tribes it is still a long step to the universal practice of it by all totem tribes, and from that again it is a still longer stride to the deduction therefrom of animal sacrifice in general. These two steps I am not yet prepared to take. No one will welcome further evidence of the wide prevalence of a totem sacrament more warmly than I shall, but until it is forthcoming I shall continue to agree with Professor E. B. Tylor that it is unsafe to make the custom the base of far-reaching speculations.

To conclude this subject, I will add that the doctrine of the universality of totemism, which Messrs. Hubert and Mauss have implicitly attributed to me, is one which I have never enunciated or assumed, and that, so far as my knowledge and opinion go, the worship of trees and cereals, which occupies so large a space in these volumes, is neither identical with nor derived from a system of totemism. It is possible that further enquiry may lead me to regard as probable the universality of totemism and the derivation from it of sacrifice and of the whole worship both of plants and animals. I hold myself ready to follow the evidence wherever it may lead ; but in the present state of our knowledge I consider that to accept these conclusions would be, not to follow the evidence, but very seriously to outrun it, In thinking so I am happy to be at one with Messrs. Hubert and Mauss.

When I am on this theme I may as well say that I am by no means prepared to stand by everything in my little apprentice work, *Totemism.* That book was a rough piece of pioneering in a field that, till then, had been but little explored, and some inferences in it were almost certainly too hasty. In particular there was a tendency, perhaps not unnatural in the circumstances, to treat as totems, or as connected with totemism, things which probably were neither the one nor the other. If ever I republish the volume, as I hope one day to do, I shall have to retrench it in some directions as well as to enlarge it in others.

Such as it is, with all its limitations, which I have tried to indicate clearly, and with all its defects, which I leave to the critics to discover, I offer my book in its new form as a contribution to that still youthful science which seeks to trace the growth of human thought and institutions in those dark ages which lie beyond the range of history. The progress of that science must needs be slow and painful, for the evidence, though clear and abundant on some sides, is lamentably obscure and scanty on others, so that the cautious enquirer is every now and then brought up sharp on the edge of some yawning chasm across which he may be quite unable to find a way. All he can do in such a case is to mark the pitfall plainly on his chart and to hope that others in time may be able to fill it up or bridge it over. Yet the very difficulty and novelty of the investigation, coupled with the extent of the intellectual prospect which suddenly opens

up before us whenever the mist rises and unfolds the far
horizon, constitute no small part of its charm. The position
of the anthropologist of to-day resembles in some sort the
position of classical scholars at the revival of learning. To
these men the rediscovery of ancient literature came like a
revelation, disclosing to their wondering eyes a splendid
vision of the antique world, such as the cloistered student
of the Middle Ages never dreamed of under the gloomy
shadow of the minster and within the sound of its solemn
bells. To us moderns a still wider vista is vouchsafed, a
greater panorama is unrolled by the study which aims at
bringing home to us the faith and the practice, the hopes
and the ideals, not of two highly gifted races only, but of all
mankind, and thus at enabling us to follow the long march,
the slow and toilsome ascent, of humanity from savagery to
civilisation. And as the scholar of the Renaissance found
not merely fresh food for thought but a new field of labour
in the dusty and faded manuscripts of Greece and Rome, so
in the mass of materials that is steadily pouring in from
many sides—from buried cities of remotest antiquity as well
as from the rudest savages of the desert and the jungle—we
of to-day must recognise a new province of knowledge which
will task the energies of generations of students to master.
The study is still in its rudiments, and what we do now
will have to be done over again and done better, with fuller
knowledge and deeper insight, by those who come after us.
To recur to a metaphor which I have already made use of,
we of this age are only pioneers hewing lanes and clearings
in the forest where others will hereafter sow and reap.

But the comparative study of the beliefs and institutions
of mankind is fitted to be much more than a means of satis-
fying an enlightened curiosity and of furnishing materials
for the researches of the learned. Well handled, it may
become a powerful instrument to expedite progress if it lays
bare certain weak spots in the foundations on which modern

society is built—if it shews that much which we are wont
to regard as solid rests on the sands of superstition rather
than on the rock of nature.   It is indeed a melancholy and
in some respects thankless task to strike at the foundations
of beliefs in which, as in a strong tower, the hopes and
aspirations of humanity through long ages have sought a
refuge from the storm and stress of life.   Yet sooner or
later it is inevitable that the battery of the comparative
method should breach these venerable walls, mantled over
with the ivy and mosses and wild flowers of a thousand
tender and sacred associations.   At present we are only
dragging the guns into position : they have hardly yet
begun to speak.   The task of building up into fairer and
more enduring forms the old structures so rudely shattered
is reserved for other hands, perhaps for other and happier
ages.   We cannot foresee, we can hardly even guess, the
new forms into which thought and society will run in the
future.   Yet this uncertainty ought not to induce us, from
any consideration of expediency or regard for antiquity, to
spare the ancient moulds, however beautiful, when these are
proved to be out-worn.   Whatever comes of it, wherever
it leads us, we must follow truth alone.   It is our only
guiding star : *hoc signo vinces*.

    To a passage in my book it has been objected by a
distinguished scholar that the church-bells of Rome cannot
be heard, even in the stillest weather, on the shores of the
Lake of Nemi.   In acknowledging my blunder and leaving
it uncorrected, may I plead in extenuation of my obduracy
the example of an illustrious writer ?   In *Old Mortality* we
read how a hunted Covenanter, fleeing before Claverhouse's
dragoons, hears the sullen boom of the kettledrums of the
pursuing cavalry borne to him on the night wind.   When
Scott was taken to task for this description, because the
drums are not beaten by cavalry at night, he replied in
effect that he liked to hear the drums sounding there, and

that he would let them sound on so long as his book might last. In the same spirit I make bold to say that by the Lake of Nemi I love to hear, if it be only in imagination, the distant chiming of the bells of Rome, and I would fain believe that their airy music may ring in the ears of my readers after it has ceased to vibrate in my own.

J. G. FRAZER.

CAMBRIDGE,
18th September 1900.

CONTENTS

CHAPTER VI.—MAGICIANS AS KINGS   .   Pp. 332-372

CHAPTER VII.—INCARNATE HUMAN GODS Pp. 373-421

CHAPTER I

THE KING OF THE WOOD

" The still glassy lake that sleeps
Beneath Aricia's trees—
Those trees in whose dim shadow
The ghastly priest doth reign,
The priest who slew the slayer,
And shall himself be slain."
MACAULAY.

§ 1. *Diana and Virbius*

WHO does not know Turner's picture of the Golden Bough ? The lake The scene, suffused with the golden glow of imagination in of Nemi. which the divine mind of Turner steeped and transfigured even the fairest natural landscape, is a dream-like vision of the little woodland lake of Nemi—" Diana's Mirror," as it was called by the ancients. No one who has seen that calm water, lapped in a green hollow of the Alban hills, can ever forget it. The two characteristic Italian villages which slumber on its banks, and the equally Italian palace whose terraced gardens descend steeply to the lake, hardly break the stillness and even the solitariness of the scene. Dian herself might still linger by this lonely shore, still haunt these woodlands wild.

In antiquity this sylvan landscape was the scene of a Its tragic strange and recurring tragedy. In order to understand it memories aright we must try to form in our minds an accurate picture of the place where it happened ; for, as we shall see later on, a subtle link subsisted between the natural beauty of the spot and the dark crimes which under the mask of religion were often perpetrated there, crimes which after the lapse of so many ages still lend a touch of melancholy to these quiet woods and waters, like a chill breath of autumn on one of those bright September days "while not a leaf seems faded."

The Alban hills.

The Alban hills are a fine bold group of volcanic mountains which rise abruptly from the Campagna in full view of Rome, forming the last spur sent out by the Apennines towards the sea. Two of the extinct craters are now filled by two beautiful waters, the Alban lake and its lesser sister the lake of Nemi. Both lie far below the monastery-crowned top of Monte Cavo, the summit of the range, but yet so high above the plain that standing on the rim of the larger crater at Castel Gandolfo, where the Popes had their summer palace, you look down on the one hand into the Alban lake, and on the other away across the Campagna to where, on the western horizon, the sea flashes like a broad sheet of burnished gold in the sun.

The sanctuary of Diana Nemorensis.

The lake of Nemi is still as of old embowered in woods, where in spring the wild flowers blow as fresh as no doubt they did two thousand springs ago. It lies so deep down in the old crater that the calm surface of its clear water is seldom ruffled by the wind. On all sides but one the banks, thickly mantled with luxuriant vegetation, descend steeply to the water's edge. Only on the north a stretch of flat ground intervenes between the lake and the foot of the hills. This was the scene of the tragedy. Here, in the very heart of the wooded hills, under the abrupt declivity now crested by the village of Nemi, the sylvan goddess Diana had an old and famous sanctuary, the resort of pilgrims from all parts of Latium. It was known as the sacred grove of Diana Nemorensis, that is, Diana of the Wood, or, perhaps more exactly, Diana of the Woodland Glade.[1] Sometimes the lake and grove were called, after the nearest town, the lake

[1] Strictly speaking, *nemus* is a natural opening or glade in a forest. Thus Lucan says (*Pharsal.* i. 453 *sq.*) that the Druids inhabited "deep glades in sacred groves far from the haunts of men" ("*nemora alta remotis incolitis lucis*"), as the words are rendered by Haskins in his edition, who compares Propertius v. 9. 24, "*lucus ubi umbroso fecerat orbe nemus.*" But commonly *nemus* means no more than a wood or grove. See for example Lucan, *Pharsal.* iii. 396, "*procumbunt nemora et spoliantur robora silvae.*" At Nemi the sacred grove (*lucus*) formed part of the woodlands (*nemus*), as we learn from Cato, quoted by Priscian, *Inst.* iv. 21 (vol. i. p. 129, ed. M. Hertz), "*lucum Dianium in nemore Aricino,*" etc. As to the thick woods of Nemi in antiquity see Ovid, *Fasti*, iii. 263 *sq.*; *id.*, *Metam.* xv. 485.

and grove of Aricia.[1] But the town, the modern Ariccia,
lay three miles away at the foot of the mountains, and
separated from the lake by a long and steep descent. A
spacious terrace or platform contained the sanctuary. On
the north and east it was bounded by great retaining walls
which cut into the hillsides and served to support them.
Semicircular niches sunk in the walls and faced with columns
formed a series of chapels, which in modern times have
yielded a rich harvest of votive offerings. On the side of
the lake the terrace rested on a mighty wall, over seven
hundred feet long by thirty feet high, built in triangular
buttresses, like those which we see in front of the piers of
bridges to break floating ice. At present this terrace-wall
stands back some hundred yards from the lake ; in other
days its buttresses may have been lapped by the water.
Compared with the extent of the sacred precinct, the temple
itself was not large ; but its remains prove it to have been
neatly and solidly built of massive blocks of peperino, and
adorned with Doric columns of the same material. Elaborate
cornices of marble and friezes of terra-cotta contributed to
the outward splendour of the edifice, which appears to have
been further enhanced by tiles of gilt bronze.[2]

[1] Cato, *loc. cit.* ; Ovid, *Fasti*, vi.
756 ; Statius, *Sylvae*, iii. 1. 56 ;
Philostratus, *Vit. Apollon.* iv. 36. A
loose expression of Appian (*Bellum
Civile*, v. 24) has sometimes given rise
to the notion that there was a town
called Nemus. But this is a mistake.
See E. Desjardins, *Essai sur la Topographie du Latium* (Paris, 1854), p. 214,
and on the other side, A. Bormann,
Altitalische Chorographie (Halle, 1852),
pp. 135 *sq.*

[2] The site was excavated in 1885
and 1886 by Sir John Savile Lumley,
now Lord Savile, who was then English
ambassador at Rome. Further excava-
tions were conducted in 1886-1888 by
Signor Luigi Boccanera, and again in
1895 by Signor Eliseo Borghi. See
Notizie degli Scavi, 1885, pp. 159 *sq.*,
192 *sq.*, 227 *sq.*, 254 *sq.*, 317-321,
344, 428 *sq.*, 478 *sq. ; id.* 1887, pp.
23-25, 120 *sq.*, 195-198 ; *id.* 1888,
pp. 193 *sq.*, 392 *sq : id.* 1889, pp.

20-22 ; *id.* 1895, pp. 106-108, 206,
232, 324, 424-438 ; *Bulletino del-
l' Instituto di Corrispondenza Archeologica*, 1885, pp. 149-157, 225-242 ;
R. Lanciani, in the *Athenaeum*,
October 10, 1885, pp. 477 *sq.* ; R. P.
Pullan, in *Archaeologia : Miscellaneous
Tracts relating to Antiquity*, l. (1887)
pp. 58-65 ; O. Rossbach, in *Verhandlungen der vierzigsten Versammlung
deutscher Philologen und Schulmänner
in Görlitz* (Leipsic, 1890), pp. 147-
164 ; G. H. Wallis, *Illustrated Catalogue of Classical Antiquities from the
Site of the Temple of Diana, Nemi,
Italy* (preface dated 1893). The
temple measured 30 metres in length
by 15.90 in breadth (*Notizie degli
Scavi*, 1885, p. 193). It had columns
on either side of the *pronaos* (Vitruvius,
iv. 7. 4). A few votive offerings found
on the site in earlier times are described
in Graevius's *Thesaurus Antiquitatum
Romanarum*, xii. col. 752-757, 808.

Wealth
and
popularity
of the
shrine.

The great wealth and popularity of the sanctuary in antiquity are attested by ancient writers as well as by the remains which have come to light in modern times. In the civil war its sacred treasures went to replenish the empty coffers of Octavian,[1] who well understood the useful art of thus securing the divine assistance, if not the divine blessing, for the furtherance of his ends. But we are not told that he treated Diana on this occasion as civilly as his divine uncle Julius Caesar once treated Capitoline Jupiter himself, borrowing three thousand pounds' weight of solid gold from the god, and scrupulously paying him back with the same weight of gilt copper.[2] However, the sanctuary at Nemi recovered from this drain on its resources, for two centuries later it was still reputed one of the richest in Italy.[3] Ovid has described the walls hung with fillets and commemorative tablets ;[4] and the abundance of cheap votive offerings and copper coins, which the site has yielded in our own day, speaks volumes for the piety and numbers, if not for the opulence and liberality, of the worshippers. Swarms of beggars used to stream forth daily from the slums of Aricia and take their stand on the long slope up which the labouring horses dragged well-to-do pilgrims to the shrine ; and according to the response which their whines and importunities met with they blew kisses or hissed curses after the carriages as they swept rapidly down hill again.[5]

For the inscriptions of Nemi and Aricia see Corpus Inscriptionum Latinarum, xiv. Nos. 2156-2226, 4180-4210, 4268-4275a ; W. Henzen, in Hermes, vi. (1872) pp. 6-13 ; G. Tomassetti, in Museo Italiano di Antichità Classica, ii. (1888) coll. 481 sqq. Among these inscriptions the many dedications to Diana serve to identify the site beyond a doubt. The evidence of ancient writers is collected by Cluverius, Italia Antiqua, ii. pp. 920-935. See also H. Nissen, Italische Landeskunde, ii. (Berlin, 1902) pp. 588-592 ; and for the topography, Sir W. Gell, The Topography of Rome and its Vicinity (London, 1834), i. pp. 182-191, ii. pp. 112-117.

[1] Appian, Bellum Civile, v. 24.

[2] Suetonius, Divus Julius, 54. Serv-ing his own gods thus, he naturally felt no compunction at relieving the barbarous Gaulish gods of their little savings (Suetonius, ib.).

[3] Appian, loc. cit.

[4] Fasti, iii. 267 sq.

[5] Juvenal, Sat. iv. 117 sq. ; Persius, Sat. vi. 56, with the scholiast's note ; Martial, Epigr. ii. 19. 3, xii. 32. 10. Persius calls this part of the road the slope of Virbius. Juvenal and Martial call it the Arician slope. But the former was probably the correct name, for at Rome also there was a "slope of Virbius" on the Esquiline, near a sanctuary of Diana (Livy, i. 48. 6). The double coincidence with Aricia is probably significant, as has been acutely pointed out by Mr. A. B. Cook (Classical Review, xvi. (1902)

Even peoples and potentates of the East did homage to the lady of the lake by setting up monuments in her sanctuary; and within the precinct stood shrines of the Egyptian goddesses Isis and Bubastis, with a store of gorgeous jewellery.[1]

The retirement of the spot and the beauty of the land- Roman villas at scape naturally tempted some of the luxurious Roman Nemi. nobles to fix their summer residences by the lake.[2] Here Lucius Caesar had a house to which, on a day in early summer, only two months after the murder of his illustrious namesake, he invited Cicero to meet the assassin Brutus.[3] The emperors themselves appear to have been partial to a retreat where they could find repose from the cares of state and the bustle of the great city in the fresh air of the lake and the stillness of the woods. Here Julius Caesar built himself a costly villa, but pulled it down because it was not to his mind.[4] Here Caligula had two magnificent barges, or rather floating palaces, launched for him on the lake;[5] and it was while dallying in the woods of Nemi that the sluggard Vitellius received the tidings of revolt which woke him from his dream of pleasure and called him to arms.[6] Vespasian had a monument dedicated to his honour in the

p. 380, n. 3). We shall return to this later on. As to Virbius, we shall hear more of him presently.

[1] W. Henzen, in *Hermes*, vi. (1872) pp. 6-12; *Corpus Inscriptionum Latinarum*, xiv., Nos. 2215, 2216, 2218.

[2] At the place called S. Maria, in the commune of Nemi, there have been found remains of a magnificent villa of the first or second century, built in terraces just above the lake and adorned with variegated marbles, frescoes, and works of art. See *Notizie degli Scavi*, 1888, pp. 194-196, 393 *sq.* The place is near the mouth of the ancient emissary, below the village of Genzano; the vineyards beside the lake are here littered with fragments of fine marbles. In January 1901 I visited the site in the company of Mr. St. Clair Baddeley, who has kindly furnished me with some notes on the subject.

[3] Cicero, *Ad Atticum*, xv. 4. 5.

[4] Suetonius, *Divus Julius*, 46. From a letter of Cicero to Atticus (vi. 1. 25) we infer that the house was building in 50 B.C.

[5] Some of the timbers and fittings of these vessels were fished up from the bottom of the lake in 1895. Especially remarkable are the beautiful bronze heads of lions and wolves with mooring-rings in their mouths. Caligula's name (C . CAESARIS . AVG . GERMANICI) is stamped on the leaden water-pipes, and the style of the bronzes is that of the first century. See *Notizie degli Scavi*, 1895, pp. 361-396, 461-474; J. C. G. Boot, in *Verslagen en Mededeelingen der kon. Akademie van Wetenschappen, Afdeeling Letterkunde*, III. Reeks, xii. deel (Amsterdam, 1895), pp. 278-285; R. Lanciani, *New Tales of Old Rome* (London, 1901), pp. 205-214.

[6] Tacitus, *Histor.* iii. 36.

grove by the senate and people of Aricia : Trajan condescended to fill the chief magistracy of the town ; and
Hadrian indulged his taste for architecture by restoring a
structure which had been erected in the precinct by a prince
of the royal house of Parthia.[1]

Diana as the mistress of wild animals. Such, then, was the sanctuary of Diana at Nemi, a
fitting home for the "mistress of mountains, and forests
green, and lonely glades, and sounding rivers," as Catullus
calls her.[2] Multitudes of her statuettes, appropriately clad
in the short tunic and high buskins of a huntress, with the
quiver slung over her shoulder, have been found on the
spot. Some of them represent her with her bow in her
hand or her hound at her side.[3] Bronze and iron spears,
and images of stags and hinds, discovered within the precinct,[4] may have been offerings of huntsmen to the huntress
goddess for success in the chase. Similarly the bronze
tridents, which have also come to light at Nemi, were
perhaps presented by fishermen who had speared fish in the
lake, or maybe by hunters who had stabbed boars in the
forest.[5] The wild boar was still hunted in Italy down
to the end of the first century of our era ; for the younger
Pliny tells us how, with his usual charming affectation, he
sat meditating and reading by the nets, while three fine
boars fell into them.[6] Indeed, some fourteen - hundred
years later boar-hunting was a favourite pastime of Pope

[1] *Corpus Inscriptionum Latinarum,*
xiv., Nos. 2213, 2216, 4191. Hadrian
also had a monument in the grove dedicated to him by the senate and people
of Aricia (*Notizie degli Scavi*, 1895,
pp. 430 *sq.*). A bust of Caesar and a
statue of Tiberius have been found on
the spot. See G. H. Wallis, *Illustrated Catalogue*, p. 31 ; O. Rossbach,
in *Verhandlungen der vierzig. Ver-
samml. aeutscher Philologen*, p. 159.

[2] Catullus, xxxiv. 9 *sqq.*

[3] *Bulletino dell' Instituto di Corrispondenza Archeologica*, 1885, pp. 228
sq.; *Notizie degli Scavi*, 1887, pp. 24,
195 ; *id.* 1888, p. 393 ; O. Rossbach, in *Verhandl. d. vierzig. Ver-
samml. deutscher Philologen*, pp. 150
note, 161 ; G. H. Wallis, *Illustrated
Catalogue*, pp. 4, 15, 34 *sq.*

[4] *Notizie degli Scavi*, 1887, p. 195 ;

id. 1888, p. 393 ; *Bulletino di Corr.
Archeol.* 1885, p. 230 ; O. Rossbach,
op. cit., pp. 150 note, 151 note, 163 ;
G. H. Wallis, *Illustrated Catalogue*,
pp. 35, 40. Greek hunters dedicated
spears and javelins to Pan (*Anthologia
Palatina*, vi. 57, 177). Compare W.
H. D. Rouse, *Greek Votive Offerings*
(Cambridge, 1902), p. 71.

[5] W. Helbig, in *Bulletino dell' Inst.
di Corr. Archeol.* 1885, pp. 231 *sq.* ;
Notizie degli Scavi, 1887, p. 195 ; *id.*
1888, p. 393. Helbig observes that
the ancients sometimes used tridents in
boar-hunts.

[6] Pliny, *Epist.* i. 6. In the second
century of our era the mountains and
oak woods of Greece harboured numbers of wild boars. See Pausanias, i.
32. 1, iii. 20. 4, v. 6. 6, vii. 26. 10,
viii. 23. 9, ix. 23. 7.

Leo the Tenth.[1] A frieze of painted reliefs in terra-cotta, which was found in the sanctuary at Nemi, and may have adorned Diana's temple, portrays the goddess in the character of what is called the Asiatic Artemis, with wings sprouting from her waist and a lion resting its paws on each of her shoulders.[2] A few rude images of cows, oxen, horses, and pigs dug up on the site may perhaps indicate that Diana was here worshipped as the patroness of domestic animals as well as of the wild creatures of the wood.[3] In like manner her Greek counterpart Artemis was a goddess not only of game but of herds. Thus her sanctuary in the highlands of north-western Arcadia, between Clitor and Cynaethae, owned sacred cattle which were driven off by Aetolian freebooters on one of their forays.[4] When Xenophon returned from the wars and settled on his estate among the wooded hills and green meadows of the rich valley through which the Alpheus flows past Olympia, he dedicated to Artemis a little temple on the model of her great temple at Ephesus, surrounded it with a grove of all kinds of fruit-trees, and endowed it not only with a chase but also with a sacred pasture. The chase abounded in fish and game of all sorts, and the pasture sufficed to rear swine, goats, oxen, and horses ; and on her yearly festival the pious soldier sacrificed to the goddess a tithe both of the cattle from the sacred pasture and of the game from the sacred chase.[5] Again, the people of Hyampolis in Phocis worshipped Artemis and thought that no cattle throve like those which they dedicated to her.[6] Perhaps then the images of cattle found in Diana's precinct at Nemi were offered to her by herdsmen to ensure her blessing on their herds. In Catholic Germany at the present time the great patron of cattle, horses, and pigs is St. Leonhard, and models of cattle, horses, and pigs are dedicated to him, sometimes in order to ensure the health and increase of the flocks and herds through the coming year, sometimes in order to

Diana as the patroness of cattle.

Analogy of St. Leonhard in Germany.

[1] W. Roscoe, *Life and Pontificate of Leo the Tenth,*[3] iv. 376.

[2] O. Rossbach, *op. cit.* pp. 157 *sq.* ; G. H. Wallis, *Illustrated Catalogue,* pp. 3, 31, with the plate facing p. 43.

[3] *Bulletino dell' Inst. di Corr. Archeol.* 1885, p. 153 ; G. H. Wallis, *Illustrated Catalogue,* p. 23.

[4] Polybius, *Hist.* iv. 18 and 19.

[5] Xenophon, *Anabasis,* v. 3. 4-13.

[6] Pausanias, x. 35. 7.

obtain the recovery of sick animals.[1]   And, curiously enough,
like Diana of Aricia, St. Leonhard is also expected to help
women in travail and to bless barren wives with offspring.[2]
Nor do these points exhaust the analogy between St.
Leonard and Diana of Aricia ; for like the goddess the
saint heals the sick ; he is the patron of prisoners, as she
was of runaway slaves ; and his shrines, like hers, enjoyed
the right of asylum.[3]

Nemi an
image of
Italy in the
olden time.

So to the last, in spite of a few villas peeping out here
and there from among the trees, Nemi seems to have remained in some sense an image of what Italy had been in
the far-off days when the land was still sparsely peopled
with tribes of savage hunters or wandering herdsmen, when
the beechwoods and oakwoods, with their deciduous foliage,
reddening in autumn and bare in winter, had not yet begun,
under the hand of man, to yield to the evergreens of the
south, the laurel, the olive, the cypress, and the oleander,
still less to those intruders of a later age, which nowadays
we are apt to think of as characteristically Italian, the
lemon and the orange.[4]

Rule of
succession
to the
priesthood
of Diana
at Nemi.

However, it was not merely in its natural surroundings
that this ancient shrine of the sylvan goddess continued to
be a type or miniature of the past.   Down to the decline of
Rome a custom was observed there which seems to trans-
port us at once from civilisation to savagery.   In the
sacred grove there grew a certain tree round which at any
time of the day, and probably far into the night, a grim
figure might be seen to prowl.   In his hand he carried a
drawn sword, and he kept peering warily about him as if

[1] R. Andree, *Votive und Weihegaben des Katholischen Volks in Süddeutschland* (Brunswick, 1904), pp.
37, 50, 152 *sqq.*

[2] R. Andree, *op. cit.* p. 41.

[3] R. Andree, *op. cit.* pp. 41-50.

[4] See V. Hehn, *Kulturpflanzen und
Haustiere in ihrem übergang aus
Asien*[7] (Berlin, 1902), pp. 520 *sq.* :
" In the course of history the flora
of the Italian peninsula assumed more
and more a southern character. When
the first Greeks landed in lower Italy
the forests consisted predominantly of
deciduous trees, the beeches reached
lower down than now, when they are
confined to the highest mountain
regions. Centuries later in the land-
scapes on the walls of Pompeii we see
nothing but evergreen trees, the *Laurus
nobilis*, the olive, the cypress, the
oleander ; in the latest times of the
empire and in the Middle Ages the
lemon-trees and orange-trees appear,
and since the discovery of America
the magnolias, the agaves, and the
Indian figs. There can be no question
that this revolution has been wrought
mainly by the hand of man."

at every instant he expected to be set upon by an enemy.[1]
He was a priest and a murderer; and the man for whom
he looked was sooner or later to murder him and hold the
priesthood in his stead. Such was the rule of the sanctuary.
A candidate for the priesthood could only succeed to office
by slaying the priest, and having slain him, he retained
office till he was himself slain by a stronger or a craftier.

The post which he held by this precarious tenure carried *The priest*
with it the title of king; but surely no crowned head ever *who slew the slayer.*
lay uneasier, or was visited by more evil dreams, than his.
For year in year out, in summer and winter, in fair weather
and in foul, he had to keep his lonely watch, and whenever
he snatched a troubled slumber it was at the peril of his life.
The least relaxation of his vigilance, the smallest abatement
of his strength of limb or skill of fence, put him in jeopardy;
grey hairs might seal his death-warrant. His eyes probably
acquired that restless, watchful look which, among the
Esquimaux of Bering Strait, is said to betray infallibly
the shedder of blood; for with that people revenge is a
sacred duty, and the manslayer carries his life in his hand.[2]
To gentle and pious pilgrims at the shrine the sight of
him might well seem to darken the fair landscape, as
when a cloud suddenly blots the sun on a bright day. The
dreamy blue of Italian skies, the dappled shade of summer
woods, and the sparkle of waves in the sun, can have accorded
but ill with that stern and sinister figure. Rather we picture
to ourselves the scene as it may have been witnessed by a
belated wayfarer on one of those wild autumn nights when
the dead leaves are falling thick, and the winds seem to
sing the dirge of the dying year. It is a sombre picture,
set to melancholy music—the background of forest shewing
black and jagged against a lowering and stormy sky, the
sighing of the wind in the branches, the rustle of the
withered leaves under foot, the lapping of the cold water
on the shore, and in the foreground, pacing to and fro, now
in twilight and now in gloom, a dark figure with a glitter

---

[1] ξιφήρης οὖν ἐστιν ἀεί, περισκοπῶν
τὰς ἐπιθέσεις, ἕτοιμος ἀμύνεσθαι, is
Strabo's description (v. 3. 12), who
may have seen him "pacing there
alone."

[2] E. W. Nelson, "The Eskimo
about Bering Strait," *Eighteenth
Annual Report of the Bureau of
American Ethnology*, Part I. (Washington, 1899) p. 293.

of steel at the shoulder whenever the pale moon, riding clear of the cloud-rack, peers down at him through the matted boughs.

Possibility of explaining the rule of succession by the comparative method.

The strange rule of this priesthood has no parallel in classical antiquity, and cannot be explained from it. To find an explanation we must go farther afield. No one will probably deny that such a custom savours of a barbarous age, and, surviving into imperial times, stands out in striking isolation from the polished Italian society of the day, like a primaeval rock rising from a smooth-shaven lawn. It is the very rudeness and barbarity of the custom which allow us a hope of explaining it. For recent researches into the early history of man have revealed the essential similarity with which, under many superficial differences, the human mind has elaborated its first crude philosophy of life. Accordingly, if we can shew that a barbarous custom, like that of the priesthood of Nemi, has existed elsewhere; if we can detect the motives which led to its institution; if we can prove that these motives have operated widely, perhaps universally, in human society, producing in varied circumstances a variety of institutions specifically different but generically alike; if we can shew, lastly, that these very motives, with some of their derivative institutions, were actually at work in classical antiquity; then we may fairly infer that at a remoter age the same motives gave birth to the priesthood of Nemi. Such an inference, in default of direct evidence as to how the priesthood did actually arise, can never amount to demonstration. But it will be more or less probable according to the degree of completeness with which it fulfils the conditions I have indicated. The object of this book is, by meeting these conditions, to offer a fairly probable explanation of the priesthood of Nemi.

Legend of the origin of the Nemi worship : Orestes and the Tauric Diana.

I begin by setting forth the few facts and legends which have come down to us on the subject. According to one story the worship of Diana at Nemi was instituted by Orestes, who, after killing Thoas, King of the Tauric Chersonese (the Crimea), fled with his sister to Italy, bringing with him the image of the Tauric Diana hidden in a faggot of sticks. After his death his bones were transported from Aricia to Rome and buried in front of the temple of Saturn, on the

Capitoline slope, beside the temple of Concord.   The bloody
ritual which legend ascribed to the Tauric Diana is familiar
to classical readers ; it is said that every stranger who landed
on the shore was sacrificed on her altar.   But transported
to Italy, the rite assumed a milder form.   Within the sanctuary at Nemi grew a certain tree of which no branch might
be broken.   Only a runaway slave was allowed to break off,
if he could, one of its boughs.   Success in the attempt   The King
entitled him to fight the priest in single combat, and if he of the
                                                             Wood.
slew him he reigned in his stead with the title of King of
the Wood (*Rex Nemorensis*).   According to the public
opinion of the ancients the fateful branch was that Golden
Bough which, at the Sibyl's bidding, Aeneas plucked before
he essayed the perilous journey to the world of the dead.
The flight of the slave represented, it was said, the flight of
Orestes ; his combat with the priest was a reminiscence of
the human sacrifices once offered to the Tauric Diana.   This
rule of succession by the sword was observed down to
imperial times ; for amongst his other freaks Caligula, thinking that the priest of Nemi had held office too long, hired
a more stalwart ruffian to slay him ; and a Greek traveller,
who visited Italy in the age of the Antonines, remarks that
down to his time the priesthood was still the prize of victory
in a single combat.[1]

[1] Servius on Virgil, *Aen*. vi. 136,
"*Licet de hoc ramo hi qui de sacris
Proserpinae scripsisse dicuntur, quid-
dam esse mysticum adfirment, publica
tamen opinio hoc habet.   Orestes post
occisum regem Thoantem*," etc. ; *id.* on
Virgil, *Aen*. ii. 116 ; Valerius Flaccus,
Argonaut. ii. 304 *sq*. ; Strabo, v. 3.
12 ; Pausanias, ii. 27. 4 ; Solinus, ii.
11 ; Suetonius, *Caligula*, 35.   The
custom of breaking the branch, and its
supposed connexion with the Golden
Bough of Virgil, are recorded by Servius alone (on Virgil, *Aen*. vi. 136).
For the title "King of the Wood" see
Suetonius, *l.c.* ; and compare Statius,
Sylv. iii. 1. 55 *sq*.—

"*Jamque dies aderat, profugis cum
        regibus aptum
    Fumat Aricinum Triviae nemus*" ;

Ovid, *Fasti*, iii. 271 *sq*.—

"Regna *tenent fortesque manu, pedi-
        busque fugaces ;
    Et perit exemplo postmodo quisque
        suo*" ;

id., *Ars am*. i. 259 *sq*.—

"*Ecce suburbanae templum nemorale
        Dianae,
    Partaque per gladios* regna *nocente
        manu*" ;

Valerius Flaccus, *Argon*. ii. 304 *sq*.—

"*Jam nemus Egeriae, jam te ciet altus
        ab alba
    Juppiter et soli non mitis Aricia
        regi.*"

An archaic Greek relief, found in 1791
near the outlet of the lake, in the Valle-
riccia, has been sometimes thought to
portray the combat between a priest
and a candidate for the office.   But

Chief
features
of the
worship of
Diana at
Nemi.

Import-
ance of fire
in her
ritual.

Of the worship of Diana at Nemi some leading features can still be made out. From the votive offerings which have been found on the site, it appears that she was conceived of especially as a huntress, and further as blessing men and women with offspring, and granting expectant mothers an easy delivery.[1] Again, fire seems to have played a foremost part in her ritual. For during her annual festival, held on the thirteenth of August, at the hottest time of the year, her grove shone with a multitude of torches, whose ruddy glare was reflected by the lake ; and throughout the length and breadth of Italy the day was kept with holy rites at every domestic hearth.[2] Bronze statuettes found in her precinct represent the goddess herself holding a torch in her raised right hand ;[3] and women whose prayers had been heard by her came crowned with wreaths and bearing lighted torches to the sanctuary in fulfilment of their vows.[4] Some one unknown

the subject is rather the murder of Aegisthus by Orestes in presence of Clytaemnestra and Electra. See Sir W. Gell, *Topography of Rome*, ii. 116 *sq.* ; O. Jahn, in *Archäologische Zeitung*, vii. (1849) coll. 113-118 ; Baumeister's *Denkmäler*, p. 1112 ; O. Rossbach, *op. cit.* pp. 148 *sq.* ; R. Lanciani, *New Tales of Old Rome*, p. 204.

[1] Thus there have been found many models of the organs of generation, both male and female, including wombs ; figures of women with infants on their laps or on their arms ; and couples seated side by side, the woman pregnant or carrying a child. See *Bulletino dell' Inst. di Corrisp. Archeologica*, 1885, pp. 183 *sq.* ; *Notizie degli Scavi*, 1885, pp. 160, 254 ; *id.* 1895, p. 424 ; O. Rossbach, *op. cit.* p. 160 ; G. H. Wallis, *Illustrated Catalogue*, pp. 4, 15, 17. Another group represents a woman just after delivery, supported by the midwife, who holds the child in her lap. See Graevius, *Thesaurus Antiquitatum Romanarum*, xii. col. 808. As to the huntress Diana, see above, p. 6.

[2] Statius, *Sylvae*, iii. 1. 52-60 ; Gratius Faliscus, *Cynegeticon*, i. 484 *sq.* As to the date we know from the calendars (W. Warde Fowler, *The Roman Festivals of the Republic*, p.

198) and from Festus (p. 343 ed. Müller ; compare Plutarch, *Quaest. Rom.* 100) that the festival of Diana on the Aventine at Rome fell on the Ides, that is, the 13th of August. Further, the Ides of August was held as the birthday of Diana at Lanuvium (*Corpus Inscriptionum Latinarum*, xiv., No. 2112 ; G. Wilmanns, *Exempla Inscriptionum Latinarum*, No. 319 ; C. G. Bruns, *Fontes Juris Romani*,[7] ed. O. Gradenwitz, p. 389 ; H. Dessau, *Inscriptiones Latinae Selectae*, No. 7212). Moreover, Martial (xii. 67. 2) and Ausonius (*De feriis Romanis*, 5 *sq.*) speak of the Ides of August as Diana's day. Hence we may safely conclude that the *Hecateias idus* which Statius (*l.c.*) mentions as the date of the festival of Diana at Nemi were no other than the Ides of August, all the more that the poet describes the time as the hottest of the year. Compare G. Wissowa, *Religion und Kultus der Römer* (Munich, 1902), p. 201.

[3] O. Rossbach, *op. cit.* pp. 150 note, 161. A coin of P. Clodius Turrinus (43 B.C.) portrays Diana with a long torch in either hand. See E. Babelon, *Monnaies de la République Romaine* (Paris, 1885), i. 355.

[4] Ovid, *Fasti*, iii. 269 *sq.* ; Propertius, iii. 24. (30) 9 *sq.*, ed. Paley.

dedicated a perpetually burning lamp in a little shrine at
Nemi for the safety of the Emperor Claudius and his family.[1]
The terra-cotta lamps which have been discovered in the
grove [2] may perhaps have served a like purpose for humbler
persons.   If so, the analogy of the custom to the Catholic
practice of dedicating holy candles in churches would be
obvious.[3]   Further, the title of Vesta borne by Diana at   Diana as
Nemi [4] points clearly to the maintenance of a perpetual   Vesta.
holy fire in her sanctuary.   A large circular basement at
the north-east corner of the temple, raised on three steps and
bearing traces of a mosaic pavement, probably supported a
round temple of Diana in her character of Vesta, like the
round temple of Vesta in the Roman Forum.[5]   Here the
sacred fire would seem to have been tended by Vestal
Virgins, for the head of a Vestal in terra-cotta was found on
the spot,[6] and the worship of a perpetual fire, cared for by
holy maidens, appears to have been common in Latium
from the earliest to the latest times.[7]   Thus we know that
among the ruins of Alba the Vestal fire was kept burning
by Vestal Virgins, bound to strict chastity, until the end
of the fourth century of our era.[8]   There were Vestals at

[1] *Notizie degli Scavi*, 1888, p. 193
sq.; O. Rossbach, *op. cit.* p. 164.
[2] *Bulletino dell' Inst. di Corrisp.
Archeologica*, 1885, p. 157; *Notizie
degli Scavi*, 1888, p. 393; G. H.
Wallis, *Illustrated Catalogue*, pp. 24-26.
[3] On the dedication of burning lamps
and candles in antiquity, see M. P.
Nilsson, *Griechische Feste* (Leipsic,
1906), p. 345, note 5.   As to the derivation of the Catholic from the old
heathen custom, see R. Andree, *Votive
und Weihegaben des Katholischen Volks
in Süddeutschland* (Brunswick, 1904),
p. 77.
[4] *Corpus Inscriptionum Latinarum*,
xiv., No. 2213; G. Wilmanns, *Exempla Inscriptionum Latinarum*, No.
1767; H. Dessau, *Inscriptiones Latinae
Selectae*, No. 3243.
[5] *Notizie degli Scavi*, 1885, p. 478;
O. Rossbach, *op. cit.* p. 158; G. H.
Wallis, *Illustrated Catalogue*, pp. 9 *sq.*
The true character of this circular
basement was first pointed out by Mr.
A. B. Cook (*Classical Review*, xvi.

(1902) p. 376).   Previous writers had
taken it for an altar or a pedestal.
But the mosaic pavement and the
bases of two columns which were
found in position on it exclude the
hypothesis of an altar and cannot easily
be reconciled with that of a pedestal,
for which, moreover, it appears to be too
large.   A rain-water gutter runs round
it and then extends in the direction of
the larger temple.   As to the temple
of Vesta at Rome see J. H. Middleton,
The Remains of Ancient Rome, i.
297 *sq.*; O. Richter, *Topographie der
Stadt Rom* [2] (Munich, 1902), pp. 88
sq.; G. Boni, in *Notizie degli Scavi*,
May 1900, pp. 159 *sqq.*
[6] G. H. Wallis, *Illustrated Catalogue*, p. 30.
[7] J. Marquardt, *Römische Staatsverwaltung*, iii.[2] 336.
[8] Juvenal, iv. 60 *sq.*; Asconius,
In Milonianam, p. 35, ed. Kiesse-
ling and Schoell; Symmachus, *Epist.*
ix. 128 and 129 (Migne's *Patrologia
Latina*, xviii. col. 355); *Corpus In-*

Tibur[1] and doubtless also at Lavinium, for the Roman consuls, praetors, and dictators had to sacrifice to Vesta at that ancient city when they entered on or laid down their office.[2]

Diana's festival on August 13 converted by the Christian Church into the festival of the Assumption of the Virgin on August 15.

At her annual festival, which, as we have just seen, was celebrated all over Italy on the thirteenth of August, hunting dogs were crowned and wild beasts were not molested; young people went through a purificatory ceremony in her honour; wine was brought forth, and the feast consisted of a kid, cakes served piping hot on plates of leaves, and apples still hanging in clusters on the boughs.[3] The Christian Church appears to have sanctified this great festival of the virgin goddess by adroitly converting it into the festival of the Assumption of the Blessed Virgin on the fifteenth of August.[4] The discrepancy of two days between the dates of the festivals is not a fatal argument against their identity; for a similar displacement of two days occurs in the case of St. George's festival on the twenty-third of April, which is probably identical with the ancient Roman festival of the Parilia on April twenty-first.[5] On the reasons which prompted this conversion of the festival of the Virgin Diana into the festival of the Virgin Mary, some light is thrown by a passage in the Syriac text of *The Departure of My Lady Mary from this World*, which runs thus: "And the apostles also ordered that there should be a commemoration of the blessed one on the thirteenth of Ab [that is, August; another MS. reads the 15th of Ab], on account of the vines bearing bunches (of grapes), and on account of the trees bearing fruit, that clouds of hail, bearing stones of wrath, might not come, and the trees be broken, and their fruits, and the vines with their clusters."[6] Here the festival of

---

scriptionum Latinarum, vi., No. 2172, xiv., No. 4120; Wilmanns, *Exempla Inscriptionum Latinarum*, No. 1750. The Alban Vestals gave evidence at Milo's trial in 52 B.C. (Asconius, *l.c.*); one of them was tried for breaking her vow of chastity late in the fourth century A.D. (Symmachus, *l.c.*).

[1] *Corpus Inscriptionum Latinarum*, xiv., Nos. 3677, 3679.

[2] Servius on Virgil, *Aen.* ii. 296; Macrobius, *Saturn.* iii. 4. 11.

[3] Statius, *Sylvae*, iii. 1. 55 *sqq.*; Gratius Faliscus, *Cynegeticon*, i. 483-492.

[4] J. Rendel Harris, *The Annotators of the Codex Bezae* (London, 1901), pp. 93-102.

[5] See below, vol. ii. pp. 324 *sqq.*

[6] *Journal of Sacred Literature and Biblical Record*, New Series, vii. (London, 1865), "The Departure of my Lady Mary from this World," p. 153. The Greek original of the treatise

the Assumption of the Virgin is definitely said to have been fixed on the thirteenth or fifteenth of August for the sake of protecting the ripening grapes and other fruits. Similarly in the Arabic text of the apocryphal work *On the Passing of the Blessed Virgin Mary*, which is attributed to the Apostle John, there occurs the following passage : "Also a festival in her honour was instituted on the fifteenth day of the month Ab [that is, August], which is the day of her passing from this world, the day on which the miracles were performed, and the time when the fruits of trees are ripening."[1] Further, in the calendars of the Syrian Church the fifteenth of August is repeatedly designated as the festival of the Mother of God "for the vines" ;[2] and to this day in Greece the ripening grapes and other fruits are brought to the churches to be blest by the priests on the fifteenth of August.[3] Now we hear of vineyards and plantations dedicated to Artemis, fruits offered to her, and her temple standing in an orchard.[4] Hence we may conjecture that her Italian sister Diana was also revered as a patroness of vines and fruit-trees, and that on the thirteenth of August the

The Virgin Mary seems to have succeeded Artemis and Diana as the patroness of the ripening fruits.

---

was discovered by Tischendorf. This passage was kindly indicated to me by my learned friend Mr. J. Rendel Harris. He writes to me : "In these late Syrian calendars the festivals are simply taken over from the Greek and Roman calendars without any adjustment at all, as a study of the detailed saints' days shows."

[1] *Johanni Apostoli de transitu Beatae Mariae Virginis Liber :* ex recensione et cum interpretatione Maximiliani Engeri (Elberfeldae, 1854), pp. 101, 103. This and the preceding passage are both cited by the late Prof. E. Lucius in his book *Die Anfänge des Heiligenkultes in der christlichen Kirche* (Tübingen, 1904), pp. 488 *sq.*, 521. From them and from the entries in the Syrian calendars (see the next note), Lucius rightly inferred that the Assumption of the Virgin Mary had been assigned by the Church to the 15th of August with reference to the ripening of the grapes and other fruits, and that the Christian festival replaced an old heathen festival of first-fruits, which

must have been held about the same time. But he appears to have overlooked the occurrence of Diana's festival on the 13th of August.

[2] N. Nilles, *Kalendarium Manuale utriusque Ecclesiae Orientalis et Occidentalis*[2] (Innsbruck, 1896-7), i. pp. 249, 480. Professor Nilles compares the blessing of the herbs (*Krautweihe*), which still takes place in various parts of German-speaking lands on August 15th for the purpose of defeating the charms of witches.

[3] B. Schmidt, *Das Volksleben der Neugriechen* (Leipsic, 1871), p. 58. My learned friend Dr. W. H. D. Rouse, who is well acquainted with Greece, both ancient and modern, gave me similar information.

[4] Pauly-Wissowa, *Real-Encyclop. d. class. Wissenschaften*, ii. 1342 ; Pausanias, vii. 18. 12 ; Xenophon, *Anabasis*, v. 3. 12. On the other hand the very sight of the image of Artemis at Pellene was said to render trees barren and to blight the fruits of the earth. See Plutarch, *Aratus*, 32.

owners of vineyards and orchards paid their respects to her at Nemi along with other classes of the community. We have just seen that wine and apples still hanging on the boughs formed part of the festal cheer on that day ; in an ancient fresco found at Ostia a statue of Diana is depicted in company with a procession of children, some of whom bear clusters of grapes ; [1] and in a series of gems the goddess, is represented with a branch of fruit in one hand and a cup, which is sometimes full of fruit, in the other.[2] Catullus, too, tells us that Diana filled the husbandman's barns with a

Survivals of Diana's festival in Italy, Sicily, and Scandinavia. bounteous harvest.[3] In some parts of Italy and Sicily the day of the Assumption of the Virgin is still celebrated, like Diana's day of old, with illuminations and bonfires ; in many Sicilian parishes the corn is then brought in sacks to the churches to be blessed, and many persons, who have a favour to ask of the Virgin, vow to abstain from one or more kinds of fruit during the first fifteen days of August.[4] Even in Scandinavia a relic of the worship of Diana survived in the custom of blessing the fruits of the earth of every sort, which in Catholic times was annually observed on the festival of the Assumption of the Virgin.[5] There is no intrinsic improbability in the view that for the sake of edification the church may have converted a real heathen festival into a

The Virgin Mary and the goddess Anaitis. nominal Christian one. Similarly in the Armenian Church " according to the express evidence of the Armenian fathers of the year 700 and later, the day of the Virgin was placed on September the fifteenth, because that was the day of Anahite, the magnificence of whose feast the Christian doctors hoped thereby to transfer to Mary." [6] This Anahite or Anaitis, as the Greeks called her, the Armenian predecessor of the Virgin Mary, was a great Oriental goddess,

---

[1] A. Dieterich, "Sommertag," *Archiv für Religionswissenschaft*, viii. (1905) Beiheft, pp. 108 *sqq.*, with fig. 2.

[2] Furtwängler, *Die antiken Gemmen*, iii. 231, with plates XX. 66, XXII. 18, 26, 30, 32, all cited by Mr. A. B. Cook, *Classical Review*, xvi. (1902) p. 378, note 4. Furtwängler held that these gems portray Diana of Nemi herself.

[3] Catullus, xxxiv. 17 *sqq.*

[4] G. Pitrè, *Spettacoli e Feste popolari Siciliane* (Palermo, 1881), pp. 356, 358, 360, 361, 362 ; G. Finamore, *Credenze, Usi e Costumi Abruzzesi* (Palermo, 1890), p. 176 ; G. Amalfi, *Tradizioni ed Usi nella peninsola Sorrentina* (Palermo, 1890), p. 50.

[5] Olaus Magnus, *Historia de Gentium Septentrionalium variis conditionibus*, xvi. 9.

[6] Note of Mr. F. C. Conybeare.

whose worship was exceedingly popular not only in Armenia
but in the adjoining countries.   The loose character of her
rites is plainly indicated by Strabo, himself a native of
these regions.[1]

Among the ancient Celts of Gaul, who, to judge by their
speech, were near kinsmen of the ancient Latins, the thirteenth
of August appears to have been the day when the harvest
was dedicated to the harvest-god Rivos.[2] If that was so, we
may conjecture that the choice of a day in mid-August for the
solemn celebration of the harvest-home dates from the remote
time when the ancestors of the Celtic and Italian peoples,
having renounced the wandering life of the huntsman and
herdsman, had settled down together in some land of fertile
soil and temperate climate, where harvest fell neither so late
as after the cool rainy summers of the North nor so early as
before the torrid and rainless summers of southern Europe.

The 13th of August a harvest festival among the Celts of Gaul.

But Diana did not reign alone in her grove at Nemi.[3]
Two lesser divinities shared her forest sanctuary.   One was
Egeria, the nymph of the clear water which, bubbling from
the basaltic rocks, used to fall in graceful cascades into the
lake at the place called Le Mole, because here were established the mills of the modern village of Nemi.   The purling
of the stream as it ran over the pebbles is mentioned by
Ovid, who tells us that he had often drunk of its water.[4]

Egeria, water-nymph and wife of Numa.

[1] Strabo, xi. 8. 12, xi. 14. 16, xii. 3. 37.

[2] This is inferred from entries in the ancient Celtic calendar of which numer-ous fragments, engraved on bronze, were found in 1897 at Coligny near Lyons. In this calendar the month Rivros seems to mean "the harvest month" and to correspond to August. Sir John Rhys believes that the harvest-god Rivos, who is only known from this calendar, answers to the better-known Celtic god Lug. See Sir John Rhys, in *Transactions of the Third International Congress for the History of Religion* (Oxford, 1908), ii. 222 *sqq.*; and as to the Coligny calendar in general see further Sir John Rhys, "Celtae and Galli," *Proceedings of the British Academy, 1905-1906*, pp. 71 *sqq.*; *id.* "Notes on the Coligny Cal-endar," *Proceedings of the British*

Academy, vol. iv.

[3] Dedications to Juno and Venus have been found in the grove (*Notizie degli Scavi*, 1888, p. 393 ; G. H. Wallis, *Illustrated Catalogue*, p. 44), also a bronze statuette of Jupiter (O. Rossbach, *op. cit.* p. 162), and a muti-lated or unfinished bust supposed to represent that deity (*Notizie degli Scavi*, 1885, p. 344 ; G. H. Wallis, *op. cit.* p. 54).

[4] Virgil, *Aen.* vii. 762 *sqq.*; Ovid, *Fasti*, iii. 273 *sqq.*; *id.*, *Metam.* xv. 482 *sqq.* ; Strabo, v. 3. 12. As to the stream, see P. Rosa, in *Monumenti ed Annali pubblic. dall' Instituto di Corrispondenza Archeologica nel 1856*, p. 7 ; R. Lanciani, in *Athenaeum*, October 10, 1885, p. 477. The water was diverted some years ago to supply Albano.

Women with child used to sacrifice to Egeria, because she was believed, like Diana, to be able to grant them an easy delivery.[1] Tradition ran that the nymph had been the wife or mistress of the wise king Numa, that he had consorted with her in the secrecy of the sacred grove, and that the laws which he gave the Romans had been inspired by communion with her divinity.[2] Plutarch compares the legend with other tales of the loves of goddesses for mortal men, such as the love of Cybele and the Moon for the fair youths Attis and Endymion.[3] According to some, the trysting-place of the lovers was not in the woods of Nemi but in a grove outside the dripping Porta Capena at Rome, where another sacred spring of Egeria gushed from a dark cavern.[4] Every day the Roman Vestals fetched water from this spring to wash the temple of Vesta, carrying it in earthenware pitchers on their heads.[5] In Juvenal's time the natural rock had been encased in marble, and the hallowed spot was profaned by gangs of poor Jews, who were suffered to squat, like gypsies, in the grove. We may suppose that the spring which fell into the lake of Nemi was the true original Egeria, and that when the first settlers moved down from the Alban hills to the banks of the Tiber they brought

---

[1] Festus, p. 77, ed. C. O. Müller.

[2] Ovid, *Fasti*, iii. 273 *sqq.*; *id.*, *Metam.* xv. 482 *sqq.*; Cicero, *De legibus*, i. 1. 4; Livy, i. 19. 5, i. 21. 3; Plutarch, *Numa*, 4, 8, 13, 15; Dionysius Halicarn. *Antiquit. Roman.* ii. 60 *sq.*; Juvenal, *Sat.* iii. 12; Lactantius, *Divin. Inst.* i. 22; Augustine, *De civitate Dei*, vii. 35; Servius on Virgil, *Aen.* vii. 763. Ovid, Livy, Lactantius, and Augustine speak of Egeria as the wife of Numa, whereas Juvenal and Servius call her his mistress. The language of Plutarch is somewhat ambiguous, but he uses the phrase γάμων θείων ἠξιωμένος (c. 4).

[3] Plutarch, *Numa*, 4.

[4] Juvenal, *Sat.* iii. 10 *sqq.*; Livy, i. 21. 3. As to the position of this grove and spring see O. Gilbert, *Geschichte und Topographie der Stadt Rom im Altertum*, i. 109 *sqq.*, ii. pp. 152 *sqq.*; O. Richter, *Topographie der Stadt Rom* [2] (Munich, 1902), pp. 342 *sq.* According to the latter writer, the valley of Egeria was outside the Servian wall, at the foot of the Caelian Mount, and is now traversed by the streets Via delle Mole di S. Sisto and Via della Ferratella. He identifies the sacred spring with a copious source at the Villa Fonseca. On the other hand, Statius (*Sylvae*, v. 3. 290 *sq.*), Lactantius (*Divin. Inst.* iii. 22), and Servius (on Virgil, vii. 763) held that Numa's Egeria was not at Rome but at Nemi. The grove of Egeria is now popularly identified with a little wood called the *Bosco Sacro*, which stands in a commanding situation to the left of the Appian Way, about a mile and a half from Rome (Baedeker's *Central Italy and Rome*,[13] p. 378).

[5] Plutarch, *Numa*, 13. That they carried the water in pitchers on their heads may be inferred from Propertius, v. 4. 15 *sq.*; Ovid, *Fasti*, iii. 11-14.

the nymph with them and found a new home for her in a grove outside the gates.[1] The remains of baths which have been discovered within the sacred precinct,[2] together with many terra-cotta models of various parts of the human body,[3] suggest that the waters of Egeria were used to heal the sick, who may have signified their hopes or testified their gratitude by dedicating likenesses of the diseased members to the goddess, in accordance with a custom which is still observed in many parts of Europe.[4] To this day it would seem that the spring retains medicinal virtues.[5]

The other of the minor deities at Nemi was Virbius. Legend had it that Virbius was the young Greek hero Hippolytus, chaste and fair, who learned the art of venery from the centaur Chiron, and spent all his days in the greenwood chasing wild beasts with the virgin huntress Artemis (the Greek counterpart of Diana) for his only comrade. Proud of her divine society, he spurned the love of women,[6] and this proved his bane. For Aphrodite, stung by his scorn, inspired his stepmother Phaedra with love of him; and when he disdained her wicked advances she falsely accused him to his father Theseus. The slander was believed, and Theseus prayed to his sire Poseidon to avenge the imagined wrong. So while Hippolytus drove in a chariot by the shore of the Saronic Gulf, the sea-god

Virbius, the male companion of Diana.

---

[1] This is the view of A. Schwegler (*Römische Geschichte*, i. 548 note), O. Gilbert (*Geschichte und Topographie der Stadt Rom im Altertum*, i. 111), and G. Wissowa (in W. H. Roscher's *Lexikon der griech. und röm. Mythologie, s.v.* "Egeria").

[2] O. Rossbach, *op. cit.* p. 151. "The old bath" is mentioned in an inscription found on the spot (*Corpus Inscriptionum Latinarum*, xiv., No. 4190).

[3] *Notizie degli Scavi*, 1885, pp. 159 *sq.*, 192, 254; *id.* 1888, p. 193; *Bulletino dell' Inst. di Corrisp. Archeologica*, 1885, pp. 153, 154 *sq.*; O. Rossbach, *op. cit.* p. 160; *Archaeologia: or Miscellaneous Tracts relating to Antiquity*, l. (1887), Pt. I. pp. 61 *sq.*, 64; G. H. Wallis, *Illustrated Catalogue*, pp. 2, 4, 22. Amongst these models may be specially noted the

torso of a woman clad in a long robe, with her breast cut open so as to expose the bowels. It may be the offering of a woman who suffered from some internal malady.

[4] For an example of the custom in modern times see J. J. Blunt, *Vestiges of Ancient Manners and Customs discoverable in Modern Italy and Sicily* (London, 1823), p. 135. The custom is still widespread among the Catholic population of Southern Germany. See R. Andree, *Votive und Weihegaben des Katholischen Volks in Süddeutschland* (Brunswick, 1904), pp. 94 *sqq.*, 112 *sqq.*, 123 *sqq.*

[5] R. Lanciani, in *Athenaeum*, October 10, 1885, p. 477.

[6] Xenophon, *Cyneget.* i. 2 and 11; Euripides, *Hippolytus*, 10-19. 1092 *sq.*

sent a fierce bull forth from the waves. The terrified horses bolted, threw Hippolytus from the chariot, and dragged him at their hoofs to death.[1] But Diana, for the love she bore Hippolytus, persuaded the leech Aesculapius to bring her fair young hunter back to life by his simples. Jupiter, indignant that a mortal man should return from the gates of death, thrust down the meddling leech himself to Hades. But Diana hid her favourite from the angry god in a thick cloud, disguised his features by adding years to his life, and then bore him far away to the dells of Nemi, where she entrusted him to the nymph Egeria, to live there, unknown and solitary, under the name of Virbius, in the depth of the Italian forest. There he reigned a king, and there he dedicated a precinct to Diana. He had a comely son, Virbius, who, undaunted by his father's fate, drove a team of fiery steeds to join the Latins in the war against Aeneas and the Trojans.[2] Virbius was worshipped as a god not only at Nemi but elsewhere; for in Campania we hear of a special priest devoted to his service.[3] Horses were excluded from the Arician grove and sanctuary because horses had killed Hippolytus.[4] It was unlawful to touch his image. Some thought that he was the sun.[5] "But the

---

[1] Euripides, *Hippolytus*, 20 *sqq.*; Apollodorus, *Epitoma*, i. 18 *sq.*, ed. R. Wagner; Hyginus, *Fabulae*, 47; Ovid, *Metam.* xv. 497 *sqq.*

[2] Virgil, *Aen.* vii. 761 *sqq.*, with the commentary of Servius; Ovid, *Fasti*, iii. 263 *sqq.*, vi. 735 *sqq.*; *id.*, *Metam.* xv. 497 *sqq.*; Scholiast on Persius, *Sat.* vi. 56, p. 347 *sq.*, ed. O. Jahn; Lactantius, *Divin. Inst.* i. 17; Pausanias, ii. 27. 4; Apollodorus, iii. 10. 3; Scholiast on Pindar, *Pyth.* iii. 96. It was perhaps in his character of a serpent that Aesculapius was said to have brought the dead Hippolytus to life. See my note on Pausanias, ii. 10. 3.

[3] An inscription in the public museum at Naples mentions a *flamen Virbialis* (*Corpus Inscriptionum Latinarum*, x., No. 1493). Another inscription mentions a similar priesthood at Aricia, but the inscription is forged (Orelli, *Inscript. Latin.* No. 1457; compare H. Dessau on *Corpus Inscriptionum*

Latinarum, xiv., No. 2213). The same title *flamen Virbialis* has sometimes been wrongly read in an inscription of Gratianopolis, in Narbonensian Gaul (*Corpus Inscriptionum Latinarum*, xii., No. 2238; Orelli, *Inscript. Latin.* Nos. 2212, 4022). For the worship of Virbius we have also the testimony of Servius, on Virgil, *Aen.* vii. 776: "*Nam et Virbius inter deos colitur.*"

[4] Virgil, *Aen.* vii. 779 *sq.*; Ovid, *Fasti*, iii. 265 *sq.*

[5] Servius on Virgil, *Aen.* vii. 776. Helbig proposed to identify as Virbius some bronze statuettes found at Nemi, which represent a young man naked except for a cloak thrown over his left arm, holding in his extended right hand a shallow bowl, while in his raised left hand he seems to have held a spear or staff on which he leaned. See *Bulletino dell' Inst. di Corrisp. Archeologica*, 1885, p. 229. But to this it has been objected by Rossbach (*op. cit.* p. 162) that Virbius appears to have

truth is," says Servius, "that he is a deity associated with
Diana, as Attis is associated with the Mother of the Gods,
and Erichthonius with Minerva, and Adonis with Venus." [1]
What the nature of that association was we shall enquire
presently. Here it is worth observing that in his long
and chequered career this mythical personage has displayed
a remarkable tenacity of life. For we can hardly doubt
that the Saint Hippolytus of the Roman calendar, who was
dragged by horses to death on the thirteenth of August,
Diana's own day, is no other than the Greek hero of the
same name, who after dying twice over as a heathen sinner
has been happily resuscitated as a Christian saint. [2]

It needs no elaborate demonstration to convince us that The
the stories told to account for Diana's worship at Nemi legends
of Nemi
are unhistorical. Clearly they belong to that large class of invented
myths which are made up to explain the origin of a religious to explain
the ritual.
ritual and have no other foundation than the resemblance,
real or imaginary, which may be traced between it and some
foreign ritual. The incongruity of these Nemi myths is
indeed transparent, since the foundation of the worship is
traced now to Orestes and now to Hippolytus, according as

been portrayed as an older, probably
bearded man (Ovid, *Metam.* xv. 538
sqq.).

[1] Servius on Virgil, *Aen.* vii. 761 ;
compare *id.* on *Aen.* vii. 84. See also
Ovid, *Metam.* xv. 545 *sq.*—

"*Hoc nemus inde colo de disque mi-
   noribus unus
Nomine sub dominae lateo atque ac-
   censeor illi.*"

[2] P. Ribadeneira, *Flos Sanctorum*
(Venice, 1763), ii. 93 *sq.*; *Acta Sanctorum*, August 13, pp. 4 *sqq.* (Paris
and Rome, 1867). The merit of
tracing the saint's pedigree belongs to
Mr. J. Rendel Harris. See his *Annotators of Codex Bezae* (London,
1901), pp. 101 *sq.* Prudentius has
drawn a picture of the imaginary
martyrdom which might melt the
stoniest heart (*Peristeph.* xi. p. 282 *sqq.*,
ed. Th. Obbarius). According to the
Acta Sanctorum the saint shared the
crown of martyrdom with twenty members of his household, of whom nineteen were beheaded, while one of

them, his nurse *Concordia*, was scourged
to death ("*plumbatis caesa*"). It is an
odd coincidence that his Greek proto-
type Hippolytus dedicated just twenty
horses to Aesculapius (Pausanias, ii. 27.
4) ; and it is another odd coincidence,
if it is nothing worse, that the bones
of Orestes, the other mythical hero of
Nemi, were buried beside the temple
of *Concordia* in Rome, and that Servius,
who mentions this tradition (on Virgil,
Aen. ii. 116), should immediately afterwards quote the words "*virgine caesa.*"
If we knew why the hero Hippolytus
dedicated just twenty horses to the god
who raised him from the dead, we
might perhaps know why the saint
Hippolytus went to heaven attended
by a glorious company of just twenty
martyrs. Bunsen courageously stood
out for the historical reality of the
martyr, whom he would fain identify
with his namesake the well-known
writer of the third century (*Hippolytus
and his Age*, London, 1852, i. pp.
212 *sqq.*).

this or that feature of the ritual has to be accounted for. The real value of such tales is that they serve to illustrate the nature of the worship by providing a standard with which to compare it; and further, that they bear witness indirectly to its venerable age by shewing that the true origin was lost in the mists of a fabulous antiquity. In the latter respect these Nemi legends are probably more to be trusted than the apparently historical tradition, vouched for by Cato the Elder, that the sacred grove was dedicated to Diana by a certain Egerius Baebius or Laevius of Tusculum, a Latin dictator, on behalf of the peoples of Tusculum, Aricia, Lanuvium, Laurentum, Cora, Tibur, Pometia, and Ardea.[1] This tradition indeed speaks for the great age of the sanctuary, since it seems to date its foundation sometime before 495 B.C., the year in which Pometia was sacked by the Romans and disappears from history.[2] But we cannot suppose that so barbarous a rule as that of the Arician priesthood was deliberately instituted by a league of civilised communities, such as the Latin cities undoubtedly were. It must have been handed down from a time beyond the memory of man, when Italy was still in a far ruder state than any known to us in the historical period. The credit of the tradition is rather shaken than confirmed by another story which ascribes the foundation of the sanctuary to a certain Manius Egerius, who gave rise to the saying, "There are many Manii at Aricia." This proverb some explained by alleging that Manius Egerius was the ancestor of a long and distinguished line, whereas others thought it meant that there were many ugly and deformed people at Aricia, and they derived the name Manius from *Mania*, a bogey or bugbear to frighten children.[3] A Roman satirist uses the name Manius as typical of the beggars who lay in wait for pilgrims on the Arician slopes.[4] These differences of opinion, together with the discrepancy between Manius Egerius of Aricia and Egerius Laevius of Tusculum, as well as the resemblance of both names to the mythical Egeria,[5] excite

Tradition that the grove of Nemi was dedicated by a Latin dictator.

---

[1] Cato, *Origines*, i., quoted by Priscian, *Inst.* iv. 21, vol. i. p. 129, ed. Hertz; *M. Catonis praeter librum de re rustica quae extant*, ed. H. Jordan, p. 12.

[2] Livy, ii. 25; Dionysius Halicarnas. *Antiquit. Roman.* vi. 29.

[3] Festus, p. 145, ed. C. O. Müller.

[4] Persius, *Sat.* vi. 55 *sqq.*

[5] Wissowa suggests that Manius

our suspicion. Yet the tradition recorded by Cato seems too circumstantial, and its sponsor too respectable, to allow us to dismiss it as an idle fiction.[1] Rather we may suppose that it refers to some ancient restoration or reconstruction of the sanctuary, which was actually carried out by the confederate states.[2] At any rate it testifies to a belief that the grove had been from early times a common place of worship for many of the oldest cities of the country, if not for the whole Latin confederacy.[3]

Another argument of antiquity may be drawn from some of the votive offerings found on the spot, such as a sacrificial ladle of bronze bearing Diana's name in archaic Greek letters,[4] and pieces of the oldest kind of Italian money, being merely shapeless bits of copper, unstamped and valued by weight.[5] But as the use of such old-fashioned money

Evidence of the antiquity of the grove.

Egerius was a half-forgotten male counterpart of Egeria (W. H. Roscher's *Lexikon d. griech. und röm. Mythologie, s.v.* "Egeria"); and Dessau observes that the name Egerius "*sine dubio cohaeret cum Egerio fonte*" (*Corpus Inscriptionum Latinarum*, xiv. p. 204). The same view is taken by Messrs. A. B. Cook and E. Pais. Mr. Cook holds that the original form of the names was Aegerius and Aegeria, which he would interpret as "the Oak God" and "the Oak Goddess." See A. B. Cook, "The European Sky-God," *Folk-lore*, xvi. (1905) pp. 291 *sq.*; E. Pais, *Ancient Legends of Roman History* (London, 1906), p. 142.

[1] As Cluverius seems to do (*Italia Antiqua*, p. 931).

[2] This is substantially the view of Prof. Wissowa, who holds that the reference is to the foundation of a common altar in the grove by all the members of the league (*Religion und Kultus der Römer*, p. 199).

[3] Scholars are not agreed as to whether the list of confederate Latin cities in Cato is complete, and whether the Latin dictator he mentions was the head of the league or only of Tusculum. In regard to the former question we must remember that the passage of Cato is known to us only from Priscian, who seems to have quoted no more than suited his purpose, which was merely

to illustrate a grammatical termination (*Ardeatis* for the later *Ardeas*). Probably, therefore, the original passage contained many more names of towns which Priscian did not think it needful to cite. This is the view of H. Dessau (in *Corpus Inscriptionum Latinarum*, xiv. p. 204). With regard to the second question, Mommsen held that the dictatorship in question was merely the chief magistracy of Tusculum, the presidency of the Latin league being vested in two praetors, not in a dictator (Livy, viii. 3. 9). Most scholars, however, appear to be of opinion that the dictator referred to was head of the league. See H. Jordan, *M. Catonis praeter librum de re rustica quae extant*, pp. xli. *sqq.*; J. Beloch, *Der italische Bund unter Roms Hegemonie* (Leipsic, 1880), p. 188; H. Nissen, *Italische Landeskunde*, ii. (Berlin, 1902) pp. 557 *sq.*

[4] G. H. Wallis, *Illustrated Catalogue*, pp. 5, 36; *Corpus Inscriptionum Latinarum*, xiv., No. 4186.

[5] *Bulletino di Corrisp. Archeologica*, 1885, p. 232; *Notizie degli Scavi*, 1885, pp. 255, 320; *id.* 1895, p. 108; G. H. Wallis, *Illustrated Catalogue*, pp. 5, 55. The use of this rude currency is said to have been superseded in the reign of Servius Tullius, who substituted stamped ingots of copper (Pliny, *Nat. Hist.* xxxiii. 43).

survived in offerings to the gods long after it vanished from daily life,[1] no great stress can be laid on its occurrence at Nemi as evidence of the age of the shrine.

§ 2. *Artemis and Hippolytus*

Origin of the Arician myths of Orestes and Hippolytus.

I have said that the Arician legends of Orestes and Hippolytus, though worthless as history, have a certain value in so far as they may help us to understand the worship at Nemi better by comparing it with the ritual and myths of other sanctuaries. We must ask ourselves, Why did the authors of these legends pitch upon Orestes and Hippolytus in order to explain Virbius and the King of the Wood? In regard to Orestes, the answer is obvious. He and the image of the Tauric Diana, which could only be appeased with human blood,[2] were dragged in to render intelligible the murderous rule of succession to the Arician priesthood. In regard to Hippolytus the case is not so plain. The manner of his death suggests readily enough a reason for the exclusion of horses from the grove; but this by itself seems hardly enough to account for the identification. We must try to probe deeper by examining the worship as well as the legend or myth of Hippolytus.

Worship of Hippolytus at Troezen.

He had a famous sanctuary at his ancestral home of Troezen, situated on that beautiful, almost landlocked bay, where groves of oranges and lemons, with tall cypresses soaring like dark spires above the garden of the Hesperides, now clothe the strip of fertile shore at the foot of the rugged mountains. Across the blue water of the tranquil bay, which it shelters from the open sea, rises Poseidon's sacred island, its peaks veiled in the sombre green of the pines. On this fair coast Hippolytus was worshipped. Within his sanctuary stood a temple with an ancient image. His service was performed by a priest who held office for life: every year a sacrificial festival was held in his honour; and his untimely fate was yearly mourned, with weeping and

[1] Livy, xxvi. 11. 9; Tacitus, *Historiae*, iv. 53; E. Babelon, *Monnaies de la République romaine*, i. pp. ii. *sq.*
[2] Herodotus, iv. 103; Euripides, *Iphigenia in Tauris*, 38 *sqq.*; Strabo, vi. 4. 2, p. 308; Pausanias, iii. 16. 7-10; K. O. Müller, *Die Dorier*,[2] i. 385 *sqq.*

doleful chants, by unwedded maids, who also dedicated locks of their hair in his temple before marriage.[1] His grave existed at Troezen, though the people would not shew it.[2] It has been suggested, with great plausibility, that in the handsome Hippolytus, beloved of Artemis, cut off in his youthful prime, and yearly mourned by damsels, we have one of those mortal lovers of a goddess who appear so often in ancient religion, and of whom Adonis is the most familiar type. The rivalry of Artemis and Phaedra for the affection of Hippolytus reproduces, it is said, under different names, the rivalry of Aphrodite and Proserpine for the love of Adonis, for Phaedra is merely a double of Aphrodite.[3] Certainly in the *Hippolytus* of Euripides the tragedy of the hero's death is traced directly to the anger of Aphrodite at his contempt for her power, and Phaedra is nothing but a tool of the goddess. Moreover, within the precinct of Hippolytus at Troezen there stood a temple of Peeping Aphrodite, which was so named, we are told, because from this spot the amorous Phaedra used to watch Hippolytus at his manly sports. Clearly the name would be still more appropriate if it was Aphrodite herself who peeped. And beside this temple of Aphrodite grew a myrtle-tree with pierced leaves, which the hapless Phaedra, in the pangs of love, had pricked with her bodkin.[4] Now the myrtle, with its glossy evergreen leaves, its red and white blossom, and its fragrant perfume, was Aphrodite's own tree, and legend associated it with the birth of Adonis.[5] At Athens also Hippolytus was intimately associated with Aphrodite, for on the south side of the Acropolis, looking towards Troezen, a barrow or sepulchral mound in his memory was shewn, and beside it stood a temple of Aphrodite, said to have been founded by Phaedra, which bore the name of the temple of Aphrodite at Hippo-

Hippolytus a mythical being of the Adonis type.

---

[1] Pausanias, ii. 32. 1; Euripides, *Hippolytus*, 1423-1430, with Paley's comment. Diodorus Siculus speaks (iv. 62) of the "godlike honours" accorded to Hippolytus at Troezen.

[2] Pausanias, i. 22. 1, ii. 32. 1.

[3] S. Wide, *De sacris Troezeniorum, Hermionensium, Epidauriorum* (Upsala, 1898), pp. 86 *sq.* C. Boetticher thought that "the whole legend of Hippolytus represents simply the con-flict of the worship of Aphrodite with that of Artemis at Troezen" (*Der Baumkultus der Hellenen*, p. 445, n. 2).

[4] Pausanias, ii. 32. 3.

[5] Servius on Virgil, *Aen.* v. 72; Pausanias, vi. 24. 7. As to the myrtle and Aphrodite, see C. Boetticher, *Der Baumkultus der Hellenen*, pp. 444 *sqq.*; V. Hehn, *Kulturpflanzen und Haustiere*[7] (Berlin, 1902), pp. 220 *sqq.*

lytus.[1] The conjunction, both in Troezen and in Athens, of his grave with a temple of the goddess of love is significant. Later on we shall meet with mounds in which the lovers of the great Asiatic goddess were said to lie buried.

The divine mistresses of Hippolytus associated with oaks.

If this view of the relation of Hippolytus to Artemis and Aphrodite is right, it is somewhat remarkable that both his divine mistresses appear to have been associated at Troezen with oaks. For Aphrodite was here worshipped under the title of Askraia, that is, she of the Fruitless Oak ;[2] and Hippolytus was said to have met his death not far from a sanctuary of Saronian Artemis, that is, Artemis of the Hollow Oak, for here the wild olive-tree was shewn in which the reins of his chariot became entangled, and so brought him to the ground.[3]

Orestes at Troezen.

It may not be without significance that Orestes, the other mythical hero of Nemi, also appears in the legendary history of Troezen. For at Troezen there was a temple of Wolfish Artemis, said to have been dedicated by Hippolytus, and in front of the temple stood a sacred stone upon which nine men, according to the legend, had cleansed Orestes from the guilt of his mother's murder. In the solemn rite they made use of water drawn from the Horse's Fount ; and as late as the second century of our era their descendants dined together on certain set days in a building called the Booth of Orestes. Before the building there grew a laurel-tree which was said to have sprung on the spot where the things used in purifying the matricide were buried. The old traveller Pausanias, to whom we owe so much of our knowledge of ancient Greece, could not learn why Hippo-

---

[1] Pausanias, i. 22. 1 ; Euripides, *Hippolytus*, 30 *sqq.*, with the scholiast's note ; Diodorus Siculus, iv. 62 ; J. Tzetzes, *Scholia on Lycophron*, 1329.

[2] Pausanias, ii. 32. 6 Ἀφροδίτης Ἀσκραίας, where Bekker and all subsequent editors have changed Ἀσκραίας into Ἀκραίας. But Ἀσκραίας has the better manuscript authority. The title is derived from *askra*, "a fruitless oak" (Hesychius, *s.v.* ἄσκρα). See Mr. A. B. Cook, "Zeus, Jupiter, and the Oak," *Classical Review*, xvii. (1903) pp. 415 *sq.*

[3] Pausanias, ii. 32. 10. In Greek *saronis* is a hollow oak. See Callimachus, *Hymn to Zeus*, 22 ; Hesychius and *Etymologicum Magnum*, *s.v.* σαρωνίδες ; A. B. Cook, "Zeus, Jupiter, and the Oak," *Classical Review*, xviii. (1904) p. 370. Mythology derived the name Saronian from a certain Saron, an ancient king of Troezen and a mighty hunter, who had been drowned while swimming after a doe (Pausanias, ii. 30. 7). In this mythical hunter associated with Artemis we may perhaps detect a duplicate of Hippolytus.

lytus dedicated a temple to Wolfish Artemis ; but he conjectured that it might have been because he extirpated the packs of wolves that used to scour the country.[1]

Another point in the myth of Hippolytus which deserves attention is the frequent recurrence of horses in it. His name signifies either " horse-loosed " or " horse-looser " ;[2] he consecrated twenty horses to Aesculapius at Epidaurus ;[3] he was killed by horses ; the Horse's Fount probably flowed not far from the temple which he built for Wolfish Artemis ; and horses were sacred to his grandsire Poseidon, who had an ancient sanctuary in the wooded island across the bay, where the ruins of it may still be seen in the pine-forest.[4] Lastly, Hippolytus's sanctuary at Troezen was said to have been founded by Diomede, whose mythical connexion both with horses and wolves is attested. For the Veneti, at the head of the Adriatic, were famed for their breed of horses, and they had a sacred grove of Diomede, at the spot where many springs burst forth from the foot of a lofty cliff, forming at once the broad and deep river Timavus (the modern Timao), which flows with a still and tranquil current into the neighbouring sea. Here the Veneti sacrificed a white horse to Diomede ; and associated with his grove were two others, sacred to Argive Hera and Aetolian Artemis. In these groves wild beasts were reported to lose their ferocity, . and deer to herd with wolves. Moreover, the horses of the district, famed for their speed, were said to have been branded with the mark of a wolf.[5] Thus Hippolytus was associated with the horse in many ways, and this association may have been used to explain more features of the Arician ritual than the mere exclusion of the animal from the sacred grove.[6]

Hippolytus in relation to horses and wolves.

---

[1] Pausanias, ii. 31. 4, 8, and 9.

[2] See Kühner-Blass, *Grammatik der griech. Sprache*, ii. 288 *sq.*

[3] Pausanias, ii. 27. 4.

[4] Pausanias, ii. 33. 2 with my commentary, vol. iii. pp. 285 *sq.*, vol. v. pp. 596 *sqq.*

[5] Strabo, v. 1. 4, 8, and 9, pp. 212, 214 *sq.* As to the topography, see Bunbury in Smith's *Dictionary of Greek and Roman Geography*, *s.v.* "Timavus" ; H. Nissen, *Italische Landeskunde*, ii. 233. I have to thank my friend Mr. A. B. Cook for drawing

my attention to the association of the horse and wolf in the early cults of Greece and Italy.

[6] M. Salomon Reinach would explain Hippolytus at Troezen as a sacred horse, which was torn to pieces by his worshippers at a solemn sacrifice, just as Dionysus Zagreus was said to have been rent in pieces by his worshippers. See S. Reinach, " Hippolyte," *Archiv für Religionswissenschaft*, x. (1907) pp. 47 - 60 ; *id. Cultes, Mythes, et Religions*, iii. (Paris, 1908) pp. 54-67.

To this point we shall return later on. Whether his relation to wolves was also invoked to account for any other aspect of the worship at Nemi we cannot say, since the wolf plays no part in the scanty notices of that worship which have come down to us.[1] But doubtless, as one of the wild creatures of the wood, the beast would be under the special care of Diana.

Hair offered before marriage to Hippolytus and others. The custom observed by Troezenian girls of offering tresses of their hair to Hippolytus before their wedding brings him into a relation with marriage, which at first sight seems out of keeping with his reputation as a confirmed bachelor. According to Lucian, youths as well as maidens at Troezen were forbidden to wed till they had shorn their hair in honour of Hippolytus, and we gather from the context that it was their first beard which the young men thus polled.[2] However we may explain it, a custom of this sort appears to have prevailed widely both in Greece and the East. Plutarch tells us that formerly it was the wont of boys at puberty to go to Delphi and offer of their hair to Apollo; Theseus, the father of Hippolytus, complied with the custom,[3] which lasted down into historical times.[4] Argive maidens, grown to womanhood, dedicated their tresses to Athena before marriage.[5] On the same occasion Megarian girls poured libations and laid clippings of their hair on the tomb of the maiden Iphinoe.[6] At the entrance to the temple of Artemis in Delos the grave of two maidens was shewn under an olive-tree. It was said that long ago they had come as pilgrims from a far northern land with offerings to Apollo, and dying in the sacred isle were buried there. The Delian virgins before marriage used to cut off a lock of their hair, wind it on a spindle, and lay it on the maidens' grave. The young men did the same, except that they twisted the down of their first beard round a wisp of grass or a green shoot.[7] In some places it was Artemis who

---

[1] No argument can be drawn from the bronze wolf-heads of Caligula's ships (above, p. 5, note 5), since these may have been purely ornamental.

[2] Lucian, *De dea Syria*, 60.

[3] Plutarch, *Theseus*, 5.

[4] Athenaeus, xiii. 83, p. 605A. For dedications of hair to Apollo see *Anthologia Palatina*, vi. 198, 279.

[5] Statius, *Theb*. ii. 253 *sqq*.

[6] Pausanias, i. 43. 4.

[7] Herodotus, iv. 33 *sq*.; Callimachus, *Hymn to Delos*, 291 *sqq*.; Pausanias, i. 43. 4.

received the offering of a maiden's hair before marriage.[1] At Panamara in Caria men dedicated locks of their hair in the temple of Zeus. The locks were enclosed in little stone boxes, some of them fitted with a marble lid or shutter, and the name of the dedicator was engraved on a square sinking in the stone, together with the name of the priest for the time being. Many of these inscribed boxes have been found of late years on the spot. None of them bear the names of women ; some of them are inscribed with the names of a father and his sons. All the dedications are to Zeus alone, though Hera was also worshipped with him at Panamara.[2] At Hierapolis, on the Euphrates, youths offered of their beards and girls of their tresses to the great Syrian goddess, and left the shorn hair in caskets of gold or silver, inscribed with their names, and nailed to the walls of the temple.[3] The custom of dedicating the first beard seems to have been common at Rome under the Empire.[4] Thus Nero consecrated his first beard in a golden box, studded with costly pearls, on the Capitol.[5]

Some light is perhaps thrown on the meaning of these practices by two ancient Oriental customs, the one Egyptian, the other Phoenician. When Egyptian boys or girls had recovered from sickness, their parents used to shave the children's heads, weigh the hair against gold or silver, and give the precious metal to the keepers of the sacred beasts, who bought food with it for the animals according to their tastes. These tastes varied with the nature of the beast, and the beast varied with the district. Where hawks were worshipped, the keepers chopped up flesh, and calling the birds in a loud voice, flung the gobbets up into the air, till the hawks stooped and caught them. Where cats, or ichneumons, or

Such offerings intended to communicate strength and fertility.

Egyptian practice.

---

[1] *Anthologia Palatina*, vi. 276, 277 ; Pollux, iii. 38 ; Hesychius, *s.v.* γάμων ἔθη. Pollux seems to imply that the hair was dedicated to Hera and the Fates as well as to Artemis.

[2] G. Deschamps and G. Cousin, in *Bulletin de Correspondance hellénique*, xi. (1887) pp. 390 *sq.* ; *id.* xii. (1888) pp. 97 *sq.*, 249 *sqq.*, 479-490.

[3] Lucian, *De dea Syria*, 60.

[4] J. Marquardt, *Privatleben der Römer*, pp. 599 *sq.*

[5] Suetonius, *Nero*, 12. On hair-offerings in general see G. A. Wilken, *Ueber das Haaropfer* (Amsterdam, 1886) (reprinted from the *Revue Coloniale Internationale*). On the hair-offerings of the Greeks see Fr. Wieseler, in *Philologus*, ix. (1854), pp. 711-715 ; G. Deschamps and G. Cousin, in *Bulletin de Correspondance hellénique*, xii. (1888) pp. 479 - 490 ; W. H. D. Rouse, *Greek Votive Offerings* (Cambridge, 1902), pp. 240-245.

fish were the local deities, the keepers crumbled bread in milk and set it before them, or threw it into the Nile. And similarly with the rest of the divine menagery.[1] Thus in Egypt the offerings of hair went to feed the worshipful animals.

In the sanctuary of the great Phoenician goddess Astarte at Byblus the practice was different. Here, at the annual mourning for the dead Adonis, the women had to shave their heads, and such of them as refused to do so were bound to prostitute themselves to strangers and to sacrifice to the goddess with the wages of their shame.[2] Though Lucian, who mentions the custom, does not say so, there are some grounds for thinking that the women in question were generally maidens, of whom this act of devotion was required as a preliminary to marriage.[3] In any case, it is clear that the goddess accepted the sacrifice of chastity as a substitute for the sacrifice of hair.[4] Why? By many people, as we shall afterwards see, the hair is regarded as in a special sense the seat of strength; and at puberty it might well be thought to contain a double portion of vital energy, since at that season it is the outward sign and manifestation of the newly-acquired power of reproducing the species. For that reason, we may suppose, the beard rather than the hair of the head is offered by males on this occasion. Thus the substitution permitted at Byblus becomes intelligible: the women gave of their fecundity to the goddess, whether they offered their hair or their chastity. But why, it may be asked, should they make such an offering to Astarte, who was herself the great goddess of love and fertility? What need had she to receive fecundity from

---

[1] Herodotus, ii. 65; Diodorus Siculus, i. 83. The latter writer's account is the fuller, and has been followed in the text.

[2] Lucian, *De dea Syria*, 6.

[3] W. Robertson Smith, *Religion of the Semites*,[2] p. 329. He refers to Sozomenus, *Histor. Eccles.* v. 10. 7; Socrates, *Histor. Eccles.* i. 18; and Eusebius, *Vita Constant.* iii. 58, from whose testimonies we learn that at Heliopolis, in Syria, it was the custom to prostitute maidens to strangers before marriage. Eusebius speaks of the religious prostitution of married women as well as of maidens. Constantine destroyed the temple of the goddess in which these impure rites seem to have been performed. To moderns, Heliopolis (the City of the Sun) is better known as Baalbec; its magnificent ruins are the finest remains of Greek architecture in the East.

[4] This is recognised by G. A. Wilken (*Ueber das Haaropfer*, p. 105).

her worshippers? Was it not rather for her to bestow it on them? Thus put, the question overlooks an important side of polytheism, perhaps we may say of ancient religion in general. The gods stood as much in need of their worshippers as the worshippers in need of them. The benefits conferred were mutual. If the gods made the earth to bring forth abundantly, the flocks and herds to teem, and the human race to multiply, they expected that a portion of their bounty should be returned to them in the shape of tithe or tribute. On this tithe, indeed, they subsisted, and without it they would starve. Their divine bellies had to be filled, and their divine reproductive energies to be recruited; hence men had to give of their meat and drink to them, and to sacrifice for their benefit what is most manly in man and womanly in woman. Sacrifices of the latter kind have too often been overlooked or misunderstood by the historians of religion. Other examples of them will meet us in the course of our enquiry. At the same time it may well be that the women who offered their hair to Astarte hoped to benefit through the sympathetic connexion which they thus established between themselves and the goddess; they may in fact have expected to fecundate themselves by contact with the divine source of fecundity. And it is probable that a similar motive underlay the sacrifice of chastity as well as the sacrifice of hair.

If the sacrifice of hair, especially of hair at puberty, is sometimes intended to strengthen the divine beings to whom it is offered by feeding or fertilising them, we can the better understand, not only the common practice of offering hair to the shadowy dead,[1] but also the Greek usage of shearing it for rivers, as the Arcadian boys of Phigalia did for the stream that runs in the depths of the tremendous woody glen below the city.[2] For next perhaps to rain and sunshine, nothing in nature so obviously contributes to fertilise a country as its rivers. Again, this view may set in a clearer light the custom of the Delian youths and maidens,

Hair offered to rivers as sources of fertility.

---

[1] G. A. Wilken, *Das Haaropfer*, pp. 61 *sqq.*; W. Robertson Smith, *Religion of the Semites*,[2] pp. 323 *sqq.*; I. Goldziher, *Muhammedanische Studien*, i. (Halle a. S. 1888) pp. 247 *sqq.* See also below, p. 102.

[2] Pausanias, viii. 41. 3. To the references given in my note on the passage add Pollux, ii. 30.

Delos and
Delphi as
centres of
fertilisa-
tion and
of fire.

who offered their hair on the maidens' tomb under the olive-tree. For at Delos, as at Delphi, one of Apollo's many functions was to make the crops grow and to fill the husbandman's barns; hence at the time of harvest tithe-offerings poured in to him from every side in the form of ripe sheaves, or, what was perhaps still more acceptable, golden models of them, which went by the name of the "golden summer."[1] The festival at which these first-fruits were dedicated may have been the 6th and 7th of the harvest-month Thargelion, corresponding to the 24th and 25th of May, for these were the birthdays of Artemis and Apollo respectively.[2] In Hesiod's day the corn-reaping began at the morning rising of the Pleiades, which then answered to our 9th of May,[3] and in Greece the wheat is still ripe about that time.[4] In return for these offerings the god sent out a sacred new fire from both his great sanctuaries at Delos and Delphi, thus radiating from them, as from central suns, the divine blessings of heat and light. A ship brought the new fire every year from Delos to Lemnos, the sacred island of the fire-god Hephaestus, where all fires were put out before its arrival, to be afterwards rekindled at the pure flame.[5] The fetching of the new fire from Delphi to Athens appears to have been a ceremony of great solemnity and pomp. All the chief Athenian magistrates repaired to Delphi for the purpose. The holy fire blazed or smouldered in a sacred

[1] Callimachus, *Hymn to Delos*, 278 *sqq.*; Pliny, *Nat. Hist.* iv. 91; Strabo, vi. 1. 15, p. 264; Plutarch, *De Pythiae oraculis*, 16. In Apollo's temple at Delphi there were dedicated a radish of gold, a beet of silver, and a turnip of lead, which was thought to signify the respective value of these vegetables (Pliny, *Nat. Hist.* xix. 86). A poet speaks of tithes and first-fruits hung up for Apollo on a high pillar at Delphi (Clement of Alexandria, *Strom.* i. 24. 164, p. 419, ed. Potter).

[2] Diogenes Laertius, *Vit. Philos.* ii. 44, iii. 2; Plutarch, *Quaest. Conviv.* viii. 1. 2; J. T. Wood, *Discoveries at Ephesus: Inscriptions from the great Theatre*, pp. 4, 16. Apollo's birthday (the 7th of Thargelion) was probably the festival known in the Delian calendar as the Apollonia, not the Delia as

was formerly supposed. The Delia seems to have fallen in early spring, not in early summer. See C. Robert in *Hermes*, xxi. (1886) pp. 161-169; Aug. Mommsen, *Feste der Stadt Athen* (Leipsic, 1898), p. 451. On this harvest-festival at Delos see W. Mannhardt, *Antike Wald- und Feldkulte*, pp. 232 *sqq.*, who, however, took the festival to be the Delia.

[3] Hesiod, *Works and Days*, 383 *sq.*; L. Ideler, *Handbuch der mathematischen und technischen Chronologie*, i. 242.

[4] *Folk-lore*, i. (1890) p. 518. As to the season of the ripening of the corn in Greece both in ancient and modern times, see G. Busolt's discussion of the evidence, *Griechische Geschichte*, iii. 2 (Gotha, 1904), pp. 909 *sqq.*, note.

[5] Philostratus, *Heroica*, xx. 24.

tripod borne on a chariot and tended by a woman who was
called the Fire-bearer.   Soldiers, both horse and foot, escorted
it ; magistrates, priests, and heralds accompanied it ; and
the procession moved to the music of trumpet and fife.[1]
We do not know on what occasion the fire was thus solemnly
sent from Delphi to Athens, but we may conjecture that
it was when the Pythaists at Athens, watching from the
hearth of Lightning Zeus, saw lightning flash over Harma
on Mount Parnes, for then they sent a sacrifice to Delphi
and may have received the fire in return.[2]   After the great
defeat of the Persians at Plataea, the people of that city
extinguished all the fires in the country, deeming them
defiled by the presence of the barbarians.   Having done so
they relit them at a pure new fire fetched by a runner from
the altar of the common hearth at Delphi.[3]

Now the maidens on whose grave the Delian youths
and damsels laid their shorn locks before marriage, were
said to have died in the island after bringing the harvest
offering, wrapt in wheaten straw, from the land of the
Hyperboreans in the far north.[4]   Thus they were in
popular opinion the mythical representatives of those bands
of worshippers who bore, year by year, the yellow sheaves
with dance and song to Delos.   But in fact they had once
been much more than this.   For an examination of their
names, which are commonly given as Hekaerge and Opis,
has led modern scholars to conclude, with every appearance
of probability, that these maidens were originally mere
duplicates of Artemis herself.[5]   Perhaps indeed we may

The graves
of Apollo
and
Artemis
at Delos.

---

[1] *Bulletin de Correspondance hellénique*, xviii. (1894) pp. 87-93 ; *id.*
xx. (1896) pp. 639-641 ; E. Curtius
in *Archäologischer Anzeiger*, 1895, pp.
109 *sq.* ; Dittenberger, *Sylloge Inscriptionum Graecarum*,[2] Nos. 611, 665,
718.

[2] Strabo, ix. 2. 11, p. 404.

[3] Plutarch, *Aristides*, 20.   Probably
the custom of sending out new fire
from Delos and Delphi was common,
though the existing evidence of it is
scanty.   The same remark applies to
the practice of bringing tithes of the
harvest to these sanctuaries.

[4] Herodotus, iv. 33 ; Callimachus,

Hymn to Delos, 278 *sqq.*   Herodotus
does not tell us in what the sacred
offerings consisted ; Pausanias says
(i. 31. 2) that no one knew what
they were.   But from the evidence
of Callimachus, compared with that
of Pliny (*Nat. Hist.* iv. 91) and Mela
(iii. 37), it appears that they were
believed to be the first-fruits of the
corn.

[5] H. Stein on Herodotus, iv. 33 ;
O. Crusius in W. H. Roscher's *Lexikon
der griech. und röm. Mythologie*, i.
2813, 2831 ; Preller-Robert, *Griechische
Mythologie*, i. 298 *sq.* ; Wernicke, in
Pauly-Wissowa, *Real-Encyclopädie der*

go a step farther. For sometimes one of this pair of
Hyperboreans appears as a male, not a female, under the
name of the Far-shooter (Hekaergos), which was a common
epithet of Apollo.[1] This suggests that the two were
originally the heavenly twins themselves, Apollo and
Artemis, and that the two graves which were shewn at
Delos, one before and the other behind the sanctuary of
Artemis, may have been at first the tombs of these great
deities, who were thus laid to their rest on the spot where
they had been born. As the one grave received offerings
of hair, so the other received the ashes of the victims which
were burned on the altar.[2] Both sacrifices, if I am right,
were designed to strengthen and fertilise the divine powers
who made the earth to wave with the golden harvest, and
whose mortal remains, like the miracle-working bones of
saints in the Middle Ages, brought wealth to their fortunate
possessors. Ancient piety was not shocked by the sight
of the tomb of a dead god. The grave of Apollo himself
was shewn at his other great sanctuary of Delphi,[3] and
this perhaps explains its disappearance at Delos. The
priests of the rival shrines may have calculated that one
tomb sufficed even for a god, and that two might prove a
stumbling-block to any but the most robust faith. Acting
on this prudent conviction, they may have adjusted their
respective claims to the possession of the holy sepulchre

class. Altertumswissenschaft, ii. coll.
1355, 1356, 1357, 1358, 1359, 1380,
1383, 1393, 1402. The names of
the maidens were variously given as
Hyperoche and Laodice (Herodotus,
iv. 33), or Hekaerge and Opis,
(Pausanias, i. 43. 4, v. 7. 8 ; Servius
on Virgil, *Aen.* xi. 532), or Upis,
Loxo, and Hekaerge (Callimachus,
Hymn to Delos, 292). Herodotus
further mentions (iv. 35) another pair
of Hyperborean maidens, Arge and
Opis by name, who came with Apollo
and Artemis to Delos, and were buried
behind the sanctuary of Artemis in
the island. They are clearly the
equivalents of the Hekaerge and Opis
or Upis of the other writers. For
Hekaerge as an epithet of Artemis
see Servius, *loc. cit.* ; Clement of

Alexandria, *Strom.* v. 8. 49, p. 674,
ed. Potter, quoting Apollodorus of
Corcyra : μέλπετε ὦ παῖδες ἑκάεργον καὶ
ἑκαέργαν. For Opis or Upis as a
name of Artemis see Macrobius, *Saturn.*
v. 22. 3-6 ; Callimachus, *Hymn to
Artemis*, 204 ; Palaephatus, *De in-
credib.* 32.

[1] Pseudo-Plato, *Axiochus*, p. 371A ;
Servius on Virgil, *Aen.* xi. 532 :
" *Alii putant Opim et Hecaergon
nutritores Apollinis et Dianae fuisse ;
hinc itaque Opim ipsam Dianam
cognominatam, quod supra dictum est,
Apollinem vero Hecaergon.*"

[2] Herodotus, iv. 34 *sq.* According
to Herodotus, each grave contained
the dust of a pair of Hyperborean
damsels.

[3] Porphyry, *Vita Pythagorae*, 16.

by leaving Apollo to sleep undisturbed at Delphi, while his
grave at Delos was dexterously converted into the tomb
of a blessed virgin by the easy grammatical change of
Hekaergos into *Hekaerge*.

But how, it may be asked, does all this apply to Hip- Hippolytus
and
Artemis.
polytus? Why attempt to fertilise the grave of a bachelor who
paid all his devotions to a barren virgin? What seed could
take root and spring up in so stony a soil? The question
implies the popular modern notion of Diana or Artemis as
the pattern of a straight-laced maiden lady with a taste for
hunting. No notion could well be further from the truth.
To the ancients, on the contrary, she was the ideal and Artemis a
goddess of
the wild
life of
nature.
embodiment of the wild life of nature—the life of plants,
of animals, and of men—in all its exuberant fertility and
profusion. As a recent German writer has admirably put
it : " From of old a great goddess of nature was everywhere
worshipped in Greece. She was revered on the mountain
heights as in the swampy lowlands, in the rustling woods
and by the murmuring spring. To the Greek her hand
was everywhere apparent. He saw her gracious blessing
in the sprouting meadow, in the ripening corn, in the
healthful vigour of all living things on earth, whether the
wild creatures of the wood and the fell, or the cattle which
man has tamed to his service, or man's own offspring from
the cradle upward. Her destroying anger he perceived in
the blight of vegetation, in the inroads of wild beasts on
his fields and orchards, as well as in the last mysterious
end of life, in death. No empty personification, like the
earth conceived as a goddess, was this deity, for such
abstractions are foreign to every primitive religion ; she
was an all-embracing power of nature, everywhere the
object of a similar faith, however her names differed with the
place in which she was believed to abide, with the emphasis
laid on her gloomy or kindly aspect, or with the particular
side of her energy which was specially revered. And as
the Greek divided everything in animated nature into male
and female, he could not imagine this female power of
nature without her male counterpart. Hence in a number Artemis
not
originally
regarded as
a virgin.
of her older worships we, find Artemis associated with a
nature-god of similar character, to whom tradition assigned

different names in different places. In Laconia, for instance, she was mated with the old Peloponnesian god Karneios, in Arcadia more than once with Poseidon, elsewhere with Zeus, Apollo, Dionysus, and so on."[1] The truth is, that the word *parthenos* applied to Artemis, which we commonly translate virgin, means no more than an unmarried woman,[2] and in early days the two things were by no means the same. With the growth of a purer morality among men a stricter code of ethics is imposed by them upon their gods; the stories of the cruelty, deceit, and lust of these divine beings are glossed lightly over or flatly rejected as blasphemies, and the old ruffians are set to guard the laws which before they broke. In regard to Artemis, even the ambiguous *parthenos* seems to have been merely a popular epithet, not an official title. As Dr. Farnell has well pointed out, there was no public worship of Artemis the chaste; so far as her sacred titles bear on the relation of the sexes, they shew that, on the contrary, she was, like Diana in Italy, specially concerned with the

[1] Wernicke, in Pauly - Wissowa's *Real-Encyclopädie der class. Altertumswissenschaft,* ii. 1339. This general statement the writer supports with a wealth of detailed evidence, to which I can only refer the reader.

[2] This appears from the name *Partheniai* applied at Sparta to the men who were born of the *parthenoi* (unmarried women) during the absence of the married men at the Messenian war. See Ephorus, cited by Strabo, vi. 3. 3, p. 279. Whether this explanation was historically correct or not (and other explanations of it were given, see W. L. Newman on Aristotle, *Politics,* vii. (v.) 7, p. 1306 b 29), it proves that in Greek of the best period *parthenos* did not connote chastity. Compare what Herodotus says of the Thracians (v. 6): τὰς δὲ παρθένους οὐ φυλάσσουσι, ἀλλ' ἐῶσι τοῖσι αὐταὶ βούλονται ἀνδράσι μίσγεσθαι. As to the worship of unmarried goddesses in Western Asia, Sir W. M. Ramsay observes: "It is, in fact, probable, though with our present knowledge not susceptible of proof, that the term Parthenos in connection with the Anatolian system should be rendered simply as 'the Unmarried,' and should be regarded as evidence of the religious existence of the pre-Greek social system. The Parthenos goddess was also the Mother; and however much the Parthenoi who formed part of her official retinue may have been modified by Greek feeling, it is probable that originally the term indicated only that they were not cut off by marriage from the divine life" (*Cities and Bishoprics of Phrygia,* i. p. 96). Similarly in a celebrated passage of Isaiah (vii. 14) the Hebrew word (עַלְמָה) which is translated "virgin" in our English version means no more than "young woman." A correct translation would have obviated the necessity for the miracle which so many generations of devout but unlearned readers have discovered in the text; for while it would unquestionably be a miracle if a virgin were to conceive and bear a son, there is nothing whatever miraculous or even unusual about a young woman doing so.

loss of virginity and with child-bearing, and that she not only assisted but encouraged women to be fruitful and multiply; indeed, if we may take Euripides's word for it, in her capacity of midwife she would not even speak to childless women. Further, it is highly significant that while her titles and the allusions to her functions mark her out clearly as the patroness of childbirth, we find none that recognise her distinctly as a deity of marriage.[1] Nothing, however, sets the true character of Artemis as a goddess of fecundity, though not of wedlock, in a clearer light than her constant identification with the unmarried, but not chaste, Asiatic goddesses of love and fertility, who were worshipped with rites of notorious profligacy at their popular sanctuaries.[2] At Ephesus, the most celebrated of all the seats of her worship,[3] her universal motherhood was set forth unmistakably in her sacred image. Copies of it have come down to us which agree in their main features, though they differ from each other in some details. They represent the goddess with a multitude of protruding breasts; the heads of animals of many kinds, both wild and tame, spring from the front of her body in a series of bands that extend from the breasts to the feet; bees, roses,

Artemis a goddess of childbirth.

The Ephesian Artemis.

---

[1] L. R. Farnell, *The Cults of the Greek States*, ii. 444. The whole of Dr. Farnell's treatment of this subject is excellent (pp. 442-449). He suggests doubtfully that the epithets *Peitho*, *Hegemone*, and *Eukleia* may possibly refer to marriage. But clearly "persuasion," "leader," and "good fame" do not in themselves imply any allusion to wedlock. The passage of Euripides referred to in the text is *Supplices*, 958 *sq.*: οὐδ᾽ Ἄρτεμις λοχία προσφθέγ-ξαιτ᾽ ἂν τὰς ἀτέκνους.

[2] Thus she was identified with Anaitis (Plutarch, *Artoxerxes*, 27; Dittenberger, *Sylloge Inscr. Graec.*[2] No. 775), and with Nana (*Corpus Inscriptionum Atticarum*, iii. 131), or Nanaea, the goddess of Elymais (2 Maccabees, i. 13 and 15, compared with Polybius, xxxi. 11, and Josephus, *Antiquit. Jud.* xii. 9). This Nanaea was sometimes identified with Aphrodite instead of with Artemis (Appian, *Syriace*, 66). She seems to have

been the old Babylonian goddess Nana, Nanai, or Nannaia, who was identical with the Ishtar (Astarte) of Erech. See H. Zimmern, in Schrader's *Die Keilinschriften und das Alte Testament*,[3] p. 422; R. F. Harper, *Assyrian and Babylonian Literature* (New York, 1901), pp. 116 *sq.*, 245; W. H. Roscher's *Lexikon der griech. und röm. Mythologie*, iii. 4 *sq. s.v.* "Nana." For the identification of Artemis with another Semitic mother-goddess, see W. Robertson Smith, *Kinship and Marriage in Early Arabia*[2] (London, 1903), p. 298. As to the dissolute worship of Anaitis, see Strabo, xi. 14, 16, p. 532. And as to the identification of Artemis with Asiatic goddesses of this type see L. R. Farnell, *Cults of the Greek States*, ii. 478 *sqq.*; Wernicke, in Pauly-Wissowa, *Encycl. d. class. Alter.* ii. 1369 *sqq.*

[3] Pausanias, iv. 31. 8; Dittenberger, *Sylloge Inscript. Graecarum*,[2] No. 656.

and sometimes butterflies, decorate her sides from the hips downward. The animals that thus appear to issue from her person vary in the different copies of the statue; they include lions, bulls, stags, horses, goats, and rams. Moreover, lions rest on her upper arms; in at least one copy, serpents twine round her lower arms; her bosom is festooned with a wreath of blossoms, and she wears a necklace of acorns. In one of the statues the breast of her robe is decorated with two winged male figures, who hold sheaves in both hands.[1] It would be hard to devise a more expressive symbol of exuberant fertility, of prolific maternity, than these remarkable images. No doubt the Ephesian Artemis, with her eunuch priests and virgin priestesses,[2] was an Oriental, whose worship the Greek colonists took over from the aborigines.[3] But that they should have adopted it and identified the goddess with their own Artemis is proof enough that the Grecian divinity, like her Asiatic sister, was at bottom a personification of the teeming life of nature.

Hippolytus the male consort of Artemis.
To return now to Troezen, we shall probably be doing no injustice either to Hippolytus or to Artemis if we suppose that the relation between them was once of a tenderer nature

[1] The statues on which this description is based are in the Vatican, the Lateran, and the Palazzo dei Conservatori on the Capitol at Rome. The first of these is figured and described in Baumeister's *Denkmäler*, i. 130 *sq.*, and the second is described by O. Benndorf and R. Schoene, *Die antiken Bildwerke des Lateranischen Museums*, pp. 260 *sq.* See also Roscher's *Lexik. d. griech. und röm. Myth.* i. 588 *sqq.*; S. Reinach, *Répertoire de la Statuaire grecque et romaine*, i. pp. 298, 299, 300, 302, ii. pp. 321 *sq.* Both the Vatican and the Lateran statues have the necklace of acorns, and the Lateran copy (No. 768) has in addition a circlet of acorns hanging on the bosom. The acorns probably refer to the oak-tree under which the Amazons were said to have set up the image of the goddess at Ephesus (Callimachus, *Hymn to Artemis*, 237 *sqq.*). The statue in the Palazzo dei Conservatori (No. 47) has serpents twined round the arms. The many breasts of the Ephesian Artemis are mentioned by Minucius Felix (*Octavius*, xxii. 5). On the worship of the Ephesian Artemis continued as that of the Virgin Mary see Sir W. M. Ramsay, "The Worship of the Virgin Mary at Ephesus," *The Expositor*, June 1905, pp. 401 *sqq.*

[2] Strabo, xiv. 1. 23, p. 641. That a goddess of fertility should be served by such ministers may strike us as a contradiction. Yet it is typical of the Oriental worship of the great Mother Goddess. I have suggested an explanation of the custom elsewhere. See *Adonis, Attis, Osiris*, Second Edition, pp. 236 *sqq.*

[3] Pausanias, vii. 2. 7 *sq.*; Preller-Robert, *Griechische Mythologie*, i. 329; L. R. Farnell, *The Cults of the Greek States*, ii. 480 *sqq.*

than appears in classical literature. We may conjecture that
if he spurned the love of women, it was because he enjoyed
the love of a goddess.[1] On the principles of early religion,
she who fertilises nature must herself be fertile, and to be
that she must necessarily have a male consort. If I am
right, Hippolytus was the consort of Artemis at Troezen,
and the shorn tresses offered to him by the Troezenian
youths and maidens before marriage were designed to
strengthen his union with the goddess, and so to promote the
fruitfulness of the earth, of cattle, and of mankind. It is
some confirmation of this view that within the precinct of
Hippolytus at Troezen there were worshipped two female
powers named Damia and Auxesia, whose connexion with
the fertility of the ground is unquestionable. When
Epidaurus suffered from a dearth, the people, in obedience
to an oracle, carved images of Damia and Auxesia out of
sacred olive wood, and no sooner had they done so and set
them up than the earth bore fruit again. Moreover, at
Troezen itself, and apparently within the precinct of Hippolytus, a curious festival of stone-throwing was held in honour
of these maidens, as the Troezenians called them ; and it is
easy to show that similar customs have been practised in
many lands for the express purpose of ensuring good crops.[2]
In the story of the tragic death of the youthful Hippolytus we
may discern an analogy with similar tales of other fair but
mortal youths who paid with their lives for the brief rapture
of the love of an immortal goddess. These hapless lovers
were probably not always mere myths, and the legends which
traced their spilt blood in the purple bloom of the violet, the
scarlet stain of the anemone, or the crimson flush of the
rose were no idle poetic emblems of youth and beauty fleet-

---

[1] Indeed the eloquent church father
Lactantius let the cat out of the bag
when he bluntly called Hippolytus the
lover of Artemis (*Divin. Institut.*
i. 17).

[2] Herodotus, v. 82-87 ; Pausanias,
ii. 30. 4, ii. 32. 2 ; Schol. on Aristides,
vol. iii. pp. 598 *sq.*, ed. Dindorf. As
H. Stein (on Herodotus, v. 82) rightly
observes, Damia and Auxesia were

"goddesses of tilth and of the fruitful field, agrarian deities who were
accordingly compared and identified
with Demeter and Kora [Proserpine],
but who were in truth only separate
personifications of the two sides of
Demeter's character." See further my
note on Pausanias, ii. 30. 4. We
shall return hereafter to the custom of
stone-throwing as a charm to fertilise
the fields.

ing as the summer flowers. Such fables contain a deeper philosophy of the relation of the life of man to the life of nature—a sad philosophy which gave birth to a tragic practice. What that philosophy and that practice were we shall learn later on.

§ 3. *Recapitulation*

Virbius the male consort of Diana.

We can now perhaps understand why the ancients identified Hippolytus, the consort of Artemis, with Virbius, who, according to Servius, stood to Diana as Adonis to Venus, or Attis to the Mother of the Gods. For Diana, like Artemis, was a goddess of fertility in general, and of childbirth in particular.[1] As such she, like her Greek counterpart, needed a male partner. That partner, if Servius is right, was Virbius. In his character of the founder of the sacred grove and first king of Nemi, Virbius is clearly the mythical predecessor or archetype of the line of priests who served Diana under the title of Kings of the Wood, and who came, like him, one after the other, to a violent end.[2] It is natural, therefore, to conjecture that they stood to the goddess of the grove in the same relation in which Virbius stood to her ; in short, that the mortal King of the Wood had for his queen the woodland Diana herself.[3] If the sacred tree which he guarded with his life was supposed, as seems probable, to be her special embodiment, her priest may not only have worshipped it as his goddess but embraced it as his wife. There is at least nothing absurd in the supposition, since even in the time of Pliny a noble Roman used thus to treat a beautiful beech-tree in another sacred grove of Diana on the Alban hills. He embraced it, he kissed it, he lay under its shadow, he poured wine on its trunk. Apparently he took the tree for the goddess.[4] The custom of physically marrying men and women to trees is still practised in India and other

[1] See, for example, Catullus's fine poem on her (No. xxxiv.).

[2] This was pointed out long ago by P. Buttmann (*Mythologus*, ii. 151).

[3] Seneca speaks of Diana as "*regina nemorum*" or "Queen of the Woods" (*Hippolytus*, 406), perhaps with a reminiscence of the *Rex Nemorensis*, as Mr. A. B. Cook has suggested (*Classical Review*, xvi. (1902) p. 373, note 4).

[4] Pliny, *Nat. Hist.* xvi. 242, pointed out to me by Mr. A. B. Cook, who compares Herodotus, vii. 31.

parts of the East.[1]   Why should it not have obtained in ancient Latium ?

Reviewing the evidence as a whole, we may conclude Summary of results. that the worship of Diana in her sacred grove at Nemi was of great importance and immemorial antiquity ; that she was revered as the goddess of woodlands and of wild creatures, probably also of domestic cattle and of the fruits of the earth ; that she was believed to bless men and women with offspring and to aid mothers in childbed ; that her holy fire, tended by chaste virgins, burned perpetually in a round temple within the precinct ; that associated with her was a water-nymph Egeria who discharged one of Diana's own functions by succouring women in travail, and who was popularly supposed to have mated with an old Roman king in the sacred grove ; further, that Diana of the Wood herself had a male companion Virbius by name, who was to her what Adonis was to Venus, or Attis to Cybele ; and, lastly, that this mythical Virbius was represented in historical times by a line of priests known as Kings of the Wood, who regularly perished by the swords of their successors, and whose lives were in a manner bound up with a certain tree in the grove, because so long as that tree was uninjured they were safe from attack.

A curious monument of the ill-fated dynasty appears The double-headed bust at Nemi probably a portrait of the King of the Wood and his successor. to have come down to us in a double-headed bust which was found in the sanctuary at Nemi. It represents two men of heavy and somewhat coarse features and a grim expression. The type of face is similar in both heads, but there are marked differences between them ; for while the one is young and beardless with shut lips and a steadfast gaze, the other is a man of middle life with a tossed and matted beard, wrinkled brows, a wild anxious look in the eyes, and an open grinning mouth. But perhaps the most singular thing about the two heads are the leaves with scalloped edges which are plastered, so to say, on the necks of both busts and apparently also under the eyes of the younger figure. The leaves have been interpreted as oak leaves, and this interpretation, which is not free from doubt, is confirmed by the resemblance to an oak leaf which the

[1] See below, vol. ii. pp. 26 *sq*., 56 *sq*., 100 *sq*., 316 *sqq*.

moustache of the older figure clearly presents when viewed
in profile. Various explanations of this remarkable monument have been proposed ; but the most probable theory
appears to be that the older figure represents the priest of
Nemi, the King of the Wood, in possession, while the other
face is that of his youthful adversary and possible successor.
This theory would explain the coarse heavy type of both
faces, which is neither Greek nor Roman but apparently
barbarian ; for as the priest of Nemi had always to be a
runaway slave, he would commonly be a member of an
alien and barbarous race. Further, it would explain the
striking contrast between the set determined gaze of the
younger man and the haggard, scared look of the older ; on
the one face we seem to read the resolution to kill, on the
other the fear to die. Lastly, it would explain very simply
the leaves that cling like cerements to the necks and breasts
of both ; for we shall see later on that the priest was probably regarded as an embodiment of the tree which he
guarded, and human representatives of tree spirits are most
naturally draped in the foliage of the tree which they
personate. Hence if the leaves on the two heads are indeed
oak leaves, as they have been thought to be, we should have
to conclude that the tree which the King of the Wood
guarded and personated was an oak. There are independent reasons for holding that this was so, but the
consideration of them must be deferred for the present.[1]

A wider
survey re-
quired to
solve the
problem
of Nemi.

Clearly these conclusions do not of themselves suffice to
explain the peculiar rule of succession to the priesthood.
But perhaps the survey of a wider field may lead us to

[1] As to the double-headed bust see
W. Helbig, in *Notizie degli Scavi*,
1885, p. 227 ; O. Rossbach, *op. cit.*
p. 159 ; G. H. Wallis, *Illustrated
Catalogue of Classical Antiquities from
the Site of the Temple of Diana, Nemi*,
pp. 32 *sq.* ; A. B. Cook, in *Classical
Review*, xvi. (1902) p. 373 ; *id.* "The
European Sky-God," *Folk-lore*, xvi.
(1905) pp. 289 *sqq.* ; F. Granger,
"A Portrait of the Rex Nemorensis,"
Classical Review, xxi. (1907) pp. 194-
197 ; *id.* in *Classical Review*, xxii.
(1908) p. 217 ; J. G. Frazer, "The
Leafy Bust at Nemi," *Classical Review*,

xxii. (1908) pp. 147-149. The interpretation adopted in the text is that
of Professor F. Granger. The way
had been prepared for it by Mr. A. B.
Cook's suggestion that the busts represent "the double form of Diana's
favourite, Hippolytus-Virbius." Previous writers took the view that the
heads were those of water-gods. As
to the identification of the leaves on
the busts, about which botanists are
not agreed, see Mr. Francis Darwin's
letter to me, quoted in my article,
"The Leafy Bust at Nemi" (*l.c.*).

think that they contain in germ the solution of the problem. To that wider survey we must now address ourselves. It will be long and laborious, but may possess something of the interest and charm of a voyage of discovery, in which we shall visit many strange foreign lands, with strange foreign peoples, and still stranger customs. The wind is in the shrouds: we shake out our sails to it, and leave the coast of Italy behind us for a time.

CHAPTER II

PRIESTLY KINGS

The two questions to be answered.

THE questions which we have set ourselves to answer are mainly two : first, why had Diana's priest at Nemi, the King of the Wood, to slay his predecessor ? second, why before doing so had he to pluck the branch of a certain tree which the public opinion of the ancients identified with Virgil's Golden Bough ? The two questions are to some extent distinct, and it will be convenient to consider them separately. We begin with the first, which, with the preliminary enquiries, will occupy this and several following volumes. In the last part of the book I shall suggest an answer to the second question.

The first point on which we fasten is the priest's title. Why was he called the King of the Wood ? Why was his office spoken of as a kingdom ?

Priestly kings in ancient Italy and Greece.

The union of a royal title with priestly duties was common in ancient Italy and Greece. At Rome and in other cities of Latium there was a priest called the Sacrificial King or King of the Sacred Rites, and his wife bore the title of Queen of the Sacred Rites.[1] In republican Athens the second annual magistrate of the state was called the King, and his wife the Queen ; the functions of both were religious. For example, the king superintended the celebration of the Eleusinian mysteries, the Lenaean festival of Dionysus, and the torch-races, which were held at several of

---

[1] J. Marquardt, *Römische Staatsverwaltung*, iii.² 321 *sqq.* Kings of the Sacred Rites are known from inscriptions to have existed at Lanuvium, Bovillae, and Tusculum. See *Corpus Inscriptionum Latinarum*, xiv., Nos. 2089, 2413, 2634. At Rome the Sacrificial King held office for life (Dionysius Halicarn. *Antiquit. Rom.* iv. 74. 4).

the great Athenian festivals.   Moreover, he presided at the
curious trials of animals and inanimate objects, which had
caused the death of a human being.   To him in short were
assigned, in the words of Plato, " the most solemn and most
truly ancestral rites of the ancient sacrifices." [1]   Many other
Greek democracies had titular kings, whose duties, so far as
they are known, seem to have been priestly, and to have
centred round the Common Hearth of the state.[2]   For
example, in Cos the King sacrificed to Hestia, the goddess of
the hearth, the equivalent of the Italian Vesta ; and he
received the hide and one leg of the victim as his perquisite.[3]
In Mytilene the kings, of whom there were several, invited to
banquets at the Common Hearth those guests whom the
state delighted to honour.[4]   In Chios, if any herdsman or
shepherd drove his cows, his sheep, or his swine to pasture in
a sacred grove, the first person who witnessed the trans-
gression was bound to denounce the transgressor to the
kings, under pain of incurring the wrath of the god and,
what was perhaps even worse, of having to pay a fine to the
offended deity.[5]   In the same island the king was charged
with the duty of pronouncing the public curses,[6] a spiritual
weapon of which much use was made by the ancients.[7]
Every eighth year the King at Delphi took part in a quaint

---

[1] Plato, *Politicus*, p. 290 E ; Aristotle, *Constitution of Athens*, 57 ;
Lysias, *Or.* vi. 4 ; G. Gilbert, *Handbuch der griechischen Staatsalter-
thümer*,[2] i. 281 *sqq.*

[2] Aristotle, *Politics*, viii. (vi.) 8. 20,
p. 1322 b 26 *sqq.* ; G. Gilbert, *op. cit.*
ii. 323 *sq.* ; G. F. Schömann, *Griechische Alterthümer*,[4] i. 145 *sq.*, ii.
423 *sq.*

[3] Dittenberger, *Sylloge Inscrip-
tionum Graecarum*,[2] No. 616 ; Ch.
Michel, *Recueil d'Inscriptions grecques*,
No. 716.

[4] P. Cauer, *Delectus Inscriptionum
Graecarum*,[2] No. 431, lines 46 *sqq.*
Another inscription in the same collection (No. 428) also refers to the kings
of Mytilene.   Both inscriptions are
printed in Ch. Michel's *Recueil*, Nos.
356, 357.

[5] Dittenberger, *Sylloge Inscriptionum*

Graecarum,[2] No. 570; Ch. Michel,
Recueil, No. 707.

[6] P. Cauer, *Delectus Inscriptionum
Graecarum*,[2] No. 496 ; Ch. Michel,
Recueil, No. 1383.

[7] G. F. Schömann, *Handbuch der
griech. Alterthümer*,[4] ii. 270 *sqq.* ; E.
Ziebarth, "Der Fluch im griechischen
Recht," *Hermes*, xxx. (1895) pp.
57-70; Miss J. E. Harrison, *Prolego-
mena to the Study of Greek Religion*[2]
(Cambridge, 1908), pp. 138-145 ; and
my note on Pausanias, iii. 2. 7.   For
example, the people of Teos cursed
poisoners and all persons who hindered
the importation of corn (Cauer, *op. cit.*
No. 480; Ch. Michel, *op. cit.* No.
1318).   On the other hand, at Athens
in the time of Solon public curses were
levelled at all who exported anything
but olive oil (Plutarch, *Solon*, 24).
These particular curses may interest
students of the history of free trade.

ceremony. He sat in public distributing barley-meal and pulse to all who chose to apply for the bounty, whether citizens or strangers. Then an image of a girl was brought to him, and he slapped it with his shoe. After that the president of the Thyiads, a college of women devoted to the orgiastic worship of Bacchus, carried away the image to a ravine and there buried it with a rope round its neck. The ceremony was said to be an expiation for the death of a girl who in a time of famine had been publicly buffeted by the king and, smarting under the insult, had hanged herself.[1] In some cities, such as Megara, Aegosthena, and Pagae, the kingship was an annual office and the years were dated by the kings' names.[2] The people of Priene appointed a young man king for the purpose of sacrificing a bull to Poseidon at the Panionian festival.[3] Some Greek states had several of these titular kings, who held office simultaneously.[4] At Rome the tradition was that the Sacrificial King had been appointed after the abolition of the monarchy in order to offer the sacrifices which before had been offered by the kings.[5] A similar view as to the origin of the priestly kings appears to have prevailed in Greece.[6] In itself the opinion is not improbable, and it is borne out by the example of Sparta, almost the only purely Greek state which retained the kingly form of government in historical times. For in Sparta all state sacrifices were offered by the kings as descendants of the god.[7] One of the two Spartan kings held

Traditional origin of these priestly kings.

---

[1] Plutarch, *Quaest. Graec.* 12. Aug. Mommsen(*Delphika*, pp. 250 *sq.*) is probably right in comparing this ceremony with the swinging-festival (*Aiora*) at Athens, as to which see *The Golden Bough*, Second Edition, ii. 453 *sqq.*

[2] *Corpus Inscriptionum Graecarum Graeciae Septentrionalis*, i. Nos. 1, 2, 3, 10, 11, 12, 13, 14, 188, 223 ; G. F. Schömann, *op. cit.* i. 146 ; G. Gilbert, *op. cit.* ii. 323 *sq.*

[3] Strabo, viii. 7. 2, p. 384. In this passage the word βασιλέα is omitted in some editions, but has the authority of several MSS. (Strabo ed. C. Müller, p. 998), and is probably right.

[4] This was the case at Elis (H. Roehl, *Inscriptiones Graecae antiquissimae*, No. 112 ; P. Cauer, *op. cit.* No. 253 ;

E. S. Roberts, *Introduction to Greek Epigraphy*, i. No. 292), in Cos (Dittenberger, *op. cit.* No. 616), in Chios (*ib.* No. 570), at Mytilene (Cauer, *op. cit.* Nos. 428, 431), at Cyme (Plutarch, *Quaest. Graec.* 2), and perhaps in Siphnos (Isocrates, *Or.* xix. 36). The Kings of Elis may have been the officials called *Basilai* who sacrificed on the top of Mount Cronius at Olympia at the spring equinox (Pausanias, vi. 20. 1).

[5] Livy, ii. 2. 1; Dionysius Halicarn., *Antiquit. Rom.* iv. 74. 4.

[6] Aristotle, *Politics*, iii. 14. 13, p. 1285 b 14 *sqq.*; Demosthenes, *Contra Neaer.* § 74 *sqq.* p. 1370 ; Plutarch, *Quaest. Rom.* 63.

[7] Xenophon, *Repub. Lacedaem.* 15,

the priesthood of Zeus Lacedaemon, the other the priesthood of Heavenly Zeus.[1] Sometimes the descendants of the old kings were allowed to retain this shadowy royalty after the real power had departed from them. Thus at Ephesus the descendants of the Ionian kings, who traced their pedigree to Codrus of Athens, kept the title of king and certain privileges, such as the right to occupy a seat of honour at the games, to wear a purple robe and carry a staff instead of a sceptre, and to preside at the rites of Eleusinian Demeter.[2] So at Cyrene, when the monarchy was abolished, the deposed King Battus was assigned certain domains and allowed to retain some priestly functions.[3] Thus the classical evidence points to the conclusion that in prehistoric ages, before the rise of the republican form of government, the various tribes or cities were ruled by kings, who discharged priestly duties and probably enjoyed a sacred character as reputed descendants of deities

This combination of priestly functions with royal authority is familiar to every one. Asia Minor, for example, was the seat of various great religious capitals peopled by thousands of sacred slaves, and ruled by pontiffs who wielded at once temporal and spiritual authority, like the popes of mediaeval Rome. Such priest-ridden cities were Zela and Pessinus.[4] Teutonic kings, again, in the old heathen days seem to have stood in the position, and to have exercised the powers, of high priests.[5] The Emperors of China offer public sacrifices, the details of which are regulated by the ritual books.[6] The King of Madagascar was

Priestly kings in various parts of the world.

---

compare *id.* 13; Aristotle, *Politics*, iii. 14. 3, p. 1285 a 3 *sqq.* Argos was governed, at least nominally, by a king as late as the time of the great Persian war (Herodotus, vii. 149); and at Orchomenus, in the secluded highlands of Northern Arcadia, the kingly form of government persisted till towards the end of the fifth century B.C. (Plutarch, *Parallela*, 32). As to the kings of Thessaly in the sixth and fifth centuries B.C., see F. Hiller von Gaertringen in *Aus der Anomia* (Berlin, 1890), pp. 1-16.

[1] Herodotus, vi. 56.

[2] Strabo, xiv. 1. 3, pp. 632 *sq.*

These Ephesian kings, who probably held office for life, are not to be confounded with the purely priestly functionaries called Essenes or King Bees, whose tenure of office was annual. See below, vol. ii. p. 135.

[3] Herodotus, iv. 162.

[4] Strabo, xii. 3. 37, 5. 3; compare xi. 4. 7, xii. 2. 3, 2. 6, 3. 31 *sq.*, 3. 34, 8. 9, 8. 14. But see *Encyclopaedia Britannica*, 9th ed. art. "Priest," xix. 729.

[5] J. Grimm, *Deutsche Rechtsalterthümer*, p. 243.

[6] See the *Lî-Kî* (Legge's transla-

high-priest of the realm. At the great festival of the new year, when a bullock was sacrified for the good of the kingdom, the king stood over the sacrifice to offer prayer and thanksgiving, while his attendants slaughtered the animal.[1] In the monarchical states which still maintain their independence among the Gallas of Eastern Africa, the king sacrifices on the mountain tops and regulates the immolation of human victims;[2] and the dim light of tradition reveals a similar union of temporal and spiritual power, of royal and priestly duties, in the kings of that delightful region of Central America whose ancient capital, now buried under the rank growth of the tropical forest, is marked by the stately and mysterious ruins of Palenque.[3] Among the Matabeles the king is high-priest. Every year he offers sacrifices at the great and the little dance, and also at the festival of the new fruits, which ends the dances. On these occasions he prays to the spirits of his forefathers and likewise to his own spirit; for it is from these higher powers that he expects every blessing.[4]

Divinity of kings.

This last example is instructive because it shews that the king is something more than a priest. He prays not only to the spirits of his fathers but to his own spirit. He is clearly raised above the standard of mere humanity; there is something divine about him. Similarly we may suppose that the Spartan kings were thought not only to be descended from the great god Zeus but also to partake of his holy spirit. This is indeed indicated by a curious Spartan belief which has been recorded by Herodotus. The old historian tells us that formerly both of the Spartan kings went forth with the army to battle, but that in later times a rule was made that when one king marched out to fight the other should stay at home. "And accordingly," says

The Spartan kings supposed to be attended by Castor and Pollux, who were thought to manifest themselves in certain electric lights.

tion), *passim* (*Sacred Books of the East*, vols. xxvii., xxviii.).

[1] W. Ellis, *History of Madagascar* (London, N.D.), i. 359 *sq.*

[2] Ph. Paulitschke, *Ethnographie Nordost-Afrikas: die geistige Cultur der Danâkil, Galla und Somâl* (Berlin, 1896), p. 129.

[3] Brasseur de Bourbourg, *Histoire des nations civilisées du Mexique et de*

l'Amérique-Centrale, i. 94. As to the ruins of Palenque, see H. H. Bancroft, *Native Races of the Pacific States*, iv. 288 *sqq.*; T. Maler, "Mémoire sur l'état de Chiapa (Mexique)," *Revue d'Ethnographie*, iii. (1885) pp. 327 *sqq.*

[4] Father Croonenberghs, "La Mission du Zambèze," *Missions Catholiques*, xiv. (1882) p. 453.

Herodotus, " one of the kings remaining at home, one of the
Tyndarids is left there too ; for hitherto both of them were
invoked and followed the kings."[1] The Tyndarids are, of
course, the heavenly twins Castor and Pollux, the sons of
Zeus ; and it should be remembered that the two Spartan
kings themselves were believed to be descended from twins[2]
and hence may have been credited with the wondrous powers
which superstition often associates with twins.[3] The belief
described by Herodotus plainly implies that one of the
heavenly twins was supposed to be in constant attendance on
each of their human kinsmen the two Spartan kings, staying
with them where they stayed and going with them wherever
they went ; hence they were probably thought to aid the
kings with their advice in time of need. Now Castor and
Pollux are commonly represented as spearmen, and they
were constantly associated or identified, not only with stars,
but also with those lurid lights which, in an atmosphere
charged with electricity, are sometimes seen to play round
the masts of ships under a murky sky.[4] Moreover, similar
lights were observed by the ancients to glitter in the darkness on the points of spears. Pliny tells us that he had
seen such lambent flames on the spears of Roman sentinels

---

[1] Herodotus, v. 75.

[2] Pausanias, iii. 1. 5.

[3] J. Rendel Harris, *The Dioscuri in
the Christian Legends* (London, 1903) ;
id., The Cult of the Heavenly Twins
(Cambridge, 1906). See also below,
pp. 262 *sqq.* With the Spartan custom
we may compare the use which the
Zulus made of twins in war. See
Dudley Kidd, *Savage Childhood, a
Study of Kafir Children* (London,
1906), p. 47 *sq.* : " In war time a
twin used to be hunted out and made
to go right in front of the attacking
army, some few paces in front of the
others. He was supposed to be fear-
less and wild. His twin, if a sister,
and if surviving, was compelled to tie
a cord very tightly round her loins
during the fight, and had to starve
herself ; she was also expected to
place the twin brother's sleeping-mat
in that part of the hut which the

itongo [ancestral spirits] loved to haunt.
This brought success in war. But the
great chief Tshaka stopped this practice, for he said that the wild twin did
foolhardy things and brought the army
into needless danger."

[4] Pliny, *Nat. Hist.* ii. 101 ; Diodorus Siculus, iv. 43 ; Seneca, *Natur.
Quaest.* i. 1. 13 ; Lucian, *Dial.
deorum*, xxvi. 2 ; Ovid, *Fasti*, v. 720;
Plutarch, *De defect. oraculorum*, 30 ;
Lactantius Placidus, *Comment. in Statii
Theb.* viii. 792 ; Th. Henri Martin,
in *Revue Archéologique*, N.S. xiii.
(1866) pp. 168 - 174 ; P. Sébillot,
*Légendes, Croyances et Superstitions de la
Mer* (Paris, 1886), ii. 87-109. Seafar-
ing men in different parts of the world
still see and draw omens from these
weird lights on the masts. See Edward
FitzGerald, quoted in *County Folk-lore,
Suffolk* (London, 1893), pp. 121 *sq.* ;
W. W. Skeat, *Malay Magic* (London,
1900), p. 279.

as they paced their rounds by night in front of the camp ;[1] and it is said that Cossacks riding across the steppes on stormy nights perceive flickerings of the same sort at their lance-heads.[2] Since, therefore, the divine brothers Castor and Pollux were believed to attend the Spartan kings, it seems not impossible that they may have been thought to accompany the march of a Spartan army in a visible form, appearing to the awe-stricken soldiers in the twilight or the darkness either as stars in the sky or as the sheen of spears on earth. Perhaps the stories of the appearance of the heavenly twins in battle, charging on their milk-white steeds at the head of the earthly chivalry, may have originated in similar lights seen to glitter in the gloaming on a point here and there in the long hedge of levelled or ported spears ; for any two riders on white horses whose spear-heads happened to be touched by the mystic light might easily be taken for Castor and Pollux in person. If there is any truth in this conjecture, we should conclude that the divine brothers were never seen in broad day, but only at dusk or in the darkness of night. Now their most famous appearance was at the battle of Lake Regillus, as to which we are expressly told that it was late in the evening of a summer day before the fighting was over.[3] Such statements should not be lightly dismissed as late inventions of a rhetorical historian. The memories of great battles linger long among the peasantry of the neighbourhood.

The divinity of kings in early society.

But when we have said that the ancient kings were commonly priests also, we are far from having exhausted the religious aspect of their office. In those days the divinity that hedges a king was no empty form of speech, but the expression of a sober belief. Kings were revered, in many cases not merely as priests, that is, as intercessors between man and god, but as themselves gods, able to bestow upon their subjects and worshippers those blessings which are commonly supposed to be beyond the reach of mortals, and are sought, if at all, only by prayer and sacrifice

---

[1] Pliny, *Nat. Hist.* ii. 101. Compare Seneca, *Natur. Quaest.* i. 1. 14.

[2] Potocki, *Voyages dans les Steps d'Astrakhan et du Caucase*, i. 143.

[3] Dionysius Halicarn. *Antiquit. Roman.* vi. 13 ; Cicero, *De natura deorum*, ii. 2. 6.

offered to superhuman and invisible beings. Thus kings
are often expected to give rain and sunshine in due season,
to make the crops grow, and so on. Strange as this expectation appears to us, it is quite of a piece with early
modes of thought. A savage hardly conceives the distinction
commonly drawn by more advanced peoples between the
natural and the supernatural. To him the world is to a
great extent worked by supernatural agents, that is, by
personal beings acting on impulses and motives like his own,
liable like him to be moved by appeals to their pity, their
hopes, and their fears. In a world so conceived he sees no
limit to his power of influencing the course of nature to his
own advantage. Prayers, promises, or threats may secure
him fine weather and an abundant crop from the gods; and
if a god should happen, as he sometimes believes, to become
incarnate in his own person, then he need appeal to no
higher being; he, the savage, possesses in himself all the
powers necessary to further his own well-being and that of
his fellow-men.

This is one way in which the idea of a man-god is Sympa-
reached. But there is another. Along with the view of thetic
magic.
the world as pervaded by spiritual forces, savage man has
a different, and probably still older, conception in which we
may detect a germ of the modern notion of natural law or
the view of nature as a series of events occurring in an
invariable order without the intervention of personal agency.
The germ of which I speak is involved in that sympathetic
magic, as it may be called, which plays a large part in most
systems of superstition. In early society the king is frequently a magician as well as a priest; indeed he appears
to have often attained to power by virtue of his supposed
proficiency in the black or white art. Hence in order to
understand the evolution of the kingship and the sacred
character with which the office has commonly been invested
in the eyes of savage or barbarous peoples, it is essential to
have some acquaintance with the principles of magic and to
form some conception of the extraordinary hold which that
ancient system of superstition has had on the human mind
in all ages and all countries. Accordingly I propose to
consider the subject in some detail.

CHAPTER III

SYMPATHETIC MAGIC

§ 1. *The Principles of Magic*

The two principles of Sympathetic Magic are the Law of Similarity and the Law of Contact or Contagion.

If we analyse the principles of thought on which magic is based, they will probably be found to resolve themselves into two : first, that like produces like, or that an effect resembles its cause ; and, second, that things which have once been in contact with each other continue to act on each other at a distance after the physical contact has been severed. The former principle may be called the Law of Similarity, the latter the Law of Contact or Contagion. From the first of these principles, namely the Law of Similarity, the magician infers that he can produce any effect he desires merely by imitating it : from the second he infers that whatever he does to a material object will affect equally the person with whom the object was once in contact, whether it formed part of his body or not. Charms based on the Law of Similarity may be called Homoeopathic or Imitative Magic.[1] Charms based on the Law of Contact or Contagion may be called Contagious Magic. To denote the first of these branches of magic the term Homoeopathic is perhaps preferable, for the alternative term Imitative or Mimetic suggests, if it does not imply, a conscious agent who imitates, thereby limiting the scope of magic too narrowly. For the same principles

---

[1] The expression Homoeopathic Magic was first used, so far as I am aware, by Mr. Y. Hirn (*Origins of Art* (London, 1900), p. 282). The expression Mimetic Magic was suggested by a writer in *Folk-lore* (viii. 1897, p. 65), whom I believe to be Mr. E. S. Hartland. The expression Imitative Magic was used incidentally by me in the first edition of *The Golden Bough* (vol. ii. p. 268).

which the magician applies in the practice of his art are implicitly believed by him to regulate the operations of inanimate nature ; in other words, he tacitly assumes that the Laws of Similarity and Contact are of universal application and are not limited to human actions. In short, magic is a spurious system of natural law as well as a fallacious guide of conduct ; it is a false science as well as an abortive art. Regarded as a system of natural law, that is, as a statement of the rules which determine the sequence of events throughout the world, it may be called Theoretical Magic : regarded as a set of precepts which human beings observe in order to compass their ends, it may be called Practical Magic. At the same time it is to be borne in mind that the primitive magician knows magic only on its practical side ; he never analyses the mental processes on which his practice is based, never reflects on the abstract principles involved in his actions. With him, as with the vast majority of men, logic is implicit, not explicit : he reasons just as he digests his food in complete ignorance of the intellectual and physiological processes which are essential to the one operation and to the other. In short, to him magic is always an art, never a science ; the very idea of science is lacking in his undeveloped mind. It is for the philosophic student to trace the train of thought which underlies the magician's practice ; to draw out the few simple threads of which the tangled skein is composed ; to disengage the abstract principles from their concrete applications ; in short, to discern the spurious science behind the bastard art.

If my analysis of the magician's logic is correct, its two great principles turn out to be merely two different misapplications of the association of ideas.[1] Homoeopathic magic is founded on the association of ideas by similarity : contagious magic is founded on the association of ideas by contiguity. Homoeopathic magic commits the mistake of assuming that things which resemble each other are the same : contagious magic commits the mistake of assuming that things which have once been in contact with

The two principles are misapplications of the association of ideas.

---

[1] That magic is based on a mistaken association of ideas was pointed out long ago by Professor E. B. Tylor (*Primitive Culture*,[2] i. 116), but he did not analyse the different kinds of association.

each other are always in contact. But in practice the two branches are often combined ; or, to be more exact, while homoeopathic or imitative magic may be practised by itself, contagious magic will generally be found to involve an application of the homoeopathic or imitative principle. Thus generally stated the two things may be a little difficult to grasp, but they will readily become intelligible when they are illustrated by particular examples. Both trains of thought are in fact extremely simple and elementary. It could hardly be otherwise, since they are familiar in the concrete, though certainly not in the abstract, to the crude intelligence not only of the savage, but of ignorant and dull-witted people everywhere. Both branches of magic, the homoeopathic and the contagious, may conveniently be comprehended under the general name of Sympathetic Magic, since both assume that things act on each other at a distance through a secret sympathy, the impulse being transmitted from one to the other by means of what we may conceive as a kind of invisible ether, not unlike that which is postulated by modern science for a precisely similar purpose, namely, to explain how things can physically affect each other through a space which appears to be empty.

Table of the branches of Sympathetic Magic.

It may be convenient to tabulate as follows the branches of magic according to the laws of thought which underlie them :—

Sympathetic Magic
(*Law of Sympathy*)

Homoeopathic Magic
(*Law of Similarity*)

Contagious Magic [1]
(*Law of Contact*)

I will now illustrate these two great branches of sympathetic magic by examples, beginning with homoeopathic magic.

[1] It has been ingeniously suggested by Mr. Y. Hirn that magic by similarity may be reduced to a case of magic by contact. The connecting link, on his hypothesis, is the old doctrine of emanations, according to which everything is continually sending out in all directions copies of itself in the shape of thin membranes, which appear to the senses not only as shadows, reflections, and so forth, but also as sounds and names. See Y. Hirn, *Origins of Art* (London, 1900), pp. 293 *sqq.* This hypothesis certainly furnishes a point of union for the two apparently distinct sides of sympathetic magic, but whether it is one that would occur to the savage mind may be doubted.

§ 2. *Homoeopathic or Imitative Magic*

Perhaps the most familiar application of the principle that like produces like is the attempt which has been made by many peoples in many ages to injure or destroy an enemy by injuring or destroying an image of him, in the belief that, just as the image suffers, so does the man, and that when it perishes he must die. A few instances out of many may be given to prove at once the wide diffusion of the practice over the world and its remarkable persistence through the ages. For thousands of years ago it was known to the sorcerers of ancient India, Babylon, and Egypt, as well as of Greece and Rome,[1] and at this day it is still resorted to by cunning and malignant savages in Australia, Africa, and Scotland. Thus the North American Indians, we are told, believe that by drawing the figure of a person in sand, ashes, or clay, or by considering any object as his body, and then pricking it with a sharp stick or doing it any other injury, they inflict a corresponding injury on the person represented.[2] For example, when an Ojebway Indian desires to work evil on any one, he makes a little wooden image of his enemy and runs a needle into its head or heart, or he shoots an arrow into it, believing that wherever the needle pierces or the arrow strikes the image, his foe will the same instant be seized with a sharp pain in the corresponding part of his body; but if he intends to kill the person outright, he burns or buries the puppet, uttering certain magic words as he does so.[3] So when a Cora Indian

Magical images among the American Indians.

---

[1] For the Greek and Roman practice, see Theocritus, *Id.* ii.; Virgil, *Ecl.* viii. 75-82; Ovid, *Heroides*, vi. 91 *sq.*; *id. Amores*, iii. 7. 29 *sq.*; R. Wünsch, "Eine antike Rachepuppe," *Philologus*, lxi. (1902) pp. 26-31.

[2] Henry's *Travels among the Northern and Western Indians*, quoted by the Rev. Jedediah Morse, *Report to the Secretary of War of the United States on Indian Affairs* (Newhaven, 1822), Appendix, p. 102. I have not seen Henry's book.

[3] Peter Jones, *History of the Ojebway Indians*, p. 146; W. H. Keat-ing, *Narrative of an Expedition to the Source of St. Peter's River* (London, 1825), ii. 159; J. G. Kohl, *Kitschi-Gami*, ii. 80. Similar practices are reported among the Illinois, the Mandans, and the Hidatsas of North America (Charlevoix, *Histoire de la Nouvelle France*, vi. 88; Maximilian, Prinz zu Wied, *Reise in das Innere Nord-America*, ii. 188; Washington Matthews, *Ethnography and Philology of the Hidatsa Indians*, p. 50), and the Aymaras of Bolivia and Peru (D. Forbes, "On the Aymara Indians of Bolivia and Peru," *Journal of the Ethnological Society of London*. ii. (1870) p. 236).

of Mexico wishes to kill a man, he makes a figure of him out of burnt clay, strips of cloth, and so forth, and then, muttering incantations, runs thorns through the head or stomach of the figure to make his victim suffer correspondingly. Sometimes the Cora Indian makes a more beneficent use of this sort of homoeopathic magic. When he wishes to multiply his flocks or herds, he models a figure of the animal he wants in wax or clay, or carves it from tuff, and deposits it in a cave of the mountains ; for these Indians believe that the mountains are masters of all riches, including cattle and sheep. For every cow, deer, dog, or hen he wants, the Indian has to sacrifice a corresponding image of the creature.[1] This may help us to understand the meaning of the figures of cattle, deer, horses, and pigs which were dedicated to Diana at Nemi.[2] They may have been the offerings of farmers or huntsmen who hoped thereby to multiply the cattle or the game. Similarly when the Todas of Southern India desire to obtain more buffaloes, they offer silver images of these animals in the temples.[3] The Peruvian Indians moulded images of fat mixed with grain to imitate the persons whom they disliked or feared, and then burned the effigy on the road where the intended victim was to pass. This they called burning his soul. But they drew a delicate distinction between the kinds of materials to be used in the manufacture of these images, according as the victim was an Indian or a Viracocha, that is, a Spaniard. To kill an Indian they employed maize and the fat of a llama, to kill a Spaniard they used wheat and the fat of a pig, because Viracochas did not eat llamas and preferred wheat to maize.[4]

[1] C. Lumholtz, *Unknown Mexico* (London, 1903), i. 485 *sq.*

[2] Above, p. 7.

[3] W. H. R. Rivers, *The Todas* (London, 1906), p. 458. Among the Kusavans or potters of Southern India "if a male or female recovers from cholera, small-pox, or other severe illness, a figure of the corresponding sex is offered. A childless woman makes a vow to offer up the figure of a baby, if she brings forth offspring. Figures of animals — cattle, sheep, horses, etc.—are offered at the temple when they recover from sickness, or are recovered after they have been stolen " (E. Thurston, *Castes and Tribes of Southern India*, iv. 192 ; *id.*, *Ethnographic Notes in Southern India*, p. 349). The analogy of these offerings to the various votive figures found in the sanctuary of Diana at Nemi is obvious.

[4] P. J. de Arriaga, *Extirpacion de la Idolatria del Piru* (Lima, 1621), pp. 25 *sq.* The meaning and origin of the

A Malay charm of the same sort is as follows. Take parings of nails, hair, eyebrows, spittle, and so forth of your intended victim, enough to represent every part of his person, and then make them up into his likeness with wax from a deserted bees' comb. Scorch the figure slowly by holding it over a lamp every night for seven nights, and say :

Magical images among the Malays.

> " *It is not wax that I am scorching,*
> *It is the liver, heart, and spleen of So-and-so that I scorch.*"

After the seventh time burn the figure, and your victim will die. This charm obviously combines the principles of homoeopathic and contagious magic ; since the image which is made in the likeness of an enemy contains things which once were in contact with him, namely, his nails, hair, and spittle. Another form of the Malay charm, which resembles the Ojebway practice still more closely, is to make a corpse of wax from an empty bees' comb and of the length of a footstep ; then pierce the eye of the image, and your enemy

name Viracocha, as applied by the Peruvians to the Spaniards, is explained with great frankness by the Italian historian G. Benzoni, who had himself travelled in America at the time of the conquest. He says (*History of the New World*, pp. 252 *sq.*, Hakluyt Society) : " When the Indians saw the very great cruelties which the Spaniards committed everywhere on entering Peru, not only would they never believe us to be Christians and children of God, as boasted, but not even that we were born on this earth, or generated by a man and born of a woman ; so fierce an animal they concluded must be the offspring of the sea, and therefore called us *Viracocchie*, for in their language they call the sea *cocchie* and the froth *vira* ; thus they think that we are a congelation of the sea, and have been nourished by the froth ; and that we are come to destroy the world, with other things in which the Omnipotence of God would not suffice to undeceive them. They say that the winds ruin houses and break down trees, and the fire burns them ; but the *Viracocchie* devour everything, they consume the very earth, they force the rivers, they are never quiet, they never rest, they are always rushing about, sometimes in one direction and sometimes in the other, seeking for gold and silver ; yet never contented, they game it away, they make war, they kill each other, they rob, they swear, they are renegades, they never speak the truth, and they deprive us of our support. Finally, the Indians curse the sea for having cast such very wicked and harsh beings on the land. Going about through various parts of this kingdom I often met some natives, and for the amusement of hearing what they would say, I used to ask them where such and such a *Christian* was, when not only would they refuse to answer me, but would not even look me in the face : though if I asked them where such and such a *Viracocchie* was, they would reply directly." An explanation of the name much more flattering to Spanish vanity is given by Garcilasso de la Vega, himself half a Spaniard (*Royal Commentaries of the Yncas*, vol. ii. pp. 65 *sqq.*, Hakluyt Society, Markham's translation).

is blind ; pierce the stomach, and he is sick ; pierce the head, and his head aches ; pierce the breast, and his breast will suffer. If you would kill him outright, transfix the image from the head downwards ; enshroud it as you would a corpse ; pray over it as if you were praying over the dead ; then bury it in the middle of a path where your victim will be sure to step over it. In order that his blood may not be on your head, you should say :

> "*It is not I who am burying him,*
> *It is Gabriel who is burying him.*"

Thus the guilt of the murder will be laid on the shoulders of the archangel Gabriel, who is a great deal better able to bear it than you are.[1] In eastern Java an enemy may be killed by means of a likeness of him drawn on a piece of paper, which is then incensed or buried in the ground.[2] Among the Minangkabauers of Sumatra a man who is tormented by the passion of hate or of unrequited love will call in the help of a wizard in order to cause the object of his hate or love to suffer from a dangerous ulcer known as a *tinggam*. After giving the wizard the necessary instructions as to the name, bodily form, dwelling, and family of the person in question, he makes a puppet which is supposed to resemble his intended victim ; and repairs with it to a wood, where he hangs the image on a tree that stands quite by itself. Muttering a spell, he then drives an instrument through the navel of the puppet into the tree, till the sap of the tree oozes through the hole thus made. The instrument which inflicts the wound bears the same name (*tinggam*) as the ulcer which is to be raised on the body of the victim, and the oozing sap is believed to be his or her life-spirit. Soon afterwards the person against whom the charm is directed begins to suffer from an ulcer, which grows worse and worse till he dies, unless a friend can procure a piece of the wood of the tree to which the image is attached.[3]

1 W. W. Skeat, *Malay Magic* (London, 1900), pp. 570-572.

2 J. Kreemer, " Regenmaken, Oedjoeng, Tooverij onder de Javanen," *Mededeelingen van wege het Nederlandsche Zendelinggenootschap*, xxx.

(1886) pp. 117 *sq.*

3 J. L. van der Toorn, " Het animisme bij den Minangkabauer der Padangsche Bovenlanden," *Bijdragen tot de Taal- Land- en Volkenkunde van Nederlandsch Indië*, xxxix.(1890) p. 56.

The sorcerers of Mabuiag or Jervis Island, in Torres Straits, kept an assortment of effigies in stock ready to be operated on at the requirement of a customer. Some of the figures were of stone; these were employed when short work was to be made of a man or woman. Others were wooden; these gave the unhappy victim a little more rope, only, however, to terminate his prolonged sufferings by a painful death. The mode of operation in the latter case was to put poison, by means of a magical implement, into a wooden image, to which the name of the intended victim had been given. Next day the person aimed at would feel chilly, then waste away and die, unless the same wizard who had wrought the charm would consent to undo it.[1] If the sorcerer pulled off an arm or leg of the image, the human victim felt pain in the corresponding limb of his body; but if the sorcerer restored the severed arm or leg to the figure, the man recovered. Another mode of compassing a man's death in Torres Straits was to prick a wax effigy of him or her with the spine of a sting-ray; so when the man whose name had been given to the waxen image next went afishing on the reef a sting-ray would sting him in the exact part of his body where the waxen image had been pierced. Or the sorcerer might hang the effigy on the bough of a tree, and as it swayed to and fro in the wind the person represented by it would fall sick. However, he would get well again if a friend of his could induce the magician to steady the figure by sticking it firmly in the sandy bottom of the sea.[2] When the Lerons of Borneo wish to be revenged on an enemy, they make a wooden image of him and leave it in the jungle. As it decays, he dies.[3] More elaborate is the proceeding adopted by the Kenyahs of Borneo in similar circumstances. The operator retires with the image to a quiet spot on the river bank, and when a hawk appears in a certain part of the sky, he kills a fowl, smears its blood on the image, and puts a bit of fat in the mouth of the figure, saying, "Put fat in his mouth." By that he means, "May

Magical images in Torres Straits and Borneo.

[1] A. C. Haddon, "The Ethnography of the Western Tribe of Torres Straits," *Journal of the Anthropological Institute,* xix. (1890) pp. 399 *sq.*

[2] *Reports of the Cambridge Anthro-pological Expedition to Torres Straits,* v. (Cambridge, 1904) pp. 324 *sq.*

[3] W. H. Furness, *The Home-life of Borneo Head-hunters* (Philadelphia, 1902), pp. 93.

his head be cut off, hung up in an enemy's house, and fed with fat in the usual way." Then he strikes at the breast of the image with a small wooden spear, throws it into a pool of water reddened with red earth, and afterwards takes it out and buries it in the ground.[1]

Magical images in Japan and China. If an Aino of Jápan desires to compass the destruction of an enemy, he will make a likeness of him out of mug-wort or the guelder-rose and bury it in a hole upside down or under the trunk of a rotten tree, with a prayer to a demon to carry off the man's soul or to make his body rot away with the tree. Sometimes an Aino woman will attempt to get rid of her husband in this fashion by wrapping up his head-dress in the shape of a corpse and burying it deep in the ground, while she breathes a prayer that her husband may rot and die with the head-dress.[2] The Japanese themselves are familiar with similar modes of enchant-ment. In one of their ancient books we read of a rebellious minister who made figures of the heir to the throne with intent, no doubt, to do him grievous bodily harm thereby ; and sometimes a woman who has been deserted by her lover will make a straw effigy of the faithless gallant and nail it to a sacred tree, adjuring the gods to spare the tree and to visit the sacrilege on the traitor. At a shrine of Kompira there stood a pine-tree studded with nails which had been thus driven in for the purpose of doing people to death.[3] The Chinese also are perfectly aware that you can harm a man by maltreating or cursing an image of him, especially if you have taken care to write on it his name and horoscope. This mode of venting spite on an enemy is said to be commonly practised in China. In Amoy such images, roughly made of bamboo splinters and paper, are called "substitutes of persons" and may be bought very cheap for a cash or so apiece at any shop which sells paper articles for the use of the dead or the gods ; for the frugal Chinese are in the habit of palming off paper imitations of all kinds of valuables on the simple-minded ghosts and gods, who take them in all good faith for the genuine articles. As

---

[1] C. Hose and W. McDougall, in *Journal of the Anthropological Institute*, xxxi. (1901) p. 178.

[2] J. Batchelor, *The Ainu and their*

Folklore (London, 1901), pp. 329-331.

[3] W. G. Aston, *Shinto (the Way of the Gods)* (London, 1905), pp. 331 *sq.*

usual, the victim suffers a hurt corresponding to the hurt done to his image. Thus if you run a nail or a needle into the eyes of the puppet, your man will go more or less blind ; if you stick a pin in its stomach, he will be doubled up with colic ; a stab in the heart of the effigy may kill him outright ; and in general the more you prick it and the louder you speak the spell, the more certain is the effect. To make assurance doubly sure it is desirable to impregnate the effigy, so to say, with the personal influence of the man by passing it clandestinely beforehand over him or hiding it, unbeknown to him, in his clothes or under his bed. If you do that, he is quite sure to die sooner or later.[1] Naturally these nefarious practices are no new thing in the Chinese empire. There is a passage in the Chinese *Book of Rewards and Penalties* which illustrates their prevalence in days gone by. There, under the rubric " To hide an effigy of a man for the purpose of giving him the nightmare," we read as follows : " This means hiding the carved wooden effigy of a man somewhere with intent to give him the nightmare. Kong-sun-tcho having died suddenly some time after he had succeeded to the post of treasurer, he appeared in a dream to the governor of his district and said unto him : ' I have been the victim of an odious crime, and I am come, my lord, to pray you to avenge me. My time to die had not yet come; but my servants gave me the nightmare, and I was choked in my sleep. If you will send secretly some dauntless soldiers, not one of the varlets will escape you. Under the seventh tile of the roof of my house will be found my image carved of wood. Fetch it and punish the criminals.' Next day the governor of the district had all the servants arrested, and sure enough, after some search, they found under the aforesaid tile the figure of a man in wood, a foot high, and bristling all over with nails. Bit by bit the wood changed into flesh and uttered inarticulate cries when it was struck. The governor of the district immediately reported to the prefect of the department, who condemned several of the servants to suffer the extreme rigour of the law." [2]

---

[1] J. J. M. de Groot, *The Religious System of China,* v. (Leyden, 1907) pp. 920 *sq.*

[2] *Le Livre des Récompenses et des Peines, traduit du Chinois,* par Stanislas Julien (Paris, 1835), p. 345.

Magical
images in
Australia.
When some of the aborigines of Victoria desired to
destroy an enemy, they would occasionally retire to a
lonely spot, and drawing on the ground a rude likeness of
the victim would sit round it and devote him to destruction with cabalistic ceremonies. So dreaded was this
incantation that men and women, who learned that it had
been directed against them, have been known to pine away
and die of fright.[1] On the Bloomfield River in Queensland
the natives think they can doom a man by making a rough
wooden effigy of him and burying it in the ground, or by
painting his likeness on a bull-roarer ; and they believe that
persons whose portraits are carved on a tree at Cape Bedford
will waste away.[2] When the wife of a Central Australian
native has eloped from him and he cannot recover her, the
disconsolate husband repairs with some sympathising friends
to a secluded spot, where a man skilled in magic draws on
the ground a rough figure supposed to represent the woman
lying on her back. Beside the figure is laid a piece of
green bark, which stands for her spirit or soul, and at it the
men throw miniature spears which have been made for the
purpose and charmed by singing over them. This barken
effigy of the woman's spirit, with the little spears sticking in
it, is then thrown as far as possible in the direction which
she is supposed to have taken. During the whole of the
operation the men chant in a low voice, the burden of their
song being an invitation to the magic influence to go out
and enter her body and dry up all her fat. Sooner or later
—often a good deal later—her fat does dry up, she dies,
and her spirit is seen in the sky in the form of a shooting
star.[3]

Magical
images in
Burma,
and Africa.
In Burma a rejected lover sometimes resorts to a sorcerer
and engages him to make a small image of the scornful fair
one, containing a piece of her clothes, or of something which
she has been in the habit of wearing. Certain charms or
medicines also enter into the composition of the doll, which
is then hung up or thrown into the water. As a conse-

---

[1] E. M. Curr, *The Australian Race,*
iii. 547.

[2] W. E. Roth, *North Queensland
Ethnography : Bulletin* No. 5 (Brisbane,

1903), p. 31.

[3] Baldwin Spencer and F. J. Gillen,
The Native Tribes of Central Australia
(London, 1899), pp. 549 *sq.*

quence the girl is supposed to go mad.[1]   In this last
example, as in the first of the Malay charms noticed above,
homoeopathic or imitative magic is blent with contagious
magic in the strict sense of the word, since the likeness of the
victim contains something which has been in contact with
her person.   A Matabele who wishes to avenge himself on
an enemy makes a clay figure of him and pierces it with a
needle ; next time the man thus represented happens to
engage in a fight he will be speared, just as his effigy was
stabbed.[2] The Ovambo of South-western Africa believe
that some people have the power of bewitching an absent
person by gazing into a vessel full of water till his image
appears to them in the water ; then they spit at the image
and curse the man, and that seals his fate.[3]

The ancient books of the Hindoos testify to the use of Magical
similar enchantments among their remote ancestors.   To images in
destroy his foe a man would fashion a figure of him in clay India.
and transfix it with an arrow which had been barbed with a ancient
thorn and winged with an owl's feathers.   Or he would mould
the figure of wax and melt it in a fire.   Sometimes effigies
of the soldiers, horses, elephants, and chariots of a hostile
army were modelled in dough, and then pulled in pieces.[4]
Again, to destroy an enemy the magician might kill a red-
headed lizard with the words, " I am killing So-and-so,"
smear it with blood, wrap it in a black cloth, and having
pronounced an incantation burn it.[5]   Another way was to
grind up mustard into meal, with which a figure was made of
the person who was to be overcome or destroyed.   Then
having muttered certain spells to give efficacy to the rite,
the enchanter chopped up the image, anointed it with melted
butter, curds, or some such thing, and finally burnt it in
a sacred pot.[6]   In the so-called " sanguinary chapter " of
the *Calica Puran* there occurs the following passage : " On

[1] C. J. F. S. Forbes, *British Burma*
(London, 1878), p. 232.
[2] L. Decle, *Three Years in Savage
Africa* (London, 1898), p. 153.
[3] H. Schinz, *Deutsch-Südwest-Afri-
ka*, p. 314.
[4] A. Hillebrandt, *Vedische Opfer
und Zauber* (Strasburg, 1897), p. 177;
W. Caland, *Aitindisches Zauberritual*

(Amsterdam, 1900), pp. 121, 166,
173, 184.   Compare H. Oldenberg,
Die Religion des Veda (Berlin, 1894),
p. 508.
[5] W. Caland, *op. cit.* p. 164.
[6] H. W. Magoun, " The Asuri-
Kalpa ; a Witchcraft Practice of the
Atharva-Veda," *American Journal of
Philology*, x. (1889) pp. 165-197.

the autumnal *Maha-Navami*, or when the month is in the lunar mansion *Scanda*, or *Bishácủ*, let a figure be made, either of barley-meal or earth, representing the person with whom the sacrificer is at variance, and the head of the figure be struck off; after the usual texts have been used, the following text is to be used in invoking an axe on the occasion : ' Effuse, effuse blood ; be terrific, be terrific ; seize, destroy, for the love of *Ambica*, the head of this enemy.' "[1]

Magical images in modern India.

In modern India the practices described in these old books are still carried on with mere variations of detail. The magician compounds the fatal image of earth taken from sixty-four filthy places, and mixed up with clippings of hair, parings of nails, bits of leather, and so on. Upon the breast of the image he writes the name of his enemy ; then he pierces it through and through with an awl, or maims it in various ways, hoping thus to maim or kill the object of his vengeance.[2] Among the Nambutiris of Malabar a figure representing the enemy to be destroyed is drawn on a small sheet of metal, gold by preference, on which some mystic diagrams are also inscribed. The sorcerer then declares that the bodily injury or death of the person shall take place at a certain time. After that he wraps up the little sheet in another sheet or leaf of metal (gold if possible), and buries it in a place where the victim is expected to pass. Sometimes instead of a small sheet of metal he buries a live frog or lizard enclosed in a coco-nut shell, after sticking nails into its eyes and stomach. At the same moment that the animal dies the person expires also.[3] Among the Mohammedans of Northern India the proceeding is as follows. A doll is made of earth taken from a grave or from a place where bodies are cremated, and some sentences of the Coran are read backwards over twenty-one small wooden pegs. These pegs the operator next strikes into various parts of the body of the image, which is afterwards shrouded like a corpse, carried to a graveyard, and buried in the name of the enemy whom it is intended to injure. The man, it is

[1] *Asiatick Researches*, v. (Fourth Edition, London, 1807) p. 389.

[2] J. A. Dubois, *Mœurs, institutions, et cérémonies des peuples de l'Inde* (Paris,

1825), ii. 63.

[3] Fr. Fawcett, in *Madras Government Museum, Bulletin*, iii. No. 1 (Madras, 1900), p. 85.

believed, will die without fail after the ceremony.[1] A
slightly different form of the charm is observed by the
Bâm-Margi, a very degraded sect of Hindoos in the North-
West Provinces. To kill an enemy they make an image
of flour or earth, and stick razors into the breast, navel, and
throat, while pegs are thrust into the eyes, hands, and feet.
As if this were not enough, they next construct an image
of Bhairava or Durga holding a three-pronged fork in her
hand ; this they place so close to the effigy of the person
to whom mischief is meant that the fork penetrates its
breast.[2] To injure a person a Singhalese sorcerer will procure a lock of his intended victim's hair, a paring of his
nails, or a thread of his garment. Then he fashions an
image of him and thrusts nails made of five metals into the
joints. All these he buries where the unfortunate man is
likely to pass. No sooner has he done so than the victim falls
ill with swelling or stiffness of joints, or burning sensations
in the body, or disfigurements of the mouth, legs, and arms.[3]

Similar enchantments are wrought by the Moslem peoples
of North Africa. Thus an Arabic treatise on magic directs
that if you wish to deprive a man of the use of his limbs
you should make a waxen image of him, and engrave his
name and his mother's name on it with a knife of which
the handle must be made of the same wax ; then smite
the limb of the image which answers to the particular
limb of the man which you desire to disable ; at the same
moment the limb of flesh and blood will be paralysed.[4]
The following is another extract from the same treatise :
" To injure the eyes of an enemy, take a taper and fashion
it into the likeness of him whom you would harm. Write
on it the seven signs, along with the name of your enemy
and the name of his mother and gouge out the two eyes of
the figure with two points. Then put it in a pot with quick-

Magical images among the Arabs of North Africa.

[1] W. Crooke, *Popular Religion and
Folklore of Northern India* (Westminster, 1896), ii. 278 *sq.*
[2] *Id.*, *The Tribes and Castes of the
North - Western Provinces and Oudh*
(Calcutta, 1896), i. 137.
[3] A. A. Perera, " Glimpses of Singhalese Social Life," *Indian Antiquary*, xxxiii. (1904) p. 57. For

more evidence of such practices in
India, see E. Thurston, *Ethnographic
Notes in Southern India*, pp. 328 *sqq.* ;
id., *Castes and Tribes of Southern
India*, iv. 489 *sq.*, vi. 124 ; W. Crooke,
Natives of Northern India, pp. 248 *sq.*
[4] E. Doutté, *Magie et Religion dans
l'Afrique du Nord* (Algiers, 1908), pp.
61 *sq.*

lime on which you must throw a little *chârib el h'amâm*, and bury the whole near the fire. The fire will make your victim to shriek and will hurt his eyes so that he will see nothing, and that the pain will cause him to utter cries of distress. But do not prolong the operation more than seven days, for he would die and you would have to answer for it at the day of the last judgment. If you wish to heal him, withdraw the figure and throw it into water. He will recover, with God's leave." [1]

Magical images in ancient Egypt and Babylon.
　　　Nowhere, perhaps, were the magic arts more carefully cultivated, nowhere did they enjoy greater esteem or exercise a deeper influence on the national life than in the land of the Pharaohs. Little wonder, therefore, that the practice of enchantment by means of images was familiar to the wizards of Egypt. A drop of a man's blood, some clippings of his hair or parings of his nails, a rag of the garment which he had worn, sufficed to give a sorcerer complete power over him. These relics of his person the magician kneaded into a lump of wax, which he moulded into the likeness and dressed after the fashion of his intended victim, who was then at the mercy of his tormentor. If the image was exposed to the fire, the person whom it represented straightway fell into a burning fever ; if it were stabbed with a knife, he felt the pain of the wound. [2] Thus, for instance, a certain superintendent of the king's cattle was once prosecuted in an Egyptian court of law for having made figures of men and women in wax, thereby causing paralysis of their limbs and other grievous bodily harm. He had somehow obtained a book of magic which contained the spells and directions how to act in reciting them. Armed with this powerful instrument the rogue had shut himself up in a secret chamber, and there proceeded to cast spells over the people of his town. [3] In ancient Babylonia also it was

[1] E. Doutté, *op. cit.* p. 299.

[2] G. Maspero, *Histoire ancienne des peuples de l'Orient classique : les origines* (Paris, 1895), pp. 213 *sq.*

[3] F. Chabas, *Le Papyrus magique Harris* (Chalon-sur-Saône, 1860), pp. 169 *sqq.* ; E. A. Wallis Budge, in *Archaeologia*, Second Series, vol. ii.

(1890) pp. 428 *sq.* ; *id.*, *Egyptian Magic* (London, 1899), pp. 73 *sqq.* The case happened in the reign of Rameses III., about 1200 B.C. Compare A. Erman, *Aegypten und aegyptisches Leben im Altertum*, p. 475. As to Egyptian magic in general see A. Erman, *Die ägyptische Religion* (Berlin, 1905), pp. 148 *sqq.*

a common practice to make an image of clay, pitch, honey, fat, or other soft material in the likeness of an enemy, and to injure or kill him by burning, burying, or otherwise ill-treating it.   Thus in a hymn to the fire-god Nusku we read :

> *"Those who have made images of me, reproducing my features,*
> *Who have taken away my breath, torn my hairs,*
> *Who have rent my clothes, have hindered my feet from treading the*
> * dust,*
> *May the fire-god, the strong one, break their charm."* [1]

But both in Babylon and in Egypt this ancient tool of superstition, so baneful in the hands of the mischievous and malignant, was also pressed into the service of religion and turned to glorious account for the confusion and overthrow of demons.   In a Babylonian incantation we meet with a long list of evil spirits whose effigies were burnt by the magician in the hope that, as their images melted in the fire, so the fiends themselves might melt away and disappear.[2]   Every night when the sun-god Ra sank down to his home in the glowing west he was assailed by hosts of demons under the leadership of the arch-fiend Apepi. All night long he fought them, and sometimes by day the powers of darkness sent up clouds even into the blue Egyptian sky to obscure his light and weaken his power. To aid the sun-god in this daily struggle, a ceremony was daily performed in his temple at Thebes.   A figure of his foe Apepi, represented as a crocodile with a hideous face or a serpent with many coils, was made of wax, and on it the demon's name was written in green ink.   Wrapt in a papyrus case, on which another likeness of Apepi had been drawn in green ink, the figure was then tied up with black hair, spat upon, hacked with a stone knife, and cast on the ground.   There the priest trod on it with his left foot again and again, and then burned it in a fire made of a certain plant or grass.   When Apepi himself had thus been effectually disposed of, waxen effigies of each of his principal demons, and of their fathers, mothers, and children, were

(marginal note: Magical images in Babylon and Egypt for the discomfiture of demons)

[1] M. Jastrow, *The Religion of Babylonia and Assyria* (Boston, U.S.A., 1898), pp. 268, 286, compare pp. 270, 272, 276, 278 ; R. F. Harper, *Assyrian and Babylonian Literature* (New York, 1901), pp. 375, 376, 377 *sqq* : C. Fossey, *La Magie assyrienne* (Paris, 1902), pp. 77-81.

[2] M. Jastrow, *op. cit.* pp. 286 *sq.* ; C. Fossey, *op. cit.* p. 78.

made and burnt in the same way. The service, accompanied by the recitation of certain prescribed spells, was repeated not merely morning, noon, and night, but whenever a storm was raging, or heavy rain had set in, or black clouds were stealing across the sky to hide the sun's bright disc. The fiends of darkness, clouds, and rain felt the injuries inflicted on their images as if they had been done to themselves ; they passed away, at least for a time, and the beneficent sun-god shone out triumphant once more.[1]

Magical images in Scotland.

From the azure sky, the stately fanes, and the solemn ritual of ancient Egypt we have to travel far in space and time to the misty mountains and the humble cottages of the Scottish Highlands of to-day ; but at our journey's end we shall find our ignorant countrymen seeking to attain the same end by the same means and, unhappily, with the same malignity as the Egyptian of old. To kill a person whom he hates, a modern Highlander will still make a rude clay image of him, called a *corp chre* or *corp chreadh* (" clay body "), stick it full of pins, nails, and broken bits of glass, and then place it in a running stream with its head to the current. As every pin is thrust into the figure an incantation is uttered, and the person represented feels a pain in the corresponding part of his body. If the intention is to make him die a lingering death, the operator is careful to stick no pins into the region of the heart, whereas he thrusts them into that region deliberately if he desires to rid himself of his enemy at once. And as the clay puppet crumbles away in the running water, so the victim's body is believed to waste away and turn to clay. In Islay the spell spoken over the *corp chre*, when it is ready to receive the pins, is as follows : " From behind you are like a ram with an old fleece." And as the pins are being thrust in, a long incantation is pronounced, beginning " As you waste away, may she waste away ; as this wounds you, may it wound her." Sometimes, we are told, the effigy is set before a blazing fire on a door which has been taken off its hinges ; there it is toasted and

---

[1] E. A. Wallis Budge, " On the Hieratic Papyrus of Nesi-Amsu, a scribe in the temple of Amen-Rā at Thebes, about B.C. 305," *Archaeologia*, Second Series, ii. (1890) pp. 393-601 ; *id.*, *Egyptian Magic*, pp. 77 *sqq.* ; *id.*, *The Gods of the Egyptians* (London, 1904), i. 270-272.

turned to make the human victim writhe in agony. The *corp chre* is reported to have been employed of late years in the counties of Inverness, Ross, and Sutherland. A specimen from Inverness-shire may be seen in the Pitt-Rivers Museum at Oxford.[1] It is remarkable, however, that in the High-lands this form of magic has no power over a man who has lost any of his members. For example, though Ross-shire witches made a clay figure of "Donald of the Ear," they could not destroy him, because he had lost an ear in battle.[2] A similar form of witchcraft, known as "bury-ing the sheaf," seems still to linger in Ireland among the dwellers in the Bog of Ardee. The person who works the charm goes first to a chapel and says certain prayers with his back to the altar; then he takes a sheaf of wheat, which he fastens into the likeness of a human body, sticking pins in the joints of the stems and, according to one account, shaping a heart of plaited straw. This sheaf he buries in the devil's name near the house of his enemy, who will, it is supposed, gradually pine away as the sheaf decays, dying when it finally decomposes. If the enchanter desires his foe to perish speedily, he buries the sheaf in wet ground, where it will soon moulder away; but if on the other hand his wish is that his victim should linger in pain, he chooses a dry spot, where decomposition will be slow.[3] However, in Scotland, as in Babylon and Egypt, the destruction of an image has also been employed for the discomfiture of fiends. When Shetland fishermen wish to disenchant their boat, they

---

[1] See an article by R. M. O. K. entitled "A Horrible Rite in the High-lands," in the *Weekly Scotsman*, Saturday, August 24, 1889; Pro-fessor J. Rhys in *Folklore*, iii. (1892) p. 385; R. C. Maclagan, "Notes on Folklore Objects collected in Argyle-shire," *Folklore*, vi. (1895) pp. 144-148; J. Macdonald, *Religion and Myth* (London, 1893), pp. 3 *sq.*; J. G. Campbell, *Witchcraft and Second Sight in the Highlands and Islands of Scot-land* (Glasgow, 1902), pp. 46-48. Many older examples of the practice of this form of enchantment in Scotland are collected by J. G. Dalyell in his *Darker Superstitions of Scotland* (Edin-

burgh, 1834), pp. 328 *sqq.*

[2] J. G. Campbell, *op. cit.* pp. 47, 48.

[3] Bryan J. Jones, in *Folklore*, vi. (1895) p. 302. For evidence of the custom in the Isle of Man see J. Train, *Historical and Statistical Account of the Isle of Man*, ii. 168; in England, see Brand, *Popular Antiquities*, iii. 10 *sqq.*; in Germany, see J. Grimm, *Deutsche Mythologie*,[4] ii. 913 *sq.*; F. Panzer, *Beitrag zur deutschen Mytho-logie*, ii. 272 *sq.* As to the custom in general, see E. B. Tylor, *Researches into the Early History of Mankind*,[3] pp. 106 *sqq.*; R. Andree, "Sympathie-Zauber," *Ethnographische Parallelen und Vergleiche*, Neue Folge, pp. 8 *sqq.*

row it out to sea before sunrise, and as the day is dawning they burn a waxen figure in the boat, while the skipper exclaims, "Go hence, Satan."[1]

Magical images to procure offspring in America and Africa. If homoeopathic or imitative magic, working by means of images, has commonly been practised for the spiteful purpose of putting obnoxious people out of the world, it has also, though far more rarely, been employed with the benevolent intention of helping others into it. In other words, it has been used to facilitate childbirth and to procure offspring for barren women. Thus among the Esquimaux of Bering Strait a barren woman desirous of having a son will consult a shaman, who commonly makes, or causes her husband to make, a small doll-like image over which he performs certain secret rites, and the woman is directed to sleep with it under her pillow.[2] Amongst the many ceremonies which a Thompson Indian girl of British Columbia had formerly to perform at puberty was the following. She had to run four times in the morning, carrying two small stones which had been obtained from underneath the water. These were put in her bosom ; and as she ran, they slipped down between her body and her clothes and fell to the ground. While she ran, she prayed to the Dawn that when she should be with child she might be delivered as easily as she had been delivered of these stones.[3] Similarly among the Haida Indians of the Queen Charlotte Islands a pregnant woman would let round stones, eels, chips, or other small objects slip down over her abdomen for the sake of facilitating her delivery.[4] Among the Nishinam Indians of California, when a woman is childless, her female friends sometimes make out of grass a rude image of a baby and tie it in a small basket after the Indian fashion. Some day, when the woman is from home, they lay this grass baby in her hut. On finding it she holds it to her breast, pretends

[1] Ch. Rogers, *Social Life in Scotland*, iii. 220.

[2] E. W. Nelson, "The Eskimo about Bering Strait," *Eighteenth Annual Report of the Bureau of American Ethnology*, Part I. (Washington, 1899) p. 435.

[3] J. Teit, "The Thompson Indians of British Columbia," *Memoir of the American Museum of Natural History, The Jesup North Pacific Expedition*, vol. i. No. 4 (April 1900), p. 314.

[4] J. R. Swanton, "Contributions to the Ethnology of the Haida" (Leyden and New York, 1905), pp. 47 *sq*. (*The Jesup North Pacific Expedition*, vol. v.).

to nurse it, and sings it lullabies.   This is done as a charm
to make her conceive.[1]   The Huichol Indians of Mexico
believe in a certain Mother who is the goddess of conception
and childbirth, and lives in a cave near Santa Catarina.   A
woman desirous of offspring deposits in this cave a doll
made of cotton cloth to represent the baby on which her
heart is set.   After a while she goes back to the cave, puts
the doll under her girdle, and soon afterwards is supposed
to be pregnant.[2]   With a like intent Indian women in Peru
used to wrap up stones like babies and leave them at the
foot of a large stone, which they revered for this purpose.[3]
Among the Makatisses, a Caffre tribe of South Africa, a
traveller observed a woman carefully tending a doll made
out of a gourd, adorned with necklaces of glass beads, and
heavily weighted with iron ore.   On enquiry he learned that
she had been directed by the medicine-man to do this as a
means of obtaining a child.[4]   Among the Basutos childless
wives make rude effigies of clay, and give them the name of
some tutelar deity.   They treat these dolls as if they were real
children, and beseech the divinity to whom they have dedicated
them to grant them the power of conception.[5]   In Anno, a
district of West Africa, women may often be seen carrying
wooden dolls strapped, like babies, on their backs as a cure
for sterility.[6]   In Japan, when a marriage is unfruitful, the
old women of the neighbourhood come to the house and go
through a pretence of delivering the wife of a child.   The
infant is represented by a doll.[7]   The Maoris had a household
god whose image was in the form of an infant.   The image
was very carefully made, generally life-size, and adorned with
the family jewels.   Barren women nursed it and addressed it
in the most endearing terms in order to become mothers.[8]

Among the Battas of Sumatra a barren woman, who
would become a mother, will make a wooden image of a

[1] S. Powers, *Tribes of California* (Washington, 1877), p. 318.

[2] C. Lumholtz, "Symbolism of the Huichol Indians," *Memoirs of the American Museum of Natural History*, vol. iii. (May 1900) p. 52.

[3] P. J. de Arriaga, *Extirpacion de la Idolatria del Piru* (Lima, 1621), p. 37.

[4] A. Delegorgue, *Voyage dans l'Afrique Australe* (Paris, 1847), ii. 325 *sq.*

[5] E. Casalis, *The Basutos*, p. 251.

[6] Binger, *Du Niger au Golfe de Guinée* (Paris, 1892), ii. 230.

[7] W. G. Aston, *Shinto (the Way of the Gods)* (London, 1905), p. 331.

[8] R. Taylor, *Te Ika A Maui, or New Zealand and its Inhabitants* (London, 1870), p. 213.

Magical
images to
procure
offspring
in the
Eastern
Archi-
pelago.

child and hold it in her lap, believing that this will lead to
the fulfilment of her wish.[1]   In the Babar Archipelago, when
a woman desires to have a child, she invites a man who is
himself the father of a large family to pray on her behalf to
Upulero, the spirit of the sun.   A doll is made of red cotton,
which the woman clasps in her arms as if she would suckle
it.   Then the father of many children takes a fowl and holds
it by the legs to the woman's head, saying, " O Upulero,
make use of the fowl ; let fall, let descend a child, I beseech
you, I entreat you, let a child fall and descend into my hands
and on my lap."   Then he asks the woman, " Has the child
come ? " and she answers, " Yes, it is sucking already."
After that the man holds the fowl on the husband's head,
and mumbles some form of words.   Lastly, the bird is killed
and laid, together with some betel, on the domestic place of
sacrifice.   When the ceremony is over, word goes about in
the village that the woman has been brought to bed, and
her friends come and congratulate her.[2]   Here the pretence
that a child has been born is a purely magical rite designed
to secure, by means of imitation or mimicry, that a child
really shall be born ; but an attempt is made to add to the
efficacy of the rite by means of prayer and sacrifice.   To
put it otherwise, magic is here blent with and reinforced by
religion.   In Saibai, one of the islands in Torres Straits, a
similar custom of purely magical character is observed,
without any religious alloy.   Here, when a woman is pregnant, all the other women assemble.   The husband's sister
makes an image of a male child and places it before the
pregnant woman ; afterwards the image is nursed until the
birth of the child in order to ensure that the baby shall be
a boy.   To secure male offspring a woman will also press to
her abdomen a fruit resembling the male organ of generation,
which she then passes to another woman who has borne
none but boys.   This, it is clear, is imitative magic in a
slightly different form.[3]   In the seventh month of a woman's

[1] J. B. Neumann, "Het Pane- en
Bila-Stroomgebied op het eiland Sum-
atra," *Tijdschrift van het Nederlandsch
Aardrijkskundig Genootschap*, Tweede
Serie, deel iii. (1886) Afdeeling, meer
uitgebreide artikelen, No. 3, p. 515.

[2] J. G. F. Riedel, *De sluik- en
kroesharige rassen tusschen Selebes en
Papua* (The Hague, 1886), p. 343.

[3] Dr. MacFarlane, quoted by A. C.
Haddon, in *Journal of the Anthropological Institute*, xix. (1890) pp. 389 *sq.*

pregnancy common people in Java observe a ceremony which is plainly designed to facilitate the real birth by mimicking it. Husband and wife repair to a well or to the bank of a neighbouring river. The upper part of the woman's body is bare, but young banana leaves are fastened under her arms, a small opening, or rather fold, being left in the leaves in front. Through this opening or fold in the leaves on his wife's body the husband lets fall from above a weaver's shuttle. An old woman receives the shuttle as it falls, takes it up in her arms and dandles it as if it were a baby, saying, " Oh, what a dear little child ! Oh, what a beautiful little child ! " Then the husband lets an egg slip through the fold, and when it lies on the ground as an emblem of the afterbirth, he takes his sword and cuts through the banana leaf at the place of the fold, obviously as if he were severing the navel-string.[1] Persons of high rank in Java observe the ceremony after a fashion in which the real meaning of the rite is somewhat obscured. The pregnant woman is clothed in a long robe, which her husband, kneeling before her, severs with a stroke of his sword from bottom to top. Then he throws his sword on the ground and runs away as fast as he can.[2] According to another account, the woman is wrapt round with white thread ; her husband cuts it with his sword, throws away an oblong white gourd, dashes a fowl's egg to the ground, rolls along a young coco-nut on which the figures of a man and woman have been painted, and so departs in haste.[3] Among some of the Dyaks of Borneo, when a woman is in hard labour, a wizard is called in, who essays to facilitate the delivery in a rational manner by manipulating the body of the sufferer. Meantime another wizard outside the room exerts himself to attain the same

[1] C. Poensen, "Iets over de kleeding der Javanen," *Mededeelingen van wege het Nederlandsche Zendelinggenootschap*, xx. (1876) pp. 274 *sq.* ; C. M. Pleyte, " Plechtigheden en gebruiken uit den cyclus van het familienleven der volken van den Indischen Archipel," *Bijdragen tot de Taal- Land- en Volkenkunde van Nederlandsch Indië*, xli. (1892) p. 578. A slightly different account of the ceremony is given by J. Kreemer ("Hoe

de Javaan zijne zieken verzorgt," *Mededeelingen van wege het Nederlandsche Zendelinggenootschap*, xxxvi. (1892) p. 116).

[2] S. A. Buddingh, "Gebruiken bij Javaansche Grooten," *Tijdschrift voor Neêrlands Indië*, 1840, deel ii. pp. 239-243.

[3] J. Knebel, "Varia Javanica," *Tijdschrift voor Indische Taal- Land- en Volkenkunde*, xliv. (1901) pp. 34-37.

end by means which we should regard as wholly irrational.
He, in fact, pretends to be the expectant mother ; a large
stone attached to his stomach by a cloth wrapt round his
body represents the child in the womb, and, following the
directions shouted to him by his colleague on the real scene
of operations, he moves this make-believe baby about on his
body in exact imitation of the movements of the real baby
till the infant is born.[1]

Simulation
of birth at
adoption,
and after
supposed
death.   The same principle of make-believe, so dear to children,
has led other peoples to employ a simulation of birth as a
form of adoption, and even as a mode of restoring a supposed
dead person to life.   If you pretend to give birth to a boy,
or even to a great bearded man who has not a drop of your
blood in his veins, then, in the eyes of primitive law and
philosophy, that boy or man is really your son to all intents
and purposes.   Thus Diodorus tells us that when Zeus
persuaded his jealous wife Hera to adopt Hercules, the
goddess got into bed, and clasping the burly hero to her
bosom, pushed him through her robes and let him fall to the
ground in imitation of a real birth ; and the historian adds
that in his own day the same mode of adopting children
was practised by the barbarians.[2]   At the present time it is
said to be still in use in Bulgaria and among the Bosnian
Turks.   A woman will take a boy whom she intends to
adopt and push or pull him through her clothes ; ever afterwards he is regarded as her very son, and inherits the whole
property of his adoptive parents.[3]   Among the Berawans of
Sarawak, when a woman desires to adopt a grown-up man
or woman, a great many people assemble and have a feast.
The adopting mother, seated in public on a raised and
covered seat, allows the adopted person to crawl from behind
between her legs.   As soon as he appears in front he is

[1] F. W. Leggat, quoted by H. Ling
Roth, *The Natives of Sarawak and
British North Borneo* (London, 1896),
i. 98 *sq.*

[2] Diodorus Siculus, iv. 39.

[3] Stanislaus Ciszewski, *Künstliche
Verwandtschaft bei den Südslaven*
(Leipsic, 1897), pp. 103 *sqq.*   In the
Middle Ages a similar form of adoption
appears to have prevailed, with the

curious variation that the adopting
parent who simulated the act of birth
was the father, not the mother.   See
J. Grimm, *Deutsche Rechtsalterthümer*,
pp. 160, 464 *sq.* ; J. J. Bachofen, *Das
Mutterrecht*, pp. 254 *sq.* F. Liebrecht,
however, quotes a mediaeval case in
which the ceremony was performed by
the adopting mother (*Zur Volkskunde*,
p. 432).

stroked with the sweet-scented blossoms of the areca palm, and tied to the woman. Then the adopting mother and the adopted son or daughter, thus bound together, waddle to the end of the house and back again in front of all the spectators. The tie established between the two by this graphic imitation of childbirth is very strict; an offence committed against an adopted child is reckoned more heinous than one committed against a real child.[1] In Central Africa "the Bahima practise adoption; the male relatives always take charge of a brother's children. When a man dies his brother takes any children of the deceased and places them one by one in his wife's lap. Then he binds round her waist the thong used for tying the legs of restive cows during milking, just as is done after childbirth. The children are then brought up with his own family."[2] In ancient Greece any man who had been supposed erroneously to be dead, and for whom in his absence funeral rites had been performed, was treated as dead to society till he had gone through the form of being born again. He was passed through a woman's lap, then washed, dressed in swaddling-clothes, and put out to nurse. Not until this ceremony had been punctually performed might he mix freely with living folk.[3] In ancient India, under similar circumstances, the supposed dead man had to pass the first night after his return in a tub filled with a mixture of fat and water; there he sat with doubled-up fists and without uttering a syllable, like a child in the womb, while over him were performed all the sacraments that were wont to be celebrated over a pregnant woman. Next morning he got out of the tub and went through once more all the other sacraments he had formerly partaken of from his youth up; in particular, he married a wife or espoused his old one over again with due solemnity.[4]

Amongst the Akikuyu of British East Africa every member of the tribe, whether male or female, has to go

---

[1] For this information I have to thank Dr. C. Hose, formerly Resident Magistrate of the Baram district, Sarawak.

[2] Rev. J. Roscoe, "The Bahima," *Journal of the R. Anthropological Institute*, xxxvii. (1907) p. 104.

[3] Plutarch, *Quaestiones Romanae*, 5;

Hesychius, *s.v.* Δευτερόποτμος.

[4] W. Caland, *Die altindischen Todten- und Bestattungsgebräuche* (Amsterdam, 1896), p. 89. Among the Hindoos of Kumaon the same custom is reported to be still observed. See Major Reade in *Panjab Notes and Queries*, ii. p. 74, § 452.

Simulation
of birth
among the
Akikuyu. through a pretence of being born again. The age at
which the ceremony is performed varies with the ability
of the father to provide the goat or sheep which is required
for the due observance of the rite; but it seems that the
new birth generally takes place when a child is about ten
years old or younger. If the child's father or mother
is dead, a man or woman acts as proxy on the occasion,
and in such a case the woman is thenceforth regarded by
the child as its own mother. A goat or sheep is killed
in the afternoon and the stomach and intestines are reserved.
The ceremony takes place at evening in a hut; none but
women are allowed to be present. A circular piece of the
goat-skin or sheep-skin is passed over one shoulder and
under the other arm of the child who is to be born again;
and the animal's stomach is similarly passed over the child's
other shoulder and under its other arm. The mother, or
the woman who acts as mother, sits on a hide on the floor
with the child between her knees. The sheep's or goat's
gut is passed round her and brought in front of the child.
She groans as if in labour, another woman cuts the gut
as if it were the navel-string, and the child imitates the
cry of a new-born infant. Until a lad has thus been born
again in mimicry, he may not assist at the disposal of his
father's body after death, nor help to carry him out into the
wilds to breathe his last. Formerly the ceremony of the new
birth was combined with the ceremony of circumcision; but
the two are now kept separate.[1] In origin we may suppose
that this curious pretence of being born again regularly
formed part of the initiatory rites through which every
Kikuyu lad and every Kikuyu girl had to pass before
he or she was recognised as a full-grown member of the
tribe;[2] for in many parts of the world a simulation of death
and resurrection has been enacted by candidates on such
occasions as well as on admission to the membership of
certain secret societies.[3] The intention of the mock birth

[1] W. S. Routledge and K. Routledge, *With a Prehistoric People, the
Akikuyu of British East Africa* (London, 1910), pp. 151 *sq.* The ceremony
was briefly described by me on Dr.
Crawford's authority in *Totemism and*

Exogamy, iv. 228.

[2] As to these rites among the Akikuyu see W. S. Routledge and K
Routledge, *op. cit.* pp. 154 *sqq.*

[3] *The Golden Bough*, Second Edition,
iii. 422 *sqq.* ; *Totemism and Exogamy,*

or mock resurrection is not clear ; but we may conjecture that it is designed, on the principles of homoeopathic or imitative magic, either to impart to the candidate the powers of a ghost or to enable him to be reborn again into the world whenever he shall have died in good earnest.

Magical images have often been employed for the amiable purpose of winning love. Thus to shoot an arrow into the heart of a clay image was an ancient Hindoo mode of securing a woman's affection ; only the bow-string must be of hemp, the shaft of the arrow must be of black *ala* wood, its plume an owl's feather, and its barb a thorn.[1] No doubt the wound inflicted on the heart of the clay image was supposed to make a corresponding impression on the woman's heart. Among the Chippeway Indians there used to be few young men or women who had not little images of the persons whose love they wished to win. They pricked the hearts of the images and inserted magical powders in the punctures, while they addressed the effigies by the names of the persons whom they represented, bidding them requite their affection.[2] Ancient witches and wizards melted wax in the fire in order to make the hearts of their sweethearts to melt of love.[3] And as the wound of love may be inflicted by an image, so by an image it may be healed. How that can be done is told by Heine in a poem based on the experience of one of his own schoolfellows. It is called *The Pilgrimage to Kevlaar,* and describes how sick people offer waxen models of their ailing members to the Virgin Mary at Kevlaar in order that she may heal them of their infirmities. In the poem a lover, wasting away for love and sorrow at the death of his sweetheart, offers to the Virgin the waxen model of a heart with a prayer that she would heal his heart-ache.[4] Such customs, still commonly

Magical images to procure love.

i. 44, iii. 463 *sqq.*, 485, 487 *sq.*, 489 *sq.*, 505, 532, 542, 545, 546, 549.

[1] W. Caland, *Altindisches Zauberritual* (Amsterdam, 1900), p. 119 ; M. Bloomfield, *Hymns of the Atharva-Veda* (Oxford, 1897), pp. 358 *sq.* (*Sacred Books of the East,* vol. xlii.).

[2] W. H. Keating, *Narrative of an Expedition to the Source of St. Peter's River* (London, 1825), ii. 159.

[3] Theocritus, *Id.* ii. 28 *sq.* ; Virgil, *Ecl.* viii. 81 *sq.* In neither of these passages is the wax said to have been fashioned in the likeness of the beloved one, but it may have been so.

[4] As to the waxen models of the human body, or parts of it, which are still dedicated to the Virgin Mary at Kevelaer, see R. Andree, *Votive und Weihegaben des Katholischen Volks in*

observed in some parts of Catholic Europe, are interesting because they shew how in later times magic comes to be incorporated with religion. The moulding of wax images of ailing members is in its origin purely magical: the prayer to the Virgin or to a saint is purely religious: the combination of the two is a crude, if pathetic, attempt to turn both magic and religion to account for the benefit of the sufferer.

Magical images to maintain domestic harmony.

The natives of New Caledonia make use of effigies to maintain or restore harmony between husband and wife. Two spindle-shaped bundles, one representing the man and the other the woman, are tied firmly together to symbolise and ensure the amity of the couple. They are made up of various plants, together with some threads from the woman's girdle and a piece of the man's apron; a bone needle forms the axis of each. The talisman is meant to render the union of the spouses indissoluble, and is carefully treasured by them both. If, nevertheless, a domestic jar should unfortunately take place, the husband repairs to the family burying-ground with the precious packet. There he lights a fire with a wood of a particular kind, fumigates the talisman, sprinkles it with water from a prescribed source, waves it round his head, and then stirring the needle in the bundle which represents himself he says, " I change the heart of this woman, that she may love me." If the wife still remains obdurate, he ties a sugar-cane to the bundle, and presents it to her through a third person. If she eats of the sugar-cane, she feels her love for her husband revive. On her side she has the right to operate in like manner on the bundle which represents herself, always provided that she does not go to the burying-ground, which is strictly forbidden to women.[1]

Homoeopathic magic in medicine.

Another beneficent use of homoeopathic magic is to heal or prevent sickness. In ancient Greece, when a man died of dropsy, his children were made to sit with their feet in water until the body was burned. This was supposed to prevent the disease from attacking them.[2] Similarly, on

---

Süddeutschland (Brunswick, 1904) p. 85 ; and as to votive images of hearts in general, see *id.* pp. 127 *sq.*

[1] Father Lambert, in *Missions Catho-*

liques, xii. (1880) p. 41 ; *id., Mœurs et Superstitions des Néo - Calédoniens* (Nouméa, 1900), pp. 97 *sq.*

[2] Plutarch, *De sera numinis vindicta*, 14.

the principle of water to water, among the natives of the
hills near Rajamahall in India, the body of a person who
has died of dropsy is thrown into a river; they think that
if the corpse were buried, the disorder would return and
carry off other people.[1]

The ancient Hindoos performed an elaborate ceremony, Homoeo-
based on homoeopathetic magic, for the cure of jaundice. pathic
Its main drift was to banish the yellow colour to yellow of jaundice
creatures and yellow things, such as the sun, to which it
properly belongs, and to procure for the patient a healthy
red colour from a living, vigorous source, namely a red bull.
With this intention, a priest recited the following spell:
" Up to the sun shall go thy heart-ache and thy jaundice:
in the colour of the red bull do we envelop thee! We
envelop thee in red tints, unto long life. May this person
go unscathed and be free of yellow colour! The cows
whose divinity is Rohini, they who, moreover, are themselves red (*rohinih*)—in their every form and every strength
we do envelop thee. Into the parrots, into the thrush, do
we put thy jaundice, and, furthermore, into the yellow wagtail do we put thy jaundice." While he uttered these words,
the priest, in order to infuse the rosy hue of health into the
sallow patient, gave him water to sip which was mixed with
the hair of a red bull; he poured water over the animal's
back and made the sick man drink it; he seated him on the
skin of a red bull and tied a piece of the skin to him. Then
in order to improve his colour by thoroughly eradicating the
yellow taint, he proceeded thus. He first daubed him from
head to foot with a yellow porridge made of turmeric or
curcuma (a yellow plant), set him on a bed, tied three yellow
birds, to wit a parrot, a thrush, and a yellow wagtail, by
means of a yellow string to the foot of the bed; then
pouring water over the patient, he washed off the yellow
porridge, and with it no doubt the jaundice, from him to
the birds. After that, by way of giving a final bloom to his
complexion, he took some hairs of a red bull, wrapt them
in gold leaf, and glued them to the patient's skin.[2] The

---

[1] Th. Shaw, "The Inhabitants of
the Hills near Rajamahall," *Asiatic
Researches*, iv. 69 (8vo edition, London,

1807).

[2] M. Bloomfield, *Hymns of the
Atharva-Veda* (Oxford, 1897), pp. 7

Homoeo-
pathic
treatment
of jaundice. ancients held that if a person suffering from jaundice looked sharply at a stone-curlew, and the bird looked steadily at him, he was cured of the disease. "Such is the nature," says Plutarch, "and such the temperament of the creature that it draws out and receives the malady which issues, like a stream, through the eyesight."[1] So well recognised among bird - fanciers was this valuable property of the stone-curlew that when they had one of these birds for sale they kept it carefully covered, lest a jaundiced person should look at it and be cured for nothing.[2] The virtue of the bird lay not in its colour but in its large golden eye, which, if it do not pass for a tuft of yellow lichen, is the first thing that strikes the searcher, as the bird cowers, to escape observation, on the sandy, flint-strewn surface of the ground which it loves to haunt, and with which its drab plumage blends so well that only a practised eye can easily detect it.[3] Thus the yellow eye of the bird drew out the yellow jaundice. Pliny tells of another, or perhaps the same, bird, to which the Greeks gave their name for jaundice, because if a jaundiced man saw it, the disease left him and slew the bird.[4] He mentions also a stone which was supposed to cure jaundice because its hue resembled that of a jaundiced skin.[5] In modern Greece jaundice goes by the name of the Golden Disease, and very naturally it can be healed by gold. To effect a perfect cure all that you have to do is this. Take a piece of gold (best of all an English sovereign, since English gold is the purest) and put it in a measure of wine. Expose the wine with the gold to the stars for three nights ; then drink three glasses of it daily till it is used up. By that time the jaundice will be quite washed out of your system. The cure is, in the strictest sense of the word, a sovereign one.[6]

sq., 263 *sq.* ; W. Caland, *Altindisches Zauberritual* (Amsterdam, 1900), pp. 75 *sq.*

[1] Plutarch, *Quaest. conviv.* v. 7. 2, 8 *sq.* ; Aelian, *Nat. animalium*, xvii. 13.

[2] Schol. on Aristophanes, *Birds*, 266; Schol. on Plato, *Gorgias*, p. 494 B.

[3] Alfred Newton, *Dictionary of Birds* (London, 1893-1896), p. 129.

[4] Pliny, *Nat. Hist.* xxx. 94. The Greek name for jaundice, and for this singular bird, was *ikteros*. The Romans called jaundice "the king's malady" (*morbus regius*). See below, p. 371, note [4].

[5] *Nat. Hist.* xxxvii. 170.

[6] This precious remedy was communicated to me by my colleague and friend Professor R. C. Bosanquet of

A Wend cure for jaundice, like the modern Greek one, is to drink a glass of water in which a gold coin has been left overnight.[1] A remedy based on the principle of contraries is to look steadily at pitch or other black substances.[2] In South Russia a Jewish remedy for jaundice is to wear golden bracelets.[3] Here the great homoeopathic principle is clearly the same as in the preceding cases, though its application is different. In Germany yellow turnips, gold coins, gold rings, saffron, and other yellow things are still esteemed remedies for jaundice, just as a stick of red sealing - wax carried on the person cures the red eruption popularly known as St. Anthony's fire, or the blood-stone with its blood-red spots allays bleeding.[4] Another popular remedy in Germany for the red St. Anthony's fire and also for bleeding is supplied by the common crossbills. In this bird "after the first moult the difference between the sexes is shewn by the hens inclining to yellowish-green, while the cocks become diversified by orange-yellow and red, their plumage finally deepening into a rich crimson-red, varied in places by a flame-colour."[5] The smallest reflection may convince us that these gorgeous hues must be endowed with very valuable medical properties. Accordingly in some parts of Bavaria, Saxony, and Bohemia people keep crossbills in cages in order that the red birds may draw the red St. Antony's fire and the inflammation of fever to themselves and so relieve the human patient. Often in a peasant's cottage you may see the red bird in its cage hanging beside a sick-bed and drawing to itself the hectic flush from the cheeks of the hot and restless patient, who lies tossing under the blankets. And the dried body of a crossbill has only to be placed on a wound to stop the bleeding at once. It is not the colour only of the feathers which produces this salutary effect; the peculiar

Homoeopathic treatment of St. Anthony's fire.

Liverpool. The popular Greek name for jaundice is χρυσῆ.

[1] W. von Schulenburg, *Wendische Volkssagen und Gebräuche* (Leipsic, 1880), p. 223.

[2] J. Grimm, *Deutsche Mythologie,*[4] ii. 981; G. Lammert, *Volksmedizin und medizinischer Aberglaube in Bayern* (Würzburg, 1869), p. 248.

[3] Dr. S. Weissenberg, "Krankheit und Tod bei den südrussischen Juden," *Globus,* xci. (1907) p. 358.

[4] K. Freiherr von Leoprechting, *Aus dem Lechrain* (Munich, 1855), p. 92 ; A. Wuttke, *Der deutsche Volksaberglaube,*[2] p. 302, § 477.

[5] Alfred Newton, *Dictionary of Birds,* p. 115.

shape of the bill, which gives the bird its English and German name, is a contributory cause. For the horny sheaths of the bill cross each other obliquely, and this formation undoubtedly enables the bird to draw diseases to itself more readily than a beak of the common shape could possibly do. Curious observers have even remarked that when the upper bill crosses the lower to the right, the bird will attract the diseases of men, whereas if the upper bill crosses the lower to the left, it will attract the diseases of women. But I cannot vouch for the accuracy of this particular observation. However that may be, certain it is that no fire will break out in a house where a crossbill is kept in a cage, neither will lightning strike the dwelling; and this immunity can only be ascribed to the protective colouring of the bird, the red hue of its plumage serving to ward off the red lightning and to nip a red conflagration in the bud. However, the poor bird seldom lives to old age; nor could this reasonably be expected of a creature which has to endure so much vicarious suffering. It generally falls a victim to one or other of the maladies of which it has relieved our ailing humanity. The causes which have given the crossbill its remarkable colour and the peculiar shape of its bill have escaped many naturalists, but they are familiar to children in Germany. The truth is that when Jesus Christ hung on the cross a flight of crossbills fluttered round him and tugged with their bills at the nails in his hands and feet to draw them out, till their feathers, which were grey before, were all bedabbled with blood, and their beaks, which had been straight, were twisted awry. So red have been their feathers and twisted their beaks from that day to this.[1] Another cure prescribed in Germany for St. Anthony's fire is to rub the patient with ashes from a house that has been burned down;[2] for it is easy to see that as the fire died out in that house, so St. Anthony's fire will die out in that man.

A curious application of homoeopathic magic to the

[1] Dr. J. Gengler, "Der Kreuzschnabel als Hausarzt," *Globus*, xci. (1907) pp. 193 *sq.*; A. Wuttke, *Der deutsche Volksaberglaube*,[2] p. 117, § 164; Alois John, *Sitte, Brauch und Volksglaube im deutschen Westböhmen* (Prague, 1905), p. 218; P. Drechsler, *Sitte, Brauch und Volksglaube in Schlesien*, ii. (Leipsic, 1906) p. 231.

[2] A. Wuttke, *Der deutsche Volksaberglaube*,[2] p. 302, § 477.

cure of disease is founded on the old English superstition
that if a shrew-mouse runs over a beast, be it horse, cow,
or sheep, the animal suffers cruelly and may lose the use
of its limb. Against this accident the farmer used to
keep a shrew-ash at hand as a remedy. A shrew-ash was
prepared thus. A deep hole was bored in the tree, and a
shrew-mouse was thrust in alive and plugged in, probably
with some incantations which have been forgotten.[1] An
ancient Indian cure for a scanty crop of hair was to pour
a solution of certain plants over the head of the patient ;
this had to be done by a doctor who was dressed in black
and had eaten black food, and the ceremony must be performed in the early morning, while the stars were fading in
the sky, and before the black crows had risen cawing from
their nests.[2] The exact virtue of these plants has escaped
our knowledge, but we can hardly doubt that they were dark
and hairy ; while the black clothes of the doctor, his black
food, and the swarthy hue of the crows unquestionably combined to produce a crop of black hair on the patient's head.
A more disagreeable means of attaining the same end is
adopted by some of the tribes of Central Australia. To
promote the growth of a boy's hair a man with flowing locks
bites the youth's scalp as hard as he can, being urged thereto
by his friends, who sit round watching him at his task, while
the sufferer howls aloud with pain.[3] Clearly, on the principle
of capillary attraction, if I may say so, he thus imparts of
his own mature abundance to the scarcity of his youthful
friend.

One of the great merits of homoeopathic magic is that it
enables the cure to be performed on the person of the doctor
instead of on that of his victim, who is thus relieved of all
trouble and inconvenience, while he sees his medical man
writhe in anguish before him. For example, the peasants of

The shrew-mouse and the shrew-ash.

Homoeopathic prescriptions to make the hair grow.

Various homoeopathic remedies.

[1] Gilbert White, *The Natural History
and Antiquities of Selborne*, part ii.
letter 28.

[2] M. Bloomfield, *Hymns of the
Atharva-Veda*, pp. 31, 536 *sq.* ; W.
Caland, *Altindisches Zauberritual*, p.
103. In ancient Indian magic it is
often prescribed that charms to heal
sickness should be performed at the

hour when the stars are vanishing in
the sky. See W. Caland, *op. cit.* pp.
85, 86, 88, 96. Was this in order
that the ailment might vanish with the
stars?

[3] Spencer and Gillen, *Northern
Tribes of Central Australia* (London,
1904), p. 352 ; *id.*, *Native Tribes of
Central Australia*, p. 251.

Perche, in France, labour under the impression that a prolonged fit of vomiting is brought about by the patient's
stomach becoming unhooked, as they call it, and so falling
down.　Accordingly, a practitioner is called in to restore
the organ to its proper place.　After hearing the symptoms
he at once throws himself into the most horrible contortions,
for the purpose of unhooking his own stomach.　Having
succeeded in the effort, he next hooks it up again in another
series of contortions and grimaces, while the patient experiences a corresponding relief.　Fee five francs.[1]　In like
manner a Dyak medicine-man, who has been fetched in
a case of illness, will lie down and pretend to be dead.　He
is accordingly treated like a corpse, is bound up in mats,
taken out of the house, and deposited on the ground.　After
about an hour the other medicine-men loose the pretended
dead man and bring him to life ; and as he recovers, the
sick person is supposed to recover too.[2]　A cure for a
tumour, based on the principle of homoeopathic magic, is prescribed by Marcellus of Bordeaux, court physician to Theo-
dosius the First, in his curious work on medicine.　It is as
follows.　Take a root of vervain, cut it across, and hang
one end of it round the patient's neck, and the other in the
smoke of the fire.　As the vervain dries up in the smoke, so
the tumour will also dry up and disappear.　If the patient
should afterwards prove ungrateful to the good physician,
the man of skill can avenge himself very easily by throwing
the vervain into water ; for as the root absorbs the moisture
once more, the tumour will return.[3]　The same sapient writer
recommends you, if you are troubled with pimples, to watch
for a falling star, and then instantly, while the star is still
shooting from the sky, to wipe the pimples with a cloth or
anything that comes to hand.　Just as the star falls from
the sky, so the pimples will fall from your body ; only you
must be very careful not to wipe them with your bare hand,
or the pimples will be transferred to it.[4]

[1] F. Chapiseau, *Le Folk-lore de la
Beuce et du Perche* (Paris, 1902), i.
172 *sq.*

[2] J. Perham, "Manangism in Borneo,"
*Journal of the Straits Branch of the
Royal Asiatic Society*, No. 19 (1887),
p. 100 ; H. Ling Roth, *The Natives of
Sarawak and British North Borneo*,
i. 280.

[3] Marcellus, *De medicamentis*, xv.
82.

[4] Marcellus, *op. cit.* xxxiv. 100.

Further, homoeopathic and in general sympathetic magic Sympa- plays a great part in the measures taken by the rude hunter thetic magic to or fisherman to secure an abundant supply of food. On ensure the the principle that like produces like, many things are done food supply. by him and his friends in deliberate imitation of the result which he seeks to attain ; and, on the other hand, many things are scrupulously avoided because they bear some more or less fanciful resemblance to others which would really be disastrous.

Nowhere is the theory of sympathetic magic more sys- Systematic tematically carried into practice for the maintenance of the use of sympa- food supply than in the barren regions of Central Australia. thetic Here the tribes are divided into a number of totem clans, magic in Central each of which is charged with the duty of propagating and Australia. multiplying their totem for the good of the community by means of magical ceremonies and incantations. The great majority of the totems are edible animals and plants, and the general result supposed to be accomplished by these magical totemic ceremonies or *intichiuma*, as the Arunta call them, is that of supplying the tribe with food and other necessaries.. Often the rites consist of an imitation of the effect which the people desire to produce ; in other words, their magic is of the homoeopathic or imitative sort.

Thus among the Arunta the men of the witchetty grub *In-* totem perform a series of elaborate ceremonies for multi- *tichiuma,* or magical plying the grub which the other members of the tribe use ceremonies as food. One of the ceremonies is a pantomime represent- for the increase of ing the fully-developed insect in the act of emerging from the totemic the chrysalis. A long narrow structure of branches is animals and plants set up to imitate the chrysalis case of the grub. In this in Central structure a number of men, who have the grub for their Australia. Witchetty totem, sit and sing of the creature in its various stages. grub Then they shuffle out of it in a squatting posture, and as ceremony. they do so they sing of the insect emerging from the chrysalis. This is supposed to multiply the numbers of the grubs.[1] Again, in order to multiply emus, which are an Emu important article of food, the men of the emu totem in the ceremony. Arunta tribe proceed as follows. They clear a small spot of level ground, and opening veins in their arms they let the

[1] Spencer and Gillen, *Native Tribes of Central Australia*, p. 176.

blood stream out until the surface of the ground, for a space of about three square yards, is soaked with it. When the blood has dried and caked, it forms a hard and fairly impermeable surface, on which they paint the sacred design of the emu totem, especially the parts of the bird which they like best to eat, namely, the fat and the eggs. Round this painting the men sit and sing. Afterwards performers, wearing head-dresses to represent the long neck and small head of the emu, mimic the appearance of the bird as it stands

Hakea
flower
ceremony. aimlessly peering about in all directions.[1] Again, men of the hakea flower totem in the Arunta tribe perform a ceremony to make the hakea tree burst into blossom. The scene oi the ceremony is a little hollow, by the side of which grows an ancient hakea tree. In the middle of the hollow is a small worn block of stone, supposed to represent a mass of hakea flowers. Before the ceremony begins, an old man of the totem carefully sweeps the ground clean, and then strokes the stone all over with his hands. After that the men sit round the stone and chant invitations to the tree to flower much and to the blossoms to be filled with honey. Finally, at the request of the old leader, one of the young men opens a vein in his arm and lets the blood flow freely over the stone, while the rest continue to sing. The flow of blood is supposed to represent the preparation of the favourite drink of the natives, which is made by steeping the hakea flower in water. As soon as the stone

Kangaroo
ceremony. is covered with blood the ceremony is complete.[2] Again, the men of the kangaroo totem in the Arunta tribe perform ceremonies for the multiplication of kangaroos at a certain rocky ledge, which, in the opinion of the natives, is full of the spirits of kangaroos ready to go forth and inhabit kangaroo bodies. A little higher up on the hillside are two blocks of stone, which represent a male and female kangaroo respectively. At the ceremony these two blocks are rubbed with a stone by two men. Then the rocky ledge below is decorated with alternate vertical stripes of red and white, to indicate the red fur and white bones of the kangaroo. After that a number of young men sit on the ledge, open veins in

[1] Spencer and Gillen, *op. cit.* pp. 179 *sqq.*

[2] Spencer and Gillen, *op. cit.* pp 184 *sq.*

their arms, and allow the blood to spurtle over the edge of
the rock on which they are seated.   This pouring out of the
blood of the kangaroo men on the rock is thought to drive
out the spirits of the kangaroos in all directions, and so to
increase the number of the animals.   While it is taking
place, the other men sit below watching the performers and
singing songs which refer to the expected increase of
kangaroos.[1]   In the Kaitish tribe, when the headman of   Grass seed
the grass seed totem wishes to make the grass grow, he   ceremony.
takes two sacred sticks or stones (*churinga*) of the well-
known bull-roarer pattern, smears them with red-ochre, and
decorates them with lines and dots of down to represent
grass seed.   Then he rubs the sticks or stones together so

---

[1] Spencer and Gillen, *op. cit.* pp.
193 *sqq.*, 199 *sqq.*, 206 *sq.*   In the
south of France and in the Pyrenees a
number of caves have been found
adorned with paintings or carvings of
animals which have long been extinct
in that region, such as the mammoth,
the reindeer, and the bison.   All the
beasts thus represented appear to be
edible, and none of them to be fierce
carnivorous creatures.   Hence it has
been ingeniously suggested by M. S.
Reinach that the intention of these
works of art may have been to multiply
by magic the animals so represented,
just as the Central Australians seek to
increase kangaroos and emus in the
manner described above.   He infers
that the comparatively high development of prehistoric art in Europe
among men of the reindeer age may
have been due in large measure to the
practice of sympathetic magic.   See
S. Reinach, "L'Art et la magie,"
L'Anthropologie, xiv. (1903) pp. 257-
266 ; *id.*, *Cultes, Mythes et Religions*,
i. (Paris, 1905) pp. 125-136.   Paintings and carvings executed in caves
and on rocks by the aborigines have
been described in various parts of
Australia.   See G. Grey, *Journals of
two Expeditions of Discovery* (London,
1841), i. 201-206 ; R. Brough Smyth,
The Aborigines of Victoria, i. 289-294,
ii. 309 ; E. M. Curr, *The Australian
Race*, ii. 476 ; Spencer and Gillen,
Native Tribes of Central Australia,
pp. 614-618 ; J. F. Mann, in *Proceedings of the Geographical Society
of Australia*, i. (1885) pp. 50 *sq.*,
with illustrations ; W. E. Roth,
*Ethnological Studies among the North-
west-central Queensland Aborigines*,
p. 116.   We may conjecture that
the Hebrew prohibition to make
"the likeness of any beast that is on
the earth, the likeness of any winged
fowl that flieth in the heaven, the likeness of anything that creepeth on the
ground, the likeness of any fish that is
in the water under the earth" (Deuter-
onomy iv. 17 *sq.*), was primarily directed
rather against magic than idolatry
in the strict sense.   Ezekiel speaks
(viii. 10-12) of the elders of Israel
offering incense to "every form of
creeping things, and abominable
beasts," portrayed on the walls of their
chambers.   If hieroglyphs originated,
as seems possible, in representations of
edible animals and plants which had
long been in use for the purpose of
magically multiplying the species, we
could readily understand why, for
example, dangerous beasts of prey
should be conspicuously absent from
the so-called Hittite system of hieroglyphs, without being forced to have
recourse to the rationalistic explanation
of their absence which has been adopted
by Professors G. Hirschfeld and W. M.
Ramsay.   See W. M. Ramsay, *The
Cities and Bishoprics of Phrygia*, i.
p. xv.   On the relations of art and
magic, see Y. Hirn, *Origins of Art*
(London, 1900), pp. 278-297.

that the down flies off in all directions. The down is supposed to carry with it some virtue from the sacred stick or stone whereby the grass seed is made to grow. For days afterwards the headman walks about by himself in the bush singing the grass seed and carrying one of the sacred bull-roarers (*churinga*) with him. At night he hides the implement in the bush and returns to camp, where he may have no intercourse with his wife. For during all this time he is believed to be so full of magic power, derived from the bull-roarer, that if he had intercourse with her the grass seed would not grow properly and his body would swell up when he tasted of it. When the seed begins to grow, he still goes on singing to make it grow more, but when it is fully grown he brings back the sacred implement to his camp hidden in bark ; and having gathered a store of the seed he leaves it with the men of the other half of the tribe, saying, "You eat the grass seed in plenty, it is very good and grows in my country."[1]

Manna ceremony.

A somewhat similar ceremony is performed by men of the manna totem in the Arunta tribe for the increase of their totem. This manna is a product of the mulga tree (*Acacia aneura*), and resembles the better-known sugar-manna of gum trees. When the men of the totem wish to multiply the manna, they resort to a great boulder of grey rock, curiously streaked with black and white seams, which is thought to represent a mass of manna deposited there long ago by a man of the totem. The same significance is attributed to other smaller stones which rest on the top of the boulder. The headman of the totem begins the ceremony by digging up a sacred bull-roarer (*churinga*), which is buried in the earth at the foot of the boulder. It is supposed to represent a lump of manna and to have lain there ever since the remote *alcheringa* or dream time, the farthest past of which these savages have any conception. Next the headman climbs to the top of the boulder and rubs it with the bull-roarer, and after that he takes the smaller stones and with them rubs the same spot on the boulder. Meantime the other men, sitting round about, chant loudly an invitation to the dust produced by

---

[1] Spencer and Gillen, *Northern Tribes of Central Australia*, pp. 291-294.

the rubbing of the stones to go out and generate a plentiful supply of manna on the mulga-trees. Finally, with twigs of the mulga the leader sweeps away the dust which has gathered on the surface of the stone ; his intention is to cause the dust to settle on the mulga-trees and so produce manna.[1]

Again, in a rocky gorge of the Murchison Range there are numbers of little heaps of rounded, water-worn stones, carefully arranged on beds of leaves and hidden away under piles of rougher quartzite blocks. In the opinion of the Warramunga tribe, these rounded stones represent euros, that is, a species of kangaroo. According to their size they stand for young or old, male or female euros. Any old man of the euro totem who happens to pass the spot may take the stones out, smear them with red ochre and rub them well. This is supposed to cause the spirits of euros to pass out from the stones and to be born as animals, thus increasing the food supply.[2] Again, in the Warramunga tribe Messrs. Spencer and Gillen saw and heard a ceremony which was believed to multiply white cockatoos to a wonderful extent. From ten o'clock one evening until after sunrise next morning the headman of the white cockatoo totem held in his hand a rude effigy of the cockatoo and imitated the harsh cry of the bird, with exasperating monotony, all night long. When his voice failed him, his son took up the call and relieved the old man until such time as his father was rested enough to begin again.[3]

Euro ceremony.

Cockatoo ceremony.

In this last ceremony the homoeopathic or imitative character of the rite is particularly plain : the shape of the bird which is to be multiplied is mimicked by an effigy, its cry is imitated by the human voice. In others of the ceremonies just described the homoeopathic principle works by means of stones, which resemble in shape the edible animals or plants that the natives desire to increase. We shall see presently that the Melanesians similarly attribute fertilising virtues to stones of certain shapes.[4] Meantime it

Homoeopathic or imitative character of these rites.

---

[1] Spencer and Gillen, *Native Tribes of Central Australia*, pp. 185 *sq.*

[2] Spencer and Gillen, *Northern Tribes of Central Australia*, p. 310.

[3] Spencer and Gillen, *Northern Tribes of Central Australia*, pp. 309 *sq.*

[4] See below, pp. 162-164.

deserves to be noticed that in some of these Australian rites
for the multiplication of the totemic animals the blood of the
men of the totem plays an important part. Similarly in a
ceremony performed by men of the Dieri tribe for the multiplication of carpet-snakes and iguanas the performers wound
themselves and the blood that drips from their wounds is
poured on a sandhill in which a mythical ancestor is believed
to be buried and from which carpet-snakes and iguanas are
confidently expected to swarm forth.[1] Again, when the
headman of the fish totem in the Wonkgongaru tribe desires
to make fish plentiful, he paints himself all over with red
ochre, and, taking little pointed bones, goes into a pool.
There he pierces his scrotum and the skin around the navel
with the bones, and sits down in the water. The blood
from the wounds, as it mingles with the water, is supposed
to give rise to fish.[2] In all these cases clearly a fertilising
virtue is ascribed to human blood. The ascription is interesting and may possibly go some way to explain the widely-
spread custom of voluntary wounds and mutilations in religious
or magical rites. It may therefore be worth while, even at
the cost of a digression, to enquire a little more closely
into the custom as it is practised by the rude savages
of Australia.[3]

In the first place, then, the Dieri custom of pouring blood
over the supposed remains of the ancestor in his sandhill
closely resembles the custom observed by some of the Australian aborigines at the graves of their relatives. Thus among
the tribes on the River Darling several men used to stand by
the open grave and cut each other's heads with a boomerang,
and then hold their bleeding heads over the grave so that
the blood dripped on the corpse at the bottom of it. If the
deceased was highly esteemed, the bleeding was repeated
after some earth had been thrown on the corpse.[4]   Among

---

[1] A. W. Howitt, *Native Tribes of
South-East Australia* (London, 1904),
p. 798.

[2] Spencer and Gillen, *Northern
Tribes of Central Australia*, pp. 287
sq.

[3] With what follows compare my
article "The Origin of Circumcision,"
The Independent Review, November

1904, pp. 204 *sqq.*; *Totemism and
Exogamy*, iv. 181-184.

[4] F. Bonney, "On some Customs
of the Aborigines of the River Darling,
New South Wales," *Journal of the
Anthropological Institute*, xiii. (1884)
pp. 134 *sq.* Compare J. Fraser, "The
Aborigines of New South Wales,"
Journal and Proceedings of the Royal

the Arunta it is customary for the women kinsfolk to cut
themselves at the grave so that blood flows upon it.[1]   Again,
at the Vasse River, in Western Australia, before the body
was lowered into the grave, the natives used to gash their
thighs, and at the flowing of the blood they all said, " I
have brought blood," and they stamped the foot forcibly on
the ground, sprinkling the blood around them ; then wiping
the wounds with a wisp of leaves, they threw it, all
bloody, on the dead man.   After that they let the body
down into the grave.[2]   Further, it is a common practice with **Blood**
the Central Australians to give human blood to the sick **given to the sick**
and aged for the purpose of strengthening them ; and in **and aged**
order that the blood may have this effect it need not always
be drunk by the infirm person, it is enough to sprinkle it on
his body.   For example, a young man will often open a
vein in his arm and let the blood trickle over the body of
an older man in order to strengthen his aged friend ; and
sometimes the old man will drink a little of the blood.[3]   So
in illness the blood is sometimes applied outwardly as well
as inwardly, the patient both drinking it and having it
rubbed over his body ; sometimes apparently he only drinks
it.   The blood is drawn from a man or woman who is
related to the sufferer either by blood or marriage, and the
notion always is to convey to the sick person some of the
strength of the blood-giver.[4]   In the Wiimbaio tribe, if a
man had nearly killed his wife in a paroxysm of rage, the
woman was laid out on the ground, and the husband's arms
being tightly bound above the elbows, the medicine-man
opened the veins in them and allowed the blood to flow on
the prostrate body of the victim till the man grew faint.[5]
The intention of thus bleeding the man over the woman

Society of New South Wales, xvi.
(1882) pp. 229, 231 ; A. W. Howitt,
Native Tribes of South-East Australia,
pp. 451, 465.

[1] Spencer and Gillen, *Native Tribes
of Central Australia*, pp. 507, 509 *sq.*

[2] Mr. Bussel in Sir G. Grey's *Journals of Two Expeditions of Discovery
in North-West and Western Australia*
(London, 1841), ii. 330.

[3] Spencer and Gillen, *Native Tribes
of Central Australia*, pp. 382, 461 ;

id., *Northern Tribes of Central Australia*, p. 598.

[4] Spencer and Gillen, *Native Tribes
of Central Australia*, p. 464 ; *id.*,
Northern Tribes of Central Australia,
pp. 599 *sqq.* ; W. E. Roth, *Ethnological Studies*, p. 162, § 283.   In North-
Western Queensland the blood may be
drawn for this purpose from any healthy
man, not necessarily from a kinsman.

[5] A. W. Howitt, *Native Tribes of
South-East Australia*, p. 380.

was apparently to restore her to life by means of the blood
drawn from her assailant. Again, before an avenging party
starts to take the life of a distant enemy, all the men stand
up, open veins in their genital organs with sharp flints or
pointed sticks, and allow the blood to spurtle over each
other's thighs. This ceremony is supposed to strengthen
the men mutually, and also to knit them so closely together
that treachery henceforth becomes impossible. Sometimes
for the same purpose blood is drawn from the arm and
drunk by the men of the avenging party, and if one of them
refuses thus to pledge himself the others will force his mouth
open and pour the blood into it. After that, even if he
wishes to play the traitor and to give the doomed man
warning, he cannot do so ; he is bound by a physical
necessity to side with the avengers whose blood he has
swallowed.[1]

Blood used by an avenging party.

     Further, it is worth while to notice some uses made of
human blood in connexion with the ceremonies of circumcision and subincision, which all lads of the Central Australian
tribes have to undergo before they are recognised as full-
grown men. For example, the blood drawn from them at
these operations is caught in a hollow shield and taken to
certain kinsmen or kinswomen, who drink it or have it
smeared on their breasts and foreheads.[2] The motive of
this practice is not mentioned, but on the analogy of the
preceding customs we may conjecture that it is to strengthen
the relatives who partake of the blood. This interpretation
is confirmed by an analogous use in Queensland of the
blood drawn from a woman at the operation which in the
female sex corresponds to subincision in the male ; for that
blood, mixed with another ingredient, is kept and drunk as
a medicine by any sick person who may be in the camp at
the time.[3] Moreover, it is corroborated by a similar use
of the foreskin which has been removed at circumcision ; for
among the southern Arunta this piece of skin is given to
the younger brother of the circumcised lad and he swallows

Blood of circum- cision and sub- incision ; uses made of it.

[1] Spencer and Gillen, *Native Tribes of Central Australia*, pp. 461 *sq.* ; *id.*, *Northern Tribes of Central Australia*, pp. 560, 562, 598.
[2] Spencer and Gillen, *Native Tribes*

of Central Australia, pp. 251, 463 ; *id.*, *Northern Tribes of Central Aus- tralia*, pp. 352, 355.
[3] W. E. Roth, *Ethnological Studies*, p. 174, § 305.

it, in the belief that it will make him grow strong and tall.[1]
In the tribe at Fowler's Bay, who practise both circumcision
and subincision, the severed foreskin is swallowed by the
operator,[2] perhaps in order to strengthen the lad sympathetically.   In some tribes of North-West Australia it is the lad
himself who swallows his own foreskin mixed with kangaroo
flesh ; while in other tribes of the same region the severed
portion is taken by the relations and deposited under the
bark of a large tree.[3] The possible significance of this latter
treatment of the foreskin will appear presently.   Among
the Kolkodoons of Cloniny, in Northern Queensland,
the foreskin is strung on twine made of human hair,
and is then tied round the mother's neck "to keep off
the devil." [4]   In the Warramunga tribe the old men draw
blood from their own subincised urethras in presence of the
lads who a few days before have undergone the operation
of subincision.   The object of this custom, we are told, is
to promote the healing of the young men's wounds and to
strengthen them generally.[5]   It does not appear that the
blood of the old men is drunk by or smeared upon the
youths ; seemingly it is supposed to benefit them sympathetically without direct contact.   A similar action of blood   Anodynes
at a distance may partly explain a very singular custom   based on
observed by the Arunta women at the moment when a lad   ciple of
is being subincised.   The operation is performed at a dis-   pathic
tance from, but within hearing of, the women's camp.   When   magic.
the boy is seized in order to be operated on, the men of the

[1] Spencer and Gillen, *Native Tribes
of Central Australia*, pp. 250 *sq.*
Among the northern Arunta the foreskin is buried, along with the blood,
in a hole (*ib.* p. 268).

[2] A. W. Howitt, *Native Tribes of
South-East Australia*, p. 667.

[3] E. Clement, " Ethnographical
Notes on the Western Australian
Aborigines," *Internationales Archiv
für Ethnographie*, xvi. (1904) p. 11.
Among the western coastal tribes of
the Northern Territory of South Australia the foreskin is held against the
bellies of those who have been present
at the operation, then it is placed in a
bag which the operator wears round

his neck till the wound has healed,
when he throws it into the fire.   See
H. Basedow, *Anthropological Notes on
the Western Coastal Tribes of the
Northern Territory of South Australia*,
p. 12 (printed by Hussey and Gilling-
ham, Adelaide).

[4] B. H. Purcell, "Rites and Customs of the Australian Aborigines,"
*Verhandlungen der Berliner Gesellschaft
für Anthropologie*, p. (287) (*Zeitschrift
für Ethnologie*, xxv. 1893).   Cloniny
is perhaps a misprint for Cloncurry.

[5] Spencer and Gillen, *Northern
Tribes of Central Australia*, pp. 360
sq., 599.   Compare *id.*, *Native Tribes
of Central Australia*, p. 257.

party raise a loud shout of "Pirr-rr." At that sound the women immediately assemble in their camp, and the boy's mother cuts gashes across the stomach and shoulders of the boy's sisters, her own elder sisters, an old woman who furnished the boy with a sacred fire at circumcision, and all the women whose daughters he would be allowed to marry ; and while she cuts she imitates the sound made by the men who are subincising her son. These cuts generally leave behind them a definite series of scars ; they have a name of their own (*urpma*), and are often represented by definite lines on the bull-roarers.[1] What the exact meaning of this extraordinary ceremony may be, I cannot say ; but perhaps one of its supposed effects may be to relieve the boy's pain by transferring it to his women-kind. In like manner, when the Warramunga men are fighting each other with blazing torches, the women burn themselves with lighted twigs in the belief that by so doing they prevent the men from inflicting serious injuries on each other.[2] The theory further receives some support from certain practices formerly observed by the natives inhabiting the coast of New South Wales. Before lads had their noses bored, the medicine men threw themselves into contortions on the ground, and after pretending to suffer great pain were delivered of bones, which were to be used at the ceremony of nose-boring. The lads were told that the more the medicine men suffered, the less pain they themselves would feel.[3] Again, among the same natives, when a woman was in labour, a female friend would tie one end of a cord round the sufferer's neck and rub her own gums with the other end till they bled,[4] probably in order to draw away the pain from the mother to herself. For a similar reason, perhaps, in Samoa, while blood was being drawn from a virgin bride, her friends, young and old, beat their heads with stones till they bled.[5]

Lastly, in some tribes the blood shed at the circumcision

[1] Spencer and Gillen, *Native Tribes of Central Australia*, pp. 256 sq.

[2] Spencer and Gillen, *Northern Tribes of Central Australia*, p. 391.

[3] Lieut.-Colonel D. Collins, *Account of the English Colony in New South Wales*, Second Edition (London, 1804), p. 366.

[4] D. Collins, *op. cit.* p. 363.

[5] G. Turner, *Samoa*, p. 94 ; compare W. T. Pritchard, "Notes on certain Anthropological Matters respecting the South Sea Islanders (the Samoans)," *Memoirs of the Anthropological Society of London*, i. (1863-4), pp. 324-326.

and subincision of lads is collected in paper bark and buried
in the bank of a pool where water-lilies grow ; this is supposed to promote the growth of the lilies.[1]   Needless to say,
this rude attempt at horticulture is not prompted by a
simple delight in contemplating these beautiful bright blue
flowers which bloom in the Australian wilderness, decking
the surface of pools by countless thousands.   The savages feed
on the stems and roots of the lilies ; that is why they desire
to cultivate them.[2]   In this last practice a fertilising virtue
is clearly attributed to the blood of circumcision and subincision.   The Anula tribe, who among others observe the
custom, obviously ascribe the same virtue to the severed
foreskin, for they bury it also by the side of a pool.[3]   The
Warramunga entertain the same opinion of this part of the
person, for they place the foreskin in a hole made by a
witchetty grub in a tree, believing that it will cause a plentiful supply of these edible grubs.[4]   Among the Unmatjera
the custom is somewhat different, but taken in connexion
with their traditions it is even more significant.   The boy
puts his severed foreskin on a shield, covers it up with a
broad spear-thrower, and then carries it in the darkness of
night, lest any woman should see what he is doing, to a
hollow tree in which he deposits it.   He tells no one where
he has hidden it, except a man who stands to him in the
relation of father's sister's son.   Nowadays there is no
special relation between the boy and the tree, but formerly
the case seems to have been different.   For according to

Fertilising virtue attributed to blood of circumcision and subincision.

Fertilising virtue attributed to foreskin.

---

[1] Spencer and Gillen, *Northern Tribes of Central Australia*, pp. 367, 368, 599.

[2] Spencer and Gillen, *Northern Tribes of Central Australia*, pp. 9, 368, 552, 553, 554 *sq.*   See further E. Palmer, "On Plants used by the Natives of North Queensland," *Journal and Proceedings of the Royal Society of New South Wales for 1883*, xvii. 101. The seeds of the splendid pink water-lily (the sacred lotus) are also eaten by the natives of North Queensland.   The plant grows in lagoons on the coast. See E. Palmer, *loc. cit.*

[3] Spencer and Gillen, *Northern Tribes of Central Australia*, p. 372.

[4] Spencer and Gillen, *Northern Tribes of Central Australia*, pp. 353 *sq.*   Some of the dwarf tribes of the Gaboon, who practise circumcision, place the severed foreskins in the trunks of a species of nut-tree (*Kula edulis*), which seems to be their totem ; for the tree is said to have a certain sanctity for them, and some groups take their name from it, being called *A-Kula*, "the people of the nut-tree."   They eat the nuts, and have a special cere-mony at the gathering of the first nuts of the season.   See Mgr. Le Roy, " Les Pygmées," *Missions Catholiques*, xxix. (1897) pp. 222 *sq.*, 237.

tradition the early mythical ancestors of the tribe placed their foreskins in their *nanja* trees, that is, in their local totem centres, the trees from which their spirits came forth at birth and to which they would return after death.[1] If, as seems highly probable, such a custom as that recorded by the tradition ever prevailed, its intention could hardly be any other than that of securing the future birth and reincarnation of the owner of the foreskin when he should have died and

Belief of the Central Australian tribes in the reincarnation of the dead.

his spirit returned to its abode in the tree. For among all these Central tribes the belief is firmly rooted that the human soul undergoes an endless series of reincarnations, the living men and women of one generation being nothing but the spirits of their ancestors come to life again, and destined to be themselves reborn in the persons of their descendants. During the interval between two incarnations the souls live in their *nanja* spots or local totem centres, which are always natural objects such as trees or rocks. Each totem clan has a number of such totem centres scattered over the country. There the souls of the dead men and women of the totem, but of no other, congregate during their disembodied state, and thence they issue and are born again in human form when a favourable opportunity presents itself.[2] It might well be thought that a man's new birth would be facilitated if, in his lifetime, he could lay up a stock of vital energy for the use of his disembodied spirit after death. That he did, apparently, by detaching a portion of himself, namely the foreskin, and depositing it in his *nanja* tree, or rock, or whatever it might be.

Circumcision perhaps intended to ensure reincarnation.

Is it possible that in this belief and this practice we have the long lost key to the meaning of circumcision ? In other words, can it be that circumcision was originally intended to ensure the rebirth at some future time of the circumcised man by disposing of the severed portion of his body in such a way as to provide him with a stock of energy on which his disembodied spirit could draw when the critical moment of reincarnation came round ? The conjecture is confirmed by the observation that among the Akikuyu of

[1] Spencer and Gillen, *Northern Tribes of Central Australia*, p. 341.

[2] Spencer and Gillen, *Native Tribes of Central Australia*, pp. 123 *sqq.*

British East Africa the ceremony of circumcision used to be regularly combined with a graphic pretence of rebirth enacted by the novice.[1] If this should prove to be indeed the clue to the meaning of circumcision, it would be natural to look for an explanation of subincision along the same lines. Now we have seen that the blood of subincision is used both to strengthen relatives and to make water-lilies grow. Hence we may conjecture that the strengthening and fertilising virtue of the blood was applied, like the foreskin at circumcision, to lay up a store of energy in the *nanja* spot against the time when the man's feeble ghost would need it. The intention of both ceremonies would thus be to ensure the future reincarnation of the individual by quickening the local totem centre, the home of his disembodied spirit, with a vital portion of himself. That portion, whether the foreskin or the blood, was in a manner seed sown to grow up and provide his immortal spirit with a new body when his old body should have mouldered in the dust.

Subincision possibly also designed to secure rebirth.

Perhaps the same theory may serve to explain another initiatory rite practised by some of the Australian aborigines, namely, the knocking out of teeth. This is the principal ceremony of initiation amongst the tribes of eastern and south-eastern Australia; and it is often practised, though not as an initiatory rite, by the Central tribes, with whom the essential rites of initiation are circumcision and subincision.[2] On the hypothesis here suggested, we should expect to find the tooth regarded as a vital part of the man which was sacrificed to ensure another life for him after death. The durability of the teeth, compared to the corruptible nature of the greater part of the body, might be a sufficient reason with a savage philosopher for choosing this portion of the corporeal frame on which to pin his hope of immortality. The evidence at our disposal certainly does not suffice to establish this explanation of the rite; but there are some facts which seem to point in that direction. In the first

Knocking out of teeth in Australia perhaps practised for the same purpose.

---

[1] See above, pp. 75-77.
[2] A. W. Howitt, *Native Tribes of South-East Australia*, pp. 538 *sqq.*, 563, 564, 565, 566, 569, 571, 576, 586 *sq.*, 588, 589, 592, 613, 616, 641, 655 *sq.*, 675 *sq.*; Spencer and Gillen, *Native Tribes of Central Australia*, pp. 213 *sq.*, 450 *sqq.*; *id.*, *Northern Tribes of Central Australia*, pp. 18, 329, 588 *sqq.*

place, the extracted tooth is supposed to remain in sympathetic connexion with the man from whom it has been removed ; and if proper care is not taken of it, he may fall ill.[1] With some Victorian tribes the practice was for the mother of the lad to choose a young gum-tree and to insert her son's teeth in the bark, at the fork of two of the topmost boughs. Ever afterwards the tree was held in a sense sacred. It was made known only to certain persons of the tribe, and the youth himself was never allowed to learn where his teeth had been deposited. When he died, the tree was killed by fire.[2] Thus in a fashion the tree might be said to be bound up with the life of the man whose teeth it contained, since when he died it was destroyed. Further, among some of the Central tribes the extracted tooth is thrown away as far as possible in the direction of the spot where the man's mother is supposed to have had her camp in the far-off legendary time which is known as the *alcheringa*.[3] May not this be done to secure the rebirth of the man's spirit in that place ? In the Gnanji tribe the extracted tooth is buried by the man's or woman's mother beside a pool, for the purpose of stopping the rain and increasing the number of water-lilies that grow in the pool.[4] Thus the same fertilising virtue is ascribed to the tooth which is attributed to the foreskin severed at circumcision and to the blood

Extraction of teeth associated with rain. drawn at subincision. Why the drawing of teeth should be supposed to stop rain, I cannot guess. Curiously enough, among the Central tribes generally, the extraction of teeth has a special association with rain and water. Thus among the Arunta it is practised chiefly by the members of the rain or water totem ; and it is nearly if not quite obligatory on all the men and women of that totem, whereas it is merely optional with members of the other clans. Further, the ceremony is always performed among the

[1] See below, pp. 176 *sq.*

[2] W. Blandowski, " Personal Observations made in an Excursion towards the Central Parts of Victoria," *Transactions of the Philosophical Society of Victoria*, i. (Melbourne, 1855) p. 72. Compare R. Brough Smyth, *Aborigines of Victoria*, i. 61 ; Spencer and Gillen,

Native Tribes of Central Australia, pp. 453 *sq.*

[3] Spencer and Gillen, *Native Tribes of Central Australia*, pp. 452 *sq.*

[4] Spencer and Gillen, *Northern Tribes of Central Australia*, pp. 594, 596.

Arunta immediately after the magical ceremony for the making of rain.[1] In the Warramunga tribe the knocking out of the teeth generally takes place towards the end of the wet season, when the water-holes are full, and the natives do not wish any more rain to fall. Moreover, it is always performed on the banks of a water-hole. The persons to be operated on enter the pool, fill their mouths with water, spit it out in all directions, and splash the water over themselves, taking care to wet thoroughly the crown of the head. Immediately afterwards the tooth is knocked out. The Chingilli also knock out teeth towards the close of the wet season, when they think they have had enough of rain. The extracted tooth is thrown into a water-hole, in the belief that it will drive rain and clouds away.[2] I merely note, without attempting to account for, this association between the extraction of teeth and the stopping of rain.

The natives of the Cape York Peninsula in Queensland use the extraction of the tooth to determine both a man's totem and the country to which he belongs. While the tooth is being knocked out, they mention the various districts owned or frequented by the lad's mother, her father, or other of her relatives. The one which happens to be mentioned at the moment when the tooth breaks away is the country to which the lad belongs in future, that is, the country where he will have the right to hunt and to gather roots and fruits. Further, the bloody spittle which he ejects after the extraction of the tooth is examined by the old men, who trace some likeness between it and a natural object, such as an animal, a plant, or a stone. Henceforth that object will be the young man's *ari* or totem.[3] Some light is thrown on this ceremony by a parallel custom which the natives of the Pennefather River in Queensland observe at the birth of a child. They believe that every person's spirit undergoes a series of reincarnations, and that during the interval between two

Extraction of tooth used to determine a man's country and totem.

---

[1] Spencer and Gillen, *Native Tribes of Central Australia*, p. 451.

[2] Spencer and Gillen, *Northern Tribes of Central Australia*, pp. 592-594.

[3] A. C. Haddon, *Head-hunters*, p. 193 ; *Reports of the Cambridge Anthropological Expedition to Torres Straits*, v. 193, 221.

Belief in re-
incarnation
among the
natives of
the Penne-
father River
in Queens-
land.
successive reincarnations the spirit stays in one or other
of the haunts of Anjea, the being who causes conception
in women by putting mud babies into their wombs. Hence,
in order to determine where the new baby's spirit resided
since it was last in the flesh, they mention Anjea's haunts
one after the other while the grandmother is cutting the
child's navel-string; and the place which happens to be
mentioned when the navel-string breaks is the spot where
the spirit lodged since its last incarnation. That is the
country to which the child belongs; there he will have
the right of hunting when he grows up. Hence, according
to the home from which its spirit came to dwell among
men, a child may be known as a baby obtained from a
tree, a rock, or a pool of fresh water. Anjea, with whom
the souls of the dead live till their time comes to be born
again, is never seen; but you may hear him laughing in
the depths of the woods, among the rocks, down in the
lagoons, and along the mangrove swamps.[1]   Hence we may
fairly infer that the country assigned to a man of the Cape
York Peninsula at the extraction of his tooth is the one
where his spirit tarried during the interval which elapsed
since its last incarnation. His totem, which is determined
at the same time, may possibly be the animal, plant, or other
natural object in which his spirit resided since its last embodiment in human form, or perhaps rather in which a part of his
spirit may be supposed to lodge outside of his body during life.
The latter view is favoured by the belief of the tribe of the
Pennefather River, whose practice at childbirth so closely
resembles that of the Cape York natives at puberty; for
the Pennefather people hold that during a man's life a
portion of his spirit lodges outside of his body in his afterbirth.[2]   However that may be, it seems probable that
among the Cape York natives the custom of knocking out
the tooth is closely associated with a theory of reincarna-

[1] W. E. Roth, *North Queensland
Ethnography*, *Bulletin* No. 5 (Brisbane, 1903), pp. 18, 23, §§ 68, 83.
We are reminded of the old Greek
saying to be born "of an oak or a
rock" (Homer, *Odyssey*, xix. 163).
See A. B. Cook, "Oak and Rock,"
Classical Review, xv. (1901) pp. 322-
326. In Samoa, a child sometimes
received as his god for life the deity
who chanced to be invoked at the
moment of his birth, whether that
was his father's or his mother's god.
See G. Turner, *Samoa*, p. 79.

[2] See below, pp. 183 *sq.*

tion. Perhaps the same theory explains a privilege enjoyed
by the Kamilaroi tribe of New South Wales. They claimed
a superiority over the surrounding tribes, and enforced their
claim by exacting from them the teeth knocked out at
puberty. The exaction of this tribute might have passed
for a mere assertion of suzerainty, were it not that the
Kamilaroi knocked out their own teeth also.[1] Perhaps the
extracted teeth were believed to secure to their present
possessors a magical control over their former owners, not
only during life but after death, so that armed with them
the Kamilaroi could help or hinder the rebirth of their
departed friends or enemies.[2]

Thus, if I am right, the essential feature in all the three
great initiatory rites of the Australians is the removal of
a vital part of the person which shall serve as a link between two successive incarnations by preparing for the
novice a new body to house his spirit when its present
tabernacle shall have been worn out. Now, if there is any
truth in this suggestion, we should expect to find that
measures to ensure reincarnation are also taken at death
and burial. This seems in fact to be done. For, in the
first place, the practice of pouring the blood of kinsmen
and kinswomen into the grave is obviously susceptible of
this explanation, since, in accordance with the Australian
usages which I have cited, the blood might well be thought

Australian initiatory rites meant to secure rebirth.

Certain funeral rites also intended to ensure reincarnation.

---

[1] Lieut.-Colonel D. Collins, *Account of the English Colony of New South Wales*, Second Edition (London, 1804), pp. 353, 372 *sqq*. The Cammeray of whom Collins speaks are no doubt the tribe now better known as the Kamil-aroi. *Carrahdy*, which he gives as the native name for a high-priest, is clearly the Kamilaroi *kuradyi*, "medicine-man" (W. Ridley, *Kamilaroi and other Australian Languages*, Sydney, 1875, p. 158).

[2] If the possession of the foreskin conferred on the possessor a like power over the person to whom it had be-longed, we can readily understand why the Israelites coveted the foreskins of their enemies the Philistines (1 Samuel xviii. 25-27, 2 Samuel iii. 14). Pro-fessor H. Gunkel interprets a passage

of Ezekiel (xxxii. 18-32) as contrasting the happy lot of the circumcised warrior in the under world with the misery of his uncircumcised foe in the same place, and confesses himself unable to see why circumcision should be thought to benefit the dead. See H. Gunkel, "Über die Beschneidung im alten Testament," *Archiv für Papyrusfor-schung*, ii. (1903) p. 21. (Prof. Gun-kel's paper was pointed out to me by my friend Mr. W. Wyse.) The benefit, on the theory here suggested, was very sub-stantial, since it allowed the dead to come to life again, the grave being a bourne from which only uncircumcised travellers fail, sooner or later, to return. But I confess that Prof. Gunkel's explanation of the passage seems to me rather far-fetched.

Australian funeral ceremonies intended to ensure the reincarnation of the dead.

to strengthen the feeble ghost for a new birth. The same may be said of the Australian custom of depositing hair with the dead,[1] for it is a common notion that the hair is the seat of strength.[2] Again, it has been a rule with some Australian tribes to bury their dead on the spot where they were born.[3] This was very natural if they desired the dead man to be born again. Further, the common Australian practice of depositing the dead in trees[4] may, in some cases at least, have been designed to facilitate rebirth; for trees are often the places in which the souls of the dead reside, and from which they come forth to be born again in human shape. Thus the Unmatjera and Kaitish tribes bury very aged women and decrepit old men in the ground; but the bodies of children, young women, and men in the prime of life are laid on platforms among the boughs of trees; and in regard to children we are definitely told that this is done in the hope that "before very long its spirit may come back again and enter the body of a woman—in all probability that of its former mother."[5] Further, the Arunta, who bury their dead, are careful to leave a low depression on one side of the mound, in order that the spirit may pass out and in; and this depression always faces towards the dead man's or woman's camping-ground in the *alcheringa* or remote past, that is, the spot which he or she inhabited in spirit form.[6] Is not this done to let the spirit rid itself of its decaying tabernacle and repair to the place where in due time it will find a new and better body? In this connexion the final burial rites in the Binbinga, Anula, and Mara tribes are worthy of remark. Among these people the bones of the dead are, after a series of ceremonies, deposited in a hollow log, on which the dead man's totem is painted. This log is then placed, with the

[1] G. Grey, *Journals of Two Expeditions of Discovery,* ii. 335.

[2] See above, pp. 28 *sqq.*

[3] J. Dawson, *Australian Aborigines,* p. 62; J. F. Mann, in *Proceedings of the Geographical Society of Australia,* i. (1885) p. 48.

[4] E. J. Eyre, *Journals of Expeditions of Discovery into Central Australia* (London, 1845), ii. 345 *sq.*; W. E. Roth, *Ethnological Studies,* pp. 165

sq.; J. Mathew, *Eaglehawk and Crow,* p. 122; Spencer and Gillen, *Native Tribes of Central Australia,* p. 498; *id., Northern Tribes of Central Australia,* pp. 505 *sqq.*

[5] Spencer and Gillen, *Northern Tribes of Central Australia,* p. 506.

[6] Spencer and Gillen, *Native Tribes of Central Australia,* p. 497. Compare *id., Northern Tribes of Central Australia,* p. 506.

bones, in the boughs of a tree beside a pool, so that if possible it overhangs the water. For about three wet seasons the father and son of the deceased, who placed the log there, are alone allowed to eat water-lilies out of that pool, and no woman is permitted to go near the spot. There the bones of the dead man remain till the log rots and they fall into the water or are carried away by a flood. When the burial rites are all over, the spirit of the deceased returns to its *mungai* spot, that is, to the place where it dwells in the interval between two successive incarnations. Sooner or later it will be born again.[1] These rites seem, therefore, clearly to be a preparation for the new birth.

As the belief in reincarnation is shared by many peoples besides the Australians, it is natural to suppose that funeral rites intended to facilitate the rebirth of the deceased may be found in other parts of the world. Elsewhere I have cited examples of these rites:[2] here I will add a few more. It is especially the bodies of dead infants which are the object of such ceremonies ; for since their lives have been cut prematurely short, it seems reasonable to give their souls a chance of beginning again and lengthening out their existence on earth to its natural close. But it is not always dead babies only whom the living seek thus to bring back to life. For example, we read that round about Mount Elgon in East Africa "the custom of throwing out the dead is universal among all the clans of Bagishu, except in the case of the youngest child or the old grandfather or grandmother, for whom, like the child, a prolonged life on earth is desired. . . . When it is desired to perpetuate on the earth the life of some old man or woman, or that of some young baby, the corpse is buried inside the house or just under the eaves, until another child is born to the nearest relation of the corpse. This child, male or female, takes the name of the corpse, and the Bagishu firmly believe that the spirit of the dead has passed into this new child and lives again on earth. The remains are then dug up and thrown out into the open."[3] Similarly among the

Belief in reincarnation and measures taken to secure it among other peoples.

Reincarnation among the Bagishu of Mount Elgon.

---

[1] Spencer and Gillen, *Northern Tribes of Central Australia*, pp. 552 *sqq.*

[2] *Adonis, Attis, Osiris*, Second Edition (1907), pp. 77 *sqq.*

[3] J. B. Purvis, *Through Uganda to Mount Elgon* (London, 1909), pp. 302 *sq.*

Reincarna-
tion among
the tribes
of the
Lower
Congo. tribes of the Lower Congo "a baby is always buried near the house of its mother, never in the bush. They think that, if the child is not buried near its mother's house, she will be unlucky and never have any more children. It is believed that the only new thing about a child is its body. The spirit is old and formerly belonged to some deceased person, or it may have the spirit of some living person. They have two reasons for believing this. The child speaks early of strange things the mother has never taught it, so that they believe the old spirit is talking in the child. Again, if the child is like its mother, father, or uncle, they think it has the spirit of the person it resembles, and that that person will soon die. Hence a parent will resent it if you say that the baby is like him or her." [1] Thus it appears that the argument for the pre-existence of the human soul, which Plato and Wordsworth [2] drew from reminiscence, is fully

Reincarna-
tion in
India. accepted by some negro tribes of West Africa. In the Bilaspore district of India "a still-born child, or one who has passed away before the *Chhatti* (the sixth day, the day of purification) is not taken out of the house for burial, but is placed in an earthen vessel (a *gharā*) and is buried in the doorway or in the yard of the house. Some say that this is done in order that the mother may bear another child." [3] It is said that among the Kondhs of India, on the day after a death, some boiled rice and a small fowl are taken to the place where the body was burned ; there the fowl is split down the breast and placed on the spot, after which it is eaten and the soul of the departed is invited to enter a new-born child. [4] On the fifth day after a death the Gonds perform the ceremony of bringing back the soul. They go to the riverside and call aloud the name of the deceased.

[1] J. H. Weeks, "Notes on some Customs of the Lower Congo People," *Folk-lore*, xix. (1908) p. 422.

[2] Plato, *Phaedo*, 18, p. 72 E καὶ μήν, ἔφη ὁ Κέβης ὑπολαβών, καὶ κατ᾽ ἐκεῖνόν γε τὸν λόγον, ὦ Σώκρατες, εἰ ἀληθής ἐστιν, ὃν σὺ εἴωθας θαμὰ λέγειν, ὅτι ἡμῖν ἡ μάθησις οὐκ ἄλλο τι ἢ ἀνάμνησις τυγχάνει οὖσα, καὶ κατὰ τοῦτον ἀνάγκη που ἡμᾶς ἐν προτέρῳ τινὶ χρόνῳ μεμαθηκέναι ἃ νῦν ἀναμιμνησκόμεθα. τοῦτο δὲ ἀδύνατον, εἰ μὴ ἦν που ἡμῶν ἡ ψυχὴ πρὶν ἐν τῷδε τῷ ἀνθρωπίνῳ εἴδει γενέσθαι· ὥστε καὶ ταύτῃ ἀθάνατόν τι ἔοικεν ἡ ψυχὴ εἶναι. Compare Wordsworth, *Ode on Intimations of Immortality*:

Our birth is but a sleep and a forgetting.

[3] E. M. Gordon, *Indian Folk-tales* (London, 1908), p. 49.

[4] E. Thurston, *Castes and Tribes of Southern India*, iii. 398.

Then they enter the river, catch a fish or an insect, and taking it home place it among the sainted dead of the family, believing that the spirit of their lost one has thus been brought back to the house. Sometimes the fish or insect is eaten in order that the spirit which it contains may be born again as a child.[1] When a baby died within a month or two of birth, the Hurons did not dispose of its little body like those of grown people by depositing it on a scaffold; they buried it beside the road in order, so they said, that the child might enter secretly into the womb of some woman passing by and be born again into the world.[2] Some of the ancient rules observed with regard to funerals in the Greek island of Ceos have been ingeniously explained by Mr. F. B. Jevons as designed to secure the rebirth of the departed in one of the women of the family.[3] The widespread custom of burying the dead in the house was perhaps instituted for the same purpose,[4] and the ancient Greek practice of sacrificing to the dead man at the grave on his birthday may possibly have originated in the same train of thought.[5] For example, sacrifices were annually offered on their birthdays to Hippocrates by the Coans, to Aratus by the Sicyonians, and to Epicurus by his disciples.[6]

Reincarnation among the Hurons.

Reincarnation among the ancient Greeks.

Now too we can fully understand the meaning of the bloody ritual in the ceremonies for the multiplication of the totem animals and plants. We have seen that a strengthening and fertilising virtue is attributed to human blood. What

Rites to procure the rebirth of edible animals and plants.

[1] R. V. Russel, in *Census of India, 1901*, vol. xiii. *Central Provinces*, p. 93.

[2] *Relations des Jésuites*, 1636, p. 130 (Canadian Reprint).

[3] "Greek Law and Folklore," *Classical Review*, ix. (1895) pp. 247-250. For the rules themselves see H. Roehl, *Inscriptiones Graecae Antiquissimae*, No. 395; Dittenberger, *Sylloge Inscriptionum Graecarum*,² No. 877; Ch. Michel, *Recueil d'inscriptions grecques*, No. 398.

[4] This has been suggested by Mr. J. E. King for infant burial (*Classical Review*, xvii. (1903) p. 83 *sq.*); but we need not confine the suggestion to the case of infants.

[5] Herodotus, iv. 26; Hesychius, *s.v.* Γενέσια; Im. Bekker, *Anecdota Graeca*, i. pp. 86, 231; Isaeus, ii. 46; *The Oxyrhynchus Papyri*, ed. Grenfell and Hunt, part iii. (London, 1903), p. 203 εὐωχίαν ἣν ποιήσονται πλησίον τοῦ τάφου μου κατ' ἔτος τῇ γενεθλίᾳ μου ἐφ' ᾧ διέπειν ἀργυρίου δραχμὰς ἑκατόν. My attention was called to this subject by my friend Mr. W. Wyse, who supplied me with many of the Greek passages referred to, including the one in the Oxyrhynchus Papyri.

[6] *Vitarum Scriptores Graeci*, ed. A. Westermann, p. 450; Plutarch, *Aratus*, 53; Diogenes Laertius, *Vit. Philosoph.* x. 18.

more natural than that it should be poured out by the men of the totem on the spot in which the disembodied spirits of the totem animals or plants are waiting for reincarnation? Clearly the rite seems intended to enable these spirits to take bodily shape and be born again, in order that they may again serve as food, if not to the men of the totem clan, at least to all the other members of the tribe. Later on we shall find that the attempt to reincarnate the souls of dead animals, in order that their bodies may be eaten over again, is not peculiar to the Australian savages, but is practised with many curious rites by peoples in other parts of the world.

General theory of *intichiuma* and initiatory rites in Australia.

To sum up briefly the general theory to which the foregoing facts have thus far led us, I would say that just as the *intichiuma* rites of the Australians are, for the most part, magical ceremonies intended to secure the reimbodiment of the spirits of edible animals and plants, so their initiatory rites may perhaps be regarded as magical ceremonies designed mainly to ensure the reincarnation of human souls. Now the motive for procuring the rebirth of animals and plants is simply the desire to eat them. May not this have been one

Cannibalism in Australia.

motive for attempting to resuscitate the human dead? It would seem so, for all the tribes on the Gulf of Carpentaria who have been examined by Spencer and Gillen eat their dead,[1] and the ceremonies and traditions of the Arunta indicate that their ancestors also ate the bodies of their fellow tribesmen.[2] In this respect the practice of the Binbinga tribe is particularly instructive. For among them the bodies of the dead are cut up and eaten, not by men of the same tribal subclass as the deceased, but by men belonging to the subclasses which compose the other intermarrying half of the tribe.[3] This is exactly analogous to the practice which at present prevails as to the eating of the totem animal or plant among all these central and northern tribes. Among them each clan that has an edible animal or plant for its totem is supposed to provide that animal or

---

[1] Spencer and Gillen, *Northern Tribes of Central Australia*, pp. 547 *sqq.*

[2] Spencer and Gillen, *Native Tribes of Central Australia*, pp. 473-475.

[3] Spencer and Gillen, *Northern Tribes of Central Australia*, p. 548.

plant for all the other clans to eat; and similarly among
the Binbinga the men of any particular subclass do
actually provide their own bodies for the members of
the other intermarrying half of the tribe to devour.
And just as in the far past the members of a totem
clan appear to have subsisted regularly (though not
exclusively, and perhaps not even mainly) on their totem
animal or plant,[1] so at a remote time they seem regularly to
have eaten each other. Thus the Wild Dog clan of the
Arunta has many traditions that their ancestors killed and
ate Wild Dog men and women.[2] Such traditions probably
preserve a true reminiscence of a state of things still more
savage than the present practice of the Binbinga. At that
more or less remote time, if we may trust the scattered hints
of custom and legend which are the only evidence we have
to go upon, the men and women of a totem clan, in defiance
of the customs of a later age, regularly cohabited with each
other,[3] ate their totems, and devoured each other's dead
bodies. In such a state of things there was no sharp line
of distinction drawn, either in theory or in practice, between
a man and his totem; and this confusion is again confirmed
by the legends, from which it is often difficult to make out
whether the totemic ancestor spoken of is a man or an
animal.[4] And if measures were taken to resuscitate both,
it may well have been primarily in order that both might be
eaten again. The system was thoroughly practical in its aim; Australian
only the means it took to compass its ends were mistaken. It totemism
was in no sense a religion, unless we are prepared to bestow not a religion.
the name of religion on the business of the grazier and the
market-gardener; for these savages certainly bred animals and
plants, and perhaps bred men, for much the same reasons that
a grazier and a market-gardener breed cattle and vegetables.

---

[1] Spencer and Gillen, *Native Tribes
of Central Australia*, pp. 207-211.

[2] Spencer and Gillen, *Native Tribes
of Central Australia*, pp. 434 *sq.*,
475.

[3] Spencer and Gillen, *Native Tribes
of Central Australia*, pp. 418 *sqq.*

[4] "In the Alcheringa lived ancestors
who, in the native mind, are so intimately associated with the animals or

plants the names of which they bear
that an Alcheringa man of, say, the
kangaroo totem may sometimes be
spoken of either as a man-kangaroo or
as a kangaroo-man. The identity of
the human individual is often sunk in
that of the animal or plant from which
he is supposed to have originated"
(Spencer and Gillen, *Native Tribes
of Central Australia*, p. 119).

But whereas the methods of the grazier and market-gardener rest upon the laws of nature, and therefore do really produce the effects they aim at, the methods of these savages are based on a mistaken conception of natural law, and therefore totally fail to bring about the intended result. Only they do not perceive their failure. Kindly nature, if we may personify her for a moment, draws a veil before their eyes, and herself works behind the veil those wonders of reproduction which the poor savage vainly fancies that he has wrought by his magical ceremonies and incantations. In short, totemism, as it exists at present among these tribes, appears to be mainly a crude, almost childlike attempt to satisfy the primary wants of man, especially under the hard conditions to which he is subject in the deserts of Central Australia, by magically creating everything that a savage stands in need of, and food first of all. But to say so is not to affirm that this has been the purpose, and the only purpose, of Australian totemism from the beginning. That beginning lies far behind us in the past, and is therefore necessarily much more obscure and uncertain than the function of totemism as a fully developed system, to which alone the preceding remarks are applicable.

Present function of totemism in Central Australia.

Our examination of the magical rites performed by the Australians for the maintenance of the food supply has led us into this digression. It is time to pass to ceremonies practised for the same purpose and on the same principles by peoples in other parts of the world.

Homoeopathic or imitative magic in fishing and hunting.

The Indians of British Columbia live largely upon the fish which abound in their seas and rivers. If the fish do not come in due season, and the Indians are hungry, a Nootka wizard will make an image of a swimming fish and put it into the water in the direction from which the fish generally appear. This ceremony, accompanied by a prayer to the fish to come, will cause them to arrive at once.[1] The islanders of Torres Straits use models of dugong and turtles to charm dugong and turtle to their destruction.[2]

[1] Franz Boas, in *Sixth Report on the North-Western Tribes of Canada*, p. 45 (separate reprint from the *Report of* the *British Association for* 1890).

[2] A. C. Haddon in *Journal of the Anthropological Institute*, xix. (1890)

The Toradjas of Central Celebes believe that things of the same sort attract each other by means of their indwelling spirits or vital ether. Hence they hang up the jawbones of deer and wild pigs in their houses, in order that the spirits which animate these bones may draw the living creatures of the same kind into the path of the hunter.[1] In the island of Nias, when a wild pig has fallen into the pit prepared for it, the animal is taken out and its back is rubbed with nine fallen leaves, in the belief that this will make nine more wild pigs fall into the pit, just as the nine leaves fell from the tree.[2] In the East Indian islands of Saparoea, Haroekoe, and Noessa Laut, when a fisherman is about to set a trap for fish in the sea, he looks out for a tree, of which the fruit has been much pecked at by birds. From such a tree he cuts a stout branch and makes of it the principal post in his fish-trap ; for he believes that just as the tree lured many birds to its fruit, so the branch cut from that tree will lure many fish to the trap.[3]

The western tribes of British New Guinea employ a charm to aid the hunter in spearing dugong or turtle. A small beetle, which haunts coco-nut trees, is placed in the hole of the spear-haft into which the spear-head fits. This is supposed to make the spear-head stick fast in the dugong or turtle, just as the beetle sticks fast to a man's skin when it bites him.[4] When a Cambodian hunter has set his nets and

Homoeo-pathic or imitative magic in fishing and hunting.

p. 427 ; *Reports of the Cambridge Anthropological Expedition to Torres Straits*, v. 333, 338.

[1] A. C. Kruyt, " Het koppen-snellen der Toradja's," *Verslagen en Mededeelingen der konink. Akademie van Wetenschappen*, Afdeeling Letter-kunde, IV. Reeks, III. Deel (Amsterdam, 1899), pp. 203 *sq.* I follow the experienced Messrs. N. Adriani and A. C. Kruijt (Kruyt) in calling the natives of Central Celebes by the name of Toradjas, though that name is not used by the people themselves, but is only applied to them in a derogatory sense by the Buginese. It means no more than "inlanders." The people are divided into a number of tribes, each with its own name, who speak for the most part one language but have no common name for themselves

collectively. See Dr. N. Adriani, " Mededeelingen omtrent de Toradjas van Midden - Celebes," *Tijdschrift voor Indische Taal- Land- en Volkenkunde*, xliv. (1901) p. 221.

[2] J. W. Thomas, " De jacht op het eiland Nias," *Tijdschrift voor Indische Taal- Land- en Volkenkunde*, xxvi. 277.

[3] Van Schmid, " Aanteekeningen nopens de zeden, gewoonten en gebruiken, benevens de vooroordeelen en bijgeloovigheden der bevolking van de eilanden Saparoea, Haroekoe, Noessa Laut," *Tijdschrift voor Neêrlands Indië*, 1843, dl. ii. pp. 601 *sq.*

[4] B. A. Hely, " Notes on Totemism, etc., among the Western Tribes," *British New Guinea, Annual Report for 1894-95*, p. 56.

Homoeo-
pathic or
imitative
magic in
fishing and
hunting. taken nothing, he strips himself naked, goes some way off, then strolls up to the net as if he did not see it, lets himself be caught in it, and cries, " Hillo ! what's this ?   I'm afraid I'm caught." After that the net is sure to catch game.[1]   A pantomime of the same sort has been acted within living memory in our Scottish Highlands.   The Rev. James Mac-donald, now of Reay in` Caithness, tells us that in his boy-hood when he was fishing with companions about Loch Aline and they had had no bites for a long time, they used to make a pretence of throwing one of their fellows over-board and hauling him out of the water, as if he were a fish ; after that the trout or silloch would begin to nibble, according as the boat was on fresh or salt water.[2]   Before a Carrier Indian goes out to snare martens, he sleeps by himself for about ten nights beside the fire with a little stick pressed down on his neck.   This naturally causes the fall-stick of his trap to drop down on the neck of the marten.[3] Among the Galelareese, who inhabit a district in the northern part of Halmahera, a large island to the west of New Guinea, it is a maxim that when you are loading your gun to go out shooting, you should always put the bullet in your mouth before you insert it in the gun ; for by so doing you practically eat the game that is to be hit by the bullet, which therefore cannot possibly miss the mark.[4]   A Malay who has baited a trap for crocodiles, and is awaiting results, is careful in eating his curry always to begin by swallowing three lumps of rice successively ; for this helps the bait to slide more easily down the crocodile's throat.   He is equally scrupulous not to take any bones out of his curry ; for, if he

[1] E. Aymonier, "Notes sur les coutumes et croyances superstitieuses des Cambodgiens," *Cochinchine fran-çaise: excursions et reconnaissances,* No. 16 (Saigon, 1883), p. 157.

[2] James Macdonald, *Religion and Myth* (London, 1893), p. 5.

[3] A. G. Morice, "Notes, archaeo-logical, industrial, and sociological, on the Western Dénés," *Transactions of the Canadian Institute,* iv. (1892-93) p. 108 ; *id., Au pays de l'Ours Noir : chez les sauvages de la Colombie Britan-nique* (Paris and Lyons, 1897), p. 71.

[4] M. J. van Baarda, "Fabelen, verhalen en overleveringen der Galel-areezen," *Bijdragen tot de Taal- Land-en Volkenkunde van Nederlandsch Indië,* xlv. (1895) p. 502. As to the district of Galela in Halmahera see G. Lafond in *Bulletin de la Société de Géographie* (Paris), ii. série, ix. (1838) pp. 77 *sqq.* (where Galeta is apparently a misprint for Galela) ; F. S. A. de Clercq, *Bijdragen tot de Kennis der Residentie Ternate* (Leyden, 1890), pp. 112 *sq.* ; W. Kükenthal, *Forschungs-reise in den Molukken und in Borneo* (Frankfort, 1896), pp. 147 *sqq.*

did, it seems clear that the sharp-pointed stick on which the bait is skewered would similarly work itself loose, and the crocodile would get off with the bait. Hence in these circumstances it is prudent for the hunter, before he begins his meal, to get somebody else to take the bones out of his curry, otherwise he may at any moment have to choose between swallowing a bone and losing the crocodile.[1]

This last rule is an instance of the things which the hunter abstains from doing lest, on the principle that like produces like, they should spoil his luck. For it is to be observed that the system of sympathetic magic is not merely composed of positive precepts ; it comprises a very large number of negative precepts, that is, prohibitions. It tells you not merely what to do, but also what to leave undone. The positive precepts are charms : the negative precepts are taboos. In fact the whole doctrine of taboo, or at all events a large part of it, would seem to be only a special application of sympathetic magic, with its two great laws of similarity and contact.[2] Though these laws

Negative magic or taboo.

---

[1] W. W. Skeat, *Malay Magic*, p. 300.

[2] The theory that taboo is a negative magic was first, I believe, clearly formulated by Messrs. Hubert and Mauss in their essay, " Esquisse d'une théorie générale de la magie," *L'Année Sociologique*, vii. (Paris, 1904) p. 56. Compare A. van Gennep, *Tabou et Totémisme à Madagascar* (Paris, 1904), pp. 19 *sqq.* I reached the same conclusion independently and stated it in my *Lectures on the Early History of the Kingship* (London, 1905), pp. 52-54, a passage which I have substantially reproduced in the text. When I wrote it I was unaware that the view had been anticipated by my friends Messrs. Hubert and Mauss. See my note in *Man*, vi. (1906) pp. 55 *sq.* The view has been criticised adversely by my friend Mr. R. R. Marett (*The Threshold of Religion*, pp. 85 *sqq.*). But the difference between us seems to be mainly one of words ; for I regard the supposed mysterious force, to which he gives the Melanesian name of *mana*, as supplying, so to say, the physical basis both of magic and of taboo, while the logical basis of both is furnished by a misapplication of the laws of the association of ideas. And with this view Mr. Marett, if I apprehend him aright, is to a certain extent in agreement (see particularly pp. 102 *sq.*, 113 *sq.* of his essay). However, in deference to his criticisms I have here stated the theory in question less absolutely than I did in my *Lectures*. As to the supposed mysterious force which I take to underlie magic and taboo I may refer particularly to what I have said in *The Golden Bough*,[2] i. 319-322, 343. In speaking of taboo I here refer only to those taboos which are protected by magical or religious sanctions, not to those of which the sanctions are purely civil or legal ; for I take civil or legal taboos to be merely a later extension of magical or religious taboos, which form the original stock of the institution. See my article " Taboo " in *Encyclopaedia Britannica*, Ninth Edition, vol. xxiii. pp. 16, 17.

are certainly not formulated in so many words nor even conceived in the abstract by the savage, they are nevertheless implicitly believed by him to regulate the course of nature quite independently of human will. He thinks that if he acts in a certain way, certain consequences will inevitably follow in virtue of one or other of these laws ; and if the consequences of a particular act appear to him likely to prove disagreeable or dangerous, he is naturally careful not to act in that way lest he should incur them. In other words, he abstains from doing that which, in accordance with his mistaken notions of cause and effect, he falsely believes would injure him ; in short, he subjects himself to a taboo. Thus taboo is so far a negative application of practical magic. Positive magic or sorcery says, " Do this in order that so and so may happen." Negative magic or taboo says, " Do not do this, lest so and so should happen." The aim of positive magic or sorcery is to produce a desired event ; the aim of negative magic or taboo is to avoid an undesirable one. But both consequences, the desirable and the undesirable, are supposed to be brought about in accordance with the laws of similarity and contact. And just as the desired consequence is not really effected by the observance of a magical ceremony, so the dreaded consequence does not really result from the violation of a taboo. If the supposed evil necessarily followed a breach of taboo, the taboo would not be a taboo but a precept of morality or common sense. It is not a taboo to say, " Do not put your hand in the fire " ; it is a rule of common sense, because the forbidden action entails a real, not an imaginary evil. In short, those negative precepts which we call taboo are just as vain and futile as those positive precepts which we call sorcery. The two things are merely opposite sides or poles of one great disastrous fallacy, a mistaken conception of the association of ideas. Of that fallacy, sorcery is the positive, and taboo the negative pole. If we give the general name of magic to the whole erroneous system, both theoretical and practical, then taboo may be defined as the negative side of practical magic., To put this in tabular form :—

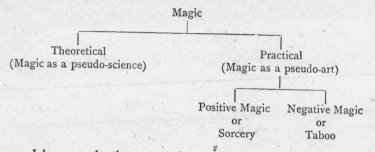

Magic

Theoretical
(Magic as a pseudo-science)

Practical
(Magic as a pseudo-art)

Positive Magic
or
Sorcery

Negative Magic
or
Taboo

I have made these remarks on taboo and its relations to magic because I am about to give some instances of taboos observed by hunters, fishermen, and others, and I wished to shew that they fall under the head of Sympathetic Magic, being only particular applications of that general theory. Thus, it is a rule with the Galelareese that when you have caught fish and strung them on a line, you may not cut the line through, or next time you go a-fishing your fishing-line will be sure to break.[1]   Among the Esquimaux of Baffin Land boys are forbidden to play cat's cradle, because if they did so their fingers might in later life become entangled in the harpoon-line.[2]   Here the taboo is obviously an application of the law of similarity, which is the basis of homoeopathic magic : as the child's fingers are entangled by the string in playing cat's cradle, so they will be entangled by the harpoon-line when he is a man and hunts whales.   Again, among the Huzuls, who inhabit the wooded north-eastern slopes of the Carpathian Mountains, the wife of a hunter may not spin while her husband is eating, or the game will turn and wind like the spindle, and the hunter will be unable to hit it.[3]   Here again the taboo is clearly derived from the law of similarity.   So, too, in most parts of ancient Italy women were forbidden by law to spin on the highroads as they walked, or even to carry their spindles openly, because any such action was believed to injure the crops.[4]   Probably the notion was that the

Taboos to be observed in fishing and hunting on the principle of sympathetic magic.

Spinning tabooed in certain cases on the principle of homoeopathic magic.

[1] M. J. van Baarda, in *Bijdragen tot de Taal- Land- en Volkenkunde van Nederlandsch Indië*, xlv. (1895) p. 507.
[2] F. Boas, "The Eskimo of Baffin Land and Hudson Bay," *Bulletin of* the *American Museum of Natural History*, xv. Part I. (1901) p. 161.
[3] R. F. Kaindl, "Zauberglaube bei den Huzulen," *Globus*, lxxvi. (1899) p. 273.
[4] Pliny, *Nat. Hist.* xxviii. 28.

twirling of the spindle would twirl the corn-stalks and prevent them from growing straight. So, too, among the Ainos of Saghalien a pregnant woman may not spin nor twist ropes for two months before her delivery, because they think that if she did so the child's guts might be entangled like the thread.[1] For a like reason in Bilaspore, a district of India, when the chief men of a village meet in council, no one present should twirl a spindle ; for they think that if such a thing were to happen, the discussion, like the spindle, would move in a circle and never be wound up.[2] In the East Indian islands of Saparoea, Haroekoe, and Noessa Laut, any one who comes to the house of a hunter must walk straight in ; he may not loiter at the door, for were he to do so, the game would in like manner stop in front of the hunter's snares and then turn back, instead of being caught in the trap.[3] For a similar reason it is a rule with the Toradjas of Central Celebes that no one may stand or loiter on the ladder of a house where there is a pregnant woman, for such delay would retard the birth of the child ;[4] and in various parts of Sumatra the woman herself in these circumstances is forbidden to stand at the door or on the top rung of the house-ladder under pain of suffering hard labour for her imprudence in neglecting so elementary a precaution.[5]

Taboos observed in the search for Malays engaged in the search for camphor eat their food dry and take care not to pound their salt fine. The reason is that the camphor occurs in the form of small grains

[1] B. Pilsudski, "Schwangerhaft, Entbindung und Fehlgeburt bei den Bewohnern der Insel Sachalin," *Anthropos*, v. (1910) p. 763.

[2] Rev. E. M. Gordon, in *Journal and Proceedings of the Asiatic Society of Bengal*, New Series, i. (1905) p. 185 ; *id.*, *Indian Folk Tales* (London, 1908), pp. 82 *sq.*

[3] Van Schmid, "Aanteekeningen nopens de zeden, gewoonten en gebruiken, benevens de vooroordeelen en bijgeloovigheden der bevolking van de eilanden Saparoea, Haroekoe, Noessa Laut," *Tijdschrift voor Neêrlands Indië*, 1843, dl. ii. p. 604.

[4] A. C. Kruijt, "Een en ander aangaande het geestelijk en maatschappelijk leven van den Poso-Alfoer," *Mededeelingen van wege het Nederlandsche Zendelinggenootschap*, xl. (1896) pp. 262 *sq* ; *id. ib.* xliv. (1900) p. 235.

[5] C. Snouck Hurgronje, *De Atjehers* (Batavia and Leyden, 1893-94), i. 409 ; E. A. Klerks, "Geographisch en ethnographisch opstal over de landschappen Korintje, Sĕrampas en Soengai Tĕnang," *Tijdschrift voor Indische Taal- Land- en Volkenkunde*, xxxix. (1897) p. 73 ; J. C. van Eerde, "Een huwelijk bij de Minangkabausche Maliers," *ib.* xliv. (1901) pp. 490 *sq.* ; M. Joustra, "Het leven, de zeden en gewoonten der Bataks," *Mededeelingen van wege het Nederlandsche Zendelinggenootschap*, xlvi. (1902) p. 406.

deposited in the cracks of the trunk of the camphor-tree. camphor
Accordingly it seems plain to the Malay that if, while seek- on the
ing for camphor, he were to eat his salt finely ground, the of homoeo
camphor would be found also in fine grains; whereas by pathic
eating his salt coarse he ensures that the grains of the cam- magic.
phor will also be large.[1] Camphor hunters in Borneo use
the leathery sheath of the leaf-stalk of the Penang palm
as a plate for food, and during the whole of the expedition
they will never ·wash the plate, for fear that the camphor
might dissolve and disappear from the crevices of the tree.[2]
Apparently they think that to wash their plates would be
to wash out the camphor crystals from the trees in which
they are imbedded.   In Laos, a province of Siam, a Taboos
rhinoceros hunter will not wash himself for fear that as a observed
consequence the wounds inflicted on the rhinoceros might on the
not be mortal, and that the animal might disappear in principle
one of the caves full of water in the mountains.[3] The pathic
chief product of some parts of Laos is lac. This is a magic.
resinous gum exuded by a red insect on the young branches
of trees, to which the little creatures have to be attached by
hand. All who engage in the business of gathering the
gum abstain from washing themselves and especially from
cleansing their heads, lest by removing the parasites from
their hair they should detach the other insects from the
boughs.[4] Some of the Brazilian Indians would never bring
a slaughtered deer into their hut without first hamstringing it,
believing that if they failed to do so, they and their children
would never be able to run down their enemies.[5] Apparently
they thought that by hamstringing the animal they at the same
stroke deprived their foemen of the use of their legs. No
Arikara Indian would break a marrow bone in a hut; for

[1] H. Lake and H. J. Kelsall, "The
Camphor-tree and Camphor Language of
Johore," *Journal of the Straits Branch
of the Royal Asiatic Society*, No. 26
(January 1894), p. 40; W. W. Skeat,
Malay Magic, p. 213.

[2] W. H. Furness, *Home - life of
Borneo Head - hunters* (Philadelphia,
1902), p. 169.

[3] E. Aymonier. *Notes sur le Laos*
(Saigon, 1885), p. 269.

[4] E. Aymonier, *Voyage dans le Laos*
(Paris, 1895-97), i. 322. As to lac
and the mode of cultivating it, see *id.*
ii. 18 *sq.* The superstition is less explicitly stated in the same writer's *Notes
sur le Laos* (Saigon, 1885), p. 110.

[5] A. Thevet, *Les Singularitez de la
France Antarctique, autrement nommée
Amerique* (Antwerp, 1558), p. 93;
id., Cosmographie Universelle (Paris,
1575), ii. 970 [wrongly numbered
936] *sq.* .

they think that were he to do so their horses would break their legs in the prairie.[1]   Again, a Blackfoot Indian who has set a trap for eagles, and is watching it, would not eat rosebuds on any account ; for he argues that if he did so, and an eagle alighted near the trap, the rosebuds in his own stomach would make the bird itch, with the result that instead of swallowing the bait the eagle would merely sit and scratch himself.   Following this train of thought the eagle hunter also refrains from using an awl when he is looking after his snares ; for surely if he were to scratch with an awl, the eagles would scratch him.   The same disastrous consequence would follow if his wives and children at home used an awl while he is out after eagles, and accordingly they are forbidden to handle the tool in his absence for fear of putting him in bodily danger.[2]

Homoeo-
pathic
taboos and
contagious
taboos.

All the foregoing taboos being based on the law of similarity may be called homoeopathic taboos.   The Cholones, an Indian tribe of eastern Peru, make use of poisoned arrows in the chase, but there are some animals, such as armadillos, certain kinds of falcons, and a species of vulture, which they would on no account shoot at with these weapons. For they believe that between the poisoned arrows which they use and the supply of poison at home there exists a sympathetic relation of such a sort that if they shot at any of these creatures with poisoned shafts, all the poison at home would be spoilt, which would be a great loss to them.[3] Here the exact train of thought is not clear ; but we may suppose that the animals in question are believed to possess a power of counteracting and annulling the effect of the poison, and that consequently if they are touched by it, all the poison, including the store of it at home, would be robbed of its virtue.   However that may be, it is plain that the superstition rests on the law of contact, on the notion, namely, that things which have once been in contact remain sympathetically in contact with each other always.   The poison with which the hunter wounds an animal has once

---

[1] Maximilian, Prinz zu Wied, *Reise in das innere Nord - America*, ii. 247.
[2] G. B. Grinnell, *Blackfoot Lodge Tales* (London, 1893), pp. 237, 238.
[3] E. Poeppig, *Reise in Chile, Peru und auf dem Amazonenstrome* (Leipsic, 1835-36), ii. 323.

been in contact with the store of poison at home ; hence if the poison in the wound loses its venom, so necessarily will all the poison at home. These may be called contagious taboos.

Among the taboos observed by savages none perhaps are more numerous or important than the prohibitions to eat certain foods, and of such prohibitions many are demonstrably derived from the law of similarity and are accordingly examples of negative magic. Just as the savage eats many animals or plants in order to acquire certain desirable qualities with which he believes them to be endowed, so he avoids eating many other animals and plants lest he should acquire certain undesirable qualities with which he believes them to be infected. In eating the former he practises positive magic ; in abstaining from the latter he practises negative magic. Many examples of such positive magic will meet us later on ;[1] here I will give a few instances of such negative magic or taboo. For example, in Madagascar soldiers are forbidden to eat a number of foods lest on the principle of homoeopathic magic they should be tainted by certain dangerous or undesirable properties which are supposed to inhere in these particular viands. Thus they may not taste hedgehog, "as it is feared that this animal, from its propensity of coiling up into a ball when alarmed, will impart a timid shrinking disposition to those who partake of it." Again, no soldier should eat an ox's knee, lest like an ox he should become weak in the knees and unable to march. Further, the warrior should be careful to avoid partaking of a cock that has died fighting or anything that has been speared to death ; and no male animal may on any account be killed in his house while he is away at the wars. For it seems obvious that if he were to eat a cock that had died fighting, he would himself be slain on the field of battle ; if he were to partake of an animal that had been speared, he would be speared himself ; if a male animal were killed in his house during his absence, he would himself be killed in like manner and perhaps at the same instant. Further, the Malagasy soldier must eschew kidneys, because in the Malagasy language the word for kidney is the same as that

(marginal notes: Foods tabooed on the principle of homoeopathic magic. Malagasy taboos on food based on the principle of homoeopathic magic.*)*

---

[1] Meanwhile I may refer the reader to *The Golden Bough*,[2] ii. 353 *sqq.*

Caffre
and Zulu
taboos on
food based
on the
principle
of homoeo-
pathic
magic.

for "shot"; so shot he would certainly be if he ate a
kidney.[1] Again, a Caffre has been known to refuse to eat
two mice caught at the same time in one trap, alleging that
were he to do so his wife would give birth to twins; yet the
same man would eat freely of mice if they were caught
singly.[2] Clearly he imagined that if he ate the two mice he
would be infected with the virus of doublets and would communicate the infection to his wife. Amongst the Zulus
there are many foods which are similarly forbidden on
homoeopathic principles. It may be well to give some
specimens of these prohibitions as they have been described
by the Zulus themselves. "There is among the black men,"
they say, "the custom of abstaining from certain foods. If
a cow has the calf taken from her dead, and the mother too
dies before the calf is taken away, young people who have
never had a child abstain from the flesh of that cow. I do
not mean to speak of girls; there is not even a thought of
whether they can eat it; for it is said that the cow will produce
a similar evil among the women, so that one of them will be
like the cow when she is in childbirth, be unable to give
birth, like the cow, and die together with her child. On this
account, therefore, the flesh of such a cow is abstained from.
Further, pig's flesh is not eaten by girls on any account; for
it is an ugly animal; its mouth is ugly, its snout is long;
therefore girls do not eat it, thinking if they eat it, a
resemblance to the pig will appear among their children.
They abstain from it on that account. There are many
things which are abstained from among black people through
fear of bad resemblance; for it is said there was a person who
once gave birth to an elephant, and a horse; but we do not
know if that is true; but they are now abstained from on
that account, through thinking that they will produce an
evil resemblance if eaten; and the elephant is said to
produce an evil resemblance, for when it is killed many
parts of its body resemble those of a female; its breasts, for
instance, are just like those of a woman. Young people,

---

[1] H. F. Standing, "Malagasy *fady*,"
*Antananarivo Annual and Madagascar
Magazine*, vol. ii. (reprint of the second
four numbers, 1881-1884) (Antanan-

arivo, 1896), p. 261.
[2] Dudley Kidd, *Savage Childhood*
(London, 1906), p. 48.

therefore, fear to eat it ; it is only eaten on account of famine, when there is no food ; and each of the young women say, 'It is no matter if I do give birth to an elephant and live ; that is better than not to give birth to it, and die of famine.' So it is eaten from mere necessity. Another thing which is abstained from is the entrails of cattle. Men do not eat them, because they are afraid if they eat them, the enemy will stab them in the bowels. Young men do not eat them ; they are eaten by old people. Another thing which is not eaten is the under lip of a bullock ; for it is said, a young person must not eat it, for it will produce an evil resemblance in the child ; the lip of the child will tremble continually, for the lower lip of a bullock moves constantly. They do not therefore eat it ; for if a child of a young person is seen with its mouth trembling, it is said, 'It was injured by its father, who ate the lower lip of a bullock.' Also another thing which is abstained from is that portion of the paunch of a bullock which is called *umtala* ; for the *umtala* has no *villi*, it has no pile ; it is merely smooth and hard. It is therefore said, if it is eaten by young people, their children will be born without hair, and their heads will be bare like a man's knee. It is therefore abstained from."[1]

The reader may have observed that in some of the fore- going examples of taboos the magical influence is supposed to operate at considerable distances ; thus among the Black- feet Indians the wives and children of an eagle hunter are forbidden to use an awl during his absence, lest the eagles should scratch the distant husband and father ;[2] and again no male animal may be killed in the house of a Malagasy soldier while he is away at the wars, lest the killing of the animal should entail the killing of the man.[3] This belief in the sympathetic influence exerted on each other by persons or things at a distance is of the essence of magic. Whatever doubts science may entertain as to the possibility of action at a distance, magic has none ; faith in telepathy is one of its first principles. A modern advocate of the influence of mind upon mind at a distance would have no difficulty in

Magical telepathy

[1] H. Callaway, *Nursery Tales, Traditions, and Histories of the Zulus*, i. (Natal and London, 1868), pp. 280-282.
[2] Above, p. 116.
[3] Above, p. 117.

convincing a savage ; the savage believed in it long ago, and what is more, he acted on his belief with a logical consistency such as his civilised brother in the faith has not yet, so far as I am aware, exhibited in his conduct. For the savage is convinced not only that magical ceremonies affect persons and things afar off, but that the simplest acts of daily life may do so too. Hence on important occasions the behaviour of friends and relations at a distance is often regulated by a more or less elaborate code of rules, the neglect of which by the one set of persons would, it is supposed, entail misfortune or even death on the absent ones. In particular when a party of men are out hunting or fighting, their kinsfolk at home are often expected to do certain things or to abstain from doing certain others, for the sake of ensuring the safety and success of the distant hunters or warriors. I will now give some instances of this magical telepathy both in its positive and in its negative aspect.

Telepathy in hunting among the Dyaks, Chams, Hottentots, etc.

In Laos when an elephant hunter is starting for the chase, he warns his wife not to cut her hair or oil her body in his absence ; for if she cut her hair the elephant would burst the toils, if she oiled herself it would slip through them.[1] When a Dyak village has turned out to hunt wild pigs in the jungle, the people who stay at home may not touch oil or water with their hands during the absence of their friends ; for if they did so, the hunters would all be " butter-fingered " and the prey would slip through their hands.[2] In setting out to look for the rare and precious eagle-wood on the mountains, Cham peasants enjoin their wives, whom they leave at home, not to scold or quarrel in their absence, for such domestic brawls would lead to their husbands being rent in pieces by bears and tigers.[3] A Hottentot woman whose husband is out hunting must do one of two things all the time he is away. Either she must light a fire and keep it burning till he comes back ; or if she does not choose to do that, she must go to the water

[1] E. Aymonier, *Notes sur le Laos*, pp. 25 *sq.* ; *id.*, *Voyage dans le Laos* (Paris, 1895-97), i. 62, 63.

[2] Chalmers, quoted by H. Ling Roth, *The Natives of Sarawak and British North Borneo*, i. 430.

[3] E. Aymonier, " Les Tchames et leurs religions," *Revue de l'Histoire des Religions*, xxiv. (1891) p. 278.

and continue to splash it about on the ground. When she is tired with throwing the water about, her place may be taken by her servant, but the exercise must in any case be kept up without cessation. To cease splashing the water or to let the fire out would be equally fatal to the husband's prospect of a successful bag.[1] In Yule Island, Torres Straits, when the men are gone to fetch sago, a fire is lit and carefully kept burning the whole time of their absence ; for the people believe that if it went out the voyagers would fare ill.[2] At the other end of the world the Lapps similarly object to extinguish a brand in water while any members of the family are out fishing, since to do so would spoil their luck.[3]

Among the Koniags of Alaska a traveller once observed a young woman lying wrapt in a bearskin in the corner of a hut. On asking whether she were ill, he learned that her husband was out whale-fishing, and that until his return she had to lie fasting in order to ensure a good catch.[4] Among the Esquimaux of Alaska similar notions prevail. The women during the whaling season remain in comparative idleness, as it is considered not good for them to sew while the men are out in the boats. If during this period any garments should need to be repaired, the women must take them far back out of sight of the sea and mend them there in little tents in which just one person can sit. And while the crews are at sea no work should be done at home which would necessitate pounding or hewing or any kind of noise ; and in the huts of men who are away in the boats no work of any kind whatever should be carried on.[5] When the Esquimaux of Aivilik and Iglulik are away hunting on the ice, the bedding may not be raised up, because they think that to do so would cause the ice to crack and drift off, and so the men might be lost. And among these people in the winter,

Telepathy in hunting among the Koniags, Esquimaux and Californian Indians.

[1] Th. Hahn, *Tsuni-‖Goam* (London, 1881), p. 77.

[2] A. C. Haddon, *Head-hunters* (London, 1901), p. 259.

[3] C. Leemius, *De Lapponibus Finmarchiae* (Copenhagen, 1767), p. 500.

[4] H. J. Holmberg, " Über die Völker des russischen Amerika," *Acta Societatis Scientiarum Fennicae,* iv. (1856) p. 392.

[5] *Arctic Papers for the Expedition of 1875* (published by the Royal Geographical Society), pp. 261 *sq.* ; *Report of the International Polar Expedition to Point Barrow, Alaska* (Washington, 1885), p. 39.

when the new moon appears, boys must run out of the snow-house, take a handful of snow, and put it into the kettle. It is believed that this helps the hunter to capture the seal and to bring it home.[1] When the Maidu Indians of California were engaged in driving deer into the snares which they had prepared for them, and which consisted of fences stretched from tree to tree, the women and children who were left behind in the village had to observe a variety of regulations. The women had to keep quiet and spend much of the time indoors, and children might not romp, shout, jump over things, kick, run, fall down, or throw stones. If these rules were broken, it was believed that the deer would become unmanageable and would jump the fence, so that the whole drive would be unsuccessful.[2]

Telepathy in hunting among the Gilyaks, Jukagirs, etc.

While a Gilyak hunter is pursuing the game in the forest, his children at home are forbidden to make drawings on wood or on sand; for they fear that if the children did so, the paths in the forest would become as perplexed as the lines in the drawings, so that the hunter might lose his way and never return. A Russian political prisoner once taught some Gilyak children to read and write; but their parents forbade them to write when any of their fathers was away from home; for it seemed to them that writing was a peculiarly complicated form of drawing, and they stood aghast at the idea of the danger to which such a drawing would expose the hunters out in the wild woods.[3] Among the Jukagirs of north-eastern Siberia, when a young man is out hunting, his unmarried sister at home may not look at his footprints nor eat certain parts of the game killed by him. If she leaves the house while he is absent at the chase, she must keep her eyes fixed on the ground, and may not speak of the chase nor ask any questions about it.[4] When a Nuba of north-eastern Africa goes to El Obeid for the first time, he tells his wife not to wash or oil herself and not to wear pearls

[1] F. Boas, "The Eskimo of Baffin Land and Hudson Bay," *Bulletin of the American Museum of Natural History*, xv. part i. (1901) pp. 149, 160.

[2] Roland B. Dixon, "The Northern Maidu," *Bulletin of the American Museum of Natural History*, xvii. part iii. (New York, 1905) p. 193.

[3] P. Labbé, *Un Bagne Russe, l'Île de Sakhaline* (Paris, 1903), p. 268.

[4] W. Jochelson, "Die Jukagiren im äussersten Nordosten Asiens," *Jahresbericht der geograph. Gesellschaft von Bern*, xvii. (1900) p. 14.

round her neck during his absence, because by doing so she would draw down on him the most terrible misfortunes.[1] When Bushmen are out hunting, any bad shots they may make are set down to such causes as that the children at home are playing on the men's beds or the like, and the wives who allow such things to happen are blamed for their husbands' indifferent marksmanship.[2]

Elephant-hunters in East Africa believe that, if their wives prove unfaithful in their absence, this gives the elephant power over his pursuer, who will accordingly be killed or severely wounded. Hence if a hunter hears of his wife's misconduct, he abandons the chase and returns home.[3] If a Wagogo hunter is unsuccessful, or is attacked by a lion, he attributes it to his wife's misbehaviour at home, and returns to her in great wrath. While he is away hunting, she may not let any one pass behind her or stand in front of her as she sits ; and she must lie on her face in bed.[4] The Moxos Indians of eastern Bolivia thought that if a hunter's wife was unfaithful to him in his absence he would be bitten by a serpent or a jaguar. Accordingly, if such an accident happened to him, it was sure to entail the punishment, and often the death, of the woman, whether she was innocent or guilty.[5] An Aleutian hunter of sea-otters thinks that he cannot kill a single animal if during his absence from home his wife should be unfaithful or his sister unchaste.[6]

The Huichol Indians of Mexico treat as a demi-god a species of cactus which throws the eater into a state of ecstasy. The plant does not grow in their country, and has to be fetched every year by men who make a journey of forty-three days for the purpose. Meanwhile the wives at home contribute to the safety of their absent husbands by never walking fast, much less running, while the men are on the road. They also do their best to ensure the benefits which, in the shape of rain,

Telepathy in hunting: supposed disastrous effect of wife's infidelity.

Telepathy in the search for the sacred cactus.

[1] *Missions Catholiques*, xiv. (1882) p. 460.

[2] W. H. I. Bleek, *A Brief Account of Bushman Folklore*, p. 19.

[3] P. Reichard, *Deutsch - Ostafrika* (Leipsic, 1892), p. 427.

[4] H. Cole, "Notes on the Wagogo of German East Africa," *Journal of the Anthropological Institute*, xxxii. (1902) pp. 318 *sq.*

[5] A. D'Orbigny, *Voyage dans l'Amérique Méridionale*, iii. part i. p. 226.

[6] I. Petroff, *Report on the Population, Industries, and Resources of Alaska*, p. 155.

good crops, and so forth, are expected to flow from the
sacred mission.   With this intention they subject themselves
to severe restrictions like those imposed upon their husbands.
During the whole of the time which elapses till the festival
of the cactus is held, neither party washes except on certain
occasions, and then only with water brought from the
distant country where the holy plant grows.   They also fast
much, eat no salt, and are bound to strict continence.   Any
one who breaks this law is punished with illness, and, moreover, jeopardises the result which all are striving for.
Health, luck, and life are to be gained by gathering the
cactus, the gourd of the God of Fire ; but inasmuch as the
pure fire cannot benefit the impure, men and women must
not only remain chaste for the time being, but must also
purge themselves from the taint of past sin.   Hence four
days after the men have started the women gather and
confess to Grandfather Fire with what men they have been
in love from childhood till now.   They may not omit a
single one, for if they did so the men would not find a
single cactus.   So to refresh their memories each one
prepares a string with as many knots as she has had
lovers.   This she brings to the temple, and, standing before
the fire, she mentions aloud all the men she has scored on
her string, name after name.   Having ended her confession,
she throws the string into the fire, and when the god has
consumed it in his pure flame, her sins are forgiven her and
she departs in peace.   From now on the women are averse
even to letting men pass near them.   The cactus-seekers
themselves make in like manner a clean breast of all their
frailties.   For every peccadillo they tie a knot on a string, and
after they have " talked to all the five winds " they deliver
the rosary of their sins to the leader, who burns it in the fire.[1]

Telepathy
in the
search for
camphor.

Many of the indigenous tribes of Sarawak are firmly
persuaded that were the wives to commit adultery while
their husbands are searching for camphor in the jungle,
the camphor obtained by the men would evaporate.[2]

[1] C. Lumholtz, *Unknown Mexico,*
ii. 126 *sqq.* ; as to the sacred cactus,
which the Indians call *hikuli*, see *id.*
i. 357 *sqq.*

[2] For this information I am indebted
to Dr. C. Hose, formerly Resident
Magistrate of the Baram district,
Sarawak.

Husbands can discover, by certain knots in the tree, when
their wives are unfaithful ; and it is said that in former days
many women were killed by jealous husbands on no better
evidence than that of these knots. Further, the wives dare
not touch a comb while their husbands are away collecting
the camphor ; for if they did so, the interstices between the
fibres of the tree, instead of being filled with the precious
crystals, would be empty like the spaces between the teeth
of a comb.[1] While men of the Toaripi or Motumotu tribe
of eastern New Guinea are away hunting, fishing, fighting,
or on any long journey, the people who remain at home
must observe strict chastity, and may not let the fire go out.
Those of them who stay in the men's club-houses must
further abstain from eating certain foods and from touching
anything that belongs to others. A breach of these rules
might, it is believed, entail the failure of the expedition.[2]
Among the tribes of Geelvink Bay, in north-western New
Guinea, when the men are gone on a long journey, as to
Ceram or Tidore, the wives and sisters left at home sing to
the moon, accompanying the lay with the booming music of
gongs. The singing takes place in the afternoons, beginning two or three days before the new moon, and lasting
for the same time after it. If the silver sickle of the moon
is seen in the sky, they raise a loud cry of joy. Asked why
they do so, they answer, " Now we see the moon, and so do
our husbands, and now we know that they are well ; if we
did not sing, they would be sick or some other misfortune
would befall them." [3] On nights when the moon is at the
full the natives of Doreh, in north-western New Guinea, go
out fishing on the lagoons. Their mode of proceeding is
to poison the water with the pounded roots of a certain
plant which has a powerful narcotic effect ; the fish are
stunned by it, and so easily caught. While the men are at
work on the moonlit water, the people on the shore must

Marginal notes: Telepathy in hunting fishing, and trading. — Telepathy in New Guinea.

[1] W. H. Furness, *Home-life of
Borneo Head-hunters*, p. 169.

[2] J. Chalmers, "Toaripi," *Journal
of the Anthropological Institute*, xxvii.
(1898) p. 327.

[3] J. L. van Hasselt, " Eenige Aanteekeningen aangaande de Bewoners

der N. Westkust van Nieuw Guinea,
meer bepaaldelijk den Stam der Noe-
foereezen," *Tijdschrift voor Indische
Taal- Land- en Volkenkunde*, xxxii.
(1889) p. 263 ; *id.*, " Die Papua-
stämme an der Geelvinkbai," *Mitteilungen der geograph. Gesellschaft zu
Jena*, ix. (1891) pp. 101 *sq.*

keep as still as death with their eyes fixed on the fishermen ;
but no woman with child may be among them, for if she
were there and looked at the water, the poison would at
once lose its effect and the fish would escape.[1]   In the Kei
Islands, to the south-west of New Guinea, as soon as a vessel
that is about to sail for a distant port has been launched,
the part of the beach on which it lay is covered as speedily
as possible with palm branches, and becomes sacred.   No
one may thenceforth cross that spot till the ship comes
home.   To cross it sooner would cause the vessel to perish.[2]
Moreover, all the time that the voyage lasts three or four
young girls, specially chosen for the duty, are supposed
to remain in sympathetic connexion with the mariners
and to contribute by their behaviour to the safety and
success of the voyage.   On no account, except for the
most necessary purpose, may they quit the room that
has been assigned to them.   More than that, so long as
the vessel is believed to be at sea they must remain absolutely motionless, crouched on their mats with their hands
clasped between their knees.   They may not turn their
heads to the left or to the right or make any other movement whatsoever.   If they did, it would cause the boat
to pitch and toss ; and they may not eat any sticky stuff,
such as rice boiled in coco-nut milk, for the stickiness
of the food would clog the passage of the boat through
the water.   When the sailors are supposed to have reached
their destination, the strictness of these rules is somewhat
relaxed ; but during the whole time that the voyage lasts
the girls are forbidden to eat fish which have sharp bones
or stings, such as the sting-ray, lest their friends at sea
should be involved in sharp, stinging trouble.[3]

Where beliefs like these prevail as to the sympathetic connexion between friends at a distance, we need not wonder
that above everything else war, with its stern yet stirring
appeal to some of the deepest and tenderest of human

(margin note) Telepathy in the Kei Islands.

(margin note) Telepathy in war.

[1] H. von Rosenberg, *Der malayi-
sche Archipel* (Leipsic, 1878), pp. 453,
462.
[2] C. M. Pleyte, " Ethnographische
Beschrijving der Kei-Eilanden," *Tijdschrift van het Nederlandsch Aardrijks-*

kundig Genootschap, Tweede Serie, x.
(1893) p. 831.
[3] H. Geurtjens, " Le Cérémonial des
Voyages aux Îles Keij," *Anthropos*, v.
(1910) pp. 337, 353. The girls bear
the title of *wat moel*.

emotions, should quicken in the anxious relations left behind a desire to turn the sympathetic bond to the utmost account for the benefit of the dear ones who may at any moment be fighting and dying far away.   Hence, to secure an end so natural and laudable, friends at home are apt to resort to devices which will strike us as pathetic or ludicrous, according as we consider their object or the means adopted to effect it.   Thus in some districts of Borneo, when a Dyak is out head-hunting, his wife or, if he is unmarried, his sister must wear a sword day and night in order that he may always be thinking of his weapons ; and she may not sleep during the day nor go to bed before two in the morning, lest her husband or brother should thereby be surprised in his sleep by an enemy.[1]   In other parts of Borneo, when the men are away on a warlike expedition, their mats are spread in their houses just as if they were at home, and the fires are kept up till late in the evening and lighted again before dawn, in order that the men may not be cold.   Further, the roofing of the house is opened before daylight to prevent the distant husbands, brothers, and sons from sleeping too late, and so being surprised by the enemy.[2]   While a Malay of the Peninsula is away at the wars, his pillows and sleeping-mat at home must be kept rolled up.   If any one else were to use them, the absent warrior's courage would fail and disaster would befall him.   His wife and children may not have their hair cut in his absence, nor may he himself have his hair shorn.[3]

Telepathy in war among the Dyaks.

Among the Sea Dyaks of Banting in Sarawak the women strictly observe an elaborate code of rules while the men are away fighting.   Some of the rules are negative and some are positive, but all alike are based on the principles of magical homoeopathy and telepathy.   Amongst them are the following.   The women must wake very early in the morning and open the windows as soon as it is light ; otherwise their absent husbands will oversleep themselves.   The women may not oil their hair, or the men will slip.   The women may neither sleep nor doze by day,

Telepathy in war among the Sea Dyaks.

[1] J. C. E. Tromp, " De Rambai en Sebroeang Dajaks," *Tijdschrift voor Indische Taal- Land- en Volkenkunde,* xxv. 118.

[2] H. Ling Roth, "Low's Natives of Borneo," *Journal of the Anthropological Institute,* xxii. (1893) p. 56.

[3] W. W. Skeat, *Malay Magic,* p. 524.

or the men will be drowsy on the march. The women must cook and scatter popcorn on the verandah every morning; so will the men be agile in their movements. The rooms must be kept very tidy, all boxes being placed near the walls; for if any one were to stumble over them, the absent husbands would fall and be at the mercy of the foe. At every meal a little rice must be left in the pot and put aside; so will the men far away always have something to eat and need never go hungry. On no account may the women sit at the loom till their legs grow cramped, otherwise their husbands will likewise be stiff in their joints and unable to rise up quickly or to run away from the foe. So in order to keep their husband's joints supple the women often vary their labours at the loom by walking up and down the verandah. Further, they may not cover up their faces, or the men would not be able to find their way through the tall grass or jungle. Again, the women may not sew with a needle, or the men will tread on the sharp spikes set by the enemy in the path. Should a wife prove unfaithful while her husband is away, he will lose his life in the enemy's country. Some years ago all these rules and more were observed by the women of Banting, while their husbands were fighting for the English against rebels. But alas! these tender precautions availed them little; for many a man, whose faithful wife was keeping watch and ward for him at home, found a soldier's grave.[1]

Telepathy in war among the Shans, the Timorese, and the Toradjas.   Among the Shans of Burma the wife of an absent warrior has to observe certain rules. Every fifth day she rests and does no work. She fills an earthen goblet with water to the brim and puts flowers into it every day. If the water sinks or the flowers fade, it is an omen of death. Moreover, she may not sleep on her husband's bed during his absence, but she sweeps the bedding clean and lays it out every night.[2] In the island of Timor, while war is being waged, the high-priest never quits the temple; his food is brought to him or cooked inside; day and night he must keep the fire burning, for if he were to let it die out, disaster would befall the warriors and would continue so

---

[1] Mrs. Hewitt, "Some Sea-Dayak Tabus," *Man*, viii. (1908) pp. 186 *sq.*   [2] *Indian Antiquary*, xxi. (1892) p. 120.

long as the hearth was cold. Moreover, he must drink
only hot water during the time the army is absent; for
every draught of cold water would damp the spirits of
the people, so that they could not vanquish the enemy.[1]
Among the Toradjas of Central Celebes, when a party
of men is out hunting for heads, the villagers who stay at
home, and especially the wives of the head-hunters, have to
observe certain rules in order not to hinder the absent men
at their task. In the first place, the entrance to the *lobo* or
spirit-house is shut. For the spirits of their fathers, who
live in that house, are now away with the warriors, watching
over and guarding them; and if any one entered their
house in their absence they would hear the noise and return
and be very angry at being thus called back from the
campaign. Moreover, the people at home have to keep
the house tidy: the sleeping-mats of the absent men must
be hung on beams, not rolled up as if they were to be away
a long time: their wives and next-of-kin may not quit the
house at night: every night a light burns in the house, and
a fire must be kept up constantly at the foot of the house-
ladder: garments, turbans, and head-dresses may not be laid
aside at night, for if the turban or head-dress were put off
the warrior's turban might drop from his head in the battle;
and the wives may sew no garments. When the spirit of
the head-hunter returns home in his sleep (which is the
Toradja expression for a soldier's dream) he must find
everything there in good order and nothing that could vex
him. By the observance of these rules, say the Toradjas,
the souls of the head-hunters are "covered" or protected.
And in order to make them strong, that they may not soon
grow weary, rice is strewed morning and evening on the
floor of the house. The women too go about constantly
with a certain plant of which the pods are so light and
feathery that they are easily wafted by the wind, for that
helps to make the men nimble-footed.[2]

[1] H. O. Forbes, "On some Tribes
of the Island of Timor," *Journal of
the Anthropological Institute*, xiii.
(1884) p. 414.

[2] A. C. Kruyt, "Het koppensnellan

der Toradja's van Midden-Celebes, en
zijne beteekenis," *Verslagen en Mededeelingen der konink. Akademie van
Wetenschappen*, Afdeeling Letterkunde,
IV. Reeks, III. Deel (Amsterdam,
1899), pp. 158 *sq.*

Telepathy
in war
among the
Galelareese
and the
Kei
Islanders.
When Galelareese men are going away to war, they
are accompanied down to the boats by the women. But
after the leave-taking is over, the women, in returning to
their houses, must be careful not to stumble or fall, and
in the house they may neither be angry nor lift up weapons
against each other; otherwise the men will fall and be
killed in battle.[1] Similarly, we saw that among the Chams
domestic brawls at home are supposed to cause the searcher
for eagle-wood to fall a prey to wild beasts on the mountains.[2]
Further, Galelareese women may not lay down the chopping knives in the house while their husbands are at the
wars; the knives must always be hung up on hooks.[3] The
reason for the rule is not given; we may conjecture that
it is a fear lest, if the chopping knives were laid down by
the women at home, the men would be apt to lay down
their weapons in the battle or at other inopportune moments.
In the Kei Islands, when the warriors have departed, the
women return indoors and bring out certain baskets containing fruits and stones. These fruits and stones they
anoint and place on a board, murmuring as they do so, "O
lord sun, moon, let the bullets rebound from our husbands,
brothers, betrothed, and other relations, just as raindrops
rebound from these objects which are smeared with oil." As
soon as the first shot is heard, the baskets are put aside, and
the women, seizing their fans, rush out of the houses. Then,
waving their fans in the direction of the enemy, they run
through the village, while they sing, "O golden fans! let
our bullets hit, and those of the enemy miss."[4] In this
custom the ceremony of anointing stones, in order that
the bullets may recoil from the men like raindrops from
the stones, is a piece of pure homoeopathic or imitative
magic; but the prayer to the sun, that he will be pleased
to give effect to the charm, is a religious and perhaps
later addition. The waving of the fans seems to be a
charm to direct the bullets towards or away from their

[1] M. J. van Baarda, "Fabelen,
verhalen en overleveringen der Galelareezen," *Bijdragen tot de Taal- Land-
en Volkenkunde van Nederlandsch-Indië*,
xlv. (1895) p. 507.
[2] See above, p. 120.

[3] M. J. van Baarda, *l.c.*
[4] C. M. Pleyte, "Ethnographische
Beschrijving der Kei-Eilanden," *Tijdschrift van het Nederlandsch Aardrijkskundig Genootschap*, Tweede Serie, x.
(1893) p. 805.

mark, according as they are discharged from the guns of
friends or foes.

An old historian of Madagascar informs us that "while
the men are at the wars, and until their return, the women
and girls cease not day and night to dance, and neither lie
down nor take food in their own houses. And although
they are very voluptuously inclined, they would not for
anything in the world have an intrigue with another man
while their husband is at the war, believing firmly that if
that happened, their husband would be either killed or
wounded. They believe that by dancing they impart
strength, courage, and good fortune to their husbands ;
accordingly during such times they give themselves no rest,
and this custom they observe very religiously." [1] Similarly
a traveller of the seventeenth century writes that in Madagascar "when the man is in battle or under march, the wife
continually dances and sings, and will not sleep or eat in
her own house, nor admit of the use of any other man,
unless she be desirous to be rid of her own ; for they entertain this opinion among them, that if they suffer themselves
to be overcome in an *intestin war* at home, their husbands
must suffer for it, being ingaged in a *forreign expedition ;*
but, on the contrary, if they behave themselves chastely, and
dance lustily, that then their husbands, by some certain
sympathetical operation, will be able to vanquish all their
combatants." [2] We have seen that among hunters in various
parts of the world the infidelity of the wife at home is
believed to have a disastrous effect on her absent husband.
In the Babar Archipelago, and among the Wagogo of East
Africa, when the men are at the wars the women at home are
bound to chastity, and in the Babar Archipelago they must
fast besides. [3] Under similar circumstances in the islands of
Leti, Moa, and Lakor the women and children are forbidden to
remain inside of the houses and to twine thread or weave. [4]

Telepathy
in war
among the
Malagasy.

[1] De Flacourt, *Histoire de la Grande
Isle Madagascar* (Paris, 1658), pp. 97 *sq.*
A statement of the same sort is made by
the Abbé Rochon, *Voyage to Madagascar
and the East Indies,* translated from the
French (London, 1792), pp. 46 *sq.*

[2] John Struys, *Voiages and Travels*
(London, 1684), p. 22. Struys may

have copied from De Flacourt.

[3] J. G. F. Riedel, *De sluik- en
kroesharige rassen tusschen Selebes en
Papua,* p. 341 ; H. Cole, "Notes on
the Wagogo of German East Africa,"
Journal of the Anthropological Institute,
xxxii. (1902) pp. 312, 317.

[4] Riedel, *op. cit.* p. 377.

Telepathy in war among the natives of West Africa.

Among the Tshi-speaking peoples of the Gold Coast the wives of men who are away with the army paint themselves white, and adorn their persons with beads and charms. On the day when a battle is expected to take place, they run about armed with guns, or sticks carved to look like guns, and taking green paw-paws (fruits shaped somewhat like a melon), they hack them with knives, as if they were chopping off the heads of the foe.[1] The pantomime is no doubt merely an imitative charm, to enable the men to do to the enemy as the women do to the paw-paws. In the West African town of Framin, while the Ashantee war was raging some years ago, Mr. Fitzgerald Marriott saw a dance performed by women whose husbands had gone as carriers to the war. They were painted white and wore nothing but a short petticoat. At their head was a shrivelled old sorceress in a very short white petticoat, her black hair arranged in a sort of long projecting horn, and her black face, breasts, arms, and legs profusely adorned with white circles and crescents. All carried long white brushes made of buffalo or horse tails, and as they danced they sang, "Our husbands have gone to Ashanteeland ; may they sweep their enemies off the face of the earth !"[2] Among the Thompson Indians of British Columbia, when the men were on the war-path, the women performed dances at frequent intervals. These dances were believed to ensure the success of the expedition. The dancers flourished their knives, threw long sharp-pointed sticks forward, or drew sticks with hooked ends repeatedly backward and forward. Throwing the sticks forward was symbolic of piercing or warding off the enemy, and drawing them back was symbolic of drawing their own men from danger. The hook at the end of the stick was particularly well adapted to serve the purpose of a life-saving apparatus. The women always pointed their weapons towards the enemy's country. They painted their faces red and sang as they danced, and they prayed to the weapons to preserve their husbands and help them to kill many foes. Some had

Telepathy in war among the American Indians.

[1] A. B. Ellis, *The Tshi-speaking Peoples of the Gold Coast*, p. 226.

[2] H. P. Fitzgerald Marriott, *The Secret Tribal Societies of West Africa*, p.

17 (reprinted from *Ars quatuor Coronatorum*, the transactions of a Masonic lodge of London). The lamented Miss Mary H. Kingsley was so kind as to lend me a copy of this work.

eagle-down stuck on the points of their sticks. When the
dance was over, these weapons were hidden. If a woman
whose husband was at the war thought she saw hair or a
piece of a scalp on the weapon when she took it out, she
knew that her husband had killed an enemy. But if she
saw a stain of blood on it, she knew he was wounded or
dead.[1] When the men of the Yuki tribe of Indians in
California were away fighting, the women at home did
not sleep ; they danced continually in a circle, chanting
and waving leafy wands. For they said that if they
danced all the time, their husbands would not grow tired.[2]
Among the Haida Indians of the Queen Charlotte
Islands, when the men had gone to war, the women at
home would get up very early in the morning and pretend
to make war by falling upon their children and feigning to
take them for slaves. This was supposed to help their
husbands to go and do likewise. If a wife were unfaithful
to her husband while he was away on the war-path, he
would probably be killed. For ten nights all the women
at home lay with their heads towards the point of the
compass to which the war-canoes had paddled away. Then
they changed about, for the warriors were supposed to
be coming home across the sea. At Masset the Haida
women danced and sang war-songs all the time their husbands were away at the wars, and they had to keep everything about them in a certain order. It was thought that a
wife might kill her husband by not observing these customs.[3]
In the Kafir district of the Hindoo Koosh, while the men are Telepathy
out raiding, the women abandon their work in the fields and in war
among the
assemble in the villages to dance day and night. The dances Kafirs of
are kept up most of each day and the whole of each night. the Hindoo
Sir George Robertson, who reports the custom, more than Koosh.
once watched the dancers dancing at midnight and in the
early morning, and could see by the fitful glow of the wood-

[1] J. Teit, "The Thompson Indians
of British Columbia," *Memoir of the
American Museum of Natural History,
The Jesup North Pacific Expedition,*
vol. i. No. 4 (April 1900), p. 356.

[2] S. Powers, *Tribes of California*
(Washington, 1877), pp. 129 *sq.*

[3] J. R. Swanton, "Contributions to
the Ethnology of the Haida" (Leyden
and New York, 1905), pp. 55 *sq.*
(*Memoir of the American Museum of
Natural History, The Jesup North
Pacific Expedition,* vol. v. part i.).

fire how haggard and tired they looked, yet how gravely and earnestly they persisted in what they regarded as a serious duty.[1]   The dances of these Kafirs are said to be performed in honour of certain of the national gods, but when we consider the custom in connexion with the others which have just been passed in review, we may reasonably surmise that it is or was originally in its essence a sympathetic charm intended to keep the absent warriors wakeful, lest they should be surprised in their sleep by the enemy. When a band of Carib Indians of the Orinoco had gone on the war-path, their friends left in the village used to calculate as nearly as they could the exact moment when the absent warriors would be advancing to attack the enemy.   Then they took two lads, laid them down on a bench, and inflicted a most severe scourging on their bare backs.   This the youths submitted to without a murmur, supported in their sufferings by the firm conviction, in which they had been bred from childhood, that on the constancy and fortitude with which they bore the cruel ordeal depended the valour and success of their comrades in the battle.[2]

Homoeo-
pathic
magic at
making
drums.

So much for the savage theory of telepathy in war and the chase.   We pass now to other cases of homoeopathic or imitative magic.   While marriageable boys of the Mekeo district in British New Guinea are making their drums, they have to live alone in the forest and to observe a number of rules which are based on the principle of homoeopathic magic.   The drums will be used in the dances, and in order that they may give out a resonant sonorous note, great care must be taken in their construction.   The boys may spend from two days to a week at the task.   Having chosen a suitable piece of wood, they scrape the outside into shape with a shell, and hollow out the inside by burning it with a hot coal till the sides are very thin.   The skin of an iguana, made supple by being steeped in coco-nut milk, is then stretched over the hollow and tightened with string and glue.   All the time a boy is at work on his drum, he must carefully avoid

[1] Sir George Scott Robertson, *The Kafirs of the Hindu Kush* (London, 1896), pp. 335, 621-626.

[2] Antonio Caulin, *Historia Coro-graphica natural y evangelica dela Nueva Andalucia de Cumana, Guayana y Vertientes del Rio Orinoco* (1779), p. 97.

women ; for if a woman or a girl were to see him, the drum would split and sound like an old cracked pot. If he ate fish, a bone would prick him and the skin of the drum would burst. If he ate a red banana it would choke him, and the drum would give a dull stifled note ; if he tasted grated coco-nut, the white ants, like the white particles of the nut, would gnaw the body of the drum ; if he cooked his food in the ordinary round-bellied pot, he would grow fat and would not be able to dance, and the girls would despise him and say, "Your belly is big ; it is a pot!" Moreover, he must strictly shun water ; for if he accidentally touched it with his feet, his hands, or his lips before the drum was quite hollowed out, he would throw the instrument away, saying : "I have touched water ; my hot coal will be put out, and I shall never be able to hollow out my drum."[1] A Highland witch can sink a ship by homoeopathic or imitative magic. She has only to set a small round dish floating in a milk-pan full of water, and then to croon her spell. When the dish upsets in the pan, the ship will go down in the sea. They say that once three witches from Harris left home at night after placing the milk-pan thus on the floor, and strictly charging a serving-maid to let nothing come near it. But while the girl was not looking a duck came in and squattered about in the water on the floor. Next morning the witches returned and asked if anything had come near the pan. The girl said "No," whereupon one of the witches said to the others, "What a heavy sea we had last night coming round Cabag head!"[2] If a wolf has carried off a sheep or a pig, the Esthonians have a very simple mode of making him drop it. They let fall anything that they happen to have at hand, such as a cap or a glove, or, what is perhaps still better, they lift a heavy stone and then let it go. By that act, on the principle of homoeopathic magic, they compel the wolf to let go his booty.[3]

Among the many beneficent uses to which a mistaken

Various applications of homoeopathic magic.

[1] Father Guis, "Les Canaques, ce qu'ils font, ce qu'ils disent," *Missions Catholiques*, xxx. (1898) p. 29 ; A. C. Haddon, *Head-hunters*, p. 257.

[2] J. G. Campbell, *Witchcraft and Second Sight in the Highlands and Islands of Scotland* (Glasgow, 1902), pp. 21 *sq.*

[3] Boecler-Kreutzwald, *Der Ehsten abergläubische Gebräuche, Weisen und Gewohnheiten*, p. 122.

Homoeo-
pathic
magic
applied to
make
plants
grow.
Magic at
sowing and
planting.

ingenuity has applied the principle of homoeopathic or imitative magic, is that of causing trees and plants to bear fruit in due season. In Thüringen the man who sows flax carries the seed in a long bag which reaches from his shoulders to his knees, and he walks with long strides, so that the bag sways to and fro on his back. It is believed that this will cause the flax to wave in the wind.[1] In the interior of Sumatra rice is sown by women who, in sowing, let their hair hang loose down their back, in order that the rice may grow luxuriantly and have long stalks.[2] Similarly, in ancient Mexico a festival was held in honour of the goddess of maize, or "the long-haired mother," as she was called. It began at the time "when the plant had attained its full growth, and fibres shooting forth from the top of the green ear indicated that the grain was fully formed. During this festival the women wore their long hair unbound, shaking and tossing it in the dances which were the chief feature in the ceremonial, in order that the tassel of the maize might grow in like profusion, that the grain might be correspondingly large and flat, and that the people might have abundance."[3] It is a Malay maxim to plant maize when your stomach is full, and to see to it that your dibble is thick; for this will swell the ear of the maize.[4] And they say that you should sow rice also with a full stomach, for then the ears will be full.[5] The eminent novelist, Mr. Thomas Hardy, was once told that the reason why certain trees in front of his house, near Weymouth, did not thrive, was that he looked at them before breakfast on an empty stomach.[6] More elaborate still are the measures taken by an Esthonian peasant woman to make her cabbages thrive. On the day when they are

[1] Aug. Witzschel, *Sagen, Sitten und Gebräuche aus Thüringen* (Vienna, 1878), p. 218, § 36.

[2] A. L. van Hasselt, *Volksbeschrijving van Midden-Sumatra* (Leyden, 1882), p. 323; J. L. van der Toorn, "Het animisme bij den Minang-kabauer der Padangsche Bovenlanden," *Bijdragen tot de Taal- Land- en Volkenkunde van Nederlandsch-Indië*, xxxix. (1890) p. 64.

[3] E. J. Payne, *History of the New World called America*, i. (Oxford,

1892) p. 421. Compare Brasseur de Bourbourg, *Histoire des nations civilisées du Mexique et de l'Amérique-Centrale*, i. 518 *sq*.

[4] W. W. Skeat, *Malay Magic*, p. 217.

[5] A. L. van Hasselt, "Nota betreffende de rijstcultuur in de Residentie Tapanoeli," *Tijdschrift voor Indische Taal- Land- en Volkenkunde*, xxxvi. (1893) p. 529.

[6] This I learned from Mr. Hardy in conversation. See also his letter in *Folklore*, viii. (1897) p. 11.

sown she bakes great pancakes, in order that the cabbages
may have great broad leaves ; and she wears a dazzling
white hood in the belief that this will cause the cabbages
to have fine white heads.   Moreover, as soon as the cabbages
are transplanted, a small round stone is wrapt up tightly in
a white linen rag and set at the end of the cabbage bed,
because in this way the cabbage heads will grow very white
and firm.[1]   Among the Huzuls of the Carpathians, when a
woman is planting cabbages, she winds many cloths about
her head, in order that the heads of the cabbages may also
be thick.   And as soon as she has sown parsley, she grasps
the calf of her leg with both hands, saying, " May it be as
thick as that ! "[2]   Among the Kurs of East Prussia, who
inhabit the long sandy tongue of land known as the
Nehrung which parts the Baltic from a lagoon, when a
farmer sows his fields in spring, he carries an axe and
chops the earth with it, in order that the cornstalks may
be so sturdy that an axe will be needed to hew them down.[3]
For much the same reason a Bavarian sower in sowing
wheat will sometimes wear a golden ring, in order that the
corn may have a fine yellow colour.[4]   The Malagasy think
that only people with a good even set of teeth should plant
maize, for otherwise there will be empty spaces in the maize
cob corresponding to the empty spaces in the planter's
teeth.[5]

In many parts of Europe dancing or leaping high
in the air are approved homoeopathic modes of making
the crops grow high.   Thus in Franche-Comté they
say that you should dance at the Carnival in order to
make the hemp grow tall.[6]   In the Vosges mountains the
sower of hemp pulls his nether garments up as far as he
can, because he imagines that the hemp he is sowing will

Dancing and leaping high as a charm to make the crops grow high.

[1] Boecler - Kreutzwald, *Der Ehsten
abergläubische Gebräuche, Weisen und
Gewohnheiten*, p. 133.   Compare F.
J. Wiedemann, *Aus dem inneren und
äusseren Leben der Ehsten*, p. 447.

[2] R. F. Kaindl, " Zauberglaube bei
den Huzulen," *Globus*, lxxvi. (1899)
p. 276.

[3] F. Tetzner, " Die Kuren in Ostpreussen," *Globus*, lxxv. (1899) p.
148.

[4] F. Panzer, *Beitrag zur deutschen
Mythologie*, ii. p. 207, § 362 ; *Bavaria,
Landes- und Volkskunde des Königreichs
Bayern*, ii. 297, iii. 343.

[5] H. F. Standing, " Malagasy *fady*,"
*Antananarivo Annual and Madagascar
Magazine*, vol. ii. (reprint of the second
four numbers, 1881-1884) (Antananarivo, 1896), p. 257.

[6] Ch. Beauquier, *Les Mois en
Franche-Comté* (Paris, 1900), p. 30.

Dancing
and leap-
ing high as
a charm
to make
the crops
grow high.
attain the precise height to which he has succeeded in
hitching up his breeches ;[1] and in the same region another
way of ensuring a good crop of hemp is to dance on the
roof of the house on Twelfth Day.[2] In Swabia and among
the Transylvanian Saxons it is a common custom for a man
who has sown hemp to leap high on the field, in the belief
that this will make the hemp grow tall.[3] All over Baden
till recently it was the custom for the farmer's wife to give
the sower a dish of eggs or a cake baked with eggs either
before or after sowing, in order that he might leap as high
as possible. This was deemed the best way of making the
hemp grow high. For the same purpose some people who
had sown hemp used to dance the hemp dance, as it was
called, on Shrove Tuesday, and in this dance also the
dancers jumped as high as they could. In some parts of
Baden the hemp seed is thrown in the air as high as
possible, and in Katzenthal the urchins leap over fires
in order that the hemp may grow tall.[4] Similarly in many
other parts of Germany and Austria the peasant imagines
that he makes the flax grow tall by dancing or leaping
high, or by jumping backwards from a table ; the higher
the leap the taller will the flax be that year. The special
season for thus promoting the growth of flax is Shrove
Tuesday, but in some places it is Candlemas or Walpurgis
Night (the eve of May Day). The scene of the performance
is the flax field, the farmhouse, or the village tavern.[5] In

[1] L. F. Sauvé, Le Folk-lore des
Hautes-Vosges (Paris, 1889), p. 142.

[2] L. F. Sauvé, op. cit. pp. 17 sq.

[3] E. Meier, Deutsche Sagen, Sitten
und Gebräuche aus Schwaben, p. 499 ;
A. Heinrich, Agrarische Sitten und
Gebräuche unter den Sachsen Siebenbürgens (Hermannstadt, 1880), p. 11.

[4] E. H. Meyer, Badisches Volksleben
im neunzehnten Jahrhundert (Strasburg, 1900), pp. 421 sq.

[5] A. Kuhn und W. Schwartz, Norddeutsche Sagen, Märchen und Gebräuche,
p. 445, § 354 ; J. V. Grohmann, Aberglauben und Gebräuche aus Böhmen
und Mähren, p. 95, § 664; A.
Peter, Volksthümliches aus österrei-
chisch-Schlesien, ii. 266 ; Von Reins-
berg-Düringsfeld, Fest-Kalender aus

Böhmen, p. 49 ; E. Sommer, Sagen,
Märchen und Gebräuche aus Sachsen
und Thüringen, p. 148 ; O. Knoop,
Volkssagen, Erzählungen, Aberglauben,
Gebräuche und Märchen aus dem
östlichen Hinterpommern, p. 176 ;
A. Witzschel, Sagen, Sitten und Gebräuche aus Thüringen, p. 191, § 13 ;
J. F. L. Woeste, Volksüberlieferun-
gen in der Grafschaft Mark, p. 56,
§ 24 ; Bavaria, Landes- und Volkskunde des Königreichs Bayern, ii.
298, iv. 2, pp. 379, 382 ; A. Heinrich,
Agrarische Sitten und Gebräuche unter
den Sachsen Siebenbürgens, pp. 11 sq.;
W. von Schulenberg, Wendische Volkssagen und Gebräuche aus dem Spreewald,
p. 252 ; J. A. E. Köhler, Volksbrauch,
Aberglauben, Sagen und andre alte

some parts of Eastern Prussia the girls dance one by one
in a large hoop at midnight on Shrove Tuesday. The
hoop is adorned with leaves, flowers, and ribbons, and
attached to it are a small bell and some flax. Strictly
speaking, the hoop should be wrapt in white linen handkerchiefs, but the place of these is often taken by many-
coloured bits of cloth, wool, and so forth. While dancing
within the hoop each girl has to wave her arms vigorously
and cry " Flax grow ! " or words to that effect. When she
has done, she leaps out of the hoop, or is lifted out of it
by her partner.[1]   In Anhalt, when the sower had sown the
flax, he leaped up and flung the seed-bag high in the air,
saying, " Grow and turn green ! You have nothing else to
do." He hoped that the flax would grow as high as he
flung the seed-bag in the air.   At Quellendorff, in Anhalt,
the first bushel of seed-corn had to be heaped up high in
order that the corn-stalks should grow tall and bear plenty
of grain.[2]   When Macedonian farmers have done digging
their fields, they throw their spades up into the air, and
catching them again, exclaim, " May the crop grow as high
as the spade has gone ! "[3]

The notion that a person can influence a plant homoeopathically by his act or condition comes out clearly in a
remark made by a Malay woman.   Being asked why she
stripped the upper part of her body naked in reaping the
rice, she explained that she did it to make the rice-husks

Plants and trees influenced homoeopathically by a person's act or state.

Überlieferungen im Voigtlande, pp. 368
sq. ; Die gestriegelte Rockenphilosophie
(Chemnitz, 1759), p. 103; M. Toeppen,
Aberglauben aus Masuren,[2] p. 68 ;
A. Wuttke, Der deutsche Volksaberglaube,[2] p. 396, § 657 ; U. Jahn, Die
deutsche Opfergebräuche bei Ackerbau
und Viehzucht, pp. 194 sq.; R. Wuttke,
Sächsische Volkskunde[2] (Dresden, 1901),
p. 370 ; E. Hoffmann - Krayer,
" Fruchtbarkeitsriten im schweizerischen Volksbrauch," Schweizerisches
Archiv für Volkskunde, xi. (1907)
p. 260. According to one account,
in leaping from the table you should
hold in your hand a long bag containing flax seed (Woeste, l.c.). The
dancing or leaping is often done
specially by girls or women (Kuhn

und Schwartz, Grohmann, Witzschel,
Heinrich, ll.cc.). Sometimes the
women dance in the sunlight (Die
gestriegelte Rockenphilosophie, l.c.) ;
but in Voigtland the leap from the
table should be made by the housewife naked and at midnight on Shrove
Tuesday (Köhler, l.c.). On Walpurgis
Night the leap is made over an alder
branch stuck at the edge of the flax
field (Sommer, l.c.).

[1] E. Lemke, Volksthümliches in
Ostpreussen, pp. 8-12 ; M. Toeppen,
l.c.

[2] O. Hartung, " Zur Volkskunde aus
Anhalt," Zeitschrift des Vereins für
Volkskunde, vii. (1897) pp. 149 sq.

[3] G. F. Abbott, Macedonian Folklore (Cambridge, 1903), p. 122.

thinner, as she was tired of pounding thick-husked rice.[1] Clearly, she thought that the less clothing she wore the less husk there would be on the rice. Among the Minangkabauers of Sumatra, when a rice barn has been built a feast is held, of which a woman far advanced in pregnancy must partake. Her condition will obviously help the rice to be fruitful and multiply.[2] Among the Zulus a pregnant woman sometimes grinds corn, which is afterwards burnt among the half-grown crops in order to fertilise them.[3] For a similar reason in Syria when a fruit-tree does not bear, the gardener gets a pregnant woman to fasten a stone to one of its branches; then the tree will be sure to bear fruit, but the woman will run a risk of miscarriage,[4] having transferred her fertility, or part of it, to the tree. The practice of loading with stones a tree which casts its fruit is mentioned by Maimonides,[5] though the Rabbis apparently did not understand it. The proceeding was most probably a homoeopathic charm designed to load the tree with fruit.[6] In Swabia they say that if a fruit-tree does not bear, you should keep it loaded with a heavy stone all summer, and next year it will be sure to bear.[7] The custom of tying stones to fruit-trees in order to ensure a crop of fruit is followed also in Sicily.[8] The magic virtue of a pregnant woman to communicate fertility is known to Bavarian and Austrian peasants, who

Fertilising influence supposed to be exercised on plants by pregnant women or by women who have borne many children.

[1] W. W. Skeat, *Malay Magic*, p. 248.

[2] J. L. van der Toorn, "Het animisme bij den Minangkabauer der Padangsche Bovenlanden," *Bijdragen tot de Taal- Land- en Volkenkunde van Nederlandsch-Indië*, xxxix. (1890) p. 67.

[3] Dudley Kidd, *Savage Childhood* (London, 1906), p. 291.

[4] Eijūb Abēla, "Beiträge zur Kenntniss abergläubischer Gebräuche in Syrien," *Zeitschrift des deutschen Palaestina-Vereins*, vii. (1884) p. 112, § 202. Compare L'Abbé B. Chémali, "Naissance et premier âge au Liban," *Anthropos*, v. (1910) pp. 734, 735.

[5] Quoted by D. Chwolsohn, *Die Ssabier und der Ssabismus* (St. Petersburg, 1856), ii. 469.

[6] W. Mannhardt (*Baumkultus*, p. 419) promised in a later investigation to prove that it was an ancient custom at harvest or in spring to load or pelt trees and plants, as well as the representatives of the spirit of vegetation, with stones, in order thereby to express the weight of fruit which was expected. This promise, so far as I know, he did not live to fulfil. Compare, however, his *Mythologische Forschungen*, p. 324.

[7] E. Meier, *Deutsche Sagen, Sitten und Gebräuche aus Schwaben*, pp. 249 *sq.* The placing of the stone on the tree is described as a punishment, but this is probably a misunderstanding.

[8] G. Pitrè, *Usi e costumi, credenze et pregiudizi del popolo siciliano*, iii. (Palermo, 1889) pp. 113 *sq.*

think that if you give the first fruit of a tree to a woman
with child to eat, the tree will bring forth abundantly next
year.[1] In Bohemia for a similar purpose the first apple of a
young tree is sometimes plucked and eaten by a woman who
has borne many children, for then the tree will be sure to bear
many apples.[2] In the Zürcher Oberland, Switzerland, they
think that a cherry-tree will bear abundantly if its first
fruit is eaten by a woman who has just given birth to her
first child.[3] In Macedonia the first fruit of a tree should
not be eaten by a barren woman but by one who has many
children.[4] The Nicobar Islanders think it lucky to get a
pregnant woman and her husband to plant seed in gardens.[5]
The Greeks and Romans sacrificed pregnant victims to
the goddesses of the corn and of the earth, doubtless
in order that the earth might teem and the corn swell in
the ear.[6] When a Catholic priest remonstrated with the
Indians of the Orinoco on allowing their women to sow the
fields in the blazing sun, with infants at their breasts, the
men answered, " Father, you don't understand these things,
and that is why they vex you. You know that women are
accustomed to bear children, and that we men are not.
When the women sow, the stalk of the maize bears two or
three ears, the root of the yucca yields two or three

---

[1] *Bavaria, Landes- und Volkskunde
des Königreichs Bayern*, ii. 299 ; T.
Vernaleken, *Mythen und Bräuche des
Volkes in Österreich*, p. 315. On
the other hand, in some parts of north-
west New Guinea a woman with child
may not plant, or the crop would be
eaten up by pigs ; and she may not
climb a tree in the rice-field, or the crop
would fail. See J. L. van Hasselt,
" Enige aanteekeningen aangaande de
Bewoners der N. Westkust van Nieuw
Guinea," *Tijdschrift voor Indische
Taal- Land- en Volkenkunde*, xxxii.
(1889) p. 264 ; *id.*, " Die Papua-
stämme an der Geelvinkbai," *Mitteilungen der Geographischen Gesellschaft
zu Jena*, ix. (1891) p. 102. Similarly
the Galelareese say that a pregnant
woman must not sweep under a
shaddock tree, or knock the fruit from
the bough, else it will taste sour instead
of sweet. See M. J. van Baarda,

" Fabelen, Verhalen en Overleveringen
der Galelareezen," *Bijdragen tot de
Taal- Land- en Volkenkunde van
Nederlandsch - Indië*, xlv. (1895) p.
457.
[2] J. V. Grohman, *Aberglauben und
Gebräuche aus Böhmen und Mähren*,
p. 143, § 1053.
[3] E.   Hoffmann-Krayer, " Fruchtbarkeitsriten im schweizerischen Volksbrauch," *Schweizerisches Archiv für
Volkskunde*, xi. (1907) p. 263.
[4] G. F. Abbott, *Macedonia Folklore*, p. 122.
[5] *Census of India, 1901*, vol. iii. p.
206.
[6] Dittenberger, *Sylloge Inscriptionum Graecarum*,[2] No. 615, line 17
ὑπὲρ καρποῦ Δήμητρι ὗν ἐνκύμονα πρωτο-
τόκον; compare *id.*, No. 616, line 61 *sq.*,
No. 617, line 3 ; Ovid, *Fasti*, iv. 633
sq. ; Macrobius, *Saturn.* i. 12. 20 ;
Arnobius, *Adversus nationes*, iv. 22.

basketfuls, and everything multiplies in proportion. Now why is that? Simply because the women know how to bring forth, and know how to make the seed which they sow bring forth also. Let them sow, then; we men don't know as much about it as they do."[1] For the same reason, probably, the Tupinambas of Brazil thought that if a certain earth-almond were planted by the men, it would not grow.[2] Among the Ilocans of Luzon the men sow bananas, but the sower must have a young child on his shoulder, or the bananas will bear no fruit.[3] When a tree bears no fruit, the Galelareese think it is a male; and their remedy is simple. They put a woman's petticoat on the tree, which, being thus converted into a female, will naturally prove prolific.[4] On the other hand the Baganda believe that a barren wife infects her husband's garden with her own sterility and prevents the trees from bearing fruit; hence a childless woman is generally divorced.[5] For a like reason, probably, the Wajagga of East Africa throw away the corpse of a childless woman, with all her belongings, in the forest or in any other place where the land is never cultivated; moreover her body is not carried out of the door of the hut, but a special passage is broken for it through the wall,[6] no doubt to prevent her dangerous ghost from finding its way back.[7]

Barren women supposed to make the fruit-trees barren.

Taboos based on the belief that persons can influence vegetation homoeopathically by their acts or states.

Thus on the theory of homoeopathic magic a person can influence vegetation either for good or for evil according to the good or the bad character of his acts or states: for example, a fruitful woman makes plants fruitful, a barren woman makes them barren. Hence this belief in the noxious and infectious nature of certain personal qualities or accidents

[1] J. Gumilla, *Histoire naturelle, civile et géographique de l'Orénoque* (Avignon, 1758), iii. 184.

[2] R. Southey, *History of Brazil*, i.[2] (London, 1822) p. 253.

[3] F. Blumentritt, "Sitten und Bräuche der Ilocanen," *Globus*, xlviii. No. 12, p. 202.

[4] M. J. van Baarda, "Fabelen, Verhalen en Overleveringen der Galelareezen," *Bijdragen tot de Taal- Land- en Volkenkunde van Nederlandsch-Indië*, xlv. (1895) p. 489.

[5] Rev. J. Roscoe, "Further Notes on the Manners and Customs of the Baganda," *Journal of the Anthropological Institute*, xxxii. (1902) p. 38.

[6] B. Guttmann, "Trauer und Begräbnissitten der Wadschagga," *Globus*, lxxxix. (1906) p. 200.

[7] J. G. Frazer, "On certain Burial Customs as illustrative of the Primitive Theory of the Soul," *Journal of the Anthropological Institute*, xv. (1886) pp. 69 *sq.*

has given rise to a number of prohibitions or rules of avoidance : people abstain from doing certain things lest they should homoeopathically infect the fruits of the earth with their own undesirable state or condition. All such customs of abstention or rules of avoidance are examples of negative magic or taboo.[1] Thus, for example, arguing from what may be called the infectiousness of personal acts or states, the Galelareese say that you ought not to shoot with a bow and arrows under a fruit-tree, or the tree will cast its fruit even as the arrows fall to the ground ;[2] and that when you are eating water-melon you ought not to mix the pips which you spit out of your mouth with the pips which you have put aside to serve as seed ; for if you do, though the pips you spat out may certainly spring up and blossom, yet the blossoms will keep falling off just as the pips fell from your mouth, and thus these pips will never bear fruit.[3] Precisely the same train of thought leads the Bavarian peasant to believe that if he allows the graft of a fruit-tree to fall on the ground, the tree that springs from that graft will let its fruit fall untimely.[4] The Indians of Santiago Tepehuacan suppose that if a single grain of the maize which they are about to sow were eaten by an animal, the birds and the wild boars would come and devour all the rest, and nothing would grow. And if any of these Indians has ever in his life buried a corpse, he will never be allowed to plant a fruit-tree, for they say that the tree would wither. And they will not let such a man go fishing with them, for the fish would flee from him.[5] Clearly these Indians imagine that anybody who has buried a corpse is thereby tainted, so to say, with an infection of death, which might prove fatal to fruits and fish. In Nias, the day after a man has made pre-parations for planting rice he may not use fire, or the crop would be parched ; he may not spread his mats on the ground, or the young plants would droop towards the earth.[6]

---

[1] As to negative magic or taboo, see above, pp. 111 *sqq.*

[2] M. J. van Baarda, *op. cit.* p. 488.

[3] M. J. van Baarda, *op.cit.* pp. 496 *sq.*

[4] *Bavaria, Landes- und Volkskunde des Königreichs Bayern*, ii. 299.

[5] "Lettre du curé de Santiago Tepehuacan," *Bulletin de la Société de Géographie* (Paris), IIme Série, ii. (1834) pp. 181 *sq.*, 183.

[6] E. Modigliani, *Un Viaggio a Nias* (Milan, 1890), p. 590.

When the Chams of Cochinchina are sowing their dry rice-fields and desire that no rain should fall, they eat their rice dry instead of moistening it, as they usually do, with the water in which vegetables and fish have been boiled. That prevents rain from spoiling the rice.[1]

 Persons in-fluenced homoeo-pathically by plants.

In the foregoing cases a person is supposed to influence vegetation homoeopathically. He infects trees or plants with qualities or accidents, good or bad, resembling and derived from his own. But on the principle of homoeo-pathic magic the influence is mutual : the plant can infect the man just as much as the man can infect the plant. In magic, as I believe in physics, action and reaction are equal and opposite. The Cherokee Indians are adepts in prac-tical botany of the homoeopathic sort. Thus wiry roots of the catgut plant or devil's shoestring (*Tephrosia*) are so tough that they can almost stop a ploughshare in the furrow. Hence Cherokee women wash their heads with a decoction of the roots to make the hair strong, and Cherokee ball-players wash themselves with it to toughen their muscles. To help them to spring quickly to their feet when they are thrown to the ground, these Indian ball-players also bathe their limbs with a decoction of the small rush (*Juncus tenuis*), which, they say, always recovers its erect position, no matter how often it is trampled down. To improve a child's memory the Cherokees beat up burs in water which has been fetched from a roaring waterfall. The virtue of the potion is threefold. The voice of the Long Man or river-god is heard in the roar of the cataract ; the stream seizes and holds things cast upon its surface ; and there is nothing that sticks like a bur. Hence it seems clear that with the potion the child will drink in the lessons taught by the voice of the waters, will seize them like the stream, and stick fast to them like a bur. For a like reason the Cherokee fisherman ties the plant called Venus' flytrap (*Dionaea*) to his fishtrap, and he chews the plant and spits it on the bait. That will be sure to make the trap and the bait catch fish, just as Venus' flytrap catches and digests the insects which alight on it.[2]

[1] Damien Grangeon, " Les Cham et leurs superstitions," *Missions Catho-*   *liques*, xxviii. (1896) p. 83.

[2] J. Mooney, " Myths of the

The Kei islanders think that certain creepers which adhere
firmly to the trunks of trees prevent voyagers at sea from
being wafted hither and thither at the mercy of the wind
and the waves ; the adhesive power of the plants enables
the mariners to go straight to their destination.[1] It is a
Galelareese belief that if you eat a fruit which has fallen
to the ground, you will yourself contract a·disposition to
stumble and fall ; and that if you partake of something
which has been forgotten (such as a sweet potato left in the
pot or a banana in the fire), you will become forgetful.[2] The
Galelareese are also of opinion that if a woman were to consume two bananas growing from a single head she would give
birth to twins.[3] The Guarani Indians of South America
thought that a woman would become a mother of twins if she
ate a double grain of millet.[4] In Vedic times a curious
application of this principle supplied a charm by which a
banished prince might be restored to his kingdom. He had
to eat food cooked on a fire which was fed with wood which
had grown out of the stump of a tree which had been cut down.
The recuperative power manifested by such a tree would in
due course be communicated through the fire to the food,
and so to the prince, who ate the food which was cooked on
the fire which was fed with the wood which grew out of the
tree.[5] Among the Lkuñgen Indians of Vancouver Island
an infallible means of making your hair grow long is to rub
it with fish oil and the pulverised fruit of a particular kind
of poplar (*Populus trichocarpa*). As the fruit grows a long
way up the tree, it cannot fail to make your hair grow long
too.[6] At Allumba, in Central Australia, there is a tree to

Cherokee," *Nineteenth Annual Report
of the Bureau of American Ethnology*
(Washington, 1900), pt. i. pp. 425-
427 ; compare *id.*, "Sacred Formulas
of the Cherokees," *Seventh Annual
Report of the Bureau of Ethnology*
(Washington, 1891), p. 329.
  [1] H. Geurtjens, "Le Cérémonial des
voyages aux Îles Keij," *Anthropos*, v.
(1910) p. 352.
  [2] M. J. van Baarda, "Fabelen,
Verhalen en Overleveringen der Galel-
areezan," *Bijdragen tot de Taal- Land-
en Volkenkunde van Nederlandsch-*

Indië, xlv. (1895) pp. 466, 468.
  [3] M. J. van Baarda, *op. cit.* p.
467.
  [4] R. Southey, *History of Brazil*, ii.
(London, 1817) p. 37.
  [5] H. Oldenberg, *Die Religion des
Veda*, p. 505 ; M. Bloomfield, *Hymns
of the Atharva - Veda*, p. 240 ; W.
Caland, *Altindisches Zauberritual*,
p. 37.
  [6] Fr. Boas, in *Sixth Report on the
North-Western Tribes of Canada*, p. 25
(separate reprint from the *Report of
the British Association for 1890*).

which the sun, in the shape of a woman, is said to have travelled from the east. The natives believe that if the tree were destroyed, they would all be burned up ; and that were any man to kill and eat an opossum from this tree, the food would burn up all his inward parts so that he would die.[1]

People supposed to be influenced homoeopathically by the nature of the timber of which their houses are built.

The Sundanese of the Indian Archipelago regard certain kinds of wood as unsuitable for use in house-building, especially such trees as have prickles or thorns on their trunks. They think that the life of people who lived in a house made of such timber would be thorny and full of trouble. Again, if a house is built of trees that have fallen, or lost their leaves through age, the inmates would die soon or would be hard put to it to earn their bread. Again, wood from a house that has been burnt down should never be used in building, for it would cause a fire to break out in the new house.[2] In Java some people would not build a house with the wood of a tree that has been uprooted by a storm, lest the house should fall down in like manner ; and they take care not to construct the upright and the horizontal parts (the standing and lying parts, as they call them) of the edifice out of the same tree. The reason for this precaution is a belief that if the standing and lying woodwork was made out of the same tree, the inmates of the house would constantly suffer from ill health ; no sooner had one of them got up from a bed of sickness than another would have to lie down on it ; and so it would go on, one up and another down, perpetually.[3] Before Cherokee braves went forth to war the medicine-man used to give each man a small charmed root which made him absolutely invulnerable. On the eve of battle the warrior bathed in a running stream, chewed a portion of the root and spat the juice on his body in order that the bullets might slide from his skin like the drops of water. Some of my readers perhaps doubt whether this really made the men bomb-proof. There is a barren and paralysing spirit of scepticism abroad at

[1] Spencer and Gillen, *Northern Tribes of Central Australia*, pp. 624 *sq.*

[2] J. Habbema, "Bijgeloof in de Praenger-Regentschappen," *Bijdragen tot de Taal- Land- en Volkenkunde van Nederlandsch-Indië*, li. (1900) p. 113.

[3] D. Louwerier, "Bijgeloovige gebruiken, die door de Javanen worden in acht genomen bij het bouwen hunner huizen," *Mededeelingen van wege het Nederlandsche Zendelinggenootschap*, xlviii. (1904) pp. 380 *sq.*

the present day which is most deplorable. However, the efficacy of this particular charm was proved in the Civil War, for three hundred Cherokees served in the army of the South ; and they were never, or hardly ever, wounded in action.[1] Near Charlotte Waters, in Central Australia, there is a tree which sprang up to mark the spot where a blind man died. It is called the Blind Tree by the natives, who think that if it were cut down all the people of the neighbourhood would become blind. A man who wishes to deprive his enemy of sight need only go to the tree by himself and rub it, muttering his wish and exhorting the magic virtue to go forth and do its baleful work.[2]

In this last example the infectious quality, though it emanates directly from a tree, is derived originally from a man—namely, the blind man—who was buried at the place where the tree grew. Similarly, the Central Australians believe that a certain group of stones at Undiara are the petrified boils of an old man who long ago plucked them from his body and left them there ; hence any man who wishes to infect his enemy with boils will go to these stones and throw miniature spears at them, taking care that the points of the spears strike the stones. Then the spears are picked up, and thrown one by one in the direction of the person whom it is intended to injure. The spears carry with them the magic virtue from the stones, and the result is an eruption of painful boils on the body of the victim. Sometimes a whole group of people can be afflicted in this way by a skilful magician.[3] These examples introduce us to a fruitful branch of homoeopathic magic, namely to that department of it which works by means of the dead ; for just as the dead can neither see nor hear nor speak, so you may on homoeopathic principles render people blind, deaf, and dumb by the use of dead men's bones or anything else that is tainted by the infection of death. Thus among the Galelareese, when a young man goes a-wooing at night, he takes a little earth from a grave and strews it on the

Homoeo-pathic magic of the dead.

[1] J. Mooney, " Sacred Formulas of the Cherokees," *Seventh Annual Report of the Bureau of Ethnology* (Washington, 1891), p. 389.

[2] Spencer and Gillen, *Native Tribes of Central Australia*, p. 552.

[3] Spencer and Gillen, *op. cit.* p. 550.

roof of his sweetheart's house just above the place where
her parents sleep.   This, he fancies, will prevent them from
waking while he converses with his beloved, since the earth
from the grave will make them sleep as sound as the dead.[1]

Homoeo-
pathic
magic of
the dead
employed
by burglars
for the
purpose
of conceal-
ment.
Burglars in all ages and many lands have been patrons of this
species of magic, which is very useful to them in the exercise
of their profession.   Thus a South Slavonian housebreaker
sometimes begins operations by throwing a dead man's bone
over the house, saying, with pungent sarcasm, " As this bone
may waken, so may these people waken"; after that not a
soul in the house can keep his or her eyes open.[2]   Similarly,
in Java the burglar takes earth from a grave and sprinkles
it round the house which he intends to rob; this throws
the inmates into a deep sleep.[3]   With the same intention a
Hindoo will strew ashes from a pyre at the door of the
house;[4] Indians of Peru scatter the dust of dead men's
bones;[5] and Ruthenian burglars remove the marrow from a
human shin-bone, pour tallow into it, and having kindled the
tallow, march thrice round the house with this candle burning,
which causes the inmates to sleep a death-like sleep.   Or
the Ruthenian will make a flute out of a human leg-bone
and play upon it; whereupon all persons within hearing are
overcome with drowsiness.[6]   The Indians of Mexico employed
for this maleficent purpose the left fore-arm of a woman who
had died in giving birth to her first child; but the arm had
to be stolen.   With it they beat the ground before they
entered the house which they designed to plunder; this caused
every one in the house to lose all power of speech and
motion; they were as dead, hearing and seeing everything,
but perfectly powerless; some of them, however, really slept
and even snored.[7]   In Europe similar properties were

[1] M. J. van Baarda, " Fabelen, Verhalen en Overleveringen der Galelareezen," *Bijdragen tot de Taal- Land- en
Volkenkunde van Nederlandsch-Indië*,
xlv. (1895) p. 462.

[2] F. S. Krauss, *Volksglaube und religiöser Brauch der Südslaven*, p. 146.

[3] J. Knebel, " Amulettes java-
naises," *Tijdschrift voor Indische Taal-
Land- en Volkenkunde*, xl. (1898) p.
506.

[4] *North Indian Notes and Queries*,

ii. 215, No. 760; W. Crooke, *Popular
Religion and Folklore of Northern
India* (Westminster, 1896), i. 261.

[5] P. J. de Arriaga, *Extirpacion de
la idolatria del Piru* (Lima, 1621),
p. 22.

[6] R. F. Kaindl, " Zauberglaube bei
den Rutenen," *Globus*, lxi. (1892)
p. 282.

[7] B. de Sahagun, *Histoire générale des
choses de la Nouvelle-Espagne* (Paris,
1880), bk. iv. ch. 31, pp. 274 *sq.* ; E.

ascribed to the Hand of Glory, which was the dried and
pickled hand of a man who had been hanged. If a candle
made of the fat of a malefactor who had also died on the
gallows was lighted and placed in the Hand of Glory as in a
candlestick, it rendered motionless all persons to whom it was
presented ; they could not stir a finger any more than if they
were dead.[1] Sometimes the dead man's hand is itself the
candle, or rather bunch of candles, all its withered fingers
being set on fire ; but should any member of the household
be awake, one of the fingers will not kindle. Such nefarious
lights can only be extinguished with milk.[2] Often it is prescribed that the thief's candle should be made of the finger
of a new-born or, still better, unborn child ; sometimes it is
thought needful that the thief should have one such candle
for every person in the house, for if he has one candle too
little somebody in the house will wake and catch him. Once
these tapers begin to burn, there is nothing but milk that will
put them out. In the seventeenth century robbers used to
murder pregnant women in order thus to extract candles from
their wombs.[3] An ancient Greek robber or burglar thought
he could silence and put to flight the fiercest watchdogs by
carrying with him a brand plucked from a funeral pyre.[4]

Again, Servian and Bulgarian women who chafe at the
restraints of domestic life will take the copper coins from
the eyes of a corpse, wash them in wine or water, and give
the liquid to their husbands to drink. After swallowing it,
the husband will be as blind to his wife's peccadilloes as the
dead man was on whose eyes the coins were laid.[5] When a

Homoeo-
pathic
magic of
the dead
employed
for various
purposes.

Seler, *Altmexikanische Studien*, ii.
(Berlin, 1899) pp. 51 *sq.* (*Veröffent-
lichungen aus dem königlichen Museum
für Völkerkunde*, vi.).

[1] J. Brand, *Popular Antiquities of
Great Britain*, iii. 278 *sq.* (Bohn's ed.).

[2] W. Henderson, *Folklore of the
Northern Counties of England*, pp. 239
sqq. ; J. W. Wolf, *Niederländische
Sagen* (Leipsic, 1843), pp. 363-365.

[3] L. Strackerjan, *Aberglaube und
Sagen aus dem Herzogthum Oldenburg*,
i. 100 *sq.* § 141 ; J. V. Grohmann,
*Aberglauben und Gebräuche aus Böhmen
und Mähren*, p. 106 § 758, p. 205
§ 1421 ; A. Wuttke, *Der deutsche

Volksaberglaube,[2] pp. 126 *sq.* § 184 ;
A. Gittée, *De hand en de vingeren in
het volksgeloof*, pp. 31 *sqq.* Compare
Tettau und Temme, *Volkssagen Ostpreussens, Litthauens und Westpreussens*, p. 266.

[4] Aelian, *Nat. Anim.* i. 38.

[5] F. S. Krauss, *Volksglaube und religiöser Brauch der Südslaven*, p. 140.
The custom of placing coins on the eyes
of a corpse to prevent them from opening is not uncommon. Its observance in
England is attested by the experienced
Mrs. Gamp : — "When Gamp was
summoned to his long home, and I
see him a-lying in Guy's Hospital with

Blackfoot Indian went out eagle-hunting, he used to take a
skull with him, because he believed that the skull would
make him invisible, like the dead person to whom it had
belonged, and so the eagles would not be able to see and
attack him.[1]   The Tarahumares of Mexico are great runners,
and parties of them engage in races with each other.   They
believe that human bones induce fatigue ; hence before a race
the friends of one side will bury dead men's bones in the
track, hoping that the runners of the other side will pass over
them and so be weakened.   Naturally they warn their own
men to shun the spot where the bones are buried.[2]   The
Belep of New Caledonia think that they can disable an
enemy from flight by means of the leg-bone of a dead foe.
They stick certain plants into the bone, and then smash it
between stones before the skulls of their ancestors.   It is
easy to see that this breaks the leg of the living enemy and
so hinders him from running away.   Hence in time of war
men fortify themselves with amulets of this sort.[3]   The
ancient Greeks seem to have thought that to set a young
male child on a tomb would be to rob him of his manhood
by infecting him with the impotence of the dead.[4]   And as
there is no memory in the grave the Arabs think that earth
from a grave can make a man forget his griefs and sorrows,
especially the sorrow of an unhappy love.[5]

Homoeo-
pathic
magic of
animals.

Again, animals are often conceived to possess qualities
or properties which might be useful to man, and homoeopathic or imitative magic seeks to communicate these
properties to human beings in various ways.   Thus some
Bechuanas wear a ferret as a charm, because, being very
tenacious of life, it will make them difficult to kill.[6]   Others

a penny piece on each eye, and his
wooden leg under his left arm, I
thought I should have fainted away.
But I bore up" (C. Dickens, *Martin
Chuzzlewit*, ch. xix.).

[1] G. B. Grinnell, *Blackfoot Lodge
Tales*, p. 238.

[2] C. Lumholtz, *Unknown Mexico*,
i. 284.

[3] Father Lambert, in *Missions Catholiques*, xi. (1879) p. 43 ; *id.*, *Mœurs
et superstitions des Néo - Calédoniens*
(Nouméa, 1900), pp. 30 *sq.*

[4] Hesiod, *Works and Days*, 750 *sqq.*
But the lines are not free from am-
biguity.   See F. A. Paley's note on the
passage.

[5] E. Doutté, *Magie et religion dans
l'Afrique du Nord* (Algiers, 1908),
pp. 302 *sq.*

[6] J. Campbell, *Travels in South
Africa, Second Journey* (London,
1822), ii. 206 ; Barnabas Shaw, *Mem-
orials of South Africa* (London, 1840),
p. 66.

wear a certain insect, mutilated, but living, for a similar purpose.[1] Yet other Bechuana warriors wear the hair of a hornless ox among their own hair, and the skin of a frog on their mantle, because a frog is slippery, and the ox, having no horns, is hard to catch ; so the man who is provided with these charms believes that he will be as hard to hold as the ox and the frog.[2] Again, it seems plain that a South African warrior who twists tufts of rats' hair among his own curly black locks will have just as many chances of avoiding the enemy's spear as the nimble rat has of avoiding things thrown at it ; hence in these regions rats' hair is in great demand when war is expected.[3] In Morocco a fowl or a pigeon may sometimes be seen with a little red bundle tied to its foot ; the bundle contains a charm, and it is believed that as the charm is kept in constant motion by the bird, a corresponding restlessness is kept up in the mind of him or her against whom the charm is directed.[4] When a Galla sees a tortoise, he will take off his sandals and step on it, believing that the soles of his feet are thereby made hard and strong like the shell of the animal.[5] The Wajaggas of Eastern Africa think that if they wear a piece of the wing-bone of a vulture tied round their leg they will be able to run and not grow weary, just as the vulture flies unwearied through the sky.[6] The Esquimaux of Baffin Land fancy that if part of the intestines of a fox is placed under the feet of a baby boy, he will become active and skilful in walking over thin ice, like a fox.[7] One of the ancient books of India prescribes that when a sacrifice is offered for victory, the earth out of which the altar is to be made should be taken from a place where a boar has been wallowing, since the strength of the boar will be in that earth.[8]

[1] E. Casalis, *The Basutos*, pp. 271 sq.

[2] E. Casalis, *op. cit.* p. 272.

[3] Rev. James Macdonald, "Manners, Customs, Religions, and Superstitions of South African Tribes," *Journal of the Anthropological Institute*, xx. (1891) p. 132.

[4] A. Leared, *Morocco and the Moors* (London, 1876), p. 272.

[5] Ph. Paulitschke, *Ethnographie Nordost-Afrikas: die geistige Cultur der Danâkil, Galla und Somâl* (Berlin, 1896), p. 27.

[6] M. Merker, *Rechtsverhältnisse und Sitten der Wadschagga* (Gotha, 1902), p. 21 (*Petermanns Mitteilungen*, Ergänzungsheft, No. 138).

[7] F. Boas, "The Eskimo of Baffin Land and Hudson Bay," *Bulletin of the American Museum of Natural History*, xv. pt. i. (1901) p. 160.

[8] H. Oldenberg, *Die Religion des Veda*, p. 505.

When you are playing the one-stringed lute, and your fingers
are stiff, the thing to do is to catch some long-legged field
spiders and roast them, and then rub your fingers with the
ashes ; that will make your fingers as lithe and nimble as
the spiders' legs—at least so think the Galelareese.[1]   As
the sea-eagle is very expert at seizing fish in its talons,
the Kei islanders use its claws as a charm to enable
them to make great gain on their trading voyages.[2]   The
children of the Baronga on Delagoa Bay are much troubled
by a small worm which burrows under their skin, where its
meanderings are visible to the eye.   To guard her little
one against this insect pest a Baronga mother will attach
to its wrist the skin of a mole which burrows just under
the surface of the ground, exactly as the worm burrows
under the infant's skin.[3]   To bring back a runaway slave
an Arab of North Africa will trace a magic circle on
the ground, stick a nail in the middle of it, and attach
a beetle by a thread to the nail, taking care that the
sex of the beetle is that of the fugitive.   As the beetle
crawls round and round it will coil the thread about the
nail, thus shortening its tether and drawing nearer to the
centre at every circuit.   So by virtue of homoeopathic magic
the runaway slave will be drawn back to his master.[4]   The
Patagonian Indians kill a mare and put a new-born boy in
its body, believing that this will make him a good horseman.[5]
The Lkuñgen Indians of Vancouver's Island believe that
the ashes of wasps rubbed on the faces of warriors going to
battle will render the men as pugnacious as wasps, and
that a decoction of wasps' nests or of flies administered
internally to barren women will make them prolific like
the insects.[6]

Among the western tribes of British New Guinea, a

[1] M. J. van Baarda, "Fabelen,
Verhalen en Overleveringen der Galelareezen," *Bijdragen tot de Taal- Land-
en Volkenkunde van Nederlandsch-Indië*,
xlv. (1895) p. 484.

[2] H. Geurtjens, "Le Cérémonial des
voyages aux Iles Keij," *Anthropos*, v.
(1910) p. 352.

[3] H. A. Junod, *Les Ba-ronga* (Neuchâtel, 1898), pp. 472 *sq.*

[4] E. Doutté, *Magie et religion dans
l'Afrique du Nord* (Algiers, 1908),
pp. 244 *sq.*

[5] *Journal of American Folk-lore*,
xvii. (1904) p. 293, referring to Hes-
keth Pritchard, *Through the Heart of
Patagonia* (London, 1902).

[6] Fr. Boas, in *Sixth Report on the
North-Western Tribes of Canada*, p.
25 (separate reprint from *Report of the
British Association for 1890*).

man who has killed a snake will burn it and smear his legs
with the ashes when he goes into the forest; for no snake
will bite him for some days afterwards.[1] The Baronga of
Delagoa Bay carry the powdered ashes of a serpent in a
little bag as a talisman which guards them from snake-
bites.[2] Among the Arabs of Moab a woman will give her
infant daughter the ashes of a scorpion mixed with milk to
drink in order to protect her against the stings of scorpions.[3]
The Cholones of eastern Peru think that to carry the poison
tooth of a serpent is a protection against the bite of a serpent,
and that to rub the cheek with the tooth of an ounce is an
infallible remedy for toothache and face-ache.[4] In order to
strengthen her teeth some Brazilian Indians used to hang
round a girl's neck at puberty the teeth of an animal which
they called *capugouare*, that is "grass-eating."[5] When a
thoroughbred mare has drunk at a trough, an Arab woman
will hasten to drink any water that remains in order that she
may give birth to strong children.[6] If a South Slavonian
has a mind to pilfer and steal at market, he has nothing to
do but to burn a blind cat, and then throw a pinch of its
ashes over the person with whom he is higgling; after that
he can take what he likes from the booth, and the owner
will not be a bit the wiser, having become as blind as the
deceased cat with whose ashes he has been sprinkled. The
thief may even ask boldly " Did I pay for it ? " and the deluded
huckster will reply, " Why, certainly."[7] Equally simple and
effectual is the expedient adopted by natives of Central
Australia who desire to cultivate their beards. They prick
the chin all over with a pointed bone, and then stroke it
carefully with a magic stick or stone, which represents a kind
of rat that has very long whiskers. The virtue of these
whiskers naturally passes into the representative stick or

[1] B. A. Hely, "Notes on Totemism, etc., among the Western Tribes," *British New Guinea: Annual Report for 1894-95*, p. 56.

[2] H. A. Junod, *Les Ba - ronga* (Neuchâtel, 1898), p. 472.

[3] A. Jaussen, *Coutumes arabes au pays de Moab* (Paris, 1908), p. 29.

[4] E. Poeppig, *Reise in Chile, Peru und auf dem Amazonenstrome*, ii. 323.

[5] A. Thevet, *Cosmographie universelle* (Paris, 1575), ii. 946 [980].

[6] A. Jaussen, " Coutumes arabes," *Revue Biblique*, April 1903, p. 245; id., *Coutumes arabes au pays de Moab*, p. 36.

[7] F. S. Krauss, *Volksglaube und religiöser Brauch der Südslaven*, p. 147.

stone, and thence by an easy transition to the chin, which, consequently, is soon adorned with a rich growth of beard.[1] When a party of these same natives has returned from killing a foe, and they fear to be attacked by the ghost of the dead man in their sleep, every one of them takes care to wear the tip of the tail of a rabbit-kangaroo in his hair. Why? Because the rabbit - kangaroo, being a nocturnal animal, does not sleep of nights; and therefore a man who wears a tip of its tail in his hair will clearly be wakeful during the hours of darkness.[2] The Unmatjera tribe of Central Australia use the tip of the tail of the same animal for the same purpose, but they draw out the sympathetic chain one link farther. For among them, when a boy has undergone subincision and is leading a solitary life in the bush, it is not he but his mother who wears the tip of the nocturnal creature's tail in order that he may be watchful at nights, lest harm should befall him from snakes and so forth.[3] The ancient Greeks thought that to eat the flesh of the wakeful nightingale would prevent a man from sleeping; that to smear the eyes of a blear-sighted person with the gall of an eagle would give him the eagle's vision; and that a raven's eggs would restore the blackness of the raven to silvery hair. Only the person who adopted this last mode of concealing the ravages of time had to be most careful to keep his mouth full of oil all the time he applied the eggs to his venerable locks, else his teeth as well as his hair would be dyed raven black, and no amount of scrubbing and scouring would avail to whiten them again.[4] The hair-restorer was in fact a shade too powerful, and in applying it you might get more than you bargained for.

Homoeo-
pathic
magic of
animals
among the
Cherokees
and other
American
Indians.

The Huichol Indians of Mexico admire the beautiful markings on the backs of serpents. Hence when a Huichol woman is about to weave or embroider, her husband catches a large serpent and holds it in a cleft stick, while the woman strokes the reptile with one hand down the whole length of its back; then she passes the same hand over her forehead

---

[1] Spencer and Gillen, *Native Tribes of Central Australia*, pp. 545 *sq.*

[2] *Ibid.* pp. 494 *sq.*

[3] Spencer and Gillen, *Northern Tribes of Central Australia*, p. 344.

[4] Aelian, *Nat. Anim.* i. 42, 43, and 48.

and eyes, that she may be able to work as beautiful patterns
in the web as the markings on the back of the serpent.[1]
Among the Tarahumares of Mexico men who run races
tie deer-hoofs to their backs in the belief that this will
make them swift-footed like the deer.[2]   Cherokee ball-
players rub their bodies with eel-skins in order to make
themselves as slippery and hard to hold as eels ; and they
also apply land-tortoises to their legs in the hope of making
them as thick and strong as the legs of these animals.   But
they are careful not to eat frogs, lest the brittleness of
the frog's bones should infect their own bones.   Moreover,
they will not eat the flesh of the sluggish hog-sucker, lest they
should lose their speed, nor the flesh of rabbits, lest, like the
rabbit, they should become confused in running.   On the
other hand, their friends sprinkle a soup made of rabbit ham-
strings along the path to be taken by their rivals, in order to
make these rivals timorous in action.   Moreover, the ball-
players will not wear the feathers of the bald-headed buzzard,
for fear of themselves becoming bald, nor turkey feathers,
lest they should suffer from a goitrous growth on the throat
like the red appendage on the throat of a turkey.[3]   The
flesh of the common grey squirrel is forbidden to Cherokees
who suffer from rheumatism, because the squirrel eats in a
cramped position, which would clearly aggravate the pangs
of the rheumatic patient.[4]   And a Cherokee woman who is
with child may not eat the flesh of the ruffed grouse,
because that bird hatches a large brood, but loses most of
them before maturity.   Strict people, indeed, will not allow a
woman to taste of the bird till she is past child-bearing.[5]
When a Cherokee is starting on a journey on a cold winter
morning he rubs his feet in the ashes of the fire and sings
four verses by means of which he can set the cold at defiance,
like the wolf, the deer, the fox, and the opossum, whose feet,
so the Indians think, are never frost-bitten.   After each
verse he imitates the cry and action of the animal, thus
homoeopathically identifying himself with the creature.   The

---

[1] C. Lumholtz, *Unknown Mexico,*
ii. 234.
[2] C. Lumholtz, *op. cit.* i. 290.
[3] J. Mooney, "Myths of the
Cherokee," *Nineteenth Annual Report*

of the Bureau of American Ethnology
(Washington, 1900), part i. pp. 262,
284, 285, 306, 308.
[4] *Id., ib.* p. 262.
[5] *Id., ib.* p. 285.

Homoeo-
pathic
magic of
animals
among the
Cherokees. song he sings may be rendered, " I become a real wolf, a real deer, a real fox, and a real opossum." After stating that he has become a real wolf, the songster utters a prolonged howl and paws the ground like a wolf with his feet. After giving notice that he has become a real deer, he imitates the call and jumping of a deer. And after announcing his identification, for all practical purposes, with a fox and an opossum, he mimicks the barking and scratching of a fox and the cry of an opossum when it is driven to bay, also throwing his head back just as an opossum does when it feigns death.[1] Some Cherokees are said to drink tea made of crickets in order to become good singers like the insects.[2] If the eyes of a Cherokee child be bathed with water in which a feather of an owl has been soaked, the child will be able, like the owl, to keep awake all night. The mole-cricket has claws with which it burrows in the earth, and among the Cherokees it is reputed to be an excellent singer. Hence when children are long of learning to speak, their tongues are scratched with the claw of a live mole-cricket in order that they may soon talk as distinctly as the insect. Grown persons also, who are slow of speech, may acquire a ready flow of eloquence, if only the inside of their throat be scratched on four successive mornings with a mole-cricket.[3] The negroes of the Maroni river in Guiana have a somewhat similar cure for stammering. Day and night the shrieks of a certain species of ape resound through the forest. Hence when the negroes kill one of these pests, they remove its larynx and make a cup out of it. If a stammering child drinks out of such a cup for a few months, it ceases to stammer.[4] Cherokee parents scratch the hands of their children with the pincers of a live red crawfish, resembling a lobster, in order to give the infants a strong grip, like that of the crawfish.[5] This may help us to understand why on the fifth day after birth a Greek child used to receive presents of octopuses and cuttle-fish from its friends and relations.[6] For the numerous arms, legs, and tentacles of

[1] *Id., ib.* p. 266.
[2] *Id., ib.* p. 309.
[3] *Id., ib.* p. 309.
[4] J. Crevaux, *Voyages dans l'Amé-*

rique du Sud (Paris, 1883), pp. 159 *sq.*
[5] J. Mooney, *op. cit.* p. 308.
[6] Scholiast on Plato, *Theaetetus,* p. 160 A.

these creatures seem well calculated to strengthen the grip
of a baby's hands and to impart the power of toddling to
its little toes.

On the principle of homoeopathic magic, inanimate
things, as well as plants and animals, may diffuse blessing or
bane around them, according to their own intrinsic nature
and the skill of the wizard to tap or dam, as the case may
be, the stream of weal or woe.   Thus, for example, the
Galelareese think that when your teeth are being filed you
should keep spitting on a pebble, for this establishes a
homoeopathic connexion between you and the pebble, by
virtue of which your teeth will henceforth be as hard and
durable as a stone.   On the other hand, you ought not to
comb a child before it has teethed, for if you do, its teeth
will afterwards be separated from each other like the teeth
of a comb.[1]   Nor should children look at a sieve, otherwise
they will suffer from a skin disease, and will have as many
sores on their bodies as there are holes in the sieve.[2]   In
Samaracand women give a baby sugar candy to suck and
put glue in the palm of its hand, in order that, when the
child grows up, his words may be sweet and precious things
may stick to his hands as if they were glued.[3]   The
Greeks thought that a garment made from the fleece of a
sheep that had been torn by a wolf would hurt the wearer,
setting up an itch or irritation in his skin.   They were also
of opinion that if a stone which had been bitten by a dog
were dropped in wine, it would make all who drank of that
wine to fall out among themselves.[4]   Among the Arabs of
Moab a childless woman often borrows the robe of a woman
who has had many children, hoping with the robe to acquire
the fruitfulness of its owner.[5]   The Caffres of Sofala, in
East Africa, had a great dread of being struck with anything hollow, such as a reed or a straw, and greatly preferred
being thrashed with a good thick cudgel or an iron bar, even
though it hurt very much.   For they thought that if a man

*Homoeo-
pathic
magic of
inanimate
things.*

[1] M. J. van Baarda, "Fabelen,
Verhalen en Overleveringen der Galelareezen," *Bijdragen tot de Taal- Land-
en Volkenkunde van Nederlandsch-Indië*,
xlv. (1895) p. 483.

[2] M. J. van Baarda, *op. cit.* p. 534.

[3] E. Chavannes, *Documents sur les
Tou-Kiue (Turcs) Occidentaux* (St.
Petersburg, 1903), p. 134.

[4] Aelian, *Nat. anim.* i. 38.

[5] A. Jaussen, *Coutumes arabes au
pays de Moab*, p. 35.

were beaten with anything hollow, his inside would waste
away till he died.[1] In eastern seas there is a large shell
which the Buginese of Celebes call the "old man" (*kadjâwo*).
On Fridays they turn these "old men" upside down and
place them on the thresholds of their houses, believing that
whoever then steps over the threshold of the house will live
to be old.[2] Again, the Galelareese think that, if you are
imprudent enough to eat while somebody is sharpening a
knife, your throat will be cut that same evening, or next
morning at latest.[3] The disastrous influence thus attributed,
under certain circumstances, to a knife in the East Indies,
finds its counterpart in a curious old Greek story. A
certain king had no child, and he asked a wise man how he
could get one. The wise man himself did not know, but
he thought that the birds of the air might, and he undertook
to enquire of them. For you must know that the sage understood the language of birds, having learned it through some
serpents whose life he had saved, and who, out of gratitude, had
cleansed his ears as he slept. So he sacrificed two bulls, and
cut them up, and prayed the fowls to come and feast on the
flesh ; only the vulture he did not invite. When the birds
came, the wise man asked them what the king must do to
get a son ; but none of them knew. At last up came the
vulture, and he knew all about it. He said that once when
the king was a child his royal father was gelding rams in the
field, and laid down the bloody knife beside his little son ;
nay, he threatened the boy with it. The child was afraid
and ran away, and the father stuck the knife in a tree, either
a sacred oak or a wild pear-tree. Meanwhile, the bark of
the tree had grown round the knife and hidden it. The
vulture said that if they found the knife, scraped the rust off
it, and gave the rust, mixed with wine, to the king to drink
for ten days, he would beget a son. They did so, and it fell
out exactly as the vulture had said.[4] In this story a knife

[1] J. Dos Santos, *Eastern Ethiopia*,
book i. ch. 20 (G. McCall Theal,
Records of South-Eastern Africa, vii.
224).

[2] One of these shells is exhibited in
the Anthropological Museum at Berlin,
with a label explaining its use. I do
not know to what species it belongs.

It appeared to me to be of a sort which
may often be seen on mantelpieces in
England.

[3] M. J. van Baarda, *op. cit.* p. 468.

[4] The king was Iphiclus ; the wise
man was Melampus. See Apollodorus,
i. 9. 12 ; Eustathius on Homer, *Od.*
xi. 292 ; Schol. on Theocritus, iii. 43.

which had gelded rams is supposed to have deprived a boy
of his virility merely by being brought near his person.
Through simple proximity it infected him, so to say, with the
same disability which it had already inflicted on the rams ;
and the loss he thus sustained was afterwards repaired by
administering to him in a potion the rust which, having been
left on the blade by the blood of the animals, might be
supposed to be still imbued with their generative faculty.

The strengthening virtue of iron is highly appreciated
by the Toradjas of Central Celebes, only they apply it
externally, not internally, as we do in Europe. For this
purpose the people of a village assemble once a year in the
smithy. The master of the ceremonies opens the proceedings by carrying a little pig and a white fowl round the
smithy, after which he kills them and smears a little of
their blood on the forehead of every person present. Next
he takes a doit, a chopping-knife, and a bunch of leaves in
his hand, and strikes with them the palm of the right
hand of every man, woman, and child, and ties a leaf of the
Dracaena terminalis to every wrist. Then a little fire is
made in the furnace and blown up with the bellows. Every
one who feels sick or unwell now steps up to the anvil, and
the master of the ceremonies sprinkles a mixture of pigs'
blood, water, and herbs on the joints of his body, and
finally on his head, wishing him a long life. Lastly, the
patient takes the chopping-knife, heats it in the furnace,
lays it on the anvil, and strikes it seven times with the
hammer. After that he has only to cool the knife in water
and the iron cure is complete. Again, on the seventh day
after a birth the Toradjas hold a little feast, at which the
child is carried down the house ladder and its feet set on a
piece of iron, in order to strengthen its feeble soul with the
strong soul of the iron.[1] At critical times the Mahakam
Dyaks of Central Borneo seek to strengthen their souls

(marginal note: Homoeo-pathic magic of iron.)

The way in which the king's impotence
was caused by the knife is clearly indicated by the scholiast on Theocritus :
συνέβη ἐπενεγκεῖν αὐτὴν [scil. τὴν
μάχαιραν] τοῖς μορίοις τοῦ παιδός. In this
scholium we must correct ἐκτέμνοντι
. . . δένδρον into ἐκτέμνοντι . . . ζῷα.
Eustathius (*l.c.*) quotes the scholium in

this latter form. The animals were
rams, according to Apollodorus.

[1] A. C. Kruijt, " Het ijzer in Midden-Celebes," *Bijdragen tot de Taal-
Land- en Volkenkunde van Nederlandsch-Indië*, liii. (1901) pp. 157 *sq.*,
159.

by biting on an old sword or setting their feet upon it.[1]

Homoeo-
pathic
magic of
stones.

At initiation a Brahman boy is made to tread with his right foot on a stone, while the words are repeated, " Tread on this stone ; like a stone be firm " ;[2] and the same ceremony is performed, with the same words, by a Brahman bride at her marriage.[3] In Madagascar a mode of counteracting the levity of fortune is to bury a stone at the foot of the heavy house-post.[4] The common custom of swearing upon a stone may be based partly on a belief that the strength and stability of the stone lend confirmation to an oath. Thus the old Danish historian Saxo Gram-maticus tells us that "the ancients, when they were to choose a king, were wont to stand on stones planted in the ground, and to proclaim their votes, in order to foreshadow from the steadfastness of the stones that the deed would be lasting."[5] There was a stone at Athens on which the nine archons stood when they swore to rule justly and according to the laws.[6] A little to the west of St. Columba's tomb in Iona "lie the black stones, which are so called, not from their colour, for that is grey, but from the effects that tradition says ensued upon perjury, if any one became guilty of it after swearing on these stones in the usual manner ; for an oath made on them was decisive in all controversies. Mac-Donald, king of the isles, de-livered the rights of their lands to his vassals in the isles and

Oaths upon
stones.

---

[1] A. W. Nieuwenhuis, *Quer durch Borneo*, ii. (Leyden, 1907) p. 173.

[2] *Grihya-Sûtras*, translated by H. Oldenberg, part ii. p. 146.

[3] *Grihya-Sûtras*, translated by H. Oldenberg, part i. pp. 168, 282 *sq.*, part ii. p. 188 (*Sacred Books of the East*, vols. xxix. and xxx.). Compare Sonnerat, *Voyage aux Indes Orientales* (Paris, 1782), ii. 81 ; E. Thurston, *Ethnographic Notes in Southern India* (Madras, 1906), p. 1. So among the Kookies of Northern Cachar in India the young couple at marriage place each a foot on a large stone in the middle of the village. See Lieut. R. Stewart, "Notes on Northern Cachar," *Journal of the Asiatic Society of Bengal*, xxiv. (1855) pp. 620 *sq.* In the old ruined church

of Balquhidder in Perthshire there is an ancient gravestone on which people used to stand barefoot at marriages and baptisms. See *The Folk-lore Journal*, vi. (1888) p. 271.

[4] Father Abinal, "Astrologie Mal-gache," *Missions Catholiques*, xi. (1879) p. 482.

[5] *The First Nine Books of the Danish History of Saxo Grammaticus*, translated by O. Elton (London, 1894), p. 16. The original runs thus : *Lecturi regem veteres affixis humo saxis insistere suffragiaque promere consueverant, subjectorum lapidum firmitate facti constantiam ominaturi* (*Historia Danica*, lib. i. p. 22, ed. P. E. Müller).

[6] Aristotle, *Constitution of Athens*, 7 and 55 ; Plutarch, *Solon*, 25 ; Pollux, viii. 86.

continent, with uplifted hands and bended knees, on the black stones ; and in this posture, before many witnesses, he solemnly swore that he would never recall those rights which he then granted : and this was instead of his great seal. Hence it is that when one was certain of what he affirmed, he said positively, I have freedom to swear this matter upon the black stones."[1] Again, in the island of Arran there was a green globular stone, about the size of a goose's egg, on which oaths were taken. It was also endowed with healing virtue, for it cured stitches in the sides of sick people if only it was laid on the affected part. They say that Macdonald, the Lord of the Isles, carried this stone about with him, and that victory was always on his side when he threw it among the enemy.[2] Once more, in the island of Fladda there was a round blue stone, on which people swore decisive oaths, and it too healed stitches in the side like the green stone of Arran.[3] When two Bogos of eastern Africa have a dispute, they will sometimes settle it at a certain stone, which one of them mounts. His adversary calls down the most dreadful curses on him if he forswears himself, and to every curse the man on the stone answers "Amen!"[4] In Laconia an unwrought stone was shewn which, according to the legend, relieved the matricide Orestes of his madness as soon as he had sat down on it ;[5] and Zeus is said to have often cured himself of his love for Hera by sitting down on a certain rock in the island of Leucadia.[6] In these cases it may have been thought that the wayward and flighty impulses of love and madness were counteracted by the steadying influence of a heavy stone.

But while a general magical efficacy may be supposed

---

[1] Martin, "Description of the Western Islands of Scotland," in Pinkerton's *Voyages and Travels*, iii. 657.

[2] Martin, *op. cit.* p. 646.

[3] Martin, *op. cit.* pp. 627 *sq.*

[4] W. Munzinger, *Sitten und Recht der Bogos* (Winterthur, 1859), pp. 33 *sq.* For an Indian example of swearing on a stone see J. Eliot, "Observations on the Inhabitants of the Garrow

Hills," *Asiatick Researches*, iii. 30 *sq.* (8vo ed.). On the custom see further my article, "Folk-lore in the Old Testament," in *Anthropological Essays presented to E. B. Tylor* (Oxford, 1907), pp. 131 *sqq.*

[5] Pausanias, iii. 22. 1 ; compare *id.* ii. 31. 4.

[6] Ptolemaeus, *Nova Historia*, in Photius, *Bibliotheca*, p. 153, ed. I. Bekker ; *id.* in *Mythographi Graeci*, ed. A. Westermann, p. 198.

Homoeo-
pathic
magic of
special
kinds of
stones.
to reside in all stones by reason of their common properties
of weight and solidity, special magical virtues are attributed
to particular stones, or kinds of stone, in accordance with
their individual or specific qualities of shape and colour.
For example, a pot-hole in a rocky gorge of Central
Australia contains many rounded boulders which, in the
opinion of the Warramunga tribe, represent the kidneys,
heart, tail, intestines, and so forth of an old euro, a species
of kangaroo. Hence the natives jump into the pool, and
after splashing the water all over their bodies rub one
another with the stones, believing that this will enable them
to catch euros.[1] Again, not very far from Alice Springs, in
Central Australia, there is a heap of stones supposed to be
the vomit of two men of the eagle-hawk totem who had
dined too copiously on eagle-hawk men, women, and
children. The natives think that if any person caught
sight of these stones he would be taken very sick on the
spot ; hence the heap is covered with sticks, to which every
passer-by adds one in order to prevent the evil magic from
coming out and turning his stomach.[2] The Indians of
Peru employed certain stones for the increase of maize,
others for the increase of potatoes, and others again for the
increase of cattle. The stones used to make maize grow
were fashioned in the likeness of cobs of maize, and the
stones destined to multiply cattle had the shape of sheep.[3]

Homoeo-
pathic
magic of
stones in
New
Caledonia.
No people perhaps employ stones more freely for the
purposes of homoeopathic magic than the natives of New
Caledonia. They have stones of the most diverse shapes
and colours to serve the most diverse ends—stones for
sunshine, rain, famine, war, madness, death, fishing, sailing,
and so forth. Thus in order to make a plantation of taro
thrive they bury in the field certain stones resembling taros,
praying to their ancestors at the same time. A stone
marked with black lines like the leaves of the coco-nut
palm helps to produce a good crop of coco-nuts. To
make bread-fruit grow they use two stones of different sizes
representing the unripe and the ripe fruit respectively.

---

[1] Spencer and Gillen, *Northern
Tribes of Central Australia*, pp. 253 *sq.*
[2] Spencer and Gillen, *op. cit.* p. 472.

[3] P. J. de Arriaga, *Extirpacion de la
idolatria del Piru* (Lima, 1621), pp.
15, 16, 25

As soon as the fruit begins to form, they bury the small stone at the foot of the tree ; and later on, when the fruit approaches maturity, they replace the small stone by the large one. The yam is the chief crop of the New Caledonians ; hence the number of stones used to foster its growth is correspondingly great. Different families have different kinds of stones which, according to their diverse shapes and colours, are supposed to promote the cultivation of the various species of yams. Before the stones are buried in the yam field they are deposited beside the ancestral skulls, wetted with water, and wiped with the leaves of certain trees. Sacrifices, too, of yams and fish are offered to the dead, with the words, " Here are your offerings, in order that the crop of yams may be good." Again, a stone carved in the shape of a canoe can make a voyage prosperous or the reverse according as it is placed before the ancestral skulls with the opening upwards or downwards, the ceremony being accompanied with prayers and offerings to the dead. Again, fish is a very important article of diet with the New Caledonians, and every kind of fish has its sacred stone, which is enclosed in a large shell and kept in the graveyard. In performing the rite to secure a good catch, the wizard swathes the stone in bandages of various colours, spits some chewed leaves on it, and, setting it up before the skulls, says, " Help us to be lucky at the fishing." [1]   In these and many similar practices of the New Caledonians the magical efficacy of the stones appears to be deemed insufficient of itself to accomplish the end in view ; it has to be reinforced by the spirits of the dead, whose help is sought by prayer and sacrifice. Moreover, the stones are regularly kept in the burial-grounds, as if to saturate them with the powerful influence of the ancestors ; they are brought from the cemetery to be buried in the fields or at the foot of trees for the sake of quickening the fruits of the earth, and they are restored to the cemetery when they

---

[1] Father Lambert, in *Missions Catholiques*, xii. (1880) pp. 273, 287, xxv. (1893) pp. 104-106, 116-118 ; *id.*, *Mœurs et Superstitions des Néo-Calédoniens* (Nouméa, 1900), pp. 217, 218, 222, 292-304. Compare Glaumont, " Usages, mœurs et coutumes des Néo-Calédoniens," *Revue d'Ethnographie*, vii. (1889) pp. 114 *sq.* (whose account of the stones is borrowed from Father Lambert).

have discharged this duty. Thus in New Caledonia magic is blent with the worship of the dead.

Homoeo-
pathic
magic of
stones in
Melanesia.In other parts of Melanesia a like belief prevails that certain sacred stones are endowed with miraculous powers which correspond in their nature to the shape of the stone. Thus a piece of water-worn coral on the beach often bears a surprising likeness to a bread-fruit. Hence in the Banks Islands a man who finds such a coral will lay it at the root of one of his bread-fruit trees in the expectation that it will make the tree bear well. If the result answers his expectation, he will then, for a proper remuneration, take stones of less-marked character from other men and let them lie near his, in order to imbue them with the magic virtue which resides in it. Similarly, a stone with little discs upon it is good to bring in money ; and if a man found a large stone with a number of small ones under it, like a sow among her litter, he was sure that to offer money upon it would bring him pigs. In these and similar cases the Melanesians ascribe the marvellous power, not to the stone itself, but to its indwelling spirit ; and sometimes, as we have just seen, a man endeavours to propitiate the spirit by laying down offerings on the stone.[1] But the conception of spirits that must be propitiated lies outside the sphere of magic, and within that of religion. Where such a conception is found, as here, in conjunction with purely magical ideas and practices, the latter may generally be assumed to be the original stock on which the religious conception has been at some later time engrafted. For there are strong grounds for thinking that, in the evolution of thought, magic has preceded religion. But to this point we shall return presently.

Homoeo-
pathic
magic
of precious
stones.The ancients set great store on the magical qualities of precious stones ; indeed it has been maintained, with great show of reason, that such stones were used as amulets long before they were worn as mere ornaments.[2] Thus the Greeks gave the name of tree-agate to a stone which exhibits tree-like markings, and they thought that if two

[1] R. H. Codrington, *The Melanesians* (Oxford, 1891), pp. 181-185.

[2] W. Ridgeway, *The Early Age of Greece* (Cambridge, 1901), i. 330 sq. ; *id.*, "The Origin of Jewellery," *Report of the British Association for 1903* (meeting at Southport), pp. 815 sq.

of these gems were tied to the horns or neck of oxen at the plough, the crop would be sure to be plentiful.[1] Again, they recognised a milk-stone which produced an abundant supply of milk in women if only they drank it dissolved in honey-mead.[2] Milk-stones are used for the same purpose by Greek women in Crete and Melos at the present day;[3] in Albania nursing mothers wear the stones in order to ensure an abundant flow of milk.[4] In Lechrain down to modern times German women have attempted to increase their milk by stroking their breasts with a kind of alum which they call a milk-stone.[5] Again, the Greeks believed in a stone which cured snake-bites, and hence was named the snake-stone; to test its efficacy you had only to grind the stone to powder and sprinkle the powder on the wound.[6] The wine-coloured amethyst received its name, which means "not drunken," because it was supposed to keep the wearer of it sober;[7] and two brothers who desired to live at unity were advised to carry magnets about with them, which, by drawing the twain together, would clearly prevent them from falling out.[8] In Albania people think that if the blood-stone is laid on a wound it will stop the flow of blood.[9]

Amongst the things which homoeopathic magic seeks to turn to account are the great powers of nature, such as the waxing and the waning moon, the rising and the setting sun, the stars, and the sea. Elsewhere I have illustrated the homoeopathic virtues ascribed to the waxing and the waning moon:[10] here I will give an Arab charm of the

Homoeopathic magic of the sun, the moon, the stars, and the sea.

---

[1] *Orphica: Lithica*, 230 *sqq.*, ed. G. Hermann. Pliny mentions (*Nat. Hist.* xxxvii. 192) a white tree-stone ("*dendritis alba*") which, if buried under a tree that was being felled, would prevent the woodman's axe from being blunted.

[2] *Orphica: Lithica*, 189 *sqq.*; compare Pliny, *Nat. Hist.* xxxvii. 162.

[3] W. Ridgeway, *The Early Age of Greece*, i. 330.

[4] J. G. von Hahn, *Albanesische Studien*, i. 158.

[5] K. Freiherr von Leoprechting, *Aus dem Lechrain* (Munich, 1855), p. 92.

[6] *Orphica: Lithica*, 335 *sqq.* This

was perhaps the "dragon-stone" which was supposed to confer extraordinary sharpness of vision on its owner. See Ptolemaeus Hephaestionis, *Nov. Hist.* v. p. 150, in Photius, *Bibliotheca*, ed. I. Bekker, p. 192 of A. Westermann's *Mythographi Graeci.*

[7] Pliny, *Nat. Hist.* xxxvii. 124.

[8] *Orphica: Lithica*, 320 *sq.*

[9] J. G. von Hahn, *Albanesische Studien*, i. 158. On the magic of precious stones see also E. Doutté, *Magie et religion dans l'Afrique du Nord*, pp. 82 *sqq.*

[10] *Adonis, Attis, Osiris*, Second Edition, pp. 361 *sqq.*, 369 *sqq.*

setting sun. When a husband is far away and his wife would bring him home to her, she procures pepper and coriander seed from a shop that faces the east, and throws them on a lighted brasier at sunset. Then turning to the east she waves a napkin with which she has wiped herself, and says : " Let the setting sun return having found such and such an one, son of such and such a woman, in grief and pain. May the grief that my absence causes him make him weep, may the grief that my absence causes him make him lament, may the grief that my absence causes him make him break the obstacles that part us and bring him back to me." If the charm is unsuccessful, she repeats it one day at sunrise, burning the same perfumes. Clearly she imagines that as the sun goes away in the west and comes back in the east, it should at its return bring the absent one home.[1]

The ancient books of the Hindoos lay down a rule that after sunset on his marriage night a man should sit silent with his wife till the stars begin to twinkle in the sky. When the pole-star appears, he should point it out to her, and, addressing the star, say, " Firm art thou ; I see thee, the firm one. Firm be thou with me, O thriving one ! " Then, turning to his wife, he should say, " To me Brihaspati has given thee ; obtaining offspring through me, thy husband, live with me a hundred autumns." [2] The intention of the ceremony is plainly to guard against the fickleness of fortune and the instability of earthly bliss by the steadfast influence of the constant star. It is the wish expressed in Keats's last sonnet :—

> Bright star ! would I were steadfast as thou art—
> Not in lone splendour hung aloft the night.

Dwellers by the sea cannot fail to be impressed by the sight of its ceaseless ebb and flow, and are apt, on the prin-

---

[1] E. Doutté, *Magie et religion dans l'Afrique du Nord*, pp. 131 *sq.*

[2] *The Grihya-Sûtras*, translated by H. Oldenberg, part i. pp. 43, 285 *sq.*, part ii. pp. 47 *sq.*, 193 *sqq.* (*Sacred Books of the East*, vols. xxix. and xxx.). In the last passage the address to the star is fuller and more explicit. A part of it runs thus :—" He who knows thee (the polar star) as the firm, immovable Brahman with its children and with its grandchildren, with such a man children and grandchildren will firmly dwell, servants and pupils, garments and woollen blankets, bronze and gold, wives and kings, food, safety, long life, glory, renown, splendour, strength, holy lustre, and the enjoyment of food. May all these things firmly and immovably dwell with me ! "

ciples of that rude philosophy of sympathy and resemblance Homoeo-
pathic
magic of
the tides. which here engages our attention, to trace a subtle relation, a secret harmony, between its tides and the life of man, of animals, and of plants.   In the flowing tide they see not merely a symbol, but a cause of exuberance, of prosperity, and of life, while in the ebbing tide they discern a real agent as well as a melancholy emblem of failure, of weakness, and of death.   The Breton peasant fancies that clover sown when the tide is coming in will grow well, but that if the plant be sown at low water or when the tide is going out, it will never reach maturity, and that the cows which feed on it will burst.[1]   His wife believes that the best butter is made when the tide has just turned and is beginning to flow, that milk which foams in the churn will go on foaming till the hour of high water is past, and that water drawn from the well or milk extracted from the cow while the tide is rising will boil up in the pot or saucepan and overflow into the fire.[2]   The Galelareese say that if you wish to make oil, you should do it when the tide is high, for then you will get plenty of oil.[3]   According to some of the ancients, the skins of seals, even after they had been parted from their bodies, remained in secret sympathy with the sea, and were observed to ruffle when the tide was on the ebb.[4]   Another ancient belief, attributed to Aristotle, was that no creature can die except at ebb tide. The belief, if we can trust Pliny, was confirmed by experience, so far as regards human beings, on the coast of France.[5] Philostratus also assures us that at Cadiz dying people never yielded up the ghost while the water was high.[6]   A like fancy still lingers in some parts of Europe.   On the Cantabrian coast of Spain they think that persons who die of chronic or acute disease expire at the moment when the tide begins to recede.[7]   In Portugal, all along the coast of Wales, and on some parts of the coast of Brittany,

[1] P. Sébillot, *Légendes, croyances et superstitions de la mer* (Paris, 1886), i. 136.

[2] P. Sébillot, *op. cit.* i. 135.

[3] M. J. van Baarda, "Fabelen, Verhalen en Overleveringen der Galelareezen," *Bijdragen tot de Taal- Land- en Volkenkunde van Nederlandsch-Indië*, xlv. (1895) p. 499.

[4] Pliny, *Nat. Hist.* ix. 42.

[5] *Ibid.* ii. 220.

[6] Philostratus, *Vit. Apollon.* v. 2.

[7] P. Sébillot, *Légendes, croyances et superstitions de la mer*, i. 132.

a belief is said to prevail that people are born when the
tide comes in, and die when it goes out.[1] Dickens attests
the existence of the same superstition in England. " People
can't die, along the coast," said Mr. Peggotty, " except
when the tide's pretty nigh out. They can't be born,
unless it's pretty nigh in—not properly born till flood." [2]
The belief that most deaths happen at ebb tide is said to
be held along the east coast of England from Northumber-
land to Kent.[3] Shakespeare must have been familiar with
it, for he makes Falstaff die " even just between twelve and
one, e'en at the turning o' the tide." [4] We meet the belief
again on the Pacific coast of North America among the
Haidas of the Queen Charlotte Islands. Whenever a good
Haida is about to die he sees a canoe manned by some of
his dead friends, who come with the tide to bid him welcome
to the spirit land. " Come with us now," they say, " for the
tide is about to ebb and we must depart." [5] At the other
extremity of America the same fancy has been noted among
the Indians of Southern Chili. A Chilote Indian in the
last stage of consumption, after preparing to die like a
good Catholic, was heard to ask how the tide was running.
When his sister told him that it was still coming in, he
smiled and said that he had yet a little while to live. It
was his firm conviction that with the ebbing tide his soul
would pass to the ocean of eternity.[6] At Port Stephens,
in New South Wales, the natives always buried their dead
at flood tide, never at ebb, lest the retiring water should
bear the soul of the departed to some distant country.[7]

Homoeo-
pathic
magic of
grave-
clothes
in China.
To ensure a long life the Chinese have recourse to certain
complicated charms, which concentrate in themselves the
magical essence emanating, on homoeopathic principles,
from times and seasons, from persons and from things.
The vehicles employed to transmit these happy influences

[1] P. Sébillot, *op. cit.* i. 129-132 ;
M. E. James in *Folklore*, ix. (1898)
p. 189.
[2] Dickens, *David Copperfield*, chap.
xxx.
[3] W. Henderson, *Folklore of the
Northern Counties of England* (London, 1879), p. 58.
[4] *Henry V.* Act ii. Scene 3.

[5] Rev. C. Harrison, "Religion and
Family among the Haidas," *Journal
of the Anthropological Institute*, xxi.
(1892) pp. 17 *sq.*
[6] C. Martin, "Über die Eingeborenen von Chiloe," *Zeitschrift für Ethnologie*, ix. (1877) p. 179.
[7] A. W. Howitt, *Native Tribes of
South-East Australia*, p. 465.

are no other than grave-clothes. These are provided by many Chinese in their lifetime, and most people have them cut out and sewn by an unmarried girl or a very young woman, wisely calculating that, since such a person is likely to live a great many years to come, a part of her capacity to live long must surely pass into the clothes, and thus stave off for many years the time when they shall be put to their proper use. Further, the garments are made by preference in a year which has an intercalary month ; for to the Chinese mind it seems plain that grave-clothes made in a year which is unusually long will possess the capacity of prolonging life in an unusually high degree. Amongst the clothes there is one robe in particular on which special pains have been lavished to imbue it with this priceless quality. It is a long silken gown of the deepest blue colour, with the word "longevity" embroidered all over it in thread of gold. To present an aged parent with one of these costly and splendid mantles, known as "longevity garments," is esteemed by the Chinese an act of filial piety and a delicate mark of attention. As the garment purports to prolong the life of its owner, he often wears it, especially on festive occasions, in order to allow the influence of longevity, created by the many golden letters with which it is bespangled, to work their full effect upon his person. On his birthday, above all, he hardly ever fails to don it, for in China common sense bids a man lay in a large stock of vital energy on his birthday, to be expended in the form of health and vigour during the rest of the year. Attired in the gorgeous pall, and absorbing its blessed influence at every pore, the happy owner receives complacently the congratulations of friends and relations, who warmly express their admiration of these magnificent cerements, and of the filial piety which prompted the children to bestow so beautiful and useful a present on the author of their being.[1]

Another application of the maxim that like produces

---

[1] J. J. M. de Groot, *The Religious System of China*, i. 60-63. Among the hairpins provided for a woman's burial is almost always one which is adorned with small silver figures of a stag, a tortoise, a peach, and a crane. These being emblems of longevity, it is supposed that the pin which is decorated with them will absorb some of their life-giving power and communicate it to the woman in whose hair it is ultimately to be fastened. See De Groot, *op. cit.* i. 55-57.

Homoeo-
pathic
magic
applied to
the sites of
cities in
China.
like is seen in the Chinese belief that the fortunes of a town
are deeply affected by its shape, and that they must vary
according to the character of the thing which that shape
most nearly resembles. Thus it is related that long ago
the town of Tsuen-cheu-fu, the outlines of which are like
those of a carp, frequently fell a prey to the depredations of
the neighbouring city of Yung-chun, which is shaped like a
fishing-net, until the inhabitants of the former town conceived the plan of erecting two tall pagodas in their midst.
These pagodas, which still tower above the city of Tsuen-
cheu-fu, have ever since exercised the happiest influence
over its destiny by intercepting the imaginary net before it
could descend and entangle in its meshes the imaginary
carp.[1] Some thirty years ago the wise men of Shanghai
were much exercised to discover the cause of a local
rebellion. On careful enquiry they ascertained that the
rebellion was due to the shape of a large new temple which
had most unfortunately been built in the shape of a tortoise,
an animal of the very worst character. The difficulty was
serious, the danger was pressing; for to pull down the
temple would have been impious, and to let it stand as it
was would be to court a succession of similar or worse
disasters. However, the genius of the local professors of
geomancy, rising to the occasion, triumphantly surmounted
the difficulty and obviated the danger. By filling up two
wells, which represented the eyes of the tortoise, they at
once blinded that disreputable animal and rendered him
incapable of doing further mischief.[2]

Homoeo-
pathic
magic to
avert
threatened
misfortune.
Sometimes homoeopathic or imitative magic is called in
to annul an evil omen by accomplishing it in mimicry. The
effect is to circumvent destiny by substituting a mock calamity
for a real one. At Kampot, a small seaport of Cambodia, a
French official saw one morning a troop of armed guards
escorting a man who was loaded with chains. They passed
his house and went away towards the country, preceded by
a man who drew lugubrious sounds from a gong, and
followed by a score of idlers. The official thought it must
be an execution and was surprised to have heard nothing

---

[1] J. J. M. de Groot, *op. cit*. iii. 977.
[2] J. J. M. de Groot, *op. cit*. iii. 1043 *sq.*

about it.   Afterwards he received from his interpreter the following lucid explanation of the affair.   " In our country it sometimes happens that a man walking in the fields has nothing but the upper part of his body visible to people at a distance.   Such an appearance is a sign that he will certainly die soon, and that is what happened last evening to the man you saw.   Going homewards across the plain he carried over his shoulder a bundle of palms with long slender stems ending in fan-like tufts of leaves.   His family, returning from their work, followed him at a distance, and soon they saw his head, shoulders, and arms moving along the road and carrying the branches, while his body and legs were invisible.   Struck with consternation at the sight, his mother and wife repaired in all haste to the magistrate and implored him to proceed against the man after the fashion customary in such cases.   The magistrate replied that the custom was ridiculous, and that he would be still more ridiculous if he complied with it.   However, the two women insisted on it so vehemently, saying it was the only way to avert the omen, that he decided to do as they wished, and gave them his word that he would have the man arrested next morning at sunrise.   So this morning the guards came to seize the poor man, telling him that he was accused of rebellion against the king, and without listening to his protestations of innocence they dragged him off to court.   His family pretended to be surprised and followed him weeping.   The judges had him clapped into irons and ordered him to instant execution.   His own entreaties and the prayers of his family being all in vain, he begged that the priests of the pagoda might come and bear witness to his innocence and join their supplications to those of his friends.   They came in haste, but receiving a hint how the wind lay they advised the condemned man to submit to his fate and departed to pray for his soul at the temple.   Then the man was led away to a rice-field, in the middle of which a banana-tree, stripped of its leaves, had been set up as a stake.   To this he was tied, and while his friends took their last leave of him, the sword of the exe-cutioner flashed through the air and at a single stroke swept off the top of the banana-tree above the head of the pretended victim. The man had given himself up for dead. His friends, while they knocked off his irons, explained to him the meaning of it all and led him away to thank the magistrates and priests for what they had done to save him from the threatened catastrophe." The writer who reports the case adds that if the magistrates had not good-naturedly lent themselves to the pious fraud, the man's family would have contrived in some other way to impress him with the terror of death in order to save his life.[1]

Homoeo-
pathic
magic to
avert
threatened
misfortune.

Again, two missionaries were journeying not long ago through Central Celebes, accompanied by some Toradjas. Unfortunately the note of a certain bird called *teka-teka* was heard to the left. This boded ill, and the natives insisted that they must either turn back or pass the night on the spot. When the missionaries refused to do either, an expedient was hit upon which allowed them to continue the journey in safety. A miniature hut was made out of a leafy branch, and in it were deposited a leaf moistened with spittle and a hair from the head of one of the party. Then one of the Toradjas said, "We shall pass the night here," and addressing the hair he spoke thus: "If any misfortune should happen through the cry of that bird, may it fall on you." In this way the evil omen was diverted from the real men and directed against their substitute the hair, and perhaps also the spittle, in the tiny hut.[2] When a Cherokee has dreamed of being stung by a snake, he is treated just in the same way as if he had really been stung; otherwise the place would swell and ulcerate in the usual manner, though perhaps years might pass before it did so. It is the ghost of a snake that has bitten him in sleep.[3] One night a Huron Indian dreamed that he had been taken and burned alive by his hereditary foes the Iroquois. Next morning a council was held on the affair, and the following measures

---

[1] *Mission Pavie, Indo-Chine, 1879-1895, Géographie et voyages,* i. (Paris, 1901) pp. 35-37. The kind of optical illusion which this mock execution was intended to expiate is probably caused by a mist or exhalation rising from damp ground.

[2] N. Adriani en A. C. Kruijt, "Van Posso naar Parigi, Sigi en Lindoe,"

Mededeelingen van wege het Neder-landsche Zendelinggenootschap, xlii. (1898) p. 524.

[3] J. Mooney, "Sacred Formulas of the Cherokees," *Seventh Annual Report of the Bureau of Ethnology* (Washington, 1891), p. 352; *id.* in *Nineteenth Annual Report, etc.,* part i. (Washington, 1900) p. 295.

were adopted to save the man's life.   Twelve or thirteen
fires were kindled in the large hut where they usually burned
their prisoners to death.   Every man seized a flaming brand
and applied it to the naked body of the dreamer, who
shrieked with pain.   Thrice he ran round the hut, escaping
from one fire only to fall into another.   As each man thrust
his blazing torch at the sufferer he said, " Courage, my
brother, it is thus that we have pity on you."   At last he
was allowed to escape.   Passing out of the hut he caught
up a dog which was held ready for the purpose, and throwing it over his shoulder carried it through the wigwams as
a sacred offering to the war-god, praying him to accept the
animal instead of himself.   Afterwards the dog was killed,
roasted, and eaten, exactly as the Indians were wont to
roast and eat their captives.[1]

In Madagascar this mode of cheating the fates is reduced   Homoeo-
to a regular system.   Here every man's fortune is deter-   pathic
mined by the day or hour of his birth, and if that happens   magic to
to be an unlucky one his fate is sealed, unless the mischief   avert mis-
can be extracted, as the phrase goes, by means of a sub-   fortune in
stitute.   The ways of extracting the mischief are various.   gascar.
For example, if a man is born on the first day of the second
month (February), his house will be burnt down when he
comes of age.   To take time by the forelock and avoid this
catastrophe, the friends of the infant will set up a shed in a
field or in the cattle-fold and burn it.   If the ceremony is to
be really effective, the child and his mother should be placed
in the shed and only plucked, like brands, from the burning
hut before it is too late.   Again, dripping November is the
month of tears, and he who is born in it is born to sorrow.
But in order to disperse the clouds that thus gather over
his future, he has nothing to do but to take the lid off a
boiling pot and wave it about.   The drops that fall from it
will accomplish his destiny and so prevent the tears from
trickling from his eyes.   Again, if fate has decreed that a
young girl, still unwed, should see her children, still unborn,
descend before her with sorrow to the grave, she can avert
the calamity as follows.   She kills a grasshopper, wraps it
in a rag to represent a shroud, and mourns over it like

[1] *Relations des Jésuites*, 1642, pp. 86 *sq.* (Canadian reprint).

Rachel weeping for her children and refusing to be com-
forted. Moreover, she takes a dozen or more other grass-
hoppers, and having removed some of their superfluous legs
and wings she lays them about their dead and shrouded
fellow. The buzz of the tortured insects and the agitated
motions of their mutilated limbs represent the shrieks and
contortions of the mourners at a funeral. After burying
the deceased grasshopper she leaves the rest to continue
their mourning till death releases them from their pain ; and
having bound up her dishevelled hair she retires from the
grave with the step and carriage of a person plunged in
grief. Thenceforth she looks cheerfully forward to seeing
her children survive her ; for it cannot be that she should
mourn and bury them twice over. Once more, if fortune
has frowned on a man at his birth and penury has marked
him for her own, he can easily eraze the mark in question
by purchasing a couple of cheap pearls, price three halfpence,
and burying them. For who but the rich of this world can
thus afford to fling pearls away ? [1]

§ 3. *Contagious Magic*

Contagious magic working by contact, not re- semblance. Thus far we have been considering chiefly that branch
of sympathetic magic which may be called homoeopathic
or imitative. Its leading principle, as we have seen, is
that like produces like, or, in other words, that an effect
resembles its cause. The other great branch of sympathetic magic, which I have called Contagious Magic, proceeds upon the notion that things which have once been
conjoined must remain ever afterwards, even when quite
dissevered from each other, in such a sympathetic relation
that whatever is done to the one must similarly affect the
other.[2] Thus the logical basis of Contagious Magic, like
that of Homoeopathic Magic, is a mistaken association of
ideas ; its physical basis, if we may speak of such a thing,

[1] W. Ellis, *History of Madagascar*,
i. 454 *sqq.* ; Father Abinal, "Astrologie
Malgache," *Missions Catholiques*, xi.
(1879) pp. 432-434, 481-483. Compare J. B. Piolet, *Madagascar et les
Hovas* (Paris, 1895), pp. 72 *sq.*

[2] The principles of contagious
magic are lucidly stated and copiously
illustrated by Mr. E. S. Hartland in
the second volume of his *Legend of
Perseus* (London, 1895).

like the physical basis of Homoeopathic Magic, is a material medium of some sort which, like the ether of modern physics, is assumed to unite distant objects and to convey impressions from one to the other. The most familiar example of Contagious Magic is the magical sympathy which is supposed to exist between a man and any severed portion of his person, as his hair or nails ; so that whoever gets possession of human hair or nails may work his will, at any distance, upon the person from whom they were cut. This superstition is world-wide ; instances of it in regard to hair and nails will be noticed later on in this work.[1] While like other superstitions it has had its absurd and mischievous consequences, it has nevertheless indirectly done much good by furnishing savages with strong, though irrational, motives for observing rules of cleanliness which they might never have adopted on rational grounds. How the superstition has produced this salutary effect will appear from a single instance, which I will give in the words of an experienced observer. Amongst the natives of the Gazelle Peninsula in New Britain " it is as a rule necessary for the efficiency of a charm that it should contain a part of the person who is to be enchanted (for example, his hair), or a piece of his clothing, or something that stands in some relation to him, such as his excrements, the refuse of his food, his spittle, his footprints, etc. All such objects can be employed as *panait*, that is, as a medium for a *papait* or charm, consisting of an incantation or murmuring of a certain formula, together with the blowing into the air of some burnt lime which is held in the hand. It need hardly, therefore, be said that the native removes all such objects as well as he can. Thus the cleanliness which is usual in the houses and consists in sweeping the floor carefully every day, is by no means based on a desire for cleanliness and neatness in themselves, but purely on the effort to put out of the way anything that might serve an ill-wisher as a charm." [2] I will now illustrate the principles of Contagious Magic by examples, beginning with its application to various parts of the human body.

Marginal notes: Magical sympathy between a man and the severed portions of his person, such as his hair or nails. Beneficial effect of this superstition in causing the removal of refuse.

---

[1] Meantime I may refer the reader to *The Golden Bough*, Second Edition, i. 367 *sqq.*

[2] R. Parkinson, *Dreissig Jähre in der Südsee* (Stuttgart, 1907), pp. 118 sq.

Among the Australian tribes it was a common practice to knock out one or more of a boy's front teeth at those ceremonies of initiation to which every male member had to submit before he could enjoy the rights and privileges of a full-grown man.[1] The reason of the practice is obscure ; a conjecture on this subject has been hazarded above.[2] All that concerns us here is the evidence of a belief that a sympathetic relation continued to exist between the lad and his teeth after the latter had been extracted from his gums. Thus among some of the tribes about the river Darling, in New South Wales, the extracted tooth was placed under the bark of a tree near a river or water-hole ; if the bark grew over the tooth, or if the tooth fell into the water, all was well ; but if it were exposed and the ants ran over it, the natives believed that the boy would suffer from a disease of the mouth.[3] Among the Murring and other tribes of New South Wales the extracted tooth was at first taken care of by an old man, and then passed from one headman to another, until it had gone all round the community, when it came back to the lad's father, and finally to the lad himself. But however it was thus conveyed from hand to hand, it might on no account be placed in a bag containing magical substances, for to do so would, they believed, put the owner of the tooth in great danger.[4] The late Dr. Howitt once acted as custodian of the teeth which had been extracted from some novices at a ceremony of initiation, and the old men earnestly besought him not to carry them in a bag in which they knew that he had some quartz crystals. They declared that if he did so the magic of the crystals would pass into the teeth, and so injure the boys. Nearly a year after Dr. Howitt's return from the ceremony he was visited by one of the principal men of the Murring tribe, who had travelled some two hundred and fifty miles from his home to fetch back the teeth. This man explained that he had been

[1] As to the diffusion of this custom in Australia see above, p. 97.

[2] See pp. 97 *sqq.*

[3] F. Bonney, "On some Customs of the Aborigines of the River Darling, New South Wales," *Journal of the*

Anthropological Institute, xiii. (1884) p. 128. For the practice of some Victorian tribes see above, p. 98.

[4] A. W. Howitt, in *Journal of the Anthropological Institute,* xiii. (1884) pp. 456 *sq.*; *id., Native Tribes of South-East Australia,* p. 561.

sent for them because one of the boys had fallen into ill health, and it was believed that the teeth had received some injury which had affected him. He was assured that the teeth had been kept in a box apart from any substances, like quartz crystals, which could influence them ; and he returned home bearing the teeth with him carefully wrapt up and concealed.[1] In the Dieri tribe of South Australia the teeth knocked out at initiation were bound up in emu feathers, and kept by the boy's father or his next-of-kin until the mouth had healed, and even for long afterwards. Then the father, accompanied by a few old men, performed a ceremony for the purpose of taking all the supposed life out of the teeth. He made a low rumbling noise without uttering any words, blew two or three times with his mouth, and jerked the teeth through his hand to some little distance. After that he buried them about eighteen inches under ground. The jerking movement was meant to shew that he thereby took all the life out of the teeth. Had he failed to do so, the boy would, in the opinion of the natives, have been liable to an ulcerated and wry mouth, impediment in speech, and ultimately a distorted face.[2] This ceremony is interesting as a rare instance of an attempt to break the sympathetic link between a man and a severed part of himself by rendering the part insensitive.

The Basutos are careful to conceal their extracted teeth, lest these should fall into the hands of certain mythical beings called *baloi*, who haunt graves, and could harm the owner of the tooth by working magic on it.[3] In Sussex some forty years ago a maid-servant remonstrated strongly against the throwing away of children's cast teeth, affirming that should they be found and gnawed by any animal, the child's new tooth would be, for all the world, like the teeth of the animal that had bitten the old one. In proof of this she named old Master Simmons, who had a

Contagious magic of teeth in Africa, Europe, America. etc.

---

[1] A. W. Howitt, in *Journal of the Anthropological Institute*, xvi. (1887) p. 55, xx. (1891) p. 81 ; *id., Native Tribes of South-East Australia*, pp. 561 *sq.*

[2] A. W. Howitt, in *Journal of the*

Anthropological Institute, xx. (1891) pp. 80 *sq.* ; *id., Native Tribes of South-East Australia*, pp. 655 *sq.*

[3] Father Porte, " Les Reminiscences d'un missionaire du Basutoland," *Missions Catholiques*, xxviii. (1896) p. 312.

very large pig's tooth in his upper jaw, a personal defect that he always averred was caused by his mother, who threw away one of his cast teeth by accident into the hog's trough.[1]   A similar belief has led to practices intended, on the principles of homoeopathic magic, to replace old teeth by new and better ones.   Thus in many parts of the world it is customary to put extracted teeth in some place where they will be found by a mouse or a rat, in the hope that, through the sympathy which continues to subsist between them and their former owner, his other teeth may acquire the same firmness and excellence as the teeth of these rodents.   Thus in Germany it is said to be an almost universal maxim among the people that when you have had a tooth taken out you should insert it in a mouse's hole.   To do so with a child's milk-tooth which has fallen out will prevent the child from having toothache.   Or you should go behind the stove and throw your tooth backwards over your head, saying, " Mouse, give me your iron tooth ; I will give you my bone tooth."   After that your other teeth will remain good.   German children say, " Mouse, mouse, come out and bring me out a new tooth " ; or " Mouse, I give you a little bone ; give me a little stone " ; or " Mouse, there is an old tooth for you ; make me a new one."   In Bavaria they say that if this ceremony be observed the child's second teeth will be as white as the teeth of mice.[2]   Amongst the South Slavonians, too, the child is taught to throw his tooth into a dark corner and say, " Mouse, mouse, there is a bone tooth ; give me an iron tooth instead."[3]   Jewish children in South Russia throw their cast teeth on the roof with the same request to the mouse to give them an iron tooth for a tooth of bone.[4]   Far away

Teeth of mice and rats.

---

[1] Charlotte Latham, " West Sussex Superstitions lingering in 1868," *Folklore Record*, i. (1878) p. 44.

[2] A. Wuttke, *Der deutsche Volksaberglaube*,[2] p. 330, § 526 ; F. Panzer, *Beitrag zur deutschen Mythologie*, ii. 307 ; E. Krause, in *Zeitschrift für Ethnologie*, xv. (1883) p. 79 ; J. Vonbun, *Volkssagen aus Vorarlberg*, p. 67 ; J. W. Wolf, *Beiträge zur deutschen Mythologie*, i. p. 208, §§ 37, 39 ; G. Lammert, *Volksmedizin und medizinischer Aberglaube in Bayern*, p. 128 ; H. Prahn, " Glaube und Brauch in der

Mark Brandenburg," *Zeitschrift des Vereins für Volkskunde*, i. (1891) p. 193 ; H. Raff, " Aberglaube in Bayern," *ibid.* viii. (1898) p. 400 ; R. Andree, *Braunschweiger Volkskunde* (Brunswick, 1896), p. 213. Compare J. V. Grohmann, *Aberglauben und Gebräuche aus Böhmen und Mähren*, p. 169, § 1197.

[3] F. S. Krauss, *Sitte und Brauch der Südslaven*, p. 546.

[4] S. Weissenberg, " Kinderfreud und -leid bei den südrussischen Juden," *Globus*, lxxxiii. (1903) p. 317.

from Europe, at Raratonga, in the Pacific, when a child's tooth was extracted, the following prayer used to be recited :—

> "*Big rat ! little rat !*
> *Here is my old tooth.*
> *Pray give me a new one.*"

Then the tooth was thrown on the thatch of the house, because rats make their nests in the decayed thatch. The reason assigned for invoking the rats on these occasions was that rats' teeth were the strongest known to the natives.[1] In the Seranglao and Gorong archipelagoes, between New Guinea and Celebes, when a child loses his first tooth, he must throw it on the roof, saying, "Mouse, I give you my tooth ; give me yours instead."[2] In Amboyna the custom is the same, and the form of words is, "Take this tooth, thrown on the roof, as the mouse's share, and give me a better one instead."[3] In the Kei Islands, to the south-west of New Guinea, when a child begins to get his second teeth, he is lifted up to the top of the roof in order that he may there deposit, as an offering to the rats, the tooth which has fallen out. At the same time some one cries aloud, "O rats, here you have his tooth ; give him a golden one instead."[4] Among the Ilocans of Luzon, in the Philippines, when children's teeth are loose, they are pulled out with a string and put in a place where rats will be likely to find and drag them away.[5] In ancient Mexico, when a child was getting a new tooth, the father or mother used to put the old one in a mouse's hole, believing that if this precaution were not taken the new tooth would not issue from the gums.[6] A different and more barbarous

---

[1] W. Wyatt Gill, *Jottings from the Pacific*, pp. 222 *sq*. On the use of roof-thatch in superstitious ceremonies see W. Caland, *Altindisches Zauberritual*, pp. 82 n.[2] 182 *sq*. In the present case the virtue of the thatch clearly depends on its harbouring rats. Some Dravidian tribes forbid a menstruous woman to touch the housethatch (W. Crooke, *Popular Religion and Folklore of Northern India*, Westminster, 1896, i. 269).

[2] J. G. F. Riedel, *De sluik- en kroesharige rassen tusschen Selebes en Papua*, p. 176.

[3] Riedel, *op. cit.* p. 75.

[4] C. M. Pleyte, "Ethnographische Beschrijving der Kei-Eilanden," *Tijdschrift van het Nederlandsch Aardrijkskundig Genootschap*, Tweede Serie, x. (1893) p. 822.

[5] F. Blumentritt, "Sitten und Bräuche der Ilocanen," *Globus*, xlviii. No. 12, p. 200.

[6] B. de Sahagun, *Histoire générale des choses de la Nouvelle Espagne*, pp. 316 *sq*.

application of the same principle is the Swabian superstition that when a child is teething you should bite off the head of a living mouse, and hang the head round the child's neck by a string, taking care, however, to make no knot in the string ; then the child will teethe easily.[1]   In Bohemia the treatment prescribed is similar, though there they recommend you to use a red thread and to string three heads of mice on it instead of one.[2]

Con-
tagious
magic of
teeth :
teeth of
squirrels,
foxes,
beavers,
etc.But it is not always a mouse or a rat that brings the child a new and stronger tooth.   Apparently any strong-toothed animal will serve the purpose.   Thus when his or her tooth drops out, a Singhalese will throw it on the roof, saying, " Squirrel, dear squirrel, take this tooth and give me a dainty tooth."[3]   In Bohemia a child will sometimes throw its cast tooth behind the stove, asking the fox to give him an iron tooth instead of the bone one.[4]   In Berlin the teeth of a fox worn as an amulet round a child's neck make teething easy for him, and ensure that his teeth will be good and lasting.[5]   Similarly, in order to help a child to cut its teeth, the aborigines of Victoria fastened to its wrist the front tooth of a kangaroo, which the child used as a coral to rub its gums with.[6]   Again, the beaver can gnaw through the hardest wood.   Hence among the Cherokee Indians, when the loosened milk tooth of a child has been pulled out or has dropped out of itself, the child runs round the house with it, repeating four times, " Beaver, put a new tooth into my jaw," after which he throws the tooth on the roof of the house.[7]   In Macedonia, a child carefully keeps for a time its first drawn tooth, and then throws it on the roof with the following invocation to the crow :—

1 E. Meier, *Deutsche Sagen, Sitten und Gebräuche aus Schwaben*, p. 510, § 415.

2 J. V. Grohmann, *Aberglauben und Gebräuche aus Böhmen und Mähren*, p. 111, § 822.

3 A. A. Perera, " Glimpses of Cinghalese Social Life," *Indian Antiquary*, xxxii. (1903) p. 435.

4 J. V. Grohmann, *Aberglauben und Gebräuche aus Böhmen und Mähren*, pp. 55 at top, p. 111, § 825.   Mr. A. P.

Goudy kindly translated the Czech words for me.

5 E. Krause, " Abergläubische Kuren und sonstiger Aberglaube in Berlin," *Zeitschrift für Ethnologie*, xv. (1883) p. 84.

6 J. Dawson, *Australian Aborigines*, p. 39.

7 J. Mooney, " Myths of the Cherokee," *Nineteenth Annual Report of the Bureau of American Ethnology* (Washington, 1900), part i. p. 266.

> "*O dear crow, here is a tooth of bone,*
>   *Take it and give me a tooth of iron instead,*
>   *That I may be able to chew beans*
>   *And to crunch dry biscuits.*" [1]

We can now understand a custom of the Thompson Indians of British Columbia, which the writer who records it is unable to explain. When a child lost its teeth, the father used to take each one as it fell out and to hide it in a piece of raw venison, which he gave to a dog to eat. The animal swallowed the venison and the tooth with it.[2] Doubtless the custom was intended to ensure that the child's new teeth should be as strong as those of a dog. In Silesia mothers sometimes swallow their children's cast teeth in order to save their offspring from toothache. The intention is perhaps to strengthen the weak teeth of the child by the strong teeth of the grown woman.[3] Amongst the Warramunga of Central Australia, when a girl's tooth has been knocked out as a solemn ceremony, it is pounded up and the fragments placed in a piece of flesh, which has to be eaten by the girl's mother. When the same rite has been performed on a man, his pounded tooth must be eaten in a piece of meat by his mother-in-law.[4] Among the heathen Arabs, when a boy's tooth fell out, he used to take it between his finger and thumb and throw it towards the sun, saying, "Give me a better for it." After that his teeth were sure to grow straight, and close, and strong. "The sun," says Tharafah, "gave the lad from his own nursery-ground a tooth like a hailstone, white and polished." [5] Thus the reason for throwing the old teeth towards the sun would seem to have been a notion that the sun sends hail, from which it naturally follows that he can send you a tooth as smooth and white and hard as a hailstone. Among the peasants of the Lebanon, when a child loses a milk tooth, he throws it

Teeth thrown towards the sun.

---

[1] G. F. Abbott, *Macedonian Folklore* (Cambridge, 1903), p. 20.

[2] J. Teit, "The Thompson Indians of British Columbia," *Memoir of the American Museum of Natural History, The Jesup North Pacific Expedition,* vol. i. part iv. (April 1900) p. 308.

[3] J. V. Grohmann, *op. cit.* p. 111,
§ 823; A. Wuttke, *Der deutsche Volksaberglaube,*[2] p. 330, § 527.

[4] Spencer and Gillen, *Northern Tribes of Central Australia,* p. 593.

[5] Rasmussen, *Additamenta ad historiam Arabum ante Islamismum,* p. 64.

towards the sun, saying, "Sun, sun, take the ass's tooth and give me the deer's tooth." They sometimes say jestingly that the child's tooth has been carried off by a mouse.[1] An Armenian generally buries his extracted teeth at the edge of the hearth with the prayer : "Grandfather, take a dog's tooth and give me a golden tooth."[2]   In the light of the preceding examples, we may conjecture that the grandfather here invoked is not so much the soul of a dead ancestor as a mouse or a rat.

Con-
tagious
magic of
navel-
string and
afterbirth
among the
Maoris
and the
aborigines
of Aus-
tralia.   Other parts which are commonly believed to remain in a sympathetic union with the body, after the physical connexion has been severed, are the navel-string and the afterbirth, including the placenta.   So intimate, indeed, is the union conceived to be, that the fortunes of the individual for good or evil throughout life are often supposed to be bound up with one or other of these portions of his person, so that if his navel-string or afterbirth is preserved and properly treated, he will be prosperous ; whereas if it be injured or lost, he will suffer accordingly.   Thus among the Maoris, when the navel-string dropped off, the child was carried to a priest to be solemnly named by him.   But before the ceremony of naming began, the navel-string was buried in a sacred place and a young sapling was planted over it.   Ever afterwards that tree, as it grew, was a *tohu oranga* or sign of life for the child.[3]   In the Upper Whakatane valley, in the North Island of New Zealand, there is a famous *hinau* tree, to which the Maoris used to attach the navel-strings of their children ; and barren women were in the habit of embracing the tree in the hope of thereby obtaining offspring.[4]   Again, among the Maoris, "the placenta is named *fenua*, which word signifies land.   It is applied by the natives to the placenta, from their supposing it to be the residence of the child : on being discharged it is immediately buried with

[1] L'Abbé B. Chémali, " Naissance et premier âge au Liban," *Anthropos*, v. (1910) p. 745.

[2] M. Abeghian, *Der armenische Volksglaube* (Leipsic, 1899), p. 68.

[3] R. Taylor, *Te Ika A Maui, or New* *Zealand and its Inhabitants* [2] (London, 1870), p. 184.

[4] Elsdon Best, quoted by W. H. Goldie, " Maori Medical Lore," *Transactions and Proceedings of the New Zealand Institute*, xxxvii. (1904) pp. 94 *sq.*

great care, as they have the superstitious idea that the
priests, if offended, would procure it ; and, by praying
over it, occasion the death of both mother and child,
by 'praying them to death,' to use their own expression." [1] Again, some of the natives of South Australia
regarded the placenta as sacred and carefully put it away
out of reach of the dogs,[2] doubtless because they thought
that harm would come to the child if this part of himself
were eaten by the animals. Certain tribes of Western
Australia believe that a man swims well or ill, according
as his mother at his birth threw the navel-string into
water or not.[3] Among the Arunta of Central Australia
the navel-string is swathed in fur-string and made into a
necklace, which is placed round the child's neck. The
necklace is supposed to facilitate the growth of the
child, to keep it quiet and contented, and to avert illness
generally.[4] In the Kaitish tribe of Central Australia the
practice and belief are similar.[5] In the Warramunga tribe,
after the string has hung round the child's neck for a
time, it is given to the wife's brother, who wears it in his
armlet, and who may not see the child till it can walk.
In return for the navel-string, the man makes a present
of weapons to the infant's father. When the child can
walk, the father gives fur-string to the man, who now
comes to the camp, sees the child, and makes another
present to the father. After that he keeps the navel-
string for some time longer, and finally places it in a
hollow tree known only to himself.[6] Among the
natives on the Pennefather river in Queensland it is

---

[1] George Bennett, *Wanderings in
New South Wales, Batavia, Pedir
Coast, Singapore and China* (London,
1834), i. 128, note *. As to *fenua* or
whenua in the sense of "placenta" and
"land," see E. Tregear, *Maori-Polynesian Comparative Dictionary* (Wellington, N.Z., 1891), pp. 620 *sq.*

[2] E. J. Eyre, *Journals of Expeditions of Discovery into Central Australia*,
ii. 323.

[3] G. F. Moore, *Descriptive Vocabulary of the Language in Common Use
amongst the Aborigines of Western*

Australia, p. 9 (published along with
the author's *Diary of Ten Years'
Eventful Life of an Early Settler in
Western Australia*, London, 1884,
but paged separately).

[4] Spencer and Gillen, *Native Tribes
of Central Australia*, p. 467.

[5] Spencer and Gillen, *Northern
Tribes of Central Australia*, p. 607.

[6] Spencer and Gillen, *op. cit.* p. 608.
The writers add that the child has no
special connexion with the tree in after
years. We may suspect that such a
connexion did exist in former times.

believed that a part of the child's spirit (*cho-i*) stays in the afterbirth. Hence the grandmother takes the afterbirth away and buries it in the sand. She marks the spot by a number of twigs which she sticks in the ground in a circle, tying their tops together so that the structure resembles a cone. When Anjea, the being who causes conception in women by putting mud babies into their wombs, comes along and sees the place, he takes out the spirit and carries it away to one of his haunts, such as a tree, a hole in a rock, or a lagoon, where it may remain for years. But sometime or other he will put the spirit again into a baby, and it will be born once more into the world.[1]

Contagious magic of navel-string in New Guinea, Fiji, the Caroline Islands, and the Gilbert Islands.

In the Yabim tribe of German New Guinea the mother ties the navel-string to the net in which she carries the child, lest any one should use the string to the child's hurt.[2] " In some parts of Fiji the navel-string of a male infant is planted together with a cocoanut, or slip of a bread-fruit tree, and the child's life is supposed to be intimately connected with that of the tree. Moreover, the planting is supposed to have the effect of making the boy a good climber. If the child be a girl, the mother or her sister will take the navel-string to the sea-water when she goes out fishing for the first time after the childbirth, and she will throw it into the sea when the nets are stretched in line. Thus the girl will grow up into a skilful fisherwoman. But the queerest use I ever saw the string put to was at Rotuma. There it has become almost obligatory for a young man, who wants the girls to respect him, to make a voyage in a white man's vessel ; and mothers come alongside ships anchored in the roadstead and fasten their boy's navel-string to the vessel's chain-plates. This will make sure of a voyage for the child when it has grown up. This, of course, must be a modern development, but it has all the strength of an ancient custom." [3]   In Ponape, one of the Caroline Islands, the

---

[1] W. E. Roth, *North Queensland Ethnography*, Bulletin No. 5 (Brisbane, 1903), p. 18. As to the mode of determining where the soul of the child has dwelt since its last incarnation, see above, pp. 99 *sq.*

[2] K. Vetter, in *Nachrichten über Kaiser Wilhelms-Land und den Bismarck-Archipel*, 1897, pp. 92 ; M. Krieger, *Neu-Guinea*, p. 165.

[3] The Rev. Lorimer Fison, in a letter to me dated May 29, 1901.

navel-string is placed in a shell and then disposed of in
such a way as shall best adapt the child for the career which
the parents have chosen for him.   Thus if they wish to
make him a good climber, they will hang the navel-string
on a tree.[1]   In the Gilbert Islands the navel-string is wrapt
by the child's father or adoptive father in a pandanus leaf,
and then worn by him as a bracelet for several months.
After that he keeps it most carefully in the hut, generally
hanging under the ridge-beam.   The islanders believe that
if the navel-string is thus preserved, the child will become a
great warrior if it is a boy, or will make a good match if
it is a girl.   But should the bracelet be lost before the child
is grown up, they expect that the boy will prove a coward
in war, and that the girl will make an unfortunate marriage.
Hence the most anxious search is made for the missing
talisman, and if it is not to be found, weeks will pass before
the relations resign themselves to its loss.   When the boy
has grown to be a youth and has distinguished himself for
the first time in war, the bracelet containing the navel-string
is taken by the villagers, on a day fixed for the purpose, far
out to sea ; the adoptive father of the lad throws the bracelet
overboard, and all the canoes begin to catch as many fish
as they can.   The first fish caught, whether large or small,
is carefully preserved apart from the rest.   Meantime the
old women at home have been busy preparing a copious
banquet for the fishermen.   When the little fleet comes to
shore, the old woman who helped at the lad's birth goes to
meet it ; the first fish caught is handed to her, and she
carries it to the hut.   The fish is laid on a new mat, the
youth and his mother take their places beside it, and they
and it are covered up with another mat.   Then the old
woman goes round the mat, striking the ground with a short
club and murmuring a prayer to the lad's god to help him
henceforth in war, that he may be brave and invulnerable, and that he may turn out a skilful fisherman.   The
navel-string of a girl, as soon as she is grown up, is thrown
into the sea with similar ceremonies ; and the ceremony on
land is the same except that the old woman's prayer is

[1] Dr. Hahl, "Mittheilungen über   Ponape," *Ethnologisches Notizblatt*,
Sitten und rechtliche Verhältnisse auf   ii. (Berlin, 1901) p. 10.

naturally different ; she asks the girl's god to grant that she
may have a happy marriage and many children. After the
mat has been removed, the fish is cooked and eaten by the
two ; if it is too large to be eaten by them alone, the
remainder is consumed by friends and relations. These
ceremonies are only observed for the children of wealthy
parents, who can defray the cost. In the case of a child
of poorer parents the bracelet containing the navel-string
simply hangs up till it disappears in one way or another.[1]

Con-
tagious
magic of
navel-
string and
afterbirth
in the
Moluccas. Among the Galelareese, to the west of New Guinea,
the mother sometimes keeps the navel-string till the child
is old enough to begin to play. Then she gives it as a
plaything to the little one, who may take it away ; otherwise the child would be idiotic. But others plant the
navel-string with a banana-bush or a coco-nut.[2] The Kei
islanders, to the south-west of New Guinea, regard the navel-
string as the brother or sister of the child, according as the
infant is a boy or a girl. They put it in a pot with ashes,
and set it in the branches of a tree, that it may keep a
watchful eye on the fortunes of its comrade.[3] In the Babar
Archipelago, between New Guinea and Celebes, the placenta
is mixed with ashes and put in a small basket, which seven
women, each of them armed with a sword, hang up on a
tree of a particular kind (*Citrus hystrix*). The women carry
swords for the purpose of frightening the evil spirits ; otherwise these mischievous beings might get hold of the placenta
and make the child sick. The navel-string is kept in a
little box in the house.[4] In the Tenimber and Timorlaut
islands the placenta is buried in a basket under a sago or
coco-nut palm, which then becomes the property of the
child. But sometimes it is hidden in the forest, or deposited
in a hole under the house with an offering of betel.[5] In the

[1] R. Parkinson, "Beiträge zur
Ethnologie der Gilbertinsulaner," *Internationales Archiv für Ethnographie*,
ii. (1889) p. 35. In these islands the
children of well-to-do parents are
always adopted by other people as soon
as they are weaned. See *ib.* p. 33.

[2] M. J. van Baarda, "Fabelen,
Verhalen en Overleveringen der Galelareezen," *Bijdragen tot de Taal- Land-
en Volkenkunde van Nederlandsch-*

Indië, xlv. (1895) p. 461.

[3] C. M. Pleyte, "Ethnographische
Beschrijving der Kei-Eilanden," *Tijdschrift van het Nederlandsch Aardrijkskundig Genootschap*, Tweede Serie, x.
(1893) pp. 816 *sq.* Compare J. G.
F. Riedel, *De sluik-en kroesharige
rassen tusschen Selebes en Papua*, p.
236.

[4] J. G. F. Riedel, *op. cit.* p. 354.

[5] Riedel, *op. cit.* p. 303.

Watubela islands the placenta is buried under a coco-nut, *mangga*, or great fig-tree along with the shell of the coco-nut, of which the pulp had been used to smear the newborn child.[1] In many of the islands between New Guinea and Celebes the placenta is put in the branches of a tree, often in the top of one of the highest trees in the neighbourhood. Sometimes the navel-string is deposited along with the placenta in the tree, but often it is kept to be used as medi-cine or an amulet by the child.[2] Thus in Ceram the child sometimes wears the navel-string round its neck as a charm to avert sickness;[3] and in the islands of Leti, Moa, and Lakor he carries it as an amulet in war or on a far journey.[4] We cannot doubt that the intention of putting the placenta in the top of a tall tree is to keep it, and with it the child, out of harm's way. In the islands of Saparoea, Haroekoe, and Noessa Laut, to the east of Amboyna, the midwife buries the afterbirth and strews flowers over it. Moreover, resin or a lamp is kept burning for seven or three nights over the buried afterbirth, in order that no harm may come to the child. Some people, however, in these islands solemnly cast the afterbirth into the sea. Being placed in a pot and closely covered up with a piece of white cotton, it is taken out to sea in a boat. A hole is knocked in the pot to allow it to sink in the water. The midwife, who is charged with the duty of heaving the pot and its contents overboard, must look straight ahead; if she were to glance to the right or left the child whose afterbirth is in the pot would squint. And the man who rows or steers the boat must make her keep a straight course, otherwise the child would grow up a gad-about. Before the pot is flung into the sea, the midwife disengages the piece of white cotton in which it is wrapt, and this cloth she takes straight back to the house and covers the baby with it. In these islands it is thought that a child born with a caul will enjoy in later years the gift of second sight—that is, that he will be able to see things which are hidden from common eyes, such as devils and evil spirits. But if his parents desire to prevent

---

[1] Riedel, *op. cit.* p. 208.
[2] Riedel, *op. cit.* pp. 23, 135, 236, 325, 391, 417, 449, 468.

[3] Riedel, *op. cit.* p. 135.

[4] Riedel, *op. cit.* p. 391

him from exercising this uncanny power, they can do so. In that case the midwife must dry the caul in the sun, steep it in water, and then wash the child with the water thrice ; further, when the child is a little older, she must grind the caul to powder, and give the child the powder to eat with its pap. Some people keep the caul ; and if the child falls ill, it is given water to drink in which the caul has been steeped.[1] Similarly in the Luang-Sermata islands a child born with a caul is counted lucky, and can perceive and recognise the spirits of his ancestors.[2] A caul, it may be said, is merely the fœtal membrane which usually forms part of the afterbirth ; occasionally a child is born with it wrapt like a hood round its head.

Contagious magic of the placenta in Celebes.
In Parigi, a kingdom on the coast of Central Celebes, the placenta is laid in a cooking-pot, and one of the mother's female relations carries the pot wrapt in white cotton and hidden under a petticoat (*sarong*) to a spot beneath the house or elsewhere, and there she buries it. A coco-nut is planted near the place. Going and coming the woman is led by another, and must keep her eyes fast shut, for if she looked right or left the child would squint, " because she is at this time closely united with a part of the child, to wit its older brother, in other words the placenta." On her return to the house she lies down on her sleeping-mat, still with closed eyes, and draws a petticoat over her head, and another woman sprinkles her with water. After that she may get up and open her eyes. The sprinkling with water is intended to sever her sympathetic connexion with the child and so prevent her from exercising any influence on it.[3] Among the Tolalaki of Central Celebes turmeric and other spices are put on the placenta,

---

[1] Van Schmidt, "Aanteekeningen nopens de zeden, gewoonten en gebruiken, etc., der bevolking van de eilanden Saparoea, Haroekoe, Noessa Laut," etc., *Tijdschrift voor Neêrlands Indië*, Batavia, 1843, dl. ii. pp. 523-526. The customs and beliefs on this subject in the adjoining island of Amboyna seem to be identical. See J. G. F. Riedel, *op. cit.* pp. 73 *sq.* According to Riedel, if the pot with the afterbirth does not sink in the water, it is a sign that the wife has been unfaithful.

[2] Riedel, *op. cit.* p. 326.

[3] N. Adriani and A. C. Kruijt, "Van Posso naar Parigi, Sigi en Lindoe," *Mededeelingen van wege het Nederlandsche Zendelinggenootschap*, xlii. (1898) pp. 434 *sq.* In Parigi after a birth the *kindspek* (?) is wrapt in a leaf and hung in a tree at some distance from the house. For the people think that if it were burned, the child would die (*ibid.* p. 434).

which is then enclosed in two coco-nut shells that fit one on
the other. These are wrapt in bark-cloth and kept in the
house. If the child falls ill, the coco-nut shells are opened
and the placenta examined. Should there be worms in it,
they are removed and fresh spices added. When the child
has grown big and strong, the placenta is thrown away.[1]
Among the Toboongkoo of Central Celebes the afterbirth
is placed in a rice-pot with various plants, which are intended
to preserve it from decay as long as possible ; it is then
carefully tied up in bark-cloth. A man and a woman of the
family carry the placenta away ; in doing so they go out and
in the house four times, and each time they enter they kiss
the child, but they take care not to look to the right or the
left, for otherwise the child would squint. Some bury the
placenta, others hang it on a tree. If the child is unwell,
they dig up the placenta or take it down from the tree, and
lay bananas, rice of four sorts, and a lighted taper beside it.
Having done so, they hang it up on a tree if it was
previously buried ; but they bury it if it was formerly hung
up.[2] The Tomori of Central Celebes wash the afterbirth,
put it in a rice-pot, and bury it under the house. Great
care is taken that no water or spittle falls on the place. For
a few days the afterbirth is sometimes fed with rice and eggs,
which are laid on the spot where it is buried. Afterwards
the people cease to trouble themselves about it.[3] In
southern Celebes they call the navel-string and afterbirth
the two brothers or sisters of the child. When the infant
happens to be a prince or princess, the navel-string and
afterbirth are placed with salt and tamarind in a new rice-
pot, which is then enveloped in a fine robe and tightly
corded up to prevent the evil spirits from making off with
the pair of brothers or sisters. For the same reason a light
is kept burning all night, and twice a day rice is rubbed on
the edge of the pot, for the purpose, as the people say, of
giving the child's little brothers or sisters something to eat.
After a while this feeding, as it is called, takes place at

[1] N. Adriani and A. C. Kruijt, "Van
Posso naar Mori," *Mededeelingen van
wege het Nederl. Zendelinggenootschap,*
xliv. (1900) pp. 161 *sq.*

[2] A. C. Kruijt, "Eenige ethno-

grafische aanteekeningen omtrent de
Toboengkoe en de Tomori," *ibid.* p.
218.

[3] *Id., ib.* p. 236.

rarer intervals, and when the mother has been again brought
to bed it is discontinued altogether. On the ninth day after
the birth a number of coco-nuts are planted, with much
ceremony, in a square enclosure, and the water which was
used in cleansing the afterbirth and navel-string is poured
upon them.   These coco-nuts are called the contemporaries
of the child and grow up with him. When the planting is
done, the rice-pot with the navel-string and afterbirth is
carried back and set beside the bed of the young prince or
princess, and when his royal highness is carried out to take
the air the rice-pot with his two "brothers" goes out with
him, swathed in a robe of state and screened from the sun
by an umbrella. If the prince or princess should die, the
afterbirth and navel-string are buried.   Among common
people in South Celebes these parts of the infant are
generally buried immediately after the birth, or they are
sunk in the deep sea, or hung in a rice-pot on a tree.[1]

Contagious
magic of
the
placenta
and navel-
string in
Timor,
Savou,
and Rotti

In the island of Timor the placenta is called the child's
companion and treated accordingly. The midwife puts it
in an earthen pot and covers it with ashes from the hearth.
After standing thus three days it is taken away and buried
by a person who must observe silence in discharging this
duty.[2] In Savou, a small island to the south-west of Timor,
the afterbirth is filled with native herbs, and having been
deposited in a new pot, which has never before been used, is
buried under the house to keep off evil spirits.   Or it is put
in a new basket and hung in a high toddy palm to fertilise
it, or thrown into the sea to secure a good catch of fish.
The person who thus disposes of the afterbirth may not
look to the right or the left; he must be joyous and, if
possible, go singing on his way.   If it is to be hung on a
tree, he must climb nimbly up, in order that the child may
always be lucky.   These islanders ascribe a similar fertilising
virtue to a caul.   It is dried and carefully kept in a box.
When rice-stalks turn black and the ears refuse to set, a
man will take the box containing the caul and run several

[1] B. F. Matthes, *Bijdragen tot de
Ethnologie van Zuid - Celebes* (The
Hague, 1875), pp. 57-60.
[2] G. Heijmering, "Zeden en gewoonten op het eiland Timor," *Tijdschrift voor Neêrland's Indië*, 1845, pp.
279 *sq.*

times round the rice-field, in order that the wind may waft the genial influence of the caul over the rice.[1] In Rotti, an island to the south of Timor, the navel-string is put in a small satchel made of leaves, and if the father of the child is not himself going on a voyage, he entrusts the bag to one of his seafaring friends and charges him to throw it away in the open sea with the express wish that, when the child grows up and has to sail to other islands, he may escape the perils of the deep. But the business of girls in these islands does not lie in the great waters, and hence their navel-strings receive a different treatment. It is their task to go afishing daily, when the tide is out, on the coral reefs which ring the islands. So when the mother is herself again, she repairs with the little satchel to the reef where she is wont to fish. Acting the part of a priestess she there eats one or two small bagfuls of boiled rice on the spot where she intends to deposit the dried navel-string of her baby daughter, taking care to leave a few grains of rice in the bags. Then she ties the precious satchel and the nearly empty rice-bags to a stick and fastens it among the stones of the reef, generally on its outer edge, within sight and sound of the breaking waves. In doing so she utters a wish that this ceremony may guard her daughter from the perils and dangers that beset her on the reef—for example, that no crocodile may issue from the lagoon and eat her up, and that the sharp corals and broken shells may not wound her feet.[2]

In the island of Flores the placenta is put in an earthen pot, along with some rice and betel, and buried by the father in the neighbourhood of the house, or else preserved in one of the highest trees.[3] The natives of Bali, an island to the east of Java, believe firmly that the afterbirth is the child's brother or sister, and they bury it in the courtyard in the half of a coco-nut from which the kernel has not been

Contagious magic of the placenta in Flores, Bali, and Java.

---

[1] J. H. Letteboer, "Eenige aanteekeningen omtrent de gebruiken bij zwangerschap en geboorte onder de Savuneezen," *Mededeelingen van wege het Nederlandsche Zendelinggenootschap*, xlvi. (1902) p. 47.

[2] G. Heijmering, "Zeden en gewoonten op het eiland Rottie," *Tijdschrift voor Neêrlands Indië*, 1843, dl. ii. pp. 637 *sq.*

[3] J. G. F. Riedel, *The Island of Flores*, p. 7 (reprinted from the *Revue Coloniale Internationale*).

removed. For forty days afterwards a light is burned, and food, water, and betel deposited on the spot,[1] doubtless in order to feed the baby's little brother or sister, and to guard him or her from evil spirits. In Java the afterbirth is also called the brother or sister of the infant; it is wrapt in white cotton, put in a new pot or a coco-nut shell, and buried by the father beside the door, outside the house if the child is a boy, but inside the house if the child is a girl. Every evening until the child's navel has healed a lamp is lit over the spot where the afterbirth is buried. If the afterbirth hangs in a rice-pot in the house, as the practice is with some people, the lamp burns under the place where the rice-pot is suspended. The purpose of the light is to ward off demons, to whose machinations the child and its supposed brother or sister are at this season especially exposed.[2] If the child is a boy, a piece of paper inscribed with the alphabet is deposited in the pot with his placenta, in order that he may be smart at his learning; if the child is a girl, a needle and thread are deposited in the pot, that she may be a good sempstress, and water with flowers in it is poured on the spot where the placenta is buried, in order that the child may always be healthy; for many Javanese think that if the placenta is not properly honoured, the child will never be well.[3] Sometimes, however, women in the interior of Java allow the placenta, surrounded with fruits and flowers and illuminated by little lamps, to float down the river in the dusk of the evening as an offering to the crocodiles, or rather to the ancestors whose souls are believed to lodge in these animals.[4]

Contagious magic of placenta and navel-string in Sumatra.

In Mandeling, a district on the west coast of Sumatra, the afterbirth is washed and buried under the house or put in an earthenware pot, which is carefully shut up and thrown

---

[1] Julius Jacobs, *Eenigen tijd onder de Baliërs* (Batavia, 1883), p. 9.

[2] C. F. Winter, "Instellingen, gewoonten en gebruiken der Javanen te Soerakarta," *Tijdschrift voor Neêrlands Indië*, 1843, dl. i. pp. 695 *sq*; P. J. Veth, *Java*, i. (Haarlem, 1875) pp. 639 *sq*.; C. Poensen, "Iets over de kleeding der Javanen," *Mededeelingen van wege het Nederlandsche Zendeling-genootschap*, xx. (1876) p. 281.

[3] D. Louwerier, "Bijgeloovige gebruiken, die door de Javanen worden in acht genomen bij de verzorging en opvoeding hunner kinderen," *Mededeelingen van wege het Nederlandsche Zendelinggenootschap*, xlix. (1905) pp. 254 *sq*.

[4] P. J. Veth, *Java*, i. 231.

into the river. This is done to avert the supposed un-
favourable influence of the afterbirth on the child, whose
hands or feet, for example, might be chilled by it. When
the navel-string drops off, it is preserved to be used as a
medicine when its former owner is ill.[1] In Mandeling, too,
the midwife prefers to cut the navel-string with a piece of a
flute on which she has first blown, for then the child will be
sure to have a fine voice.[2] Among the Minangkabau
people of Sumatra the placenta is put in a new earthenware
pot, which is then carefully closed with a banana leaf to
prevent the ants and other insects from coming at it ; for
if they did, the child would be sickly and given to squalling.[3]
In Central Sumatra the placenta is wrapt in white cotton,
deposited in a basket or a calabash, and buried in the courtyard before the house or under a rice-barn. The hole is
dug by a kinsman or kinswoman according as the baby is
a boy or a girl. Over the hole is placed a stone from the
hearth, and beside it a wooden spoon is stuck in the
ground. Both stone and spoon are sprinkled with the
juice of a citron. During the ceremony *koemajen* is burned
and a shot fired. For three evenings afterwards candles are
lighted at the spot,[4] doubtless to keep off demons. Among
the Battas of Sumatra, as among so many other peoples
of the Indian Archipelago, the placenta passes for the
child's younger brother or sister, the sex being determined
by the sex of the child, and it is buried under the house.
According to the Battas it is bound up with the child's
welfare, and seems, in fact, to be the seat of the transferable
soul, of whose wanderings outside of the body we shall
hear something later on.[5] The Karo Battas even affirm

---

[1] H. Ris, "De onderafdeeling klein
Mandailing Oeloe en Pahantan en hare
Bevolking met uitzondering van de
Oeloes," *Bijdragen tot de Taal- Land-
en Volkenkunde van Nederlandsch-
Indië*, xlvi. (1896) p. 504.

[2] A. L. Heyting, "Beschrijving der
onderafdeeling Groot Mandeling en
Batang - Natal," *Tijdschrift van het
Nederlandsch Aardrijkskundig Genootschap*, Tweede Serie, xiv. (1897), p.
292.

[3] J. C. van Eerde, "Een huwelijk

bij de Minangkabausche Maliers,"
*Tijdschrift voor Indische Taal- Land-
en Volkenkunde*, xliv. (1901) p.
493.

[4] A. L. van Hasselt, *Volksbeschrijving van Midden-Sumatra* (Leyden,
1882), p. 267.

[5] M. Joustra, "Het leven, de zeden
en gewoonten der Bataks," *Mededeelingen van wege het Nederlandsche
Zendelinggenootschap*, xlvi. (1902) pp.
407 *sq.* The transferable soul is in
Batta *tendi*, in Malay *sumangat*.

that of a man's two souls it is the true soul that lives with the placenta under the house; that is the soul, they say, which begets children.[1]

Contagious magic of placenta and navel-string in Borneo, India, and Assam.

In Pasir, a district of eastern Borneo, the afterbirth is carefully treated and kept in an earthen pot or basket in the house until the remains of the navel-string have fallen off. All the time it is in the house candles are burned and a little food is placed beside the pot. When the navel-string has fallen off, it is placed with the placenta in the pot, and the two are buried in the ground near the house. The reason why the people take this care of the afterbirth is that they believe it able to cause the child all kinds of sickness and mishaps.[2]   The Malas, a low Telugu caste of Southern India, bury the placenta in a pot with leaves in some convenient place, generally in the back yard, lest dogs or other animals should carry it off; for if that were to happen they fancy that the child would be of a wandering disposition.[3]   The Khasis of Assam keep the placenta in a pot in the house until the child has been formally named. When that ceremony is over, the father waves the pot containing the placenta thrice over the child's head, and then hangs it to a tree outside of the village.[4]   In some Malayo-Siamese families of the Patani States it is customary to bury the afterbirth under a banana-tree, the condition of which is thenceforth regarded as ominous of the child's fate for good or ill.[5]   A Chinese medical work prescribes that "the placenta should be stored away in a felicitous spot under the salutary influences of the sky or the moon, deep in the ground, and with earth piled up over it carefully, in order that the child may be ensured a long life.   If it is devoured by a swine or dog, the child loses its intellect; if insects or ants eat it, the child becomes scrofulous; if crows or magpies swallow it,

Contagious magic of placenta and navel-string in the Patani States, China, and Japan.

Mr. Joustra thinks that the placenta is, in the opinion of the Battas, the original seat of this soul.

[1] J. H. Neumann, "De *tĕndi* in verband met Si Dajang," *Mededeelingen van wege het Nederlandsche Zendelinggenootschap*, xlviii. (1904) p. 102.

[2] A. H. F. J. Nusselein, "Beschrijving van het landschap Pasir," *Bijdragen tot de Taal- Land- en Volkenkunde van Nederlandsch-Indië*, lviii. (1905) pp. 537 *sq.*

[3] E. Thurston, *Castes and Tribes of Southern India*, iv. 370.

[4] P. R. T. Gurdon, *The Khasis* (London, 1907), pp. 124 *sq.*

[5] N. Annandale, "Customs of the Malayo-Siamese," *Fasciculi Malayenses*, Anthropology, part ii. (a) (May 1904) p. 5.

the child will have an abrupt or violent death ; if it is cast
into the fire, the child incurs running sores." [1]   The Japanese
preserve the navel-string most carefully and bury it with the
dead in the grave.[2]

Among the Gallas of East Africa the navel-string
is carefully kept, sewn up in leather, and serves as an
amulet for female camels, which then become the child's
property, together with all the young they give birth to.[3]
The Baganda believe that every person is born with a
double, and this double they identify with the afterbirth,
which they regard as a second child.   Further, they think
that the afterbirth has a ghost, and that the ghost is in that
portion of the navel-string which remains attached to the
child after birth.   This ghost must be preserved if the child
is to be healthy.   Hence when the navel-string drops off, it
is rubbed with butter, swathed in bark-cloth, and kept through
life under the name of " the twin " (mulongo).   The afterbirth
is wrapt up in plantain leaves and buried by the child's
mother at the root of a plantain tree, where it is protected
against wild beasts.   If the child be a boy, the tree chosen
is of the kind whose fruit is made into beer ; if the child be
a girl, the tree is of the kind whose fruit is eaten.   The
plantain tree at whose root the afterbirth is buried becomes
sacred until the fruit has ripened and been used.   Only the
father's mother may come near it and dig about it ; all
other people are kept from it by a rope of plantain fibre
which is tied from tree to tree in a circle round about the
sacred plantain.   All the child's secretions are thrown by
the mother at the root of the tree ; when the fruit is ripe,
the father's mother cuts it and makes it into beer or cooks
it, according to the sex of the child, and the relatives of the
father's clan then come and partake of the sacred feast.
After the meal the father must go in to his own wife, for
should he neglect to do so, and should some other member of
the clan have sexual relations with his wife first, the child's
spirit would leave it and go into the other woman.   Further,

Marginal note: Contagious magic of placenta and navel-string in Africa, especially among the Baganda.

[1] J. J. M. de Groot, *The Religious System of China*, iv. (Leyden, 1901) pp. 396 *sq.*
[2] H. von Siebold, *Ethnologische Studien über die Aino* (Berlin, 1881),

p. 32.
[3] Ph. Paulitschke, *Ethnographie Nordost Afrikas : die materielle Cultur der Danâkil, Galla und Somâl* (Berlin, 1893), p. 192.

Contagious magic of the navel-string among the Baganda.

the navel-string plays a part at the ceremony of naming a child, the object of which among the Baganda is to determine whether the child is legitimate or not. For this purpose the navel-string (the so-called "twin") is dropped into a bowl containing a mixture of beer, milk, and water; if it floats, the child is legitimate and the clan accepts it as a member; if it sinks, the child is disowned by the clan and the mother is punished for adultery. Afterwards the navel-string or "twin" (*mulongo*) is either kept by the clan or buried along with the afterbirth at the root of the plantain tree. Such are the customs observed with regard to the afterbirth and navel-string of Baganda commoners. The king's navel-string or "twin," wrapt in bark-cloths and decorated with beads, is treated like a person and confided to the care of the Kimbugwe, the second officer of the country, who has a special house built for it within his enclosure. Every month, when the new moon first appears in the sky, the Kimbugwe carries the bundle containing the "twin" in procession, with fife and drums playing, to the king, while the royal drum is beating in the royal enclosure. The king examines it and hands it back to him. After that, the minister returns the precious bundle to its own house in his enclosure and places it in the doorway, where it remains all night. Next morning it is taken from its wrappings, smeared with butter, and again set in the doorway until the evening, when it is swathed once more in its bark-cloths and restored to its proper resting-place. After the king's death his "twin" is deposited, along with his jaw-bone, in the huge hut which forms his temple. The spirit of the dead king is supposed to dwell in these two relics; they are placed on the daïs when he wishes to hold his court and when he is oracularly consulted on special occasions.[1]

Contagious magic of navel-string and afterbirth in America.

The Incas of Peru preserved the navel-string with the greatest care, and gave it to the child to suck whenever it fell ill.[2] In ancient Mexico they used to give a boy's navel-

[1] J. Roscoe, "Further Notes on the Manners and Customs of the Baganda," *Journal of the Anthropological Institute*, xxxii. (1902) pp. 33, 45, 46, 63, 76; *id.* "Kibuka, the War God of the Baganda," *Man*, vii. (1907) pp. 164 *sq.*

In the former of these two accounts Mr. Roscoe speaks of the placenta, not the navel-string, as the "twin" (*mulongo*).
[2] Garcilasso de la Vega, *Royal Commentaries of the Yncas*, bk. ii. ch. 24, vol. i. p. 186, Markham's translation.

string to soldiers, to be buried by them on a field of battle, in order that the boy might thus acquire a passion for war. But the navel-string of a girl was buried beside the domestic hearth, because this was believed to inspire her with a love of home and a taste for cooking and baking.[1] Algonquin women hung the navel-string round the child's neck; if he lost it, they thought the child would be stupid and spiritless.[2] Among the Thompson Indians of British Columbia the navel-string was sewed up by the mother in a piece of buckskin embroidered with hair, quills, or beads. It was then tied to the broad buckskin band which extended round the head of the cradle on the outside. Many thongs hung from it, each carrying fawn's hoofs and beads that jingled when the cradle was moved. If the navel-string were lost, they looked on it as a calamity, for they believed that in after years the child would become foolish or would be lost in the chase or on a journey.[3] Among the Kwakiutl Indians of British Columbia the afterbirth of girls is buried at high-water mark, in the belief that this will render them expert at digging for clam. The afterbirth of boys is sometimes exposed at places where ravens will eat it, because the boys will thus acquire the raven's prophetic vision. The same Indians are persuaded that the navel-string may be the means of imparting a variety of accomplishments to its original owner. Thus, if it is fastened to a dancing mask, which is then worn by a skilful dancer, the child will dance well. If it is attached to a knife, which is thereafter used by a cunning carver, the child will carve well. Again, if the parents wish their son to sing beautifully, they tie his navel-string to the baton of a singing-master. Then the boy calls on the singing-master every morning while the artist is eating his breakfast. The votary of the Muses thereupon takes his baton and moves it twice down the right side and twice down the left side of the boy's body, after which he gives the lad some of his food to eat. That

---

[1] B. de Sahagun, *Histoire générale des choses de la Nouvelle Espagne*, p. 310; compare pp. 240, 439, 440 (Jourdanet and Simeon's translation).

[2] *Relations des Jésuites*, 1639, p. 44

(Canadian reprint).

[3] J. Teit, "The Thompson Indians of British Columbia," pp. 304 *sq.* (*Memoir of the American Museum of Natural History, The Jesup North Pacific Expedition*, vol. i. part iv.).

is an infallible way of making the boy a beautiful singer.[1]
Among the Cherokees the navel-string of an infant girl is
buried under the corn mortar, in order that the girl may
grow up to be a good baker ; but the navel-string of a boy
is hung up on a tree in the woods, in order that he may be
a hunter. Among the Kiowas the navel-string of a girl is
sewn up in a small beaded pouch and worn by her at her
belt as she grows to womanhood. If the girl's mother ever
sells the belt and pouch, she is careful to extract the navel-
string from the pouch before the bargain is struck. Should
the child die, the pouch containing her navel-string would be
fastened to a stick and set up over her grave.[2]

Contagious
magic of
navel-
string and
afterbirth
in Europe. Even in Europe many people still believe that a person's
destiny is more or less bound up with that of his navel-string
or afterbirth. Thus in Rhenish Bavaria the navel-string is
kept for a while wrapt up in a piece of old linen, and then
cut or pricked to pieces according as the child is a boy or
a girl, in order that he or she may grow up to be a skilful
workman or a good sempstress.[3] In Berlin the midwife
commonly delivers the dried navel-string to the father with
a strict injunction to preserve it carefully, for so long as
it is kept the child will live and thrive and be free from
sickness.[4] In Beauce and Perche the people are careful
to throw the navel-string neither into water nor into fire,
believing that if that were done the child would be drowned
or burned.[5] Among the Ruthenians of Bukowina and
Galicia, the owner of a cow sometimes endeavours to increase
its milk by throwing its afterbirth into a spring, " in order
that, just as the water flows from the spring, so milk may
flow in abundance from the udders of the cow."[6] Some
German peasants think that the afterbirth of a cow must be
hung up in an apple-tree, otherwise the cow would not have

[1] Fr. Boas in *Eleventh Report on
the North-Western Tribes of Canada*,
p. 5 (separate reprint from the *Report
of the British Association for 1896*).

[2] J. Mooney, " The Indian Navel
Cord," *Journal of American Folk-lore*,
xvii. (1904) p. 197.

[3] *Bavaria, Landes- und Volkskunde
des Königreichs Bayern*, iv. 2, p. 346.

[4] E. Krause, "Abergläubische Kuren
und sonstiger Aberglaube in Berlin und
nächster Umgebung," *Zeitschrift für
Ethnologie*, xv. (1883) p. 84.

[5] F. Chapiseau, *Le Folk-lore de la
Beauce et du Perche* (Paris, 1902), ii.
16.

[6] R. F. Kaindl, "Zauberglaube bei
den Rutenen in der Bukowina und
Galizien," *Globus*, lxi. (1892) p. 282.

a calf next year.[1]   Similarly at Cleveland in Yorkshire, when
a mare foals, it is the custom to hang up the placenta in a
tree, particularly in a thorn-tree, in order to secure luck with
the foal.   "Should the birth take place in the fields, this
suspension is most carefully attended to, while as for the
requirements of such events at the homestead, in not a few
instances there is a certain tree not far from the farm-
buildings still specially marked out for the reception of
these peculiar pendants.   In one instance lately, I heard of
a larch tree so devoted, but admittedly in default of the
thorn ; the old thorn-tree long employed for the purpose
having died out."[2]   Again, in Europe children born with
a caul are considered lucky ;[3] in Holland, as in the
East Indies, they can see ghosts.[4]   The Icelanders also
hold that a child born with a caul will afterwards
possess the gift of second sight, that he will never be
harmed by sorcery, and will be victorious in every contest
he undertakes, provided he has the caul dried and carries
it with him.[5]   This latter belief explains why both in ancient
and modern times advocates have bought cauls with the hope
of winning their cases by means of them.[6]   Probably they
thought that the spirit in the caul would prove an invincible
ally to the person who had purchased its services.   In like
manner the aborigines of Central Australia believe that their
sacred sticks or stones (*churinga*) are intimately associated
with the spirits of the dead men to whom they belonged,
and that in a fight a man who carries one of these sticks or
stones will certainly vanquish an adversary who has no such
talisman.[7]   Further, it is an ancient belief in Iceland that Child's
the child's guardian spirit or a part of its soul has its seat guardian
in the chorion or foetal membrane, which usually forms part associated
of the afterbirth, but is known as the caul when the child with the
chorion.

---

[1] A. Kuhn, *Märkische Sagen und Märchen* (Berlin, 1843), pp. 379 *sq.*

[2] J. C. Atkinson, in *County Folk-lore*, ii. (London, 1901) p. 68.

[3] A. Wuttke, *Der deutsche Volks-aberglaube*,[2] § 305, p. 203 ; H. Ploss, *Das Kind*,[2] i. 12 *sqq.*

[4] J. Grimm, *Deutsche Mythologie*,[4] ii. 728, note 1.   As to the East Indian belief see above, pp. 187 *sq.*

[5] M. Bartels, "Islandischer Brauch und Volksglaube in Bezug auf die Nachkommenschaft," *Zeitschrift für Ethnologie*, xxxii. (1900) pp. 70 *sq.*

[6] Aelius Lampridius, *Antoninus Diadumenus*, 4 ; J. Grimm, *loc. cit.* ; H. Ploss, *Das Kind*,[2] i. pp. 13, 14.

[7] Spencer and Gillen, *Native Tribes of Central Australia*, p. 135.

happens to be born with it.   Hence the chorion was itself
known as the *fylgia* or guardian spirit.   It might not be
thrown away under the open sky, lest demons should get
hold of it and work the child harm thereby, or lest wild
beasts should eat it up.   It might not be burned, for if it
were burned the child would have no *fylgia*, which would
be as bad as to have no shadow.   Formerly it was customary
to bury the chorion under the threshold, where the mother
stepped over it daily when · she rose from bed.   If the
chorion was thus treated, the man had in after life a guardian
spirit in the shape of a bear, an eagle, a wolf, an ox, or a
boar.   The guardian spirits of cunning men and wizards
had the shape of a fox, while those of beautiful women
appeared as swans.   In all these forms the guardian spirits
formerly announced their coming and presented themselves
to the persons to whom they belonged ; but nowadays both
the belief and the custom have changed in many respects.[1]

Afterbirth
or navel-
string a
seat of the
external
soul.

Thus in many parts of the world the navel-string, or
more commonly the afterbirth, is regarded as a living being,
the brother or sister of the infant, or as the material object
in which the guardian spirit of the child or part of its soul
resides.   This latter belief we have found among the
aborigines of Queensland, the Battas of Sumatra, and the
Norsemen of Iceland.   In accordance with such beliefs it
has been customary to preserve these parts of the body, at
least for a time, with the utmost care, lest the character, the
fate, or even the life of the person to whom they belong
should be endangered by their injury or loss.   Further,
the sympathetic connexion supposed to exist between a
person and his afterbirth or navel-string comes out very
clearly in the widespread custom of treating the afterbirth
or navel-string in ways which are supposed to influence for
life the character and career of the person, making him, if it
is a man, a swift runner, a nimble climber, a strong swimmer,
a skilful hunter, or a brave soldier, and making her, if it is
a woman, an expert fisher, a cunning sempstress, a good
cook or baker, and so forth.   Thus the beliefs and usages

[1] J. Grimm, *Deutsche Mythologie,*[4]
ii. 728 *sq.,* iii. 266 *sq.* ; M. Bartels,
op. cit. p. 70.   Grimm speaks as if it
were only the caul which became a
fylgia.   I follow Dr. Bartels.

concerned with the afterbirth or placenta, and to a less extent with the navel-string, present a remarkable parallel to the widespread doctrine of the transferable or external soul and the customs founded on it. Hence it is hardly rash to conjecture that the resemblance is no mere chance coincidence, but that in the afterbirth or placenta we have a physical basis (not necessarily the only one) for the theory and practice of the external soul. The consideration of that subject is reserved for a later part of this work.[1]

A curious application of the doctrine of contagious magic is the relation commonly believed to exist between a wounded man and the agent of the wound, so that whatever is subsequently done by or to the agent must correspondingly affect the patient either for good or evil. Thus Pliny tells us that if you have wounded a man and are sorry for it, you have only to spit on the hand that gave the wound, and the pain of the sufferer will be instantly alleviated.[2] In Melanesia, if a man's friends get possession of the arrow which wounded him, they keep it in a damp place or in cool leaves, for then the inflammation will be trifling and will soon subside. Meantime the enemy who shot the arrow is hard at work to aggravate the wound by all the means in his power. For this purpose he and his friends drink hot and burning juices and chew irritating leaves, for this will clearly inflame and irritate the wound. Further, they keep the bow near the fire to make the wound which it has inflicted hot ; and for the same reason they put the arrow-head, if it has been recovered, into the fire. Moreover, they are careful to keep the bow-string taut and to twang it occasionally, for this will cause the wounded man to suffer from tension of the nerves and spasms of tetanus.[3] Similarly when a Kwakiutl Indian of British Columbia had bitten a piece out of an enemy's arm, he used to drink hot water afterwards for the purpose of thereby inflaming the wound in his foe's

Contagious magic exemplified in the sympathetic connexion supposed to exist between a wound and the weapon which inflicted it.

---

[1] Meantime I may refer to *The Golden Bough*, Second Edition, iii. 350 *sqq.* For other superstitions concerning the afterbirth and navel-string see H. Ploss, *Das Kind*,[2] i. 15 *sqq.*, ii. 198 *sq.* The connexion of these parts of the body with the idea of the external soul has already been indicated by Mr. E. Crawley (*The Mystic Rose*, London, 1902, p. 119).

[2] Pliny, *Nat. Hist.* xxviii. 36.

[3] R. H. Codrington, *The Melanesians* (Oxford, 1891), p. 310.

body.[1] Among the Lkuñgen Indians of the same region it is a rule that an arrow, or any other weapon that has wounded a man, must be hidden by his friends, who have to be careful not to bring it near the fire till the wound is healed. If a knife or an arrow which is still covered with a man's blood were thrown into the fire, the wounded man would suffer very much.[2] In the Yerkla-mining tribe of south-eastern Australia it is thought that if any one but the medicine-man touches the flint knife with which a boy has been subincised, the boy will thereby be made very ill. So seriously is this belief held that if the lad chanced thereafter to fall sick and die, the man who had touched the knife

Bacon on the custom of anointing the weapon in order to heal the wound.

would be killed.[3] "It is constantly received and avouched," says Bacon, "that the anointing of the weapon that maketh the wound will heal the wound itself. In this experiment, upon the relation of men of credit (though myself, as yet, am not fully inclined to believe it), you shall note the points following: first, the ointment wherewith this is done is made of divers ingredients, whereof the strangest and hardest to come by are the moss upon the skull of a dead man unburied, and the fats of a boar and a bear killed in the act of generation." The precious ointment compounded out of these and other ingredients was applied, as the philosopher explains, not to the wound but to the weapon, and that even though the injured man was at a great distance and knew nothing about it. The experiment, he tells us, had been tried of wiping the ointment off the weapon without the knowledge of the person hurt, with the result that he was presently in a great rage of pain until the weapon was anointed again. Moreover, "it is affirmed that if you cannot get the weapon, yet if you put an instrument of iron or wood resembling the weapon into the wound, whereby it bleedeth, the anointing of that instrument will serve and work the effect."[4] Remedies of the

[1] Fr. Boas, "The Social Organization and the Secret Societies of the Kwakiutl Indians," *Report of the U.S. National Museum for 1895*, p. 440.

[2] Fr. Boas, in *Sixth Report on the North-Western Tribes of Canada*, p. 25 (separate reprint from the *Report of the British Association for 1890*).

[3] A. W. Howitt, *Native Tribes of South-East Australia*, p. 667.

[4] Francis Bacon, *Natural History*, cent. x. § 998. Compare J. Brand *Popular Antiquities*, iii. 305, quoting Werenfels. In Dryden's play *The Tempest* (Act v. Scene I) Ariel directs Prospero to anoint the sword which

sort which Bacon deemed worthy of his attention are still
in vogue in the eastern counties of England.   Thus in East
Suffolk if a man cuts himself with a bill-hook or a scythe Anglian practice of
he always takes care to keep the weapon bright, and oils anointing
it to prevent the wound from festering.   If he runs a the weapon instead of
thorn or, as he calls it, a bush into his hand, he oils or the wound
greases the extracted thorn.   A man came to a doctor with
an inflamed hand, having run a thorn into it while he was
hedging.   On being told that the hand was festering, he
remarked, " That didn't ought to, for I greased the bush
well arter I pulled it out."   If a horse wounds its foot by
treading on a nail, a Suffolk groom will invariably preserve
the nail, clean it, and grease it every day, to prevent the
foot from festering.   Arguing in the same way, a Suffolk
woman, whose sister had burnt her face with a flat-iron,
observed that " the face would never heal till the iron had
been put out of the way ; and even if it did heal, it would be
sure to break out again every time the iron was heated." [1]   At
Norwich in June 1902 a woman named Matilda Henry
accidentally ran a nail into her foot.   Without examining the
wound, or even removing her stocking, she caused her
daughter to grease the nail, saying that if this were done
no harm would come of the hurt.   A few days afterwards
she died of lockjaw.[2]   Similarly Cambridgeshire labourers
think that if a horse has run a nail into its foot, it is necessary
to grease the nail with lard or oil and put it away in some
safe place, or the horse will not recover.   A few years ago
a veterinary surgeon was sent for to attend a horse which
had ripped its side open on the hinge of a farm gatepost.
On arriving at the farm he found that nothing had been
done to the wounded horse, but that a man was busy trying
to pry the hinge out of the gatepost in order that it might
be greased and put away, which, in the opinion of the
Cambridge wiseacres, would conduce to the recovery of the

wounded Hippolito and to wrap it
up close from the air.   See Dryden's
Works, ed. Scott, vol. iii. p. 191 (first
edition).
    [1] W. W. Groome, " Suffolk Leech-
craft," *Folklore*, vi. (1895) p. 126.
Compare *County Folklore : Suffolk*,
edited by Lady E. C. Gurdon, pp. 25 *sq.*

A like belief and practice occur in
Sussex (C. Latham, " West Sussex
Superstitions," *Folklore Record*, i. 43
sq.).   See further E. S. Hartland, *The
Legend of Perseus*, ii. 169-172.
    [2] " Death from Lockjaw at Norwich,"
*The People's Weekly Journal for Nor-
folk*, July 19, 1902, p. 8.

Anointing
the weapon
instead of
the wound.
animal.[1] Similarly Essex rustics opine that, if a man has
been stabbed with a knife, it is essential to his recovery that
the knife should be greased and laid across the bed on which
the sufferer is lying.[2] So in Bavaria you are directed to
anoint a linen rag with grease and tie it on the edge of the
axe that cut you, taking care to keep the sharp edge
upwards. As the grease on the axe dries, your wound heals.[3]
Similarly in the Harz mountains they say that if you cut
yourself, you ought to smear the knife or the scissors with
fat and put the instrument away in a dry place in the name
of the Father, of the Son, and of the Holy Ghost. As the
knife dries, the wound heals.[4] Other people, however,
in Germany say that you should stick the knife in some
damp place in the ground, and that your hurt will heal
as the knife rusts.[5] Others again, in Bavaria, recommend
you to smear the axe or whatever it is with blood and put
it under the eaves.[6]

Further
extensions
of this
case of
contagious
magic.
The train of reasoning which thus commends itself to
English and German rustics, in common with the savages
of Melanesia and America, is carried a step further by the
aborigines of Central Australia, who conceive that under
certain circumstances the near relations of a wounded man
must grease themselves, restrict their diet, and regulate
their behaviour in other ways in order to ensure his
recovery. Thus when a lad has been circumcised and the
wound is not yet healed, his mother may not eat opossum,
or a certain kind of lizard, or carpet snake, or any kind of
fat, for otherwise she would retard the healing of the boy's
wound. Every day she greases her digging-sticks and never
lets them out of her sight; at night she sleeps with them
close to her head. No one is allowed to touch them. Every
day also she rubs her body all over with grease, as in some
way this is believed to help her son's recovery.[7] Another

---

[1] F. N. Webb, in *Folk-lore*, xvi.
(1905) p. 337.

[2] C. Partridge, *Cross River Natives*
(London, 1905), p. 295.

[3] F. Panzer, *Beitrag zur deutschen
Mythologie*, ii. 305, compare 277.

[4] H. Pröhle, *Harzbilder* (Leipsic,
1855), p. 82.

[5] J. W. Wolf, *Beiträge zur deutschen*

Mythologie, i. p. 225, § 282.

[6] *Bavaria, Landes- und Volkskunde
des Königreichs Bayern*, iv. 1, p. 223.
A further recommendation is to stroke
the wound or the instrument with a
twig of an ash-tree and then keep the
twig in a dark place.

[7] Spencer and Gillen, *Native Tribes
of Central Australia*, p. 250.

refinement of the same principle is due to the ingenuity of
the German peasant. It is said that when one of his pigs
or sheep breaks its leg, a farmer of Rhenish Bavaria or
Hesse will bind up the leg of a chair with bandages and
splints in due form. For some days thereafter no one may
sit on that chair, move it, or knock up against it ; for to do
so would pain the injured pig or sheep and hinder the cure.[1]
In this last case it is clear that we have passed wholly out
of the region of contagious magic and into the region of
homoeopathic or imitative magic ; the chair-leg, which is
treated instead of the beast's leg, in no sense belongs to the
animal, and the application of bandages to it is a mere
simulation of the treatment which a more rational surgery
would bestow on the real patient.

The sympathetic connexion supposed to exist between
a man and the weapon which has wounded him is probably
founded on the notion that the blood on the weapon continues to feel with the blood in his body. For a like reason
the Papuans of Tumleo, an island off German New Guinea,
are careful to throw into the sea the bloody bandages with
which their wounds have been dressed, for they fear that if
these rags fell into the hands of an enemy he might injure
them magically thereby. Once when a man with a wound
in his mouth, which bled constantly, came to the missionaries
to be treated, his faithful wife took great pains to collect all
the blood and cast it into the sea.[2] Strained and unnatural
as this idea may seem to us, it is perhaps less so than the
belief that magic sympathy is maintained between a person
and his clothes, so that whatever is done to the clothes will
be felt by the man himself, even though he may be far away
at the time. That is why these same Papuans of Tumleo
search most anxiously for the smallest scrap which they
may have lost of their scanty garments,[3] and why other
Papuans, travelling through the thick forest, will stop and
carefully scrape from a bough any clot of red pomade which

Sympathetic connexion between a wounded person and his spilt blood.

A sympathetic connexion is supposed to exist between a person and his clothes, so that any injury done to the clothes is felt by the man.

[1] F. Panzer, *Beitrag zur deutschen Mythologie*, ii. 302 ; W. Kolbe, *Hessische Volks- Sitten und Gebräuche im Lichte der heidnischen Vorzeit* (Marburg, 1888), p. 87.

[2] M. J. Erdweg, " Die Bewohner der Insel Tumleo, Berlinhafen, Deutsch-Neu-Guinea," *Mittheilungen der Anthropologischen Gesellschaft in Wien,* xxxii. (1902) p. 287.

[3] M. J. Erdweg, *loc. cit.*

Contagious magic of clothes. may have adhered to it from their greasy heads.[1]　In the Wotjobaluk tribe of Victoria a wizard would sometimes get hold of a man's opossum rug and tie it up with some small spindle-shaped pieces of casuarina wood, on which he had made certain marks, such as likenesses of his victim and of a poisonous snake.　This bundle he would then roast slowly in the fire, and as he did so the man who had owned the opossum rug would fall sick.　Should the patient suspect what was happening, he would send to the wizard and beg him to let him have the rug back.　If the wizard consented, "he would give the thing back, telling the sick man's friends to put it in water, so as to wash the fire out."　In such cases, we are told, the sick man would feel cooled and would most likely recover.[2]　In Tanna, one of the New Hebrides, a man who had a grudge at another and desired his death would try to get possession of a cloth which had touched the sweat of his enemy's body.　If he succeeded, he rubbed the cloth carefully over with the leaves and twigs of a certain tree, rolled and bound cloth, twigs, and leaves into a long sausage-shaped bundle, and burned it slowly in the fire.　As the bundle was consumed, the victim fell ill, and when it was reduced to ashes, he died.[3]　In this last form of enchantment, however, the magical sympathy may be supposed to exist not so much between the man and the cloth as between the man and the sweat which issued from his body.　But in other cases of the same sort it seems that the garment by itself is enough to give the sorcerer a hold upon his victim.　The witch in Theocritus, while she melted an image or lump of wax in order that her faithless lover might melt with love of her, did not forget to throw into the fire a shred of his cloak which he had dropped in her house.[4]　In Prussia they say that if you cannot catch a thief, the next best thing you can do is to get hold of a garment which he may have shed in his flight; for it

Prussian custom of beating the garments

---

[1] B. Hagen, *Unter den Papua's* (Wiesbaden, 1899), p. 269.

[2] A. W. Howitt, "On Australian Medicine Men," *Journal of the Anthropological Institute*, xvi. (1887) pp. 28 *sq.* ; id., *Native Tribes of South-East Australia*, pp. 363-365.

[3] B. T. Somerville, "Notes on some Islands of the New Hebrides," *Journal of the Anthropological Institute*, xxiii. (1894) p. 19.

[4] Theocritus, *Id.* ii. 53 *sq.* Similarly the witch in Virgil (*Eclog.* viii. 92 *sqq.*) buries under her threshold certain personal relics (*exuviae*) which her lover had left behind.

you beat it soundly, the thief will fall sick.   This belief is which a
thief has
dropped.
firmly rooted in the popular mind.   Some seventy or eighty
years ago, in the neighbourhood of Berend, a man was
detected trying to steal honey, and fled, leaving his coat
behind him.   When he heard that the enraged owner of
the honey was mauling his lost coat, he was so alarmed
that he took to his bed and died.[1]   But in Germany it is
not every stick that is good enough to beat an absent man
with.   It should be a hazel rod cut before sunrise on Good
Friday.   Some say it should be a one-year-old hazel-sapling,
and that you should cut it with three strokes, looking to
the east, in the name of the Father, the Son, and the Holy
Ghost.   Others think the best time for cutting the rod is at
the new moon on a Tuesday morning before sunrise.   Once
you have got this valuable instrument, you have only to
spread a garment on a mole-hill or on the threshold, and
to lay on with hearty goodwill, mentioning the name of
the person whom you desire to injure.   Though he may
be miles off, he will feel every whack as if it descended on
his body.[2]

Again, magic may be wrought on a man sympathetic- Contagious
magic may
be wrought
on a man
through
the impres-
sions left
by his
body in
sand or
earth, par-
ticularly
through his
footprints.
ally, not only through his clothes and severed parts of
himself, but also through the impressions left by his body
in sand or earth.   In particular, it is a world-wide superstition that by injuring footprints you injure the feet that
made them.   Thus the natives of south-eastern Australia
think that they can lame a man by placing sharp pieces of
quartz, glass, bone, or charcoal in his footprints.   Rheumatic
pains are often attributed by them to this cause.   Seeing a
Tatungolung man very lame, Mr. Howitt asked him what
was the matter.   He said, "Some fellow has put *bottle* in
my foot."   He was suffering from rheumatism, but believed
that an enemy had found his foot-track and had buried in
it a piece of broken bottle, the magical influence of which

[1] Tettau und Temme, *Volkssagen
Ostpreussens, Litthauens und Westpreussens* (Berlin, 1837), pp. 283 *sq.*
For more evidence of the same sort see
E. S. Hartland, *Legend of Perseus*, ii.
86 *sqq.*
[2] E. Meier, *Deutsche Sagen, Sitten
und Gebräuche aus Schwaben*, pp. 245

sq. ; A. Kuhn, *Sagen, Gebräuche und
Märchen aus Westfalen*, ii. 192 ; *id.*,
Die Herabkunft des Feuers,[2] pp. 200
sq. ; W. Mannhardt, *Die Götterwelt
der deutschen und nordischen Völker*,
i. 203 note.   Compare Montanus, *Die
deutsche Volksfeste, Volksbräuche und
deutscher Volksglaube*, p. 117.

had entered his foot. On another occasion Mr. Howitt's party was followed by a number of strange natives who looked with great interest at the footprints of the horses and camels. A black fellow with Mr. Howitt was much alarmed, and declared that the strangers were putting poison in his footsteps.[1] The Wyingurri, a tribe on the border of western Australia, have a magical instrument made of resin and rats' teeth which they call a sun, because it is supposed to contain the solar heat. By placing it on a man's tracks they think they can throw him into a violent fever, which will soon burn him up.[2] In the Unmatjera tribe of Central Australia, when a boy has been circumcised he must hide in the bush, and if he should see a woman's tracks he must be very careful to jump over them. For if his foot were to touch them, the spirit of the louse which lives in the woman's hair would go to him, and his head would be full of lice.[3] In New Britain it is thought that you can cause the sickness or death of a man by pricking his footprints with the sting of a sting-ray.[4] The Maoris imagine that they can work grievous harm to an enemy by taking up earth from his footprints, depositing it in a sacred place, and performing a ceremony over it.[5] In Savage Island a common form of witchcraft was to take up the soil on which an enemy had set his foot, and to carry it to a sacred place, where it was solemnly cursed, in order that the man might be afflicted with lameness.[6] The Galelareese think that if anybody sticks something sharp into your footprints while you are walking, you will be wounded in your feet.[7] In Japan, if a house has been robbed by night

[1] Fison and Howitt, *Kamilaroi and Kurnai*, p. 250 ; A. W. Howitt, "On Australian Medicine Men," *Journal of the Anthropological Institute*, xvi. (1887) pp. 26 *sq.* ; *id.*, *Native Tribes of South-East Australia*, pp. 366 *sq.* According to one account a cross should be made in the footprint with a piece of quartz, and round the footprint thus marked the bones of kangaroos should be stuck in the ground. See R. Brough Smyth, *Aborigines of Victoria*, i. 476 *sq.* These and many of the following examples were cited by me in *Folklore*, i. (1890) pp. 157

sqq. For more instances of the same sort see E. S. Hartland, *The Legend of Perseus*, ii. (London, 1895) 78-83.

[2] Spencer and Gillen, *Native Tribes of Central Australia*, p. 541.

[3] *Id.*, *Northern Tribes of Central Australia*, pp. 340 *sq.*

[4] R. Parkinson, *Dreissig Jahre in der Südsee* (Stuttgart, 1907), p. 605.

[5] Elsdon Best, "Spiritual Concepts of the Maori," *Journal of the Polynesian Society*, ix. (1900) p. 196.

[6] Basil C. Thomson, *Savage Island* (London, 1902), p. 97.

[7] M. J. van Baarda, "Fabelen, Ver-

and the burglar's footprints are visible in the morning,
the householder will burn mugwort on them, hoping
thereby to hurt the robber's feet so that he cannot run
far, and the police may easily overtake him.[1]   Among
the Karens of Burma some people are said to keep poison
fangs for the purpose of killing their enemies. These they
thrust into the footprints of the person whom they wish to
destroy, and soon he finds himself with a sore foot, as if a
dog had bitten it. The sore rapidly grows worse till death
follows.[2] Peasants of northern India commonly attribute
all sorts of pains and sores to the machinations of a witch
or sorcerer who has meddled with their footprints.[3] For
example, with the Chero, a Dravidian race of labourers in
the hill country of Mirzapur, a favourite mode of harming an
enemy is to measure his footprints in the dust with a straw
and then mutter a spell over them ; that brings on wounds
and sores in his feet.[4] Such magical operations have been
familiar to the Hindoos from of old. In the *Kausika Sutra*,
a book of sorcery, it is directed that, while your foe is
walking southward, you should make cuts in his footprint
with the leaf of a certain tree or with the blade of an axe
(it is not quite clear which is to be used) ; then you must
tie dust from the footprint in the leaf of a certain tree
(*Butea frondosa*) and throw it into a frying-pan ; if it crackles
in the pan, your enemy is undone.[5] Another old Hindoo
charm was to obtain earth from the footprint of a beleaguered
king and scatter it in the wind.[6] The Herero of South
Africa take earth from the footprints of a lion and throw it
on the track of an enemy, with the wish, " May the lion kill
you." [7] The Ovambo of the same region believe that they
can be bewitched by an enemy through the dust or sand

halen en Overleveringen der Galelareezen," *Bijdragen tot de Taal- Land-
en Volkenkunde van Nederlandsch-
Indië*, xlv. (1895) p. 512.
    [1] L. Hearn, *Glimpses of unfamiliar
Japan* (London, 1894), ii. 604.
    [2] F. Mason, " On Dwellings, Works
of Art, Laws, etc., of the Karens,"
Journal of the Asiatic Society of Bengal,
xxxvii. (1868) part ii. p. 149.
    [3] W. Crooke, *Popular Religion and
Folklore of Northern India* (West-

minster, 1896), ii. 280.
    [4] *Id., Tribes and Castes of the
North-Western Provinces and Oudh*,
ii. 221.
    [5] M. Bloomfield, *Hymns of the
Atharva-Veda*, p. 295 ; W. Caland,
Altindisches Zauberritual, pp. 162 *sq.*
    [6] A. Hillebrandt, *Vedische Opfer
und Zauber* (Strasburg, 1897), p. 173.
    [7] Josaphat Hahn, "Die Ovaherero,"
*Zeitschrift der Gesellschaft für Erd-
kunde zu Berlin*, iv. (1869) p. 503.

of their footprints. Hence a man who has special reason to dread the spite of a foe will carefully efface his footprints with a branch as fast as he makes them.[1] The Ewe-speaking people of West Africa fancy they can drive an enemy mad by throwing a magic powder on his footprints.[2] Among the Shuswap and Carrier Indians of North-west America shamans used to bewitch a man by taking earth from the spot on which he had stood and placing it in their medicine-bags ; then their victim fell sick or died.[3] In North Africa the magic of the footprints is sometimes used for more amiable purposes. A woman who wishes to attach her husband or lover to herself will take earth from the print of his right foot, tie it up with some of his hairs in a packet, and wear the packet next her skin.[4]

Contagious magic of footprints in Europe.
Similar practices prevail in various parts of Europe. Thus in Mecklenburg it is thought that if you drive a nail into a man's footprint he will fall lame ; sometimes it is required that the nail should be taken from a coffin.[5] A like mode of injuring an enemy is resorted to in some parts of France.[6] It is said that there was an old woman who used to frequent Stow in Suffolk, and she was a witch. If, while she walked, any one went after her and stuck a nail or a knife into her footprint in the dust, the dame could not stir a step till it was withdrawn.[7] More commonly, it would seem, in Germany earth from the footprint is tied up in a cloth and hung in the chimney smoke ; as it dries up, so the man withers away or his foot shrivels up.[8] The same practice and the same belief are said to be common in Matogrosso, a province of Brazil.[9] A Bohemian

[1] H. Schinz, *Deutsch - Südwest-Afrika*, pp. 313 *sq.*

[2] A. B. Ellis, *The Ewe-speaking Peoples of the Slave Coast*, p. 94.

[3] J. Teit, "The Shuswap" (Leyden and New York, 1909) p. 613 (*Memoir of the American Museum of Natural History, The Jesup North Pacific Expedition*, vol. ii. part vii.).

[4] E. Doutté, *Magie et religion dans l'Afrique du Nord*, p. 59.

[5] K. Bartsch, *Sagen, Märchen und Gebräuche aus Meklenburg*, ii. 329 *sq.*, §§ 1597, 1598, 1601ª.

[6] J. L. M. Noguès, *Les Mœurs d'autrefois en Saintonge et en Aunis* (Saintes, 1891), pp. 169 *sq.* ; C. de Mensignac, *Recherches ethnographiques sur la salive et le crachat* (Bordeaux, 1892), p. 45 note.

[7] *County Folklore : Suffolk*, edited by Lady E. C. Gurdon, p. 201.

[8] Josaphat Hahn, *loc. cit.* ; K. Bartsch, *op. cit.* ii. 330, 334, §§ 1599, 1611ᵃᵇᶜ, compare p. 332, § 1607 ; R. Andree, *Ethnographische Parallelen und Vergleiche*, Neue Folge (Leipsic, 1889), pp. 8, 11.

[9] K. von den Steinen, *Unter den Naturvölkern Zentral-Brasiliens*, p. 558.

variation of the charm is to put the earth from the footprint
in a pot with nails, needles, broken glass, and so forth, then set
the pot on the fire and let it boil till it bursts. After that the
man whose footprint has been boiled will have a lame leg for
the rest of his life.[1] Among the Lithuanians the proceeding
is somewhat different. They dig up the earth from the
person's footprint and bury it, with various incantations, in
a graveyard. That causes the person to sicken and die.[2]
A similar practice is reported from Mecklenburg.[3] The
Esthonians of the island of Oesel measure the footprint with
a stick and bury the stick, thereby undermining the health
of the man or woman whose foot made the mark.[4] Among
the South Slavs a girl will dig up the earth from the footprints of the man she loves and put it in a flower-pot.
Then she plants in the pot a marigold, a flower that is
thought to be fadeless. And as its golden blossom grows
and blooms and never fades, so shall her sweetheart's love
grow and bloom, and never, never fade.[5] Thus the love-
spell acts on the man through the earth he trod on. An old
Danish mode of concluding a treaty was based on the same
idea of the sympathetic connexion between a man and his
footprints : the covenanting parties sprinkled each other's
footprints with their own blood, thus giving a pledge of
fidelity.[6] In ancient Greece superstitions of the same sort
seem to have been current, for it was thought that if a horse
stepped on the track of a wolf he was seized with numb-
ness ;[7] and a maxim ascribed to Pythagoras forbade people
to pierce a man's footprints with a nail or a knife.[8]

The same superstition is turned to account by hunters
in many parts of the world for the purpose of running down
the game. Thus a German huntsman will stick a nail
taken from a coffin into the fresh spoor of the quarry,

*The con-
tagious
magic of
footprints
is used by
hunters for*

---

[1] J. V. Grohmann, *Aberglauben und
Gebräuche aus Böhmen und Mähren*,
p. 200, § 1402.

[2] Tettau and Temme, *Die Volkssagen Ostpreussens, Litthauens und
Westpreussens*, p. 267 ; A. Bezzen-
berger, *Litauische Forschungen* (Göttingen, 1882), p. 69.

[3] K. Bartsch, *op. cit.* ii. 330, §
1599.

[4] Holzmayer, " Osiliana," *Verhand-*

*lungen der gelehrten Estnischen Gesell-
schaft zu Dorpat*, vii. (1872) p. 79.

[5] F. S. Krauss, *Sitte und Brauch
der Südslaven*, p. 165.

[6] Saxo Grammaticus, *Historia Danica*, i. p. 40, ed. P. E. Müller (pp. 28
sq., O. Elton's English translation).

[7] Aelian, *De natura animalium*, i.
36.

[8] *Fragmenta Philosophorum Graecorum*, ed. F. G. A. Mullach, i. 510.

the pur-
pose of
running
down the
game.

believing that this will hinder the animal from escaping.[1] The aborigines of Victoria put hot embers in the tracks of the animals they were pursuing.[2] Hottentot hunters throw into the air a handful of sand taken from the footprints of the game, believing that this will bring the animal down.[3] Thompson Indians used to lay charms on the tracks of wounded deer ; after that they deemed it superfluous to pursue the animal any further that day, for being thus charmed it could not travel far and would soon die.[4] Similarly, Ojebway Indians placed "medicine" on the track of the first deer or bear they met with, supposing that this would soon bring the animal into sight, even if it were two or three days' journey off ; for this charm had power to compress a journey of several days into a few hours.[5] Ewe hunters of West Africa stab the footprints of game with a sharp-pointed stick in order to maim the quarry and allow them to come up with it.[6] If Esthonian peasants find a wolf's dung on a beast's tracks, they burn it and scatter the ashes to the wind. This gives the wolf a pain in his stomach and makes him lose his way.[7] The Aino think that hares bewitch people. Hence if one of them sees the track of a hare in the snow near his hut, he should carefully scoop it up with a water-ladle and then turn it upside down, saying as he does so that he buries the soul of the hare under the snow, and expressing a wish that the animal may sicken and die.[8] In order to recover strayed cattle, the Zulus take the animals' dung and earth from their footprints and place both in the chief's vessel, round which a magic circle is drawn. Then the chief says : "I have now conquered them. Those cattle are now here ; I am now sitting upon them. I do not know in what way they will escape."[9]

[1] A. Wuttke, *Der deutsche Volks-aberglaube*,[2] p. 127, § 186.

[2] J. Dawson, *Australian Aborigines*, p. 54.

[3] Theophilus Hahn, *Tsuni- Goam* (London, 1881), pp. 84 *sq.*

[4] J. Teit, "The Thompson Indians of British Columbia," p. 371 (*The Jesup North Pacific Expedition*, vol. i. part iv.).

[5] Peter Jones, *History of the Ojeb-way Indians*, p. 154.

[6] J. Spieth, *Die Ewe-Stämme* (Berlin, 1906), p. 389.

[7] Boecler-Kreutzwald, *Der Ehsten abergläubische Gebräuche, Weisen und Gewohnheiten*, pp. 121 *sq.*

[8] J. Batchelor, *The Ainu and their Folklore* (London, 1901), p. 516.

[9] H. Callaway, *The Religious System of the Amazulu*, part iii. pp. 345 *sq.*

But though the footprint is the most obvious it is not the only impression made by the body through which magic may be wrought on a man. The aborigines of south-eastern Australia believe that a man may be injured by burying sharp fragments of quartz, glass, and so forth in the mark made by his reclining body ; the magical virtue of these sharp things enters his body and causes those acute pains which the ignorant European puts down to rheumatism.[1] Sometimes they beat the place where the man sat with a pointed stick of the he-oak (*Casuarina leptoclada*), chanting an appropriate song at the same time ; the stick will enter his person and kill him, provided the place operated on is still warm with the heat of his body.[2] At Delena, in British New Guinea, a man will sometimes revenge himself on a girl who has rejected his love by thrusting the spine of a sting-ray into the spot where she has been sitting ; afterwards he puts it in the sun for a day or two and finally heats it over a fire. In a couple of days the girl dies.[3] The natives of Tumleo, an island off German New Guinea, efface the marks they have left on the ground where they sat, lest magic should be wrought on them thereby.[4] Before they leave a camping-place some of the natives of German New Guinea are careful to stab the ground thoroughly with spears, in order to prevent a sorcerer from making any use of a drop of sweat or any other personal remains which they may chance to leave behind.[5] We can now understand why it was a maxim with the Pythagoreans that in rising from bed you should smooth away the impression left by your body on the bed-clothes.[6] The rule was simply an old precaution against magic, forming part of a whole code of superstitious maxims which

[1] A. W. Howitt, "On Australian Medicine Men," *Journal of the Anthropological Institute*, xvi. (1887) pp. 26 *sq.* ; *id.*, *Native Tribes of South-East Australia*, p. 366.

[2] R. Brough Smyth, *Aborigines of Victoria*, i. 475.

[3] A. C. Haddon, *Head-hunters* (London, 1901), p. 202.

[4] M. J. Erdweg, "Die Bewohner der Insel Tumleo, Berlinhafen, Deutsch-Neu-Guinea," *Mitteilungen der an-thropologischen Gesellschaft in Wien*, xxxii. (1902) p. 287.

[5] K. Vetter, *Komm herüber und hilf uns! oder die Arbeit der Neuen Dettelsauer Mission*, Heft iii. (Barmen, 1898) p. 10.

[6] Jamblichus, *Adhortatio ad philosophiam*, 21 ; Plutarch, *Quaest. conviv.* viii. 7 ; Clement of Alexandria, *Strom.* v. 5, p. 661, ed. Potter. Compare Diogenes Laertius, *Vit. philos.* viii. 1. 17 ; Suidas, *s.v.* "Pythagoras."

antiquity fathered on Pythagoras, though doubtless they were familiar to the barbarous forefathers of the Greeks long before the time of that philosopher.[1] To ensure the good behaviour of an ally with whom they have just had a conference, the Basutos will cut and preserve the grass on which the ally sat during the interview.[2] Probably they regard the grass as a hostage for the observance of the treaty, since through it they could punish the man who sat on the grass if he should break faith. Moors who write on the sand are superstitiously careful to obliterate all the marks they made, never leaving a stroke or a dot in the sand when they have done writing.[3] Another of the so-called maxims of Pythagoras bade people in lifting a pot always to smooth away the imprint it left on the ashes.[4] So in Cambodia they say that when you lift a pot from the fire you should not set it down on the ashes; but that, if you must do so, you should be careful, in lifting the pot from the ashes, to efface the impression it has made. Otherwise they think that want will knock at your door.[5] But this seems to be an afterthought, devised to explain a rule of which the original meaning was forgotten. The old notion probably was that a magician could sympathetically injure any person who ate out of a pot by means of the impression which the pot had left on the ashes; or, to be more explicit, contagious magic was supposed to work through the impression of the pot to the pot itself, through the pot to the meat contained in it, and finally through the meat to the eater.

§ 4. *The Magician's Progress*

We have now concluded our examination of the general principles of sympathetic magic. The examples by which I have illustrated them have been drawn for the most part from what may be called private magic, that is from magical

---

[1] For detailed proof of this I may refer to my article, "Some popular Superstitions of the Ancients," *Folklore*, i. (1890) pp. 147 *sqq.*

[2] E. Casalis, *The Basutos*, p. 273.

[3] J. Richardson, *Travels in the Great Desert of Sahara* (London, 1848), ii. 65.

[4] Jamblichus, Plutarch, Clement of Alexandria, Diogenes Laertius, Suidas, *ll.cc.*

[5] É. Aymonier, "Notes sur les coutumes et croyances superstitieuses des Cambodgiens," *Cochinchine Fran-çaise: excursions et reconnaissances*, No. 16 (Saigon, 1883), p. 163.

rites and incantations practised for the benefit or the injury
of individuals.   But in savage society there is commonly to
be found in addition what we may call public magic, that is,
sorcery practised for the benefit of the whole community.
Wherever ceremonies of this sort are observed for the common
good, it is obvious that the magician ceases to be merely
a private practitioner and becomes to some extent a public
functionary.   The development of such a class of functionaries is of great importance for the political as well as the
religious evolution of society.   For when the welfare of the
tribe is supposed to depend on the performance of these
magical rites, the magician rises into a position of much
influence and repute, and may readily acquire the rank and
authority of a chief or king.   The profession accordingly
draws into its ranks some of the ablest and most ambitious
men of the tribe, because it holds out to them a prospect of
honour, wealth, and power such as hardly any other career
could offer.   The acuter minds perceive how easy it is to
dupe their weaker brother and to play on his superstition for
their own advantage.   Not that the sorcerer is always a
knave and impostor ; he is often sincerely convinced that he
really possesses those wonderful powers which the credulity
of his fellows ascribes to him.   But the more sagacious he
is, the more likely he is to see through the fallacies which
impose on duller wits.   Thus the ablest members of the
profession must tend to be more or less conscious deceivers ;
and it is just these men who in virtue of their superior ability
will generally come to the top and win for themselves
positions of the highest dignity and the most commanding
authority.   The pitfalls which beset the path of the professional sorcerer are many, and as a rule only the man of
coolest head and sharpest wit will be able to steer his way
through them safely.   For it must always be remembered
that every single profession and claim put forward by the
magician as such is false ; not one of them can be maintained
without deception, conscious or unconscious.   Accordingly
the sorcerer who sincerely believes in his own extravagant
pretensions is in far greater peril and is much more likely to
be cut short in his career than the deliberate impostor.   The
honest wizard always expects that his charms and incanta-

*who prac-
tises his
art for the
good of the
whole com-
munity,
enjoys
great in-
fluence and
may rise
to be a
chief or
king.*

tions will produce their supposed effect ; and when they fail, not only really, as they always do, but conspicuously and disastrously, as they often do, he is taken aback : he is not, like his knavish colleague, ready with a plausible excuse to account for the failure, and before he can find one he may be knocked on the head by his disappointed and angry employers.

Tendency of supreme power to fall into the hands of the ablest and most un- scrupulous men. The general result is that at this stage of social evolution the supreme power tends to fall into the hands of men of the keenest intelligence and the most unscrupulous character.   If we could balance the harm they do by their knavery against the benefits they confer by their superior sagacity, it might well be found that the good greatly out- weighed the evil.   For more mischief has probably been wrought in the world by honest fools in high places than by intelligent rascals.   Once your shrewd rogue has attained the height of his ambition, and has no longer any selfish end to further, he may, and often does, turn his talents, his experience, his resources, to the service of the public.   Many men who have been least scrupulous in the acquisition of power have been most beneficent in the use of it, whether the power they aimed at and won was that of wealth, political authority, or what not.   In the field of politics the wily intriguer, the ruthless victor, may end by being a wise and magnanimous ruler, blessed in his lifetime, lamented at his death, admired and applauded by posterity.   Such men, to take two of the most conspicuous instances, were Julius Caesar and Augustus.   But once a fool always a fool, and the greater the power in his hands the more disastrous is likely to be the use he makes of it.   The heaviest calamity in English history, the breach with America, might never have occurred if George the Third had not been an honest dullard.

The eleva- tion of magicians to power tends to substitute a monarchy for that primitive democracy, Thus, so far as the public profession of magic affected the constitution of savage society, it tended to place the control of affairs in the hands of the ablest man : it shifted the balance of power from the many to the one : it substi- tuted a monarchy for a democracy, or rather for an oligarchy of old men ; for in general the savage community is ruled, not by the whole body of adult males, but by a council of

elders. The change, by whatever causes produced, and
whatever the character of the early rulers, was on the whole
very beneficial. For the rise of monarchy appears to be an
essential condition of the emergence of mankind from savagery.
No human being is so hidebound by custom and tradition
as your democratic savage; in no state of society consequently is progress so slow and difficult. The old notion
that the savage is the freest of mankind is the reverse of the
truth. He is a slave, not indeed to a visible master, but to
the past, to the spirits of his dead forefathers, who haunt his
steps from birth to death, and rule him with a rod of iron.
What they did is the pattern of right, the unwritten law to
which he yields a blind unquestioning obedience. The least
possible scope is thus afforded to superior talent to change
old customs for the better. The ablest man is dragged
down by the weakest and dullest, who necessarily sets the
standard, since he cannot rise, while the other can fall. The
surface of such a society presents a uniform dead level, so
far as it is humanly possible to reduce the natural inequali-
ties, the immeasurable real differences of inborn capacity and
temper, to a false superficial appearance of equality. From
this low and stagnant condition of affairs, which demagogues
and dreamers in later times have lauded as the ideal state,
the Golden Age, of humanity, everything that helps to raise
society by opening a career to talent and proportioning the
degrees of authority to men's natural abilities, deserves to
be welcomed by all who have the real good of their fellows
at heart. Once these elevating influences have begun to
operate—and they cannot be for ever suppressed—the progress of civilisation becomes comparatively rapid. The rise
of one man to supreme power enables him to carry through
changes in a single lifetime which previously many generations might not have sufficed to effect; and if, as will often
happen, he is a man of intellect and energy above the
common, he will readily avail himself of the opportunity.
Even the whims and caprices of a tyrant may be of service
in breaking the chain of custom which lies so heavy on the
savage. And as soon as the tribe ceases to be swayed by
the timid and divided counsels of the elders, and yields to
the direction of a single strong and resolute mind, it

or rather oligarchy of old men, which is character-istic of savage society; and the rise of monarchy seems to be an essential condition of the emergence of mankind from savagery.

becomes formidable to its neighbours and enters on a career of aggrandisement, which at an early stage of history is often highly favourable to social, industrial, and intellectual progress. For extending its sway, partly by force of arms, partly by the voluntary submission of weaker tribes, the community soon acquires wealth and slaves, both of which, by relieving some classes from the perpetual struggle for a bare subsistence, afford them an opportunity of devoting themselves to that disinterested pursuit of knowledge which is the noblest and most powerful instrument to ameliorate the lot of man.

Intellectual progress dependent on economic progress, which is often furthered by conquest and empire.

Intellectual progress, which reveals itself in the growth of art and science and the spread of more liberal views, cannot be dissociated from industrial or economic progress, and that in its turn receives an immense impulse from conquest and empire. It is no mere accident that the most vehement outbursts of activity of the human mind have followed close on the heels of victory, and that the great conquering races of the world have commonly done most to advance, and spread civilisation, thus healing in peace the wounds they inflicted in war. The Babylonians, the Greeks, the Romans, the Arabs are our witnesses in the past : we may yet live to see a similar outburst in Japan. Nor, to remount the stream of history to its sources, is it an accident that all the first great strides towards civilisation have been made under despotic and theocratic governments, like those of Egypt, Babylon, and Peru, where the supreme ruler claimed and received the servile allegiance of his subjects in the double character of a king and a god. It is hardly too much to say that at this early epoch despotism is the best friend of humanity and, paradoxical as it may sound, of liberty. For after all there is more liberty in the best sense —liberty to think our own thoughts and to fashion our own destinies—under the most absolute despotism, the most grinding tyranny, than under the apparent freedom of savage life, where the individual's lot is cast from the cradle to the grave in the iron mould of hereditary custom.

Benefits rendered to civilisation by magic.

So far, therefore, as the public profession of magic has been one of the roads by which the ablest men have passed to supreme power, it has contributed to emancipate mankind from the thraldom of tradition and to elevate them into a larger, freer life, with a broader outlook on the world. This is no small service rendered to humanity. And when we remember further that in another direction magic has paved the way for science, we are forced to admit that if the black art has done much evil, it has also been the source of much good ; that if it is the child of error, it has yet been the mother of freedom and truth.

CHAPTER IV

MAGIC AND RELIGION

Magic like
science
postulates
the order
and uni-
formity of
nature ;
hence the
attraction
both of
magic and
of science,
which open
up a
boundless
vista to
those who
can pene-
trate to the
secret
springs of
nature. THE examples collected in the last chapter may suffice to illustrate the general principles of sympathetic magic in its two branches, to which we have given the names of Homoeopathic and Contagious respectively. In some cases of magic which have come before us we have seen that the operation of spirits is assumed, and that an attempt is made to win their favour by prayer and sacrifice. But these cases are on the whole exceptional ; they exhibit magic tinged and alloyed with religion.[1] Wherever sympathetic magic occurs in its pure unadulterated form, it assumes that in nature one event follows another necessarily and invariably without the intervention of any spiritual or personal agency. Thus its fundamental conception is identical with that of modern science ; underlying the whole system is a faith, implicit but real and firm, in the order and uniformity of nature. The magician does not doubt that the same causes will always produce the same effects, that the performance of the proper ceremony, accompanied by the appropriate spell, will inevitably be attended by the desired results, unless, indeed, his incantations should chance to be thwarted and foiled by the more potent charms of another sorcerer. He supplicates no higher power : he sues the favour of no fickle and wayward

---

[1] Malay magic in particular is deeply tinctured with a belief in spirits, to whom the magician appeals by kindly words and small gifts of food, drink, and even money. See R. J. Wilkinson, *Malay Beliefs* (London and Leyden, 1906), pp. 67 *sqq.* Here, therefore, religion is encroaching on magic, as it might naturally be expected to do in a race so comparatively advanced as the Malays.

being : he abases himself before no awful deity. Yet his power, great as he believes it to be, is by no means arbitrary and unlimited. He can wield it only so long as he strictly conforms to the rules of his art, or to what may be called the laws of nature as conceived by him. To neglect these rules, to break these laws in the smallest particular is to incur failure, and may even expose the unskilful practitioner himself to the utmost peril. If he claims a sovereignty over nature, it is a constitutional sovereignty rigorously limited in its scope and exercised in exact conformity with ancient usage. Thus the analogy between the magical and the scientific conceptions of the world is close. In both of them the succession of events is perfectly regular and certain, being determined by immutable laws, the operation of which can be foreseen and calculated precisely ; the elements of caprice, of chance, and of accident are banished from the course of nature. Both of them open up a seemingly boundless vista of possibilities to him who knows the causes of things and can touch the secret springs that set in motion the vast and intricate mechanism of the world. Hence the strong attraction which magic and science alike have exercised on the human mind ; hence the powerful stimulus that both have given to the pursuit of knowledge. They lure the weary enquirer, the footsore seeker, on through the wilderness of disappointment in the present by their endless promises of the future : they take him up to the top of an exceeding high mountain and shew him, beyond the dark clouds and rolling mists at his feet, a vision of the celestial city, far off, it may be, but radiant with unearthly splendour, bathed in the light of dreams.

The fatal flaw of magic lies not in its general assumption of a sequence of events determined by law, but in its total misconception of the nature of the particular laws which govern that sequence. If we analyse the various cases of sympathetic magic which have been passed in review in the preceding pages, and which may be taken as fair samples of the bulk, we shall find, as I have already indicated, that they are all mistaken applications of one or other of two great fundamental laws of thought, namely, the association of ideas by similarity and the associa-

The fatal flaw of magic lies not in its general assumption of the uniformity of nature, but in its misapprehension of the particular laws which govern the

tion of ideas by contiguity in space or time. A mistaken association of similar ideas produces homoeopathic or imitative magic : a mistaken association of contiguous ideas produces contagious magic. The principles of association are excellent in themselves, and indeed absolutely essential to the working of the human mind. Legitimately applied they yield science ; illegitimately applied they yield magic, the bastard sister of science. It is therefore a truism, almost a tautology, to say that all magic is necessarily false and barren ; for were it ever to become true and fruitful, it would no longer be magic but science. From the earliest times man has been engaged in a search for general rules whereby to turn the order of natural phenomena to his own advantage, and in the long search he has scraped together a great hoard of such maxims, some of them golden and some of them mere dross. The true or golden rules constitute the body of applied science which we call the arts ; the false are magic.

If magic is thus next of kin to science, we have still to enquire how it stands related to religion. But the view we take of that relation will necessarily be coloured by the idea which we have formed of the nature of religion itself ; hence a writer may reasonably be expected to define his conception of religion before he proceeds to investigate its relation to magic. There is probably no subject in the world about which opinions differ so much as the nature of religion, and to frame a definition of it which would satisfy every one must

Religion
defined :
it is a pro-
pitiation or
concilia-
tion of
super-
human
powers
which are
believed to
control
nature and
man.
Thus reli-
gion com-

obviously be impossible. All that a writer can do is, first, to say clearly what he means by religion, and afterwards to employ the word consistently in that sense throughout his work. By religion, then, I understand a propitiation or conciliation of powers superior to man which are believed to direct and control the course of nature and of human life.[1] Thus defined, religion consists of two elements, a theoretical and a practical, namely, a belief in powers higher than man and an attempt to propitiate or please them. Of the two, belief clearly comes first, since we must believe in the existence of a divine being before we can attempt to please

---

[1] " *Religio est, quae superioris cujus-dam naturae, quam divinam vocant, curam caerimoniamque adfert,*" Cicero, *De inventione,* ii. 161.

him.   But unless the belief leads to a corresponding practice, *prises two elements, a theoretical*
it is not a religion but merely a theology ; in the language *and a practical,*
of St. James, " faith, if it hath not works, is dead, being *or faith and works,*
alone." [1]   In other words, no man is religious who does not *and it does not exist*
govern his conduct in some measure by the fear or love *without both. But*
of God.[2]   On the other hand, mere practice, divested of all *religious practice*
religious belief, is also not religion.   Two men may behave *need not consist in*
in exactly the same way, and yet one of them may be *ritual ; it may con-*
religious and the other not.   If the one acts from the love or *sist in ethical*
fear of God, he is religious ; if the other acts from the love *conduct, if that is*
or fear of man, he is moral or immoral according as his *believed to be well-*
behaviour comports or conflicts with the general good. *pleasing to the deity.*
Hence belief and practice or, in theological language, faith
and works are equally essential to religion, which cannot
exist without both of them.   But it is not necessary that
religious practice should always take the form of a ritual ;
that is, it need not consist in the offering of sacrifice, the
recitation of prayers, and other outward ceremonies.   Its
aim is to please the deity, and if the deity is one who
delights in charity and mercy and purity more than in
oblations of blood, the chanting of hymns, and the fumes of
incense, his worshippers will best please him, not by prostrating themselves before him, by intoning his praises, and by
filling his temples with costly gifts, but by being pure and
merciful and charitable towards men, for in so doing they
will imitate, so far as human infirmity allows, the perfections
of the divine nature.   It was this ethical side of religion
which the Hebrew prophets, inspired with a noble ideal of
God's goodness and holiness, were never weary of inculcating.
Thus Micah says : [3] " He hath shewed thee, O man, what is
good ; and what doth the Lord require of thee, but to do
justly, and to love mercy, and to walk humbly with thy
God ? "   And at a later time much of the force by which

---

[1] James ii. 17.
[2] " Piety is not a religion, though it is the soul of all religions.   A man has not a religion simply by having pious inclinations, any more than he has a country simply by having philanthropy. A man has not a country until he is a citizen in a state, until he undertakes to follow and uphold certain laws, to

obey certain magistrates, and to adopt certain ways of living and acting. Religion is neither a theology nor a theosophy ; it is more than all this ; it is a discipline, a law, a yoke, an indis- soluble engagement" (Joubert, quoted by Matthew Arnold, *Essays in Criticism*, First Series, London, 1898, p. 288).
[3] Micah vi. 8.

Christianity conquered the world was drawn from the same high conception of God's moral nature and the duty laid on men of conforming themselves to it. "Pure religion and undefiled," says St. James, "before God and the Father is this, To visit the fatherless and widows in their affliction, and to keep himself unspotted from the world."[1]

By assuming the order of nature to be elastic or variable religion is opposed in principle alike to magic and to science, both of which assume the order of nature to be rigid and invariable. But if religion involves, first, a belief in superhuman beings who rule the world, and, second, an attempt to win their favour, it clearly assumes that the course of nature is to some extent elastic or variable, and that we can persuade or induce the mighty beings who control it to deflect, for our benefit, the current of events from the channel in which they would otherwise flow. Now this implied elasticity or variability of nature is directly opposed to the principles of magic as well as of science, both of which assume that the processes of nature are rigid and invariable in their operation, and that they can as little be turned from their course by persuasion and entreaty as by threats and intimidation. The distinction between the two conflicting views of the universe turns on their answer to the crucial question, Are the forces which govern the world conscious and personal, or unconscious and impersonal? Religion, as a conciliation of the superhuman powers, assumes the former member of the alternative. For all conciliation implies that the being conciliated is a conscious or personal agent, that his conduct is in some measure uncertain, and that he can be prevailed upon to vary it in the desired direction by a judicious appeal to his interests, his appetites, or his emotions. Conciliation is never employed towards things which are regarded as inanimate, nor towards persons whose behaviour in the particular circumstances is known to be determined with absolute certainty. Thus in so far as religion assumes the world to be directed by conscious agents who may be turned from their purpose by persuasion, it stands in fundamental antagonism to magic as well as to science, both of which take for granted that the course of nature is determined, not by the passions or caprice of personal beings, but by the operation of immutable laws acting mechanically.[2] In

[1] James i. 27.
[2] The opposition of principle between magic and religion is well brought out by Sir A. C. Lyall in his

magic, indeed, the assumption is only implicit, but in science it is explicit. It is true that magic often deals with spirits, which are personal agents of the kind assumed by religion ; but whenever it does so in its proper form, it treats them exactly in the same fashion as it treats inanimate agents, that is, it constrains or coerces instead of conciliating or propitiating them as religion would do. Thus it assumes that all personal beings, whether human or divine, are in the last resort subject to those impersonal forces which control all things, but which nevertheless can be turned to account by any one who knows how to manipulate them by the appropriate ceremonies and spells. In ancient Egypt, for example, the magicians claimed the power of compelling even the highest gods to do their bidding, and actually threatened them with destruction in case of disobedience.[1] Sometimes, without going quite so far as that, the wizard declared that he would scatter the bones of Osiris or reveal his sacred legend, if the god proved contumacious.[2] Similarly in India at the present day the great Hindoo trinity itself of Brahma, Vishnu, and Siva is subject to the sorcerers, who, by means of their spells, exercise such an ascendency over the mightiest deities, that these are bound submissively to execute on earth below, or in heaven above, whatever commands their masters the magicians may please to issue.[3] There is a saying everywhere current in

Claim of Egyptian and Indian magicians to control the gods.

Asiatic Studies, First Series (London, 1899), i. 99 *sqq.* It is also insisted on by Mr. F. B. Jevons in his *Introduction to the History of Religion* (London, 1896). The distinction is clearly apprehended and sharply maintained by Professor H. Oldenberg in his notable book *Die Religion des Veda* (Berlin, 1894) ; see especially pp. 58 *sq.*, 311 *sqq.*, 476 *sqq.* Lord Avebury has courteously pointed out to me that the fundamental difference between magic and religion was dwelt on by him many years ago. See his *Origin of Civilisation* (London, 1870), pp. 116, 164 *sq.*, and the Preface to the sixth edition of that work (London, 1902), p. vi. I am glad to find myself in agreement with Lord Avebury on this subject, and only regret that in preparing my second edition I was unaware that the view here taken has the support of his high authority. When I wrote this book originally I failed to realise the extent of the opposition between magic and religion, because I had not formed a clear general conception of the nature of religion, and was disposed to class magic loosely under it.

[1] A. Wiedemann, *Die Religion der alten Ägypter* (Münster i. W., 1890), pp. 142-145, 148 ; G. Maspero, *Histoire ancienne des peuples de l'Orient classique: les origines* (Paris, 1895), pp. 212 *sq.*

[2] Augustine, *De civitate Dei*, x. 11, quoting Porphyry.

[3] J. A. Dubois, *Mœurs, institutions et cérémonies des peuples de l'Inde* (Paris, 1825), ii. 60 *sqq.*

India : " The whole universe is subject to the gods ; the gods are subject to the spells (*mantras*); the spells to the Brahmans; therefore the Brahmans are our gods." [1]

Hostility of religion to magic in history.

This radical conflict of principle between magic and religion sufficiently explains the relentless hostility with which in history the priest has often pursued the magician. The haughty self-sufficiency of the magician, his arrogant demeanour towards the higher powers, and his unabashed claim to exercise a sway like theirs could not but revolt the priest, to whom, with his awful sense of the divine majesty, and his humble prostration in presence of it, such claims and such a demeanour must have appeared an impious and blasphemous usurpation of prerogatives that belong to God alone. And sometimes, we may suspect, lower motives concurred to whet the edge of the priest's hostility. He professed to be the proper medium, the true intercessor between God and man, and no doubt his interests as well as his feelings were often injured by a rival practitioner, who preached a surer and smoother road to fortune than the rugged and slippery path of divine favour.

This hostility comparatively late : at an earlier time magic co-operated, and was partly confused, with religion.

Yet this antagonism, familiar as it is to us, seems to have made its appearance comparatively late in the history of religion. At an earlier stage [2] the functions of priest and sorcerer were often combined or, to speak perhaps more correctly, were not yet differentiated from each other. To serve his purpose man wooed the good-will of gods or spirits by prayer and sacrifice, while at the same time he had recourse to ceremonies and forms of words which he hoped would of themselves bring about the desired result without the help of god or devil. In short, he performed religious and magical rites simultaneously; he uttered prayers and incantations almost in the same breath, knowing or

[1] Monier Williams, *Religious Thought and Life in India* (London, 1883), pp. 201 *sq.*

[2] To prevent misconception I would ask the reader to observe that the earlier stage here spoken of, in which magic is confused with religion, is not, in my opinion, the earliest of all, having been preceded by a still earlier stage in which magic existed alone. See below, pp. 233 *sqq.* On my view, the evolution of thought on this subject has passed through three stages : first, a stage in which magic existed without religion ; second, a stage in which religion, having arisen, co-operated, and was to some extent confused, with magic ; and third, a stage in which, the radical difference of principle between the two having been recognised, their relation was that of open hostility.

recking little of the theoretical inconsistency of his behaviour, so long as by hook or crook he contrived to get what he wanted. Instances of this fusion or confusion of magic with religion have already met us in the practices of Melanesians and of other peoples.[1] So far as the Melanesians are concerned, the general confusion cannot be better described than in the words of Dr. R. H. Codrington :—" That invisible power which is believed by the natives to cause all such effects as transcend their conception of the regular course of nature, and to reside in spiritual beings, whether in the spiritual part of living men or in the ghosts of the dead, being imparted by them to their names and to various things that belong to them, such as stones, snakes, and indeed objects of all sorts, is that generally known as *mana*. Without some understanding of this it is impossible to understand the religious beliefs and practices of the Melanesians ; and this again is the active force in all they do and believe to be done in magic, white or black. By means of this men are able to control or direct the forces of nature, to make rain or sunshine, wind or calm, to cause sickness or remove it, to know what is far off in time and space, to bring good luck and prosperity, or to blast and curse." " By whatever name it is called, it is the belief in this supernatural power, and in the efficacy of the various means by which spirits and ghosts can be induced to exercise it for the benefit of men, that is the foundation of the rites and practices which can be called religious ; and it is from the same belief that everything which may be called Magic and Witchcraft draws its origin. Wizards, doctors, weather - mongers, prophets, diviners, dreamers, all alike, everywhere in the islands, work by this power. There are many of these who may be said to exercise their art as a profession ; they get their property and influence in this way. Every considerable village or settlement is sure to have some one who can control the weather and the waves, some one who knows how to treat sickness, some one who can work mischief with various charms. There may be one whose skill extends to all these branches ; but generally one man knows how to do one thing and one another. This various knowledge is handed down from father

Confusion of magic and religion in Melanesia.

---

[1] See above, pp. 72, 77 *sq.*, 130, 163 *sq.*

to son, from uncle to sister's son, in the same way as is the knowledge of the rites and methods of sacrifice and prayer; and very often the same man who knows the sacrifice knows also the making of the weather, and of charms for many purposes besides. But as there is no order of priests, there is also no order of magicians or medicine-men. Almost every man of consideration knows how to approach some ghost or spirit, and has some secret of occult practices."[1]

Confusion of magic and religion in ancient India.

The same confusion of magic and religion has survived among peoples that have risen to higher levels of culture. It was rife in ancient India and ancient Egypt; it is by no means extinct among European peasantry at the present day. With regard to ancient India we are told by an eminent Sanscrit scholar that "the sacrificial ritual at the earliest period of which we have detailed information is pervaded with practices that breathe the spirit of the most primitive magic."[2] Again, the same writer observes that "the ritual of the very sacrifices for which the metrical prayers were composed is described in the other Vedic texts as saturated from beginning to end with magical practices which were to be carried out by the sacrificial priests." In particular he tells us that the rites celebrated on special occasions, such as marriage, initiation, and the anointment of a king, "are complete models of magic of every kind, and in every case the forms of magic employed bear the stamp of the highest antiquity."[3] Speaking of the sacrifices prescribed in the *Brâhmaṇas*, Professor Sylvain Lévi says: "The sacrifice has thus all the characteristics of a magical operation, independent of the divinities, effective by its own energy, and capable of producing evil as well as good. It is hardly distinguished from magic strictly so called, except by being regular and obligatory; it can easily be adapted

---

[1] R. H. Codrington, *The Melanesians*, pp. 191 *sq.* The word *mana* is Polynesian as well as Melanesian. In the Maori language it means "authority," especially "supernatural power," "divine authority," "having qualities which ordinary persons or things do not possess." See E. Tregear, *Maori-Polynesian Comparative Dictionary* (Wellington, N.Z., 1891), p. 203. Compare R. Taylor, *Te Ika A Maui*, or *New Zealand and its Inhabitants*,[2] p. 184, "the *mana*, virtue of the god."

[2] H. Oldenberg, *Die Religion des Veda*, p. 59.

[3] H. Oldenberg, *op. cit.* p. 477. For particular examples of the blending of magical with religious ritual in ancient India see pp. 311 *sqq.*, 369 *sq.*, 476 *sqq.*, 522 *sq.* of the same work.

to different objects, but it exists of necessity, independently
of circumstances. That is the sole fairly clear line of
distinction which can be drawn between the two domains;
in point of fact they are so intimately interfused with each
other that the same class of works treats of both matters.
The *Sâmavidhâna Brâhmana* is a real handbook of incantations and sorcery; the *Adbhuta Brâhmana*, which forms a
section of the *Ṣaḍviṃça Brâhmana*, has the same character." [1]
Similarly Professor M. Bloomfield writes: " Even witchcraft
is part of the religion; it has penetrated and has become
intimately blended with the holiest Vedic rites; the broad
current of popular religion and superstition has infiltrated
itself through numberless channels into the higher religion
that is presented by the Brahman priests, and it may be
presumed that the priests were neither able to cleanse their
own religious beliefs from the mass of folk-belief with which
it was surrounded, nor is it at all likely that they found it
in their interest to do so." [2]   Again, in the introduction to
his translation of the *Kausika Sūtra*, Dr. W. Caland
observes: " He who has been wont to regard the ancient
Hindoos as a highly civilised people, famed for their
philosophical systems, their dramatic poetry, their epic lays,
will be surprised when he makes the acquaintance of their
magical ritual, and will perceive that hitherto he has known
the old Hindoo people from one side only. He will find
that he here stumbles on the lowest strata of Vedic culture,
and will be astonished at the agreement between the magic
ritual of the old Vedas and the shamanism of the so-called
savage. If we drop the peculiar Hindoo expressions and
technical terms, and imagine a shaman instead of a Brahman,
we could almost fancy that we have before us a magical
book belonging to one of the tribes of North American red-
skins." [3]   Some good authorities hold that the very name of
Brahman is derived from *brahman*, " a magical spell"; so
that, if they are right, the Brahman would seem to have
been a magician before he was a priest.[4]

[1] S. Lévi, *La Doctrine du sacrifice
dans les Brâhmaṇas* (Paris, 1898), p.
129.
[2] M. Bloomfield, *Hymns of the
Atharva-Veda*, pp. xlv. *sq.* (*Sacred*

Books of the East, vol. xlii.).
[3] W. Caland, *Altindisches Zauberritual*, p. ix.
[4] O. Schrader, *Reallexikon der indo-
germanischen Altertumskunde* (Stras-

Confusion of magic and religion in ancient Egypt.

Speaking of the importance of magic in the East, and especially in Egypt, Professor Maspero remarks that " we ought not to attach to the word magic the degrading idea which it almost inevitably calls up in the mind of a modern. Ancient magic was the very foundation of religion. The faithful who desired to obtain some favour from a god had no chance of succeeding except by laying hands on the deity, and this arrest could only be effected by means of a certain number of rites, sacrifices, prayers, and chants, which the god himself had revealed, and which obliged him to do what was demanded of him." [1] According to another distinguished Egyptologist " the belief that there are words and actions by which man can influence all the powers of nature and all living things, from animals up to gods, was inextricably interwoven with everything the Egyptians did and everything they left undone. Above all, the whole system of burial and of the worship of the dead is completely dominated by it. The wooden puppets which relieved the dead man from toil, the figures of the maidservants who baked bread for him, the sacrificial formulas by the recitation of which food was procured for him, what are these and all the similar practices but magic? And as men cannot help themselves without magic, so neither can the gods ; the gods also wear amulets to protect themselves, and use magic spells to constrain each other." [2] " The whole doctrine of magic," says Professor Wiedemann, " formed in the valley of the Nile, not a part of superstition, but an essential constituent of religious faith, which to a

burg, 1901), pp. 637 *sq.* In ancient Arabia the *kâhin* (etymologically equivalent to the Hebrew *kôhen,* " priest ") seems to have been rather a soothsayer than a priest. See J. Wellhausen, *Reste arabischen Heidentums* [2] (Berlin, 1897), pp. 134, 143. The confusion of magic with religion, of spell with prayer, may also be detected in the incantations employed by Toda sorcerers at the present day. See W. H. R. Rivers, *The Todas,* pp. 272 *sq.* : " The formulae of magic and of the dairy ritual are of the same nature, though the differentiation between the sorcerer and the priest who

use them is even clearer than that between the sorcerer and the medicineman. It is probable that the names of the gods with the characteristic formulae of the prayer are later additions to the magical incantation ; that at some time the sorcerer has added the names of the most important of his deities to the spells and charms which at one time were thought to be sufficient for his purpose."

[1] G. Maspero, *Études de mythologie et d'archéologie égyptienne* (Paris, 1893), i. 106.

[2] A. Erman, *Ägypten und ägyptisches Leben im Altertum,* p. 471.

great extent rested directly on magic, and always remained most closely bound up with it." [1]   But though we can perceive the union of discrepant elements in the faith and practice of the ancient Egyptians, it would be rash to assume that the people themselves did so.   " Egyptian religion," says the same scholar, " was not one and homogeneous ; it was compounded of the most heterogeneous elements, which seemed to the Egyptian to be all equally justified.   He did not care whether a doctrine or a myth belonged to what, in modern scholastic phraseology, we should call faith or superstition ; it was indifferent to him whether we should rank it as religion or magic, as worship or sorcery.   All such classifications were foreign to the Egyptian.   To him no one doctrine seemed more or less justified than another. Nay, he went so far as to allow the most flagrant contradictions to stand peaceably side by side." [2]

Among the ignorant classes of modern Europe the same confusion of ideas, the same mixture of religion and magic, crops up in various forms.   Thus we are told that in France " the majority of the peasants still believe that the priest possesses a secret and irresistible power over the elements. By reciting certain prayers which he alone knows and has the right to utter, yet for the utterance of which he must afterwards demand absolution, he can, on an occasion of pressing danger, arrest or reverse for a moment the action of the eternal laws of the physical world.   The winds, the storms, the hail, and the rain are at his command and obey his will.   The fire also is subject to him, and the flames of a conflagration are extinguished at his word." [3]   For example, French peasants used to be, perhaps are still, persuaded that the priests could celebrate, with certain special rites, a " Mass of the Holy Spirit," of which the efficacy was so miraculous that it never met with any opposition from the divine will ;

Confusion of magic and religion in modern Europe.

Mass of the Holy Spirit.

---

[1] A. Wiedemann, *Die Religion der alten Ägypter* (Münster i. W., 1890), p. 154.

[2] A. Wiedemann, " Ein altägyptischer Weltschöpfungsmythus," *Am Urquell*, N.F. ii. (1898) pp. 95 *sq.*

[3] J. Lecœur, *Esquisses du Bocage Normand* (Condé-sur-Noireau, 1883-

1887), ii. 78.   In Beauce and Perche it was especially conflagrations caused by lightning which the priest was supposed to extinguish by the recitation of certain secret formulas.   There was a regular expression for this procedure, namely, " barring the fire."   See F. Chapiseau, *Le Folk-lore de la Beauce et du Perche*, i. 216.

God was forced to grant whatever was asked of Him in this form, however rash and importunate might be the petition. No idea of impiety or irreverence attached to the rite in the minds of those who, in some of the great extremities of life, sought by this singular means to take the kingdom of heaven by storm. The secular priests generally refused to say the "Mass of the Holy Spirit"; but the monks, especially the Capuchin friars, had the reputation of yielding with less scruple to the entreaties of the anxious and distressed.[1] In the constraint thus supposed by Catholic peasantry to be laid by the priest upon the deity we seem to have an exact counterpart of the power which, as we saw, the ancient Egyptians ascribed to their magicians.[2] Again, to take another example, in many villages of Provence the priest is still reputed to possess the faculty of averting storms. It is not every priest who enjoys this reputation; and in some villages, when a change of pastors takes place, the parishioners are eager to learn whether the new incumbent has the power (*pouder*), as they call it. At the first sign of a heavy storm they put him to the proof by inviting him to exorcise the threatening clouds; and if the result answers to their hopes, the new shepherd is assured of the sympathy and respect of his flock. In some parishes, where the reputation of the curate in this respect stood higher than that of his rector, the relations between the two have been so strained in consequence that the bishop has had to translate the rector to another benefice.[3] Again, Gascon peasants believe that to revenge themselves on their enemies bad men will sometimes induce a priest to say a mass called the Mass of Saint Sécaire. Very few priests know this mass, and three-fourths of those who do know it would not say it for love or money. None but wicked priests dare to perform the gruesome ceremony, and you may be quite sure that they will have a very heavy account to render for it at the last day. No curate or bishop, not even the archbishop of

Mass of
Saint
Sécaire.

---

[1] Amélie Bosquet, *La Normandie romanesque et merveilleuse* (Paris and Rouen, 1845), p. 308.

[2] See above, p. 225.

[3] L. J. B. Bérenger-Féraud, *Superstitions et survivances* (Paris, 1896),

i. 455 *sq.*, iii. 217 *sq.*, 222 *sqq.* Compare *id.*, *Reminiscences populaires de la Provence* (Paris, 1885), pp. 288 *sqq.*; D. Monnier, *Traditions populaires comparées* (Paris, 1854), pp. 31 *sqq.*

Auch, can pardon them ; that right belongs to the pope of
Rome alone.   The Mass of Saint Sécaire may be said only
in a ruined or deserted church, where owls mope and hoot,
where bats flit in the gloaming, where gypsies lodge of
nights, and where toads squat under the desecrated altar.
Thither the bad priest comes by night with his light o' love,
and at the first stroke of eleven he begins to mumble the
mass backwards, and ends just as the clocks are knelling
the midnight hour.   His leman acts as clerk.   The host he
blesses is black and has three points ; he consecrates no
wine, but instead he drinks the water of a well into which
the body of an unbaptized infant has been flung.   He makes
the sign of the cross, but it is on the ground and with his
left foot.   And many other things he does which no good
Christian could look upon without being struck blind and
deaf and dumb for the rest of his life.   But the man for
whom the mass is said withers away little by little, and
nobody can say what is the matter with him ; even the
doctors can make nothing of it.   They do not know that he
is slowly dying of the Mass of Saint Sécaire.[1]

Yet though magic is thus found to fuse and amalgamate
with religion in many ages and in many lands, there are
some grounds for thinking that this fusion is not primitive,
and that there was a time when man trusted to magic alone
for the satisfaction of such wants as transcended his immediate animal cravings.   In the first place a consideration
of the fundamental notions of magic and religion may incline
us to surmise that magic is older than religion in the history
of humanity.   We have seen that on the one hand magic is
nothing but a mistaken application of the very simplest and
most elementary processes of the mind, namely the association of ideas by virtue of resemblance or contiguity ; and
that on the other hand religion assumes the operation of conscious or personal agents, superior to man, behind the visible
screen of nature.   Obviously the conception of personal
agents is more complex than a simple recognition of the
similarity or contiguity of ideas ; and a theory which
assumes that the course of nature is determined by conscious

*The early
confusion
of magic
with
religion
was prob-
ably pre-
ceded by a
still earlier
phase of
thought,
when
magic
existed
without
religion.*

[1] J. F. Bladé, *Quatorze superstitions populaires de la Gascogne* (Agen, 1883),
pp. 16 *sq.*

agents is more abstruse and recondite, and requires for its apprehension a far higher degree of intelligence and reflection, than the view that things succeed each other simply by reason of their contiguity or resemblance. The very beasts associate the ideas of things that are like each other or that have been found together in their experience; and they could hardly survive for a day if they ceased to do so. But who attributes to the animals a belief that the phenomena of nature are worked by a multitude of invisible animals or by one enormous and prodigiously strong animal behind the scenes? It is probably no injustice to the brutes to assume that the honour of devising a theory of this latter sort must be reserved for human reason. Thus, if magic be deduced immediately from elementary processes of reasoning, and be, in fact, an error into which the mind falls almost spontaneously, while religion rests on conceptions which the merely animal intelligence can hardly be supposed to have yet attained to, it becomes probable that magic arose before religion in the evolution of our race, and that man essayed to bend nature to his wishes by the sheer force of spells and enchantments before he strove to coax and mollify a coy, capricious, or irascible deity by the soft insinuation of prayer and sacrifice.

Among the Australian aborigines magic is universal, but religion almost unknown.

The conclusion which we have thus reached deductively from a consideration of the fundamental ideas of religion and magic is confirmed inductively by the observation that among the aborigines of Australia, the rudest savages as to whom we possess accurate information, magic is universally practised, whereas religion in the sense of a propitiation or conciliation of the higher powers seems to be nearly unknown. Roughly speaking, all men in Australia are magicians, but not one is a priest; everybody fancies he can influence his fellows or the course of nature by sympathetic magic, but nobody dreams of propitiating gods by prayer and sacrifice.[1]

Magic is probably older than religion, and faith in it is, still universal

But if in the most backward state of human society now known to us we find magic thus conspicuously present and religion conspicuously absent, may we not reasonably conjecture that the civilised races of the world have also at some period of their history passed through a similar in-

[1] For the evidence see my *Totemism and Exogamy*, vol. i. pp. 141 *sqq.*

tellectual phase, that they attempted to force the great among the
powers of nature to do their pleasure before they thought ignorant
of courting their favour by offerings and prayer—in short stitious.
that, just as on the material side of human culture there
has everywhere been an Age of Stone, so on the intellectual
side there has everywhere been an Age of Magic?[1]   There
are reasons for answering this question in the affirmative.
When we survey the existing races of mankind from Greenland to Tierra del Fuego, or from Scotland to Singapore,
we observe that they are distinguished one from the other
by a great variety of religions, and that these distinctions
are not, so to speak, merely coterminous with the broad
distinctions of race, but descend into the minuter sub-
divisions of states and commonwealths, nay, that they
honeycomb the town, the village, and even the family, so
that the surface of society all over the world is cracked
and seamed, sapped and mined with rents and fissures
and yawning crevasses opened up by the disintegrating
influence of religious dissension.   Yet when we have
penetrated through these differences, which affect mainly
the intelligent and thoughtful part of the community, we
shall find underlying them all a solid stratum of intellectual
agreement among the dull, the weak, the ignorant, and the
superstitious, who constitute, unfortunately, the vast majority
of mankind.   One of the great achievements of the nineteenth century was to run shafts down into this low mental
stratum in many parts of the world, and thus to discover
its substantial identity everywhere.   It is beneath our feet
—and not very far beneath them—here in Europe at the
present day, and it crops up on the surface in the heart of
the Australian wilderness and wherever the advent of a
higher civilisation has not crushed it under ground.   This
universal faith, this truly Catholic creed, is a belief in the

---

[1] The suggestion has been made by
Prof. H. Oldenberg (*Die Religion des
Veda*, p. 59), who seems, however, to
regard a belief in spirits as part of the
raw material of magic. If the view
which I have put forward tentatively
is correct, faith in magic is probably
older than a belief in spirits. The
same view as to the priority of magic
to religion, and apparently also as to
the absence of spirits from primitive
magic, was held by Hegel. It was
not until long after the discussion in
the text had been written that I became aware that my conclusions had
been to a large extent anticipated by
the German philosopher. See Appendix at the end of this volume.

efficacy of magic.   While religious systems differ not only
in different countries, but in the same country in different
ages, the system of sympathetic magic remains everywhere
and at all times substantially alike in its principles and
practice.   Among the ignorant and superstitious classes of
modern Europe it is very much what it was thousands of
years ago in Egypt and India, and what it now is among
the lowest savages surviving in the remotest corners of the
world.   If the test of truth lay in a show of hands or a
counting of heads, the system of magic might appeal, with
far more reason than the Catholic Church, to the proud
motto, " *Quod semper, quod ubique, quod ab omnibus,*" as the
sure and certain credential of its own infallibility.

Latent
superstition
a danger to
civilisation.
　　　　It is not our business here to consider what bearing the
permanent existence of such a solid layer of savagery
beneath the surface of society, and unaffected by the superficial changes of religion and culture, has upon the future of
humanity.   The dispassionate observer, whose studies have
led him to plumb its depths, can hardly regard it otherwise
than as a standing menace to civilisation.[1]   We seem to
move on a thin crust which may at any moment be rent by
the subterranean forces slumbering below.   From time to
time a hollow murmur underground or a sudden spirt of
flame into the air tells of what is going on beneath our feet.
Now and then the polite world is startled by a paragraph in
a newspaper which tells how in Scotland an image has been
found stuck full of pins for the purpose of killing an
obnoxious laird or minister, how a woman has been slowly
roasted to death as a witch in Ireland, or how a girl has
been murdered and chopped up in Russia to make those
candles of human tallow by whose light thieves hope to
pursue their midnight trade unseen.[2]   But whether the
influences that make for further progress, or those that
threaten to undo what has already been accomplished, will

---

[1] After a visit to the ruined Greek
temples of Paestum, whose beauty and
splendour impressed him all the more
by contrast with the savagery of the
surrounding peasantry, Renan wrote :
"*J'ai tremblé pour la civilisation, en la
voyant si limitée, assise sur une faible
assiette, reposant sur si peu d'individus*

dans le pays même où elle est regnante."
See E. Renan et M. Berthelot, *Correspondance* (Paris, 1898), pp. 75 *sq.*

[2] See above, pp. 68 *sq.*; "The Witch-
burning at Clonmel," *Folklore,* vi.
(1895) pp. 373-384 ; F. S. Krauss,
*Volksglaube und religiöser Brauch der
Südslaven,* pp. 144 *sqq.*

ultimately prevail; whether the impulsive energy of the minority or the dead weight of the majority of mankind will prove the stronger force to carry us up to higher heights or to sink us into lower depths, are questions rather for the sage, the moralist, and the statesman, whose eagle vision scans the future, than for the humble student of the present and the past. Here we are only concerned to ask how far the uniformity, the universality, and the permanence of a belief in magic, compared with the endless variety and the shifting character of religious creeds, raises a presumption that the former represents a ruder and earlier phase of the human mind, through which all the races of mankind have passed or are passing on their way to religion and science.

If an Age of Religion has thus everywhere, as I venture to surmise, been preceded by an Age of Magic, it is natural that we should enquire what causes have led mankind, or rather a portion of them, to abandon magic as a principle of faith and practice and to betake themselves to religion instead. When we reflect upon the multitude, the variety, and the complexity of the facts to be explained, and the scantiness of our information regarding them, we shall be ready to acknowledge that a full and satisfactory solution of so profound a problem is hardly to be hoped for, and that the most we can do in the present state of our knowledge is to hazard a more or less plausible conjecture. With all due diffidence, then, I would suggest that a tardy recognition of the inherent falsehood and barrenness of magic set the more thoughtful part of mankind to cast about for a truer theory of nature and a more fruitful method of turning her resources to account. The shrewder intelligences must in time have come to perceive that magical ceremonies and incantations did not really effect the results which they were designed to produce, and which the majority of their simpler fellows still believed that they did actually produce. This great discovery of the inefficacy of magic must have wrought a radical though probably slow revolution in the minds of those who had the sagacity to make it. The discovery amounted to this, that men for the first time recognised their inability to manipulate at pleasure certain natural forces which hitherto they had believed to be completely within

The change from magic to religion may have been brought about by the discovery of the inefficacy of magic.

their control.   It was a confession of human ignorance and
weakness.   Man saw that he had taken for causes what
were no causes, and that all his efforts to work by means of
these imaginary causes had been vain.   His painful toil had
been wasted, his curious ingenuity had been squandered to
no purpose.   He had been pulling at strings to which
nothing was attached ; he had been marching, as he thought,
straight to the goal, while in reality he had only been treading in a narrow circle.   Not that the effects which he had
striven so hard to produce did not continue to manifest
themselves.   They were still produced, but not by him.
The rain still fell on the thirsty ground : the sun still
pursued his daily, and the moon her nightly journey across
the sky : the silent procession of the seasons still moved in
light and shadow, in cloud and sunshine across the earth :
men were still born to labour and sorrow, and still, after a
brief sojourn here, were gathered to their fathers in the long
home hereafter.   All things indeed went on as before, yet
all seemed different to him from whose eyes the old scales
had fallen.   For he could no longer cherish the pleasing
illusion that it was he who guided the earth and the
heaven in their courses, and that they would cease to perform their great revolutions were he to take his feeble hand
from the wheel.   In the death of his enemies and his friends
he no longer saw a proof of the resistless potency of his own
or of hostile enchantments ; he now knew that friends and
foes alike had succumbed to a force stronger than any that
he could wield, and in obedience to a destiny which he was
powerless to control.

Recognis-
ing their
own in-
ability to
control
nature,
men came
to think
that it was
controlled
by super-
natural
beings.

Thus cut adrift from his ancient moorings and left to
toss on a troubled sea of doubt and uncertainty, his old
happy confidence in himself and his powers rudely shaken,
our primitive philosopher must have been sadly perplexed
and agitated till he came to rest, as in a quiet haven after a
tempestuous voyage, in a new system of faith and practice,
which seemed to offer a solution of his harassing doubts and
a substitute, however precarious, for that sovereignty over
nature which he had reluctantly abdicated.   If the great
world went on its way without the help of him or his fellows,
it must surely be because there were other beings, like him-

self, but far stronger, who, unseen themselves, directed its course and brought about all the varied series of events which he had hitherto believed to be dependent on his own magic. It was they, as he now believed, and not he himself, who made the stormy wind to blow, the lightning to flash, and the thunder to roll; who had laid the foundations of the solid earth and set bounds to the restless sea that it might not pass; who caused all the glorious lights of heaven to shine; who gave the fowls of the air their meat and the wild beasts of the desert their prey; who bade the fruitful land to bring forth in abundance, the high hills to be clothed with forests, the bubbling springs to rise under the rocks in the valleys, and green pastures to grow by still waters; who breathed into man's nostrils and made him live, or turned him to destruction by famine and pestilence and war. To these mighty beings, whose handiwork he traced in all the gorgeous and varied pageantry of nature, man now addressed himself, humbly confessing his dependence on their invisible power, and beseeching them of their mercy to furnish him with all good things, to defend him from the perils and dangers by which our mortal life is compassed about on every hand, and finally to bring his immortal spirit, freed from the burden of the body, to some happier world, beyond the reach of pain and sorrow, where he might rest with them and with the spirits of good men in joy and felicity for ever.

In this, or some such way as this, the deeper minds may be conceived to have made the great transition from magic to religion. But even in them the change can hardly ever have been sudden; probably it proceeded very slowly, and required long ages for its more or less perfect accomplishment. For the recognition of man's powerlessness to influence the course of nature on a grand scale must have been gradual; he cannot have been shorn of the whole of his fancied dominion at a blow. Step by step he must have been driven back from his proud position; foot by foot he must have yielded, with a sigh, the ground which he had once viewed as his own. Now it would be the wind, now the rain, now the sunshine, now the thunder, that he confessed himself unable to wield at will; and as province after province of

The change from magic to religion must have been gradual.

nature thus fell from his grasp, till what had once seemed a kingdom threatened to shrink into a prison, man must have been more and more profoundly impressed with a sense of his own helplessness and the might of the invisible beings by whom he believed himself to be surrounded. Thus religion, beginning as a slight and partial acknowledgment of powers superior to man, tends with the growth of knowledge to deepen into a confession of man's entire and absolute dependence on the divine ; his old free bearing is exchanged for an attitude of lowliest prostration before the mysterious powers of the unseen, and his highest virtue is to submit his will to theirs : *In la sua volontade è nostra pace.* But this deepening sense of religion, this more perfect submission to the divine will in all things, affects only those higher intelligences who have breadth of view enough to comprehend the vastness of the universe and the littleness of man. Small minds cannot grasp great ideas ; to their narrow comprehension, their purblind vision, nothing seems really great and important but themselves. Such minds hardly rise into religion at all. They are, indeed, drilled by their betters into an outward conformity with its precepts and a verbal profession of its tenets ; but at heart they cling to their old magical superstitions, which may be discountenanced and forbidden, but cannot be eradicated by religion, so long as they have their roots deep down in the mental framework and constitution of the great majority of mankind.

The belief that the gods are magicians may mark the transition from magic to religion.

A vestige of the transition from magic to religion may perhaps be discerned in the belief, shared by many peoples, that the gods themselves are adepts in magic, guarding their persons by talismans and working their will by spells and incantations. Thus the Egyptian gods, we are told, could as little dispense with the help of magic as could men ; like men they wore amulets to protect themselves, and used spells to overcome each other. Above all the rest Isis was skilled in sorcery and famous for her incantations.[1] In Babylonia the great god Ea was reputed to be the inventor of magic, and his son Marduk, the chief deity of Babylon, inherited the art from his father. Marduk is described as " the master of exorcism, the magician of the gods."

[1] A. Erman, *Ägypten und ägyptisches Leben im Altertum*, p. 471.

Another text declares that "the incantation is the incantation of Marduk, the exorcist is the image of Marduk."[1]   In
the legend of the creation it is related that when Marduk
was preparing to fight the monster Tiamat he gave a proof
of his magical powers to the assembled gods by causing a
garment to disappear and reappear again at the word of his
mouth.   And the other Babylonian deities had in like
manner recourse to magic, especially to magical words or
spells.   "The word is above all the instrument of the gods ;
it seems to suit the high conception of their power better
than mere muscular effort; the hymns celebrate the irresistible might of their word ; it is by their word that they
compel both animate and inanimate beings to answer their
purposes ; in short, they employ almost exclusively the oral
rites of magic."   And like men they made use of amulets
and talismans.[2]   In the Vedic religion the gods are often
represented as attaining their ends by magical means ; in
particular the god Br̥haspati, "the creator of all prayers," is
regarded as "the heavenly embodiment of the priesthood, in
so far as the priesthood is invested with the power, and
charged with the task, of influencing the course of things by
prayers and spells"; in short, he is "the possessor of the
magical power of the holy word."[3]   So too in Norse mythology Odin is said to have owed his supremacy and his
dominion over nature to his knowledge of the runes or
magical names of all things in earth and heaven.   This
mystical lore he acquired as follows.   The runic names of
all things were scratched on the things themselves, then
scraped off and mixed in a magical potion, which was compounded of honey and the blood of the slain Kvasir, the
wisest of beings.   A draught of this wonderful mead
imparted to Odin not only the wisdom of Kvasir, but also
a knowledge of all things, since he had swallowed their
runic or mystical names along with the blood of the sage.[4]

---

[1] C. Fossey, *La Magie Assyrienne*
(Paris, 1902), pp. 123, 125.
[2] C. Fossey, *op. cit.* pp. 137-139.
For the incident of the magical disappearance and reappearance of the
garment, see P. Jensen, *Assyrisch-
Babylonische Mythen und Epen* (Berlin, 1900), p. 23 ; R. F. Harper,

Assyrian and Babylonian Literature
(New York, 1901), p. 291.
[3] H. Oldenberg, *Die Religion des
Veda*, pp. 66-68, 514-517.
[4] Fr. Kauffmann, *Balder, Mythus
und Sage* (Strasburg, 1902), pp. 177-
203.   Compare J. Grimm, *Deutsche
Mythologie,*[4] ii. 1024-1026.

Hence by the utterance of his spells he could heal sickness, deaden the swords of his enemies, loose himself from bonds, stop the flight of an arrow in mid-air, stay the raging of the flames, still the winds and lull the sea ; and by graving and painting certain runes he could make the corpse of a hanged man come down from the gallows-tree and talk with him.[1] It is easy to conceive how this ascription of magical powers to the gods may have originated. When a savage sorcerer fails to effect his purpose, he generally explains his want of success by saying that he has been foiled by the spells of some more potent magician. Now if it began to be perceived that certain natural effects, such as the making of rain or wind or sunshine, were beyond the power of any human magician to accomplish, the first thought would naturally be that they were wrought by the more powerful magic of some great invisible beings, and these superhuman magicians might readily develop into gods of the type of Odin, Isis, and Marduk. In short, many gods may at first have been merely deified sorcerers.

The fallacy of magic is not easy to detect, because nature herself generally produces, sooner or later, the effects which the magician fancies he produces by his art. The reader may well be tempted to ask, How was it that intelligent men did not sooner detect the fallacy of magic? How could they continue to cherish expectations that were invariably doomed to disappointment? With what heart persist in playing venerable antics that led to nothing, and mumbling solemn balderdash that remained without effect? Why cling to beliefs which were so flatly contradicted by experience? How dare to repeat experiments that had failed so often? The answer seems to be that the fallacy was far from easy to detect, the failure by no means obvious, since in many, perhaps in most cases, the desired event did actually follow, at a longer or shorter interval, the performance of the rite which was designed to bring it about ; and a mind of more than common acuteness was needed to perceive that, even in these cases, the rite was not necessarily the cause of the event. A ceremony intended to make the wind blow or the rain fall, or to work the death of an enemy, will always be followed, sooner or later, by the occurrence it is meant to bring to pass ; and primitive man may be excused for regarding the occurrence as a direct result of the ceremony, and

[1] G. Vigfusson and F. York Powell, *Corpus Poeticum Boreale*, i. 24 *sqq.*

the best possible proof of its efficacy. Similarly, rites observed in the morning to help the sun to rise, and in spring to wake the dreaming earth from her winter sleep, will invariably appear to be crowned with success, at least within the temperate zones ; for in these regions the sun lights his golden lamp in the east every morning, and year by year the vernal earth decks herself afresh with a rich mantle of green. Hence the practical savage, with his conservative instincts, might well turn a deaf ear to the subtleties of the theoretical doubter, the philosophic radical, who presumed to hint that sunrise and spring might not, after all, be direct consequences of the punctual performance of certain daily or yearly ceremonies, and that the sun might perhaps continue to rise and trees to blossom though the ceremonies were occasionally intermitted, or even discontinued altogether. These sceptical doubts would naturally be repelled by the other with scorn and indignation as airy reveries subversive of the faith and manifestly contradicted by experience. "Can anything be plainer," he might say, "than that I light my twopenny candle on earth and that the sun then kindles his great fire in heaven? I should be glad to know whether, when I have put on my green robe in spring, the trees do not afterwards do the same? These are facts patent to everybody, and on them I take my stand. I am a plain practical man, not one of your theorists and splitters of hairs and choppers of logic. Theories and speculation and all that may be very well in their way, and I have not the least objection to your indulging in them, provided, of course, you do not put them in practice. But give me leave to stick to facts; then I know where I am." The fallacy of this reasoning is obvious to us, because it happens to deal with facts about which we have long made up our minds. But let an argument of precisely the same calibre be applied to matters which are still under debate, and it may be questioned whether a British audience would not applaud it as sound, and esteem the speaker who used it a safe man—not brilliant or showy, perhaps, but thoroughly sensible and hard-headed. If such reasonings could pass muster among ourselves, need we wonder that they long escaped detection by the savage?

CHAPTER V

THE MAGICAL CONTROL OF THE WEATHER

§ 1. *The Public Magician*

THE patient reader may remember that we were led to plunge into the labyrinth of magic, in which we have wandered for so many pages, by a consideration of two different types of man-god. This is the clue which has guided our devious steps through the maze, and brought us out at last on higher ground, whence, resting a little by the way, we can look back over the path we have already traversed and forward to the longer and steeper road we have still to climb.

Two types of man-god, the religious and the magical.

As a result of the foregoing discussion, the two types of human gods may conveniently be distinguished as the religious and the magical man-god respectively. In the former, a being of an order different from and superior to man is supposed to become incarnate, for a longer or a shorter time, in a human body, manifesting his superhuman power and knowledge by miracles wrought and prophecies uttered through the medium of the fleshly tabernacle in which he has deigned to take up his abode. This may also appropriately be called the inspired or incarnate type of man-god. In it the human body is merely a frail earthly vessel filled with a divine and immortal spirit. On the other hand, a man-god of the magical sort is nothing but a man who possesses in an unusually high degree powers which most of his fellows arrogate to themselves on a smaller scale; for in rude society there is hardly a person who does not dabble in magic. Thus, whereas a man-god of the former or inspired type derives his divinity from a deity who has stooped to hide his heavenly radiance behind a dull mask of earthly mould, a man-god of the latter type draws his extraordinary power from a certain physical sympathy with nature. He is not merely the receptacle of a divine spirit. His whole being, body and soul, is so delicately attuned to the harmony of the world that a touch of his hand or a turn of his head may send a thrill vibrating through the universal framework of things ; and conversely his divine organism is acutely sensitive to such slight changes of environment as would leave ordinary mortals wholly unaffected. But the line between these two types of man-god, however sharply we may draw it in theory, is seldom to be traced with precision in practice, and in what follows I shall not insist on it.

We have seen that in practice the magic art may be employed for the benefit either of individuals or of the whole community, and that according as it is directed to one or other of these two objects it may be called private or public magic.[1] Further, I pointed out that the public magician occupies a position of great influence, from which, if he is a prudent and able man, he may advance step by step to the rank of a chief or king. Thus an examination of public magic conduces to an understanding of the early kingship, since in savage and barbarous society many chiefs and kings appear to owe their authority in great measure to their reputation as magicians. *Public and private magic : the public magician often a king.*

Among the objects of public utility which magic may be employed to secure, the most essential is an adequate supply of food. The examples cited in preceding pages prove that the purveyors of food—the hunter, the fisher, the farmer—all resort to magical practices in the pursuit of their various callings ; but they do so as private individuals for the benefit of themselves and their families, rather than as public functionaries acting in the interest of the whole people. It is otherwise when the rites are performed, not by the hunters, the fishers, the farmers themselves, but by professional magicians on their behalf. In primitive society, where uniformity of occupation is the rule, and the distribution of the community into various classes of workers has hardly begun, every man is more or less his own magician ; he practises charms and *The rise of a class of public or professional magicians is a great step in social and intellectual progress.*

---

[1] See above, pp. 214 *sq.*

incantations for his own good and the injury of his enemies. But a great step in advance has been taken when a special class of magicians has been instituted ; when, in other words, a number of men have been set apart for the express purpose of benefiting the whole community by their skill, whether that skill be directed to the healing of diseases, the forecasting of the future, the regulation of the weather, or any other object of general utility. The impotence of the means adopted by most of these practitioners to accomplish their ends ought not to blind us to the immense importance of the institution itself. Here is a body of men relieved, at least in the higher stages of savagery, from the need of earning their livelihood by hard manual toil, and allowed, nay, expected and encouraged, to prosecute researches into the secret ways of nature. It was at once their duty and their interest to know more than their fellows, to acquaint themselves with everything that could aid man in his arduous struggle with nature, everything that could mitigate his sufferings and prolong his life. The properties of drugs and minerals, the causes of rain and drought, of thunder and lightning, the changes of the seasons, the phases of the moon, the daily and yearly journeys of the sun, the motions of the stars, the mystery of life, and the mystery of death, all these things must have excited the wonder of these early philosophers, and stimulated them to find solutions of problems that were doubtless often thrust on their attention in the most practical form by the importunate demands of their clients, who expected them not merely to understand but to regulate the great processes of nature for the good of man. That their first shots fell very far wide of the mark could hardly be helped. The slow, the never-ending approach to truth consists in perpetually forming and testing hypotheses, accepting those which at the time seem to fit the facts and rejecting the others. The views of natural causation embraced by the savage magician no doubt appear to us manifestly false and absurd ; yet in their day they were legitimate hypotheses, though they have not stood the test of experience. Ridicule and blame are the just meed, not of those who devised these crude theories, but of those who obstinately adhered to them after better had been propounded.

Certainly no men ever had stronger incentives in the pursuit of truth than these savage sorcerers.   To maintain at least a show of knowledge was absolutely necessary ; a single mistake detected might cost them their life.   This no doubt led them to practise imposture for the purpose of concealing their ignorance ; but it also supplied them with the most powerful motive for substituting a real for a sham knowledge, since, if you would appear to know anything, by far the best way is actually to know it.   Thus, however justly we may reject the extravagant pretensions of magicians and condemn the deceptions which they have practised on mankind, the original institution of this class of men has, take it all in all, been productive of incalculable good to humanity.   They were the direct predecessors, not merely of our physicians and surgeons, but of our investigators and discoverers in every branch of natural science.   They began the work which has since been carried to such glorious and beneficent issues by their successors in after ages ; and if the beginning was poor and feeble, this is to be imputed to the inevitable difficulties which beset the path of knowledge rather than to the natural incapacity or wilful fraud of the men themselves.

§ 2. *The Magical Control of Rain*

Of the things which the public magician sets himself to do for the good of the tribe, one of the chief is to control the weather and especially to ensure an adequate fall of rain. Water is the first essential of life, and in most countries the supply of it depends upon showers.   Without rain vegetation withers, animals and men languish and die.   Hence in savage communities the rain-maker is a very important personage ; and often a special class of magicians exists for the purpose of regulating the heavenly water-supply.   The methods by which they attempt to discharge the duties of their office are commonly, though not always, based on the principle of homoeopathic or imitative magic.   If they wish to make rain they simulate it by sprinkling water or mimicking clouds : if their object is to stop rain and cause drought, they avoid water and resort to warmth and fire for the sake of drying up the too abundant moisture.   Such attempts are by no means confined, as the cultivated reader might

One of the chief tasks which the public magician has to perform is to control the weather, and especially to ensure an adequate supply of rain.   The method adopted by the rain-maker is commonly based on homoeopathic or imitative magic : he seeks to produce rain by imitating it.

imagine, to the naked inhabitants of those sultry lands like Central Australia and some parts of Eastern and Southern Africa, where often for months together the pitiless sun beats down out of a blue and cloudless sky on the parched and gaping earth. They are, or used to be, common enough among outwardly civilised folk in the moister climate of Europe. I will now illustrate them by instances drawn from the practice both of public and private magic.

Examples of making rain by homoeopathic or imitative magic.

Thus, for example, in a village near Dorpat, in Russia, when rain was much wanted, three men used to climb up the fir-trees of an old sacred grove. One of them drummed with a hammer on a kettle or small cask to imitate thunder ; the second knocked two fire-brands together and made the sparks fly, to imitate lightning ; and the third, who was called "the rain-maker," had a bunch of twigs with which he sprinkled water from a vessel on all sides.[1] To put an end to drought and bring down rain, women and girls of the village of Ploska are wont to go naked by night to the boundaries of the village and there pour water on the ground.[2] In Halmahera, or Gilolo, a large island to the west of New Guinea, a wizard makes rain by dipping a branch of a particular kind of tree in water and then scattering the moisture from the dripping bough over the ground.[3] In Ceram it is enough to dedicate the bark of a certain tree to the spirits, and lay it in water.[4] A Javanese mode of making rain is to imitate the pattering sound of rain-drops by brushing a coco-nut leaf over the sheath of a betel-nut in a mortar.[5] In New Britain the rain-maker wraps some leaves of a red and green striped creeper

---

[1] W. Mannhardt, *Antike Wald- und Feldkulte*, p. 342, note. The heathen Swedes appear to have mimicked thunder, perhaps as a rain-charm, by means of large bronze hammers, which they called Thor's hammers. See Saxo Grammaticus, *Historia Danica*, lib. xiii. p. 630, ed. P. E. Müller ; Olaus Magnus, *Historia*, iii. 8.

[2] K. v. Bruchhausen, in *Globus*, lxxvi. (1899) p. 253. There seem to be two villages in Wallachia that bear the name of Ploska. The reference may be to one of them.

[3] C. F. H. Campen, "De Godsdienstbegrippen der Halmaherasche Alfoeren," *Tijdschrift voor Indische Taal- Land- en Volkenkunde*, xxvii. (1882) p. 447.

[4] J. G. F. Riedel, *De sluik- en kroesharige rassen tusschen Selebes en Papua*, p. 114.

[5] G. A. J. Hazeu, "Kleine bijdragen tot de ethnografie en folklore van Java," *Tijdschrift voor Indische Taal- Land - en Volkenkunde*, xlvi. (1903) p. 298.

in a banana-leaf, moistens the bundle with water, and buries it in the ground; then he imitates with his mouth the plashing of rain.[1] Amongst the Omaha Indians of North America, when the corn is withering for want of rain, the members of the sacred Buffalo Society fill a large vessel with water and dance four times round it. One of them drinks some of the water and spirts it into the air, making a fine spray in imitation of a mist or drizzling rain. Then he upsets the vessel, spilling the water on the ground; whereupon the dancers fall down and drink up the water, getting mud all over their faces. Lastly, they squirt the water into the air, making a fine mist. This saves the corn.[2] In spring-time the Natchez of North America used to club together to purchase favourable weather for their crops from the wizards. If rain was needed, the wizards fasted and danced with pipes full of water in their mouths. The pipes were perforated like the nozzle of a watering-can, and through the holes the rain-maker blew the water towards that part of the sky where the clouds hung heaviest. But if fine weather was wanted, he mounted the roof of his hut, and with extended arms, blowing with all his might, he beckoned to the clouds to pass by.[3] In time of drought the Tarahumares Indians of Mexico will sometimes throw water towards the sky in order that God may replenish his supply. And in the month of May they always burn the grass, so that the whole country is then wrapt in smoke and travelling becomes very difficult. They think that this is necessary to produce rain, clouds of smoke being, in their opinion, equivalent to rain-clouds.[4] Among the Swazies and Hlubies of South-Eastern Africa the rain-doctor draws water from a river with various mystic ceremonies, and carries it into a cultivated field. Here he throws it in jets from his vessel high into the air, and the falling spray is believed to draw down the clouds and to make rain by sympathy.[5] To squirt water

[1] R. Parkinson, *Im Bismarck Archipel*, p. 143. Compare Joachim Graf Pfeil, *Studien und Beobachtungen aus der Südsee* (Brunswick, 1899), pp. 139 *sq.*

[2] J. Owen Dorsey, "Omaha Sociology," *Third Annual Report of the Bureau of Ethnology* (Washington, 1884), p. 347. Compare Charlevoix,

Voyage dans l'Amérique septentrionale, ii. 187.

[3] *Lettres édifiantes et curieuses*, Nouvelle Edition, vii. 29 *sq.*

[4] C. Lumholtz, *Unknown Mexico* (London, 1903), i. 180, 330.

[5] J. Macdonald, *Religion and Myth* (London, 1893), p. 10.

Making
rain by
homoeo-
pathic or
imitative
magic.

from the mouth is a West African mode of making rain,[1] and it is practised also by the Wajaggas of Kilimanjaro.[2] Among the Wahuma, on the Albert Nyanza Lake, the rain-maker pours water into a vessel in which he has first placed a dark stone as large as the hand. Pounded plants and the blood of a black goat are added to the water, and with a bunch of magic herbs the sorcerer sprinkles the mixture towards the sky.[3] In this charm special efficacy is no doubt attributed to the dark stone and the black goat, their colour being chosen from its resemblance to that of the rain-clouds, as we shall see presently. When the rains do not come in due season the people of Central Angoniland repair to what is called the rain-temple. Here they clear away the grass, and the leader pours beer into a pot which is buried in the ground, while he says, " Master *Chauta*, you have hardened your heart towards us, what would you have us do? We must perish indeed. Give your children the rains, there is the beer we have given you." Then they all partake of the beer that is left over, even the children being made to sip it. Next they take branches of trees and dance and sing for rain. When they return to the village they find a vessel of water set at the doorway by an old woman ; so they dip their branches in it and wave them aloft, so as to scatter the drops. After that the rain is sure to come driving up in heavy clouds.[4] In these practices we see a combination of religion with magic ; for while the scattering of the water-drops by means of branches is a purely magical ceremony, the prayer for rain and the offering of beer are purely religious rites. At Takitount in Algeria, when the drought is severe, the people prepare a sacrificial banquet (*zerda*), in the course of which they dance, and filling their mouths with water spirt it into the air crying, " The rain and abundance ! " Elsewhere in the course of these banquets it is customary for the same purpose to sprinkle water on children. At Tlemcen in time of drought water is thrown from terraces and windows on

[1] J. B. Labat, *Relation historique de l'Éthiopie occidentale*, ii. 180.

[2] M. Merker, *Rechtsverhältnisse und Sitten der Wadschagga* (Gotha, 1902), p. 34 (*Petermanns Mitteilungen*, Ergänzungsheft, No. 138).

[3] Fr. Stuhlmann, *Mit Emin Pascha ins Herz von Afrika* (Berlin, 1894), p. 588.

[4] R. Sutherland Rattray, *Some Folklore Stories and Songs in Chinyanja* (London, 1907), pp. 118 *sq.*

small girls, who pass singing.[1]   During the summer months
frequent droughts occur among the Japanese alps.   To procure rain a party of hunters armed with guns climb to the top
of Mount Jonendake, one of the most imposing peaks in the
range.   By kindling a bonfire, discharging their guns, and
rolling great masses of rocks down the cliffs, they represent
the wished-for storm ; and rain is supposed always to follow
within a few days.[2]   To make rain a party of Ainos will
scatter water by means of sieves, while others will take a
porringer, fit it up with sails and oars as if it were a boat,
and then push or draw it about the village and gardens.[3]
In Laos the festival of the New Year takes place about the
middle of April and lasts three days.   The people assemble
in the pagodas, which are decorated with flowers and illuminated.   The Buddhist monks perform the ceremonies, and
when they come to the prayers for the fertility of the earth
the worshippers pour water into little holes in the floor of
the pagoda as a symbol of the rain which they hope Buddha
will send down on the rice-fields in due time.[4]   In the Mara
tribe of Northern Australia the rain-maker goes to a pool
and sings over it his magic song.   Then he takes some of
the water in his hands, drinks it, and spits it out in various
directions.   After that he throws water all over himself,
scatters it about, and returns quietly to the camp.   Rain is
supposed to follow.[5]   In the Wotjobaluk tribe of Victoria
the rain-maker dipped a bunch of his own hair in water,
sucked out the water and squirted it westward, or he twirled

---

[1] E. Doutté, *Magie et Religion dans l'Afrique du Nord*, p. 583.

[2] W. Weston, in *The Geographical Journal*, vii. (1896) p. 143; *id.*, in *Journal of the Anthropological Institute*, xxvi. (1897) p. 30; *id.*, *Mountaineering and Exploration in the Japanese Alps*, p. 161.   The ceremony is not purely magical, for it is intended to attract the attention of the powerful spirit who has a small shrine on the top of the mountain.

[3] J. Batchelor, *The Ainu and their Folklore* (London, 1901), p. 333. Some of the ancient processions with ships may perhaps have been rain-charms.   See J. Grimm, *Deutsche*

Mythologie,[4] i. 213-220; Pausanias, i. 29. 1, with my note.

[4] Tournier, *Notice sur le Laos Français* (Hanoi, 1900), p. 80.   In the temple of the Syrian goddess at Hierapolis on the Euphrates there was a chasm into which water was poured twice a year by people who assembled for the purpose from the whole of Syria and Arabia.   See Lucian, *De dea Syria*, 12 *sq.*   The ceremony was perhaps a rain-charm.   Compare Pausanias, i. 18. 7, with my notes.

[5] Spencer and Gillen, *Northern Tribes of Central Australia*, pp. 313 *sq.*

the ball round his head, making a spray like rain.[1] Other Australian tribes employ human hair as a rain-charm in other ways. In Western Australia the natives pluck hair from their arm-pits and thighs and blow them in the direction from which they wish the rain to come. But if they wish to prevent rain, they light a piece of sandal wood, and beat the ground with the burning brand.[2] When the rivers were low and water scarce in Victoria, the wizard used to place human hair in the stream, accompanying the act with chants and gesticulation. But if he wished to make rain, he dropped some human hair in the fire. Hair was never burnt at other times for fear of causing a great fall of rain.[3] The Arab historian Makrizi describes a method of stopping rain which is said to have been resorted to by a tribe of nomads called Alqamar in Hadramaut. They cut a branch from a certain tree in the desert, set it on fire, and then sprinkled the burning brand with water. After that the vehemence of the rain abated,[4] just as the water vanished when it fell on the glowing brand. Some of the Eastern Angamis of Manipur are said to perform a somewhat similar ceremony for the opposite purpose, in order, namely, to produce rain. The head of the village puts a burning brand on the grave of a man who has died of burns, and quenches the brand with water, while he prays that rain may fall.[5] Here the putting out the fire with water, which is an imitation of rain, is reinforced by the influence of the dead man, who, having been burnt to death, will naturally be anxious for the descent of rain to cool his scorched body and assuage his pangs.

Other people besides the Arabs have used fire as a means of stopping rain. Thus the Sulka of New Britain heat stones red hot in the fire and then put them out in the

---

[1] A. W. Howitt, " On Australian Medicine-Men," *Journal of the Anthropological Institute,* xvi. (1887) p. 35 ; *id., Native Tribes of South - East Australia,* p. 398.

[2] R. Salvado, *Mémoires historiques sur l'Australie* (Paris, 1854), p. 262.

[3] W. Stanbridge, " On the Aborigines of Victoria," *Transactions of the Ethnological Society of London,* N.S., i. (1861) p. 300. This use of fire to make rain is peculiar. By analogy we should expect it rather to be resorted to as a mode of stopping rain. See below.

[4] P. B. Noskowÿj, *Maqrizii de valle Hadhramaut libellus arabice editus et illustratus* (Bonn, 1866), pp. 25 *sq.*

[5] T. C. Hodson, " The Native Tribes of Manipur," *Journal of the Anthropological Institute,* xxxi. (1901) p. 308.

rain, or they throw hot ashes in the air. They think that the rain will soon cease to fall, for it does not like to be burned by the hot stones or ashes.[1] The Telugus send a little girl out naked into the rain with a burning piece of wood in her hand, which she has to shew to the rain. That is supposed to stop the downpour.[2] At Port Stevens in New South Wales the medicine-men used to drive away rain by throwing fire-sticks into the air, while at the same time they puffed and shouted.[3] Any man of the Anula tribe in Northern Australia can stop rain by simply warming a green stick in the fire, and then striking it against the wind.[4] When a Thompson Indian of British Columbia wished to put an end to a spell of heavy rain, he held a stick in the fire, then described a circle with it, beginning at the east and following the sun's course till it reached the east again, towards which quarter he held the stick and addressed the rain as follows: "Now then, you must stop raining; the people are miserable. Ye mountains, become clear." The ceremony was repeated for all the other quarters of the sky.[5] To bring on rain the Ainos of Japan wash their tobacco-boxes and pipes in a stream,[6] and the Toradjas of Central Celebes dip rice-spoons in water.[7] On the contrary, during heavy rain the Indians of Guiana are careful not to wash the inside of their pots, lest by so doing they should cause the rain to fall still more heavily.[8] In Bilaspore it is believed that the grain-dealer, who has stored large quantities of grain and wishes to sell it dear, resorts to nefarious means of preventing the rain from falling, lest the abundance of rice which would follow a copious rainfall should cheapen his wares. To do this he collects rain-drops from the eaves of his house in an earthen vessel and buries the vessel under the grinding-mill.

Various ways of making and stopping rain.

[1] Rascher, "Die Sulka," *Archiv für Anthropologie*, xxix. (1904) p. 225; R. Parkinson, *Dreissig Jahre in der Südsee*, pp. 196 *sq.*
[2] *Indian Antiquary*, xxiv. (1895) p. 359.
[3] A. W. Howitt, *Native Tribes of South-East Australia*, p. 398.
[4] Spencer and Gillen, *Northern Tribes of Central Australia*, p. 315.
[5] J. Teit, "The Thompson Indians of British Columbia," p. 345 (*Memoirs*

of the *American Museum of Natural History, The Jesup North Pacific Expedition*, vol. i. part iv.).
[6] J. Batchelor, *The Ainu and their Folklore*, p. 333.
[7] A. C. Kruijt, "Regen lokken en regen verdrijven bij de Toradja's van Midden Celebes," *Tijdschrift voor Indische Taal- Land- en Volkenkunde*, xliv. (1901) p. 2.
[8] J. Crevaux, *Voyages dans l'Amérique du Sud* (Paris, 1883), p. 276.

After that you shall hear thunder rumbling in the distance like the humming sound of the mill at work, but no rain will fall, for the wicked dealer has shut it up and it cannot get out.[1]

Rain-making in Queensland.

In the torrid climate of Queensland the ceremonies necessary for wringing showers from the cloudless heaven are naturally somewhat elaborate. A prominent part in them is played by a " rain-stick." This is a thin piece of wood about twenty inches long, to which three " rain-stones " and hair cut from the beard have been fastened. The " rain-stones " are pieces of white quartz-crystal. Three or four such sticks may be used in the ceremony. About noon the men who are to take part in it repair to a lonely pool, into which one of them dives and fixes a hollow log vertically in the mud. Then they all go into the water, and, forming a rough circle round the man in the middle, who holds the rain-stick aloft, they begin stamping with their feet as well as they can, and splashing the water with their hands from all sides on the rain-stick. The stamping, which is accompanied by singing, is sometimes a matter of difficulty, since the water may be four feet deep or more. When the singing is over, the man in the middle dives out of sight and attaches the rain-stick to the hollow log under water. Then coming to the surface, he quickly climbs on to the bank and spits out on dry land the water which he imbibed in diving. Should more than one of these rain-sticks have been prepared, the ceremony is repeated with each in turn. While the men are returning to camp they scratch the tops of their heads and the inside of their shins from time to time with twigs ; if they were to scratch themselves with their fingers alone, they believe that the whole effect of the ceremony would be spoiled. On reaching the camp they paint their faces, arms, and chests with broad bands of gypsum. During the rest of the day the process of scratching, accompanied by the song, is repeated at intervals, and thus the performance comes to a close. No woman may set eyes on the rain-stick or witness the ceremony of its submergence ; but the wife of the chief rain-maker is privileged to take part in the subse-

[1] E. M. Gordon, *Indian Folk Tales* (London, 1908), p. 20 ; *id.* in *Journal* *and Proceedings of the Asiatic Society of Bengal,* New Series, i. (1905) p. 183.

quent rite of scratching herself with a twig. When the rain does come, the rain-stick is taken out of the water : it has done its work.[1] At Roxburgh, in Queensland, the ceremony is somewhat different. A white quartz-crystal which is to serve as the rain-stone is obtained in the mountains and crushed to powder. Next a tree is chosen of which the stem runs up straight for a long way without any branches. Against its trunk saplings from fifteen to twenty feet long are then propped in a circle, so as to form a sort of shed like a bell-tent, and in front of the shed an artificial pond is made in the ground. The men, who have collected within the shed, now come forth and, dancing and singing round the pond, mimic the cries and antics of various aquatic birds and animals, such as ducks and frogs. Meanwhile the women are stationed some twenty yards or so away. When the men have done pretending to be ducks, frogs, and so forth, they march round the women in single file, throwing the pulverised quartz-crystals over them. On their side the women hold up wooden troughs, shields, pieces of bark, and so on over their heads, making believe that they are sheltering themselves from a heavy shower of rain.[2] Both these ceremonies are cases of mimetic magic ; the splashing of the water over the rain-stick is as clearly an imitation of a shower as the throwing of the powdered quartz-crystal over the women.

The Dieri of Central Australia enact a somewhat similar pantomime for the same purpose. In a dry season their lot is a hard one. No fresh herbs or roots are to be had, and as the parched earth yields no grass, the emus, reptiles, and other creatures which generally furnish the natives with food grow so lean and wizened as to be hardly worth eating. At such a time of severe drought the Dieri, loudly lamenting the impoverished state of the country and their own half-starved condition, call upon the spirits of their remote predecessors, whom they call Mura-muras, to grant them power to make a heavy rainfall. For they believe that the clouds are bodies in which rain is generated by their own ceremonies or those

Rain-making among the Dieri of Central Australia.

---

[1] W. E. Roth, *Ethnological Studies among the North-West-Central Queensland Aborigines* (Brisbane and London, 1897), p. 167.

[2] W. E. Roth, *op. cit.* p. 168 ; *id., North Queensland Ethnography, Bulletin No.* 5 (Brisbane, 1903), p. 10.

of neighbouring tribes, through the influence of the Mura-muras. The way in which they set about drawing rain from the clouds is this. A hole is dug about twelve feet long and eight or ten broad, and over this hole a conical hut of logs and branches is made. Two wizards, supposed to have received a special inspiration from the Mura-muras, are bled by an old and influential man with a sharp flint; and the blood, drawn from their arms below the elbow, is made to flow on the other men of the tribe, who sit huddled together in the hut. At the same time the two bleeding men throw handfuls of down about, some of which adheres to the blood-stained bodies of their comrades, while the rest floats in the air. The blood is thought to represent the rain, and the down the clouds. During the ceremony two large stones are placed in the middle of the hut; they stand for gathering clouds and presage rain. Then the wizards who were bled carry away the two stones for about ten or fifteen miles, and place them as high as they can in the tallest tree. Meanwhile the other men gather gypsum, pound it fine, and throw it into a water-hole. This the Mura-muras see, and at once they cause clouds to appear in the sky. Lastly, the men, young and old, surround the hut, and, stooping down, butt at it with their heads, like so many rams. Thus they force their way through it and reappear on the other side, repeating the process till the hut is wrecked. In doing this they are forbidden to use their hands or arms; but when the heavy logs alone remain, they are allowed to pull them out with their hands. " The piercing of the hut with their heads symbolises the piercing of the clouds; the fall of the hut, the fall of the rain." [1] Obviously, too, the act of placing high up in trees the two stones, which stand for clouds, is a way of making the real clouds to mount up in the sky. The Dieri also

imagine that the foreskins taken from lads at circumcision have a great power of producing rain. Hence the Great Council of the tribe always keeps a small stock of fore-

---

[1] S. Gason, " The Dieyerie Tribe," *Native Tribes of South Australia*, pp. 276 *sqq.*; A. W. Howitt, " The Dieri and other Kindred Tribes of Central Australia," *Journal of the Anthropological Institute*, xx. (1891) pp. 91 *sq.*; *id.*, *Native Tribes of South - East Australia*, pp. 394-396. As to the Mura-muras, see A. W. Howitt, *Native Tribes of South-East Australia*, pp. 475 *sqq.*, 779 *sqq.*

skins ready for use. They are carefully concealed, being wrapt up in feathers with the fat of the wild dog and of the carpet snake. A woman may not see such a parcel opened on any account. When the ceremony is over, the foreskin is buried, its virtue being exhausted. After the rains have fallen, some of the tribe always undergo a surgical operation, which consists in cutting the skin of their chest and arms with a sharp flint. The wound is then tapped with a flat stick to increase the flow of blood, and red ochre is rubbed into it. Raised scars are thus produced. The reason alleged by the natives for this practice is that they are pleased with the rain, and that there is a connexion between the rain and the scars. Apparently the operation is not very painful, for the patient laughs and jokes while it is going on. Indeed, little children have been seen to crowd round the operator and patiently take their turn ; then after being operated on, they ran away, expanding their little chests and singing for the rain to beat upon them. However, they were not so well pleased next day, when they felt their wounds stiff and sore.[1] The tribes of the Karamundi nation, on the River Darling, universally believe that rain can be produced as follows. A vein in the arm of one of the men is opened, and the blood allowed to flow into a piece of hollow bark till it forms a little pool. Powdered gypsum and hair from the man's beard are then added to the blood, and the whole is stirred into a thick paste. Afterwards the mixture is placed between two pieces of bark and put under water in a river or lagoon, pointed stakes being driven into the ground to keep it down. When it has all dissolved away, the natives think that a great cloud will come bringing rain. From the time the ceremony is performed until rain falls, the men must abstain from intercourse with their wives, or the charm would be spoiled.[2] In this custom the bloody paste seems to be an imitation of a rain-cloud. In Java, when rain is wanted, two men will sometimes thrash each other with supple rods

Use of human blood in rain-making ceremonies.

----

[1] A. W. Howitt, "The Dieri and other Kindred Tribes of Central Australia," *Journal of the Anthropological Institute*, xx. (1891) pp. 92 *sq.* ; *id.*, *Native Tribes of South-East Australia*, pp. 396, 744.

[2] A. W. Howitt, *Native Tribes of South-East Australia*, pp. 396 *sq.*

till the blood flows down their backs; the streaming blood represents the rain, and no doubt is supposed to make it fall on the ground.[1]　The people of Egghiou, a district of Abyssinia, used to engage in sanguinary conflicts with each other, village against village, for a week together every January for the purpose of procuring rain.　A few years ago the emperor Menelik forbade the custom.　However, the following year the rain was deficient, and the popular outcry so great that the emperor yielded to it, and allowed the murderous fights to be resumed, but for two days a year only.[2]　The writer who mentions the custom regards the blood shed on these occasions as a propitiatory sacrifice offered to spirits who control the showers; but perhaps, as in the Australian and Javanese ceremonies, it is an imitation of rain.　The prophets of Baal, who sought to procure rain by cutting themselves with knives till the blood gushed out,[3] may have acted on the same principle.

Rain-making among the Kaitish. The Kaitish tribe of Central Australia believe that the rainbow is the son of the rain, and with filial regard is always anxious to prevent his father from falling down. Hence if it appears in the sky at a time when rain is wanted, they "sing" or enchant it in order to send it away.　When the head man of the rain totem in this tribe desires to make rain he goes to the sacred store-house of his local group.　There he paints the holy stones with red ochre and sings over them, and as he sings he pours water from a vessel on them and on himself. Moreover, he paints three rainbows in red ochre, one on the ground, one on his own body, and one on a shield, which he also decorates with zigzag lines of white clay to represent lightning.　This shield may only be seen by men of the

[1] J. Kreemer, "Regenmaken, Oed-joeng, Tooverij onder de Javanen," *Mededeelingen van wege het Nederland-sche Zendelinggenootschap*, xxx. (1886) p. 113.

[2] Coulbeaux, "Au pays de Menelik : à travers l'Abyssinie," *Missions Catho-liques*, xxx. (1898) p. 455.

[3] 1 Kings xviii. 28.　From the whole tenour of the narrative it appears that the real contest between Elijah and the prophets of Baal was as to which of them should make rain in a time of drought.　The prophets of Baal wrought magic by cutting them-selves with knives; Elijah wrought magic by pouring water on the altar. Both ceremonies alike were rain-charms.　Compare my note on the passage in *Passages of the Bible chosen for their Literary Beauty and Interest*, Second Edition (London, 1909), pp. 476 *sq.*

same exogamous half of the tribe as himself; if men of the other half of the tribe were to see it, the charm would be spoilt. Hence after bringing the shield away from the sacred place, he hides it in his own camp until the rain has fallen, after which he destroys the rainbow drawings. The intention seems to be to keep the rainbow in custody, and prevent it from appearing in the sky until the clouds have burst and moistened the thirsty ground. To ensure that event the rain-maker, on his return from the sacred storehouse, keeps a vessel of water by his side in camp, and from time to time scatters white down about, which is thought to hasten the rain. Meantime the men who accompanied him to the holy place go away and camp by themselves, for neither they nor he may have any inter- course with the women. The leader may not even speak to his wife, who absents herself from the camp at the time of his return to it. When later on she comes back, he imitates the call of the plover, a bird whose cry is always associated with the rainy season in these parts. Early next morning he returns to the sacred storehouse and covers the stones with bushes. After another night passed in silence, he and the other men and women go out in separate directions to search for food. When they meet on their return to camp, they all mimic the cry of the plover. Then the leader's mouth is touched with some of the food that has been brought in, and thus the ban of silence is removed. If rain follows, they attribute it to the magical virtue of the ceremony; if it does not, they fall back on their standing excuse, that some one else has kept off the rain by stronger magic.[1]

Among the Arunta tribe of Central Australia a cele- brated rain-maker resides at the present day in what is called by the natives the Rain Country (*Kartwia quatcha*), a district about fifty miles to the east of Alice Springs. He is the head of a group of people who have water for their totem, and when he is about to engage in a ceremony for the making of rain he summons other men of the water totem from neighbouring groups to come and help him.

Rain- making among the Arunta.

---

[1] Spencer and Gillen, *Northern Tribes of Central Australia*, pp. 294-296, 630 *sq.*

When all are assembled, they march into camp, painted with
red and yellow ochre and pipeclay, and wearing bunches of
eagle-hawk feathers on the crown and sides of the head.
At a signal from the rain-maker they all sit down in a line
and, folding their arms across their breasts, chant certain
words for a time.   Then at another signal from the master
of the ceremonies they jump up and march in single file to
a spot some miles off, where they camp for the night.   At
break of day they scatter in all directions to look for game,
which is then cooked and eaten ; but on no account may
any water be drunk, or the ceremony would fail.   When
they have eaten, they adorn themselves again in a different
style, broad bands of white bird's down being glued by
means of human blood to their stomach, legs, arms, and
forehead.   Meanwhile a special hut of boughs has been
made by some older men not far from the main camp.   Its
floor is strewn with a thick layer of gum leaves to make it
soft, for a good deal of time has to be spent lying down
here.   Close to the entrance of the hut a shallow trench,
some thirty yards long, is excavated in the ground.   At
sunset the performers, arrayed in all the finery of white
down, march to the hut.   On reaching it the young men go
in first and lie face downwards at the inner end, where they
have to stay till the ceremony is over ; none of them is
allowed to quit it on any pretext.   Meanwhile, outside the
hut the older men are busy decorating the rain-maker.
Hair girdles, covered with white down, are placed all over
his head, while his cheeks and forehead are painted with
pipeclay; and two broad bands of white down pass across
the face, one over the eyebrows and the other over the nose.
The front of his body is adorned with a broad band of pipeclay fringed with white down, and rings of white down
encircle his arms.   Thus decorated, with patches of bird's
down adhering by means of human blood to his hair and the
whole of his body, the disguised man is said to present a
spectacle which, once seen, can never be forgotten.   He now
takes up a position close to the opening of the hut.   Then
the old men sing a song, and when it is finished, the rain-
maker comes out of the hut and stalks slowly twice up and
down the shallow trench, quivering his body and legs in a

most extraordinary way, every nerve and fibre seeming to tremble. While he is thus engaged the young men, who had been lying flat on their faces, get up and join the old men in chanting a song with which the movements of the rain-maker seem to accord. But as soon as he re-enters the hut, the young men at once prostrate themselves again ; for they must always be lying down when he is in the hut. The performance is repeated at intervals during the night, and the singing goes on with little intermission until, just when the day is breaking, the rain-maker executes a final quiver, which lasts longer than any of the others, and seems to exhaust his remaining strength completely. Then he declares the ceremony to be over, and at once the young men jump to their feet and rush out of the hut, screaming in imitation of the spur-winged plover. The cry is heard by the men and women who have been left at the main camp, and they take it up with weird effect.[1]

Although we cannot, perhaps, divine the meaning of all the details of this curious ceremony, the analogy of the Queensland and the Dieri ceremonies, described above, suggests that we have here a rude attempt to represent the gathering of rain-clouds and the other accompaniments of a rising storm. The hut of branches, like the structure of logs among the Dieri, and perhaps the conical shed in Queensland, may possibly stand for the vault of heaven, from which the rain-clouds, represented by the chief actor in his quaint costume of white down, come forth to move in ever-shifting shapes across the sky, just as he struts quivering up and down the trench. The other performers, also adorned with bird's down, who burst from the tent with the cries of plovers, probably imitate birds that are supposed to harbinger or accompany rain.[2] This interpretation is confirmed by other ceremonies in which the performers definitely assimilate

Rain-making by imitation of clouds and storm.

---

[1] F. J. Gillen, in *Report of the Work of the Horn Scientific Expedition to Central Australia*, part iv., Anthropology (London and Melbourne, 1896), pp. 177-179; Spencer and Gillen, *Native Tribes of Central Australia*, pp. 189-193.

[2] As to the connexion of the plover with rain in Central Australia, see above, p. 259. It is curious that the same association has procured for the bird its name in English, French (*pluvier*, from the Latin *pluvia*), and German (*Regenpfeifer*). Ornithologists are not agreed as to the reason for this association in the popular mind. See Alfred Newton, *Dictionary of Birds* (London, 1893-1896), pp. 730 *sq.*

themselves to the celestial or atmospheric phenomena which they seek to produce. Thus in Mabuiag, a small island in Torres Straits, when a wizard desired to make rain, he took some bush or plant and painted himself black and white, " All along same as clouds, black behind, white he go first." He further put on a large woman's petticoat to signify raining clouds. On the other hand, when he wished to stop the rain, he put red paint on the crown of his head, " to represent the shining sun," and he inserted a small ball of red paint in another part of his person. By and by he expelled this ball, " Like breaking a cloud so that sun he may shine." He then took some bushes and leaves of the pandanus, mixed them together, and placed the compound in the sea. Afterwards he removed them from the water, dried them, and burnt them so that the smoke went up, thereby typifying, as Dr. Haddon was informed, the evaporation and dispersal of the clouds.[1] Again, it is said that if a Malay woman puts upon her head an inverted earthenware pan, and then, setting it upon the ground, fills it with water and washes the cat in it till the animal is nearly drowned, heavy rain will certainly follow. In this performance the inverted pan is intended, as Mr. Skeat was told, to symbolise the vault of heaven.[2]

Belief that twins can control the weather. There is a widespread belief that twin children possess magical powers over nature, especially over rain and the weather. This curious superstition prevails among some of the Indian tribes of British Columbia, and has led them often to impose certain singular restrictions or taboos on the parents of twins, though the exact meaning of these restrictions is generally obscure. Thus the Tsimshian Indians of British Columbia believe that twins control the weather; therefore they pray to wind and rain, " Calm down, breath of the twins." Further, they think that the wishes of twins are always fulfilled; hence twins are feared, because they can harm the man they hate. They can also call the salmon and the olachen or candle-fish, and so they are

Supersti-
tions as to
twins
among the
Indians of
British
Columbia.

---

[1] A. C. Haddon, "The Ethnography of the Western Tribe of Torres Straits," *Journal of the Anthropological Institute*, xix. (1890) p. 401 ; *Reports of the* *Cambridge Anthropological Expedition to Torres Straits*, v. 350.

[2] W. W. Skeat, *Malay Magic*, p. 108.

known by a name which means "making plentiful."[1] In the opinion of the Kwakiutl Indians of British Columbia twins are transformed salmon; hence they may not go near water, lest they should be changed back again into the fish. In their childhood they can summon any wind by motions of their hands, and they can make fair or foul weather, and also cure diseases by swinging a large wooden rattle. Their parents must live secluded in the woods for sixteen months after the birth, doing no work, borrowing nobody's canoes, paddles, or dishes, and keeping their faces painted red all the time. If the father were to catch salmon, or the mother were to dig clams, the salmon and the clams would disappear. Moreover the parents separate from each other, and must pretend to be married to a log, with which they lie down every night. They are forbidden to touch each other, and even their own hair. A year after the birth they drive wedges into a tree in the woods, asking it to let them work again when four more months have passed.[2] The Nootka Indians of British Columbia also believe that twins are somehow related to salmon. Hence among them twins may not catch salmon, and they may not eat or even handle the fresh fish. They can make fair or foul weather, and can cause rain to fall by painting their faces black and then washing them, which may represent the rain dripping from the dark clouds.[3] Conversely, among the Angoni of Central Africa there is a woman who stops rain by tying a strip of white calico round her black head,[4] probably in imitation of the sky clearing after a heavy storm. The parents of twins among the Nootkas must build a small hut in the woods on the bank of a river, far from the village, and there they must live for two years, avoiding other people; they may not eat or even touch fresh food, particularly salmon.

---

[1] Fr. Boas, in *Fifth Report on the North-Western Tribes of Canada*, p. 51 (separate reprint from the *Report of the British Association for 1889*).

[2] Fr. Boas, *loc. cit.*; *id.* in *Sixth Report on the North-Western Tribes of Canada*, pp. 58, 62 (separate reprint from the *Report of the British Association for 1890*); *id.* in *Eleventh Report on the North-Western Tribes of Canada*, p. 5 (separate reprint from the *Report of the British Association for 1896*).

[3] Fr. Boas, in *Sixth Report on the North-Western Tribes of Canada*, pp. 39 *sq.* (separate reprint from the *Report of the British Association for 1890*).

[4] *British Central Africa Gazette*, No. 86 (vol. v. no. 6), 30th April 1898, p. 3.

Supersti-
tions as to
twins
among the
Indians of
British
Columbia.
Wooden images and masks of birds and fish are placed round the hut, and others, representing fish, are set near the river for the purpose of inviting all birds and fish to come and see the twins, and be friendly to them. Moreover the father sings a special song praising the salmon, and asking them to come. And the fish do come in great numbers to see the twins. Therefore the birth of twins is believed to prognosticate a good year for salmon.[1] But though a Nootka father of twins has thus to live in seclusion for two years, abstaining from fresh meat, and attending none of the ordinary feasts, he is, by a singular exception, invited to banquets which consist wholly of dried provisions, and at them he is treated with great respect and seated among the chiefs, even though he be himself a mere commoner. The birth of twins among the Nootkas is said to be very rare, but one occurred while Jewitt lived with the tribe. He reports that the father always appeared very thoughtful and gloomy, and never associated with other people. " His dress was very plain, and he wore around his head the red fillet of bark, the symbol of mourning and devotion. It was his daily practice to repair to the mountain, with a chief's rattle in his hand, to sing and pray, as Maquina informed me, for the fish to come into their waters. When not thus employed, he kept continually at home, except when sent for to sing and perform his ceremonies over the sick, being considered as a sacred character, and one much in favour with their gods."[2] Among the Thompson Indians of British Columbia twins were called " grizzly-bear children " or " hairy feet," because they were thought to be under the protection of the grizzly bear, and to be endowed by him with special powers, such as that of making fair or foul weather. After their birth the parents moved away from other people, and lived in a lodge made of fir-boughs and bark till the children were about four years old. During all this time great care was taken of the twins. They might not come into contact with other people, and were washed with fir-twigs dipped in water. While they were being

[1] Fr. Boas, *loc. cit.*

[2] *Narrative of the Adventures and* *Sufferings of John R. Jewitt* (Middletown, 1820), pp. 173 *sq.* (p. 198, Edinburgh, 1824).

washed, the father described circles round them with fir-boughs, singing the song of the grizzly bear.[1] With these American beliefs we may compare an African one. The negroes of Porto Novo, on the Bight of Benin, hold that twins have for their companions certain spirits or genii like those which animate a kind of small ape, which abounds in the forests of Guinea. When the twins grow up, they will not be allowed to eat the flesh of apes, and meantime the mother carries offerings of bananas and other dainties to the apes in the forest.[2] Precisely similar beliefs and customs as to twins prevail in the Ho tribe of German Togo-land. There the twins are called "children of apes"; neither they nor their parents may eat the flesh of the particular species of apes with which they are associated ; and if a hunter kills one of these animals, the parents must beat him with a stick.[3] But to return to America. The Shuswap Indians of British Columbia, like the Thompson Indians, associate twins with the grizzly bear, for they call them "young grizzly bears." According to them, twins remain throughout life endowed with supernatural powers. In particular they can make good or bad weather. They produce rain by spilling water from a basket in the air ; they make fine weather by shaking a small flat piece of wood attached to a stick by a string ; they raise storms by strewing down on the ends of spruce branches.[4]

The Indians of Peru entertained similar notions as to

[1] J. Teit, "The Thompson Indians of British Columbia," pp. 310 sq. (Memoir of the American Museum of Natural History, The Jesup North Pacific Expedition, vol. i. part iv.). The Lillooet Indians of British Columbia also believed that twins were the real offspring of grizzly bears. Many of them said that twins were grizzly bears in human form, and that when a twin died his soul went back to the grizzly bears and became one of them. See J. Teit, "The Lillooet Indians," (Leyden and New York, 1906), p. 263 (Memoir of the American Museum of Natural History, The Jesup North Pacific Expedition, vol. ii. part v.).

[2] Father Baudin, "Le Fétichisme ou la religion des Nègres de la Guinée,"

Missions Catholiques, xvi. (1884) p. 250.

[3] J. Spieth, Die Ewe Stämme (Berlin, 1906), pp. 204, 206.

[4] Fr. Boas, in Sixth Report on the North-Western Tribes of Canada, p. 92 (separate reprint from the Report of the British Association for 1890). The instrument by which the twins make fine weather appears to be a bull-roarer. Compare J. Teit, "The Shuswap" (Leyden and New York, 1909), pp. 586 sq. (Memoir of the American Museum of Natural History, The Jesup North Pacific Expedition, vol. ii. part vii.) : "Twins were believed to be endowed with powers over the elements, especially over rain and snow. If a twin bathed in a lake or stream, it would rain."

Supersti-
tions as
to twins
among the
Indians of
Peru.
the special relation in which twins stand to the rain and the weather. For they said that one of each pair of twins was a son of the lightning; and they called the lightning the lord and creator of rain, and prayed to him to send showers. The parents of twins had to fast for many days after the birth, abstaining from salt and pepper, and they might not have intercourse with each other. In some parts of Peru this period of fasting and abstinence lasted six months. In other parts both the father and mother had to lie down on one side, with one leg drawn up, and a bean placed in the hollow of the ham. In this position they had to lie without moving for five days, till with the heat and sweat of their bodies the beans began to sprout. Then they changed over to the other side, and lay on it in like manner for other five days, fasting in the way described. When the ten days were up, their relations went out to hunt, and having killed and skinned a deer they made a robe of its hide, under which they caused the parents of the twins to pass, with cords about their necks which they afterwards wore for many days. If the twins died young, their bodies, enclosed in pots, were kept in the house as sacred things. But if they lived, and it happened that a frost set in, the priests sent for them, together with all persons who had hare-lips or had been born feet foremost, and rated them soundly for being the cause of the frost, in that they had not fasted from salt and pepper. Wherefore they were ordered to fast for ten days in the usual manner, and to abstain from their wives, and to wash themselves, and to acknowledge and confess their sins. After their nominal conversion to Christianity, the Peruvian Indians retained their belief that one of twins was always the son of the lightning, and oddly enough they regularly gave him the name of St. James (Santiago). The Spanish Jesuit, who reports the custom, was at a loss to account for it. It could not, he thought, have originated in the name of Boanerges, or "sons of thunder," which Christ applied to the two brothers James and John.[1] He suggests two explanations.

---

[1] Mark iii. 17. If James and John had been twins, we might have suspected that their name of Boanerges had its origin in a superstition like that of the Peruvian Indians. Was it in the character of "sons of thunder"

The Indians may have adopted the name because they had
heard a phrase used by Spanish children when it thunders,
" The horse of Santiago is running." Or it may have been
because they saw that the Spanish infantry in battle, before
they fired their arquebuses, always cried out " Santiago !
Santiago ! " For the Indians called an arquebuse *illapa*,
that is, " lightning," and they might easily imagine that the
name which they heard shouted just before the flash and
roar of the guns was that of the Spanish god of thunder
and lightning. However they came by the name, they
made such frequent and superstitious use of it that the
church forbade any Indian to bear the name of Santiago.[1]

The same power of influencing the weather is attributed ^{Supersti-}
to twins by the Baronga, a tribe of Bantu negroes who ^{tions as to twins in}
inhabit the shores of Delagoa Bay in south-eastern Africa. ^{Africa.}
They bestow the name of *Tilo*—that is, the sky—on a
woman who has given birth to twins, and the infants
themselves are called the children of the sky. Now
when the storms which generally burst in the months
of September and October have been looked for in
vain, when a drought with its prospect of famine is
threatening, and all nature, scorched and burnt up by a sun
that has shone for six months from a cloudless sky, is
panting for the beneficent showers of the South African
spring, the women perform ceremonies to bring down the
longed-for rain on the parched earth. Stripping themselves
of all their garments, they assume in their stead girdles and
head-dresses of grass, or short petticoats made of the leaves
of a particular sort of creeper. Thus attired, uttering
peculiar cries and singing ribald songs, they go about from
well to well, cleansing them of the mud and impurities which
have accumulated in them. The wells, it may be said, are
merely holes in the sand where a little turbid unwholesome
water stagnates. Further, the women must repair to the
house of one of their gossips who has given birth to twins,
and must drench her with water, which they carry in little
pitchers. Having done so they go on their way, shrieking

that the brothers proposed to call
down fire from heaven on a Samaritan
village (Luke ix. 54)?

[1] P. J. de Arriaga, *Extirpacion de
la idolatria del Piru* (Lima, 1621), pp.
16 *sq.*, 32, 33, 119, 130, 132.

out their loose songs and dancing immodest dances. No man may see these leaf-clad women going their rounds. If they meet a man, they maul him and thrust him aside. When they have cleansed the wells, they must go and pour water on the graves of their ancestors in the sacred grove. It often happens, too, that at the bidding of the wizard they go and pour water on the graves of twins. For they think that the grave of a twin ought always to be moist, for which reason twins are regularly buried near a lake. If all their efforts to procure rain prove abortive, they will remember that such and such a twin was buried in a dry place on the side of a hill. " No wonder," says the wizard in such a case, " that the sky is fiery. Take up his body and dig him a grave on the shore of the lake." His orders are at once obeyed, for this is supposed to be the only means of bringing down the rain. The Swiss missionary who reports this strange superstition has also suggested what appears to be its true explanation. He points out that as the mother of twins is called by the Baronga " the sky," they probably think that to pour water on her is equivalent to pouring water on the sky itself ; and if water be poured on the sky, it will of course drip through it, as through the nozzle of a gigantic watering-pot, and fall on the earth beneath. A slight extension of the same train of reasoning explains why the desired result is believed to be expedited by drenching the graves of twins, who are the Children of the Sky.[1] Among the Zulus twins are supposed to be able to foretell the weather, and people who want rain will go to a twin and say, " Tell me, do you feel ill to-day ? " If he says he feels quite well, they know it will not rain.[2] The Wanyamwesi, a large tribe of Central Africa, to the south of the Victoria Nyanza, also believe in the special association of twins with water. For amongst them, when a twin is about to cross a river, stream, or lake, he must fill his mouth full of water and spirt it out over the surface of the river or lake, adding, " I am a twin " (*nänä mpassa*).

---

[1] H. A. Junod, *Les Ba-ronga* (Neuchâtel, 1898), pp. 412, 416 *sqq*. The reason for calling twins " Children of the Sky " is obscure. Are they supposed in some mysterious way to stand for the sun and moon ?

[2] Dudley Kidd, *Savage Childhood* (London, 1906), p. 47.

And he must do the same if a storm arises on a lake over which he is sailing. Were he to omit the ceremony, some harm might befall him or his companions. In this tribe the birth of twins is comparatively common and is attended by a number of ceremonies. Old women march about the village collecting gifts for the infants, while they drum with a hoe on a piece of ox-hide and sing an obscene song in praise of the father. Further, two little fetish huts are built for the twins before their mother's house, and here people sacrifice for them in season and out of season, especially when somebody is sick or about to go on a journey or to the wars. If one or both twins die, two aloes are planted beside the little fetish hut.[1] Lastly, the Hindoos of the Central Provinces in India believe that a twin can save the crops from the ravages of hail and heavy rain if he will only paint his right buttock black and his left buttock some other colour, and thus adorned go and stand in the direction of the wind.[2]

Many of the foregoing facts strongly support an interpretation which Professor Oldenberg has given of the rules to be observed by a Brahman who would learn a particular hymn of the ancient Indian collection known as the Samaveda. The hymn, which bears the name of the Sakvarī song, was believed to embody the might of Indra's weapon, the thunderbolt ; and hence, on account of the dreadful and dangerous potency with which it was thus charged, the bold student who essayed to master it had to be isolated from his fellow-men, and to retire from the village into the forest. Here for a space of time, which might vary, according to different doctors of the law, from one to twelve years, he had to observe certain rules of life, among which were the following. Thrice a day he had to touch water ; he must wear black

The rain-maker assimilates himself to rain.

---

[1] P. Reichard, " Die Wanjamuesi," *Zeitschrift der Gesellschaft für Erdkunde zu Berlin*, xxiv. (1889), pp. 256 *sq.* Another African superstition as to twins may here be mentioned. On the Slave Coast when a woman has brought forth stillborn twins, she has a statue made with two faces and sets it up in a corner of her house. There she offers it fowls, bananas, and palm-oil in order to obtain the accomplishment of her wishes, and especially a knowledge of the future. See *Missions Catholiques*, vii. (1875) p. 592. This suggests that elsewhere two-faced images, like those of Janus, may have been intended to represent twins.

[2] M. N. Venketswami, " Superstitions among Hindus in the Central Provinces," *Indian Antiquary*, xxviii. (1899) p. 111.

The rain-maker assimilates himself to rain.

garments and eat black food; when it rained, he might not seek the shelter of a roof, but had to sit in the rain and say, "Water is the Ṣakvarī song"; when the lightning flashed he said, "That is like the Ṣakvarī song"; when the thunder pealed he said, "The Great One is making a great noise." He might never cross a running stream without touching water; he might never set foot on a ship unless his life were in danger, and even then he must be sure to touch water when he went on board; "for in water," so ran the saying, "lies the virtue of the Ṣakvarī song." When at last he was allowed to learn the song itself, he had to dip his hands in a vessel of water in which plants of all sorts had been placed. If a man walked in the way of all these precepts, the rain-god Parjanya, it was said, would send rain at the wish of that man. It is clear, as Professor Oldenberg well points out, that "all these rules are intended to bring the Brahman into union with water, to make him, as it were, an ally of the water powers, and to guard him against their hostility. The black garments and the black food have the same significance; no one will doubt that they refer to the rain-clouds when he remembers that a black victim is sacrificed to procure rain; 'it is black, for such is the nature of rain.' In respect of another rain-charm it is said plainly, 'He puts on a black garment edged with black, for such is the nature of rain.' We may therefore assume that here in the circle of ideas and ordinances of the Vedic schools there have been preserved magical practices of the most remote antiquity, which were intended to prepare the rain-maker for his office and dedicate him to it."[1]

On the contrary, the maker of dry weather must himself be dry.

It is interesting to observe that where an opposite result is desired, primitive logic enjoins the weather-doctor to observe precisely opposite rules of conduct. In the tropical island of Java, where the rich vegetation attests the abundance of the rainfall, ceremonies for the making of rain are rare, but ceremonies for the prevention of it are not uncommon. When a man is about to give a great feast in the rainy season and has invited many people, he goes to a

[1] The Grihya-Sûtras, translated by H. Oldenberg, part ii. (Oxford, 1892) pp. 72 sq. (Sacred Books of the East, vol. xxx.); H. Oldenberg, Die Religion des Veda, pp. 420 sq.

weather-doctor and asks him to " prop up the clouds that
may be lowering."   If the doctor consents to exert his
professional powers, he begins to regulate his behaviour by
certain rules as soon as his customer has departed.   He
must observe a fast, and may neither drink nor bathe ; what
little he eats must be eaten dry, and in no case may he touch
water.   The host, on his side, and his servants, both male
and female, must neither wash clothes nor bathe so long as
the feast lasts, and they have all during its continuance to
observe strict chastity.   The doctor seats himself on a new
mat in his bedroom, and before a small oil-lamp he murmurs,
shortly before the feast takes place, the following prayer or
incantation : " Grandfather and Grandmother Sroekoel" (the
name seems to be taken at random ; others are sometimes
used), " return to your country.   Akkemat is your country.
Put down your water-cask, close it properly, that not a drop
may fall out."   While he utters this prayer the sorcerer looks
upwards, burning incense the while.[1]   So among the Toradjas
of Central Celebes the rain-doctor (*sando*), whose special
business it is to drive away rain, takes care not to touch
water before, during, or after the discharge of his professional duties.   He does not bathe, he eats with unwashed
hands, he drinks nothing but palm wine, and if he has to
cross a stream he is careful not to step in the water.
Having thus prepared himself for his task he has a small
hut built for himself outside of the village in a rice-field, and
in this hut he keeps up a little fire, which on no account may
be suffered to go out.   In the fire he burns various kinds of
wood, which are supposed to possess the property of driving
off rain ; and he puffs in the direction from which the rain
threatens to come, holding in his hand a packet of leaves
and bark which derive a similar cloud-compelling virtue, not
from their chemical composition, but from their names, which
happen to signify something dry or volatile.   If clouds
should appear in the sky while he is at work, he takes lime
in the hollow of his hand and blows it towards them.   The
lime, being so very dry, is obviously well adapted to disperse
the damp clouds.   Should rain afterwards be wanted, he

---

[1] G. G. Batten, *Glimpses of the Eastern Archipelago* (Singapore, 1894), pp.
68 *sq.*

has only to pour water on his fire, and immediately the rain will descend in sheets.[1] So in Santa Cruz and Reef islands, when the man who has power over rain wishes to prevent it from falling, he will abstain from washing his face for a long time and will do no work, lest he should sweat and his body be wet; "for they think that if his body be wet it will rain." On the other hand when he desires to bring on rain, he goes into the house where the spirit or ghost of the rain is believed to reside, and there he sprinkles water at the head of the ghost-post (*duka*) in order that showers may fall.[2]

To make wet weather you must be wet; to make dry weather you must be dry.

The reader will observe how exactly the Javanese and Toradja observances, which are intended to prevent rain, form the antithesis of the Indian observances, which aim at producing it. The Indian sage is commanded to touch water thrice a day regularly as well as on various special occasions; the Javanese and Toradja wizards may not touch it at all. The Indian lives out in the forest, and even when it rains he may not take shelter; the Javanese and the Toradja sit in a house or a hut. The one signifies his sympathy with water by receiving the rain on his person and speaking of it respectfully; the others light a lamp or a fire and do their best to drive the rain away. Yet the principle on which all three act is the same; each of them, by a sort of childish make-believe, identifies himself with the phenomenon which he desires to produce. It is the old fallacy that the effect resembles its cause : if you would make wet weather, you must be wet; if you would make dry weather, you must be dry.

Rain-making in south-eastern Europe by drenching with water a leaf-clad girl or boy who represents vegetation.

In south-eastern Europe at the present day ceremonies are observed for the purpose of making rain which not only rest on the same general train of thought as the preceding, but even in their details resemble the ceremonies practised with the same intention by the Baronga of Delagoa Bay. Among the Greeks of Thessaly and Macedonia, when a drought has lasted a long time, it is customary to send a

---

[1] A. C. Kruijt, "Regen lokken en regen verdrijven bij de Toradja's van Midden Celebes," *Tijdschrift voor Indische Taal- Land- en Volkenkunde,* xliv. (1901) pp. 8-10.

[2] Rev. W. O'Ferrall, "Native Stories from Santa Cruz and Reef Islands," *Journal of the Anthropological Institute,* xxxiv. (1904), p. 225.

procession of children round to all the wells and springs of the neighbourhood.   At the head of the procession walks a girl adorned with flowers, whom her companions drench with water at every halting-place, while they sing an invocation, of which the following is part :—

> *Perperia, all fresh bedewed,*
> *Freshen all the neighbourhood;*
> *By the woods, on the highway,*
> *As thou goest, to God now pray :*
> *O my God, upon the plain,*
> *Send thou us a still, small rain;*
> *That the fields may fruitful be,*
> *And vines in blossom we may see;*
> *That the grain be full and sound,*
> *And wealthy grow the folks around.*[1]

In time of drought the Servians strip a girl to her skin and clothe her from head to foot in grass, herbs, and flowers, even her face being hidden behind a veil of living green. Thus disguised she is called the Dodola, and goes through the village with a troop of girls.   They stop before every house ; the Dodola keeps turning herself round and dancing, while the other girls form a ring about her singing one of the Dodola songs, and the housewife pours a pail of water over her.   One of the songs they sing runs thus :—

Rain-making in Servia.

> *We go through the village;*
> *The clouds go in the sky;*
> *We go faster,*
> *Faster go the clouds;*
> *They have overtaken us,*
> *And wetted the corn and the vine.*

A similar custom is observed in Greece and Roumania.[2] In Roumania the rain-maker is called Paparuda or Babaruda.   She is a gypsy girl, who goes naked except for a short skirt of dwarf elder (*Sambucus ebulus*) or of corn and vines.   Thus scantily attired the girls go in procession from house to house, singing for rain, and are drenched by

Rain-making in Roumania.

---

[1] Lucy M. J. Garnett, *The Women of Turkey and their Folklore: The Christian Women*, pp. 123 *sq.*

[2] W. Mannhardt, *Baumkultus*, pp. 329 *sqq.*; J. Grimm, *Deutsche Mythologie*,[4] i. 493 *sq.*; W. R. S. Ralston, *Songs of the Russian People*, pp. 227 *sqq.*; W. Schmidt, *Das Jahr und seine Tage in Meinung und Brauch der Romänen Siebenbürgens*, p. 17 ; E. Gerard, *The Land beyond the Forest*, ii. 13 ; *Folk-lore*, i. (1890) p. 520.

the people with buckets of water. The ceremony regularly takes place all over Roumania on the third Tuesday after Easter, but it may be repeated at any time of drought during the summer. But the Roumanians have another way of procuring rain. They make a clay figure to represent Drought, cover it with a pall, and place it in an open coffin. Girls crouch round the coffin and lament, saying, " Drought (*Scaloi*) is dead ! Lord, give us rain ! " Then the coffin is carried by children in funeral procession, with a burning wax candle before it, while lamentations fill the air. Finally, they throw the coffin and the candle into a stream or a well.[1] When rain is wanted in Bulgaria the people dress up a girl in branches of nut-trees, flowers, and the green stuff of beans, potatoes, and onions. She carries a nosegay of flowers in her hand, and is called Djuldjul or Peperuga. Attended by a train of followers she goes from house to house, and is received by the goodman with a kettleful of water, on which flowers are swimming. With this water he drenches her, while a song is sung :—

Rain-making in Bulgaria.

> *The Peperuga flew ;*
> *God give rain,*
> *That the corn, the millet, and the wheat may thrive.*

Rain-making in Macedonia and Dalmatia.

Sometimes the girl is dressed in flax to the girdle.[2] At Melenik, a Greek town in Macedonia, a poor orphan boy parades the streets in time of drought, decked with ferns and flowers, and attended by other boys of about the same age. The women shower water and money on him from the windows. He is called Dudulé, and as they march along the boys sing a song, which begins : " Hail, hail, Dudulé, (bring us) both maize and wheat." [3] In Dalmatia also the custom is observed. The performer is a young unmarried man, who is dressed up, dances, and has water poured over him. He goes by the name of Prpats, and is attended by companions called Prporushe, who are young bachelors like himself.[4] In such customs the leaf-clad person appears to

---

[1] *The Graphic*, September 9, 1905, p. 324 ; Dr. Emil Fischer, " Paparuda und Scaloian," *Globus*, xciii. (1908) pp. 14 *sq.*

[2] W. Mannhardt, *Baumkultus*, p. 329.

[3] G. F. Abbott, *Macedonian Folklore* (Cambridge, 1903), pp. 118 *sq.*

[4] W. R. S. Ralston, *Songs of the Russian People*, p. 228 ; W. Mannhardt, *Baumkultus*, pp. 329 *sq.*

personify vegetation, and the drenching of him or her with water is certainly an imitation of rain. The words of the Servian song, however, taken in connexion with the constant movement which the chief actress in the performance seems expected to keep up, points to some comparison of the girl or her companions to clouds moving through the sky. This again reminds us of the odd quivering movement kept up by the Australian rain-maker, who, in his disguise of white down, may perhaps represent a cloud.[1] At Poona in India, The King when rain is needed, the boys dress up one of their number of Rain in in nothing but leaves and call him King of Rain (*Mrüj raja*). India. Then they go round to every house in the village, where the householder or his wife sprinkles the Rain King with water, and gives the party food of various kinds. When they have thus visited all the houses, they strip the Rain King of his leafy robes and feast upon what they have gathered.[2]

Similar rain-charms are practised in Armenia, except Rain- that there the representative of vegetation is an effigy or making in doll, not a person. The children dress up a broomstick as Armenia. a girl and carry it from house to house. Before every house they sing a song, of which the following is one version :—

> *Nurin, Nurin is come,*
> *The wondrous maiden is come.*
> *A shirt of red stuff has she put on,*
> *With a red girdle is she girded.*
> *Bring water to pour on her head,*
> *Bring butter to smear on her hair.*
> *Let the blessed rain fall,*
> *Let the fields of your fathers grow green.*
> *Give our Nurin her share,*
> *And we will eat and drink and be merry.*

The children are asked, "Will you have it from the door or from the garret-window?" If they choose the door, the water is poured on Nurin from the window ; and if they choose the window, it is poured on her from the door. At each house they receive presents of butter, eggs, rice, and so

---

[1] See above, pp. 260 *sq.* This per- petual turning or whirling movement is required of the actors in other European ceremonies of a superstitious character. See below, vol. ii. pp. 74, 80, 81, 87. I am far from feeling sure that the explanation of it suggested in the text is the true one. But I do not remember to have met with any other.

[2] Father H. S. Moore, in *The Cowley Evangelist*, May 1908, pp. 111 *sq.*

forth. Afterwards they take Nurin to a river and throw her into the water. Sometimes the figure has the head of a pig or a goat, and is covered with boughs.[1] At Egin in Armenia, when rain is wanted, boys carry about an effigy which they call Chi-chi Mama or "the drenched Mother," as they interpret the phrase. As they go about they ask, "What does Chi-chi Mother want?" The answer is, "She wants wheat in her bins, she wants bread on her bread-hooks, and she wants rain from God!" The people pour water on her from the roofs, and rich people make presents to the children.[2] At Ourfa in Armenia the children in time of drought make a rain-bride, which they call Chimché-gelin. They say this means in Turkish "shovel-bride." While they carry it about they say, "What does Chimché-gelin want? She wishes mercy from God: she wants offerings of lambs and rams." And the crowd responds, "Give, my God, give rain, give a flood." The rain-bride is then thrown into the water.[3] At Kerak in Palestine, whenever there is a drought, the Greek Christians dress up a winnowing-fork in women's clothes. They call it "the bride of God." The girls and women carry it from house to house, singing doggerel songs.[4] We are not told that "the bride of God" is drenched with water or thrown into a stream, but the charm would hardly be complete without this feature. Similarly, when rain is much wanted, the Arabs of Moab attire a dummy in the robes and ornaments of a woman and call it "the Mother of the Rain." A woman carries it in procession past the houses of the village or the tents of the camp, singing:—

Rain-making in Palestine and Moab.

> *O Mother of the Rain, O Immortal, moisten our sleeping seeds.*
> *Moisten the sleeping seeds of the sheikh, who is ever generous.*
> *She is gone, the Mother of the Rain, to bring the storm; when she comes back, the crops are as high as the walls.*
> *She is gone, the Mother of the Rain, to bring the winds; when she comes back, the plantations have attained the height of lances.*
> *She is gone, the Mother of the Rain, to bring the thunders; when she comes back, the crops are as high as camels.*

And so on.[5]

[1] M. Abeghian, *Der armenische Volksglaube* (Leipsic, 1899), pp. 93 *sq.*

[2] J. Rendel Harris, MS. notes of folklore collected in the East.

[3] Rendel Harris, *op. cit.*

[4] S. I. Curtiss, *Primitive Semitic Religion To-day*, p. 114.

[5] A. Jaussen, *Coutumes des Arabes au pays de Moab* (Paris, 1908), pp. 326, 328.

Bathing is practised as a rain-charm in some parts of southern and western Russia. Sometimes after service in church the priest in his robes has been thrown down on the ground and drenched with water by his parishioners. Sometimes it is the women who, without stripping off their clothes, bathe in crowds on the day of St. John the Baptist, while they dip in the water a figure made of branches, grass, and herbs, which is supposed to represent the saint.[1] In Kursk, a province of southern Russia, when rain is much wanted, the women seize a passing stranger and throw him into the river, or souse him from head to foot.[2] Later on we shall see that a passing stranger is often taken for a deity or the personification of some natural power. It is recorded in official documents that during a drought in 1790 the peasants of Scheroutz and Werboutz collected all the women and compelled them to bathe, in order that rain might fall.[3] An Armenian rain-charm is to throw the wife of a priest into the water and drench her.[4] The Arabs of North Africa fling a holy man, willy-nilly, into a spring as a remedy for drought.[5] In Minahassa, a province of North Celebes, the priest bathes as a rain-charm.[6] In Central Celebes when there has been no rain for a long time and the rice-stalks begin to shrivel up, many of the villagers, especially the young folk, go to a neighbouring brook and splash each other with water, shouting noisily, or squirt water on one another through bamboo tubes. Sometimes they imitate the plump of rain by smacking the surface of the water with their hands, or by placing an inverted gourd on it and drumming on the gourd with their fingers.[7] The Karo-Bataks of Sumatra have a rain-making ceremony which lasts a week. The men go about with bamboo squirts and the women with

Rain-making by bathing and sprinkling of water.

---

[1] J. Polek, "Regenzauber in Osteuropa," *Zeitschrift des Vereins für Volkskunde*, iii. (1893) p. 85. For the bathing of the priest compare W. Mannhardt, *Baumkultus*, p. 331, note 2.

[2] W. Mannhardt, *Baumkultus*, p. 331.

[3] R. F. Kaindl, "Zauberglaube bei den Rutenen in der Bukowina und Galizien," *Globus*, lxi. (1892) p. 281.

[4] M. Abeghian, *Der armenische Volksglaube* (Leipsic, 1899), p. 93.

[5] E. Doutté, *Magie et religion dans l'Afrique du Nord*, p. 584.

[6] J. G. F. Riedel, "De Minahasa in 1825," *Tijdschrift voor Indische Taal- Land- en Volkenkunde*, xviii. 524.

[7] A. C. Kruijt, "Regen lokken en regen verdrijven bij de Toradja's van Midden Celebes," *Tijdschrift voor Indische Taal- Land- en Volkenkunde*, xliv. (1901) pp. 1 *sq.*

Rain-
making by
bathing
and sprink-
ling of
water.

bowls of water, and they drench each other or throw the water into the air and cry, "The rain has come," when it drips down on them.[1] In Kumaon, a district of north-west India, when rain fails they sink a Brahman up to his lips in a tank or pond, where he repeats the name of a god of rain for a day or two. When this rite is duly performed, rain is sure to fall.[2] For the same purpose village girls in the Punjaub will pour a solution of cow-dung in water upon an old woman who happens to pass; or they will make her sit down under the roof-spout of a house and get a wetting when it rains.[3] In the Solok district of Sumatra, when a drought has lasted a long time, a number of half-naked women take a half-witted man to a river; and there besprinkle him with water as a means of compelling the rain to fall.[4] In some parts of Bengal, when drought threatens the country, troops of children of all ages go from house to house and roll and tumble in puddles which have been prepared for the purpose by pouring water into the courtyards. This is supposed to bring down rain. Again, in Dubrajpur, a village in the Birbhum district of Bengal, when rain has been looked for in vain, people will throw dirt or filth on the houses of their neighbours, who abuse them for doing so. Or they drench the lame, the halt, the blind, and other infirm persons, and are reviled for their pains by the victims. This vituperation is believed to bring about the desired result by drawing down showers on the parched earth.[5] Similarly, in the Shahpur district of the Punjaub it is said to be customary in time of drought to spill a pot of filth on the threshold of a notorious old shrew, in order that the fluent stream of foul language in which she vents her feelings may accelerate the lingering rain.[6]

Curses sup-
posed to
cause rain.

[1] M. Joustra, "De Zending onder de Karo-Batak's," *Mededeelingen van wege het Nederlandsche Zendeling-genootschap*, xli. (1897) p. 158.

[2] *North Indian Notes and Queries*, iii. p. 134, § 285.

[3] W. Crooke, *Popular Religion and Folklore of Northern India* (Westminster, 1896), i. 73 *sq.*

[4] J. L. van der Toorn, "Het animisme bij den Minangkabauer der

Padangsche Bovenlanden," *Bijdragen tot de Taal- Land- en Volkenkunde van Nederlandsch-Indië*, xxxix. (1890) p. 93.

[5] Sarat Chandra Mitra, "On some Ceremonies for producing Rain," *Journal of the Anthropological Society of Bombay*, iii. (1893) pp. 25, 27; *id.*, in *North Indian Notes and Queries*, v. p. 136, § 373.

[6] *Panjab Notes and Queries*, i. p. 102, § 791.

In these latter customs the means adopted for bringing Beneficial about the desired result appear to be not so much imitative effect of curses and magic as the beneficent effect which, curiously enough, is abuse. often attributed to curses and maledictions.[1] Thus in the Indian district of Behar much virtue is ascribed to abuse, which is supposed in some cases to bring good luck. People, for example, who accompany a marriage procession to the bride's house are often foully abused by the women of the bride's family in the belief that this contributes to the good fortune of the newly-married pair. So in Behar on Jamad-witiya Day, which falls on the second day of the bright period of the moon next to that during which the Dussera festival takes place, brothers are reviled by sisters to their heart's content because it is thought that this will prolong the lives of the brothers and bring them good luck.[2] Further, in Behar and Bengal it is deemed very unlucky to look at the new moon of Bhadon (August); whoever does so is sure to meet with some mishap, or to be falsely accused of some-thing. To avert these evils people are commonly advised to throw stones or brickbats into their neighbours' houses; for if they do so, and are reviled for their pains, they will escape the threatened evils, and their neighbours who abused them will suffer in their stead. Hence the day of the new moon in this month is called the Day of Stones. At Benares a regular festival is held for this purpose on the fourth day of Bhadon, which is known as " the clod festival of the fourth."[3] On the Khurda estate in Orissa gardens and fruit-trees are conspicuously absent. The peasants explain their absence by saying that from time immemorial they have held it lucky to be annoyed and abused by their neighbours at a certain festival, which answers to the Nashti-Chandra in Bengal. Hence in order to give ample ground of offence they mutilate the fruit-trees and trample down the gardens of their neigh-bours, and so court fortune by drawing down on themselves

[1] W. Crooke, *Popular Religion and Folklore of Northern India* (West-minster, 1896), i. 74 *sq.*

[2] Sarat Chandra Mitra, "On Vestiges of Moon-worship in Behar and Bengal," *Journal of the Anthropological Society of Bombay*, ii. 598 *sq.*

[3] *Panjab Notes and Queries*, ii. p.

42, § 256; W. Crooke, *Popular Religion and Folklore of Northern India* (Westminster, 1896), i. 16 *sq.*; Sarat Chandra Mitra, in *Journal of the Anthropological Society of Bombay*, ii. 597 *sq.*; *id.*, in *Journal of the Royal Asiatic Society*, N.S. xxix. (1897) p. 482.

Beneficial
effect of
curses and
abuse.
the wrath of the injured owners.[1] At Cranganore, in the
Native State of Cochin, there is a shrine of the goddess
Bhagavati, which is much frequented by pilgrims in the
month of Minam (March–April). From all parts of Cochin,
Malabar, and Travancore crowds flock to attend the festival
and the highroads ring with their shouts of *Nada nada*,
"March! march!" They desecrate the shrine of the goddess
in every conceivable way, discharge volleys of stones and
filth, and level the most opprobrious language at the goddess
herself. These proceedings are supposed to be acceptable
to her. The intention of the pilgrimage is to secure
immunity from disease during the succeeding year.[2] In
some cases a curse may, like rags and dirt, be supposed
to benefit a man by making him appear vile and con-
temptible, and thus diverting from him the evil eye and
other malignant influences, which are attracted by beauty
and prosperity but repelled by their opposites. Among
the Huzuls of the Carpathians, if a herdsman or cattle-owner
suspects himself of having the evil eye, he will charge one of
his household to call him a devil or a robber every time he
goes near the cattle ; for he thinks that this will undo the
effect of the evil eye.[3] Among the Chams of Cambodia and
Annam, while a corpse is being burned on the pyre, a man
who bears the title of the Master of Sorrows remains in the
house of the deceased and loads it with curses, after which
he beseeches the ghost not to come back and torment his
family.[4] These last curses are clearly intended to make his
old home unattractive to the spirit of the dead. Esthonian
fishermen believe that they never have such good luck as
when some one is angry with them and curses them. Hence
before a fisherman goes out to fish, he will play a rough
practical joke on a comrade in order to be abused and
execrated by him. The more his friend storms and curses,
the better he is pleased ; every curse brings at least three

[1] W. W. Hunter, *Orissa* (London,
1872), ii. 140 *sq.* ; W. Crooke, *op. cit.*
i. 17.

[2] W. Logan, *Malabar* (Madras,
1887), i. 161 *sq.* ; E. Thurston, *Castes
and Tribes of Southern India*, vii. 287;
L. K. Anantha Krishna Iyer, *The
Cochin Tribes and Castes*, i. (Madras,
1909) p. 238.

[3] R. F. Kaindl, *Die Huzulen*
(Vienna, 1894), p. 63 ; *id.*, "Viehzucht und Viehzauber in den Ostkar-
paten," *Globus*, lxix. (1896) p. 386.

[4] A. Cabaton, *Nouvelles Recherches
sur les Chams* (Paris, 1901), p. 48.

fish into his net.[1]   There is a popular belief in Berlin and Beneficial
the neighbourhood that if you wish a huntsman good luck effect of curses and
when he is going out to shoot deer he will be certain never abuse.
to get a shot at all.   To avert the ill luck caused by such a
wish the hunter must throw a broomstick at the head of his
well-wisher.   If he is really to have luck, you must wish
that he may break his neck, or both his neck and his legs.
The wish is expressed with pregnant brevity in the phrase,
" Now then, neck and leg ! "[2]   The intention of such curses
may be to put the fish or the deer off their guard ; for, as
we shall see later on, animals are commonly supposed to
understand human speech, and even to overhear what is said
of them many miles off.   Accordingly if they hear a fisherman or a hunter flouted and vituperated, they will think too
meanly of him to go out of his way, and so will fall an easy
prey to his net or his gun.   When a Greek sower sowed
cummin he had to curse and swear, or the crop would not
turn out well.[3]   Roman writers mention a similar custom
observed by the sowers of rue and basil ;[4] and hedge doctors
in ancient Greece laid it down as a rule that in cutting black
hellebore you should face eastward and curse.[5]   Perhaps the
bitter language was supposed to strengthen the bitter taste,
and hence the medicinal virtue, of these plants.   At Lindus
in the island of Rhodes it was customary to sacrifice one or
two plough oxen to Hercules with curses and imprecations ;
indeed we are told that the sacrifice was deemed invalid if
a good word fell from any one's lips during the rite.   The
custom was explained by a legend that Hercules had laid
hands on the oxen of a ploughman and cooked and devoured
them, while their owner, unable to defend his beasts, stood
afar off and vented his anger in a torrent of abuse and
execration.   Hercules received his maledictions with a roar
of laughter, appointed him his priest, and bade him always
sacrifice with the very same execrations, for he had never

[1] Boecler-Kreutzwald, *Der Ehsten abergläubische Gebräuche, Weisen und Gewohnheiten*, pp. 90 *sq.*

[2] E. Krause, "Abergläubische Kuren und sonstiger Aberglaube in Berlin und nächster Umgebung," *Zeitschrift für Ethnologie*, xv. (1883) p. 87.

[3] Theophrastus, *Historia plantarum*,

vii. 3. 3, ix. 8. 8 ; Plutarch, *Quaest. Conviv.* vii. 2. 3 ; Pliny, *Nat. Hist.* xix. 120.

[4] Palladius, *De re rustica*, iv. 9 ; Pliny, *Nat. Hist.* xix. 120.

[5] Theophrastus, *Historia plantarum* ix. 8. 8.

dined better in his life.[1] The legend is plainly a fiction devised to explain the ritual. We may conjecture that the curses were intended to palliate the slaughter of a sacred animal. The subject will be touched on in a later part of this work. Here we must return to rain-making.

Rain-making by ploughing.

Women are sometimes supposed to be able to make rain by ploughing, or pretending to plough. Thus the Pshaws and Chewsurs of the Caucasus have a ceremony called "ploughing the rain," which they observe in time of drought. Girls yoke themselves to a plough and drag it into a river, wading in the water up to their girdles.[2] In the same circumstances Armenian girls and women do the same. The oldest woman, or the priest's wife, wears the priest's dress, while the others, dressed as men, drag the plough through the water against the stream.[3] In the Caucasian province of Georgia, when a drought has lasted long, marriage-able girls are yoked in couples with an ox-yoke on their shoulders, a priest holds the reins, and thus harnessed they wade through rivers, puddles, and marshes, praying, scream-ing, weeping, and laughing.[4] In a district of Transylvania, when the ground is parched with drought, some girls strip themselves naked, and, led by an older woman, who is also naked, they steal a harrow and carry it across the fields to a brook, where they set it afloat. Next they sit on the harrow and keep a tiny flame burning on each corner of it for an hour. Then they leave the harrow in the water and go home.[5] A similar rain-charm is resorted to in some parts of India; naked women drag a plough across a field by night, while the men keep carefully out of the way, for their presence would break the spell.[6] As performed at

[1] Lactantius, *Divin. Institut.* i. 21; Apollodorus, *Bibliotheca*, ii. 5. 11. 8; Philostratus, *Imagines*, ii. 24; Conon, in Photius, *Bibliotheca*, p. 132, ed. Bekker. Lactantius speaks of the sacri-fice of a pair of oxen, Philostratus of the sacrifice of a single ox.

[2] "Die Pschawen und Chewsurier im Kaukasus," *Zeitschrift für allge-meine Erdkunde*, N.F. ii. (1857) p. 75.

[3] M. Abeghian, *Der armenische Volksglaube* (Leipsic, 1899), p. 93.

[4] J. Reinegg, *Beschreibung des Kau-* kasus, ii. (Hildesheim and St. Peters-burg, 1797), p. 114. Among the Abchases of the Western Caucasus girls make rain by driving an ass into a river, placing a puppet dressed as a woman on a raft, and letting the raft float down stream. See N. von Seid-litz, "Die Abchasen," *Globus*, lxvi. (1894) pp. 75 *sq.*

[5] W. Mannhardt, *Baumkultus*, p. 553; E. Gerard, *The Land beyond the Forest*, ii. 40.

[6] *Panjab Notes and Queries*, iii. pp. 41, 115, §§ 173, 513.

Rain-making by ploughing.

Chunar in Bengal on the twenty-fourth of July 1891 the
ceremony was this. Between nine and ten in the evening
a barber's wife went from door to door and invited the
women to engage in ploughing. They all assembled in a
field from which men were excluded. Three women of a
husbandman's family then stripped themselves naked ; two
of them were yoked like oxen to the plough, while the third
held the handle. They next began to imitate the operation
of ploughing. The one who held the plough cried out,
" O mother earth ! bring parched grain, water, and chaff.
Our stomachs are breaking to pieces from hunger and
thirst." Then the landlord and accountant approached
them and laid down some grain, water, and chaff in the
field. After that the women dressed and returned home.
" By the grace of God," adds the gentleman who reports the
ceremony, " the weather changed almost immediately, and
we had a good shower."[1] Sometimes as they draw the
plough the women sing a hymn to Vishnu, in which they
seek to enlist his sympathy by enumerating the ills which
the people are suffering from the want of rain. In some
cases they discharge volleys of abuse at the village officials,
and even at the landlord, whom they compel to drag the
plough.[2] These ceremonies are all the more remarkable
because in ordinary circumstances Hindoo women never
engage in agricultural operations like ploughing and har-
rowing. Yet in drought it seems to be women of the
highest or Brahman caste who are chosen to perform what
at other times would be regarded as a menial and degrading
task. Occasionally, when hesitation is felt at subjecting
Brahman ladies to this indignity, they are allowed to get
off by merely touching the plough early in the morning,
before people are astir ; the real work is afterwards done by
the ploughmen.[3] In Manipur the prosperity of all classes

[1] North Indian Notes and Queries,
i. p. 210, § 1161.
[2] Sarat Chandra Mitra, " On the
Har Parauri, or the Behari Women's
Ceremony for producing Rain," Journal
of the Royal Asiatic Society of Great
Britain and Ireland, N.S. xxix. (1897)
pp. 471-484 ; id., in Journal of the
Anthropological Society of Bombay, iv.

No. 7 (1898), pp. 384-388.
[3] Sarat Chandra Mitra, " On some
Ceremonies for producing Rain," Journal
of the Anthropological Society of Bombay, iii. 25. On these Indian rain-
charms compare W. Crooke, Popular
Religion and Folklore of Northern
India (Westminster, 1896), i. 68 sqq.
Mr. E. S. Hartland suggests that such

depends on the abundance and regularity of the rainfall; hence the people have many rites and ceremonies for the making of rain. Thus in time of drought one hundred and eight girls milk one hundred and eight cows in the temple of Govindji, the most popular incarnation of Krishna in the country. If this fails, the women throw their *dhan*-pounders into the nearest pool, and at the dead of night strip themselves naked and plough.[1] There is a Burmese superstition that if a harrow has a flaw in it no rain will fall till the faulty harrow has been decked with flowers, broken, and thrown into the river. Further, the owner should have his hair cropped, and being adorned with flowers should dance and carry the harrow to the water. Otherwise the country is sure to suffer from drought.[2] The Tarahumare Indians of Mexico dip the plough in water before they use it, that it may draw rain.[3]

Making rain by means of the dead.

Sometimes the rain-charm operates through the dead. Thus in New Caledonia the rain-makers blackened themselves all over, dug up a dead body, took the bones to a cave, jointed them, and hung the skeleton over some taro leaves. Water was poured over the skeleton to run down on the leaves. They believed that the soul of the deceased took up the water, converted it into rain, and showered it down again.[4] In some parts of New Caledonia the cere-

customs furnish the key to the legend of Lady Godiva (*Folklore*, i. (1890) pp. 223 *sqq.*). Some of the features of the ceremonies, though not the ploughing, reappear in a rain-charm practised by the Rajbansis of Bengal. The women make two images of Hudum Deo out of mud or cow-dung, and carry them away into the fields by night. There they strip themselves naked, and dance round the images singing obscene songs. See (Sir) H. H. Risley, *The Tribes and Castes of Bengal: Ethnographic Glossary* (Calcutta, 1891-92), i. 498. Again, in time of drought the Kapu women of Southern India mould a small figure of a naked human being to represent Jokumara, the rain-god. This they place in a mock palanquin and go about for several days from door to door, singing indecent songs and collecting alms. Then they abandon the figure in a field, where the Malas find it and go about with it in their turn for three or four days, singing ribald songs and collecting alms. See E. Thurston, *Castes and Tribes of Southern India*, iii. 244 *sq.* We have seen (pp. 267 *sq.*) that lewd songs form part of an African rain-charm. The link between ribaldry and rain is not obvious to the European mind.

[1] T. C. Hodson, "The Native Tribes of Manipur," *Journal of the Anthropological Institute*, xxxi. (1901) pp. 302 *sq.*

[2] B. Houghton, in *Indian Antiquary*, xxv. (1896) p. 112.

[3] C. Lumholtz, *Unknown Mexico* (London, 1903), i. 330.

[4] G. Turner, *Samoa*, pp. 345 *sq.*

mony is somewhat different.   A great quantity of provisions
is offered to the ancestors, being laid down before their
skulls in the sacred place.   In front of the skulls a number
of pots full of water are set in a row, and in each pot there
is deposited a sacred stone which has more or less the shape
of a skull.   The rain-maker then prays to the ancestors to
send rain.   After that he climbs a tree with a branch in his
hand, which he waves about to hasten the approach of the
rain-clouds.[1]   The ceremony is a mixture of magic and
religion ; the prayers and offerings to the ancestors are
purely religious, while the placing of the skull-like stones in
water and the waving of the branch are magical.   In Russia,
if common report may be believed, it is not long since the
peasants of any district that chanced to be afflicted with
drought used to dig up the corpse of some one who had
drunk himself to death and sink it in the nearest swamp or
lake, fully persuaded that this would ensure the fall of the
needed rain.   In 1868 the prospect of a bad harvest, caused
by a prolonged drought, induced the inhabitants of a village
in the Tarashchansk district to dig up the body of a
Raskolnik, or Dissenter, who had died in the preceding
December.   Some of the party beat the corpse, or what was
left of it, about the head, exclaiming, " Give us rain ! " while
others poured water on it through a sieve.[2]   Here the pouring of water through a sieve seems plainly an imitation of a
shower, and reminds us of the manner in which Strepsiades
in Aristophanes imagined that rain was made by Zeus.[3]
An Armenian rain-charm is to dig up a skull and throw
it into running water.[4]   At Ourfa for this purpose they
prefer the skull of a Jew, which they cast into the Pool of
Abraham.[5]   In Mysore people think that if a leper is buried,
instead of being burnt, as he ought to be, rain will not fall.
Hence they have been known to disinter buried lepers in
time of drought.[6]   In Halmahera there is a practice of

[1] Father Lambert, in *Missions Catholiques*, xxv. (1893) p. 116; *id.*, *Mœurs
et superstitions des Néo-Calédoniens*
(Nouméa, 1900), pp. 297 *sq.*

[2] W. R. S. Ralston, *The Songs of
the Russian People*, pp. 425 *sq.*; P. v.
Stenin, " Ueber den Geisterglauben
in Russland," *Globus*, lvii. (1890) p.

285.

[3] Aristophanes, *Clouds*, 373.

[4] M. Abeghian, *Der armenische
Volksglaube*, p. 93.

[5] J. Rendel Harris, MS. notes.

[6] R. H. Elliot, *Experiences of a
Planter in the Jungles of Mysore* (London, 1871), i. 76 *sq.*

Making
rain by
means of
the dead.
throwing stones on a grave, in order that the ghost may fall
into a passion and avenge the disturbance, as he imagines,
by sending heavy rain.[1] This may explain a rain-charm
which seems to have been practised by the Mauretanians in
antiquity. A mound in the shape of a man lying on his
back was pointed out as the grave of the giant Antaeus;
and if any earth were dug up and removed from it, rain
fell till the soil was replaced.[2] Perhaps the rain was the
revenge the surly giant took for being wakened from his long
sleep. Sometimes, in order to procure rain, the Toradjas
of Central Celebes make an appeal to the pity of the
dead. Thus, in the village of Kalingooa, in Kadombookoo,
there is the grave of a famous chief, the grandfather of the
present ruler. When the land suffers from unseasonable
drought, the people go to this grave, pour water on it, and
say, " O grandfather, have pity on us ; if it is your will that
this year we should eat, then give rain." After that they
hang a bamboo full of water over the grave ; there is a
small hole in the lower end of the bamboo, so that the
water drips from it continually. The bamboo is always re-
filled with water until rain drenches the ground.[3] Here, as
in New Caledonia, we find religion blent with magic, for
the prayer to the dead chief, which is purely religious, is
eked out with a magical imitation of rain at his grave.
We have seen that the Baronga of Delagoa Bay drench
the tombs of their ancestors, especially the tombs of twins,
as a rain-charm.[4] In Zululand the native girls form a
procession and carry large pots of water to a certain tree
which chances to be on a mission station. When the girls
were asked why they did this, they said that an old ancestor
of theirs had been buried under the tree, and as he was a
great rain-maker in his life, they always came and poured
water on his grave in time of drought, in order that he
might send them rain.[5] This ceremony partakes of the
nature of religion, since it implies an appeal for help to a
deceased ancestor. Purely religious, on the other hand, are

[1] A. C. Kruijt, " Regen lokken en
regen verdrijving bij de Toradja's van
Central Celebes," *Tijdschrift voor
Indische Taal- Land- en Volkenkunde*,
xliv. (1901) p. 6, citing v. Baarda.

[2] Mela, *Chorographia*, iii. 106.
[3] A. C. Kruijt, *op. cit.* pp. 3 *sq.*
[4] Above, p. 268.
[5] Dudley Kidd, *The Essential Kafir*
(London, 1904), p. 115.

some means adopted by the Herero of south-western Africa to procure rain. If a drought has lasted long, the whole tribe goes with its cattle to the grave of some eminent man ; it may be the father or grandfather of the chief. They lay offerings of milk and flesh on the grave and utter their plaint: " Look, O Father, upon your beloved cattle and children ; they suffer distress, they are so lean, they are dying of hunger. Give us rain." The ears of the spectator are deafened by the lowing and bleating of herds and flocks, the shouts of herdsmen, the barking of dogs, and the screams of women.[1] Among some of the Indian tribes in the region of the Orinoco it was customary for the relations of a deceased person to disinter his bones a year after burial, burn them, and scatter the ashes to the winds, because they believed that the ashes were changed into rain, which the dead man sent in return for his obsequies.[2] The Chinese are convinced that when human bodies remain unburied, the souls of their late owners feel the discomfort of rain, just as living men would do if they were exposed without shelter to the inclemency of the weather. These wretched souls, therefore, do all in their power to prevent the rain from falling, and often their efforts are only too successful. Then drought ensues, the most dreaded of all calamities in China, because bad harvests, dearth, and famine follow in its train. Hence it has been a common practice of the Chinese authorities in time of drought to inter the dry bones of the unburied dead for the purpose of putting an end to the scourge and conjuring down the rain.[3]

Animals, again, often play an important part in these weather-charms. The Anula tribe of northern Australia associate the dollar-bird with rain, and call it the rain-bird. A man who has the bird for his totem can make rain at a certain pool. He catches a snake, puts it alive into the pool, and after holding it under water for a time takes it

Making rain by means of animals.

---

[1] Missionar P. H. Brincker, " Beobachtungen über die Deisidämonie der Eingeborenen Deutsch-Südwest-Afrikas," *Globus*, lviii. (1890) p. 323 ; *id.*, in *Mitteilungen des Seminars für orientalische Sprachen zu Berlin*, iii. (1900) Dritte Abteilung, p. 89.

[2] A. Caulin, *Historia coro-graphica natural y evangelica dela Nueva Andalucia, Provincias de Cumaña, Guayana y Vertientes del Rio Orinoco*, p. 92.

[3] J. J. M. de Groot, *The Religious System of China*, iii. 918 *sqq.*

out, kills it, and lays it down by the side of the creek.   Then
he makes an arched bundle of grass stalks in imitation of
a rainbow, and sets it up over the snake.   After that all
he does is to sing over the snake and the mimic rainbow;
sooner or later the rain will fall.   They explain this procedure by saying that long ago the dollar-bird had as a
mate at this spot a snake, who lived in the pool and used
to make rain by spitting up into the sky till a rainbow and
clouds appeared and rain fell.[1]   The Tjingilli of northern
Australia make rain in an odd way.   One of them will
catch a fat bandicoot and carry it about, singing over it till
the animal grows very thin and weak.   Then he lets it go,
and rain will follow.[2]   When some of the Blackfoot Indians
were at war in summer and wished to bring on a tempest,
they would take a kit-fox skin and rub it with dirt and
water, which never failed to be followed by a storm of rain.[3]
The Thompson Indians of British Columbia think that when
the loon calls loud and often, it will soon rain, and that to
mimic the cry of the bird may bring the rain down.[4]   The
fish called the small sculpin, which abounds along the rocky
shore of Norton Sound, is called by the Esquimaux the
rain-maker ; they say that if a person takes one of these fish
in his hand heavy rain will follow.[5]   If Aino fishermen
desire to bring on rain and wind, they pray to the skulls of
racoons and then throw water over each other.   Should they
wish the storm to increase they put on gloves and caps of
racoon-skin and dance.   Then it blows great guns.[6]   In
Ma-hlaing, a district of Upper Burma, when rain is scarce,
the people pray to a certain fish called *nga-yan* to send it.
They also catch some fish and put them in a tub, while
offerings of plantains and other food are made to the monks
in the name of the fish.   After that the fish are let loose in

[1] Spencer and Gillen, *Northern Tribes of Central Australia*, pp. 314 sq.

[2] Spencer and Gillen, *op. cit.* p. 311.

[3] G. B. Grinnell, *Blackfoot Lodge Tales*, p. 262.

[4] J. Teit, "The Thompson Indians," p. 374 (*Memoir of the American Museum of Natural History, The Jesup North Pacific Expedition*, vol. i. part iv.).

[5] E. W. Nelson, "The Eskimo about Bering Strait," *Eighteenth Annual Report of the Bureau of American Ethnology*, part i. (Washington, 1899) p. 446.

[6] J. Batchelor, *The Ainu and their Folklore* (London, 1901), p. 334.

a stream or pond, with gold-leaf stuck on their heads. If
live fish are not to be had, wooden ones are used and answer
the purpose just as well.[1] When the Chirus of Manipur
wish to make rain they catch a crab and put it in a pot of
water. Then the headman goes to the gate of the village
and keeps lifting the crab out of the water and putting it
back into it till he is tired.[2] An ancient Indian mode of
making rain was to throw an otter into the water.[3] If the
sky refuses rain and the cattle are perishing, an Arab sheikh
will sometimes stand in the middle of the camp and cry,
" Redeem yourselves, O people, redeem yourselves ! " At
these words every family sacrifices a sheep, divides it in two,
and hanging the pieces on two poles passes between them.
Children too young to walk are carried by their mother.[4]
But this custom has rather the appearance of a sacrifice
than of a charm. In southern Celebes people try to make
rain by carrying a cat tied in a sedan chair thrice round the
parched fields, while they drench it with water from bamboo
squirts. When the cat begins to miaul, they say, " O lord,
let rain fall on us." [5] A common way of making rain in
many parts of Java is to bathe a cat or two cats, a male
and a female ; sometimes the animals are carried in procession with music. Even in Batavia you may from time
to time see children going about with a cat for this purpose ;
when they have ducked it in a pool, they let it go.[6]

Making rain by means of animals.

[1] (Sir) J. G. Scott, *Gazetteer of Upper Burma and the Shan States*, part ii. vol. ii. (Rangoon, 1901) p. 280.

[2] T. C. Hodson, " The Native Tribes of Manipur," *Journal of the Anthropological Institute*, xxxi. (1901) p. 308.

[3] H. Oldenberg, *Die Religion des Veda*, p. 507.

[4] Fr. A. Jaussen, " Coutumes arabes," *Revue Biblique*, April 1903, p. 248. Elsewhere the same writer describes this ceremony as a mode of putting a stop to cholera. See his *Coutumes des Arabes au pays de Moab* (Paris, 1908), p. 362. To pass be- tween the pieces of a sacrificial victim is a form of oath (Genesis xv. 9 *sqq.* ; Jeremiah xxxiv. 18 ; Dictys Cretensis, *Bell. Trojan.* i. 15 ; R. Moffat, *Missionary Labours and Scenes in Southern*

Africa, p. 278) or of purification (Plutarch, *Quaestiones Romanae*, 111 ; Apollodorus, *Bibliotheca*, iii. 13. 7 ; Livy, xl. 6 ; E. Casalis, *The Basutos*, p. 256; S. Krascheninnikow, *Beschreibung des Landes Kamtschatka*, pp. 277 *sq.*). Compare my note on Pausanias, iii. 20. 9.

[5] B. F. Matthes, " Over de *ādā's* of gewoonten der Makassaren en Boegineezen," *Verslagen en Mededeelingen der Koninklijke Akademie van Wetenschappen*, Afdeeling Letterkunde, Derde Reeks, ii. (Amsterdam, 1885) p. 169.

[6] G. A. J. Hazeu, " Kleine bijdragen tot de ethnografie en folklore van Java," *Tijdschrift voor Indische Taal- Land- en Volkenkunde*, xlvi. (1903) p. 298.

Often in order to give effect to the rain-charm the animal must be black. Thus an ancient Indian way of bringing on rain was to set a black horse with his face to the west and rub him with a black cloth till he neighed.[1] In the Beni-Chougran tribe of North Africa women lead a black cow in procession, while other women sprinkle the whole group with water as a means of wringing a shower from the sky.[2] To procure rain the Peruvian Indians used to set a black sheep in a field, poured *chica* over it, and gave the animal nothing to eat until rain fell.[3] Once when a drought lasting five months had burnt up their pastures and withered the corn, the Caffres of Natal had recourse to a famous witch, who promised to procure rain without delay. A black sheep having been produced, an incision was made in the animal near the shoulder and the gall taken out. Part of this the witch rubbed over her own person, part she drank, part was mixed with medicine. Some of the medicine was then rubbed on her body; the rest of it, attached to a stick, was fixed in the fence of a calves' pen. The woman next harangued the clouds. When the sheep was to be cooked, a new fire was procured by the friction of fire-sticks; in ordinary circumstances a brand would have been taken from one of the huts.[4] Among the Wambugwe, a Bantu people of eastern Africa, when the sorcerer desires to make rain he takes a black sheep and a black calf in bright sunshine, and has them placed upon the roof of the large common hut in which the people live together. Then he slits open the stomachs of the animals and scatters their contents in all directions. After that he pours water and medicine into a vessel; if the charm has succeeded, the water boils up and rain follows. On the other hand, if the sorcerer wishes to prevent rain from falling, he withdraws into the interior of the hut, and there heats a rock-crystal in a calabash.[5] In order to procure rain the Wagogo of German East Africa sacrifice black fowls, black sheep, and black cattle at the

[1] A. Hillebrandt, *Vedische Opfer und Zauber* (Strasburg, 1897), p. 120.

[2] E. Doutté, *Magie et religion dans l'Afrique du Nord*, p. 583.

[3] Acosta, *History of the Indies*, bk. v. ch. xxviii. (vol. ii. p. 376, Hakluyt Society).

[4] J. Shooter, *The Kafirs of Natal and the Zulu Country* (London, 1857), pp. 212 *sqq.*

[5] O. Baumann, *Durch Massailand zur Nilquelle* (Berlin, 1894), p. 188.

graves of dead ancestors, and the rain-maker wears black
clothes during the rainy season.[1]　Among the Matabele the
rain-charm employed by sorcerers was made from the blood
and gall of a black ox.[2]　In a district of Sumatra, in order
to procure rain, all the women of the village, scantily clad,
go to the river, wade into it, and splash each other with the
water.　A black cat is thrown into the stream and made to
swim about for a while, then allowed to escape to the bank,
pursued by the splashing of the women.[3]　The Garos of
Assam offer a black goat on the top of a very high mountain in time of drought.[4]　In all these cases the colour of
the animal is part of the charm ; being black, it will darken
the sky with rain-clouds.　So the Bechuanas burn the
stomach of an ox at evening, because they say, " The black
smoke will gather the clouds and cause the rain to come." [5]
The Timorese sacrifice a black pig to the Earth-goddess for
rain, a white or red one to the Sun-god for sunshine.[6]　The
Angoni, a tribe of Zulu descent to the north of the Zambesi,
sacrifice a black ox for rain and a white one for fine weather.[7]
Among the high mountains of Japan there is a district in
which, if rain has not fallen for a long time, a party of
villagers goes in procession to the bed of a mountain torrent,
headed by a priest, who leads a black dog.　At the chosen
spot they tether the beast to a stone, and make it a target
for their bullets and arrows.　When its life-blood bespatters
the rocks, the peasants throw down their weapons and lift
up their voices in supplication to the dragon divinity of the

(margin note) Making rain by means of black animals.

---

[1] H. Cole, " Notes on the Wagogo
of German East Africa," *Journal of the
Anthropological Institute,* xxxii. (1902)
p. 325.

[2] L. Decle, *Three Years in Savage
Africa* (London, 1898), p. 154.

[3] A. L. van Hasselt, *Volksbeschrij-
ving van Midden-Sumatra,* pp. 320 *sq.*;
J. L. van der Toorn, " Het animisme
bij den Minangkabauer der Padangsche
Bovenlanden," *Bijdragen tot de Taal-
Land- en Volkenkunde van Nederlandsch-
Indië,* xxxix. (1890) p. 93.

[4] E. T. Dalton, *Descriptive Ethnology
of Bengal,* p. 88.

[5] *Folklore Journal,* edited by the
Working Committee of the South African

Folklore Society, i. (1879) p. 34.

[6] J. S. G. Gramberg, " Eene maand
in de binnenlanden van Timor," *Verhandelingen van het Bataviaasch Genootschap van Kunsten en Wetenschappen,* xxxvi. p. 209 ; H. Zondervan,
" Timor en de Timoreezen," *Tijdschrift
van het Nederlandsch Aardrijkskundig
Genootschap.* Tweede Serie, v. (1888)
Afdeeling, meer uitgebreide artikelen,
pp. 402 *sq.*

[7] C. Wiese, " Beiträge zur Geschichte der Zulu im Norden des
Zambesi, namentlich der Angoni,"
Zeitschrift für Ethnologie, xxxii. (1900)
p. 198.

stream, exhorting him to send down forthwith a shower to cleanse the spot from its defilement. Custom has prescribed that on these occasions the colour of the victim shall be black, as an emblem of the wished-for rain-clouds. But if fine weather is wanted, the victim must be white, without a spot.[1]

Frogs and toads in relation to rain.

The intimate association of frogs and toads with water has earned for these creatures a widespread reputation as custodians of rain ; and hence they often play a part in charms designed to draw needed showers from the sky. Some of the Indians of the Orinoco held the toad to be the god or lord of the waters, and for that reason feared to kill the creature, even when they were ordered to do so. They have been known to keep frogs under a pot and to beat them with rods when there was a drought.[2] It is said that the Aymara Indians of Peru and Bolivia often make little images of frogs and other aquatic animals and place them on the tops of the hills as a means of bringing down rain.[3] In some parts of south-eastern Australia, where the rainfall is apt to be excessive, the natives feared to injure Tidelek̦, the frog, or Bluk, the bull-frog, because they were said to be full of water instead of intestines, and great rains would follow if one of them were killed. The frog family was often referred to as Bunjil Willung or Mr. Rain. A tradition ran that once upon a time long ago the frog drank up all the water in the lakes and rivers, and then sat in the dry

---

[1] W. Weston, *Mountaineering and Exploration in the Japanese Alps* (London, 1896), pp. 162 *sq.* ; *id.*, in *Journal of the Anthropological Institute*, xxvi. (1897) p. 30 ; *id.*, in *The Geographical Journal*, vii. (1896) pp. 143 *sq.*

[2] A. Caulin, *Historia Coro-graphica natural y evangelica dela Nueva Andalucia, Provincias de Cumaña, Guayana y Vertientes del Rio Orinoco*, p. 96 ; *Colombia, being a geographical, etc., account of the country*, i. 642 *sq.* ; A. Bastian, *Die Culturländer des alten Amerika*, ii. 216.

[3] D. Forbes, "On the Aymara Indians of Bolivia and Peru," *Journal of the Ethnological Society of London*, ii. 237, note. On the supposed relation of the frog or toad to water in America, see further E. J. Payne, *History of the New World called America*, i. 420 *sq.*, 425 *sqq.* He observes that "throughout the New World, from Florida to Chile, the worship of the frog or toad, as the offspring of water and the symbol of the water-spirit, accompanied the cultivation of maize" (p. 425). A species of water toad is called by the Araucanians of Chili *genco*, "which signifies lord of the water, as they believe that it watches over the preservation and contributes to the salubrity of the waters" (J. I. Molina, *Geographical, Natural, and Civil History of Chili*, London, 1809, i. 179).

reed beds swollen to an enormous size, saying, "Bluk! bluk!" in a deep gurgling voice. All the other animals wandered about gaping and gasping for a drop of moisture, but finding none, they agreed that they must all die of thirst unless they could contrive to make the frog laugh. So they tried one after the other, but for a long time in vain. At last the conger eel and his relations, hung round with lake grass and gay sea-weed, reared themselves on their tails and pranced round the fire. This was too much for the frog. He opened his mouth and laughed till the water ran out and the lakes and streams were full once more.[1] We have seen that some of the Queensland aborigines imitate the movements and cries of frogs as part of a rain-charm.[2] The Thompson River Indians of British Columbia and some people in Europe think that to kill a frog brings on rain.[3] In order to procure rain people of low caste in the Central Provinces of India will tie a frog to a rod covered with green leaves and branches of the *nîm* tree (*Azadirachta Indica*) and carry it from door to door singing—

Frogs used in rain-charms.

> Send soon, O frog, the jewel of water!
> And ripen the wheat and millet in the field.[4]

In Kumaon, a district of north-western India, one way of bringing on rain when it is needed is to hang a frog with its mouth up on a tall bamboo or on a tree for a day or two. The notion is that the god of rain, seeing the creature in trouble, will take pity on it and send the rain.[5] In the district of Muzaffarpur in India the vulgar believe that the cry of a frog is most readily heard by the God of

[1] Mary E. B. Howitt, *Folklore and Legends of some Victorian Tribes* (in manuscript). The story is told in an abridged form by Dr. A. W. Howitt (*Journal of the Anthropological Institute*, xviii. (1889) pp. 54 *sq.*).

[2] Above, p. 255.

[3] J. Teit, "The Thompson Indians of British Columbia," *Memoirs of the American Museum of Natural History, The Jesup North Pacific Expedition*, vol. i. part iv. (April 1900) p. 346; A. Kuhn, *Sagen, Gebräuche und Märchen aus Westfalen*, ii. p. 80,

§ 244; E. Gerard, *The Land beyond the Forest*, ii. 13.

[4] M. N. Venketswami, "Superstitions among Hindus in the Central Provinces," *Indian Antiquary*, xxviii. (1899) p. 111. Compare E. Thurston, *Castes and Tribes of Southern India*, iv. 387.

[5] *North Indian Notes and Queries*, iii. p. 134, § 285; W. Crooke, *Popular Religion and Folklore of Northern India* (Westminster, 1896), i. 73.

Rain. Hence in a year of drought the low-caste females of a village assemble at evening and put a frog in a small earthen pot together with water taken from five different houses. The pot with the frog is then placed in the hollow wooden cup into which the lever used for pounding rice falls. Being raised with the foot and then allowed to drop, the lever crushes the frog to death ; and while the creature emits his dying croak the women sing songs in a loud voice about the dearth of water.[1] The Kapus or Reddis are a large and prosperous caste of cultivators and landowners in the Madras Presidency. When rain fails, women of the caste will catch a frog and tie it alive to a new winnowing fan made of bamboo. On this fan they spread a few margosa leaves and go from door to door singing, " Lady frog must have her bath. Oh ! rain-god, give a little water for her at least." While the Kapu women sing this song, the woman of the house pours water over the frog and gives an alms, convinced that by so doing she will soon bring rain down in torrents.[2] Again, in order to procure rain the Malas, who are the pariahs of the Telugu country in Southern India, tie a live frog to a mortar and put a mud figure of Gontiyalamma over it. Then they carry the mortar, frog, and all in procession, singing, " Mother frog, playing in water, pour rain by pots full," while the villagers of other castes pour water over them.[3] Beliefs like these might easily develop into a worship of frogs regarded as personifying the powers of water and rain. In the Rig Veda there is a hymn about frogs which appears to be substantially a rain-charm.[4] The Newars, the aboriginal inhabitants of Nepaul, worship the frog as a creature associated with the demi-god Nagas in the production and control of rain and the water-supply, on which the welfare of the crops depends. A sacred character is attributed to the little animal, and every care is taken not to molest or injure it. The worship of the frog is performed on the seventh day of the month Kartik (October), usually at a

---

[1] *Journal of the Asiatic Society of Bengal*, lxxii., part 3, Anthropology (Calcutta, 1904), p. 39.

[2] E. Thurston, *Castes and Tribes of Southern India*, iii. 245.

[3] E. Thurston, *op. cit.* iv. 387.

[4] M. Bloomfield, " On the ' Frog-hymn,' Rig Veda, vii. 103," *Journal of the American Oriental Society*, xvii. (1896) pp. 173-179.

pool which is known to be frequented by frogs, although it is not essential to the efficacy of the rite that a frog should be actually seen at the time. After carefully washing his face and hands, the priest takes five brazen bowls and places in them five separate offerings, namely, rice, flowers, milk and vermilion, ghee and incense, and water. Lighting the pile of ghee and incense, the priest says, " Hail, Paremêsvara Bhûmînâtha! I pray you receive these offerings and send us timely rain, and bless our crops!" [1]

Some of these customs and beliefs may be, at least in part, based on the frog's habit of storing up water in its body against seasons of drought ; when it is caught at such times, it squirts the water out in a jet.[2] On seeing a frog emit a gush of water when all around was dry and parched, savages might easily infer that the creature had caused the drought by swallowing all the water, and that in order to restore its moisture to the thirsty ground they had only to make the frog disgorge its secret store of the precious liquid. *Suggested explanation of connexion of frog with rain.*

Among some tribes of South Africa, when too much rain falls, the wizard, accompanied by a large crowd, repairs to the house of a family where there has been no death for a very long time, and there he burns the skin of a coney. As it burns he shouts, " The rabbit is burning," and the cry is taken up by the whole crowd, who continue shouting till they are exhausted.[3] This no doubt is supposed to stop the rain. Equally effective is a method adopted by gypsies in Austria. When the rain has continued to pour steadily for a long time, to the great discomfort of these homeless vagrants, the men of the band assemble at a river and divide themselves into two parties. Some of them cut branches with which to make a raft, while the others collect hazel leaves and cover the raft with them. A witch thereupon lays a dried serpent, wrapt *Stopping rain by means of rabbits and serpents.*

---

[1] A. L. Waddell, "Frog-Worship among the Newars," *The Indian Antiquary*, xxii. (1893) pp. 292-294. The title Bhûmînâtha, "Lord or Protector of the Soil," is specially reserved for the frog. The title Paremêsvara is given to all the Newar divinities.

[2] *Encyclopaedia Britannica*, 9th edition, *s.v.* " Frog," ix. 796. For an instance of a frog thus caught in a drought and made to disgorge its hoard of water, see E. Aymonier, *Voyage dans le Laos* (Paris, 1895-1897), ii. 284 *sq.*

[3] J. Macdonald, "Manners, Customs, Superstitions, and Religions of South African Tribes," *Journal of the Anthropological Institute*, xix. (1890) p. 295.

in white rags, on the raft, which is then carried by several men to the river. Women are not allowed to be present at this part of the ceremony. While the procession moves towards the river, the witch marches behind the raft singing a song, of which the burden is a statement that gypsies do not like water, and have no urgent need of serpents' milk, coupled with the expression of a hope that the serpent may see his way to swallow the water, that he may run to his mother and drink milk from her breasts, and that the sun may shine out, bringing back mirth and jollity to gypsy hearts. Transylvanian gypsies will sometimes expose the dried carcase of a serpent to the pouring rain, " in order that the serpent may convince himself of the inclemency of the weather, and so grant the people's wish." [1]

Doing violence to the being who controls the weather.
This last custom is an example of an entirely different mode of procuring rain, to which people sometimes have recourse in extreme cases, when the drought is long and their temper short. At such times they will drop the usual hocus-pocus of imitative magic altogether, and being far too angry to waste their breath in prayer they seek by threats and curses or even downright physical force to extort the waters of heaven from the supernatural being who has, so to say, cut them off at the main. Thus, in Muzaffarnagar, a town of the Punjaub, when the rains are excessive, the people draw a figure of a certain Muni or Rishi Agastya on a loin-cloth and put it out in the rain, or they paint his figure on the outside of the house and let the rain wash it off. This Muni or Rishi Agastya is a great personage in the native folklore, and enjoys the reputation of being able to stop the rain. It is supposed that he will exercise his power as soon as he is thus made to feel in effigy the misery of wet weather.[2] On the other hand, when rain is wanted at Chhatarpur, a native state in Bundelcund, they paint two figures with their legs up and their heads down on a wall that faces east; one of the figures represents Indra, the other Megha Raja, the lord of rain. They think that in this uncomfortable position these powerful beings will soon be glad to send

[1] H. von Wlislocki, *Volksglaube und religiöser Brauch der Zigeuner* (Münster i. W., 1891), pp. 64 *sq.*

[2] W. Crooke, *Popular Religion and Folklore of Northern India* (Westminster, 1896), i. 76.

the much-needed showers.[1]   In a Japanese village, when the guardian divinity had long been deaf to the peasants' prayers for rain, they at last threw down his image and, with curses loud and long, hurled it head foremost. into a stinking rice-field.   "There," they said, "you may stay yourself for a while, to see how *you* will feel after a few days' scorching in this broiling sun that is burning the life from our cracking fields."[2]   In the like circumstances the Feloupes of Senegambia cast down their fetishes and drag them about the fields, cursing them till rain falls.[3]   In Okunomura, a Japanese village not far from Tokio, when rain is wanted, an artificial dragon is made out of straw, reeds, bamboos, and magnolia leaves. Preceded by a Shinto priest, attended by men carrying paper flags, and followed by others beating a big drum, the dragon is carried in procession from the Buddhist temple and finally thrown into a waterfall.[4]   When the spirits withhold rain or sunshine, the Comanches whip a slave ; if the gods prove obstinate, the victim is almost flayed alive.[5]

The Chinese are adepts in the art of taking the kingdom of heaven by storm.   Thus, when rain is wanted they make a huge dragon of paper or wood to represent the rain-god, and carry it about in procession ; but if no rain follows, the mock-dragon is execrated and torn to pieces.[6]   At other times they threaten and beat the god if he does not give rain ; sometimes they publicly depose him from the rank of deity.   On the other hand, if the wished-for rain falls, the god is promoted to a higher rank by an imperial decree.[7] It is said that in the reign of Kia-King, fifth emperor of the

Chinese modes of compelling the gods to give rain.

---

[1] W. Crooke, *op. cit.* i. 74.

[2] W. Weston, *Mountaineering and Exploration in the Japanese Alps* (London, 1896), p. 162.

[3] L. J. B. Bérenger - Féraud, *Les Peuplades de la Sénégambie* (Paris, 1879), p. 291.

[4] R. Lange, "Bitten um Regen in Japan," *Zeitschrift des Vereins für Volkskunde*, iii. (1893) pp. 334 *sq.* Compare W. G. Aston, *Shinto* (London, 1905), p. 153. However, the throwing of the dragon into the waterfall may be a homoeopathic charm

rather than a punishment.

[5] H. H. Bancroft, *Native Races of the Pacific States*, i. 520.

[6] Huc, *L'Empire chinois*[4] (Paris, 1862), i. 241.

[7] Mgr Rizzolati, in *Annales de la Propagation de la Foi*, xvi. (1844) p. 350 ; Mgr Retord, *ib.* xxviii. (1856) p. 102.   In Tonquin also a mandarin has been known to whip an image of Buddha for not sending rain.   See *Annales de l'Association de la Propagation de la Foi*, iv. (1830) p. 330.

Manchu dynasty, a long drought desolated several provinces of northern China. Processions were of no avail; the rain-dragon hardened his heart and would not let a drop fall. At last the emperor lost patience and condemned the recalcitrant deity to perpetual exile on the banks of the river Illi in the province of Torgot. The decree was in process of execution; the divine criminal, with a touching resignation, was already traversing the deserts of Tartary to work out his sentence on the borders of Turkestan, when the judges of the High Court of Peking, moved with compassion, flung themselves at the feet of the emperor and implored his pardon for the poor devil. The emperor consented to revoke his doom, and a messenger set off at full gallop to bear the tidings to the executors of the imperial justice. The dragon was reinstated in his office on condition of performing his duties a little better in future.[1] About the year 1710 the island of Tsong-ming, which belongs to the province of Nanking, was afflicted with a drought. The viceroy of the province, after the usual attempts to soften the heart of the local deity by burning incense-sticks had been made in vain, sent word to the idol that if rain did not fall by such and such a day, he would have him turned out of the city and his temple razed to the ground. The threat had no effect on the obdurate divinity; the day of grace came and went, and yet no rain fell. Then the indignant viceroy forbade the people to make any more offerings at the shrine of this unfeeling deity, and commanded that the temple should be shut up and seals placed on the doors. This soon produced the desired effect. Cut off from his base of supplies, the idol had no choice but to surrender at discretion. Rain fell in a few days, and thus the god was restored to the affections of the faithful.[2] In some parts of China the mandarins procure rain or fine weather by shutting the southern or the northern gates of the city. For the south wind brings drought and the north wind brings showers. Hence by closing the southern and opening the northern gates you clearly exclude drought and admit rain; whereas contrariwise by shutting the northern and opening the

[1] Huc, *L'Empire chinois*,[4] i. 241 *sq.*
[2] *Lettres édifiantes et curieuses*, Nouvelle Édition, xviii. 210.

southern gates you bar out the clouds and the wet and let
in sunshine and genial warmth.[1]   In April 1888 the mandarins of Canton prayed to the god Lung-wong to stop the
incessant downpour of rain ; and when he turned a deaf ear to
their petitions they put him in a lock-up for five days.   This
had a salutary effect.   The rain ceased and the god was restored to liberty.   Some years before, in time of drought, the
same deity had been chained and exposed to the sun for days
in the courtyard of his temple in order that he might feel for
himself the urgent need of rain.[2]   So when the Siamese need *Siamese
modes of constraining the gods to give rain.*
rain, they set out their idols in the blazing sun ; but if they
want dry weather, they unroof the temples and let the rain
pour down on the idols.   They think that the inconvenience
to which the gods are thus subjected will induce them to grant
the wishes of their worshippers.[3]   When the rice-crop is
endangered by long drought, the governor of Battambang, a
province of Siam, goes in great state to a certain pagoda
and prays to Buddha for rain.   Then, accompanied by his
suite and followed by an enormous crowd, he adjourns to a
plain behind the pagoda.   Here a dummy figure has been
made up, dressed in bright colours, and placed in the middle
of the plain.   A wild music begins to play ; maddened by
the din of drums and cymbals and crackers, and goaded on
by their drivers, the elephants charge down on the dummy
and trample it to pieces.   After this, Buddha will soon give
rain.[4]

The reader may smile at the meteorology of the Far *Compelling the saints to give rain in Sicily.*
East ; but precisely similar modes of procuring rain have
been resorted to in Christian Europe within our own lifetime.   By the end of April 1893 there was great distress
in Sicily for lack of water.   The drought had lasted six
months.   Every day the sun rose and set in a sky of
cloudless blue.   The gardens of the Conca d'Oro, which
surround Palermo with a magnificent belt of verdure, were

[1] J. Bertrand, in *Annales de la
Propagation de la Foi*, xxii. (1850)
pp. 351-355 ; W. W. Rockhill, *The
Land of the Lamas* (London, 1891),
p. 311.
[2] Rev. E. Z. Simmons, "Idols and
Spirits," *Chinese Recorder and Missionary Journal*, xix. (1888) p. 502.

[3] Mgr Bruguière, in *Annales de
l'Association de la Propagation de la
Foi*, v. (1831), p. 131.

[4] Brien, "Aperçu sur la province de
Battambang," *Cochinchine Française :
excursions et reconnaissances*, No. 25
(Saigon, 1886), pp. 6 *sq.*

withering. Food was becoming scarce. The people were
in great alarm. All the most approved methods of procuring rain had been tried without effect. Processions had
traversed the streets and the fields. Men, women, and
children, telling their beads, had lain whole nights before
the holy images. Consecrated candles had burned day
and night in the churches. Palm branches, blessed on
Palm Sunday, had been hung on the trees. At Solaparuta,
in accordance with a very old custom, the dust swept from
the churches on Palm Sunday had been spread on the
fields. In ordinary years these holy sweepings preserve the
crops ; but that year, if you will believe me, they had no
effect whatever. At Nicosia the inhabitants, bare-headed
and bare-foot, carried the crucifixes through all the wards
of the town and scourged each other with iron whips.
It was all in vain. Even the great St. Francis of Paola
himself, who annually performs the miracle of rain and
is carried every spring through the market-gardens, either
could not or would not help. Masses, vespers, concerts,
illuminations, fire-works—nothing could move him. At
last the peasants began to lose patience. Most of the
saints were banished. At Palermo they dumped St.
Joseph in a garden to see the state of things for
himself, and they swore to leave him there in the
sun till rain fell. Other saints were turned, like naughty
children, with their faces to the wall. Others again,
stripped of their beautiful robes, were exiled far from their
parishes, threatened, grossly insulted, ducked in horse-
ponds. At Caltanisetta the golden wings of St. Michael
the Archangel were torn from his shoulders and replaced
with wings of pasteboard ; his purple mantle was taken
away and a clout wrapt about him instead. At Licata
the patron saint, St. Angelo, fared even worse, for he was
left without any garments at all ; he was reviled, he was
put in irons, he was threatened with drowning or hanging.
"Rain or the rope!" roared the angry people at him, as
they shook their fists in his face.[1]

[1] G. Vuillier, "La Sicile, impressions du présent et du passé," *Tour du
monde*, lxvii. (1894) pp. 54 *sq.* Compare G. Pitrè, *Usi e costumi, credenze
e pregiudizi del popolo siciliano*, iii.
(Palermo, 1889) pp. 142-144. As to

Another way of constraining the rain-god is to disturb Disturbing the rain-god in his haunts.
him in his haunts. This seems to be the reason why rain is
supposed to follow the troubling of a sacred spring. The
Dards believe that if a cow-skin or anything impure is placed
in certain springs, storms will follow.[1] In the mountains of
Farghana there was a place where rain began to fall as soon
as anything dirty was thrown into a certain famous well.[2]
Again, in Tabaristan there was said to be a cave in the
mountain of Tak which had only to be defiled by filth or
milk for the rain to begin to fall, and to continue falling till
the cave was cleansed.[3] Gervasius mentions a spring, into
which if a stone or a stick were thrown, rain would at once
issue from it and drench the thrower.[4] There was a fountain
in Munster such that if it were touched or even looked at by
a human being, it would at once flood the whole province
with rain.[5] In Normandy a wizard will sometimes repair
to a spring, sprinkle flour on it, and strike the water with
a hazel rod, while he chants his spell. A mist then rises
from the spring and condenses in the shape of heavy clouds,
which discharge volleys of hail on the orchards and corn-
fields.[6] When rain was long of coming in the Canary
Islands, the priestesses used to beat the sea with rods to
punish the water-spirit for his niggardliness.[7] Among the
natural curiosities of Annam are the caves of Chua-hang

St. Francis of Paola, who died in 1507 and was canonised by Leo X. in 1519, see P. Ribadeneira, *Flos Sanctorum, cioè Vite de' Santi* (Venice, 1763), i. 252 *sq.* ; Th. Trede, *Das Heidentum in der römischen Kirche*, iii. 45-47 ; G. Pitrè, *Feste patronali in Sicilia* (Turin and Palermo, 1900), pp. 49 *sqq.* He was sent for by Louis XI. of France, and his fame as a worker of miracles is still spread over all the south of Italy. With the entertain-ments given in honour of St Francis of Paola to wheedle rain out of him we may compare the shadow-plays or puppet-shows given by the Javanese and the comedies played by the Chinese for the same purpose. See T. S. Raffles, *History of Java* (London, 1817), i. 477 ; G. A. J. Hazeu, "Kleine bijdragen tot de ethnografie en de folk-lore van Java," *Tijdschrift voor Indische Taal- Land- en Volkenkunde*, xlvi. (1903) pp. 299 *sq.* ; Huc, *L'Empire chinois* [4] (Paris, 1862), i. 241.

[1] J. Biddulph, *Tribes of the Hindoo Koosh* (Calcutta, 1880), p. 95.

[2] Albîrûnî, *The Chronology of Ancient Nations*, translated and edited by C. E. Sachau (London, 1879), p 235. This and the following passage were pointed out to me by my late friend, W. Robertson Smith.

[3] Albîrûnî, *loc. cit.*

[4] Gervasius von Tilbury, *Otia Imperialia*, ed. F. Liebrecht, pp. 41 *sq.*

[5] Giraldus Cambrensis, *Topography of Ireland*, ch. 7. Compare W. Mann-hardt, *Antike Wald- und Feldkulte*, p. 341 note.

[6] J. Lecœur, *Esquisses du Bocage Normand*, ii. 79.

[7] L. J. B. Bérenger-Féraud, *Super-stitions et survivances*, i. 473.

or Troc. You may sail into them in a boat underground for a distance of half a mile, and a little way further in you come to the remains of an ancient altar among magnificent stalactite columns. The Annamites worship the spirit of the cave and offer sacrifices at its mouth in time of drought. From all the villages in the neighbourhood come boats, the boatmen singing, " Let it rain! let it rain ! " in time to the measured dip of their oars in the water. Arrived at the mouth of the cave, they offer rice and wine to the spirit, prostrating themselves four times before him. Then the master of the ceremonies recites a prayer, ties a written copy of it to the neck of a dog, and flings the animal into the stream which flows from the grotto. This is done in order to provoke the spirit of the cave to anger by defiling his pure water ; for he will then send abundant rains to sweep far away the carcase of the dead dog which pollutes the sacred grotto.[1]

Putting compulsion on the rain-god.

Two hundred miles to the east of the land of the Huichol Indians in Mexico there is a sacred spring, and away to the west of their country stretches the Pacific Ocean. To ensure the fall of rain these Indians carry water from the spring to the sea, and an equal quantity of sea-water from the sea to the spring. The two waters thus transferred will, they think, feel strange in their new surroundings and will seek to return to their old homes. Hence they will pass in the shape of clouds across the Huichol country and meeting there will descend as rain.[2] Sometimes an appeal is made to the pity of the gods. When their corn is being burnt up by the sun, the Zulus look out for a " heaven bird," kill it, and throw it into a pool. Then the heaven melts with tenderness for the death of the bird ; " it wails for it by raining, wailing a funeral wail."[3] In Zululand women sometimes bury their children up to the neck in the ground, and then retiring to a distance keep up a dismal·howl for a long time. The sky is supposed to melt with pity at the sight. Then the women dig the children out and feel sure

Exciting the pity of the beings who control the rain.

[1] Le R. P. Cadière, " Croyances et dictons populaires de la Vallée du Nguôn-son, Province de Quang-binh (Annam)," *Bulletin de l'École Française d'Extrême-Orient*, i. (Hanoi, 1901)

pp. 204 *sq.*

[2] C. Lumholtz, *Unknown Mexico*, ii. 194.

[3] H. Callaway, *Religious System of the Amazulu*, part. iv. (1870), pp. 407 *sq*

that rain will soon follow. They say that they call to "the lord above" and ask him to send rain. If it comes they declare that "Usondo rains."[1] In times of drought the Guanches of Teneriffe led their sheep to sacred ground, and there they separated the lambs from their dams, that their plaintive bleating might touch the heart of the god.[2] In Kumaon a way of stopping rain is to pour hot oil in the left ear of a dog. The animal howls with pain, his howls are heard by Indra, and out of pity for the beast's sufferings the god stops the rain.[3] Sometimes the Toradjas of Central Celebes attempt to procure rain as follows. They place the stalks of certain plants in water, saying. "Go and ask for rain, and so long as no rain falls I will not plant you again, but there shall you die." Also they string some fresh-water snails on a cord, and hang the cord on a tree, and say to the snails, "Go and ask for rain, and so long as no rain comes, I will not take you back to the water." Then the snails go and weep and the gods take pity and send rain.[4] However, the foregoing ceremonies are religious rather than magical, since they involve an appeal to the compassion of higher powers. A peculiar mode of making rain was adopted by some of the heathen Arabs. They tied two sorts of bushes to the tails and hind legs of their cattle, and, setting fire to the bushes, drove the cattle to the top of a mountain, praying for rain.[5] This may be, as Wellhausen suggests, an imitation of lightning on the horizon;[6] but it may also be a way of threatening the sky, as some West African rain-makers put a pot of inflammable materials on the fire and blow up the flames, threatening that if heaven does not soon give rain they will send up a blaze which will set the sky on fire.[7] In time of drought the priests of the Muyscas in New Granada ascended a mountain and there burned billets

[1] Dudley Kidd, *The Essential Kafir,* pp. 117 *sq.*

[2] E. Reclus, *Nouvelle Géographie Universelle,* xii. 100.

[3] *North Indian Notes and Queries,* iii. p. 135, § 285; W. Crooke, *Popular Religion and Folklore of Northern India* (Westminster, 1896), i. 77.

[4] A. C. Kruijt, "Regen lokken en regen verdrijven bij de Toradja's van Midden Celebes," *Tijdschrift voor Indische Taal- Land- en Volkenkunde,* xliv. (1901) p. 2.

[5] Rasmussen, *Additamenta ad historiam Arabum ante Islamismum,* pp. 67 *sq.* ; I. Goldziher, *Muhammedanische Studien* (Halle a. S., 1888-1890), i. 34 *sq.*

[6] J. Wellhausen, *Reste arabischen Heidentums,* p. 157 (first edition).

[7] J. B. Labat, *Relation historique de l'Éthiopie occidentale,* ii. 180.

of wood smeared with resin. The ashes they scattered in the air, thinking thus to condense the clouds and bring rain.[1]

Making rain by means of stones.

Stones are often supposed to possess the property of bringing on rain, provided they be dipped in water or sprinkled with it, or treated in some other appropriate manner. In a Samoan village a certain stone was carefully housed as the representative of the rain-making god, and in time of drought his priests carried the stone in procession and dipped it in a stream.[2] Among the Ta-ta-thi tribe of New South Wales, the rain-maker breaks off a piece of quartz-crystal and spits it towards the sky ; the rest of the crystal he wraps in emu feathers, soaks both crystal and feathers in water, and carefully hides them.[3] In the Keramin tribe of New South Wales the wizard retires to the bed of a creek, drops water on a round flat stone, then covers up and conceals it.[4] Among some tribes of north-western Australia the rain-maker repairs to a piece of ground which is set apart for the purpose of rain-making. There he builds a heap of stones or sand, places on the top of it his magic stone, and walks or dances round the pile chanting his incantations for hours, till sheer exhaustion obliges him to desist, when his place is taken by his assistant. Water is sprinkled on the stone and huge fires are kindled. No layman may approach the sacred spot while the mystic ceremony is being performed.[5] When the Sulka of New Britain wish to procure rain they blacken stones with the ashes of certain fruits and set them out, along with certain other plants and buds, in the sun. Then a handful of twigs is dipped in water and weighted with stones, while a spell is chanted. After that rain should follow.[6] In Manipur, on a lofty hill to the east of the capital, there is a stone which the popular imagination likens to an umbrella,

[1] H. Ternaux-Compans, *Essai sur l'ancien Cundinamarca* (Paris, n.d.), p. 42.

[2] G. Turner, *Samoa*, p. 145.

[3] A. L. P. Cameron, "Notes on some Tribes of New South Wales," *Journal of the Anthropological Institute*, xiv. (1885) p. 362. For other uses of quartz-crystal in ceremonies for the making of rain, see above, pp. 254, 255.

[4] A. L. P. Cameron, *loc. cit.* Com-

pare E. M. Curr, *The Australian Race*, ii. 377.

[5] E. Clement, "Ethnographical Notes on the Western Australian Aborigines," *Internationales Archiv für Ethnographie*, xvi. (1904) pp. 5 sq.

[6] Rascher, "Die Sulka," *Archiv für Anthropologie*, xxix. (1904) p. 225. Compare R. Parkinson, *Dreissig Jahre in der Südsee*, p. 196.

When rain is wanted, the rajah fetches water from a spring below and sprinkles it on the stone.[1] At Sagami in Japan there is a stone which draws down rain whenever water is poured on it.[2] When the Wakondyo, a tribe of Central Africa, desire rain, they send to the Wawamba, who dwell at the foot of snowy mountains, and are the happy possessors of a "rain-stone." In consideration of a proper payment, the Wawamba wash the precious stone, anoint it with oil, and put it in a pot full of water. After that the rain cannot fail to come.[3] In Behar people think to put an end to drought by keeping a holy stone named Náráyan-chakra in a vessel of water.[4] The Turks of Armenia make rain by throwing pebbles into the water. At Egin the pebbles are hung in two bags in the Euphrates; there should be seventy thousand and one of them.[5] At Myndus in Asia Minor the number of the stones used for this purpose is seventy-seven thousand, and each of them should be licked before it is cast into the sea.[6] In some parts of Mongolia, when the people desire rain, they fasten a bezoar stone to a willow twig, and place it in pure water, uttering incantations or prayers at the same time.[7] At Yakutsk all classes used firmly to believe they could make rain by means of one of these bezoar stones, provided it had really been found in the stomach of an animal, and the fiercer the beast the more powerful the charm. The rain-maker had to dip the stone in spring water just as the sun rose, and then holding it between the thumb and fore-finger of the right hand to present it to the luminary, after which he made three turns contrary to the direction of the sun. The virtue of a bezoar stone lasted only nine days.[8] Conversely, when Dr. Radloff's Mongolian guide wished to stop the rain, he tied a rock-crystal by a short string to a stick, held the stone over the fire, and then swung the stick

Bezoar stones as instruments of rain.

---

[1] T. C. Hodson, "The *genna* amongst the Tribes of Assam," *Journal of the Anthropological Institute*, xxxvi. (1906) p. 96.

[2] W. G. Aston, *Shinto* (London, 1905), p. 330.

[3] Fr. Stuhlmann, *Mit Emin Pascha ins Herz von Afrika* (Berlin, 1894), p. 654.

[4] *Indian Notes and Queries*, iv. p. 218, § 776; W. Crooke, *Popular Religion and Folklore of Northern India* (Westminster, 1896), i. 75 *sq.*

[5] J. Rendel Harris, MS. notes.

[6] W. R. Paton, in *Folklore*, xii. (1901) p. 216.

[7] G. Timkowski, *Travels of the Russian Mission through Mongolia to China* (London, 1827), i. 402 *sq.*

[8] C. H. Cottrell, *Recollections of Siberia* (London, 1842), p. 140.

about in all directions, while he chanted an incantation.[1] Water is scarce with the fierce Apaches, who roam the arid wastes of Arizona and New Mexico ; for springs are few and far between in these torrid wildernesses, where the intense heat would be unendurable were it not for the great dryness of the air. The stony beds of the streams are waterless in the plains ; but if you ascend for some miles the profound cañons that worm their way into the heart of the wild and rugged mountains, you come in time to a current trickling over the sand, and a mile or two more will bring you to a stream of a tolerable size flowing over boulders and screened from the fierce sun by walls of rock that tower on either hand a thousand feet into the air, their parched sides matted with the fantastic forms of the prickly cactus, and their summits crested far overhead with pine woods, like a black fringe against the burning blue of the sky. In such a land we need not wonder that the thirsty Indians seek to procure rain by magic. They take water from a certain spring and throw it on a particular point high up on a rock ; the welcome clouds then soon gather, and rain begins to fall.[2] In the district of Varanda, in Armenia, there is a rock with a hole in it near a sacred place. Women light candles on the rock and pour water into the hole in order to bring on rain. And in the same district there is another rock on which water is poured and milk boiled as an offering in time of drought.[3]

Making rain by means of stones in Europe.

But customs of this sort are not confined to the wilds of Africa and Asia or the torrid deserts of Australia and the New World. They have been practised in the cool air and under the grey skies of Europe. There is a fountain called Barenton, of romantic fame, in those "wild woods of Broceliande," where, if legend be true, the wizard Merlin still sleeps his magic slumber in the hawthorn shade. Thither the Breton peasants used to resort when they

[1] W. Radloff, *Aus Sibirien* (Leipsic, 1884), ii. 179 *sq.*

[2] *The American Antiquarian*, viii. 339. Vivid descriptions of the scenery and climate of Arizona and New Mexico will be found in Captain J. G. Bourke's *On the Border with Crook* (New York, 1891) ; see, for example, pp. 1 *sq.*, 12 *sq.*, 23 *sq.*, 30 *sq.*, 34 *sq.*, 41 *sqq.*, 185, 190 *sq.* See also C. Mindeleff, in *Seventeenth Annual Report of the Bureau of American Ethnology*, part 2 (Washington, 1898), pp. 477-481.

[3] M. Abeghian, *Der armenische Volksglaube*, p. 94.

needed rain. They caught some of the water in a tankard and threw it on a slab near the spring.[1] On Snowdon there is a lonely tarn called Dulyn, or the Black Lake, lying "in a dismal dingle surrounded by high and dangerous rocks." A row of stepping-stones runs out into the lake, and if any one steps on the stones and throws water so as to wet the farthest stone, which is called the Red Altar, "it is but a chance that you do not get rain before night, even when it is hot weather."[2] In these cases it appears probable that, as in Samoa, the stone is regarded as more or less divine. This appears from the custom sometimes observed of dipping the cross in the Fountain of Barenton to procure rain, for this is plainly a Christian substitute for the old pagan way of throwing water on the stone.[3] At various places in France *Dipping* it is, or used till lately to be, the practice to dip the image of *images of* a saint in water as a means of procuring rain. Thus, beside *saints in* the old priory of Commagny, a mile or two to the south-west *water as* of Moulins-Engilbert, there is a spring of St. Gervais, whither *a rain-* the inhabitants go in procession to obtain rain or fine weather *charm.* according to the needs of the crops. In times of great drought they throw into the basin of the fountain an ancient stone image of the saint that stands in a sort of niche from which the fountain flows.[4] At Collobrières and Carpentras, both in Provence, a similar practice was observed with the images of St. Pons and St. Gens respectively.[5] In several villages of Navarre prayers for rain used to be offered to St. Peter, and by way of enforcing them the villagers carried the image of the saint in procession to the river, where they thrice invited him to reconsider his resolution and to grant their prayers ; then, if he was still obstinate, they plunged him in the water, despite the remonstrances of the clergy, who

[1] J. Rhys, *Celtic Heathendom*, p. 184 ; J. Grimm, *Deutsche Mythologie*,[4] i. 494 ; L. J. B. Bérenger-Féraud, *Superstitions et survivances*, iii. 190 *sq.* Compare A. de Nore, *Coutumes, mythes et traditions des provinces de France*, p. 216; San Marte, *Die Arthur Sage*, pp. 105 *sq.*, 153 *sqq.*

[2] J. Rhys, *Celtic Heathendom*, pp. 185 *sq.*, quoting an earlier authority.

[3] J. Rhys, *op. cit.* p. 187. The same thing is done at the fountain of Sainte Anne, near Gevezé, in Brittany. See P. Sébillot, *Traditions et superstitions de la Haute-Bretagne*, i. 72.

[4] G. Herve, "Quelques superstitions de Morvan," *Bulletins de la Société d'Anthropologie de Paris*, 4me série, iii. (1892) p. 530.

[5] Bérenger-Féraud and de Mortillet, in *Bulletins de la Société d'Anthropologie de Paris*, 4me série, ii. (1891) pp. 306, 310 *sq.* ; L. J. B. Bérenger-Féraud, *Superstitions et survivances*, i. 427.

pleaded with as much truth as piety that a simple caution or admonition administered to the image would produce an equally good effect. After this the rain was sure to fall within twenty-four hours.[1] Catholic countries do not enjoy a monopoly of making rain by ducking holy images in water. In Mingrelia, when the crops are suffering from want of rain, they take a particularly holy image and dip it in water every day till a shower falls;[2] and in the Far East the Shans drench the images of Buddha with water when the rice is perishing of drought.[3] In all such cases the practice is probably at bottom a sympathetic charm, however it may be disguised under the appearance of a punishment or a threat.

Various rain-charms by means of stones.

The application of water to a miraculous stone is not the only way of securing its good offices in the making of rain. In the island of Uist, one of the Outer Hebrides, there is a stone cross opposite to St. Mary's church, which the natives used to call the Water-cross. When they needed rain, they set the cross up; and when enough rain had fallen, they laid it flat on the ground.[4] In Aurora, one of the New Hebrides islands, the rain-maker puts a tuft of leaves of a certain plant in the hollow of a stone; over it he lays some branches of a pepper-tree pounded and crushed, and to these he adds a stone which is believed to possess the property of drawing down showers from the sky. All this he accompanies with incantations, and finally covers the whole mass up. In time it ferments, and steam, charged with magical virtue, goes up and makes clouds and rain. The wizard must be careful, however, not to pound the pepper too hard, as otherwise the wind might blow too strong.[5] Sometimes the stone derives its magical virtue from its likeness to a real or imaginary animal. Thus, at Kota Gadang in Sumatra, there is a stone which, with the help of a powerful imagination, may perhaps be conceived to bear a faint and distant resemblance to a cat.

[1] Le Brun, *Historie critique des pratiques superstitieuses* (Amsterdam, 1733), i. 245 *sq.*; L. J. B. Bérenger-Féraud, *Superstitions et survivances*, i. 477. For more examples of such customs in France see P. Sébillot, *Le Folk-lore de France*, ii. 376-378.

[2] Lamberti, "Relation de la Colchide ou Mingrélie," *Voyages au Nord*, vii. 174 (Amsterdam, 1725).

[3] H. S. Hallett, *A Thousand Miles on an Elephant in the Shan States* (Edinburgh and London, 1890), p. 264.

[4] Martin, "Description of the Western Islands of Scotland," in Pinkerton's *Voyages and Travels*, iii. 594.

[5] R. H. Codrington, *The Melanesians*, p. 201.

Naturally, therefore, it possesses the property of eliciting showers from the sky, since in Sumatra, as we have seen, a real black cat plays a part in ceremonies for the production of rain. Hence the stone is sometimes smeared with the blood of fowls, rubbed, and incensed, while a charm is uttered over it.[1]   At Eneti, in Washington State, there is an irregular basaltic rock on which a face, said to be that of the thunder-bird, has been hammered. The Indians of the neighbourhood long believed that to shake the rock would cause rain by exciting the wrath of the thunder-bird.[2]

Like other peoples, the Greeks and Romans sought to obtain rain by magic, when prayers and processions[3] had proved ineffectual. For example, in Arcadia, when the corn and trees were parched with drought, the priest of Zeus dipped an oak branch into a certain spring on Mount Lycaeus. Thus troubled, the water sent up a misty cloud, from which rain soon fell upon the land.[4]   A similar mode of making rain is still practised, as we have seen, in Halmahera near New Guinea.[5]   The people of Crannon in Thessaly had a bronze chariot which they kept in a temple. When they desired a shower they shook the chariot and the shower fell.[6]   Probably the rattling of the chariot was meant to imitate thunder ; we have already seen that mock thunder and lightning form part of a rain-charm in Russia and

Rain-charms in classical antiquity.

---

[1] J. L. van der Toorn, "Het animisme bij den Minangkabauer der Padangsche Bovenlanden," *Bijdragen tot de Taal- Land- en Volkenkunde van Nederlandsch Indië,* xxxix. (1890) p. 86. As to the cat in rain-making ceremonies, see above, pp. 289, 291.

[2] Myron Eels, "The Twana, Chemakum, and Klallam Indians of Washington Territory," *Annual Report of the Smithsonian Institute for 1887,* p. 674.

[3] As to such prayers, see Pausanias, ii. 25. 10 ; Marcus Antoninus, v. 7 ; Petronius, 44 ; Tertullian, *Apolog.* 40, compare 22 and 23 ; P. Cauer, *Delectus Inscriptionum Graecarum,*[2] No. 162 ; H. Collitz und F. Bechtel, *Sammlung der griechischen Dialekt - Inschriften,* No. 3718 ; Ch. Michel, *Recueil d'inscriptions grecques,* No. 1004 ; O. Luders, *Die dionysischen Künstler*

(Berlin, 1873), pp. 26 *sq.*

[4] Pausanias, viii. 38. 4.

[5] See above, p. 248.

[6] Antigonus, *Histor. mirab.* 15 (*Scriptores rerum mirabilium Graeci,* ed. A. Westermann, pp. 64 *sq.*). Antigonus mentions that the badge of the city was a representation of the chariot with a couple of ravens perched on it. This badge appears on existing coins or Crannon, with the addition of a pitcher resting on the chariot (B. V. Head, *Historia Numorum,* p. 249). Hence A. Furtwängler conjectured, with great probability, that a pitcher full of water was placed on the real chariot when rain was wanted, and that the spilling of the water, as the chariot shook, was intended to imitate a shower of rain. See A. Furtwängler, *Meisterwerke der griechischen Plastik,* pp. 257-263.

Japan.[1] The legendary Salmoneus, King of Elis, made mock thunder by dragging bronze kettles behind his chariot, or by driving over a bronze bridge, while he hurled blazing torches in imitation of lightning. It was his impious wish to mimic the thundering car of Zeus as it rolled across the vault of heaven. Indeed he declared that he was actually Zeus, and caused sacrifices to be offered to himself as such.[2] Near a temple of Mars, outside the walls of Rome, there was kept a certain stone known as the *lapis manalis.* In time of drought the stone was dragged into Rome, and this was supposed to bring down rain immediately.[3] There were Etruscan wizards who made rain or discovered springs of water, it is not certain which. They were thought to bring the rain or the water out of their bellies.[4] The legendary Telchines in Rhodes are described as magicians who could change their shape and bring clouds, rain, and snow.[5] The Athenians sacrificed boiled, not roast meat to the Seasons, begging them to avert drought and dry heat and to send due warmth and timely rain.[6] This is an interesting example of the admixture of religion with sorcery, of sacrifice with magic. The Athenians dimly conceived that in some way the water in the pot would be transmitted through the boiled meat to the deities, and then sent down again by them in the form of rain.[7] In a similar spirit

[1] Above, pp. 248, 251.

[2] Apollodorus, i. 9. 7 ; Virgil, *Aen.* vi. 585 *sqq.*; Servius on Virgil, *l.c.*

[3] Festus, *s.vv. aquaelicium* and *manalem lapidem,* pp. 2, 128, ed. C. O. Müller ; Nonius Marcellus, *s.v. trullum,* p. 637, ed. Quicherat; Servius on Virgil, *Aen.* iii. 175; Fulgentius, "Expos. serm. antiq." *s.v. manales lapides, Mythogr. Lat.* ed. Staveren, pp. 769 *sq.* It has been suggested that the stone derived its name and its virtue from the *manes* or spirits of the dead (E. Hoffmann, in *Rheinisches Museum für Philologie,* N.F. l. (1895), pp. 484-486). Mr. O. Gilbert supposes that the stone was hollow and filled with water which was poured out in imitation of rain. See O. Gilbert, *Geschichte und Topographie der Stadt Rom im Altertum,* ii. (Leipsic, 1885) p. 154 note. His suggestion

is thus exactly parallel to that of Furtwängler as to the pitcher at Crannon (above, p. 309 note 6). Compare W. Warde Fowler, *Roman Festivals of the Period of the Republic* (London, 1899), pp. 232 *sq.*

[4] Nonius Marcellus, *s.v. aquilex,* p. 69, ed. Quicherat. In favour of taking *aquilex* as rain-maker is the use of *aquaelicium* in the sense of rain-making. Compare K. O. Müller, *Die Etrusker,* ed. W. Deecke, ii. 318 *sq.*

[5] Diodorus Siculus, v. 55.

[6] Philochorus, cited by Athenaeus, xiv. 72, p. 656 A.

[7] Among the Barotse, on the upper Zambesi, "the sorcerers or witch-doctors go from village to village with remedies which they cook in great cauldrons to make rain" (A. Bertrand, *The Kingdom of the Barotsi,* London, 1899, p. 277).

the prudent Greeks made it a rule always to pour honey, but never wine, on the altars of the sun-god, pointing out, with great show of reason, how expedient it was that a god on whom so much depended should keep strictly sober.[1]

§ 3. The Magical Control of the Sun

The rule of total abstinence which Greek prudence and piety imposed on the sun-god introduces us to a second class of natural phenomena which primitive man commonly supposes to be in some degree under his control and dependent on his exertions. As the magician thinks he can make rain, so he fancies he can cause the sun to shine, and can hasten or stay its going down. At an eclipse the Ojebways used to imagine that the sun was being extinguished. So they shot fire-tipped arrows in the air, hoping thus to rekindle his expiring light.[2] The Sencis of eastern Peru also shot burning arrows at the sun during an eclipse, but apparently they did this not so much to relight his lamp as to drive away a savage beast with which they supposed him to be struggling.[3] Conversely during an eclipse of the moon some Indian tribes of the Orinoco used to bury lighted brands in the ground; because, said they, if the moon were to be extinguished, all fire on earth would be extinguished

Making the sun to shine.

Magical control of the sun.

Attempts to help the sun at an eclipse.

---

[1] Phylarchus, cited by Athenaeus, xv. 48, p. 693 E F. If the conjectural reading τοῖς Ἐμεσηνοῖς were adopted in place of the manuscript reading τοῖς Ἕλλησιν, we should have to suppose that the custom was not observed by the Greeks, but by the people of Emesa in Syria, where there was a famous worship of the sun. But Polemo, the highest authority in such matters, tells us that the Athenians offered "sober" sacrifices to the sun and to other deities (Schol. on Sophocles, *Oed. Colon,* 100); and in a Greek inscription found at Piraeus we read of offerings to the sun and of three "sober altars," by which no doubt are meant altars on which wine was not poured. See Ch. Michel, *Recueil d'inscriptions grecques,* No. 672; Dittenberger, *Sylloge inscriptionum Graecorum,*[2] No. 631; E. S. Roberts, *Introduction to Greek Epi-*

graphy, ii. No. 133; *Leges Graecorum sacrae,* ed. J. de Prott et L. Ziehen, ii. No. 18. In the passage of Athenaeus, accordingly, the reading τοῖς Ἐμεσηνοῖς, which has been rashly adopted by the latest editor of Athenaeus (G. Kaibel), may be safely rejected in favour of the manuscript reading.

[2] Peter Jones, *History of the Ojebway Indians,* p. 84.

[3] W. Smyth and F. Lowe, *Narrative of a Journey from Lima to Para* (London, 1836), p. 230. An eclipse either of the sun or the moon is commonly supposed by savages to be caused by a monster who is trying to devour the luminary, and accordingly they discharge missiles and raise a clamour in order to drive him away. See E. B. Tylor, *Primitive Culture,*[2] i. 328 *sqq.*

with her, except such as was hidden from her sight.[1]
During an eclipse of the sun the Kamtchatkans were wont
to bring out fire from their huts and pray the great luminary
to shine as before.[2]   But the prayer addressed to the sun
shews that this ceremony was religious rather than magical.
Purely magical, on the other hand, was the ceremony
observed on similar occasions by the Chilcotin Indians of
north-western America.   Men and women tucked up their
robes, as they do in travelling, and then leaning on staves, as if
they were heavy laden, they continued to walk in a circle till
the eclipse was over.[3]   Apparently they thought thus to
support the failing steps of the sun as he trod his weary round
in the sky.   Similarly in ancient Egypt the king, as the
representative of the sun, walked solemnly round the walls of
a temple in order to ensure that the sun should perform his
daily journey round the sky without the interruption of an
eclipse or other mishap.[4]   And after the autumnal equinox
the ancient Egyptians held a festival called " the nativity of
the sun's walking-stick," because, as the luminary declined
daily in the sky, and his light and heat diminished, he was
supposed to need a staff on which to lean.[5]   In New
Caledonia when a wizard desires to make sunshine, he
takes some plants and corals to the burial - ground, and
fashions them into a bundle, adding two locks of hair cut
from a living child of his family, also two teeth or an entire
jawbone from the skeleton of an ancestor.   He then climbs
a mountain whose top catches the first rays of the morning
sun.   Here he deposits three sorts of plants on a flat stone,
places a branch of dry coral beside them, and hangs the
bundle of charms over the stone.   Next morning he returns
to the spot and sets fire to the bundle at the moment when

Various charms to cause the sun to shine.

---

[1] J. Gumilla, *Histoire de l'Orénoque*
(Avignon, 1758), iii. 243 *sq.*

[2] S. Krascheninnikow, *Beschreibung
des Landes Kamtschatka* (Lemgo,
1766), p. 217.

[3] A. G. Morice, "The Western
Dénés, their Manners and Customs,"
*Proceedings of the Canadian Institute,
Toronto,* Third Series, vii. (1888-89)
p. 154.

[4] A. Moret, *Le Rituel du culte divin
journalier en Égypte* (Paris, 1902),

pp. 90 *sq.*; *id., Du caractère religieux
de la royauté pharaonique* (Paris,
1902), p. 98.

[5] Plutarch, *Isis et Osiris,* 52. The
Esquimaux of Bering Strait give the
name of "the sun's walking-stick" to
the vertical bar in a parhelion. See
E. W. Nelson, "The Eskimo about
Bering Strait," *Eighteenth Annual
Report of the Bureau of American
Ethnology,* part i. (Washington, 1899)
p. 449.

the sun rises from the sea.   As the smoke curls up, he rubs
the stone with the dry coral, invokes his ancestors and says :
" Sun ! I do this that you may be burning hot, and eat up
all the clouds in the sky."   The same ceremony is repeated
at sunset.[1]   The New Caledonians also make a drought by
means of a disc-shaped stone with a hole in it.   At the
moment when the sun rises, the wizard holds the stone in
his hand and passes a burning brand repeatedly into the
hole, while he says : " I kindle the sun, in order that he
may eat up the clouds and dry up our land, so that it may
produce nothing." [2]   When the sun rises behind clouds—a
rare event in the bright sky of southern Africa—the Sun
clan of the Bechuanas say that he is grieving their heart.   All
work stands still, and all the food of the previous day is given
to matrons or old women.   They may eat it and may share
it with the children they are nursing, but no one else may
taste it.   The people go down to the river and wash themselves all over.   Each man throws into the river a stone
taken from his domestic hearth, and replaces it with one
picked up in the bed of the river.   On their return to the
village the chief kindles a fire in his hut, and all his subjects
come and get a light from it.   A general dance follows.[3]
In these cases it seems that the lighting of the flame on
earth is supposed to rekindle the solar fire.   Such a belief
comes naturally to people who, like the Sun clan of the
Bechuanas, deem themselves the veritable kinsmen of the
sun.   When the sun is obscured by clouds, the Lengua
Indians of the Gran Chaco hold burning sticks towards
him to encourage the luminary,[4] or rather perhaps to

---

[1] Father Lambert, in *Missions
Catholiques*, xii. (1880) p. 216 ; *id.*,
*Mœurs et superstitions des Néo-Calé-
doniens* (Nouméa, 1900), pp. 193 *sq.* ;
Glaumont, " Usages, mœurs et coutumes des Néo-Calédoniens," *Revue
d'ethnographie*, vii. (1889) p. 116.

[2] Father Lambert, in *Missions
Catholiques*, xxv. (1893) p. 116 ; *id.*,
*Mœurs et superstitions des Néo-Calé-
doniens* (Nouméa, 1900), pp. 296 *sq.*
The magic formula differs slightly in
the two passages ; in the text I have
followed the second.

[3] T. Arbousset et F. Daumas,

*Voyage d'exploration au nord-est de
la Colonie du Cap de Bonne-Espérance*
(Paris, 1842), pp. 350 *sq.*   For the
kinship with the sacred object (totem)
from which the clan takes its
name, see *ibid.* pp. 350, 422, 424.
Other people have claimed kindred
with the sun, as the Natchez of North
America (*Voyages au nord*, v. 24) and
the Incas of Peru.

[4] G. Kurze, " Sitten und Gebräuche
der Lengua-Indianer," *Mitteilungen
der Geographischen Gesellschaft zu
Jena*, xxiii. (1905) p. 17.

rekindle his seemingly expiring light.   The Banks Islanders make sunshine by means of a mock sun.   They take a very round stone, called a *vat loa* or sunstone, wind red braid about it, and stick it with owls' feathers to represent rays, singing the proper spell in a low voice. Then they hang it on some high tree, such as a banyan or a casuarina, in a sacred place.   Or the stone is laid on the ground with white rods radiating from it to imitate sunbeams.[1]   Sometimes the mode of making sunshine is the converse of that of making rain.   Thus we have seen that a white or red victim is sacrificed for sunshine, while a black one is sacrificed for rain.[2]   Some of the New Caledonians drench a skeleton to make rain, but burn it to make sunshine.[3]

Sun-
charms
among the
American
Indians.   When the mists lay thick on the Sierras of Peru, the Indian women used to rattle the silver and copper ornaments which they wore on their breasts, and they blew against the fog, hoping thus to disperse it and make the sun shine through.   Another way of producing the same effect was to burn salt or scatter ashes in the air.[4]   The Guarayo Indians also threw ashes in the air for the sake of clearing up the clouded evening sky.[5]   In Car Nicobar, when it has rained for several days without stopping, the natives roll long bamboos in leaves of various kinds and set them up in the middle of the village.   They call these bamboos "rods inviting the sun to shine."[6]   The offering made by the Brahman in the morning is supposed to produce the sun, and we are told that "assuredly it would not rise, were he not to make that offering."[7]   The ancient Mexicans conceived the sun as the source of all vital force; hence they named him Ipalnemohuani, "He by whom men live." But if he bestowed life on the world, he needed also to receive

Human
sacrifices
offered to
the sun by
the Mexi-
cans.

[1] R. H. Codrington, in *Journal of the Anthropological Institute*, x. (1881) p. 278; *id.*, *The Melanesians* (Oxford, 1891), p. 184.

[2] Above, pp. 291 *sq.*

[3] G. Turner, *Samoa*, p. 346. See above, p. 284.

[4] P. J. Arriaga, *Extirpacion de la idolatria del Piru* (Lima, 1621), p. 37.

[5] A. d'Orbigny, *Voyage dans l'Amé-rique Méridionale*, iii. (Paris and Strasburg, 1844) p. 24.

[6] V. Solomon, "Extracts from Diaries kept in Car Nicobar," *Journal of the Anthropological Institute*, xxxii. (1902) p. 213.

[7] *Satapatha - Brâhmana*, translated by J. Eggeling, part i. p. 328 (*Sacred Books of the East*, vol. xii.).

life from it. And as the heart is the seat and symbol of
life, bleeding hearts of men and animals were presented to
the sun to maintain him in vigour and enable him to run
his course across the sky. Thus the Mexican sacrifices to
the sun were magical rather than religious, being designed,
not so much to please and propitiate him, as physically to
renew his energies of heat, light, and motion. The constant
demand for human victims to feed the solar fire was met
by waging war every year on the neighbouring tribes and
bringing back troops of captives to be sacrificed on the altar.
Thus the ceaseless wars of the Mexicans and their cruel
system of human sacrifices, the most monstrous on record,
sprang in great measure from a mistaken theory of the solar
system. No more striking illustration could be given of
the disastrous consequences that may flow in practice from
a purely speculative error.[1] The ancient Greeks believed Greek
that the sun drove in a chariot across the sky ; hence the sacrifices
of horses
Rhodians, who worshipped the sun as their chief deity, to the sun
annually dedicated a chariot and four horses to him, and
flung them into the sea for his use. Doubtless they thought
that after a year's work his old horses and chariot would be
worn out.[2] From a like motive, probably, the idolatrous
kings of Judah dedicated chariots and horses to the sun,[3]
and the Spartans,[4] Persians,[5] and Massagetae[6] sacrificed
horses to him. The Spartans performed the sacrifice on the

[1] E. J. Payne, *History of the New
World called America*, i. (Oxford,
1892) pp. 520-523 ; K. Th. Preuss,
in *Verhandlungen der Berliner anthropologischen Gesellschaft*, November 15,
1902, pp. (449) *sq.*, (457) *sq.* ; *id.*,
"Die Feuergötter als Ausgangspunkt
zum Verständnis der mexikanischen
Religion," *Mitteilungen der anthropo-
log. Gesellschaft in Wien*, xxxiii. (1903)
pp. 157 *sq.*, 163. A Mexican legend
relates how in the beginning the gods
sacrificed themselves by fire in order to
set the sun in motion. See B. de Sahagun,
*Histoire générale des choses de la Nou-
velle Espagne*, bk. vii. ch. 2, pp. 478
sqq. (French trans. by Jourdanet and
Simeon).

[2] Festus, *s.v.* "October equus," p.
181, ed. C. O. Müller.

[3] 2 Kings xxiii. 11. Compare H.
Zimmern, in E. Schrader's *Die Keil-
inschriften und das Alte Testament*[3]
(Berlin, 1902), pp. 369 *sq.*

[4] Pausanias, iii. 20. 4.

[5] Xenophon, *Cyropaed.* viii. 3. 24 ;
Philostratus, *Vit. Apollon.* i. 31. 2 ;
Ovid, *Fasti*, i. 385 *sq.* ; Pausanias,
iii. 20. 4. Compare Xenophon,
Anabasis, iv. 5. 35 ; Trogus Pompeius,
i. 10. 5.

[6] Herodotus, i. 216 ; Strabo, xi.
8. 6. On the sacrifice of horses see
further S. Bochart, *Hierozoicon*, i. coll.
175 *sqq.* ; Negelein, in *Zeitschrift für
Ethnologie*, xxxiii. (1901), pp. 62-66.
Many Asiatics held that the sun rode a
horse, not a chariot. See Dittenberger,
Sylloge inscriptionum Graecarum,[2] No.
754, with note [4].

top of Mount Taygetus, the beautiful range behind which they saw the great luminary set every night. It was as natural for the inhabitants of the valley of Sparta to do this as it was for the islanders of Rhodes to throw the chariot and horses into the sea, into which the sun seemed to them to sink at evening. For thus, whether on the mountain or in the sea, the fresh horses stood ready for the weary god where they would be most welcome, at the end of his day's journey.

Staying the sun by means of a net or string. As some people think they can light up the sun or speed him on his way, so others fancy they can retard or stop him. In a pass of the Peruvian Andes stand two ruined towers on opposite hills. Iron hooks are clamped into their walls for the purpose of stretching a net from one tower to the other. The net is intended to catch the sun.[1] On a small hill in Fiji grew a patch of reeds, and travellers who feared to be belated used to tie the tops of a handful of reeds together to prevent the sun from going down.[2] As to this my late friend the Rev. Lorimer Fison wrote to me : " I have often seen the reeds tied together to keep the sun from going down. The place is on a hill in Lakomba, one of the eastern islands of the Fijian group. It is on the side —not on the top—of the hill. The reeds grow on the right side of the path. I asked an old man the meaning of the practice, and he said, ' We used to think the sun would see us, and know we wanted him not to go down till we got past on our way home again.' "[3] But perhaps the original intention was to entangle the sun in the reeds, just as the Peruvians try to catch him in the net. Stories of men who have caught the sun in a noose are widely spread.[4] When the sun is going southward in the autumn, and sinking lower and lower in the Arctic sky, the Esquimaux of Iglulik play the game of cat's cradle in order to catch him in the meshes of the string and so prevent his

---

[1] A. Bastian, *Die Völker des östlichen Asien*, iv. 174. The name of the place is Andahuayllas.

[2] Th. Williams, *Fiji and the Fijians*[2], i. 250.

[3] Mr. Fison's letter is dated August 26, 1898.

[4] H. R. Schoolcraft, *The American Indians* (Buffalo, 1851), pp. 97 *sqq.* ; *id.*, *Oneota* (New York and London, 1845), pp. 75 *sqq.* ; W. W. Gill, *Myths and Songs of the South Pacific*, pp. 61 *sq.* ; G. Turner, *Samoa*, pp. 200 *sq.*

disappearance. On the contrary, when the sun is moving northward in the spring, they play the game of cup-and-ball to hasten his return.[1] Means like those which the Esquimaux take to stop the departing sun are adopted by the Ewe negroes of the Slave Coast to catch a runaway slave. They take two sticks, unite them by a string, and then wind the string round one of them, while at the same time they pronounce the name of the fugitive. When the string is quite wound about the stick, the runaway will be bound fast and unable to stir.[2] In New Guinea, when a Motu man is hunting or travelling late in the afternoon and fears to be overtaken by darkness, he will sometimes take a piece of twine, loop it, and look through the loop at the sun. Then he pulls the loop into a knot and says, "Wait until we get home, and we will give you the fat of a pig." After that he passes the string to the man behind him, and then it is thrown away. In a similar case a Motumotu man of New Guinea says, "Sun, do not be in a hurry; just wait until I get to the end." And the sun waits. The Motumotu do not like to eat in the dark; so if the food is not yet ready, and the sun is sinking, they say, "Sun, stop; my food is not ready, and I want to eat by you."[3] Here the looking at the sinking sun through a loop and then drawing the loop into a knot appears to be a purely magical ceremony designed to catch the sun in the mesh; but the request that the luminary would kindly stand still till home is reached or the dinner cooked, coupled with the offer of a slice of fat bacon as an inducement to him to comply with the request, is thoroughly religious. Jerome of Prague, travelling among the heathen Lithuanians early in the fifteenth century, found a tribe who worshipped the sun and venerated a large iron hammer. The priests told him that once the sun had been invisible for several months, because a powerful king had shut it up in a strong tower; but the signs of the zodiac

---

[1] Fr. Boas, "The Eskimo of Baffin Land and Hudson Bay," *Bulletin of the American Museum of Natural History*, xv. (1901) p. 151.

[2] G. Zündel, "Land und Volk der Eweer auf der Sclavenküste in West-afrika," *Zeitschrift der Gesellschaft für Erdkunde zu Berlin*, xii. (1877) p. 411. We have met with a somewhat similar charm in North Africa to bring back a runaway slave. See above, p. 152.

[3] J. Chalmers, *Pioneering in New Guinea* (London, 1887), p. 172.

had broken open the tower with this very hammer and released the sun. Therefore they adored the hammer.[1]

When an Australian blackfellow wishes to stay the sun from going down till he gets home, he puts a sod in the fork of a tree, exactly facing the setting sun.[2] For the same purpose an Indian of Yucatan, journeying westward, places a stone in a tree or pulls out some of his eyelashes and blows them towards the sun.[3] When the Golos, a tribe of the Bahr-el-Ghazal, are on the march, they will sometimes take a stone or a small ant-heap, about the size of a man's head, and place it in the fork of a tree in order to retard the sunset.[4] South African natives, in travelling, will put a stone in a fork of a tree or place some grass on the path with a stone over it, believing that this will cause their friends to keep the meal waiting till their arrival.[5] In this, as in previous examples, the purpose apparently is to retard the sun. But why should the act of putting a stone or a sod in a tree be supposed to effect this? A partial explanation is suggested by another Australian custom. In their journeys the natives are accustomed to place stones in trees at different heights from the ground in order to indicate the height of the sun in the sky at the moment when they passed the particular tree. Those who follow are thus made aware of the time of day when their friends in advance passed the spot.[6] Possibly the natives, thus accustomed to mark the sun's progress, may have slipped into the confusion of imagining that to mark the sun's progress was to arrest it at the point marked. On the other hand, to make it go

[1] Aeneas Sylvius, *Opera* (Bâle, 1571), p. 418 [wrongly numbered 420]; A. Thevet, *Cosmographie universelle* (Paris, 1575), ii. 851.

[2] R. Brough Smyth, *Aborigines of Victoria*, ii. 334; E. M. Curr, *The Australian Race*, i. 50.

[3] Fancourt, *History of Yucatan*, p. 118; Brasseur de Bourbourg, *Histoire des nations civilisées du Mexique et de l'Amérique-Centrale*, ii. 51.

[4] S. L. Cummins, "Sub-tribes of the Bahr-el-Ghazal Dinkas," *Journal of the Anthropological Institute*, xxxiv. (1904) p. 164.

[5] (*South African*) *Folklore Journal*,

vol. i. part i. (Capetown, 1879) p. 34; Dudley Kidd, *Savage Childhood* (London, 1906), pp. 147 *sq.*; Rev. E. Gottschling, "The Bawenda," *Journal of the Anthropological Institute*, xxxv. (1905) p. 381.

[6] E. J. Eyre, *Journals of Expeditions of Discovery into Central Australia* (London, 1845), ii. 365. The Ova-kumbi of Angola place a stone in the fork of a tree as a memorial at any place where they have learned something which they wish to remember. See Ch. Wunenberger, "La Mission et le royaume de Humbé," *Missions Catholiques*, xx. (1888) p. 270.

down faster, the Australians throw sand into the air and blow with their mouths towards the sun,[1] perhaps to waft the lingering orb westward and bury it under the sands into which it appears to sink at night.

As some people imagine they can hasten the sun, so others fancy they can jog the tardy moon. The natives of German New Guinea reckon months by the moon, and some of them have been known to throw stones and spears at the moon, in order to accelerate its progress and so to hasten the return of their friends, who were away from home for twelve months working on a tobacco plantation.[2] The Malays think that a bright glow at sunset may throw a weak person into a fever. Hence they attempt to extinguish the glow by spitting out water and throwing ashes at it.[3] The Shuswap Indians of British Columbia believe that they can bring on cold weather by burning the wood of a tree that has been struck by lightning. The belief may be based on the observation that in their country cold follows a thunder-storm. Hence in spring, when these Indians are travelling over the snow on high ground, they burn splinters of such wood in the fire in order that the crust of the snow may not melt.[4]

Accelerating the moon.

§ 4. *The Magical Control of the Wind*

Once more, the savage thinks he can make the wind to blow or to be still. When the day is hot and a Yakut has a long way to go, he takes a stone which he has chanced to find in an animal or fish, winds a horse-hair several times round it, and ties it to a stick. He then waves the stick about, uttering a spell. Soon a cool breeze begins to blow.[5] In order to procure a cool wind for nine days the stone should first be dipped in the blood of a bird or beast and

Making the wind to blow or be still.

---

[1] E. M. Curr, *The Australian Race*, iii. 145.

[2] K. Vetter, *Komm herüber und hilf uns! oder die Arbeit der Neuen-Dettelsauer Mission in Deutsch Neu-Guinea*, ii. (Barmen, 1898) p. 29; *id.*, in B. Hagen's *Unter den Papua's* (Wiesbaden, 1899), p. 287.

[3] W. W. Skeat, *Malay Magic*, pp. 92 *sq.*

[4] G. M. Dawson, "Notes on the Shuswap People of British Columbia," *Transactions of the Royal Society of Canada*, ix. (1901, pub. 1902) section ii. p. 38.

[5] J. G. Gmelin, *Reise durch Sibirien* (Göttingen, 1751-52), ii. 510.

Making
the wind
to blow or
be still.

then presented to the sun, while the sorcerer makes three turns contrary to the course of the luminary.[1] The Wind clan of the Omahas flap their blankets to start a breeze which will drive away the mosquitoes.[2] When a Haida Indian wishes to obtain a fair wind, he fasts, shoots a raven, singes it in the fire, and then going to the edge of the sea sweeps it over the surface of the water four times in the direction in which he wishes the wind to blow. He then throws the raven behind him, but afterwards picks it up and sets it in a sitting posture at the foot of a spruce-tree, facing towards the required wind. Propping its beak open with a stick, he requests a fair wind for a certain number of days; then going away he lies covered up in his mantle till another Indian asks him for how many days he has desired the wind, which question he answers.[3] When a sorcerer in New Britain wishes to make a wind blow in a certain direction, he throws burnt lime in the air, chanting a song all the time. Then he waves sprigs of ginger and other plants about, throws them up and catches them. Next he makes a small fire with these sprigs on the spot where the lime has fallen thickest, and walks round the fire chanting. Lastly, he takes the ashes and throws them on the water.[4] If a Hottentot desires the wind to drop, he takes one of his fattest skins and hangs it on the end of a pole, in the belief that by blowing the skin down the wind will lose all its force and must itself fall.[5] Fuegian wizards throw shells against the wind to make it drop.[6] On the other hand, when a Persian peasant desires a strong wind to winnow his corn, he rubs a kind of bastard saffron and throws it up into the air; after that the breeze soon begins to blow.[7] Some of the Indians of Canada believed that the winds were caused by a fish like a lizard. When one of

[1] C. H. Cottrell, *Recollections of Siberia* (London, 1842), p. 140.

[2] J. Owen Dorsey, " Omaha Sociology," *Third Annual Report of the Bureau of Ethnology* (Washington, 1884), p. 241; *id.*, " A Study of Siouan Cults," *Eleventh Annual Report of the Bureau of Ethnology* (Washington, 1894), p. 410.

[3] G. M. Dawson, " On the Haida Indians of the Queen Charlotte Islands,"

Geological Survey of Canada, Report of Progress for 1878-1879, p. 124 B.

[4] W. Powell, *Wanderings in a Wild Country* (London, 1883), p. 169.

[5] O. Dapper, *Description de l' Afrique* (Amsterdam, 1686), p. 389.

[6] *Mission scientifique du Cap Horn,* vii. (Paris, 1891) p. 257.

[7] J. Richardson, *A Dictionary of Persian, Arabic, and English,* New Edition (London, 1829), pp. liii. *sq.*

these fish had been caught, the Indians advised the Jesuit Making the missionaries to put it back into the river as fast as possible wind to blow or be in order to calm the wind, which was contrary.[1] If a still. Cherokee wizard desires to turn aside an approaching storm, he faces it and recites a spell with outstretched hand. Then he gently blows towards the quarter to which he wishes it to go, waving his hand in the same direction as if he were pushing away the storm.[2] The Ottawa Indians fancied they could calm a tempest by relating the dreams they had dreamed during their fast, or by throwing tobacco on the troubled water.[3] When the Kei Islanders wish to obtain a favourable wind for their friends at sea, they dance in a ring, both men and women, swaying their bodies to and fro, while the men hold handkerchiefs in their hands.[4] In Melanesia there are everywhere weather-doctors who can control the powers of the air and are willing to supply wind or calm in return for a proper remuneration. For instance, in Santa Cruz the wizard makes wind by waving the branch of a tree and chanting the appropriate charm.[5] In another Melanesian island a missionary observed a large shell filled with earth, in which an oblong stone, covered with red ochre, was set up, while the whole was surrounded by a fence of sticks strengthened by a creeper which was twined in and out the uprights. On asking a native what these things meant, he learned that the wind was here fenced or bound round, lest it should blow hard ; the imprisoned wind would not be able to blow again until the fence that kept it in should have rotted away.[6] In South Africa, when the Caffres wish to stop a high wind, they call in a " wind-doctor," who takes a pot with a spout and points the spout towards the quarter from which the wind is blowing. He then places medicines

[1] *Relations des Jésuites*, 1636, p. 38 (Canadian reprint). On the other hand, some of the New South Wales aborigines thought that a wished-for wind would not rise if shell-fish were roasted at night (D. Collins, *Account of the English Colony in New South Wales*, London, 1804, p. 382).

[2] J. Mooney, "Sacred Formulas of the Cherokees," *Seventh Annual Report of the Bureau of Ethnology* (Washington, 1891), pp. 387 *sq.*

[3] *Annales de l'Association de la Propagation de la Foi*, iv. (1830) p. 482.

[4] C. M. Pleyte, "Ethnographische Beschrijving der Kei Eilanden," *Tijdschrift van het Nederlandsch Aardrijkskundig Genootschap*, Tweede Serie, x. (1893) p. 827.

[5] R. H. Codrington, *The Melanesians*, pp. 200, 201.

[6] J. Palmer, quoted by R. H. Codrington, *The Melanesians*, p. 201, note.

and some of the dust blown by the wind in the vessel, and seals up every opening of the pot with damp clay. Thereupon the doctor declares, " The head of the wind is now in my pot, and the wind will cease to blow." [1] The natives of the island of Bibili, off German New Guinea, are reputed to make wind by blowing with their mouths. In stormy weather the Bogadjim people say, " The Bibili folk are at it again, blowing away." [2] Another way of making wind which is practised in New Guinea is to strike a "windstone " lightly with a stick ; to strike it hard would bring on a hurricane.[3] So in Scotland witches used to raise the wind by dipping a rag in water and beating it thrice on a stone, saying :

> " *I knok this rag upone this stane*
> *To raise the wind in the divellis name,*
> *It sall not lye till I please againe.*" [4]

Raising the wind.

At Victoria, the capital of Vancouver's Island, there are a number of large stones not far from what is called the Battery. Each of them represents a certain wind. When an Indian wants any particular wind, he goes and moves the corresponding stone a little ; were he to move it too much, the wind would blow very hard.[5] The natives of Murray Island in Torres Straits used to make a great wind blow from the south-east by pointing coco-nut leaves and other plants at two granitic boulders on the shore. So long as the leaves remained there the wind sat in that quarter. But, significantly enough, the ceremony was only performed during the prevalence of the south-east monsoon. The natives knew better than to try to raise a south-east wind while the north-west monsoon was blowing.[6] On the altar of Fladda's chapel, in the island of Fladdahuan (one of the Hebrides), lay a round bluish stone which was always moist. Windbound fishermen walked sunwise round the chapel and

[1] Dudley Kidd, *Savage Childhood* (London, 1906), p. 151.

[2] B. Hagen, *Unter den Papua's* (Wiesbaden, 1899), p. 269.

[3] W. Monckton, " Some Recollections of New Guinea Customs," *Journal of the Polynesian Society,* v. (1896) p. 186.

[4] J. G. Dalyell, *The Darker Super-*

stitions of Scotland, p. 248.

[5] Fr. Boas, in *Sixth Report on the North-Western Tribes of Canada,* p. 26 (separate reprint from the *Report of the British Association for 1890*).

[6] A. C. Haddon, *Head-hunters,* p. 60 ; *Reports of the Cambridge Anthropological Expedition to Torres Straits,* vi. (Cambridge, 1908) pp. 201 *sq.*

then poured water on the stone, whereupon a favourable breeze was sure to spring up.[1] In Gigha, an island off the western coast of Argyleshire, there is a well named Tobarrath Bhuathaig or "The lucky well of Beathag," which used to be famous for its power of raising the wind. It lies at the foot of a hill facing north-east near an isthmus called Tarbat. Six feet above where the water gushes out there is a heap of stones which forms a cover to the sacred spring. When a person wished for a fair wind, either to leave the island or to bring home his absent friends, this part was opened with great solemnity, the stones were carefully removed, and the well cleaned with a wooden dish or a clam shell. This being done, the water was thrown several times in the direction from which the wished-for wind was to blow, and this action was accompanied by a certain form of words which the person repeated every time he threw the water. When the ceremony was over, the well was again carefully shut up to prevent fatal consequences, it being firmly believed that, were the place left open, a storm would arise which would overwhelm the whole island.[2] The Esthonians have various odd ways of raising a wind. They scratch their finger, or hang up a serpent, or strike an axe into a house-beam in the direction from which they wish the wind to blow, while at the same time they whistle. The notion is that the gentle wind will not let an innocent being or even a beam suffer without coming and breathing softly to assuage the pain.[3]

In Mabuiag, an island between New Guinea and Australia, there were men whose business was to make wind for such as wanted it. When engaged in his professional duties the wizard painted himself black behind and red on his face and chest. The red in front typified the red cloud of morning, the black represented the dark blue sky of night. Thus arrayed he took some bushes, and, when the tide was low, fastened them at the edge of the reef so that the flowing

Winds raised by wizards and witches.

---

[1] Martin, "Description of the Western Islands of Scotland," in Pinkerton's *Voyages and Travels*, iii. 627 ; Miss C. F. Gordon Cumming, *In the Hebrides*, pp. 166 *sq.*

[2] W. Fraser, in Sir John Sinclair's *Statistical Account of Scotland*, viii. (Edinburgh, 1793) p. 52, note.

[3] Boecler-Kreutzwald, *Der Ehsten abergläubische Gebräuche, Weisen und Gewohnheiten* (St. Petersburg, 1854), pp. 105 *sq.*

tide made them sway backwards and forwards. But if only a gentle breeze was needed, he fastened them nearer to the shore. To stop the wind he again painted himself red and black, the latter in imitation of the clear blue sky, and then removing the bushes from the reef he dried and burnt them. The smoke as it curled up was believed to stop the wind : " Smoke he go up and him clear up on top."[1] In some islands of Torres Straits the wizard made wind by whirling a bull-roarer ; [2] the booming sound of the instrument probably seemed to him like the roar or the whistling of the wind. Amongst the Kurnai tribe of Gippsland in Victoria there used to be a noted raiser of storms who went by the name of Bunjil Kraura or " Great West Wind." This wind makes the tall slender trees of the Gippsland forests to rock and sway so that the natives could not climb them in search of opossums. Hence the people were forced to propitiate Bunjil Kraura by liberal offerings of weapons and rugs whenever the tree-tops bent before a gale. Having received their gifts, Bunjil Kraura would bind his head with swathes of stringy bark, and lull the storm to rest with a song which consisted of the words " Wear—string—Westwind," repeated again and again.[3] Apparently the wizard identified himself with the wind, and fancied that he could bind it by tying string round his own head. The Kwakiutl Indians of British Columbia, as we have seen, believe that twins can summon any wind by merely moving their hands.[4] In Greenland a woman in child-bed and for some time after delivery is supposed to possess the power of laying a storm. She has only to go out of doors, fill her mouth with air, and coming back into the house blow it out again.[5] In antiquity there was a family at Corinth which enjoyed the reputation of being able to still the raging wind ; but we do not know in what manner its members exercised a useful function.

[1] A. C. Haddon, " The Ethnography of the Western Tribe of Torres Straits," *Journal of the Anthropological Institute,* xix. (1890), pp. 401 *sq.* ; *Reports of the Cambridge Anthropological Expedition to Torres Straits,* v. (Cambridge, 1904), pp. 351 *sq.*

[2] *Reports of the Cambridge Anthropological Expedition to Torres Straits,* v. 352.

[3] Mary E. B. Howitt, *Folklore and Legends of some Victorian Tribes* (in manuscript).

[4] See above, p. 263.

[5] H. Egede, *Description of Greenland,* second edition (London, 1818), p. 196, note.

which probably earned for them a more solid recompense Winds
than mere repute among the seafaring population of the raised by
wizards and
isthmus.[1] Even in Christian times, under the reign of witches.
Constantine, a certain Sopater suffered death at Constanti-
nople on a charge of binding the winds by magic, because
it happened that the corn-ships of Egypt and Syria were
detained afar off by calms or head-winds, to the rage and
disappointment of the hungry Byzantine rabble.[2] An
ancient charm to keep storms from damaging the crops was
to bury a toad in a new earthen vessel in the middle of the
field.[3] Finnish wizards used to sell wind to storm-stayed
mariners. The wind was enclosed in three knots; if they
undid the first knot, a moderate wind sprang up; if the
second, it blew half a gale ; if the third, a hurricane.[4] Indeed
the Esthonians, whose country is divided from Finland only
by an arm of the sea, still believe in the magical powers of
their northern neighbours. The bitter winds that blow in
spring from the north and north-east, bringing ague and
rheumatic inflammations in their train, are set down by the
simple Esthonian peasantry to the machinations of the
Finnish wizards and witches. In particular they regard with
special dread three days in spring to which they give the
name of Days of the Cross; one of them falls on the Eve of
Ascension Day. The people in the neighbourhood of Fellin
fear to go out on these days lest the cruel winds from Lappland should smite them dead. A popular Esthonian song
runs :

> " *Wind of the Cross ! rushing and mighty !*
> *Heavy the blow of thy wings sweeping past !*
> *Wild wailing wind of misfortune and sorrow,*
> *Wizards of Finland, ride by on the blast.*"[5]

It is said, too, that sailors, beating up against the wind
in the Gulf of Finland, sometimes see a strange sail heave
in sight astern and overhaul them hand over hand. On she

[1] Hesychius and Suidas, *s.v.* ἀνεμο-
κοῖται; Eustathius, on Homer, *Od*. x.
22, p. 1645. Compare J. Töpffer,
Attische Genealogie, p. 112, who con-
jectures that the Eudanemi or Heuda-
nemi at Athens may also have claimed
the power of lulling the winds.

[2] Eunapius, *Vitae sophistarum :*

Aedesius, p. 463, Didot edition.

[3] Pliny, *Nat. Hist.* xviii. 294.
Compare *Geoponica*, ii. 18.

[4] Olaus Magnus, *Gentium septentr.
hist*. iii. 15.

[5] Boecler-Kreutzwald, *Der Ehsten
abergläubische Gebräuche, Weisen und
Gewohnheiten*, pp. 107 *sq*.

comes with a cloud of canvas—all her studding-sails out—right in the teeth of the wind, forging her way through the foaming billows, dashing back the spray in sheets from her cutwater, every sail swollen to bursting, every rope strained to cracking. Then the sailors know that she hails from Finland.[1]

The art of tying up the wind in three knots, so that the more knots are loosed the stronger will blow the wind, has been attributed to wizards in Lappland and to witches in Shetland, Lewis, and the Isle of Man. Shetland seamen still buy winds in the shape of knotted handkerchiefs or threads from old women who claim to rule the storms. There are said to be ancient crones in Lerwick now who live by selling wind.[2] In the early part of the nineteenth century Sir Walter Scott visited one of these witches at Stromness in the Orkneys. He says : " We clomb, by steep and dirty lanes, an eminence rising above the town, and commanding a fine view. An old hag lives in a wretched cabin on this height, and subsists by selling winds. Each captain of a merchantman, between jest and earnest, gives the old woman sixpence, and she boils her kettle to procure a favourable gale. She was a miserable figure ; upwards of ninety, she told us, and dried up like a mummy. A sort of clay-coloured cloak, folded over her head, corresponded in colour to her corpse-like complexion. Fine light-blue eyes, and nose and chin that almost met, and a ghastly expression of cunning, gave her quite the effect of Hecate." [3] A Norwegian witch has boasted of sinking a ship by opening a bag in which she had shut up a wind.[4] Ulysses received the winds in a leathern bag from Aeolus, King of the Winds.[5] The

---

[1] Dana, *Two Years before the Mast*, ch. vi.

[2] J. Scheffer, *Lapponia* (Frankfort, 1673), p. 144 ; J. Train, *Account of the Isle of Man*, ii. 166 ; Miss C. F. Gordon Cumming, *In the Hebrides*, pp. 254 *sq.* ; Ch. Rogers, *Social Life in Scotland*, iii. 220 ; Sir W. Scott, *Pirate*, note to ch. vii. ; Miss M. Cameron, in *Folklore*, xiv. (1903) pp. 301 *sq.* Compare Shakespeare, *Macbeth*, Act i. Sc. 3, line 11. " But, my loving master, if any wind will not

serve, then I wish I were in Lapland, to buy a good wind of one of the honest witches, that sell so many winds there and so cheap" (Izaac Walton, *Compleat Angler*, ch. v.).

[3] J. G. Lockhart, *Memoirs of the Life of Sir Walter Scott*, iii. 203 (first edition).

[4] C. Leemius, *De Lapponibus Finmarchiae, etc., commentatio* (Copenhagen, 1767), p. 454.

[5] Homer, *Odyssey*, x. 19 *sqq.* It is said that Perdoytus, the Lithuanian

Motumotu in New Guinea think that storms are sent by an Oiabu sorcerer ; for each wind he has a bamboo which he opens at pleasure.[1] On the top of Mount Agu in Togo, a district of German West Africa, resides a fetish called Bagba, who is supposed to control the wind and the rain. His priest is said to keep the winds shut up in great pots.[2]

Often the stormy wind is regarded as an evil being who may be intimidated, driven away, or killed. When the darkening of the sky indicates the approach of a tornado, a South African magician will repair to a height whither he collects as many people as can be hastily summoned to his assistance. Directed by him, they shout and bellow in imitation of the gust as it swirls roaring about the huts and among the trees of the forest. Then at a signal they mimic the crash of the thunder, after which there is a dead silence for a few seconds; then follows a screech more piercing and prolonged than any that preceded, dying away in a tremulous wail. The magician fills his mouth with a foul liquid which he squirts in defiant jets against the approaching storm as a kind of menace or challenge to the spirit of the wind ; and the shouting and wailing of his assistants are meant to frighten the spirit away. The performance lasts until the tornado either bursts or passes away in another direction. If it bursts, the reason is that the magician who sent the storm was more powerful than he who endeavoured to avert it.[3] When storms and bad weather have lasted long and food is scarce with the Central Esquimaux, they endeavour to conjure the tempest by making a long whip of seaweed, armed with which they go down to the beach and strike out in the direction of the wind, crying, " *Taba* (it is enough) ! "[4] Once when north-westerly winds had kept the ice long on the coast and food was becoming scarce, the Esquimaux

Marginal note: Frightening, driving away, and killing the spirit of the wind.

Aeolus, keeps the winds enclosed in a leathern bag; when they escape from it he pursues them, beats them, and shuts them up again. See E. Vecken-stedt, *Die Mythen, Sagen und Legenden der Zamaiten* (Litauer), i. 153. The statements of this writer, however, are to be received with caution.

[1] J. Chalmers, *Pioneering in New Guinea*, p. 177.

[2] Lieut. Herold, in *Mitteilungen aus den deutschen Schutzgebieten*, v. (1892) pp. 144 *sq.* ; H. Klose, *Togo unter deutscher Flagge* (Berlin, 1899), p. 189.

[3] Rev. J. Macdonald, *Religion and Myth* (London, 1893), p. 7.

[4] Fr. Boas, "The Central Eskimo," *Sixth Annual Report of the Bureau of Ethnology* (Washington, 1888), p. 593.

performed a ceremony to make a calm. A fire was kindled on the shore, and the men gathered round it and chanted. An old man then stepped up to the fire and in a coaxing voice invited the demon of the wind to come under the fire and warm himself. When he was supposed to have arrived, a vessel of water, to which each man present had contributed, was thrown on the flames by an old man, and immediately a flight of arrows sped towards the spot where the fire had been. They thought that the demon would not stay where he had been so badly treated. To complete the effect, guns were discharged in various directions, and the captain of a European vessel was invited to fire on the wind with cannon.[1] On the twenty-first of February 1883 a similar ceremony was performed by the Esquimaux of Point Barrow, Alaska, with the intention of killing the spirit of the wind. Women drove the demon from their houses with clubs and knives, with which they made passes in the air ; and the men, gathering round a fire, shot him with their rifles and crushed him under a heavy stone the moment that steam rose in a cloud from the smouldering embers, on which a tub of water had just been thrown.[2]

Confronting the storm with swords and drums.

In ancient India the priest was directed to confront a storm, armed to the teeth with a bludgeon, a sword, and a firebrand, while he chanted a magical lay.[3] During a tremendous hurricane the drums of Kadouma, near the Victoria Nyanza, were heard to beat all night. When next morning a missionary enquired the cause, he was told that the sound of the drums is a charm against storms.[4] The Sea Dyaks and Kayans of Borneo beat gongs when a tempest is raging ; but the Dyaks, and perhaps the Kayans also, do this, not so much to frighten away the spirit of the storm, as to apprise him of their whereabouts, lest he should inadvertently knock their houses down. Heard at night above the howling of the storm, the distant boom of the

---

[1] *Arctic Papers for the Expedition of* 1875 (Royal Geographical Society), p. 274.

[2] J. Murdoch, "Ethnological Results of the Point Barrow Expedition," *Ninth Annual Report of the Bureau of Ethnology* (Washington, 1892), pp. 432 *sq.*

[3] M. Bloomfield, *Hymns of the Atharva-Veda*, p. 249 (*Sacred Books of the East*, vol. xlii.) ; W. Caland, *Altindisches Zauberritual*, p. 128.

[4] Father Livinhac, in *Annales de la Propagation de la Foi*, liii. (1881) p. 209.

gongs has a weird effect; and sometimes, before the notes can be distinguished for the wind and rain, they strike fear into a neighbouring village; lights are extinguished, the women are put in a place of safety, and the men stand to their arms to resist an attack. Then with a lull in the wind the true nature of the gong-beating is recognised, and the alarm subsides.[1]

On calm summer days in the Highlands of Scotland eddies of wind sometimes go past, whirling about dust and straws, though not another breath of air is stirring. The Highlanders think that the fairies are in these eddies carrying away men, women, children, or animals, and they will fling their left shoe, or their bonnet, or a knife, or earth from a mole-hill at the eddy to make the fairies drop their booty.[2] When a gust lifts the hay in the meadow, the Breton peasant throws a knife or a fork at it to prevent the devil from carrying off the hay.[3] Similarly in the Esthonian island of Oesel, when the reapers are busy among the corn and the wind blows about the ears that have not yet been tied into sheaves, the reapers slash at it with their sickles.[4] The custom of flinging a knife or a hat at a whirlwind is observed alike by German, Slavonian, and Esthonian rustics; they think that a witch or wizard is riding on the blast, and that the knife, if it hits the witch, will be reddened by her blood or will disappear altogether, sticking in the wound it has inflicted.[5]

Attacking the whirl-wind with weapons.

---

[1] J. Perham, "Sea Dyak Religion," *Journal of the Straits Branch of the Royal Asiatic Society*, No. 10 (December 1882), pp. 241 *sq*; H. Ling Roth, *The Natives of Sarawak and British North Borneo*, i. 201; A. W. Nieuwenhuis, *In Centraal Borneo* (Leyden, 1900), ii. 180 *sq*. The people of Samarcand used to beat drums and dance in the eleventh month to demand cold weather, and they threw water on one another. See E. Chavannes, *Les Tou-Kiue* (*Turcs*) *Occidentaux* (St. Petersburg, 1903), p. 135.

[2] J. G. Campbell, *Superstitions of the Highlands and Islands of Scotland* (Glasgow, 1900), pp. 24 *sq*.

[3] P. Sébillot, *Coutumes populaires de la Haute-Bretagne*, pp. 302 *sq*.

[4] Holzmayer, "Osiliana," *Verhand-*

lungen der gelehrten Estnischen Gesellschaft zu Dorpat, vii. 2, p. 54.

[5] A. Kuhn und W. Schwartz, *Norddeutsche Sagen, Märchen und Gebräuche*, p. 454, § 406; Von Alpenburg, *Mythen und Sagen Tirols*, pp. 262, 365 *sq*.; W. Mannhardt, *Die Götter der deutschen und nordischen Völker* (Berlin, 1860), p. 99; *id., Antike Wald- und Feldkulte*, p. 85; Boecler-Kreutzwald, *Der Ehsten abergläubische Gebräuche, Weisen und Gewohnheiten*, p. 109; F. S. Krauss, *Volksglaube und religiöser Brauch der Südslaven*, p. 117. In some parts of Austria and Germany, when a storm is raging, the people open a window and throw out a handful of meal, saying to the wind, "There, that's for you, stop!" See A. Peter, *Volksthümliches aus öster-*

Sometimes Esthonian peasants run shrieking and shouting behind a whirlwind, hurling sticks and stones into
the flying dust.[1] The Lengua Indians of the Gran
Chaco ascribe the rush of a whirlwind to the passage
of a spirit and they fling sticks at it to frighten it away.[2]
When the wind blows down their huts, the Payaguas of
South America snatch up firebrands and run against the
wind, menacing it with the blazing brands, while others beat
the air with their fists to frighten the storm.[3] When the
Guaycurus are threatened by a severe storm, the men go out
armed, and the women and children scream their loudest to
intimidate the demon.[4] During a tempest the inhabitants of
a Batta village in Sumatra have been seen to rush from
their houses armed with sword and lance. The rajah placed
himself at their head, and with shouts and yells they hewed
and hacked at the invisible foe. An old woman was observed
to be specially active in the defence of her house, slashing
the air right and left with a long sabre.[5] In a violent
thunderstorm, the peals sounding very near, the Kayans
of Borneo have been seen to draw their swords threaten-
ingly half out of their scabbards, as if to frighten away
the demons of the storm.[6] In Australia the huge columns
of red sand that move rapidly across a desert tract are
thought by the natives to be spirits passing along. Once

reichisch-Schlesien, ii. 259 ; J. Grimm,
Deutsche Mythologie,[4] p. 529 ; Zingerle,
*Sitten Bräuche und Meinungen des
Tiroler Volkes,*[2] p. 118, § 1046.
Similarly an old Irishwoman has been
seen to fling handfuls of grass into a
cloud of dust blown along a road, and
she explained her behaviour by saying
that she wished to give something to
the fairies who were playing in the
dust (*Folklore,* iv. (1893) p. 352).
But these are sacrifices to appease, not
ceremonies to constrain the spirits of
the air ; thus they belong to the domain
of religion rather than to that of magic.
The ancient Greeks sacrificed to the
winds. See P. Stengel, "Die Opfer
der Hellenen an die Winde," *Hermes,*
xvi. (1881) pp. 346-350; and my
note on Pausanias, ii. 12. 1.

[1] J. G. Kohl, *Die deutsch-russischen
Ostseeprovinzen,* ii. 278.

[2] G. Kurze, "Sitten und Gebräuche
der Lengua-Indianer," *Mitteilungen der
Geographischen Gesellschaft zu Jena,*
xxiii. (1905) p. 17.

[3] F. de Azara, *Voyage dans l'Amérique Méridionale,* ii. 137.

[4] P. Lozano, *Descripcion choro-
graphica del Gran Chaco* (Cordova,
1733), p. 71 ; Charlevoix, *Histoire du
Paraguay,* ii. 74 ; Guevara, *Historia
del Paraguay,* p. 23 (in P. de Angelis's
Coleccion de obras y documentos, etc.,
ii., Buenos Ayres, 1836) ; D. de
Alvear, *Relacion geografica e historica
de la provincia de Misiones,* p. 14 (P.
de Angelis, *op. cit.* iv.).

[5] W. A. Henry, "Bijdrage tot de
Kennis der Bataklanden," *Tijdschrift
voor Indische Taal- Land- en Volkenkunde,* xvii. 23 sq.

[6] A. W. Nieuwenhuis, *Quer durch
Borneo,* i. (Leyden, 1904) p. 97.

an athletic young black ran after one of these moving columns to kill it with boomerangs. He was away two or three hours, and came back very weary, saying he had killed Koochee (the demon), but that Koochee had growled at him and he must die.[1] Of the Bedouins of eastern Africa it is said that " no whirlwind ever sweeps across the path without being pursued by a dozen savages with drawn creeses, who stab into the centre of the dusty column in order to drive away the evil spirit that is believed to be riding on the blast." [2]

In the light of these examples a story told by Herodotus, which his modern critics have treated as a fable, is perfectly credible. He says, without however vouching for the truth of the tale, that once in the land of the Psylli, the modern Tripoli, the wind blowing from the Sahara had dried up all the water-tanks. So the people took counsel and marched in a body to make war on the south wind. But when they entered the desert the simoom swept down on them and buried them to a man.[3] The story may well have been told by one who watched them disappearing, in battle array, with drums and cymbals beating, into the red cloud of whirling sand.

Fighting the simoom.

[1] R. Brough Smyth, *Aborigines of Victoria,* i. 457 *sq.* ; compare *id.,* ii. 270 ; A. W. Howitt, in *Journal of the Anthropological Institute,* xiii. (1884) p. 194, note ; Spencer and Gillen, *Northern Tribes of Central Australia,* p. 632.

[2] W. Cornwallis Harris, *The Highlands of Ethiopia* (London, 1844), i. 352. Compare Ph. Paulitschke, *Ethnographie Nord-ost-Afrikas: die geistige Cultur der Danâkil, Galla und Somâl* (Berlin, 1896), p. 28. Even where these columns or whirlwinds of dust are not attacked they are still regarded with awe. The Ainos believe them to be filled with demons ; hence they will hide behind a tree and spit profusely if they see one coming (J. Batchelor, *The Ainu and their Folklore,* p. 385). In some parts of India they are supposed to be *bhuts* going to bathe in the Ganges (Denzil C. J. Ibbetson, *Settlement Report of the Panipat, Tahsil, and Karnal Parganah of the Kar-nal District,* p. 154). The Chevas and Tumbucas of South Africa fancy them to be the wandering souls of sorcerers (*Zeitschrift für allgemeine Erdkunde,* vi. (Berlin, 1856) pp. 301 *sq.*). The Baganda and the Pawnees believe them to be ghosts (J. Roscoe in *Journal of the Anthropological Institute,* xxxii. (1902) p. 73 ; G. B. Grinnell, *Pawnee Hero-Stories and Folk-tales,* p. 357). Californian Indians think that they are happy souls ascending to the heavenly land (Stephen Powers, *Tribes of California,* p. 328). Once when a great Fijian chief died, a whirlwind swept across the lagoon. An old man who saw it covered his mouth with his hand and said in an awestruck whisper, "There goes his spirit!" (Rev. Lorimer Fison, in a letter to the author, dated August 26, 1898).

[3] Herodotus, iv. 173 ; Aulus Gellius, xvi. 11. The Cimbrians are said to have taken arms against the tide (Strabo, vii. 2. 1).

CHAPTER VI

MAGICIANS AS KINGS

Social importance of magicians and their rise to the position of chiefs or kings.
THE foregoing evidence may satisfy us that in many lands and many races magic has claimed to control the great forces of nature for the good of man. If that has been so, the practitioners of the art must necessarily be personages of importance and influence in any society which puts faith in their extravagant pretensions, and it would be no matter for surprise if, by virtue of the reputation which they enjoy and of the awe which they inspire, some of them should attain to the highest position of authority over their credulous fellows. In point of fact magicians appear to have often developed into chiefs and kings.

But magic is not the only road by which men have travelled to a throne.
Not that magic is the only or perhaps even the main road by which men have travelled to a throne. The lust of power, the desire to domineer over our fellows, is among the commonest and the strongest of human passions, and no doubt men of a masterful character have sought to satisfy it in many different ways and have attained by many different means to the goal of their ambition. The sword, for example, in a strong hand has unquestionably done for many what the magician's wand

Complexity of the social phenomena and the danger of simplifying them unduly by our hypotheses.
in a deft hand appears to have done for some. He who investigates the history of institutions should constantly bear in mind the extreme complexity of the causes which have built up the fabric of human society, and should be on his guard against a subtle danger incidental to all science, the tendency to simplify unduly the infinite variety of the phenomena by fixing our attention on a few of them to the exclusion of the rest. The propensity to excessive simplification is indeed natural to the mind of man, since it is only

332

by abstraction and generalisation, which necessarily imply the neglect of a multitude of particulars, that he can stretch his puny faculties so as to embrace a minute portion of the illimitable vastness of the universe. But if the propensity is natural and even inevitable, it is nevertheless fraught with peril, since it is apt to narrow and falsify our conception of any subject under investigation. To correct it partially— for to correct it wholly would require an infinite intelligence —we must endeavour to broaden our views by taking account of a wide range of facts and possibilities ; and when we have done so to the utmost of our power, we must still remember that from the very nature of things our ideas fall immeasurably short of the reality.

In no branch of learning, perhaps, has this proneness to an attractive but fallacious simplicity wrought more havoc than in the investigation of the early history of mankind ; in particular, the excesses to which it has been carried have done much to discredit the study of primitive mythology and religion. Students of these subjects have been far too ready to pounce on any theory which adequately explains some of the facts, and forthwith to stretch it so as to cover them all ; and when the theory, thus unduly strained, has broken, as was to be expected, in their unskilful hands, they have pettishly thrown it aside in disgust instead of restricting it, as they should have done from the outset, to the particular class of facts to which it is really applicable. So it fared in our youth with the solar myth theory, which after being unreasonably exaggerated by its friends has long been quite as unreasonably rejected altogether by its adversaries ; and in more recent times the theories of totemism, magic, and taboo, to take only a few conspicuous examples, have similarly suffered from the excessive zeal of injudicious advocates. This instability of judgment, this tendency of anthropological opinion to swing to and fro from one extreme to another with every breath of new discovery, is perhaps the principal reason why the whole study is still viewed askance by men of sober and cautious temper, who naturally look with suspicion on idols that are set up and worshipped one day only to be knocked down and trampled under foot the next. To these cool observers Max

This propensity to excessive simplification has done much to discredit the study of primitive mythology and religion.

Müller and the rosy Dawn in the nineteenth century stand
on the same dusty shelf with Jacob Bryant and Noah's ark
in the eighteenth, and they expect with a sarcastic smile
the time when the fashionable anthropological topics of the
present day will in their turn be consigned to the same peace-
ful limbo of forgotten absurdities.   It is not for the anthropologist himself to anticipate the verdict of posterity on his
labours ; still it is his humble hope that the facts which he
has patiently amassed will be found sufficiently numerous
and solid to bear the weight of some at least of the conclusions which he rests upon them, so that these can never
again be lightly tossed aside as the fantastic dreams of a
mere bookish student.   At the same time, if he is wise,
he will be forward to acknowledge and proclaim that our
hypotheses at best are but partial, not universal, solutions of
the manifold problems which confront us, and that in science
as in daily life it is vain to look for one key to open all locks.

The practice of magic explains the rise of kings in some communities, but not in all.   Therefore, to revert to our immediate subject, in putting
forward the practice of magic as an explanation of the rise
of monarchy in some communities, I am far from thinking
or suggesting that it can explain the rise of it in all, or, in
other words, that kings are universally the descendants or
successors of magicians ; and if any one should hereafter, as
is likely enough, either enunciate such a theory or attribute
it to me, I desire to enter my caveat against it in advance.
To enumerate and describe all the modes in which men have
pushed, or fought, or wormed their way by force or by fraud,
by their own courage and wisdom or by the cowardice and
folly of others, to supreme power, might furnish the theme
of a political treatise such as I have no pretension to write ;
for my present purpose it suffices if I can trace the magician's
progress in some savage and barbarous tribes from the rank
of a sorcerer to the dignity of a king.   The facts which I
am about to lay before the reader seem to exhibit various
steps of this development from simple conjuring up to
conjuring compounded with despotism.

Social importance of magicians among the aborigines of Central Australia.   Let us begin by looking at the lowest race of men as to
whom we possess comparatively full and accurate informa-
tion, the aborigines of Australia.   These savages are ruled
neither by chiefs nor kings.   So far as their tribes can be

said to have a political constitution, it is a democracy or
rather an oligarchy of old and influential men, who meet
in council and decide on all measures of importance to the
practical exclusion of the younger men.   Their deliberative
assembly answers to the senate of later times : if we had to
coin a word for such a government of elders we might call it
a *gerontocracy*.[1]   The elders who in aboriginal Australia thus
meet and direct the affairs of their tribe appear to be for the
most part the headmen of their respective totem clans.   Now
in Central Australia, where the desert nature of the country
and the almost complete isolation from foreign influences
have retarded progress and preserved the natives on the
whole in their most primitive state, the headmen of the
various totem clans are charged with the important task of
performing magical ceremonies for the multiplication of the
totems, and as the great majority of the totems are edible
animals or plants, it follows that these men are commonly
expected to provide the people with food by means of
magic.   Others have to make the rain to fall or to render
other services to the community.   In short, among the
tribes of Central Australia the headmen are public magicians.
Further, their most important function is to take charge of
the sacred storehouse, usually a cleft in the rocks or a hole in
the ground, where are kept the holy stones and sticks (*churinga*)
with which the souls of all the people, both living and dead, are
apparently supposed to be in a manner bound up.   Thus while
the headmen have certainly to perform what we should call
civil duties, such as to inflict punishment for breaches of
tribal custom, their principal functions are sacred or magical.[2]

Again, in the tribes of South-Eastern Australia the headman was often, sometimes invariably, a magician.   Thus in
the southern Wiradjuri tribe the headman was always a
wizard or a medicine-man.   There was one for each local

Social im-
portance of
magicians
among the
aborigines
of South-
Eastern
Australia.

[1] The government of the western
islanders of Torres Straits is similar.
See A. C. Haddon, in *Reports of the
Cambridge Anthropological Expedition
to Torres Straits*, v. 263 *sq.* So, too,
the Bantoc Igorot of the Philippines
have no chiefs and are ruled by councils
of old men. See A. E. Jenks, *The
Bantoc Igorot* (Manila, 1905), pp. 32

sq., 167 *sq.*

[2] Spencer and Gillen, *Native Tribes
of Central Australia*, pp. 9-15, 154,
159-205 ; *id.*, *Northern Tribes of
Central Australia*, pp. 20-27, 285-
297, 309 *sq.*, 316 ; A. W. Howitt,
Native Tribes of South-East Australia,
pp. 320-326.

Social importance of magicians among the tribes of South-Eastern Australia.

division. He called the people together for the initiation ceremonies or to discuss matters of public importance.[1] In the Yerkla-mining tribe the medicine-men are the headmen; they are called *Mobung-bai*, from *mobung*, "magic." They decide disputes, arrange marriages, conduct the ceremonies of initiation, and in certain circumstances settle the formalities to be observed in ordeals of battle. "In fact, they wield authority in the tribe, and give orders where others only make requests."[2] Again, in the Yuin tribe there was a headman for each local division, and in order to be fitted for his office he had, among other qualifications, to be a medicine-man; above all he must be able to perform magical feats at the initiation ceremonies. The greatest headman of all was he who on these occasions could bring up the largest number of things out of his inside.[3] In fact the budding statesman and king must be first and foremost a conjuror in the most literal sense of the word. Some forty or fifty years ago the principal headman of the Dieri tribe was a certain Jalina piramurana, who was known among the colonists as the Frenchman on account of his polished manners. He was not only a brave and skilful warrior, but also a powerful medicine-man, greatly feared by the neighbouring tribes, who sent him presents even from a distance of a hundred miles. He boasted of being the "tree of life," for he was the head of a totem consisting of a particular sort of seed which forms at certain times the chief vegetable food of these tribes. His people spoke of him as the plant itself (*manyura*) which yields the edible seed.[4] Again, an early writer on the tribes of South-Western Australia, near King George's Sound, tells us that "the individuals who possess most influence are the *mulgarradocks*, or doctors. . . . A *mulgarradock* is considered to possess the power of driving away wind or rain, as well as bringing down lightning or disease upon any object of their or others' hatred," and they also attempted to heal the sick.[5] On the

[1] A. W. Howitt, *op. cit.* p. 303.

[2] A. W. Howitt, *op. cit.* p. 313.

[3] A. W. Howitt, *op. cit.* p. 314.

[4] A. W. Howitt, *op. cit.* pp. 297-299. For more examples of headmen who are also magicians see *ib.* pp. 301 *sq.*, 302, 317.

[5] Scott Nind, "Description of the Natives of King George's Sound (Swan River Colony)," *Journal of the R. Geographical Society,* i. (1832) p. 41.

whole, then, it is highly significant that in the most primitive
society about which we are accurately informed it is especially
the magicians or medicine-men who appear to have been in
process of developing into chiefs.

When we pass from Australia to New Guinea we find Social im-
that, though the natives stand at a far higher level of culture portance of
than the Australian aborigines, the constitution of society in New
among them is still essentially democratic or oligarchic, and Guinea.
chieftainship exists only in embryo. Thus Sir William
MacGregor tells us that in British New Guinea no one has
ever arisen wise enough, bold enough, and strong enough to
become the despot even of a single district. " The nearest
approach to this has been the very distant one of some
person becoming a renowned wizard ; but that has only
resulted in levying a certain amount of blackmail." [1] To
the same effect a Catholic missionary observes that in New
Guinea the *nepu* or sorcerers " are everywhere. They boast
of their misdeeds ; everybody fears them, everybody accuses
them, and, after all, nothing positive is known of their secret
practices. This cursed brood is as it were the soul of the
Papuan life. Nothing happens without the sorcerer's intervention : wars, marriages, diseases, deaths, expeditions, fishing, hunting, always and everywhere the sorcerer. . . . One
thing is certain for them, and they do not regard it as an
article of faith, but as a fact patent and indisputable, and
that is the extraordinary power of the *nepu* ; he is the master
of life and of death. Hence it is only natural that they
should fear him and obey him in everything and give him
all that he asks for. The *nepu* is not a chief, but he domi-
neers over the chiefs, and we may say that the true authority,
the only effective influence in New Guinea, is that of the
nepu. Nothing can resist him." [2] We are told that in the
Toaripi or Motumotu tribe of British New Guinea chiefs have
not necessarily supernatural powers, but that a sorcerer is
looked upon as a chief. Some years ago, for example, one
man of the tribe was a chief because he was supposed to
rule the sea, calming it or rousing it to fury at his pleasure.

[1] Sir W. MacGregor, *British New*   *Les Missions Catholiques*, xxxvi. (1904)
Guinea (London, 1897), p. 41.   p. 334.
[2] Le R. P. Guis, " Les Papous,"

Another owed his power to his skill in making the rain to fall, the sun to shine, and the plantations to bear fruit.[1]   It is believed that the chief of Mowat in British New Guinea, can affect the growth of crops for good or ill, and coax the turtle and dugong to come from all parts of the sea and allow themselves to be caught.[2]   At Bartle Bay in British New Guinea there are magicians (*taniwaga*) who are expected to manage certain departments of nature for the good of the community by means of charms (*pari*) which are known only to them.   One of these men, for example, works magic for rain, another for taro, another for wallaby, and another for fish.   A magician who is believed to control an important department of nature may be the chief of his community. Thus the present chief of Wedau is a sorcerer who can make rain and raise or calm the winds.   He is greatly respected by all and receives many presents.[3]   A chief of Kolem, on Finsch Harbour, in German New Guinea, enjoyed a great reputation as a magician ; it was supposed that he could make wind and storm, rain and sunshine, and visit his enemies with sickness and death.[4]

Supposed magical or supernatural powers of chiefs in Melanesia.   Turning now to the natives of the Melanesian islands, which stretch in an immense quadrant of a circle round New Guinea and Australia on the east, we are told by Dr. Codrington that among these savages " as a matter of fact the power of chiefs has hitherto rested upon the belief in their supernatural power derived from the spirits or ghosts with which they had intercourse.   As this belief has failed, in the Banks' Islands for example some time ago, the position of a chief has tended to become obscure ; and as this belief is now being generally undermined a new kind of chief must needs arise, unless a time of anarchy is to begin." [5]   According to a native Melanesian account, the origin of the power of chiefs lies entirely in the belief that they have communication with mighty ghosts (*tindalo*), and wield that

---

[1] J. Chalmers, " Toaripi," *Journal of the Anthropological Institute*, xxvii. (1898) p. 334.

[2] E. Beardmore, " The Natives of Mowat Daudai, New Guinea," *Journal of the Anthropological Institute*, xix. (1890) p. 464.

[3] C. G. Seligmann, *The Melanesians of British New Guinea* (Cambridge, 1910), pp. 455 *sq.*

[4] M. Krieger, *Neu-Guinea* (Berlin, n.d.), p. 334.

[5] R. H. Codrington, *The Melanesians* (Oxford, 1891), p. 46.

supernatural power (*mana*) whereby they can bring the influence of the ghosts to bear. If a chief imposed a fine, it was paid because the people universally dreaded his ghostly power, and firmly believed that he could inflict calamity and sickness upon such as resisted him. As soon as any considerable number of his people began to disbelieve in his influence with the ghosts, his power to levy fines was shaken.[1] In Malo, one of the New Hebrides, the highest nobility consists of those persons who have sacrificed a thousand little pigs to the souls of their ancestors. No one ever resists a man of that exalted rank, because in him are supposed to dwell all the souls of the ancient chiefs and all the spirits who preside over the tribe.[2] In the Northern New Hebrides the son does not inherit the chieftainship, but he inherits, if his father can manage it, what gives him the chieftainship, namely, his father's supernatural power, his charms, magical songs, stones and apparatus, and his knowledge of the way to approach spiritual beings.[3] A chief in the island of Paramatta informed a European that he had the power of making rain, wind, storm, thunder and lightning, and dry weather. He exhibited as his magical instrument a piece of bamboo with some parti-coloured rags attached to it. In this bamboo, he said, were kept the devils of rain and wind, and when he commanded them to discharge their office or to lie still, they were obliged to obey, being his subjects and prisoners. When he had given his orders to these captive devils, the bamboo had to be fastened to the highest point of his house.[4] In the Marshall Bennet Islands to the east of New Guinea it was the duty of each chief of a clan to charm the gardens of his clan so as to make them productive. The charm consisted of turning up part of the soil with a long stick and muttering an appropriate spell. Each special crop, such as yams, bananas,

---

[1] R. H. Codrington, *op. cit.* p. 52. As to the *mana* or supernatural power of chiefs and others, see *ibid.* pp. 118 *sqq.*; above, pp. 227 *sq.* I have pointed out (p. 111, note 2) that this supernatural power supplies, as it were, the physical basis of magic.

[2] Father A. Deniau, "Croyances religieuses et mœurs des indigènes de l'île Malo (Nouvelles - Hébrides)," *Les Missions Catholiques*, xxxiii. (1901) p. 347.

[3] R. H. Codrington, *op. cit.* p. 56.

[4] C. Ribbe, *Zwei Jahren unter den Kannibalen der Salomo - Inseln* (Dresden - Blasewitz, 1903), pp. 173 *sq.*

sugar-cane, and coco-nuts, had its special kind of stick and its special spell.[1]

With regard to government among the Melanesians of New Britain or the Bismarck Archipelago, I may cite the evidence of an experienced missionary, the Rev. Dr. George Brown, who settled in the islands at a time when no other white man was living in the group, and who resided among the savage islanders for some five or six years. He says : " There was no government so called in New Britain except that form of jurisdiction or power represented by the secret societies and that exercised by chiefs, who were supposed to possess exceptional powers of sorcery and witchcraft. These powers were very real, owing, I think, principally to two reasons—one of which was that the men themselves thoroughly believed that they were the possessors of the powers which they claimed, and the other was that the people themselves believed that the men really possessed them. There was indeed the title of chief (*todaru*) claimed and also given to them by the people ; but this was not the result of any election or necessarily by inheritance, it was simply that a certain man claimed to · be the possessor of these powers and succeeded in convincing the people that he really possessed them." [2]   Again, Dr. Brown tells us that in New Britain " a ruling chief was always supposed to exercise priestly functions, that is, he professed to be in constant communication with the *tebarans* (spirits), and through their influence he was enabled to bring rain or sunshine, fair winds or foul ones, sickness or health, success or disaster in war, and generally to procure any blessing or curse for which the applicant was willing to pay a sufficient price. If his spells did not produce the desired effect he always had a plausible explanation ready, which was generally accepted as a sufficient excuse. I think much of the success which these men undoubtedly had was due to their keen observa- tions of natural phenomena, and to the effects of fear upon the people." [3]

[1] C. G. Seligmann, *The Melanesians of New Guinea* (Cambridge, 1910), p. 702.

[2] G. Brown, D.D., *Melanesians and Polynesians* (London, 1910), p. 270.

[3] Rev. G. Brown, *op. cit.* p. 429.

According to Dr. Turner, "The real gods at Tana may be said to be the disease-makers. It is surprising how these men are dreaded, and how firm the belief is that they have in their hands the power of life and death. There are rain-makers and thunder-makers, and fly and mosquito-makers, and a host of other 'sacred men,' but the disease-makers are the most dreaded. It is believed that these men can create disease and death by burning what is called *nahak*. *Nahak*, means rubbish, but principally refuse of food. Everything of the kind they bury or throw into the sea, lest the disease-makers should get hold of it. These fellows are always about, and consider it their special business to pick up and burn, with certain formalities, anything in the *nahak* line which comes in their way. If a disease-maker sees the skin of a banana, for instance, he picks it up, wraps it in a leaf, and wears it all day hanging round his neck. The people stare as they see him go along, and say to each other, 'He has got something; he will do for somebody by-and-by at night.' In the evening he scrapes some bark off a tree, mixes it up with the banana skin, rolls all up tightly in a leaf in the form of a cigar, and then puts the one end close enough to the fire to cause it to singe, and smoulder, and burn away very gradually. Presently he hears a shell blowing. 'There,' he says to his friends, 'there it is; that is the man whose rubbish I am now burning, he is ill; let us stop burning, and see what they bring in the morning.' When a person is taken ill he believes that it is occasioned by some one burning his rubbish. Instead of thinking about medicine, he calls some one to blow a shell, a large conch or other shell, which, when perforated and blown, can be heard two or three miles off. The meaning of it is to implore the person who is supposed to be burning the sick man's rubbish and causing all the pain to stop burning; and it is a promise as well that a present will be taken in the morning. The greater the pain the more they blow the shell, and when the pain abates they cease, supposing that the disease-maker has been kind enough to stop burning." Night after night the silence is broken by the dismal too-too-tooing of these shells; and in the morning the friends of the sufferer repair to the disease-maker with presents of pigs, mats, hatchets, beads.

whales' teeth, or such like things.[1]   Thus these sorcerers
attain to a position of immense power and influence and
acquire wealth by purely maleficent magic ; it is not by the
imaginary benefits which they confer on the community, but
by the imaginary evils which they inflict on individuals, that
they climb the steps of a throne or the ladder that leads to
heaven ; for according to Dr. Turner these rascals are on
the highroad to divinity.   The process which they employ
to accomplish their ends is a simple application of the
principles of contagious magic : whatever has once been in
contact with a person remains in sympathetic connexion
with him always, and harm done to it is therefore harm
done to him.   Side by side with the evil which this superstition produces, on the one hand by inspiring men with
baseless terrors, and on the other by leading them to neglect
effectual remedies for real evils, we must recognise the benefit
which it incidentally confers on society by causing people to
clear away and destroy the refuse of their food and other
rubbish, which if suffered to accumulate about their dwell-
ings might, by polluting the atmosphere, prove a real, not
an imaginary source of disease.   In practice, cleanliness
based on motives of superstition may be just as effective
for the preservation of health as if it were founded on the
best-ascertained principles of sanitary science.[2]

Evolution of chiefs or kings out of magicians, especially out of rain-makers, in Africa.

Still rising in the scale of culture we come to Africa,
where both the chieftainship and the kingship are fully
developed ; and here the evidence for the evolution of the
chief out of the magician, and especially out of the rain-
maker, is comparatively plentiful.   Thus among the Wambugwe, a Bantu people of East Africa, the original form of
government was a family republic, but the enormous power
of the sorcerers, transmitted by inheritance, soon raised them
to the rank of petty lords or chiefs.   Of the three chiefs
living in the country in 1894 two were much dreaded as
magicians, and the wealth of cattle they possessed came to
them almost wholly in the shape of presents bestowed for
their services in that capacity.   Their principal art was that
of rain-making.[3]   The chiefs of the Wataturu, another

Power of magicians among the Wambug-we, Wata-turu, and Wagogo of East Africa.

---

[1] G. Turner, *Samoa*, pp. 320-322.
[2] See above, p. 175.

[3] O. Baumann, *Durch Massailand
zur Nilquelle* (Berlin, 1894), pp. 187 *sq.*

people of East Africa, are said to be nothing but sorcerers
destitute of any direct political influence.[1] Again, among
the Wagogo of German East Africa the main power of the
chiefs, we are told, is derived from their art of rain-making.
If a chief cannot make rain himself, he must procure it from
some one who can.[2] Again, in the powerful Masai nation *Among the*
of the same region the medicine-men are not uncommonly *Masai the*
supreme
the chiefs, and the supreme chief of the race is almost *chief is*
invariably a powerful medicine-man. These *Laibon*, as they *always a*
powerful
are called, are priests as well as doctors, skilled in interpret- *medicine-*
ing omens and dreams, in averting ill-luck, and in making *man.*
rain.[3] The head chief or medicine-man, who has been
called the Masai pope,[4] is expected not only to make rain,
but to repel and destroy the enemies of the Masai in war
by his magic art.[5] The following is Captain Merker's
account of the Masai pope: "The most prominent clan of
the whole Masai people is the *En gidon*, because to it belong
not only the family of the chief (*ol oiboni*), but also the family
of the magicians. The designation chief is, strictly speaking,
not quite correct, since the chief (*ol oiboni*) does not govern
directly and exercises no real administrative function. He
rules only indirectly ; the firm belief of his subjects in his
prophetic gifts and in his supernatural power of sorcery gives
him an influence on the destinies of the people. Despotism
and cruelty, such as we find among all negro rulers, are alien
to him. He is not so much a ruler as a national saint or
patriarch. The people speak of his sacred person with shy
awe, and no man dares to appear before this mighty personage without being summoned. The aim of his policy is to
unite and strengthen the Masai. While he allows free play
to the predatory instincts of the warriors in raids on other
tribes, he guards his own people from the scourge of civil
war, to which the ceaseless quarrels of the various districts
with each other would otherwise continually give occasion.
This influence of his is rendered possible by the belief that

[1] O. Baumann, *op. cit.* p. 173.

[2] H. Cole, "Notes on the Wagogo
of German East Africa," *Journal of
the Anthropological Institute*, xxxii.
(1902) p. 321.

[3] Sir Harry Johnston, *The Uganda

Protectorate (London, 1902), ii. 830.

[4] O. Baumann, *Durch Massailand
zur Nilquelle*, p. 164.

[5] Baron C. C. von der Decken,
Reisen in Ost-Afrika, ii. (Leipsic and
Heidelberg, 1871) p. 24.

victory can only be achieved through the secret power of the war-medicine which none but he can compound, and that defeat would infallibly follow if he were to predict it. Neither he nor his nearest relatives march with the army to war. He supplies remedies, generally in the shape of magical medicines, for plagues and sicknesses, and he appoints festivals of prayer in honour of the Masai god *'Ng ai*. He delivers his predictions by means of an oracular game like the telling of beads."[1] And just as Samson's miraculous strength went from him when his hair was shorn, so it is believed that the head chief of the Masai would lose his supernatural powers if his chin were shaved.[2] According to one writer, the Masai pope has never more than one eye : the father knocks out his son's eye in order to qualify him for the holy office.[3]

Among the Nandi of British East Africa "the *Orkoiyot*, or principal medicine man, holds precisely the same position as the Masai *Ol-oiboni*, that is to say, he is supreme chief of the whole race." He is a diviner, and foretells the future by casting stones, inspecting entrails, interpreting dreams, and prophesying when he is drunk. The Nandi believe implicitly in his powers. He tells them when to begin planting their crops : in time of drought he procures rain for them either directly or by means of the rainmakers : he makes women and cattle fruitful ; and no war-party can expect to be successful if he has not approved of the foray. His office is hereditary and his person is usually regarded as absolutely sacred. Nobody may approach him with weapons in his hand or speak in his presence unless the great man addresses him ; and it is most important that nobody should touch his head, else it is feared that his powers of divination and so forth would depart from him. However, one of these sacred pontiffs was clubbed to death, being held responsible for several public calamities, to wit, famine, sickness, and defeat in war.[4] The Suk and Turkana,

Among the Nandi of British East Africa the principal medicine-man is the supreme chief.

---

[1] M. Merker, *Die Masai* (Berlin, 1904), pp. 18 *sq.* I have slightly abridged the writer's account.

[2] M. Merker, *Die Masai*, p. 21. As to the medicine-men of the Masai, see further A. C. Hollis, *The Masai* (Oxford, 1905), pp. 324-330.

[3] O. Baumann, *Durch Massailand zur Nilquelle*, p. 164.

[4] A. C. Hollis, *The Nandi* (Oxford, 1909), pp. 49 *sq.*

two other peoples of British East Africa, distinguish between
their chiefs and their medicine-men, who wield great power ;
but very often the medicine-man is a chief by virtue of his
skill in medicine or the occult arts.[1]

Again, among the tribes of the Upper Nile the medicine-
men are generally the chiefs.[2] Their authority rests above
all upon their supposed power of making rain, for " rain is
the one thing which matters to the people in those districts,
as if it does not come down at the right time it means untold
hardships for the community. It is therefore small wonder
that men more cunning than their fellows should arrogate to
themselves the power of producing it, or that having gained
such a reputation, they should trade on the credulity of their
simpler neighbours." Hence " most of the chiefs of these
tribes are rainmakers, and enjoy a popularity in proportion
to their powers to give rain to their people at the proper
season. . . . Rain-making chiefs always build their villages
on the slopes of a fairly high hill, as they no doubt know
that the hills attract the clouds, and that they are, therefore,
fairly safe in their weather forecasts." Each of these rain-
makers has a number of rain-stones, such as rock-crystal,
aventurine, and amethyst, which he keeps in a pot. When
he wishes to produce rain he plunges the stones in water,
and taking in his hand a peeled cane, which is split at the
top, he beckons with it to the clouds to come or waves them
away in the way they should go, muttering an incantation
the while. Or he pours water and the entrails of a sheep or
goat into a hollow in a stone and then sprinkles the water
towards the sky. Though the chief acquires wealth by the
exercise of his supposed magical powers, he often, perhaps
generally, comes to a violent end ; for in time of drought
the angry people assemble and kill him, believing that it is
he who prevents the rain from falling. Yet the office is
usually hereditary and passes from father to son. Among
the tribes which cherish these beliefs and observe these
customs are the Latuka, Bari, Laluba, and Lokoiya.[3] Thus,

Rainmakers as chiefs among the tribes of the Upper Nile.

---

[1] Sir H. Johnston, *The Uganda Protectorate*, ii. 851.

[2] Sir H. Johnston, *The Uganda Protectorate*, ii. 779.

[3] W. E. R. Cole, " African Rain-making Chiefs, the Gondokoro District, White Nile," *Man*, x. (1910) pp. 90-92 ; Yuzbashi, " Tribes on the Upper Nile," *Journal of the African Society*, No. 14 (January, 1905), pp. 228 *sq.* ;

for example, with regard to the Latuka we are told that
" amongst the most important but also the most dangerous
occupations of the greater chiefs is the procuring of rain
for their country. Almost all the greater chiefs enjoy the
reputation of being rainmakers, and the requisite knowledge
usually passes by inheritance from father to son. However,
there are also here and there among the natives persons who,
without being chiefs, busy themselves with rain-making. If
there has been no rain in a district for a long time and the
people wish to attract it for the sake of the sowing, they
apply to their chief, bringing him a present of sheep, goats,
or, in urgent cases, cattle or a girl, and if the present seems
to him sufficient he promises to furnish rain ; but if it appears
to him too little he asks for more. If some days pass
without rain, it gives the magician an opportunity for
claiming fresh presents, on the ground that the smallness of
the offered gifts hinders the coming of the rain." When the
cupidity of the rain-maker is satisfied, he goes to work in the
usual way, pouring water over two flat stones, one called the
male and the other the female, till they are covered to a
depth of three inches. The "male" stone is a common
white quartz ; the "female" is brownish. If still no rain
falls, he makes a smoky fire in the open with certain herbs,
and if the smoke mounts straight up, rain is near. Although
an unsuccessful rain-maker is often banished or killed, his
son always succeeds him in the dignity.[1] Amongst the
Bari the procedure of the rain-making chief to draw down
the water of heaven is somewhat elaborate. He has many
rain-stones, consisting of rock crystal and pink and green
granite. These are deposited in the hollows of some twenty
slabs of gneiss, and across the hollows are laid numerous iron
rods of various shapes and sizes. When rain is to be made,
these iron rods are set up in a perpendicular position, and
water is poured on the crystals and stones. Then the rain-
maker takes up the stones one by one and oils them, praying
to his dead father to send the rain. One of the iron rods is

Brun-Rollet, *Le Nil Blanc et le Soudan*
(Paris, 1855), pp. 227 *sq.* ; F. Spire,
"Rain-making in Equatorial Africa,"
Journal of the African Society, No. 17

(October, 1905), pp. 15-21.
[1] Emin Pasha, quoted by Fr. Stuhlmann, *Mit Emin Pascha ins Herz von
Afrika* (Berlin, 1894), pp. 778-780.

provided with a hook, and another is a two-headed spear. With the hook the rain-maker hooks and attracts the rain-clouds ; with the two-headed spear he attacks and drives them away. In this procedure the prayer to the dead ancestor is religious, while the rest of the ceremony is magical. Thus, as so often happens, the savage seeks to compass his object by combining magic with religion. The logical inconsistency does not trouble him, provided he attains his end. Further, the rain-maker chief of the Bari is supposed to be able to make women fruitful. For this purpose he takes an iron rod with a hollow bulb at each end, in which are small stones. Grasping the rod by the middle he shakes it over the would-be mother, rattling the stones and muttering an incantation.[1]

Again, among the Bongo, a tribe of the same region, the influence of the chiefs is said to rest in great part on a belief in their magical powers ; for the chief is credited with the knowledge of certain roots, which are the only means of communicating with the dangerous spirits of whose mischievous pranks the Bongo stand in great fear.[2] In the Dinka or Denka nation, to the north-east of the Bongo, men who are supposed to be in close communication with spirits pass for omnipotent ; it is believed that they make rain, conjure away all calamities, foresee the future, exorcise evil spirits, know all that goes on even at a distance, have the wild beasts in their service, and can call down every kind of disaster on their enemies. One of these men became the richest and most esteemed chief of the Kič tribe through his skill in ventriloquism. He kept a cage from which the roars of imaginary lions and the howls of imaginary hyaenas were heard to proceed ; and he gave out that these beasts guarded his house and were ready at his bidding to rush forth on his enemies. The dread which he infused into the tribe and its neighbours was incredible ; from all sides oxen were sent to him as presents, so that his herds were the most numerous in the country. Another of these conjurers in the Tuič tribe had a real tame

Magical powers of chiefs among the Bongo and Dinkas.

---

[1] F. Spire, " Rain-making in Equatorial Africa," *Journal of the African Society*, No. 17 (October, 1905), pp. 16-18, 21.

[2] G. Schweinfurth, *The Heart of Africa*[3] (London, 1878), i. 144 *sq.*

lion and four real fat snakes, which slept in front of his door, to the great awe of the natives, who could only attribute the pacific demeanour of these ferocious animals to sorcery.[1] But it does not appear that the real lion inspired nearly so much terror as the imaginary one ; from which we may perhaps infer that among these people ventriloquism is a more solid basis of political power even than lion-taming.

Chiefs and kings as rain-makers in Central Africa.

In Central Africa, again, the Lendu tribe, to the west of Lake Albert, firmly believe that certain people possess the power of making rain. Among them the rain-maker either is a chief or almost invariably becomes one.[2] The Banyoro also have a great respect for the dispensers of rain, whom they load with a profusion of gifts. The great dispenser, he who has absolute and uncontrollable power over the rain, is the king ; but he can depute his power to other persons, so that the benefit may be distributed and the heavenly water laid on over the various parts of the kingdom.[3] A Catholic missionary observes that " a superstition common to the different peoples of equatorial Africa attributes to the petty kings of the country the exclusive power of making the rain to fall ; in extreme cases the power is ascribed to certain kings more privileged than the rest, such as those of Huilla, Humbé, Varé, Libebé, and others. These kings profit by the superstition in order to draw to themselves many presents of cattle ; for the rain must fall after the sacrifice of an ox, and if it tarries, the king, who is never at a loss for excuses to extricate himself from the scrape, will ascribe the failure to the defects of the victim, and will seize the pretext to claim more cattle." [4] Among the Ba-Yaka, a tribe of the Kasai district in the Congo Free State, magicians are exempt from justice, and the chief is the principal magician ;[5] and among the Ba-Yanzi, another

---

[1] E. D. Pruyssenaere, "Reisen und Forschungen im Gebiete des Weissen und Blauen Nil," *Petermanns Mittheilungen, Ergänzungsheft*, No. 50 (Gotha, 1877), pp. 27 *sq.*

[2] Sir H. Johnston, *The Uganda Protectorate*, ii. 555.

[3] G. Casati, *Ten Years in Equatoria* (London and New York, 1891), ii. 57,

compare i. 134.

[4] Ch. Wunenberger, "La Mission et le royaume de Humbé, sur les bords du Cunène," *Les Missions Catholiques*, xx. (1888) p. 262.

[5] E. Torday and T. A. Joyce, "Notes on the Ethnography of the Ba-Yaka," *Journal of the Anthropological Institute*, xxxvi. (1906) pp. 48, 51.

tribe of the same district, there is, or was a few years ago, a chief who passed for the greatest magician in the country.[1]

In Western as well as in Eastern and Central Africa we meet with the same union of chiefly with magical functions. Thus in the Fan tribe the strict distinction between chief and medicine-man does not exist. The chief is also a medicine-man and a smith to boot; for the Fans esteem the smith's craft sacred, and none but chiefs may meddle with it.[2] The chiefs of the Ossidinge district in the Cameroons have as such very little influence over their subjects; but if the chief happens to be also the fetish-priest, as he generally is among the Ekois, he has not only powerful influence in all fetish matters (and most of the vital interests of the people are bound up with fetish worship), but he also enjoys great authority in general.[3] A few years ago the head chief of Etatin on the Cross River, in Southern Nigeria, was an old man whom the people had compelled to take office in order that he should look after the fetishes or jujus and work magic for the benefit of the community. In accordance with an old custom, which is binding on the head chief, he was never allowed to leave his compound, that is, the enclosure in which his house stands. He gave the following account of himself to an English official, who paid him a visit: "I have been shut up ten years, but, being an old man, I don't miss my freedom. I am the oldest man of the town, and they keep me here to look after the jujus, and to conduct the rites celebrated when women are about to give birth to children, and other ceremonies of the same kind. By the observance and performance of these ceremonies, I bring game to the hunter, cause the yam crop to be good, bring fish to the fisherman, and make rain to fall. So they bring me meat, yams, fish, etc. To make rain, I drink water, and squirt it out, and pray to our big deities. If I were to go outside this compound, I should fall down dead on returning to this hut.

Medicine-men as chiefs in Western Africa.

---

[1] E. Torday and T. A. Joyce, "On the Ethnology of the South-Western Congo Free State," *Journal of the R. Anthropological Institute*, xxxvii. (1907) p. 140.

[2] O. Lenz, *Skizzen aus Westafrika* (Berlin, 1878), p. 87.

[3] A. Mansfeld, *Urwald-Dokumente, Vier Jahre unter den Crossflussnegern Kameruns* (Berlin, 1908), p. 161.

My wives cut my hair and nails, and take great care of the parings." [1]

As to the relation between the offices of chief and rain-maker in South Africa a well-informed writer observes : " In very old days the chief was the great Rain-maker of the tribe. Some chiefs allowed no one else to compete with them, lest a successful Rain-maker should be chosen as chief. There was also another reason : the Rain-maker was sure to become a rich man if he gained a great reputation, and it would manifestly never do for the chief to allow any one to be too rich. The Rain-maker exerts tremendous control over the people, and so it would be most important to keep this function connected with royalty. Tradition always places the power of making rain as the fundamental glory of ancient chiefs and heroes, and it seems probable that it may have been the origin of chieftainship. The man who made the rain would naturally become the chief. In the same way Chaka [the famous Zulu despot] used to declare that he was the only diviner in the country, for if he allowed rivals his life would be insecure." [2] These South African rain-makers smear themselves with mud and sacrifice oxen as an essential part of the charm ; almost everything is thought to turn on the colour of the beasts. Thus Umbandine, the old king of the Swazies, had huge herds of cattle of a peculiar colour, which was particularly well adapted for the production of rain. Hence deputations came to him from distant tribes praying and bribing him to make rain by the sacrifice of his cattle ; and he used to threaten to " bind up the sky " if they did not satisfy his demands. The power

[1] Ch. Partridge, *Cross River Natives* (London, 1905), pp. 201 *sq.* The care taken of the chief's cut hair and nails is a precaution against the magical use that might be made of them by his enemies. See *The Golden Bough*, Second Edition, i. 375 *sqq.*

[2] Dudley Kidd, *The Essential Kafir* (London, 1904), p. 114. " The chief collects to himself all medicines of known power ; each doctor has his own special medicine or medicines, and treats some special form of disease, and

the knowledge of such medicines is transmitted as a portion of the inheritance to the eldest son. When a chief hears that any doctor has proved successful in treating some case where others have failed, he calls him and demands the medicine, which is given up to him. Thus the chief becomes the great medicine-man of his tribe, and the ultimate reference is to him. If he fail, the case is given up as incurable" (H. Callaway, *Religious System of the Amazulu*, part iv. pp. 419 *sq.*, note). The medicines here referred

which by this means he wielded was enormous.[1] Similarly Mablaan, a chief of the Bawenda, in the north-eastern corner of the Transvaal, enjoyed a wide reputation and was revered beyond the limits of his own tribe because he was credited with the power of rain-making, "a greater power in the eyes of natives than that of the assegai." Hence he was constantly importuned by other chiefs to exercise his power and received valuable presents of girls, oxen, and red and green beads as inducements to turn on the heavenly water-tap.[2]

Among the Matabeles of South Africa the witch-doctors are supposed to be on speaking terms with spirits, and their influence is described as tremendous; in the time of King Lo Bengula some years ago "their power was as great as, if not greater than, the king's."[3] Similarly speaking of the South African tribes in general, Dr. Moffat says that "the rain-maker is in the estimation of the people no mean personage, possessing an influence over the minds of the people superior even to that of the king, who is likewise compelled to yield to the dictates of this arch-official."[4] In Matabeleland the rainy season falls in November, December, January, and February. For several weeks before the rain sets in, the clouds gather in heavy banks, dark and lowering. Then the king is busy with his magicians compounding potions of wondrous strength to make the labouring clouds discharge their pent-up burden on the thirsty earth. He may be seen gazing at every black cloud, for his people flock from all parts to beg rain from him, "their rain-maker," for their parched fields; and they thank and praise him when a heavy rain has fallen.[5] A letter dated from Bulawayo, the twentieth of November 1880, records that Lo Bengula, king of the Matabeles, "arrived yesterday evening at his kraal of 'the White Rocks.' He brought with him the rain to his people. For according to the ideas of the Matabeles, it is the king who ought to 'make the rain

marginal notes: Power of rain-makers among the Matabeles.

The king of the Matabeles as rain-maker.

---

to are probably for the most part magical rather than medicinal in our sense of the term.

[1] Dudley Kidd, *op. cit.* p. 115.

[2] W. Grant, "Magato and his Tribe," *Journal of the Anthropological Institute*, xxxv. (1905) p. 267.

[3] L. Decle, *Three Years in Savage Africa* (London, 1898), p. 154.

[4] R. Moffat, *Missionary Labours and Scenes in Southern Africa* (London, 1842), p. 306.

[5] E. A. Maund, "Zambesia, the new British Possession in Central South Africa," *Proceedings of the Royal Geographical Society*, 1890, p. 651.

The king of the Matabeles as rain-maker.

and the good season' in all senses of the word. Now Lo Bengula had chosen well the day and the hour, for it was in the midst of a tremendous storm that the king made his solemn entrance into his capital." "You must know that the arrival of the king and of the rain gives rise every year to a little festival. For the rain is the great benefit conferred by the king, the pledge of future harvests and of plenty, after eight months of desolating drought." To bring down the needed showers the king of the Matabeles boils a magic hell-broth in a cauldron, which sends up volumes of steam to the blue sky. But to make assurance doubly sure, he has recourse to religion as well as to magic ; for he sacrifices twelve black oxen to the spirits of his fathers, and prays to them : " O great spirits of my father and grandfather, I thank you for having granted last year to my people more wheat than to our enemies the Mashonas. This year also, in gratitude for the twelve black oxen which I am about to dedicate to you, make us to be the best-fed and the strongest people in the world!"[1] Thus the king of the Matabeles acts not only as a magician but as a priest, for he prays and sacrifices to the spirits of his forefathers.

Thus in Africa kings have probably often been developed out of magicians, and especially out of rain-makers.

The foregoing evidence renders it probable that in Africa the king has often been developed out of the public magician, and especially out of the rain-maker. The unbounded fear which the magician inspires and the wealth which he amasses in the exercise of his profession may both be supposed to have contributed to his promotion. But if the career of a magician and especially of a rain-maker offers great rewards to the successful practitioner of the art, it is beset with many pitfalls into which the unskilful or unlucky artist may fall. The position of the public sorcerer is indeed a very precarious one ; for where the people firmly believe that he has it in his power to make the rain to fall, the sun to shine, and the fruits of the earth to grow, they naturally impute drought and dearth to his culpable negligence or wilful obstinacy, and they punish him accordingly. We have seen that in Africa the chief who fails to procure rain is often exiled or killed.[2] Examples of such punishments could be multiplied.

[1] Father C. Croonenberghs, in Annales de la Propagation de la Foi, liii. (1881) pp. 262 sq., 267 sq.
[2] See above, pp. 344, 345, 346.

Thus, in some parts of West Africa, when prayers and offerings presented to the king have failed to procure rain, his subjects bind him with ropes and take him by force to the grave of his forefathers that he may obtain from them the needed rain.[1] The Banjars in West Africa ascribe to their king the power of causing rain or fine weather. So long as the weather is fine they load him with presents of grain and cattle. But if long drought or rain threatens to spoil the crops, they insult and beat him till the weather changes.[2] When the harvest fails or the surf on the coast is too heavy to allow of fishing, the people of Loango accuse their king of a " bad heart " and depose him.[3] On the Grain Coast the high priest or fetish king, who bears the title of Bodio, is responsible for the health of the community, the fertility of the earth, and the abundance of fish in the sea and rivers ; and if the country suffers in any of these respects the Bodio is deposed from his office.[4] In Ussukuma, a great district on the southern bank of the Victoria Nyanza, " the rain and locust question is part and parcel of the Sultan's government. He, too, must know how to make rain and drive away the locusts. If he and his medicine-men are unable to accomplish this, his whole existence is at stake in times of distress. On a certain occasion, when the rain so greatly desired by the people did not come, the Sultan was simply driven out (in Ututwa, near Nassa). The people, in fact, hold that rulers must have power over Nature and her phenomena." [5] Again, we are told of the natives of the Nyanza region generally that " they are persuaded that rain only falls as a result of magic, and the important duty of causing it to descend devolves on the chief of the tribe. If rain does not come at the proper time, everybody complains. More than one petty king has been banished his country because of drought." [6] Similarly

[1] J. B. Labat, *Relation historique de l'Éthiopie occidentale* (Paris, 1732), ii. 172-176.

[2] H. Hecquard, *Reise an der Küste und in das Innere von West Afrika* (Leipsic, 1854), p. 78.

[3] A. Bastian, *Die deutsche Expedition an der Loango-Küste*, i. 354, ii. 230.

[4] J. Leighton Wilson, *Western Africa* (London, 1856), pp. 129 *sq.*; Miss Mary H. Kingsley, in *Journal of the Anthropological Institute*, xxix. (1899) p. 62.

[5] P. Kollmann, *The Victoria Nyanza* (London, 1899), p. 168.

[6] Mgr Livinhac, in *Annales de la Propagation de la Foi*, lx. (1888) p. 110.

among the Antimores of Madagascar the chiefs are held responsible for the operation of the laws of nature. Hence if the land is smitten with a blight or devastated by clouds of locusts, if the cows yield little milk, or fatal epidemics rage among the people, the chief is not only deposed but stripped of his property and banished, because they say that under a good chief such things ought not to happen.[1] So, too, of the Antaimorona we read that "although the chiefs of this tribe are chosen by the people, during their tenure of power they enjoy a respect which borders on adoration ; but if a crop of rice fails or any other calamity happens, they are immediately deposed, sometimes even killed ; and yet their successor is always chosen from the family."[2] Among the Latukas of the Upper Nile, when the crops are withering in the fields and all the efforts of the chief to bring down rain have proved fruitless, the people commonly attack him by night, rob him of all he possesses, and drive him away. But often they kill him.[3]

In other parts of the world kings have been punished for failing to regulate the course of nature.

In many other parts of the world kings have been expected to regulate the course of nature for the good of their people and have been punished if they failed to do so. It appears that the Scythians, when food was scarce, used to put their king in bonds.[4] In ancient Egypt the sacred kings were blamed for the failure of the crops,[5] but the sacred beasts were also held responsible for the course of nature. When pestilence and other calamities had fallen on the land, in consequence of a long and severe drought, the priests took the animals by night and threatened them, but if the evil did not abate they slew the beasts.[6] On the coral island of Niuē or Savage Island, in the South Pacific, there formerly reigned a line of kings. But as the kings were also high priests, and

---

[1] D'Unienville, *Statistique de l'Ile Maurice* (Paris, 1838) iii. 285 *sq.*

[2] A. van Gennep, *Tabou et Totémisme à Madagascar* (Paris, 1904), p. 118, quoting Leguével de Lacombe, *Voyage à Madagascar* (Paris, 1840), i. 229 *sq.* Probably the Antimoirona are identical with the Antimores.

[3] Emin Pasha, quoted by Fr. Stuhlmann, *Mit Emin Pascha ins Herz von Afrika* (Berlin, 1894), pp. 779 *sq.*

[4] Schol. on Apollonius Rhodius, *Argon.* ii. 1248 καὶ Ἡρόδωρος ξένως περὶ τῶν δεσμῶν τοῦ Προμηθέως ταῦτα. εἶναι γὰρ αὐτὸν Σκυθῶν βασιλέα φησί· καὶ μὴ δυνάμενον παρέχειν τοῖς ὑπηκόοις τὰ ἐπιτήδεια, διὰ τὸν καλούμενον Ἀετὸν ποταμὸν ἐπικλύζειν τὰ πεδία, δεθῆναι ὑπὸ τῶν Σκυθῶν.

[5] Ammianus Marcellinus, xxviii. 5. 14.

[6] Plutarch, *Isis et Osiris*, 73.

were supposed to make the food grow, the people became angry with them in times of scarcity and killed them ; till at last, as one after another was killed, no one would be king, and the monarchy came to an end.[1] Ancient Chinese writers inform us that in Corea the blame was laid on the king whenever too much or too little rain fell and the crops did not ripen. Some said that he must be deposed, others that he must be slain.[2] The Chinese emperor himself is deemed responsible if the drought is at all severe, and many are the self-condemnatory edicts on this subject published in the pages of the venerable *Peking Gazette.* In extreme cases the emperor, clad in humble vestments, sacrifices to heaven and implores its protection.[3] So, too, the kings of Tonquin used to take blame to themselves when the country was visited by such calamities as scanty harvests, dearth, floods, destructive hurricanes and cholera. On these occasions the monarch would sometimes publicly confess his guilt and impose on himself a penance as a means of appeasing the wrath of Heaven.[4] In former days it sometimes happened that when the country suffered from drought and dearth the king of Tonquin was obliged to change his name in the hope that this would turn the weather to rain. But if the drought continued even after the change of name the people would sometimes resort to stronger measures and transfer the title of king from the legitimate monarch to his brother, son, or other near relation.[5]

Among the American Indians the furthest advance towards civilisation was made under the monarchical and

[1] G. Turner, *Samoa*, pp. 304 *sq*.

[2] A. Pfizmayer, " Nachrichten von den alten Bewohnern des heutigen Corea," *Sitzungsberichte der philos.-histor. Classe der kais. Akademie der Wissenschaften* (Vienna), lvii. (1868) pp. 483 *sq*. It would seem that the Chinese reported similarly of the Roman emperors. See Hirth, *China and the Roman Orient*, pp. 41, 44, 52, 58, 70, 78.

[3] N. B. Dennis, *Folklore of China* (London and Hongkong, 1876), p. 125. An account of the *Peking Gazette*, the official publication of the Chinese government, may be read in *Lettres édifiantes et curieuses*, Nouvelle Edition, xxi. 95-182.

[4] Mgr Havard, in *Annales de la Propagation de la Foi*, vii. (1834) pp. 470-473.

[5] Gio. Filippo de Marini, *Historia et relatione del Tunchino et del Giappone* (Rome, 1665), pp. 137 *sq*. ; *Relation nouvelle et curieuse des royaumes de Tunquin et de Lao*, traduite de l'Italien du P. Mariny (*sic*) Romain (Paris, 1666), pp. 258 *sq*.

Power of
medicine-
men
among
the North
American
Indians.

theocratic governments of Mexico and Peru ; but we know too little of the early history of these countries to say whether the predecessors of their deified kings were medicine-men or not. Perhaps a trace of such a succession may be detected in the oath which the Mexican kings took when they mounted the throne : they swore that they would make the sun to shine, the clouds to give rain, the rivers to flow, and the earth to bring forth fruits in abundance.[1] Certainly, in aboriginal America the sorcerer or medicine - man, surrounded by a halo of mystery and an atmosphere of awe, was a personage of great influence and importance, and he may well have developed into a chief or king in many tribes, though positive evidence of such a development appears to be lacking. Thus Catlin tells us that in North America the medicine-men "are valued as dignitaries in the tribe, and the greatest respect is paid to them by the whole community ; not only for their skill in their *materia medica*, but more especially for their tact in magic and mysteries, in which they all deal to a very great extent. . . . In all tribes their doctors are conjurors—are magicians—are sooth-sayers, and I had like to have said high-priests, inasmuch as they superintend and conduct all their religious ceremonies ; they are looked upon by all as oracles of the nation. In all councils of war and peace, they have a seat with the chiefs, are regularly consulted before any public step is taken, and the greatest deference and respect is paid to their opinions."[2] Among the Loucheux of North-West America each band is "headed by a chief and one or more medicine-men. The latter, however, do not possess any secular power as chiefs, but they acquire an authority by shamanism to which even the chiefs themselves are subject." "The Loucheux are very superstitious, and place implicit faith in the pretended incantations of their medicine-men, for whom they entertain great fear. . . . The power of the medicine-men is very great, and they use every means they can to increase it by working on the fears and credulity of the people. Their influence exceeds even that of the chiefs. The power of the

[1] H. H. Bancroft, *The Native Races of the Pacific States*, ii. 146.
[2] Geo. Catlin, *Manners, Customs, and Conditions of the North American Indians*[4] (London, 1844), i. 40 *sq.*

latter consists in the quantity of beads they possess, their Power of
wealth and the means it affords them to work ill to those to medicine-
men
whom they may be evil-disposed ; while the power of the among
medicine-man consists in the harm they believe he is able to the North
American
do by shamanism, should they happen to displease him in Indians.
any way. It is when sickness prevails that the conjuror
rules supreme ; it is then that he fills his bead bags and
increases his riches." [1]   Amongst the Tinneh Indians of the
same region "the social standing of a medicine-man is, on
the whole, a desirable one ; but it has also its drawbacks
and its dark side.   The medicine-man is decidedly influential
among his fellow savages.   He is consulted and listened to,
on account of the superior knowledge imparted to him by
the spirits.   He is feared, on account of his power to do
evil, viz. to cause the death of a person, to ruin his under-
takings, to render him unsuccessful in the hunt by driving
away the game from his path, to cause the loss of his
property, of his strength, of his health, of his faculties, etc.
The medicine-man is rich, because his services, when
summoned, or even when accepted though uncalled for, are
generously remunerated.   He is respected on account of
his continual intercourse with the supernatural world.   His
words, when said in a peculiar low tone, with a momentary
glow in the eyes, which [he] seems able to control at will, or
when uttered during his sleep (real or feigned) are taken as
oracles, as the very words of the spirit.   In short, for these
tribes who have no chiefs, no religion, no medical knowledge,
he is the nearest approach to a chief, a priest, and a
physician." [2]   Similarly in California "the shaman was, and
still is, perhaps the most important individual among the
Maidu.   In the absence of any definite system of government, the word of a shaman has great weight : as a class
they are regarded with much awe, and as a rule are obeyed
much more than the chief." [3]   As leader of the local branch

---

[1] W. L. Hardisty, "The Loucheux Indians," *Report of the Smithsonian Institution for 1866*, pp. 312, 316.

[2] Rev. J. Jetté, "On the Medicine-Men of the Ten'a," *Journal of the R. Anthropological Institute*, xxxvii. (1907) p. 163.   By the Ten'a the writer means the tribe which is vari-ously known as the Tinneh, Déné, Dindjie, etc., according to the taste and fancy of the speller.

[3] Roland B. Dixon, "The North-ern Maidu," *Bulletin of the American Museum of Natural History*, vol. xvii. part iii. (New York, 1905) p. 267.

Power of
medicine-
men
among
the North
American
Indians.

of a secret society the most noted Maidu shaman of each district was supposed to make rain when it was needed, to ensure a good crop of edible acorns and a plentiful supply of salmon, and to drive away evil spirits, disease, and epidemics from the village. Further, it was his business to inflict disease and death on hostile villages, which he did by burning certain roots and blowing the smoke towards the doomed village, while he said, " Over there, over there, not here ! To the other place ! Do not come back this way. We are good. Make those people sick. Kill them, they are bad people." [1] Among the Yokuts, another tribe of Californian Indians, the rain-makers exercised great influence. One of them by his insinuating address, eloquence, and jugglery spread his fame to a distance of two hundred miles, and cunningly availed himself of two years of drought to levy contributions far and wide from the trembling Indians, who attributed to his magic the fall of the rain.[2] In the same tribe the wizards drew large profits from the rattle-snake dance which they danced every spring, capering about with rattlesnakes twined round their arms ; for after this exhibition many simpletons paid them for complete immunity from snake-bites, which the wizards were believed able to grant for a year.[3]

Power of
medicine-
men
among
the South
American
Indians.

In South America also the magicians or medicine-men seem to have been on the highroad to chieftainship or kingship. One of the earliest settlers on the coast of Brazil, the Frenchman Thevet, reports that the Indians " hold these *pages* (or medicine-men) in such honour and reverence that they adore, or rather idolise them. You may see the common folk go to meet them, prostrate themselves, and pray to them, saying, ' Grant that I be not ill, that I do not die, neither I nor my children,' or some such request. And he answers, ' You shall not die, you shall not be ill,' and such like replies. But sometimes if it happens that these *pages* do not tell the truth, and things turn out otherwise than they predicted, the people make no scruple of killing them as unworthy of the title and dignity

---

[1] Roland B. Dixon, *op. cit.* pp. 328, 331.

[2] S. Powers, *Tribes of California*

(Washington, 1877), pp. 372 *sq.*

[3] S. Power, *op. cit.* pp. 380 *sq.*

of *pages*." [1]   The Indians of Brazil, says a modern writer
who knew them well, "have no priests but only magicians,
who at the same time use medical help and exorcism in
order to exert influence over the superstition and the dread
of spirits felt by the rude multitude.   We may perfectly
compare them with the shamans of the north-eastern Asiatic
peoples.   But like the shamans they are not mere magicians,
fetish-men, soothsayers, interpreters of dreams, visionaries,
and casters-out of devils ; their activity has also a political
character in so far as they influence the decisions of the
leaders and of the community in public business, and exert a
certain authority, more than anybody else, as judges, sureties,
and witnesses in private affairs." [2]   Among the Lengua Indians
of the Gran Chaco every clan has its cazique or chief, but
he possesses little authority.   In virtue of his office he has
to make many presents, so he seldom grows rich and is
generally more shabbily clad than any of his subjects.   "As
a matter of fact the magician is the man who has most
power in his hands, and he is accustomed to receive presents
instead of to give them."   It is the magician's duty to bring
down misfortune and plagues on the enemies of his tribe,
and to guard his own people against hostile magic.   For
these services he is well paid and by them he acquires a
position of great influence and authority.[3]   Among the
Indians of Guiana also the magician or medicine-man (*piai,
peaiman*) is a personage of great importance.   By his magic
art he alone, it is believed, can counteract the machinations
of the great host of evil spirits, to which these savages attribute all the ills of life.   It is almost impossible, we are told,
to overestimate the dreadful sense of constant and unavoid-
able danger in which the Indian would live were it not for
his trust in the protecting power of the magician.   Every
village has one such spiritual guardian, who is physician,
priest, and magician in one.   His influence is immense.
No Indian dare refuse him anything he takes a fancy to,

---

[1] F. A. Thevet, *Les Singularitez de la France Antarctique, autrement nommée Amérique* (Antwerp, 1558), p. 65 [wrongly numbered 67].

[2] C. F. Phil. v. Martius, *Zur Ethno-graphie Amerikas, zumal Brasiliens* (Leipsic, 1867), p. 76.

[3] G. Kurze, "Sitten und Gebräuche der Lengua - Indianer," *Mitteilungen der Geographischen Gesellschaft zu Jena.* xxiii. (Jena, 1905) pp. 19, 29.

from a trifle of food up to a man's wife. Hence these
cunning fellows live in idleness on the fat of the land and
acquire a large harem ; their houses are commonly full of
women who serve them in the capacity of beasts of burden
as well as of wives, plodding wearily along under the weight
of the baggage on long journeys, while their lord and master,
fantastically tricked out in feathers and paint, strolls ahead,
burdened only with his magic rattle and perhaps his bow and
arrows.[1]

*Power of
medicine-
men
among the
pagan
tribes of
the Malay
Peninsula.*　　Among the wild pagan tribes of the Malay peninsula the
connexion between the offices of magician and chief is very
close ; indeed the two offices are often united in the same
person. Among these savages, "as among the Malays, the
accredited intermediary between gods and men is in all cases
the medicine-man or sorcerer. In the Semang tribes the
office of chief medicine-man appears to be generally combined with that of chief, but amongst the Sakai and Jakun
these offices are sometimes separated, and although the chief
is almost invariably a medicine-man of some repute, he is
not necessarily the chief medicine-man, any more than the
chief medicine-man is necessarily the administrative head of
the tribe. In both cases there is an unfailing supply of
aspirants to the office, though it may be taken for granted
that, all else being equal, a successful medicine-man would
have much the best prospect of being elected chief, and that
in the vast majority of cases his priestly duties form an
important part of a chief's work. The medicine-man is, as
might be expected, duly credited with supernatural powers.
His tasks are to preside as chief medium at all the ceremonies, to instruct the youth of the tribe, to ward off
as well as to heal all forms of sickness and trouble, to
foretell the future (as affecting the results of any given
act), to avert when necessary the wrath of heaven, and
even when re-embodied after death in the shape of a
wild beast, to extend a benign protection to his devoted
descendants. Among the Sakai and the Jakun he is
provided with a distinctive form of dress and body-

[1] Sir R. Schomburgk, *Reisen in
Britisch-Guiana*, i. 169 *sq.*, compare
id. i. 423, ii. 431 ; (Sir) Everard F.
im Thurn, *Among the Indians of
Guiana* (London, 1883), pp. 211, 223
sq., 328, 333 *sq.*, 339 *sq.*

painting, and carries an emblematic wand or staff by virtue of his office." [1]

Throughout the Malay region the rajah or king is commonly regarded with superstitious veneration as the possessor of supernatural powers, and there are grounds for thinking that he too, like apparently so many African chiefs, has been developed out of a simple magician. At the present day the Malays firmly believe that the king possesses a personal influence over the works of nature, such as the growth of the crops and the bearing of fruit-trees. The same prolific virtue is supposed to reside, though in a lesser degree, in his delegates, and even in the persons of Europeans who chance to have charge of districts. Thus in Selangor, one of the native states of the Malay Peninsula, the success or failure of the rice crops is often attributed to a change of district officers.[2] The Toorateyas of southern Celebes hold that the prosperity of the rice depends on the behaviour of their princes, and that bad government, by which they mean a government which does not conform to ancient custom, will result in a failure of the crops.[3]

The Dyaks of Sarawak believed that their famous English ruler, Rajah Brooke, was endowed with a certain magical virtue which, if properly applied, could render the rice-crops abundant. Hence when he visited a tribe, they used to bring him the seed which they intended to sow next year, and he fertilised it by shaking over it the women's necklaces, which had been previously dipped in a special mixture. And when he entered a village, the women would wash and bathe his feet, first with water, and then with the milk of a young coco-nut, and lastly with water again, and all this water which had touched his person they preserved for the purpose of distributing it on their farms, believing that it ensured an abundant harvest. Tribes which were too far

Develop-ment of kings out of magicians among the Malays.

Belief of the Dyaks in the power of the rajah to fertilise the rice.

---

[1] W. W. Skeat and C. O. Blagden, *Pagan Races of the Malay Peninsula* (London, 1906), ii. 196 *sq.*

[2] W. W. Skeat, *Malay Magic* (London, 1900), p. 36.

[3] G. Maan, " Enige mededeelingen omtrent de zeden en gewoonten der Toerateya ten opzichte van de rijst-bouw," *Tijdschrift voor Indische Taal-Land- en Volkenkunde*, xlvi. (1903) p. 339. The name Toorateya or " in-lander" is only another form of Toradja

off for him to visit used to send him a small piece of white cloth and a little gold or silver, and when these things had been impregnated by his generative virtue they buried them in their fields, and confidently expected a heavy crop. Once when a European remarked that the rice-crops of the Samban tribe were thin, the chief immediately replied that they could not be otherwise, since Rajah Brooke had never visited them, and he begged that Mr. Brooke might be induced to visit his tribe and remove the sterility of their land.[1]

Links between Malay rajahs and magicians.

Among the Malays the links which unite the king or rajah with the magician happen to be unusually plain and conspicuous. Thus the magician shares with the king the privilege of using cloth dyed yellow, the royal colour; he has considerable political influence, and he can compel people to address him in ceremonial language, of which indeed the phraseology is even more copious in its application to a magician than to a king. Moreover, and this is a fact of great significance, the Malay magician owns certain insignia which are said to be exactly analogous to the regalia of the king, and even bear the very same name (*kabĕsaran*).[2] Now the regalia of a Malay king are not mere jewelled baubles designed to impress the multitude with the pomp and splendour of royalty; they are regarded as wonder-working talismans,[3] the possession of which carries with it the right to the throne; if the king loses them, he thereby forfeits the allegiance of his subjects. It seems, therefore, to be a probable inference that in the Malay region the regalia of the kings are only the conjuring apparatus of their predecessors the magicians, and that in this part of the world accordingly the magician is the humble grub or chrysalis which in due time bursts and discloses that gorgeous butterfly the rajah or king.

In Celebes the regalia are talismans or

Nowhere apparently in the Indian Archipelago is this view of the regalia as the true fount of regal dignity carried to such lengths as in southern Celebes. Here the royal

[1] H. Low, *Sarawak* (London, 1848), pp. 259 *sq.*

[2] W. W. Skeat, *Malay Magic*, p. 59.

[3] T. J. Newbold, *Political and*

Statistical Account of the British Settlements in the Straits of Malacca, ii. 193; W. W. Skeat, *Malay Magic*, pp. 23-29.

authority is supposed to be in some mysterious fashion fetishes, the
embodied in the regalia, while the princes owe all the possession of which
power they exercise, and all the respect they enjoy, carries
to their possession of these precious objects. In short, with it the right to the
the regalia reign, and the princes are merely their repre- throne.
sentatives.   Hence whoever happens to possess the regalia
is regarded by the people as their lawful king.   For example,
if a deposed monarch contrives to keep the regalia, his
former subjects remain loyal to him in their hearts, and look
upon his successor as a usurper who is to be obeyed only in
so far as he can exact obedience by force.   And on the
other hand, in an insurrection the first aim of the rebels is
to seize the regalia, for if they can only make themselves
masters of them, the authority of the sovereign is gone.   In
short, the regalia are here fetishes, which confer a title to the
throne and control the fate of the kingdom.   Houses are
built for them to dwell in, as if they were living creatures ;
furniture, weapons, and even lands are assigned to them.
Like the ark of God, they are carried with the army to battle,
and on various occasions the people propitiate them, as if they
were gods, by prayer and sacrifice and by smearing them with
blood.   Some of them serve as instruments of divination, or
are brought forth in times of public disaster for the purpose
of staying the evil, whatever it may be.   For example, when
plague is rife among men or beasts, or when there is a
prospect of dearth, the Boogineese bring out the regalia,
smear them with buffalo's blood, and carry them about.
For the most part these fetishes are heirlooms of which the
origin is forgotten ; some of them are said to have fallen
from heaven.   Popular tradition traces the foundation of
the oldest states to the discovery or acquisition of one of
these miraculous objects—it may be a stone, a piece of wood,
a fruit, a weapon, or what not, of a peculiar shape or colour.
Often the original regalia have disappeared in course of
time, but their place is taken by the various articles of
property which were bestowed on them, and to which the
people have transferred their pious allegiance.   The oldest
dynasties have the most regalia, and the holiest regalia
consist of relics of the bodies of former princes, which are
kept in golden caskets wrapt in silk.   At Paloppo, the

Regalia as talismans in Celebes.

capital of Loowoo, a kingdom on the coast of Celebes, two toy cannons, with barrels like thin gas-pipes, are regalia ; their possession is supposed to render the town impregnable. Other regalia of this kingdom are veiled from vulgar eyes in bark-cloth. When a missionary requested to see them, the official replied that it was strictly forbidden to open the bundle ; were he to do so, the earth would yawn and swallow them up. In Bima the principal part of the regalia or public talismans consists of a sacred brown horse, which no man may ride. It is always stabled in the royal palace. When the animal passes the government fort on high days and holidays, it is saluted with the fire of five guns ; when it is led to the river to bathe, the royal spear is carried before it, and any man who does not give way to the beast, or crosses the road in front of it, has to pay a fine. But the horse is mortal, and when it goes the way of all horse-flesh, another steed chosen from the same stud reigns in its place.[1]

Magical virtue of regalia in Egypt and Africa.

But if in the Malay region the regalia are essentially wonder-working talismans or fetishes which the kings appear to have derived from their predecessors the magicians, we may conjecture that in other parts of the world the emblems of royalty may at some time have been viewed in a similar light and have had a similar origin. In ancient Egypt the two royal crowns, the white and the red, were supposed to be endowed with magical virtues, indeed to be themselves divinities, embodiments of the sun god. One text declares : " The white crown is the eye of Horus ; the red crown is the eye of Horus." Another text speaks of a crown as a "great magician." And applied to the image of a god, the crown was supposed to confirm the deity in the possession of his soul and of his form.[2] Among the Yorubas of West Africa

---

[1] G. J. Harrebomée, " Een orna- mentenfeest van Gantarang (Zuid- Celebes)," *Mededeelingen van wege het Nederlandsche Zendelinggenootschap*, xix. (1875) pp. 344 - 351 ; G. K. Niemann, " De Boegineezen en Makassaren," *Bijdragen tot de Taal- Land- en Volkenkunde van Nederlandsch- Indië*, xxxviii. (1889) pp. 270 *sq.* ; D. F. van Braam Morris, in *Tijdschrift voor Indische Taal- Land- en Volken- kunde*, xxxiv. (1891) pp. 215 *sq.* ; A.

C. Kruijt, "Van Paloppo naar Posso," *Mededeelingen van wege het Neder- landsche Zendelinggenootschap*, xlii. (1898) pp. 18, 25 *sq.* ; L. W. C. van den Berg, "De Mohammedaansche Vorsten in Nederlandsch - Indië," *Bijdragen tot de Taal- Land- en Volken- kunde van Nederlandsch - Indië*, liii. (1901) pp. 72-80.

[2] A. Moret, *Le Rituel du culte divin journalier en Égypte* (Paris 1902) pp. 94 *sq.*

at the present time the king's crown is sacred and is supposed
to be the shrine of a spirit which has to be propitiated.
When the king (*Oni*) of Ife visited Lagos some years ago,
he had to sacrifice five sheep to his crown between Ibadan
and Ife, a two days' journey on foot.[1]   Among the Ashan-
tees "the throne or chair of the king or chief is believed to
be inhabited by a spirit to which it is consecrated, and to
which human sacrifices were formerly offered : at present the
victims are sheep.   It is the personification of power ; hence
a king is not a king and a chief is not a chief until he has
been solemnly installed on the throne."[2]   Among the Hos,
a Ewe tribe of Togoland in German West Africa, the king's
proper throne is small and the king does not sit on it.
Usually it is bound round with magic cords and wrapt up
in a sheep's skin ; but from time to time it is taken out of
the wrappings, washed in a stream, and smeared all over
with the blood of a sheep which has been sacrificed for the
purpose.   The flesh of the sheep is boiled and a portion of
it eaten by every man who has been present at the ceremony.[3]

In Cambodia the regalia are regarded as a palladium on
which the existence of the kingdom depends ; they are
committed to Brahmans for safe keeping.[4]   In antiquity
the Scythian kings treasured as sacred a plough, a yoke, a
battle-axe, and a cup, all of gold, which were said to have
fallen from heaven ; they offered great sacrifices to these
sacred things at an annual festival ; and if the man in
charge of them fell asleep under the open sky, it was
believed that he would die within the year.[5]   The sceptre
of king Agamemnon, or what passed for such, was worshipped
as a god at Chaeronea ; a man acted as priest of the sceptre for
a year at a time, and sacrifices were offered to it daily.[6]   The
golden lamb of Mycenae, on the possession of which, according
to legend, the two rivals Atreus and Thyestes based their claim
to the throne,[7] may have been a royal talisman of this sort.

Regalia venerated in Cambodia, Scythia, and ancient Greece.

---

[1] Sir William MacGregor, "Lagos,
Abeokuta, and the Alake," *Journal of
the African Society*, No. 12 (July,
1904), p. 472.

[2] E. Perregaux, *Chez les Achanti*
(Neuchatel, 1906), p. 140.

[3] J. Spieth, *Die Ewe-Stämme* (Berlin,
1906), pp. 76, 78, compare pp. 101 *sq.*

[4] A. Bastian, *Völkerstämme am
Brahmaputra* (Berlin, 1883), p. xi.

[5] Herodotus, iv. 5-7.   Compare K.
Neumann, *Die Hellenen im Skythen-
lande*, i. (Berlin, 1855) pp. 269 *sq.*

[6] Pausanias, ix. 40. 11 *sq.*

[7] Apollodorus, *Bibliotheca*, ed. R.
Wagner, p. 185.   On public talismans

The belief
that kings
possess
magical
or super-
natural
powers to
control the
course of
nature for
the good
of their
subjects
seems to
have been
shared by
the ances-
tors of all
the Aryan
races from
India to
Ireland.

The belief that kings possess magical or supernatural powers by virtue of which they can fertilise the earth and confer other benefits on their subjects would seem to have been shared by the ancestors of all the Aryan races from India to Ireland, and it has left clear traces of itself in our own country down to modern times. Thus the ancient Hindoo law-book called *The Laws of Manu* describes as follows the effects of a good king's reign : " In that country where the king avoids taking the property of mortal sinners, men are born in due time and are long-lived. And the crops of the husbandmen spring up, each as it was sown, and the children die not, and no misshaped offspring is born." [1] In Homeric Greece kings and chiefs were spoken of as sacred or divine ; their houses, too, were divine and their chariots sacred ; [2] and it was thought that the reign of a good king caused the black earth to bring forth wheat and barley, the trees to be loaded with fruit, the flocks to multiply, and the sea to yield fish. [3] A Greek historian of a much later age tells us that in the reign of a very bad king of Lydia the country suffered from drought, for which he would seem to have held the king responsible. [4] There is a tradition that once when the land of the Edonians in Thrace bore no fruit, the god Dionysus intimated to the people that its fertility could be restored by putting their king Lycurgus to death. So they took him to Mount Pangaeum and there caused him to be torn in pieces by horses. [5] When the crops failed, the Burgundians used to blame their kings and depose them. [6] In the time of the Swedish king Domalde a mighty famine broke out, which lasted several years, and could be stayed by the blood neither of beasts nor of men. Therefore, in a great popular

in antiquity see Ch. A. Lobeck, *Agla-ophamus*, pp. 278 *sqq.* ; and my note on Pausanias, viii. 40. 11.

[1] *The Laws of Manu*, ix. 246 *sq.*, translated by G. Bühler, p. 385 (*Sacred Books of the East*, vol. xxv.).

[2] Homer, *Odyssey*, ii. 409, iv. 43, 691, vii. 167, viii. 2, xviii. 405 ; *Iliad*, ii. 335, xvii. 464, etc.

[3] Homer, *Odyssey*, xix. 109-114. The passage was pointed out to me by my friend Prof. W. Ridgeway. Natur-

ally this view was not shared by the enlightened Greeks of a later age. See Sophocles, *Oedipus Tyrannus*, 31 *sqq.*; Polybius, *Hist.* vi. 6 *sq.*

[4] Nicolaus Damascenus, bk. vi. frag. 49, in *Fragmenta historicorum Graecorum*, ed. C. Müller, iii. 381, Ἦν γὰρ δὴ κάκιστος, καὶ ἄλλως βασιλεύοντος αὐτοῦ ηὔχμησεν ἡ γῆ.

[5] Apollodorus, *Bibliotheca*, iii. 5. 1.

[6] Ammianus Marcellinus, xxviii. 5. 14.

assembly held at Upsala, the chiefs decided that King
Domalde himself was the cause of the scarcity and must
be sacrificed for good seasons. So they slew him and
smeared with his blood the altars of the gods. Again,
we are told that the Swedes always attributed good or
bad crops to their kings as the cause. Now, in the reign
of King Olaf, there came dear times and famine, and the
people thought that the fault was the king's, because he
was sparing in his sacrifices. So, mustering an army, they
marched against him, surrounded his dwelling, and burned
him in it, " giving him to Odin as a sacrifice for good crops." [1]
In the Middle Ages, when Waldemar I., King of Denmark,
travelled in Germany, mothers brought their infants and
husbandmen their seed for him to lay his hands on, thinking that children would both thrive the better for the royal
touch, and for a like reason farmers asked him to throw
the seed for them.[2] It was the belief of the ancient
Irish that when their kings observed the customs of their
ancestors, the seasons were mild, the crops plentiful, the
cattle fruitful, the waters abounded with fish, and the fruit
trees had to be propped up on account of the weight
of their produce. A canon attributed to St. Patrick
enumerates among the blessings that attend the reign of
a just king " fine weather, calm seas, crops abundant, and
trees laden with fruit." On the other hand, dearth, dryness
of cows, blight of fruit, and scarcity of corn were regarded
as infallible proofs that the reigning king was bad. For
example, in the reign of the usurper king Carbery Kinncat,
" evil was the state of Ireland : fruitless her corn, for there
used to be only one grain on the stalk ; fruitless her rivers ;
milkless her cattle ; plentiless her fruit, for there used to be

[1] Snorro Starleson, *Chronicle of the Kings of Norway* (trans. by S. Laing), saga i. chs. 18, 47. Compare F. Liebrecht, *Zur Volkskunde* (Heilbronn, 1879), p. 7; J. Scheffer, *Upsalia* (Upsala, 1666), p. 137. In 1814 a pestilence broke out among the Chuk-chees of north-eastern Siberia, which carried off many of the people and spread its ravages among the herds of reindeer. The shamans declared that the spirits were angry and would not stay the plague till the virtuous Kotchène, one of the most venerated chiefs, had been offered to them in sacrifice. No one was found hardy enough to raise a sacrilegious hand against him, and the shamans had to force the chief's own son to cut his father's throat. See De Wrangell, *Le Nord de la Sibérie* (Paris, 1843), i. 265-267.

[2] Saxo Grammaticus, *Historia Danica*, bk. xiv. p. 779, ed. P. E. Müller.

Magical
virtue
attributed
to the chiefs
of the
Macleods.
but one acorn on the stalk." [1] Superstitions of the same sort
seem to have lingered in the Highlands of Scotland down
to the eighteenth century ; for when Dr. Johnson travelled
in Skye it was still held that the return of the laird to
Dunvegan, after any considerable absence, produced a plentiful
capture of herring.[2] The laird of Dunvegan is chief of the
clan of the Macleods, and his family still owns a banner
which is called " Macleod's Fairy Banner," on account of the
supernatural powers ascribed to it. When it is unfurled,
victory in war attends it, and it relieves its followers from
imminent danger. But these virtues it can exert only thrice,
and already it has been twice unfurled. When the potato
crop failed, many of the common people desired that the
magical banner should be displayed, apparently in the belief
that the mere sight of it would produce a fine crop of
potatoes. Every woman with child who sees it is taken
with premature labour, and every cow casts her calf.[3]

A relic of
this belief
is the
notion that
English
kings can
heal
scrofula
by their
touch.
Perhaps the last relic of such superstitions which lingered
about our English kings was the notion that they could heal
scrofula by their touch. The disease was accordingly known
as the King's Evil. Queen Elizabeth often exercised this
miraculous gift of healing. On Midsummer Day 1633,
Charles the First cured a hundred patients at one swoop in
the chapel royal at Holyrood.[4] But it was under his son
Charles the Second that the practice seems to have attained
its highest vogue. In this respect the Merry Monarch did
not let the grass grow under his feet. It was the twenty-
ninth of May 1660 when he was brought home in triumph
from exile amid a shouting multitude and a forest of
brandished swords, over roads strewed with flowers and
through streets hung with tapestry, while the fountains ran
wine and all the bells of London rang for joy. And it was
on the sixth of July that he began to touch for the King's

[1] P. W. Joyce, *Social History of
Ancient Ireland* (London, 1903), i.
56 *sq.*; J. O'Donovan, *The Book of
Rights* (Dublin, 1847), p. 8, note.
Compare Bérenger - Féraud, *Super-
stitions et survivances*, i. 492.

[2] S. Johnson, *Journey to the Western
Islands* (Baltimore, 1815), p. 115.

[3] J. G. Campbell, *Superstitions of*

the Highlands and Islands of Scotland
(Glasgow, 1900), p. 5. As to the
banner see also Th. Pennant, " Second
Tour in Scotland," in Pinkerton's
Voyages and Travels, iii. 321 *sq.*

[4] J. G. Dalyell, *The Darker Superstitions of Scotland* (Edinburgh, 1834),
pp. 62 *sqq.*

Evil. The ceremony is thus described by Evelyn, who may Charles II. have witnessed it. " His Majestie began first to *touch for y*ᵉ *evil,* according to costome, thus: His Maᵗⁱᵉ sitting under his state in the Banquetting House, the chirurgeons cause the sick to be brought or led up to the throne, where they kneeling, yᵉ King strokes their faces or cheekes with both his hands at once, at which instant a chaplaine in his formalities says, ' He put his hands upon them and he healed them.' This is sayd to every one in particular. When they have been all touch'd they come up again in the same order, and the other chaplaine kneeling, and having angel gold strung on white ribbon on his arme, delivers them one by one to his Maᵗⁱᵉ, who puts them about the necks of the touched as they pass, whilst the first chaplaine repeats, ' That is yᵉ true light who came into yᵉ world.' Then follows an Epistle (as at first a Gospell) with the liturgy, prayers for the sick, with some alteration, lastly yᵉ blessing ; and then the Lo. Chamberlaine and the Comptroller of the Household bring a basin, ewer and towell, for his Majesty to wash." [1] Pepys witnessed the same ceremony at the same place on the thirteenth of April in the following year and he has recorded his opinion that it was " an ugly office and a simple." [2] It is said that in the course of his reign Charles the Second touched near a hundred thousand persons for scrofula. The press to get near him was sometimes terrific. On one occasion six or seven of those who came to be healed were trampled to death. While the hope of a miraculous cure attracted the pious and sanguine, the certainty of receiving angel gold attracted the needy and avaricious, and it was not always easy for the royal surgeons to distinguish between the motives of the applicants. This solemn mummery cost the state little less than ten thousand pounds a year. The cool-headed William the Third contemptuously refused to lend himself to the hocus-pocus ; and when his palace was besieged by the usual unsavoury crowd, he ordered them to be turned away

(margin note:) touching for the king's evil (scrofula).

---

[1] *Memoirs of John Evelyn, Esq.,* New Edition (London, 1827), ii. 151 *sq.,* under July 6th, 1660. Angel gold were gold coins with the figure of an angel stamped on them. As to Charles's triumphal entrance into London, see Evelyn, *op. cit.* ii. 148 *sq.*

[2] *Memoirs of Samuel Pepys, Esq.,* edited by Lord Braybrook, Second Edition (London, 1828), i. 187, compare *ib.* p. 110, iii. 192.

with a dole. On the only occasion when he was importuned into laying his hand on a patient, he said to him, "God give you better health and more sense." However, the practice was continued, as might have been expected, by the dull bigot James the Second [1] and his dull daughter Queen Anne. In his childhood Dr. Johnson was touched for scrofula by the queen, and he always retained a faint but solemn recollection of her as of a lady in diamonds with a long black hood.[2] To judge by the too faithful picture which his biographer has drawn of the doctor's appearance in later life we may conclude that the touch of the queen's hand was not a perfect remedy for the disorder; perhaps the stream of divine grace which had flowed so copiously in the veins of Charles the Second had been dried up by the interposition of the sceptical William.

Other
kings and
chiefs have
claimed
to heal
diseases by
a touch.   The kings of France also claimed to possess the same gift of healing by touch, which they are said to have derived from Clovis or from St. Louis, while our English kings inherited it from Edward the Confessor.[3] We may suspect that these estimates of the antiquity of the gift were far too modest, and that the barbarous, nay savage, predecessors both of the Saxon and of the Merovingian kings had with the same justice claimed the same powers many ages before. Down to the nineteenth century the West African tribe of the Walos, in Senegal, ascribed to their royal family a like power of healing by touch. Mothers have been seen to bring their sick children to the queen, who touched them solemnly with her foot on the back, the stomach, the head, and the legs, after which the women departed in peace, convinced that

[1] T. B. Macaulay, *History of England*, chap. xiv. vol. iii. pp. 478-481 (First Edition, London, 1855).

[2] J. Boswell, *Life of Samuel Johnson*, Ninth Edition (London, 1822), i. 18 *sq.*

[3] T. J. Pettigrew, *Superstitions connected with the History and Practice of Medicine and Surgery* (London, 1844), pp. 117-154; W. G. Black, *Folk-Medicine* (London, 1883), pp. 140 *sqq.*; W. E. H. Lecky, *History of England in the Eighteenth Century* (London, 1892), i. 84-90. Down to the end of

the eighteenth century it was believed in the Highlands of Scotland that some tribes of Macdonalds had the power of curing a certain disease by their touch and the use of a particular set of words. Hence the disease, which attacked the chest and lungs, was called "the Macdonald's disease." We are told that the faith of the people in the touch of a Macdonald was very great. See Rev. Dr. Th. Bisset, "Parish of Logierait," in Sir John Sinclair's *Statistical Account of Scotland*, iii. (Edinburgh, 1792) p. 84.

their children had been made whole.[1]   Similarly the savage
chiefs of Tonga were believed to heal scrofula and cases of in-
durated liver by the touch of their feet; and the cure was strictly
homoeopathic, for the disease as well as the cure was thought
to be caused by contact with the royal person or with anything that belonged to it.[2]   In fact royal personages in the
Pacific and elsewhere have been supposed to live in a sort of
atmosphere highly charged with what we may call spiritual
electricity, which, if it blasts all who intrude into its charmed
circle, has happily also the gift of making them whole again
by a touch.[3]   We may conjecture that similar views prevailed
in ancient times as to the predecessors of our English
monarchs, and that accordingly scrofula received its name of
the King's Evil from the belief that it was caused as well as
cured by contact with a king.[4]   In Loango palsy is called
the king's disease, because the negroes imagine it to be
heaven's punishment for treason meditated against the
king.[5]

On the whole, then, we seem to be justified in inferring
that in many parts of the world the king is the lineal
successor of the old magician or medicine-man.   When once
a special class of sorcerers has been segregated from the
community and entrusted by it with the discharge of duties
on which the public safety and welfare are believed to
depend, these men gradually rise to wealth and power, till
their leaders blossom out into sacred kings.   But the great
social revolution which thus begins with democracy and ends
in despotism is attended by an intellectual revolution which
affects both the conception and the functions of royalty.

[marginal note:] On the whole kings seem to have been often evolved out of magicians, but in course of time to have exchanged magical for religious functions, in other words,

---

[1] Baron Roger, "Notice sur le
gouvernement, les mœurs et les superstitions du pays de Walo," *Bulletin de
la Société de Géographie* (Paris), viii.
(1827) p. 351.

[2] W. Mariner, *An Account of the
Natives of the Tonga Islands*, Second
Edition (London, 1818), i. 434, note.

[3] To this subject we shall recur later
on.   Meantime I may refer the reader
to *The Golden Bough*, Second Edition,
i. 319 *sqq.*, 343; *Psyche's Task*, pp.
5 *sqq.*

[4] A Roman name for jaundice was
"the royal disease" (*morbus regius*).
See Horace, *Ars poetica*, 453; Celsus,
De medicina, iii. 24.   Can this have
been because the malady was believed
to be caused and cured by kings?   Did
the sight or touch of the king's red or
purple robe ban the yellow tinge from
the skin of the sufferer?   As to such
homoeopathic cures of jaundice, see
above, pp. 79 *sqq.*

[5] Proyart's "History of Loango,
Kakongo, and other Kingdoms in
Africa," in Pinkerton's *Voyages and
Travels*, xvi. 573.

to have
become
priests
instead of
sorcerers.

For as time goes on, the fallacy of magic becomes more and more apparent to the acuter minds and is slowly displaced by religion; in other words, the magician gives way to the priest, who renouncing the attempt to control directly the processes of nature for the good of man, seeks to attain the same end indirectly by appealing to the gods to do for him what he no longer fancies he can do for himself. Hence the king, starting as a magician, tends gradually to exchange the practice of magic for the priestly functions of prayer and sacrifice. And while the distinction between the human and the divine is still imperfectly drawn, it is often imagined that men may themselves attain to godhead, not merely after their death, but in their lifetime, through the temporary or permanent possession of their whole nature by a great and powerful spirit. No class of the community has benefited so much as kings by this belief in the possible incarnation of a god in human form. The doctrine of that incarnation, and with it the theory of the divinity of kings in the strict sense of the word, will form the subject of the following chapter.

CHAPTER VII

INCARNATE HUMAN GODS

THE instances which in the preceding chapters I have drawn from the beliefs and practices of rude peoples all over the world, may suffice to prove that the savage fails to recognise those limitations to his power over nature which seem so obvious to us. In a society where every man is supposed to be endowed more or less with powers which we should call supernatural, it is plain that the distinction between gods and men is somewhat blurred, or rather has scarcely emerged. The conception of gods as superhuman beings endowed with powers to which man possesses nothing comparable in degree and hardly even in kind, has been slowly evolved in the course of history.[1] By primitive peoples the supernatural agents are not regarded as greatly, if at all, superior to man ; for they may be frightened and coerced by him into doing his will. At this stage of thought the world is viewed as a great democracy ; all beings in it, whether natural or supernatural, are supposed to stand on a footing of tolerable equality. But with the growth of his knowledge man learns to realise more clearly the vastness of nature and his own littleness and feebleness in presence of it. The recognition of his helplessness does not, however, carry with it a corresponding belief in the impotence of those supernatural beings with which his imagination peoples the universe. On the contrary, it enhances his

---

[1] A reminiscence of this evolution is preserved in the Brahman theology, according to which the gods were at first mortal and dwelt on earth with men, but afterwards attained immortality and ascended to heaven by means of sacrifice. See S. Lévi, *La Doctrine du sacrifice dans les Brâhmanas* (Paris, 1898), pp. 37-43, 59-61, 84 *sq.*

conception of their power. For the idea of the world as a system of impersonal forces acting in accordance with fixed and invariable laws has not yet fully dawned or darkened upon him. The germ of the idea he certainly has, and he acts upon it, not only in magic art, but in much of the business of daily life. But the idea remains undeveloped, and so far as he attempts to explain the world he lives in, he pictures it as the manifestation of conscious will and personal agency. If then he feels himself to be so frail and slight, how vast and powerful must he deem the beings who

As religion grows, magic declines into a black art. control the gigantic machinery of nature! Thus as his old sense of equality with the gods slowly vanishes, he resigns at the same time the hope of directing the course of nature by his own unaided resources, that is, by magic, and looks more and more to the gods as the sole repositories of those supernatural powers which he once claimed to share with them. With the advance of knowledge, therefore, prayer and sacrifice assume the leading place in religious ritual; and magic, which once ranked with them as a legitimate equal, is gradually relegated to the background and sinks to the level of a black art. It is now regarded as an encroachment, at once vain and impious, on the domain of the gods, and as such encounters the steady opposition of the priests, whose reputation and influence rise or fall with those of their gods. Hence, when at a late period the distinction between religion and superstition has emerged, we find that sacrifice and prayer are the resource of the pious and enlightened portion of the community, while magic is the refuge of the superstitious and ignorant. But when, still later, the conception of the elemental forces as personal agents is giving way to the recognition of natural law; then magic, based as it implicitly is on the idea of a necessary and invariable sequence of cause and effect, independent of personal will, reappears from the obscurity and discredit into which it had fallen, and by investigating the causal sequences in nature, directly prepares the way for science. Alchemy leads up to chemistry.

The conception of a man-god or deity The notion of a man-god, or of a human being endowed with divine or supernatural powers, belongs essentially to that earlier period of religious history in which gods and men are still viewed as beings of much the same order, and incarnate in human form belongs to an early stage of religious history. before they are divided by the impassable gulf which, to later thought, opens out between them. Strange, therefore, as may seem to us the idea of a god incarnate in human form, it has nothing very startling for early man, who sees in a man-god or a god-man only a higher degree of the same supernatural powers which he arrogates in perfect good faith to himself. Nor does he draw any very sharp distinction between a god and a powerful sorcerer. His gods, as we have seen,[1] are often merely invisible magicians who behind the veil of nature work the same sort of charms and incantations which the human magician works in a visible and bodily form among his fellows. And as the gods are commonly believed to exhibit themselves in the likeness of men to their worshippers, it is easy for the magician, with his supposed miraculous powers, to acquire the reputation of being an incarnate deity. Thus beginning as little more than a simple conjurer, the medicine-man or magician tends to blossom out into a full-blown god and king in one. Only in speaking of him as a god we must beware of importing into the savage conception of deity those very abstract and complex ideas which we attach to the term. Our ideas on this profound subject are the fruit of a long intellectual and moral evolution, and they are so far from being shared by the savage that he cannot even understand them when they are explained to him. Much of the controversy which has raged as to the religion of the lower races has sprung merely from a mutual misunderstanding. The savage does not understand the thoughts of the civilised man, and few civilised men understand the thoughts of the savage. When the savage uses his word for god, he has in his mind a being of a certain sort: when the civilised man uses his word for god, he has in his mind a being of a very different sort; and if, as commonly happens, the two men are equally unable to place themselves at the other's point of view, nothing but confusion and mistakes can result from their discussions. If we civilised men insist on limiting the name of God to that particular conception of the divine nature which we ourselves have formed, then we must confess that

---

[1] See above, pp. 240-242.

the savage has no god at all. But we shall adhere more closely to the facts of history if we allow most of the higher savages at least to possess a rudimentary notion of certain supernatural beings who may fittingly be called gods, though not in the full sense in which we use the word. That rudimentary notion represents in all probability the germ out of which the civilised peoples have gradually evolved their own high conceptions of deity ; and if we could trace the whole course of religious development, we might find that the chain which links our idea of the Godhead with that of the savage is one and unbroken.

Examples of incarnate human deities.

With these explanations and cautions I will now adduce some examples of gods who have been believed by their worshippers to be incarnate in living human beings, whether men or women. The persons in whom a deity is thought to reveal himself are by no means always kings or descendants of kings ; the supposed incarnation may take place even in men of the humblest rank. In India, for example, one human god started in life as a cotton-bleacher and another as the son of a carpenter.[1] I shall therefore not draw my examples exclusively from royal personages, as I wish to illustrate the general principle of the deification of living men, in other words, the incarnation of a deity in human form. Such incarnate gods are common in rude society.

The incarnation either temporary or permanent.

The incarnation may be temporary or permanent. In the former case, the incarnation—commonly known as inspiration or possession—reveals itself in supernatural knowledge rather than in supernatural power. In other words, its usual manifestations are divination and prophecy rather than miracles. On the other hand, when the incarnation is not merely temporary, when the divine spirit has permanently taken up its abode in a human body, the god-man is usually expected to vindicate his character by working miracles. Only we have to remember that by men at this stage of thought miracles are not considered as breaches of natural law. Not conceiving the existence of natural law, primitive man cannot

---

[1] Monier Williams, *Religious Life and Thought in India*, p. 268. However, as to the son of the carpenter it is said that "his followers scarcely worshipped him as a god, yet they fully believed in his power of working miracles."

conceive a breach of it.   A miracle is to him merely an
unusually striking manifestation of a common power.

The belief in temporary incarnation or inspiration is Temporary
world-wide.   Certain persons are supposed to be possessed incarnation
from time to time by a spirit or deity; while the possession human
lasts, their own personality lies in abeyance, the presence of form
the spirit is revealed by convulsive shiverings and shakings the Poly-
of the man's whole body, by wild gestures and excited looks,
all of which are referred, not to the man himself, but to the
spirit which has entered into him ; and in this abnormal
state all his utterances are accepted as the voice of the god
or spirit dwelling in him and speaking through him.   Thus,
for example, in the Sandwich Islands, the king personating
the god, uttered the responses of the oracle from his con-
cealment in a frame of wicker-work.   But in the southern
islands of the Pacific the god " frequently entered the
priest, who, inflated as it were with the divinity, ceased to
act or speak as a voluntary agent, but moved and spoke as
entirely under supernatural influence.   In this respect there
was a striking resemblance between the rude oracles of the
Polynesians, and those of the celebrated nations of ancient
Greece.   As soon as the god was supposed to have entered
the priest, the latter became violently agitated, and worked
himself up to the highest pitch of apparent frenzy, the
muscles of the limbs seemed convulsed, the body swelled,
the countenance became terrific, the features distorted, and
the eyes wild and strained.   In this state he often rolled on
the earth, foaming at the mouth, as if labouring under the
influence of the divinity by whom he was possessed, and, in
shrill cries, and violent and often indistinct sounds, revealed
the will of the god.   The priests, who were attending, and
versed in the mysteries, received, and reported to the people,
the declarations which had been thus received.   When the
priest had uttered the response of the oracle, the violent
paroxysm gradually subsided, and comparative composure
ensued.   The god did not, however, always leave him as
soon as the communication had been made.   Sometimes the
same *taura*, or priest, continued for two or three days
possessed by the spirit or deity ; a piece of a native cloth,
of a peculiar kind, worn round one arm, was an indication

of inspiration, or of the indwelling of the god with the individual who wore it. The acts of the man during this period were considered as those of the god, and hence the greatest attention was paid to his expressions, and the whole of his deportment. . . . When *uruhia*, (under the inspiration of the spirit,) the priest was always considered as sacred as the god, and was called, during this period, *atua*, god, though at other times only denominated *taura* or priest." [1]

Temporary incarnation of gods in Mangaia, Fiji, Bali, and Celebes. In Mangaia, an island of the South Pacific, the priests in whom the gods took up their abode from time to time were called "god-boxes" or, for shortness, "gods." Before giving oracles as gods, they drank an intoxicating liquor, and in the frenzy thus produced their wild whirling words were received as the voice of the deity. [2] In Fiji there is in every tribe a certain family who alone are liable to be thus temporarily inspired or possessed by a divine spirit. "Their qualification is hereditary, and any one of the ancestral gods may choose his vehicle from among them. I have seen this possession, and a horrible sight it is. In one case, after the fit was over, for some time the man's muscles and nerves twitched and quivered in an extraordinary way. He was naked except for his breech-clout, and on his naked breast little snakes seemed to be wriggling for a moment or two beneath his skin, disappearing and then suddenly reappearing in another part of his chest. When the *mbete* (which we may translate 'priest' for want of a better word) is seized by the possession, the god within him calls out his own name in a stridulous tone, 'It is I! Katouivere!' or some other name. At the next possession some other ancestor may declare himself." [3] In Bali there are certain persons called *pĕrmas*, who are predestined or fitted by nature to become the temporary abode of the invisible deities. When a god is to be consulted, the villagers go and compel some of these mediums to lend their services. Sometimes the medium leaves his consciousness at home, and is then conducted with marks of honour to the temple, ready to

[1] W. Ellis, *Polynesian Researches*, Second Edition (London, 1832-36), i. 372-5.
[2] W. W. Gill, *Myths and Songs of* the South Pacific (London, 1876), p. 35.
[3] Rev. Lorimer Fison, in a letter to the author, dated August 26, 1898.

receive the godhead into his person.   Generally, however, Temporary incarnation of gods in human form.
some time passes before he can be brought into the requisite
frame of body and mind ; but the desired result may be
hastened by making him inhale the smoke of incense or
surrounding him with a band of singing men or women.
The soul of the medium quits for a time his body, which is
thus placed at the disposal of the deity, and up to the
moment when his consciousness returns all his words and
acts are regarded as proceeding not from himself but from
the god.   So long as the possession lasts he is a *dewa
kapiragan*, that is, a god who has become man, and in that
character he answers the questions put to him.   During this
time his body is believed to be immaterial and hence
invulnerable.   A dance with swords and pikes follows the
consultation of the oracle ; but these weapons could make no
impression on the ethereal body of the inspired medium.[1]   In
Poso, a district of Central Celebes, sickness is often supposed
to be caused by an alien substance, such as a piece of
tobacco, a stick, or even a chopping-knife, which has been
introduced unseen into the body of the sufferer by the
magic art of an insidious foe.   To discover and eject this
foreign matter is a task for a god, who for this purpose
enters into the body of a priestess, speaks through her
mouth, and performs the necessary surgical operation with
her hands.   An eye-witness of the ceremony has told how,
when the priestess sat beside the sick man, with her head
covered by a cloth, she began to quiver and shake and to
sing in a strident tone, at which some one observed to
the writer, " Now her own spirit is leaving her body and a
god is taking its place."   On removing the cloth from her
head she was no longer a woman but a heavenly spirit, and
gazed about her with an astonished air as if to ask how she
came from her own celestial region to this humble abode.
Yet the divine spirit condescended to chew betel and to
drink palm-wine like any poor mortal of earthly mould.
After she had pretended to extract the cause of the disease
by laying the cloth from her head on the patient's stomach
and pinching it, she veiled her face once more, sobbed,

---

[1] F. A. Liefrinck, " Bijdrage tot de   *voor Indische Taal- Land- en Volken-*
Kennis van het eiland Bali," *Tijdschrift   kunde*, xxxiii. (1890) pp. 260 *sq.*

quivered, and shook violently, at which the people said, "The human spirit is returning into her." [1]

Deification of the sacrificer in Brahman ritual.

A Brahman householder who performs the regular half-monthly sacrifices is supposed thereby to become himself a deity for a time. In the words of the *Satapatha-Brâhmana*, "He who is consecrated draws nigh to the gods and becomes one of the deities." [2] "All formulas of the consecration are *audgrabhana* (elevatory), since he who is consecrated elevates himself (*ud-grabh*) from this world to the world of the gods. He elevates himself by means of these same formulas." [3] "He who is consecrated indeed becomes both Vishnu and a sacrificer; for when he is consecrated, he is Vishnu, and when he sacrifices, he is the sacrificer." [4] After he has completed the sacrifice he becomes man again, divesting himself of his sacred character with the words, "Now I am he who I really am," which are thus explained in the *Satapatha-Brâhmana*: "In entering upon the vow, he becomes, as it were, non-human; and as it would not be becoming for him to say, 'I enter from truth into untruth'; and as, in fact, he now again becomes man, let him therefore divest himself (of the vow) with the

The new birth.

text: 'Now I am he who I really am.'" [5] The means by which the sacrificer passed from untruth to truth, from the human to the divine, was a simulation of a new birth. He was sprinkled with water as a symbol of seed. He feigned to be an embryo, and shut himself up in a special hut, which represented the womb. Under his robe he wore a belt, and over it the skin of a black antelope; the belt stood for the navel-string, and the robe and the black antelope skin represented the inner and outer membranes (the amnion and the chorion) in which an embryo is wrapt. He might not scratch himself with his nails or a stick because he was an embryo, and were an embryo scratched with nails or a stick it would die. If he moved about in

---

[1] A. C. Kruijt, "Mijne eerste ervaringen te Poso," *Mededeelingen van wege het Nederlandsche Zendelingg nootschap*, xxxvi. (1892) pp. 399-403.

[2] *Satapatha-Brâhmana*, part ii. pp. 4, 38, 42, 44, translated by J. Eggeling (*Sacred Books of the East*, vol. xxvi.).

[3] *Op. cit.* p. 20.

[4] *Op. cit.* p. 29.

[5] *Satapatha-Brâhmana*, part i. p. 4, translated by J. Eggeling (*Sacred Books of the East*, vol. xii.). On the deification of the sacrificer in the Brahman ritual see H. Hubert and M. Mauss, "Essai sur le sacrifice," *L'Année sociologique*, ii. (1897-1898), pp. 48 *sqq.*

the hut, it was because the child moves about in the womb. If he kept his fists doubled up, it was because an unborn babe does the same. If in bathing he put off the black antelope skin but retained his robe, it was because the child is born with the amnion but not with the chorion. By these practices he acquired, in addition to his old natural and mortal body, a new body that was sacramental and immortal, invested with superhuman powers, encircled with an aureole of fire. Thus, by a new birth, a regeneration of his carnal nature, the man became a god. At his natural birth, the Brahmans said, man is born but in part; it is by sacrifice that he is truly born into the world. The funeral rites, which ensured the final passage from earth to heaven, might be considered as a phase of the new birth. " In truth," they said, " man is born thrice. At first he is born of his father and mother; then when he sacrifices he is born again; and lastly, when he dies and is laid on the fire, he is born again from it, and that is his third birth. That is why they say that man is born thrice." [1]

But examples of such temporary inspiration are so common in every part of the world and are now so familiar through books on ethnology that it is needless to multiply illustrations of the general principle.[2] It may be well, however, to refer to two particular modes of producing temporary inspiration, because they are perhaps less known than some others, and because we shall have occasion to refer to them later on. One of these modes of producing inspiration is by sucking the fresh blood of a sacrificed victim. In the temple of Apollo Diradiotes at Argos, a lamb was sacrificed by night once a month; a woman, who had to observe a rule of chastity, tasted the blood of the lamb, and thus being inspired by the god she prophesied or divined.[3] At Aegira in Achaia the priestess of Earth drank the fresh blood of a

Temporary incarnation or inspiration produced by drinking blood.

[1] S. Lévi, *La Doctrine du sacrifice dans les Brâhmanas* (Paris, 1898), pp. 102-108; Hubert and Mauss, *loc. cit.*; *Satapatha - Brâhmana*, trans. by J. Eggeling, part ii. pp. 18-20, 25-35, 73, part v. pp. 23 *sq.* (*Sacred Books of the East*, vols. xxvi. and xliv.).

[2] See for examples E. B. Tylor, *Primitive Culture*,[2] ii. 131 *sq.*

[3] Pausanias, ii. 24. I. In 1902 the site of the temple was identified by means of inscriptions which mention the oracle. See *Berliner philologische Wochenschrift*, April 11, 1903, coll. 478 *sq.*

Temporary
incarnation
or inspira-
tion pro-
duced by
drinking
blood.
bull before she descended into the cave to prophesy.[1]   In
southern India a devil - dancer " cuts and lacerates his
flesh till the blood flows, lashes himself with a huge whip,
presses a burning torch to his breast, drinks the blood which
flows from his own wounds, or drinks the blood of the
sacrifice, putting the throat of the decapitated goat to his
mouth.   Then, as if he had acquired new life, he begins to
brandish his staff of bells, and to dance with a quick but
wild unsteady step.   Suddenly the afflatus descends.   There
is no mistaking that glare, or those frantic leaps.   He snorts,
he stares, he gyrates.   The demon has now taken bodily
possession of him ; and, though he retains the power of
utterance and of motion, both are under the demon's control,
and his separate consciousness is in abeyance.   The by-
standers signalize the event by raising a long shout, attended
with a peculiar vibratory noise, which is caused by the motion
of the hand and tongue, or of the tongue alone.   The
devil-dancer is now worshipped as a present deity, and every
bystander consults him respecting his disease, his wants, the
welfare of his absent relatives, the offerings to be made for
the accomplishment of his wishes, and, in short, respecting
everything for which superhuman knowledge is supposed to
be available." [2]   Similarly among the Kuruvikkarans, a class
of bird-catchers and beggars in Southern India, the goddess
Kali is believed to descend upon the priest, and he gives
oracular replies after sucking the blood which streams from
the cut throat of a goat.[3]   At a festival of the Alfoors of Minahassa, in northern Celebes, after a pig has been killed, the
priest rushes furiously at it, thrusts his head into the carcase,
and drinks of the blood.   Then he is dragged away from it
by force and set on a chair, whereupon he begins to prophesy
how the rice-crop will turn out that year.   A second time he
runs at the carcase and drinks of the blood ; a second time

[1] Pliny, *Nat. Hist.* xxviii. 147.
Pausanias (vii. 25. 13) mentions the
draught of bull's blood as an ordeal to
test the chastity of the priestess. Doubtless it was thought to serve both
purposes.

[2] Bishop R. Caldwell, " On Demon-
olatry in Southern India," *Journal of
the Anthropological Society of Bombay,*

i. 101 *sq.* For a description of a similar
rite performed at Periepatam in southern
India see *Lettres édifiantes et curieuses,*
Nouvelle Édition, x. 313 *sq.*   In this
latter case the performer was a woman,
and the animal whose hot blood she
drank was a pig.

[3] E. Thurston, *Castes and Tribes of
Southern India,* iv. 187.

he is forced into the chair and continues his predictions. It is thought that there is a spirit in him which possesses the power of prophecy.[1] At Rhetra, a great religious capital of the Western Slavs, the priest tasted the blood of the sacrificed oxen and sheep in order the better to prophesy.[2] The true test of a Dainyal or diviner among some of the Hindoo Koosh tribes is to suck the blood from the neck of a decapitated goat.[3] The Takhas on the border of Cashmeer have prophets who act as inspired mediums between the deity and his worshippers. At the sacrifices the prophet inhales the smoke of the sacred cedar in order to keep off evil spirits, and sometimes he drinks the warm blood as it spouts from the neck of the decapitated victim before he utters his oracle.[4] The heathen of Harran regarded blood as unclean, but nevertheless drank it because they believed it to be the food of demons, and thought that by imbibing it they entered into communion with the demons, who would thus visit them and lift the veil that hides the future from mortal vision.[5]

The other mode of producing temporary inspiration, to which I shall here refer, consists in the use of a sacred tree or plant. Thus in the Hindoo Koosh a fire is kindled with twigs of the sacred cedar; and the Dainyal or sibyl, with a cloth over her head, inhales the thick pungent smoke till she is seized with convulsions and falls senseless to the ground. Soon she rises and raises a shrill chant, which is

Marginal notes: Drinking blood as means of inspiration. Temporary incarnation or inspiration produced by means of a sacred tree or plant.

[1] J. G. F. Riedel, " De Minahasa in 1825," *Tijdschrift voor Indische Taal- Land- en Volkenkunde*, xviii. 517 *sq.* Compare "De godsdienst en gods-dienst-plegtigheden der Alfoeren in de Menhassa op het eiland Celebes," *Tijdschrift van Nederlandsch Indië*, 1849, dl. ii. p. 395; N. Graafland, *De Minahassa*, i. 122; J. Dumont D'Urville, *Voyage autour du monde et à la recherche de La Perouse*, v. 443.

[2] F. J. Mone, *Geschichte des Heidenthums im nördlichen Europa* (Leipsic and Darmstadt, 1822-23), i. 188.

[3] J. Biddulph, *Tribes of the Hindoo Koosh* (Calcutta, 1880), p. 96. For other instances of priests or representatives of the deity drinking the warm blood of the victim, compare

H. A. Oldfield, *Sketches from Nipal* (London, 1880), ii. 296 *sq.* ; *Asiatic Researches*, iv. pp. 40, 41, 50, 52 (8vo ed.) ; Paul Soleillet, *L'Afrique Occidentale* (Paris, 1877), pp. 123 *sq.* To snuff up the savour of the sacrifice was similarly supposed to produce inspiration (Tertullian, *Apologet.* 23).

[4] C. F. Oldham, "The Nagas," *Journal of the Royal Asiatic Society for 1901* (London, 1901), pp. 463, 465 *sq.*, 467, 470 *sq.* The Takhas worship the cobra, and Mr. Oldham believes them to be descended from the Nagas of the *Mahabharata*.

[5] Maimonides, quoted by D. Chwolsohn, *Die Ssabier und der Ssabismus* (St. Petersburg, 1856), ii. 480 *sq.*

caught up and loudly repeated by her audience.[1] So Apollo's prophetess ate the sacred laurel and was fumigated with it before she prophesied.[2] The Bacchanals ate ivy, and their inspired fury was by some believed to be due to the exciting and intoxicating properties of the plant.[3] In Uganda the priest, in order to be inspired by his god, smokes a pipe of tobacco fiercely till he works himself into a frenzy ; the loud excited tones in which he then talks are recognised as the voice of the god speaking through him.[4] In Madura, an island off the north coast of Java, each spirit has its regular medium, who is oftener a woman than a man. To prepare herself for the reception of the spirit she inhales the fumes of incense, sitting with her head over a smoking censer. Gradually she falls into a sort of trance accompanied by shrieks, grimaces, and violent spasms. The spirit is now supposed to have entered into her, and when she grows calmer her words are regarded as oracular, being the utterances of the indwelling spirit, while her own soul is temporarily absent.[5]

It is worth observing that many peoples expect the victim as well as the priest or prophet to give signs of inspiration by convulsive movements of the body ; and if the animal remains obstinately steady, they esteem it unfit for sacrifice. Thus when the Yakuts sacrifice to an evil spirit, the beast must bellow and roll about, which is considered a token that the evil spirit has entered into it.[6] Apollo's prophetess could give no oracles unless the sacrificial victim trembled in every limb when the wine was poured on its head. But for ordinary Greek sacrifices it was enough that the victim should shake its head ; to make it do so, water was poured on it.[7] Many other peoples (Tonquinese,

---

[1] J. Biddulph, *Tribes of the Hindoo Koosh*, p. 97.

[2] Lucian, *Bis accus.* 1 ; J. Tzetzes, *Schol. on Lycophron*, 6 ; Plutarch, *De E apud Delphos*, 2 ; *id.*, *De Pythiae oraculis*, 6.

[3] Plutarch, *Quaestiones Romanae*, 112.

[4] Rev. J. Roscoe, "Further Notes on the Manners and Customs of the Baganda," *Journal of the Anthropological Institute*, xxxii. (1902) p. 42.

[5] C. Lekkerkerker, "Enkele opmerkingen over sporen van Shamanisme bij Madoereezen en Javanen," *Tijdschrift voor Indische Taal- Landen Volkenkunde*, xlv. (1902) pp. 282-284.

[6] H. Vambery, *Das Türkenvolk* (Leipsic, 1885), p. 158.

[7] Plutarch, *De defect. oracul.* 46, 49, 51. The Greeks themselves seem commonly to have interpreted the shaking or nodding of the victim's

Hindoos, Chuwash, and so forth) have adopted the same test of a suitable victim ; they pour water or wine on its head ; if the animal shakes its head it is accepted for sacrifice ; if it does not, it is rejected.[1]   Among the Kafirs of the Hindoo Koosh the priest or his substitute pours water into the ear and all down the spine of the intended victim, whether it be a sheep or a goat.   It is not enough that the animal should merely shake its head to get the water out of its ear ; it must shake its whole body as a wet dog shakes himself. When it does so, a kissing sound is made by all present, and the victim is forthwith slaughtered.[2]

The person temporarily inspired is believed to acquire, Divine not merely divine knowledge, but also, at least occasionally, power divine power.   In Cambodia, when an epidemic breaks out, by tem- the inhabitants of several villages unite and go with a band porary in of music at their head to look for the man whom the local spiration. god is supposed to have chosen for his temporary incarnation.

---

head as a token that the animal consented to be sacrificed.   See Plutarch, *Quaest. conviv.* viii. 8. 7 ; Scholiast on Aristophanes, *Peace*, 960 ; Scholiast on Apollonius Rhodius, *Argon.* i. 425 ; and this explanation has been adopted by modern interpreters.   See A. Willems, *Notes sur la Paix d'Aristophane* (Brussels, 1899), pp. 30-33 ; E. Monseur, in *Bulletin de Folklore*, 1903, pp. 216-229.   But this interpretation can hardly be extended to the case of the Delphic victim which was expected to shake all over.   The theory of possession applies equally to that and to the other cases, and is therefore preferable.   The theory of consent may have been invented when the older view had ceased to be held and was forgotten.

[1] D. Chwolsohn, *Die Ssabier und der Ssabismus*, ii. 37 ; *Lettres édifiantes et curieuses*, xvi. 230 *sq.* ; E. T. Atkinson, *The Himalayan Districts of the North-Western Provinces of India*, ii. (Allahabad, 1884) p. 827 ; *Panjab Notes and Queries*, iii. p. 171, § 721 ; *North Indian Notes and Queries*, i. p. 3, § 4 ; W. Crooke, *Popular Religion and Folklore of Northern India* (Westminster, 1896), i. 263 ; *Indian*

Antiquary, xxviii. (1899) p. 161 ; *Journal of the Anthropological Society of Bombay*, i. 103 ; S. Mateer, *The Land of Charity*, p. 216 ; *id.*, *Native Life in Travancore*, p. 94 ; E. T. Thurston, *Castes and Tribes of Southern India*, iii. 466, 469 ; Sir A. C. Lyall, *Asiatic Studies*, First Series (London, 1899), p. 19 ; J. Biddulph, *Tribes of the Hindoo Koosh*, p. 131 ; P. S. Pallas, *Reisen in verschiedenen Provinzen des russischen Reiches*, i. 91 ; H. Vambery, *Das Türkenvolk*, p. 485 ; Erman, *Archiv für wissenschaftliche Kunde von Russland*, i. 377 ; " Über die Religion der heidnischen Tscheremissen im Gouvernement Kasan," *Zeitschrift für allgemeine Erdkunde*, N.F. iii. (1857) p. 153 ; *Globus*, lxvii. (1895) p. 366.   When the Rao of Kachh sacrifices a buffalo, water is sprinkled between its horns ; if it shakes its head, it is unsuitable ; if it nods its head, it is sacrificed (*Panjab Notes and Queries*, i. p. 120, § 911).   This is probably a modern misinterpretation of the old custom.

[2] Sir George Scott Robertson, *The Kafirs of the Hindu Kush* (London, 1896), p. 423.

When found, the man is conducted to the altar of the god where the mystery of incarnation takes place. Then the man becomes an object of veneration to his fellows, who implore him to protect the village against the plague.[1] A certain image of Apollo, which stood in a sacred cave at Hylae near Magnesia, was thought to impart superhuman strength. Sacred men, inspired by it, leaped down precipices, tore up huge trees by the roots, and carried them on their backs along the narrowest defiles.[2] The feats performed by inspired dervishes belong to the same class.

Human gods, or men permanently possessed by a deity. Thus far we have seen that the savage, failing to discern the limits of his ability to control nature, ascribes to himself and to all men certain powers which we should now call supernatural. Further, we have seen that, over and above this general supernaturalism, some persons are supposed to be inspired for short periods by a divine spirit, and thus temporarily to enjoy the knowledge and power of the indwelling deity. From beliefs like these it is an easy step to the conviction that certain men are permanently possessed by a deity, or in some other undefined way are endued with so high a degree of supernatural power as to be ranked as gods and to receive the homage of prayer and sacrifice. Sometimes these human gods are restricted to purely supernatural or spiritual functions. Sometimes they exercise supreme political power in addition. In the latter case they are kings as well as gods, and the government is a theocracy. *Human gods in the Pacific.* Thus in the Marquesas or Washington Islands there was a class of men who were deified in their lifetime. They were supposed to wield a supernatural power over the elements; they could give abundant harvests or smite the ground with barrenness; and they could inflict disease or death. Human sacrifices were offered to them to avert their wrath. There were not many of them, at the most one or two in each island. They lived in mystic seclusion.

---

[1] J. Moura, *Le Royaume du Cambodge* (Paris, 1883), i. 177 *sq.* The practice in Tonquin is similar, except that there the person possessed seems only to give oracles. See *Annales de l'Association de la Propagation de la Foi,* iv. (1830) pp. 331 *sq.*

[2] Pausanias, x. 32. 6. Coins of Magnesia exhibit on the reverse a man carrying an uprooted tree. See F. B. Baker, in *Numismatic Chronicle,* Third Series, xii. (1892) pp. 89 *sqq.* Mr. Baker suggests that the custom may be a relic of ancient tree-worship.

Their powers were sometimes, but not always, hereditary.
A missionary has described one of these human gods from
personal observation.   The god was a very óld man who
lived in a large house within an enclosure.   In the house
was a kind of altar, and on the beams of the house and
on the trees round it were hung human skeletons, head
down.   No one entered the enclosure except the persons
dedicated to the service of the god ; only on days when
human victims were sacrificed might ordinary people
penetrate into the precinct.   This human god received more
sacrifices than all the other gods ; often he would sit on a
sort of scaffold in front of his house and call for two or
three human victims at a time.   They were always brought,
for the terror he inspired was extreme.   He was invoked all
over the island, and offerings were sent to him from every
side.[1]   Again, of the South Sea Islands in general we are
told that each island had a man who represented or personified the divinity.   Such men were called gods, and their
substance was confounded with that of the deity.   The
man-god was sometimes the king himself ; oftener he was a
priest or subordinate chief.[2]   Tanatoa, king of Raiatea, was

---

[1] C. S. Stewart, *A Visit to the South Seas* (London, 1832), i. 244 *sq.* ; Vincendon-Dumoulin et C. Desgraz, *Îles Marquises ou Nouka-Hiva* (Paris, 1843), pp. 226, 240 *sq.* Compare Mathias G ✳ ✳ ✳ , *Lettres sur les Îles Marquises* (Paris, 1843), pp. 44 *sq.* The general name applied to these human gods was *atuas*, which, " with scarce a modification, is the term used in all the Polynesian dialects to desig-nate the ideal beings worshipped as gods, in the system of polytheism existing among the people.   At the Washington Islands, as at other groups, the atuas, or false gods of the in-habitants, are numerous and vary in their character and powers.   Besides those having dominion respectively, as is supposed, over the different elements and their most striking phenomena, there are atuas of the mountain and of the forest, of the seaside and of the interior, atuas of peace and of war, of the song and of the dance, and of all the occupations and amusements of life.   It is supposed by them that many of the departed spirits of men also become atuas : and thus the multi-plicity of their gods is such, that almost every sound in nature, from the roaring of the tempest in the mountains and the bursting of a thunderbolt in the clouds, to the sighing of a breeze through the cocoa-nut tops and the chirping of an insect in the grass or in the thatch of their huts, is interpreted into the movements of a god " (C. S. Stewart, *op. cit.* i. 243 *sq.*).   The missionary referred to in the text, who described one of the human gods from personal observation, was the Rev. Mr. Crooke of the London Missionary Society, who resided in the island of Tahuata in 1797.   On the deification of living men see Lord Avebury (Sir John Lubbock), *Origin of Civilisa-tion*[4] (London, 1882), pp. 354 *sqq.*

[2] J. A. Moerenhout, *Voyages aux Îles du Grand Océan* (Paris, 1837), i. 479 ; W. Ellis, *Polynesian Researches*, Second Edition (London, 1832-1836), iii. 94.

deified by a certain ceremony performed at the chief temple. "As one of the divinities of his subjects, therefore, the king was worshipped, consulted as an oracle and had sacrifices and prayers offered to him."[1]   This was not an exceptional case. The kings of the island regularly enjoyed divine honours, being deified at the time of their accession.[2]   At his inauguration the king of Tahiti received a sacred girdle of red and yellow feathers, "which not only raised him to the highest earthly station, but identified him with their gods."[3] A new piece, about eighteen inches long, was added to the belt at the inauguration of every king, and three human victims were sacrificed in the process.[4]   The king's houses were called the clouds of heaven; the rainbow was the name of the canoe in which he voyaged; his voice was spoken of as thunder, and the glare of the torches in his dwelling as lightning; and when the people saw them in the evening, as they passed near his house, instead of saying the torches were burning in the palace, they would remark that the lightning was flashing in the clouds of heaven.   When he moved from one district to another on the shoulders of his bearers, he was said to be flying.[5]   The natives of Futuna, an island in the South Pacific, "are not content with deifying the evils that afflict them; they place gods everywhere, and even go so far as to suppose that the greatest of all the spirits resides in the person of their prince as in a living sanctuary.   From this belief springs a strange mode of regarding their king, and of behaving under his authority.   In their eyes the sovereign is not responsible for his acts; they deem him inspired by the divine spirit whose tabernacle he is; hence his will is sacred; even his whims and rages are revered; and if it pleases him to play the tyrant, his subjects submit from conscientious motives to

[1] D. Tyerman and G. Bennet, *Journal of Voyages and Travels in the South Sea Islands, China, India, etc.* (London, 1831), i. 524; compare *ibid.* pp. 529 *sq.*

[2] Tyerman and Bennet, *op. cit.* i. 529 *sq.*

[3] W. Ellis, *Polynesian Researches,*[2] iii. 108.   The Ethnological Museum at Berlin possesses a magnificent robe of red and yellow feathers with a feather helmet, also two very handsome tippets of the same materials. They were the insignia of the royal family of Hawaii, and might be worn by no one else.

[4] J. Williams, *Narrative of Missionary Enterprises in the South Sea Islands* (London, 1838), pp. 471 *sq.*

[5] W. Ellis, *op. cit.* iii. 113 *sq.*

the vexations he inflicts on them."[1]   The gods of Samoa
generally appeared in animal form, but sometimes they
were permanently incarnate in men, who gave oracles,
received offerings (occasionally of human flesh), healed the
sick, answered prayers, and so on.[2]   In regard to the old
religion of the Fijians, and especially of the inhabitants of
Somosomo, it is said that " there appears to be no certain
line of demarcation between departed spirits and gods, nor
between gods and living men, for many of the priests and
old chiefs are considered as sacred persons, and not a few
of them will also claim to themselves the right of divinity.
' I am a god,' Tuikilakila would say ; and he believed it
too."[3]   In the Pelew Islands it is thought that every god
can take possession of a man and speak through him.
The possession may be either temporary or permanent ; in
the latter case the chosen person is called a *korong*.   The
god is free in his choice, so the position of *korong* is not
hereditary.   After the death of a *korong* the god is for some
time unrepresented, until he suddenly makes his appearance
in a new Avatar.   The person thus chosen gives signs of
the divine presence by behaving in a strange way ; he
gapes, runs about, and performs a number of senseless acts.
At first people laugh at him, but his sacred mission is in
time recognised, and he is invited to assume his proper
position in the state.   Generally this position is a distinguished one and confers on him a powerful influence over
the whole community.   In some of the islands the god is
political sovereign of the land ; and hence his new incarnation, however humble his origin, is raised to the same high
rank, and rules, as god and king, over all the other chiefs.[4]

The ancient Egyptians, far from restricting their

[1] Missionary Chevron, in *Annales de la Propagation de la Foi*, xv. (1843) p. 37.   Compare *id*. xiii. (1841) p. 378.

[2] G. Turner, *Samoa*, pp. 37, 48, 57, 58, 59, 73.

[3] Hazlewood, in J. E. Erskine's *Cruise among the Islands of the Western Pacific* (London, 1853), pp. 246 *sq*. Compare Ch. Wilkes, *Narrative of the U.S. Exploring Expedition*, New Edition (New York, 1851), iii. 87 ; Th.

Williams, *Fiji and the Fijians*,[2] i. 219 *sq*. ; R. H. Codrington, *The Melanesians*, p. 122.   "A great chief [in Fiji] really believed himself to be a god—*i.e.* a reincarnation of an ancestor who had grown into a god " (Rev. Lorimer Fison, in a letter to the author, dated August 26, 1898).

[4] J. Kubary, "Die Religion der Pelauer," in A. Bastian's *Allerlei aus Volks- und Menschenkunde* (Berlin, 1888), i. 30 *sqq*.

adoration to cats and dogs and such small deer, very liberally
extended it to men. One of these human deities resided at
the village of Anabis, and burnt sacrifices were offered to
him on the altars; after which, says Porphyry, he would eat
his dinner just as if he were an ordinary mortal.[1] In
classical antiquity the Sicilian philosopher Empedocles
gave himself out to be not merely a wizard but a god.
Addressing his fellow-citizens in verse he said :—

> " O friends, in this great city that climbs the yellow slope
> Of Agrigentum's citadel, who make good works your scope,
> Who offer to the stranger a haven quiet and fair,
> All hail! Among you honoured I walk with lofty air.
> With garlands, blooming garlands you crown my noble brow,
> A mortal man no longer, a deathless godhead now.
> Where e'er I go, the people crowd round and worship pay,
> And thousands follow seeking to learn the better way.
> Some crave prophetic visions, some smit with anguish sore
> Would fain hear words of comfort and suffer pain no more."

He asserted that he could teach his disciples how to make
the wind to blow or be still, the rain to fall and the sun to
shine, how to banish sickness and old age and to raise the
dead.[2] When Demetrius Poliorcetes restored the Athenian
democracy in 307 B.C., the Athenians decreed divine honours
to him and his father Antigonus, both of them being then
alive, under the title of the Saviour Gods. Altars were set
up to the Saviours, and a priest appointed to attend to their
worship. The people went forth to meet their deliverer
with hymns and dances, with garlands and incense and
libations; they lined the streets and sang that he was the
only true god, for the other gods slept, or dwelt far away, or
were not. In the words of a contemporary poet, which were
chanted in public and sung in private :—

---

[1] Porphyry, De abstinentia, iv. 9;
Eusebius, Praeparatio Evangelii, iii. 12;
compare Minucius Felix, Octavius, 29.
The titles of the nomarchs or provincial
governors of Egypt seem to shew that
they were all originally worshipped as
gods by their subjects (A. Wiedemann,
Die Religion der alten Ägypter, p. 93;
id. "Menschenvergötterung im alten
Ägypten," Am Urquell, N.F. i.
(1897) pp. 290 sq.).

[2] Diogenes Laertius, Vit. Philosoph.
viii. 59-62; Fragmenta philosophorum
Graecorum, ed. F. G. A. Mullach, i.
pp. 12, 14; H. Diels, Die Fragmente
der Vorsokratiker,[2] i. (Berlin, 1906),
p. 205. I owe this and the following
case of a human god to a lecture on
Greek religion by my friend Professor
H. Diels, which I was privileged to
hear at Berlin in December 1902.

" Of all the gods the greatest and the dearest
To the city are come.
For Demeter and Demetrius
Together time has brought.
She comes to hold the Maiden's awful rites,
And he joyous and fair and laughing,
As befits a god.
A glorious sight, with all his friends about him,
He in their midst,
They like to stars, and he the sun.
Son of Poseidon the mighty, Aphrodite's son,
All hail!
The other gods dwell far away,
Or have no ears,
Or are not, or pay us no heed.
But thee we present see,
No god of wood or stone, but godhead true.
Therefore to thee we pray." [1]

The ancient Germans believed that there was something Human
holy in women, and accordingly consulted them as oracles. goddesses
Their sacred women, we are told, looked on the eddying ancient
rivers and listened to the murmur or the roar of the water, Germans.
and from the sight and sound foretold what would come to
pass.[2]   But often the veneration of the men went further,
and they worshipped women as true and living goddesses.
For example, in the reign of Vespasian a certain Veleda, of
the tribe of the Bructeri, was commonly held to be a deity,
and in that character reigned over her people, her sway
being acknowledged far and wide.   She lived in a tower on
the river Lippe, a tributary of the Rhine.   When the people
of Cologne sent to make a treaty with her, the ambassadors
were not admitted to her presence ; the negotiations were
conducted through a minister, who acted as the mouthpiece
of her divinity and reported her oracular utterances.[3]   The

---

[1] Plutarch, *Demetrius*, 10-13 ;
Athenaeus, vi. 62 *sq.*, pp. 253 *sq.*
Apparently the giddy young man submitted to deification with a better
grace than his rough old father
Antigonus ; who, when a poet called
him a god and a child of the sun,
bluntly remarked, " That's not my
valet's opinion of me." See Plutarch,
Isis et Osiris, 24.   For more evidence
of the deification of living men

among the Greeks see Mr. A. B.
Cook, in *Folk-lore*, xv. (1904) pp.
299 *sqq.*
[2] Tacitus, *Germania*, 8; *id.*, *Histor.*
iv. 61 ; Clement of Alexandria, *Strom.*
i. 15. 72, p. 360, ed. Potter ; Caesar,
Bell. Gall. i. 50.
[3] Tacitus, *Germania*, 8; *id.*, *Histor.*
iv. 61, 65, v. 22.   Compare K.
Müllenhoff, *Deutsche Altertumskunde*,
iv. 208 *sqq.*

example shews how easily among our rude forefathers the ideas of divinity and royalty coalesced. It is said that among the Getae down to the beginning of our era there was always a man who personified a god and was called God by the people. He dwelt on a sacred mountain and acted as adviser to the king.[1]

Human gods in South-East Africa.   An early Portuguese historian informs us that the Quiteve or king of Sofala, in south-eastern Africa, " is a woolly-haired Kaffir, a heathen who adores nothing whatever, and has no knowledge of God ; on the contrary he esteems himself the god of all his lands, and is so looked upon and reverenced by his subjects." " When they suffer necessity or scarcity they have recourse to the king, firmly believing that he can give them all that they desire or have need of, and can obtain anything from his dead predecessors, with whom they believe that he holds converse. For this reason they ask the king to give them rain when it is required, and other favourable weather for their harvest, and in coming to ask for any of these things they bring him valuable presents, which the king accepts, bidding them return to their homes and he will be careful to grant their petitions. They are such barbarians that though they see how often the king does not give them what they ask for, they are not undeceived, but make him still greater offerings, and many days are spent in these comings and goings, until the weather turns to rain, and the Kaffirs are satisfied, believing that the king did not grant their request until he had been well bribed and importuned, as he himself affirms, in order to maintain them in their error." [2]   The Zimbas, or Muzimbas, another people of south-eastern Africa, " do not adore idols or recognise any god, but instead they venerate and honour their king, whom they regard as a divinity, and they say he is the greatest and best in the world. And the said king says of himself that he alone is god of the earth, for which reason if it rains when he does not wish it to do so, or is too hot, he shoots arrows at the sky for not obeying him." [3]   Amongst the Barotse, a tribe on the upper Zambesi, " there is an old but waning

---

[1] Strabo, vii. 3, 5, pp. 297 sq.
[2] J. Dos Santos, " Eastern Ethiopia," in G. M'Call Theal's Records of South-

Eastern Africa, vii. (1901) pp. 190 sq., 199.
[3] J. Dos Santos, op. cit. p. 295.

belief that a chief is a demigod, and in heavy thunderstorms
the Barotse flock to the chief's yard for protection from the
lightning. I have been greatly distressed at seeing them
fall on their knees before the chief, entreating him to open
the water-pots of heaven and send rain upon their gardens."
" The king's servants declare themselves to be invincible,
because they are the servants of God (meaning *the king*)." [1]

The Maraves of South Africa " have a spiritual head to
whom they ascribe supernatural powers, revering him as a
prophet and designating him by the name of Chissumpe.
Besides a considerable territory, which he owns and rules,
he receives tribute from all, even from the king (*unde*).
They believe that this being is invisible and immortal,
and they consult him as an oracle, in which case he makes
himself heard. He is personified by a *Fumo-a-Chissumpe*,
that is, by an intimate of the Chissumpe, whose dignity
is hereditary and who is revered exactly like the supposed
Chissumpe, with whom he is naturally identical. As he
names his own successor, disputes as to the succession
do not arise. His oracles are as unintelligible and ambiguous as can well be imagined. He derives great profit from
impostors of both sexes, who purchase the gift of soothsaying
from him. In the settlement (*Muzinda*) of the Chissumpe
there are women whom the people regard as his wives, but
who, according to the universal belief, cannot bear children.
If these women are convicted of an offence with a man, they
are burnt along with the partner of their guilt." [2] The
Mashona of southern Africa informed their bishop that they
had once had a god, but that the Matabeles had driven him
away. " This last was in reference to a curious custom in
some villages of keeping a man they called their god. He
seemed to be consulted by the people and had presents given
to him. There was one at a village belonging to a chief

(marginal note: Human gods in South Africa.)

---

[1] F. S. Arnot, *Garengauze; or, Seven Years' Pioneer Mission Work in Central Africa* (London, N.D., preface, dated March 1889), p. 78.

[2] *Zeitschrift für allgemeine Erdkunde*, vi. (1856) pp. 273 *sq.* This is from a German abstract (pp. 257-313, 369-420) of a work, which embodies the results of a Portuguese expedition conducted by Major Monteiro in 1831 and 1832. The territory of the Maraves is described as bounded on the south by the Zambesi and on the east by the Portuguese possessions. Probably things have changed greatly in the seventy years which have elapsed since the expedition.

Magondi, in the old days. We were asked not to fire off any guns near the village, or we should frighten him away."[1] This Mashona god was formerly bound to render an annual tribute to the king of the Matabeles in the shape of four black oxen and one dance. A missionary has seen and described the deity discharging the latter part of his duty in front of the royal hut. For three mortal hours, without a break, to the banging of a tambourine, the click of castanettes, and the drone of a monotonous song, the swarthy god engaged in a frenzied dance, crouching on his hams like a tailor, sweating like a pig, and bounding about with an agility which testified to the strength and elasticity of his divine legs.[2]

Human god of the Makalakas.

"In the Makalaka hills, to the west of Matabeleland, the natives all acknowledge there dwells a god whom they name Ngwali, much worshipped by the bushmen and Makalakas, and feared even by the Matabele : even Lo Bengula paid tribute and sent presents to him often. This individual has only been seen by a few of those who live close by, and who doubtless profit by the numberless offerings made to this strange being ; but the god never dies ; and the position is supposed to be hereditary in the one family who are the intermediaries for and connexion between Ngwali' and the outer world."[3] This Makalaka god "resides in the depth of a cave, in the midst of a labyrinth. Nobody has ever seen him, but he has sons and daughters, who are priests and priestesses and dwell in the neighbourhood of the grotto. It is rather odd that not long ago three sons of this god were put to death like common mortals for having stolen wheat from the king. Lo Bengula probably thought that they should practise justice even more strictly than other folk. . . . In the middle of the cavern, they say, there is a shaft, very deep and very black. From this gulf there issue from time to time terrible noises like the crash of thunder. On the edge of the abyss the worshippers tremblingly lay flesh and

---

[1] G. W. H. Knight-Bruce, *Memories of Mashonaland* (London and New York, 1895), p. 43 ; *id.*, in *Proceedings of the Royal Geographical Society*, 1890, pp. 346 *sq.*

[2] Father Croonenberghs, " La Mission du Zambèze," *Missions Catholiques*,

xiv. (1882) pp. 452 *sq.*

[3] Ch. L. Norris Newman, *Matabeleland and how we got it* (London, 1895), pp. 167 *sq.* These particulars were communicated to Captain Newman by Mr. W. E. Thomas, son of the first missionary to Matabeleland.

wheat, fowls, cakes, and other presents to appease the hunger
of the dreadful god and secure his favour.   After making
this offering the poor suppliants declare aloud their wishes
and the object of their application.   They ask to know
hidden things, future events, the names of those who have
cast a spell on them, the issue of such and such an enter-
prise.   After some moments of profound silence there are
heard, amid the crash of subterranean thunder, inarticulate
sounds, strange broken words, of which it is hard to make
out the sense, and which the medicine-men (*amazizis*), who
are hand in glove with the makers of thunder, explain to
these credulous devotees." [1]

The Baganda of Central Africa believed in a god of Lake
Nyanza, who sometimes took up his abode in a man or woman.
The incarnate god was much feared by all the people, including the king and the chiefs.   When the mystery of incarnation
had taken place, the man, or rather the god, removed about
a mile and a half from the margin of the lake, and there
awaited the appearance of the new moon before he engaged
in his sacred duties.   From the moment that the crescent
moon appeared faintly in the sky, the king and all his subjects
were at the command of the divine man, or *Lubare* (god),
as he was called, who reigned supreme not only in matters of
faith and ritual, but also in questions of war and state policy.
He was consulted as an oracle ; by his word he could inflict
or heal sickness, withhold rain, and cause famine.   Large
presents were made him when his advice was sought.[2]   The
chief of Urua, a large region to the west of Lake Tanganyika,
" arrogates to himself divine honours and power and pretends
to abstain from food for days without feeling its necessity ;
and, indeed, declares that as a god he is altogether above
requiring food and only eats, drinks, and smokes for the
pleasure it affords him." [3]   Among the Gallas, when a
woman grows tired of the cares of housekeeping, she

Human gods in Central and East Africa.

[1] *Annales de la Propagation de la Foi*, lii. (1880) pp. 443-445.   Com-pare Father Croonenberghs, " La Mis-sion du Zambèze," *Missions Catholiques*, xiv. (1882) p. 452.

[2] R. W. Felkin, " Notes on the Waganda Tribe of Central Africa," *Proceedings of the Royal Society of Edinburgh*, xiii. (1885-86) p. 762 ; C. T. Wilson and R. W. Felkin, *Uganda and the Egyptian Soudan*, i. 206 ; J. Macdonald, *Religion and Myth*, pp. 15 *sq.*

[3] V. L. Cameron, *Across Africa* (London, 1877), ii. 69.

begins to talk incoherently and to demean herself extravagantly. This is a sign of the descent of the holy spirit Callo upon her. Immediately her husband prostrates himself and adores her ; she ceases to bear the humble title of wife and is called " Lord " ; domestic duties have no further claim on her, and her will is a divine law.[1]

The king of Loango is honoured by his people "as though he were a god; and he is called Sambee and Pango, which mean god. They believe that he can let them have rain when he likes ; and once a year, in December, which is the time they want rain, the people come to beg of him to grant it to them." On this occasion the king, standing on his throne, shoots an arrow into the air, which is supposed to bring on rain.[2] Much the same is said of the king of Mombasa.[3] Down to a few years ago, when his spiritual reign on earth was brought to an abrupt end by the carnal weapons of English marines and bluejackets, the king of Benin was the chief object of worship in his dominions. " He occupies a higher post here than the Pope does in Catholic Europe; for he is not only God's vicegerent upon earth, but a god himself, whose subjects both obey and adore him as such, although I believe their adoration to arise rather from fear than love."[4] The king of Iddah told the English officers of the Niger Expedition, " God made me after his own image; I am all the same as God; and he appointed me a king."[5] In the language of the Hos, a Ewe tribe of Togoland, the word for god is *Mawu* and the Great God is *Mawu gã*. They personify the blessing of god and say that the Great God dwells

---

[1] Mgr. Massaja, in *Annales de la Propagation de la Foi*, xxx. (1858) p. 51.

[2] " The Strange Adventures of Andrew Battel," in Pinkerton's *Voyages and Travels*, xvi. 330 ; Proyart, " History of Loango, Kakongo, and other Kingdoms in Africa," in Pinkerton, *op. cit.* xvi. 577; O. Dapper, *Description de l'Afrique*, p. 335.

[3] Ogilby, *Africa*, p. 615 ; Dapper, *op. cit.* p. 400.

[4] J. Adams, *Sketches taken during ten Voyages to Africa*, p. 29 ; *id.*, *Remarks on the Country extending from*

Cape Palmas to the River Congo (London, 1823), p. 111. Compare " My Wanderings in Africa," by an F.R.G.S. [R. F. Burton], *Fraser's Magazine*, lxvii. (April 1863) p. 414.

[5] W. Allen and T. R. H. Thomson, *Narrative of the Expedition to the River Niger in 1841* (London, 1848), i. 288. A slight mental confusion may perhaps be detected in this utterance of the dark-skinned deity. But such confusion, or rather obscurity, is almost inseparable from any attempt to define with philosophic precision the profound mystery of incarnation.

with a rich man. " From the personification of the divine
blessing to the deification of the man himself the step is
not a long one, and as a matter of fact it is taken. The
Hos know men in whose life are to be seen so many
resemblances to the Great God that they call them simply
Mawu. In the neighbourhood of Ho there lived a good
many years ago a man who enjoyed an extraordinary
reputation in the whole of the neighbourhood, and who
accordingly named himself *Wuwo*, that is, ' more than the
others.' The people actually paid him divine honours, not
indeed in the sense that they sacrificed to him, but in the
sense that they followed his words absolutely. They worked
on his fields and brought him rich presents. On the coast
there lived a respected old chief, who called himself *Mawu.*
He was richer than all the other chiefs, and the inhabitants
of twenty-seven towns rendered him unconditional obedience.
In the circumstance that he was richer and more honoured
than all the other chiefs he saw his resemblance to the
deity." [1]

Among the Hovas and other tribes of Madagascar Divinity
there is said to be a deep sense of the divinity of of kings
kings ; and down to the acceptance of Christianity by in Mada-
the late queen, the Hova sovereigns were regularly termed gascar.
" the visible God " (*Andriamánitra híta màso*), and other
terms of similar import were also applied to them.[2] The
chiefs of the Betsileo in Madagascar " are considered as
far above the common people and are looked upon almost
as if they were gods." " For the chiefs are supposed to
have power as regards the words they utter, not, however,
merely the power which a king possesses, but power like
that of God ; a power which works of itself on account of
its inherent virtue, and not power exerted through soldiers
and strong servants." [3] " The *Ampandzaka-mandzaka* or
sovereign whom the Sakkalava of the north often call

[1] J. Spieth, *Die Ewe-Stämme* (Berlin, 1906), p. 419.
[2] Rev. J. Sibree, " Curiosities of
Words connected with Royalty and
Chieftainship," *Antananarivo Annual
and Madagascar Magazine*, No. xi.
(1887) p. 302 ; *id.* in *Journal of the*

Anthropological Institute, xxi. (1892)
p. 218.
[3] Rev. J. Sibree, in *Antananarivo
Annual and Madagascar Magazine*,
No. xi. (1887) p. 307 ; *id.* in *Journal
of the Anthropological Institute*, xxi.
(1892) p. 225.

also *Zanahari ântani,* God on earth, is surrounded by them with a veneration which resembles idolatry, and the vulgar are simple enough to attribute the creation of the world to his ancestors. The different parts of his body and his least actions are described by nouns and verbs which are foreign to the ordinary language, forming a separate vocabulary called *Voûla fâli,* sacred words, or *Voûla n' ampandzâka,* princely words. The person and the goods of the *Ampandzaka-mandzaka* are *fali,* sacred." [1]

Divine kings in the Malay region. The theory of the real divinity of a king is said to be held strongly in the Malay region. Not only is the king's person considered sacred, but the sanctity of his body is supposed to communicate itself to his regalia and to slay those who break the royal taboos. Thus it is firmly believed that any one who seriously offends the royal person, who imitates or Miraculous powers attributed to regalia. touches even for a moment the chief objects of the regalia, or who wrongfully makes use of the insignia or privileges of royalty, will be *kĕna daulat,* that is, struck dead by a sort of electric discharge of that divine power which the Malays suppose to reside in the king's person and to which they give the name of *daulat* or sanctity. [2] The regalia of every petty Malay state are believed to be endowed with super-natural powers; [3] and we are told that " the extraordinary strength of the Malay belief in the supernatural powers of the regalia of their sovereigns can only be thoroughly realised after a study of their romances, in which their kings are credited with all the attributes of inferior gods, whose birth, as indeed every subsequent act of their after-life, is attended by the most amazing prodigies." [4]

Divine kings and men in the East Indies. Among the Battas of Central Sumatra there is a prince who bears the hereditary title of Singa Mangaradja and is worshipped as a deity. He reigns over Bakara, a village on the south-western shore of Lake Toba; but his worship is diffused among the tribes both near and far. All sorts of strange stories are told of him. It is said that

---

[1] V. Noel, "Île de Madagascar: recherches sur les Sakkalava," *Bulletin de la Société de Géographie* (Paris), Deuxième Série, xx. (1843) p. 56.

[2] W. W. Skeat, *Malay Magic,* pp. 23 *sq.*

[3] T. J. Newbold, *Political and Statistical Account of the British Settlement in the Straits of Malacca,* ii. 193. See above, pp. 362-364.

[4] W. W. Skeat, *op. cit.* p. 29.

he was seven years in his mother's womb, and thus came
into the world a seven-year-old child ; that he has a black
hairy tongue, the sight of which is fatal, so that in speaking
he keeps his mouth as nearly shut as possible and gives all
his orders in writing.   Sometimes he remains seven months
without eating, or sleeps for three months together.   He
can make the sun to shine or the rain to fall at his pleasure ;
hence the people pray to him for a good harvest, and worshippers hasten to Bakara from all sides with offerings in
the hope of thereby securing his miraculóus aid.   Wherever
he goes, the gongs are solemnly beaten and the public peace
may not be broken.   He is said to eat neither pork nor
dog's flesh.[1]   The Battas used to cherish a superstitious
veneration for the Sultan of Minangkabau, and shewed a
blind submission to his relations and emissaries, real or
pretended, when these persons appeared among them for the
purpose of levying contributions.   Even when insulted and
put in fear of their lives they made no attempt at resistance ;
for they believed that their affairs would never prosper, that
their rice would be blighted and their buffaloes die, and that
they would remain under a sort of spell if they offended
these sacred messengers.[2]   In the kingdom of Loowoo the
great majority of the people have never seen the king, and
they believe that were they to see him their belly would
swell up and they would die on the spot.   The farther you
go from the capital, the more firmly rooted is this belief.[3]
In time of public calamity, as during war or pestilence, some
of the Molucca Islanders used to celebrate a festival of
heaven.   If no good result followed, they bought a slave,
took him at the next festival to the place of sacrifice, and
set him on a raised place under a certain bamboo-tree.   This
tree represented heaven, and had been honoured as its image

[1] G. K. N[iemann], " Bijdrage tot de Kennis van den Godsdienst der Bataks," *Tijdschrift voor Nederlandsch-Indië*, iii. Serie, iv. (1870) pp. 289 *sq.* ; B. Hagen, " Beiträge zur Kennt-niss der Battareligion," *Tijdschrift voor Indische Taal- Land- en Volkenkunde*, xxviii. 537 *sq.* ; G. A. Wilken, " Het animisme," *De Indische Gids*, July 1884, p. 85 ; *id.*, *Handleiding voor de vergelijkende Volkenkunde van Nederlandsch-Indië* (Leyden, 1893), pp. 369 *sq.*, 612 ; J. Freiherr von Brenner, *Besuch bei den Kannibalen Sumatras* (Würzburg, 1894), pp. 340.

[2] W. Marsden, *History of Sumatra* (London, 1811), pp. 376 *sq.*

[3] A. C. Kruijt, " Van Paloppo naar Posso," *Mededeelingen van wege het Nederlandsche Zendelinggenootschap*, xlii. (1898) p. 22.

at former festivals. The portion of the sacrifice which had previously been offered to heaven was now given to the slave, who ate and drank it in the name and stead of heaven. Henceforth he was well treated, kept for the festivals of heaven, and employed to represent heaven and receive the offerings in its name.[1] Every Alfoor village of northern Ceram has usually six priests, of whom the most intelligent discharges the duties of high priest. This man is the most powerful person in the village ; all the inhabitants, even the regent, are subject to him and must do his bidding. The common herd regard him as a higher being, a sort of demi-god. He aims at surrounding himself with an atmosphere of mystery, and for this purpose lives in great seclusion, generally in the council-house of the village, where he conceals himself from vulgar eyes behind a screen or partition.[2] However, in this case the god seems to be in process of incubation rather than full-fledged.

Divine kings in Burma and Siam.

A peculiarly bloodthirsty monarch of Burma, by name Badonsachen, whose very countenance reflected the inbred ferocity of his nature, and under whose reign more victims perished by the executioner than by the common enemy, conceived the notion that he was something more than mortal, and that this high distinction had been granted him as a reward for his numerous good works. Accordingly he laid aside the title of king and aimed at making himself a god. With this view, and in imitation of Buddha, who, before being advanced to the rank of a divinity, had quitted his royal palace and seraglio and retired from the world, Badonsachen withdrew from his palace to an immense pagoda, the largest in the empire, which he had been engaged in constructing for many years. Here he held conferences with the most learned monks, in which he sought to persuade them that the five thousand years assigned for the observance of the law of Buddha were now elapsed, and that he himself was the god who was destined to appear after that period, and to abolish the old law by

---

[1] F. Valentyn, *Oud en nieuw Oost-Indiën*, iii. 7 *sq.*

[2] J. Boot, "Korte schets der noord-kust van Ceram," *Tijdschrift van het* *Nederlandsch Aardrijkskundig Genootschap*, Tweede Serie, x. (1893) pp. 1198 *sq.*

substituting his own. But to his great mortification many of the monks undertook to demonstrate the contrary; and this disappointment, combined with his love of power and his impatience under the restraints of an ascetic life, quickly disabused him of his imaginary godhead, and drove him back to his palace and his harem.[1] The king of Siam " is venerated equally with a divinity. His subjects ought not to look him in the face; they prostrate themselves before him when he passes, and appear before him on their knees, their elbows resting on the ground." [2] There is a special language devoted to his sacred person and attributes, and it must be used by all who speak to or of him. Even the natives have difficulty in mastering this peculiar vocabulary. The hairs of the monarch's head, the soles of his feet, the breath of his body, indeed every single detail of his person, both outward and inward, have particular names. When he eats or drinks, sleeps or walks, a special word indicates that these acts are being performed by the sovereign, and such words cannot possibly be applied to the acts of any other person whatever. There is no word in the Siamese language by which any creature of higher rank or greater dignity than a monarch can be described; and the missionaries, when they speak of God, are forced to use the native word for king.[3] In Tonquin every village chooses its guardian

Divinity of the king of Siam.

---

[1] Sangermano, *Description of the Burmese Empire* (reprinted at Rangoon, 1885), pp. 63 *sq.*

[2] E. Aymonier, *Le Cambodge*, ii. (Paris, 1901) p. 25.

[3] E. Young, *The Kingdom of the Yellow Robe* (Westminster, 1898), pp. 142 *sq.* Similarly, special sets of terms are or have been used with reference to persons of royal blood in Burma (Forbes, *British Burma*, pp. 71 *sq.*; Shway Yoe, *The Burman*, ii. 118 *sqq.*), Cambodia (Lemire, *Cochinchine française et le royaume de Cambodge*, p. 447), the Malay Peninsula (W. W. Skeat, *Malay Magic*, p. 35), Travancore (S. Mateer, *Native Life in Travancore*, p. 129), the Pelew Islands (K. Semper, *Die Palau-Inseln*, pp. 309 *sq.*), Ponape, one of the Caroline Islands (Dr. Hahl, "Mitteilungen über Sitten und rechtliche Verhältnisse

auf Ponape," *Ethnologisches Notizblatt*, ii. Heft 2 (Berlin, 1901), p. 5), Samoa (L. Th. Violette, in *Missions Catholiques*, iii. (1870) p. 190; J. E. Newell, "Chief's Language in Samoa," *Transactions of the Ninth International Congress of Orientalists*, London, 1893, ii. 784-799), the Maldives (Fr. Pyrard, *Voyage to the East Indies, the Maldives, the Moluccas, and Brazil*, Hakluyt Society, i. 226), in some parts of Madagascar (J. Sibree, in *The Antananarivo Annual and Madagascar Magazine*, No. xi., Christmas 1887, pp. 310 *sqq.*; *id.*, in *Journal of the Anthropological Institute*, xxi. (1892) pp. 215 *sqq.*), among the Bawenda of the Transvaal (Beuster, "Das Volk der Vawenda," *Zeitschrift der Gesellschaft für Erdkunde zu Berlin*, xiv. (1879) p. 238), and among the Natchez Indians of North America

Divine men in Tonquin.

spirit, often in the form of an animal, as a dog, tiger, cat, or serpent. Sometimes a living person is selected as patron-divinity. Thus a beggar persuaded the people of a village that he was their guardian spirit ; so they loaded him with honours and entertained him with their best.[1] At the

Divine head of the Babites.

present day the head of the great Persian sect of the Babites, Abbas Effendi by name, resides at Acre in Syria, and is held by Frenchmen, Russians, and Americans, especially by rich American ladies, to be an incarnation of God himself. The late Professor S. I. Curtiss of Chicago had the honour of dining with "the master," as he is invariably called by his followers, when the incarnation expressed a kindly hope that he might have the pleasure of drinking tea with the professor in the kingdom of heaven.[2]

Human gods in India.

But perhaps no country in the world has been so prolific of human gods as India ; nowhere has the divine grace been poured out in a more liberal measure on all

Divine dairymen among the Todas.

classes of society from kings down to milkmen. Thus amongst the Todas, a pastoral people of the Neilgherry Hills of southern India, the dairy is a sanctuary, and the milkman who attends to it has been described as a god. On being asked whether the Todas salute the sun, one of these divine milkmen replied, "Those poor fellows do so, but I," tapping his chest, "I, a god! why should I salute the sun?" Every one, even his own father, prostrates himself before the milkman, and no one would dare to refuse him anything. No human being, except another milkman,

(Du Pratz, *History of Louisiana*, p. 328). When we remember that special vocabularies of this sort have been employed with regard to kings or chiefs who are known to have enjoyed a divine or semi-divine character, as in Tahiti (see above, p. 388), Fiji (Th. Williams, *Fiji and the Fijians*,[2] i. 37), and Tonga (W. Mariner, *Tonga Islands*, ii. 79), we shall be inclined to surmise that the existence of such a practice anywhere is indicative of a tendency to deify royal personages, who are thus marked off from their fellows. This would not necessarily apply to a custom of using a special

dialect or particular forms of speech in addressing social superiors generally, such as prevails in Java (T. S. Raffles, *History of Java*, i. 310, 366 *sqq.*, London, 1817), and Bali (R. Friederich, "Voorloopig Verslag van het eiland Bali," *Verhandelingen van het Batavia-asch Genootschap van Kunsten en Weten-schappen*, xxii. 4 ; J. Jacobs, *Eenigen tijd onder de Baliërs*, p. 36).

[1] A. Bastian, *Die Völker des östlichen Asien*, iv. 383.

[2] S. I. Curtiss, *Primitive Semitic Religion To-day* (Chicago, 1902), p. 102.

may touch him; and he gives oracles to all who consult
him, speaking with the voice of a god.[1]

Further, in India " every king is regarded as little short of Kings and
a present god." [2]   The Hindoo law-book of Manu goes farther Brahmans considered
and says that " even an infant king must not be despised from as gods
an idea that he is a mere mortal; for he is a great deity in in India.
human form." [3]   As to the Brahmans it is laid down in the
same treatise that a Brahman, " be he ignorant or learned,
is a great divinity, just as the fire, whether carried forth (for
the performance of a burnt-oblation) or not carried forth, is
a great divinity."   Further, it is said that though Brahmans
" employ themselves in all sorts of mean occupations, they
must be honoured in every way; for each of them is a very
great deity." [4]   In another ancient Hindoo book we read
that " verily, there are two kinds of gods; for, indeed, the
gods are the gods; and the Brahmans who have studied
and teach sacred lore are the human gods.   The sacrifice of
these is divided into two kinds: oblations constitute the
sacrifice to the gods; and gifts to the priests that to the
human gods, the Brahmans who have studied and teach
sacred lore." [5]   The spiritual power of a Brahman priest is
described as unbounded.   " His anger is as terrible as that
of the gods.   His blessing makes rich, his curse withers.
Nay, more, he is himself actually worshipped as a god.   No
marvel, no prodigy in nature is believed to be beyond the
limits of his power to accomplish.   If the priest were to
threaten to bring down the sun from the sky or arrest it in
its daily course in the heavens, no villager would for a
moment doubt his ability to do so." [6]   As to the *mantras*,
or sacred texts by means of which the Brahmans exercise

[1] W. E. Marshall, *Travels amongst the Todas* (London, 1873), pp. 136, 137; cp. pp. 141, 142; F. Metz, *Tribes inhabiting the Neilgherry Hills*, Second Edition (Mangalore, 1864), pp. 19 *sqq.* However, at the present day, according to Dr. W. H. R. Rivers, the *palol* or milkman of the highest class is rather a sacred priest than a god.   But there is a tradition that the gods held the office of milkman, and even now the human milkman of one particular dairy is believed to be the direct successor

of a god.   See W. H. R. Rivers, *The Todas* (London, 1906), pp. 448 *sq.*
[2] Monier Williams, *Religious Life and Thought in India*, p. 259.
[3] *The Laws of Manu*, vii. 8, p. 217, translated by G. Bühler (*Sacred Books of the East*, vol. xxv.).
[4] *Id.* ix. 317, 319, pp. 398, 399.
[5] *Satapatha-Brâhmana*, trans. by J. Eggeling, part i. pp. 309 *sq.* ; compare *id.*, part ii. p. 341 (*Sacred Books of the East*, vols. xii. and xxvi.).
[6] Monier Williams, *op. cit.* p. 457.

their miraculous powers, there is a saying everywhere current in India : " The whole universe is subject to the gods ; the gods are subject to the Mantras ; the Mantras to the Brahmans ; therefore the Brahmans are our gods." [1]   There is said to have been a sect in Orissa some years ago who worshipped the late Queen Victoria in her lifetime as their chief divinity.   And to this day in India all living persons remarkable for great strength or valour or for supposed miraculous powers run the risk of being worshipped as gods.   Thus, a sect in the Punjaub worshipped a deity whom they called Nikkal Sen.   This Nikkal Sen was no other than the redoubted General Nicholson, and nothing that the general could do or say damped the ardour of his adorers.   The more he punished them, the greater grew the religious awe with which they worshipped him.[2] At Benares a few years ago a celebrated deity was incarnate in the person of a Hindoo gentleman who rejoiced in the euphonious name of Swami Bhaskaranandaji Saraswati, and looked uncommonly like the late Cardinal Manning, only more ingenuous.   His eyes beamed with kindly human interest, and he took what is described as an innocent pleasure in the divine honours paid him by his confiding worshippers.[3]

Lingayat priests worshipped as gods. The Lingayats are the Unitarians of Hindooism, for they believe in only one god, Siva, rejecting the other two persons of the Hindoo Trinity.   Yet " they esteem the *Jangam* or priest as superior even to the deity.   They pay homage to the *Jangam* first and to Siva afterwards.   The *Jangam* is regarded as an incarnation of the deity. . . . In practice the *Jangam* is placed first and, as stated above, is worshipped as

[1] Monier Williams, *op. cit.* pp. 201 *sq.*
[2] Monier Williams, *op. cit.* pp. 259 *sq.*
[3] I have borrowed the description of this particular deity from the Rev. Dr. A. M. Fairbairn, who knew him personally (*Contemporary Review*, June 1899, p. 768).   It is melancholy to reflect that in our less liberal land the divine Swami would probably have been consigned to the calm seclusion of a gaol or a madhouse.   The difference between a god and a madman or a criminal is often merely a question of latitude and longitude.

Swami departed this life in August 1899 at the age of about seventy. It is only fair to his memory to add that the writer who records his death bears high and honourable testimony to the noble and unselfish character of the deceased, who is said to have honestly repudiated the miraculous powers ascribed to him by his followers.   He was worshipped in temples during his life, and other temples have been erected to him since his death.   See Rai Bahadur Lala Baij Nath, B.A., *Hinduism Ancient and Modern* (Meerut, 1905), pp. 94 *sq.*

god upon earth."[1] In 1900 a hill-man in Vizagapatam gave out that he was an incarnate god, and his claims to divinity were accepted by a following of five thousand people, who, when a sceptical government sent an armed force to suppress the movement, which threatened political trouble, testified to the faith that was in them by resisting even to the shedding of their blood. Two policemen who refused to bow the knee to the new god were knocked on the head. However, in the scuffle the deity himself was arrested and laid by the heels in gaol, where he died just like a common mortal.[2] At Chinchvad, a small town about ten miles from Poona in western India, there lives a family of whom one in each generation is believed by a large proportion of the Mahrattas to be an incarnation of the elephant-headed god Gunputty. That celebrated deity was first made flesh about the year 1640 in the person of a Brahman of Poona, by name Mooraba Gosseyn, who sought to work out his salvation by abstinence, mortification, and prayer. His piety had its reward. The god himself appeared to him in a vision of the night and promised that a portion of his, that is, of Gunputty's holy spirit should abide with him and with his seed after him even to the seventh generation. The divine promise was fulfilled. Seven successive incarnations, transmitted from father to son, manifested the light of Gunputty to a dark world. The last of the direct line, a heavy-looking god with very weak eyes, died in the year 1810. But the cause of truth was too sacred, and the value of the church property too considerable, to allow the Brahmans to contemplate with equanimity the unspeakable loss that would be sustained by a world which knew not Gunputty. Accordingly they sought and found a holy vessel in whom the divine spirit of the master had revealed itself anew, and the revelation has been happily continued in an unbroken succession of vessels from that time to this. But a mysterious law of spiritual economy, whose operation in the history of religion we may deplore though we cannot alter, has decreed that the miracles

Human incarnations of the elephant-headed god Gunputty.

[1] E. Thurston, *Castes and Tribes of Southern India*, iv. 236, 280.

[2] E. Thurston, *Ethnographic Notes in Southern India* (Madras, 1906), p. 301.

wrought by the god-man in these degenerate days cannot compare with those which were wrought by his predecessors in days gone by; and it is even reported that the only sign vouchsafed by him to the present generation of vipers is the miracle of feeding the multitude whom he annually entertains to dinner at Chinchvad.[1]

Worship of the Maharajas as incarnations of Krishna.

A Hindoo sect, which has many representatives in Bombay and Central India, holds that its spiritual chiefs or Maharajas, as they are called, are representatives or even actual incarnations on earth of the god Krishna. Hence in the temples where the Maharajas do homage to the idols, men and women do homage to the Maharajas, prostrating themselves at their feet, offering them incense, fruits, and flowers, and waving lights before them, as the Maharajas themselves do before the images of the gods. One mode of worshipping Krishna is by swinging his images in swings. Hence, in every district presided over by a Maharaja, the women are wont to worship not Krishna but the Maharaja by swinging him in pendulous seats. The leavings of his food, the dust on which he treads, the water in which his dirty linen is washed, are all eagerly swallowed by his devotees, who worship his wooden shoes, and prostrate themselves before his seat and his painted portraits. And as Krishna looks down from heaven with most favour on such as minister to the wants of his successors and vicars on earth, a peculiar rite called Self-devotion has been instituted, whereby his faithful worshippers make over their bodies, their souls, and, what is perhaps still more important, their worldly substance to his adorable incarnations; and women are taught to believe that the highest bliss for themselves and their families is to be attained by yielding themselves to the embraces of those beings in whom the divine nature

[1] Captain Edward Moor, "Account of an Hereditary Living Deity," *Asiatic Researches*, vii. (London, 1803) pp. 381-395; Viscount Valentia, *Voyages and Travels*, ii. 151-159; Ch. Coleman, *Mythology of the Hindus* (London, 1832), pp. 106-111; *Gazetteer of the Bombay Presidency*, xviii. part iii. (Bombay, 1885) pp. 125 *sq.* I have to thank my friend Mr. W. Crooke for calling my attention to the second and fourth of these works. To be exact, I should say that I have no information as to this particular deity later than the account given of him in the eighteenth volume of the Bombay Gazetteer, published some twenty-five years ago. But I think we may assume that the same providential reasons which prolonged the revelation down to the publication of the Gazetteer have continued it to the present time.

mysteriously coexists with the form and even the appetites of true humanity.[1]

Christianity itself has not uniformly escaped the taint of these unhappy delusions; indeed it has often been sullied by the extravagances of vain pretenders to a divinity equal to or even surpassing that of its great Founder.   In the second century Montanus the Phrygian claimed to be the incarnate Trinity, uniting in his single person God the Father, God the Son, and God the Holy Ghost.[2]   Nor is this an isolated case, the exorbitant pretension of a single ill-balanced mind.   From the earliest times down to the present day many sects have believed that Christ, nay God himself, is incarnate in every fully initiated Christian, and they have carried this belief to its logical conclusion by adoring each other.   Tertullian records that this was done by his fellow-Christians at Carthage in the second century; the disciples of St. Columba worshipped him as an embodiment of Christ; and in the eighth century Elipandus of Toledo spoke of Christ as "a god among gods," meaning that all believers were gods just as truly as Jesus himself. The adoration of each other was customary among the Albigenses, and is noticed hundreds of times in the records of the Inquisition at Toulouse in the early part of the fourteenth century.   It is still practised by the Paulicians of Armenia and the Bogomiles about Moscow.   The Paulicians, indeed, presume to justify their faith, if not their practice, by the authority of St. Paul, who said, " It is not I that speak, but Christ that dwelleth in me." [3]   Hence the members of this Russian sect are known as the Christs. "Among them men and women alike take upon themselves the calling of teachers and prophets, and in this character they lead a strict, ascetic life, refrain from the most ordinary and innocent pleasures, exhaust themselves by long fasting

Pretenders to divinity among Christians.

---

[1] Monier Williams, *op. cit.* pp. 136 *sq.*   A full account of the doctrines and practices of the sect may be found in the *History of the Sect of the Maharajas or Vallabhacharyas*, published by Trübner at London in 1865.   My attention was directed to it by my friend Mr. W. Crooke.

[2] A. Harnack, *Lehrbuch der Dogmen-* *geschichte,* i. 321.

[3] F. C. Conybeare, " The History of Christmas," *American Journal of Theology,* iii. (1899) pp. 18 *sq.*   Mr. Conybeare kindly lent me a proof of this article, and the statement in the text is based on it.   In the published article the author has made some changes.

and wild ecstatic religious exercises, and abhor marriage. Under the excitement caused by their supposed holiness and inspiration, they call themselves not only teachers and prophets, but also ' Saviours,' ' Redeemers,' ' Christs,' ' Mothers of God.' Generally speaking, they call themselves simply Gods, and pray to each other as to real gods and living Christs or Madonnas." [1]

Brethren and Sisters of the Free Spirit.

In the thirteenth century there arose a sect called the Brethren and Sisters of the Free Spirit, who held that by long and assiduous contemplation any man might be united to the deity in an ineffable manner and become one with the source and parent of all things, and that he who had thus ascended to God and been absorbed in his beatific essence, actually formed part of the Godhead, was the Son of God in the same sense and manner with Christ himself, and enjoyed thereby a glorious immunity from the trammels of all laws human and divine. Inwardly transported by this blissful persuasion, though outwardly presenting in their aspect and manners a shocking air of lunacy and distraction, the sectaries roamed from place to place, attired in the most fantastic apparel and begging their bread with wild shouts and clamour, spurning indignantly every kind of honest labour and industry as an obstacle to divine contemplation and to the ascent of the soul towards the Father of spirits. In all their excursions they were followed by women with whom they lived on terms of the closest familiarity. Those of them who conceived they had made the greatest proficiency in the higher spiritual life dispensed with the use of clothes altogether in their assemblies, looking upon decency and modesty as marks of inward corruption, characteristics of a soul that still grovelled under the dominion of the flesh and had not yet been elevated into communion with the divine spirit, its centre and source. Sometimes their progress towards this mystic communion was accelerated by the Inquisition,

---

[1] D. Mackenzie Wallace, *Russia* (London, Paris, and New York, N.D.), p. 302. The passage in the text is " a short extract from a description of the ' Khlysti ' by one who was initiated into their mysteries." As to these Russian Christs see further N. Tsakni,

La Russie sectaire (Paris, N.D.), pp. 63 *sqq.* Amongst the means which these sectaries take to produce a state of religious exaltation are wild, whirling dances like those of the dancing Dervishes.

and they expired in the flames, not merely with un-
clouded serenity, but with the most triumphant feelings of
cheerfulness and joy.[1] In the same century a Bohemian Incarna-
woman named Wilhelmina, whose head had been turned by tion of the Holy
brooding over some crazy predictions about a coming age of Ghost.
the Holy Ghost, persuaded herself and many people besides
that the Holy Ghost had actually become incarnate in her
person for the salvation of a great part of mankind.   She
died at Milan in the year 1281 in the most fragrant odour
of sanctity, and her memory was held in the highest veneration by a numerous following, and even honoured with
religious worship both public and private.[2]

   About the year 1830 there appeared, in one of the Modern in-
states of the American Union bordering on Kentucky, an carnations of Jesus
impostor who declared that he was the Son of God, Christ.
the Saviour of mankind, and that he had reappeared
on earth to recall the impious, the unbelieving, and
sinners to their duty.   He protested that if they did not
mend their ways within a certain time, he would give the
signal, and in a moment the world would crumble to ruins.
These extravagant pretensions were received with favour
even by persons of wealth and position in society.   At last
a German humbly besought the new Messiah to announce
the dreadful catastrophe to his fellow-countrymen in the
German language, as they did not understand English, and
it seemed a pity that they should be damned merely on that
account.   The would-be Saviour in reply confessed with
great candour that he did not know German.   " What ! "
retorted the German, " you the Son of God, and don't speak
all languages, and don't even know German ?   Come, come,
you are a knave, a hypocrite, and a madman.   Bedlam is
the place for you."   The spectators laughed, and went
away ashamed of their credulity.[3]   About thirty years
ago a new sect was founded at Patiala in the Punjaub
by a wretched creature named Hakim Singh, who lived
in extreme poverty and filth, gave himself out to be a

[1] J. L. Mosheim, *Ecclesiastical History* (London, 1819), iii. 278 *sqq.*
[2] J. L. Mosheim, *op. cit.* iii. 288 *sq.*
[3] Mgr Flaget, in *Annales de la
Propagation de la Foi*, vii. (1834) p.

84. Mgr Flaget was bishop of Bards-
town, and his letter is dated May 4,
1833. He says that the events happened in a neighbouring state about
three years before he wrote.

reincarnation of Jesus Christ, and offered to baptize the missionaries who attempted to argue with him. He proposed shortly to destroy the British Government, and to convert and conquer the world. His gospel was accepted by four thousand believers in his immediate neighbourhood.[1] Cases like these verge on, if they do not cross, the wavering and uncertain line which divides the raptures of religion from insanity.

Trans-migrations of human deities.

Sometimes, at the death of the human incarnation, the divine spirit transmigrates into another man. In the kingdom of Kaffa, in eastern Africa, the heathen part of the people worship a spirit called *Deòce*, to whom they offer prayer and sacrifice, and whom they invoke on all important occasions. This spirit is incarnate in the grand magician or pope, a person of great wealth and influence, ranking almost with the king, and wielding the spiritual, as the king wields the temporal power. It happened that, shortly before the arrival of a Christian missionary in the kingdom, this African pope died, and the priests, fearing lest the missionary might assume the position vacated by the deceased prelate, declared that the *Deòce* had passed into the king, who henceforth, uniting the spiritual with the temporal power, reigned as god and king.[2] Before beginning to work at the salt-pans in a Laosian village, the workmen offer sacrifice to the divinity of the salt-pans. This divinity is incarnate in a woman and transmigrates at her death into another woman.[3] In Bhotan the spiritual head of the government is a dignitary called the Dhurma Rajah, who is supposed to be a perpetual incarnation of the deity. At his death the new incarnate god shews himself in an infant by the refusal of his mother's milk and a preference for that of a cow.[4]

The Buddhist Tartars believe in a great number of living Buddhas, who officiate as Grand Lamas at the

---

[1] D. C. J. Ibbetson, *Outlines of Panjab Ethnography* (Calcutta, 1883), p. 123.

[2] G. Massaja, *I miei trentacinque anni di missione nell' alta Etiopia* (Rome and Milan, 1888), v. 53 *sq.* Compare Father Leon des Avanchers, in *Bulletin de la Société de Géographie*

(Paris), Vme Série, xvii. (1869) p. 307.

[3] E. Aymonier, *Notes sur le Laos* (Saigon, 1885), pp. 141 *sq.*; *id.*, *Voyage dans le Laos*, ii. (Paris, 1897) p. 47.

[4] W. Robinson, *Descriptive Account of Assam* (London and Calcutta, 1841), pp. 342 *sq.*; *Asiatic Researches*, xv. 146.

head of the most important monasteries. When one of Trans-
these Grand Lamas dies his disciples do not sorrow, for migrations
they know that he will soon reappear, being born in the divine
form of an infant. Their only anxiety is to discover the Lamas.
place of his birth. If at this time they see a rainbow
they take it as a sign sent them by the departed Lama to
guide them to his cradle. Sometimes the divine infant himself reveals his identity. " I am the Grand Lama," he says,
" the living Buddha of such and such a temple. Take me
to my old monastery. I am its immortal head." In whatever way the birthplace of the Buddha is revealed, whether
by the Buddha's own avowal or by the sign in the sky, tents
are struck, and the joyful pilgrims, often headed by the king
or one of the most illustrious of the royal family, set forth
to find and bring home the infant god. Generally he is
born in Tibet, the holy land, and to reach him the caravan
has often to traverse the most frightful deserts. When at
last they find the child they fall down and worship him.
Before, however, he is acknowledged as the Grand Lama
whom they seek he must satisfy them of his identity. He
is asked the name of the monastery of which he claims to be
the head, how far off it is, and how many monks live in it ;
he must also describe the habits of the deceased Grand
Lama and the manner of his death. Then various articles,
as prayer-books, tea-pots, and cups, are placed before him,
and he has to point out those used by himself in his previous
life. If he does so without a mistake his claims are
admitted, and he is conducted in triumph to the monastery.[1]
At the head of all the Lamas is the Dalai Lama of Lhasa,

---

[1] Huc, *Souvenirs d'un voyage dans la Tartarie et le Thibet*, i. 279 *sqq.*, ed. 12mo. For more details, see L. A. Waddell, *The Buddhism of Tibet* (London, 1895), pp. 245 *sqq.* Compare G. Timkowski, *Travels of the Russian Mission through Mongolia to China*, i. 23-25 ; Abbé Armand David, "Voyage en Mongolie," *Bulletin de la Société de Géographie* (Paris), VIme Série, ix. (1875) pp. 132-134 ; Mgr Bruguière, in *Annales de la Propagation de la Foi*, ix. (1836) pp. 296 *sq.* ; Father Gabet, *ib.* xx. (1848) pp. 229-231 ; G. Sandberg, *Tibet and the Tibetans* (London, 1906), pp. 128 *sqq.* In the Delta of the Niger the souls of little negro babies are identified by means of a similar test. An assortment of small wares that belonged to deceased members of the family is shewn to the new baby, and the first thing he grabs at identifies him. "Why, he's uncle John," they say ; "see ! he knows his own pipe." Or, "That's cousin Emma ; see ! she knows her market calabash" (Miss M. H. Kingsley, *Travels in West Africa*, p. 493).

Divinity of the Grand Lama of Lhasa.

the Rome of Tibet. He is regarded as a living god, and at death his divine and immortal spirit is born again in a child. According to some accounts the mode of discovering the Dalai Lama is similar to the method, already described, of discovering an ordinary Grand Lama. Other accounts speak of an election by drawing lots from a golden jar. Wherever he is born, the trees and plants put forth green leaves ; at his bidding flowers bloom and springs of water rise ; and his presence diffuses heavenly blessings. His palace stands on a commanding height ; its gilded cupolas are seen sparkling in the sunlight for miles.[1] In 1661 or 1662 Fathers Grueber and d'Orville, on their return from Peking to Europe, spent two months at Lhasa waiting for a caravan, and they report that the Grand Lama was worshipped as a true and living god, that he received the title of the Eternal and Heavenly Father, and that he was believed to have risen from the dead no less than seven times. He lived withdrawn from the business of this passing world in the recesses of his palace, where, seated aloft on a cushion and precious carpets, he received the homage of his adorers in a chamber screened from the garish eye of day, but glittering with gold and silver, and lit up by the blaze of a multitude of torches. His worshippers, with heads bowed to the earth, attested their veneration by kissing his feet, and even bribed the attendant Lamas with great sums to give them a little of the natural secretions of his divine person, which they either swallowed with their food or wore about their necks as an amulet that fortified them against the assaults of every ailment.[2]

Incarnate human gods in the Chinese empire.

But he is by no means the only man who poses as a god in these regions. A register of all the incarnate gods in the Chinese empire is kept in the Li fan yüan or Colonial

---

[1] Huc, op. cit. ii. 279, 347 sq. ; C. Meiners, Geschichte der Religionen, i. 335 sq. ; J. G. Georgi, Beschreibung aller Nationen des russischen Reichs, p. 415 ; A. Erman, Travels in Siberia, ii. 303 sqq. ; Journal of the Roy. Geogr. Soc. xxxviii. (1868) pp. 168, 169 ; Proceedings of the Roy. Geogr. Soc. N.S. vii. (1885) p. 67 ; Sarat Chandra Das, Journey to Lhasa and Central Tibet (London, 1902), pp. 159 sq. The Grand Lama's palace is called Potala. Views of it from a photograph and from a drawing are given by Sarat Chandra Das. In the Journal of the Royal Geographical Society, l.c., the Lama in question is called the Lama Gûrû ; but the context shows that he is the great Lama of Lhasa.

[2] Thevenot, Relations des divers voyages, iv. Partie (Paris, 1672), "Voyage à la Chine des PP. I. Grueber et d'Orville," pp. 1 sq., 22.

Office at Peking.   The number of gods who have thus
taken out a license is one hundred and sixty.   Tibet is
blessed with thirty of them, northern Mongolia rejoices in
nineteen, and southern Mongolia basks in the sunshine of no
less than fifty-seven. The Chinese government, with a paternal
solicitude for the welfare of its subjects, forbids the gods on
the register to be reborn anywhere but in Tibet.   They
fear lest the birth of a god in Mongolia should have serious
political consequences by stirring the dormant patriotism
and warlike spirit of the Mongols, who might rally round
an ambitious native deity of royal lineage and seek to
win for him, at the point of the sword, a temporal as well
as a spiritual kingdom.   But besides these public or licensed
gods there are a great many little private gods, or unlicensed
practitioners of divinity, who work miracles and bless their
people in holes and corners ; and of late years the Chinese
government has winked at the rebirth of these pettifogging
deities outside of Tibet.   However, once they are born, the
government keeps its eye on them as well as on the regular
practitioners, and if any of them misbehaves he is promptly
degraded, banished to a distant monastery, and strictly
forbidden ever to be born again in the flesh.[1]

At the head of Taoism, the most numerous religious Divine
sect of China, is a pope who goes by the name of the head of the
Taoist
Heavenly Master and is believed to be an incarnation and religion in
representative on earth of the god of heaven.   His official China.
title is *Chên-yen,* or "the True Man."   When one of these
pontiffs or incarnate deities departs this life, his soul passes
into a male member of his family, the ancient house of
Chang.   In order to determine the chosen vessel, all the
male members of the clan assemble at the palace, their
names are engraved on tablets of lead, the tablets are
thrown into a vase full of water, and the one which bears
the name of the new incarnation floats on the surface.   The
reputation and power of the pope are very great.   He lives
in princely style at his palace on the Dragon and Tiger

---

[1] E. Pander (professor at the University of Peking), "Das lamaische
Pantheon," *Zeitschrift für Ethnologie,*
xxi. (1889) p. 76 ; *id.,* "Geschichte
des Lamaismus," *Verhandlungen der
Berliner Gesellschaft für Anthropologie,
Ethnologie und Urgeschichte,* 1889, p.
(202).

mountains in the province of Kiang-si, about twenty-five miles to the south-west of Kuei-Ki. The road, which is kept in good repair, partly flagged, and provided at regular intervals with stone halls for the repose of weary pilgrims, leads gradually upward through a bleak and barren district, treeless and thinly peopled, to the summit of a pass, from which a beautiful prospect suddenly opens up of a wide and fertile valley watered by a little stream. The scene charms the traveller all the more by contrast with the desert country which he has just traversed. This is the beginning of the pope's patrimony, which he holds from the emperor free of taxes. The palace stands in the middle of a little town. It is new and of no special interest, having been rebuilt after the Taiping rebellion. For in their march northward the rebels devastated the papal domains with great fury. About a mile to the east of the palace lie the ruins of stately temples, which also perished in the great rising and have only in part been rebuilt. However, the principal temple is well preserved. It is dedicated to the god of heaven and contains a colossal image of that deity. The papal residence naturally swarms with monks and priests of all ranks. But the courts and gardens of the monasteries, littered with heaps of broken bricks and stones and mouldering wood, present a melancholy spectacle of decay. And the ruinous state of the religious capital reflects the decline of the papacy. The number of pilgrims has fallen off and with them the revenues of the holy see. Of old the pope ranked with viceroys and the highest dignitaries of the empire ; now he is reduced to the level of a mandarin of the third class, and wears a blue button instead of a red. Formerly he repaired every year to the imperial court at Peking or elsewhere in order to procure peace and prosperity for the whole kingdom by means of his ceremonies ; and on his journey the gods and spirits were bound to come from every quarter to pay him homage, unless he considerately hung out on his palanquin a board with the notice, " You need not trouble to salute." The people, too, gathered up the dust or mud from under his feet to preserve it as a priceless talisman. Nowadays, if he goes to court at all, it seems to be not oftener than once in three years ; and his services are seldom wanted except to ban the demons of plague. But he still exercises the right of elevating deceased mandarins to the rank of local deities, and as he receives a fee for every deification, the ranks of the celestial hierarchy naturally receive many recruits. He also draws a considerable revenue from the manufacture and sale of red and green papers inscribed with cabalistic characters, which are infallible safeguards against demons, disease, and calamities of every sort.[1]

From our survey of the religious position occupied by the king in rude societies we may infer that the claim to divine and supernatural powers put forward by the monarchs of great historical empires like those of Egypt, China, Mexico, and Peru, was not the simple outcome of inflated vanity or the empty expression of a grovelling adulation ; it was merely a survival and extension of the old savage apotheosis of living kings. Thus, for example, as children of the Sun the Incas of Peru were revered like gods ; they could do no wrong, and no one dreamed of offending against the person, honour, or property of the monarch or of any of the royal race. Hence, too, the Incas did not, like most people, look on sickness as an evil. They considered it a messenger sent from their father the Sun to call them to come and rest with him in heaven. Therefore the usual words in which an Inca announced his approaching end were these : " My father calls me to come and rest with him." They would not oppose their father's will by offering sacrifice for recovery, but openly declared that he had called them to his rest.[2] Issuing from the sultry valleys upon the lofty table-

Divine kings of Peru.

---

[1] Mgr Danicourt, " Rapport sur l'origine, les progrès et la décadence de la secte des *Tao-sse*, en Chine," *Annales de la Propagation de la Foi*, xxx. (1858) pp. 15-20 ; J. H. Gray, *China* (London, 1878), i. 103 *sq.* ; Dr. Merz, " Bericht über seine erste Reise von Amoy nach Kui-kiang," *Zeitschrift der Gesellschaft für Erdkunde zu Berlin*, xxiii. (1888) pp. 413-416.

[2] Garcilasso de la Vega, *First Part of the Royal Commentaries of the Yncas*, bk. ii. chs. 8 and 15 (vol. i. pp. 131, 155, Markham's translation). This

writer tells us that the Peruvian Indians "held their kings not only to be possessed of royal majesty, but to be gods" (*ib.* bk. iv. ch. v. vol. i. p. 303, Markham's Trans.). Mr. E. J. Payne denies that the Incas believed in their descent from the sun, and stigmatises as a ridiculous fable the notion that they were worshipped as gods (*History of the New World called America*, i. 506, 512). I content myself with reproducing the statements of Garcilasso de la Vega, who had ample means of ascertaining the truth. His good faith has been questioned, but, as I

Divine rulers among the Chibchas.

land of the Colombian Andes, the Spanish conquerors were astonished to find, in contrast to the savage hordes they had left in the sweltering jungles below, a people enjoying a fair degree of civilisation, practising agriculture, and living under a government which Humboldt has compared to the theocracies of Tibet and Japan. These were the Chibchas, Muyscas, or Mozcas, divided into two kingdoms, with capitals at Bogota and Tunja, but united apparently in spiritual allegiance to the high pontiff of Sogamozo or Iraca. By a long and ascetic novitiate, this ghostly ruler was reputed to have acquired such sanctity that the waters and the rain obeyed him, and the weather depended on his will.[1]

Divine kings of Mexico.

The Mexican kings at their accession, as we have seen,[2] took an oath that they would make the sun to shine, the clouds to give rain, the rivers to flow, and the earth to bring forth fruits in abundance.[3] We are told that Montezuma, the last king of Mexico, was worshipped by his people as a god.[4]

Divinity of the Chinese emperors.

In China, if the emperor is not himself worshipped as a deity, he is supposed by his subjects to be the lord and master of all the gods. On this subject a leading authority on Chinese religion observes : " To no son of China would it ever occur to question the supreme authority wielded by the emperor and his proxies, the mandarins, not only over mankind, but also over the gods. For the gods or *shen* are souls of intrinsically the same nature as those existing in human beings ; why then, simply because they have no human bodies, should they be placed above the emperor, who is no less than a son of Heaven, that is to say, a magnitude second to none but Heaven or the Power above

---

believe, on insufficient grounds. See below, vol. ii. p. 244 note [1].

[1] Alex. von Humboldt, *Researches concerning the Institutions and Monuments of the Ancient Inhabitants of America*, ii. 106 *sqq.* ; H. Ternaux-Compans, *Essai sur l'ancien Cundinamarca*, pp. 14 *sq.*, 19 *sq.*, 40 *sq.* ; Th. Waitz, *Anthropologie der Naturvölker*, iv. 352 *sqq.* ; J. G. Müller, *Geschichte der amerikanischen Urreligionen*, pp. 430 *sq.* ; C. F. Ph. v. Martius, *Zur Ethnographie Amerikas*, p. 455 ; A.

Bastian, *Die Culturländer des alten Amerika*, ii. 204 *sq.*

[2] See above, p. 356.

[3] H. H. Bancroft, *Native Races of the Pacific States*, ii. 146.

[4] *Manuscrit Ramirez: Histoire de l'origine des Indiens qui habitent la Nouvelle Espagne*, publié par D. Charnay (Paris, 1903), p. 107 ; J. de Acosta, *Natural and Moral History of the Indies*, ii. 505, 508 (Hakluyt Society, London, 1880).

whom there is none—who governs the universe and all that
moves and exists therein? Such absurdity could not
possibly be entertained by Chinese reason. So it is a first
article of China's political creed that the emperor, as well as
Heaven, is lord and master of all the gods, and delegates
this dignity to his mandarins, each in his jurisdiction.
With them then rests the decision which of the gods are
entitled to receive the people's worship, and which are not.
It is the imperial government which deifies disembodied
souls of men, and also divests them of their divine rank.
Their worship, if established against its will or without its
consent, can be exterminated at its pleasure, without
revenge having to be feared from the side of the god for
any such radical measure; for the power of even the
mightiest and strongest god is as naught compared with
that of the august Celestial Being with whose will and under
whose protection the Son reigns supreme over everything
existing below the empyrean, unless he forfeits this
omnipotent support through neglect of his imperial duties."[1]

As the emperor of China is believed to be a Son of
Heaven, so the Emperor of Japan, the Mikado, is supposed
to be an incarnation of the sun goddess, the deity who
rules the universe, gods and men included. Once a year
all the gods wait upon him, and spend a month at his
court. During that month, the name of which means
"without gods," no one frequents the temples, for they are
believed to be deserted.[2] *Divinity of the Mikado.*

The early Babylonian kings, from the time of Sargon
I. till the fourth dynasty of Ur or later, claimed to be
gods in their lifetime. The monarchs of the fourth dynasty
of Ur in particular had temples built in their honour; they
set up their statues in various sanctuaries and commanded
the people to sacrifice to them; the eighth month was
especially dedicated to the kings, and sacrifices were offered
to them at the new moon and on the fifteenth of each
month.[3] Again, the Parthian monarchs of the Arsacid house *Divinity of early Babylonian kings.*

[1] J. J. M. de Groot, *Sectarianism and Religious Persecution in China,* i. (Amsterdam, 1903), pp. 17 *sq.*

[2] *Manners and Customs of the Japanese in the Nineteenth Century*:

from recent Dutch visitors to Japan and the German of Dr. Ph. Fr. von Siebold (London, 1841), pp. 141 *sqq.*

[3] H. Radau, *Early Babylonian History* (New York and London,

styled themselves brothers of the sun and moon and were worshipped as deities. It was esteemed sacrilege to strike even a private member of the Arsacid family in a brawl.[1]

Divinity of Egyptian kings. The kings of Egypt were deified in their lifetime, sacrifices were offered to them, and their worship was celebrated in special temples and by special priests. Indeed the worship of the kings sometimes cast that of the gods into the shade. Thus in the reign of Merenra a high official declared that he had built many holy places in order that the spirits of the king, the ever-living Merenra, might be invoked "more than all the gods."[2] "It has never been doubted that the king claimed actual divinity; he was the 'great god,' the 'golden Horus,' and son of Ra. He claimed authority not only over Egypt, but over 'all lands and nations,' 'the whole world in its length and its breadth, the east and the west,' 'the entire compass of the great circuit of the sun,' 'the sky and what is in it, the earth and all that is upon it,' 'every creature that walks upon two or upon four legs, all that fly or flutter, the whole world offers her productions to him.' Whatever in fact might be asserted of the Sun-god, was dogmatically predicable of the king of Egypt. His titles were directly derived from those of the sun-god."[3] "In the course of his existence," we are told, "the king of Egypt exhausted all the possible conceptions of divinity which the Egyptians had framed for themselves. A superhuman god by his birth and by his royal office, he became the deified man after his death."

1900), pp. 307-317. Compare C. Brockelmann, "Wesen und Ursprung des Eponymats in Assyrien," *Zeitschrift für Assyriologie*, xvi. (1902) p. 394; H. Zimmern, in E. Schrader's *Die Keilinschriften und das Alte Testament*[3] (Berlin, 1903), pp. 379, 639 *sq.*

[1] Ammianus Marcellinus, xxiii. 6, §§ 5 and 6.

[2] C. P. Tiele, *History of the Egyptian Religion*, pp. 103 *sq.* On the worship of the kings see also E. Meyer, *Geschichte des Altertums*,[2] i. 2. § 219, pp. 142 *sq.*; A. Erman, *Ägypten und ägyptisches Leben im Altertum*, pp. 91 *sqq.*; *id.*, *Die ägyptische Religion* (Berlin, 1905), pp. 39 *sq.*; V. von Strauss und Carnen, *Die altägyptischen*

Götter und Göttersagen, pp. 467 *sqq.*; A. Wiedemann, *Die Religion der alten Ägypter*, pp. 92 *sq.*; *id.*, "Menschenvergötterung im alten Ägypten," *Am Urquelle*, N.F. i. (1897), pp. 289 *sqq.*; *id.*, *Herodots zweites Buch*, pp. 274 *sq.*; G. Maspero, *Histoire ancienne des peuples de l'Orient classique: les origines*, pp. 258-267; E. Naville, *La Religion des anciens Égyptiens* (Paris, 1906), pp. 225 *sqq.* Diodorus Siculus observed (i. 90) that "the Egyptians seem to worship and honour their kings as very gods."

[3] P. le P. Renouf, "The priestly Character of the earliest Egyptian Civilisation," *Proceedings of the Society of Biblical Archaeology*, xii. (1890) p. 355.

Thus all that was known of the divine was summed up in
him."[1] "The divinity of the king was recognised in all the
circumstances of the public life of the sovereign. It was not
enough to worship Pharaoh in the temple; beyond the limits
of the sanctuary he remained the 'good god' to whom all
men owed a perpetual adoration. The very name of the
sovereign was sacred like his person; people swore by his
name as by that of the gods, and he who took the oath in
vain was punished."[2] In particular the king of Egypt
was identified with the great sun-god Ra. "Son of the
sun, decked with the solar crowns, armed with the solar
weapons, gods and men adored him as Ra, defended him as
Ra from the attacks which menaced in him the divine being
who, in his human existence, knew the glory and the
dangers of being 'an incarnate sun' and 'the living image
on earth of his father Tum of Heliopolis.'"[3] Even the life
of the gods depended on the divine life of the king. Gods
and men, it is said, "live by the words of his mouth."[4] "O
gods," said the king before celebrating divine worship, "you
are safe, if I am safe. Your doubles are safe if my double is
safe at the head of all living doubles. All live, if I live."[5]
The king was addressed as "Lord of heaven, lord of earth,
sun, life of the whole world, lord of time, measurer of the
sun's course, Tum for men, lord of well-being, creator
of the harvest, maker and fashioner of mortals, bestower of
breath upon all men, giver of life to all the host of gods,
pillar of heaven, threshold of the earth, weigher of the equi-
poise of both worlds, lord of rich gifts, increaser of the
corn," and so forth.[6] Yet, as we should expect, the exalted
powers thus ascribed to the king differ in degree rather than
in kind from those which every Egyptian claimed for
himself. Professor Tiele observes that "as every good man
at his death became Osiris, as every one in danger or need
could by the use of magic sentences assume the form of a
deity, it is quite comprehensible how the king, not only after

---

[1] A. Moret, *Du caractère religieux de la royauté pharaonique* (Paris, 1902), pp. 278 *sq.*; compare *ib.* pp. 313.

[2] A. Moret, *op. cit.* p. 306.

[3] A. Moret, *op. cit.* p. 310.

[4] A. Mo et, *op. cit.* p. 299.

[5] A. Moret, *op. cit.* p. 233.

[6] V. von Strauss und Carnen, *op. cit.* p. 470. On the titles of the Egyptian kings see further A. Moret, *op. cit.* pp. 17-38.

death, but already during his life, was placed on a level with the deity."[1]

Evolution of sacred kings out of magicians.

We have now completed our sketch, for it is no more than a sketch, of the evolution of that sacred kingship which attained its highest form, its most absolute expression, in the monarchies of Peru and Egypt, of China and Japan. Historically, the institution appears to have originated in the order of public magicians or medicine-men ; logically it rests on a mistaken deduction from the association of ideas. Men mistook the order of their ideas for the order of nature, and hence imagined that the control which they have, or seem to have, over their thoughts, permitted them to exercise a corresponding control over things. The men who for one reason or another, because of the strength or the weakness of their natural parts, were supposed to possess these magical powers in the highest degree, were gradually marked off from their fellows and became a separate class, who were destined to exercise a most far-reaching influence on the political, religious, and intellectual evolution of mankind. Social progress, as we know, consists mainly in a successive differentiation of functions, or, in simpler language, a division of labour. The work which in primitive society is done by all alike and by all equally ill, or nearly so, is gradually distributed among different classes of workers and executed more and more perfectly ; and so far as the products, material or immaterial, of this specialised labour are shared by all, the whole com-

Magicians or medicine-men the oldest professional class.

munity benefits by the increasing specialisation. Now magicians or medicine-men appear to constitute the oldest artificial or professional class in the evolution of society.[2] For sorcerers are found in every savage tribe known to us ; and among the lowest savages, such as the Australian aborigines, they are the only professional class that exists. As time goes on, and the process of differentiation continues,

[1] C. P. Tiele, *History of the Egyptian Religion*, p. 105. Compare A. Moret, *op. cit.* pp. 71 *sq.*, 312.

[2] In regard to the natives of the western islands of Torres Straits it has been remarked by Dr. A. C. Haddon that the magicians or sorcerers "con-stituted the only professional class among these democratic islanders" (*Reports of the Cambridge Anthropological Expedition to Torres Straits*, v. 321). The same observation could be applied to many other savage tribes.

the order of medicine-men is itself subdivided into such classes as the healers of disease, the makers of rain, and so forth ;[1] while the most powerful member of the order wins for himself a position as chief and gradually develops into a sacred king, his old magical functions falling more and more into the background and being exchanged for priestly or even divine duties, in proportion as magic is slowly ousted by religion. Still later, a partition is effected between the civil and the religious aspect of the kingship, the temporal power being committed to one man and the spiritual to another. Meanwhile the magicians, who may be repressed but cannot be extirpated by the predominance of religion, still addict themselves to their old occult arts in preference to the newer ritual of sacrifice and prayer ; and in time the more sagacious of their number perceive the fallacy of magic and hit upon a more effectual mode of manipulating the forces of nature for the good of man ; in short, they abandon sorcery for science. I am far from affirming that the course of development has everywhere rigidly followed these lines : it has doubtless varied greatly in different societies. I merely mean to indicate in the broadest outline what I conceive to have been its general trend. Regarded from the industrial point of view the evolution has been from uniformity to diversity of function : regarded from the political point of view, it has been from democracy to despotism. With the later history of monarchy, especially with the decay of despotism and its displacement by forms of government better adapted to the higher needs of humanity, we are not concerned in this enquiry : our theme is the growth, not the decay, of a great and, in its time, beneficent institution.

[1] For example, amongst the Todas the medicine-man has been differentiated from the sorcerer ; yet their common origin is indicated by their both using the same kind of magical formulas or spells to accomplish their different ends. See Dr. W. H. R. Rivers, *The Todas*, p. 271 : " It seems clear that the Todas have advanced beyond the stage of human culture in which all misfortunes are produced by magic. They recognise that some ills are not due to human intervention, but yet they employ the same kind of means to remove these ills as are employed to remove those brought about by human agency. The advance of the Todas is shown most clearly by the differentiation of function between *pilikòren* and *utkòren*, between sorcerers and medicine-men, and we seem to have here a clear indication of the differentiation between magic and medicine. The two callings are followed by different men, who are entirely distinct from one another, but both use the same kind of formula to bring about the effect they desire to produce."

APPENDIX

HEGEL ON MAGIC AND RELIGION

My friend Professor James Ward has pointed out to me that the view which I have taken of the nature and historical relations of magic and religion was anticipated by Hegel in his *Lectures on the Philosophy of Religion*.[1] So far as I understand the philosopher's exposition, the agreement between us amounts to this : we both hold that in the mental evolution of humanity an age of magic preceded an age of religion, and that the characteristic difference between magic and religion is that, whereas magic aims at controlling nature directly, religion aims at controlling it indirectly through the mediation of a powerful supernatural being or beings to whom man appeals for help and protection. That I take to be the substance of Hegel's meaning in the following passages which I extract from his lectures on the philosophy of religion.

Speaking of what he calls the religion of nature he observes : "Fear of the powers of nature, of the sun, of thunder-storms, etc., is here not as yet fear which might be called religious fear, for this has its seat in freedom. The fear of God is a different fear from the fear of natural forces. It is said that 'fear is the beginning of wisdom'; this fear cannot present itself in immediate religion. It first appears in man when he knows himself to be powerless in his particularity, when his particularity trembles within him. . . . It is not, however, fear in this higher sense only that is not present here, but even the fear of the powers of nature, so far as it enters at all at this first stage of the religion of nature, changes round into its opposite, and becomes magic.

"The absolutely primary form of religion, to which we give the name of magic, consists in this, that the Spiritual is the ruling power over nature. This spiritual element does not yet exist,

[1] *Vorlesungen über die Philosophie der Religion*, i. 220 *sqq.* (vol. xi. of the first collected edition of Hegel's works, Berlin, 1832). The coincidence was also pointed out to me by my friend Dr. J. M. E. McTaggart.

423

however, as Spirit; it is not yet found in its universality, but is merely the particular, contingent, empirical self-consciousness of man, which, although it is only mere passion, knows itself to be higher in its self-consciousness than nature—knows that it is a power ruling over nature. . . . This power is a direct power over nature in general, and is not to be likened to the indirect power, which we exercise by means of implements over natural objects in their separate forms. . . . Here the power over nature acts in a direct way.   It thus is magic or sorcery.

"As regards the external mode in which this idea actually appears, it is found in a form which implies that this magic is what is highest in the self-consciousness of those peoples. But in a subordinate way magic steals up to higher standpoints too, and insinuates itself into higher religions, and thus into the popular conception of witches, although in that form it is recognised as something which is partly impotent, and partly improper and godless.

"There has been an inclination on the part of some (as, for example, in the Kantian philosophy) to consider prayer too as magic, because man seeks to make it effectual, not through media-tion, but by starting direct from Spirit.   The distinction here, however, is that man appeals to an absolute will, for which even the individual or unit is an object of care, and which can either grant the prayer or not, and which in so acting is determined by general purposes of good.   Magic, however, in the general sense, simply amounts to this,—that man has the mastery as he is in his natural state, as possessed of passions and desires.

"Such is the general character of this primal and wholly imme-diate standpoint, namely, that the human consciousness, any definite human being, is recognised as the ruling power over nature in virtue of his own will.   The natural has, however, by no means that wide range which it has in our idea of it.   For here the greater part of nature still remains indifferent to man, or is just as he is accustomed to see it.   Everything is stable.   Earthquakes, thunder-storms, floods, animals, which threaten him with death, enemies, and the like, are another matter.   To defend himself against these recourse is had to magic.[1]   Such is the oldest mode of religion, the wildest, most barbarous form. . . .

"By recent travellers, such as Captain Parry, and before him Captain Ross, this religion has been found among the Esquimaux, wholly without the element of mediation and as the crudest consciousness.   Among other peoples a mediation is already present.

---

[1] Similarly I have pointed out else-where (*Totemism and Exogamy*, i. 169 *sq.*) that it is the unstable, apparently irregular, incalculable element in nature which the magician particularly aims at controlling, while so far as the

" Captain Parry says of them [1]: '. . . They have not the slightest idea of Spirit, of a higher existence, of an essential substance as contrasted with their empirical mode of existence. . . . On the other hand, they have amongst them individuals whom they call *Angekoks,* magicians, conjurers. Those assert that they have it in their power to raise a storm, to create a calm, to bring whales near, etc., and say that they learnt these arts from old *Angekoks.* The people regard them with fear ; in every family, however, there is at least one. A young *Angekok* wished to make the wind rise, and he proceeded to do it by dint of phrases and gestures. These phrases had no meaning and were directed toward no Supreme Being as a medium, but were addressed in an immediate way to the natural object over which the *Angekok* wished to exercise power ; he required no aid from any one whatever.' . . .

" This religion of magic is very prevalent in Africa, as well as among the Mongols and Chinese ; here, however, it is no longer found in the absolute crudeness of its first form, but mediations already come in, which owe their origin to the fact that the Spiritual has begun to assume an objective form for self-consciousness.

" In its first form this religion is more magic than religion ; it is in Africa among the negroes that it prevails most extensively. . . . In this sphere of magic the main principle is the direct domination of nature by means of the will, of self-consciousness— in other words that Spirit is something of a higher kind than nature. However bad this magic may look regarded in one aspect, still in

course of nature is observed to be stable, regular, and uniform it lies comparatively outside the operations of magic. " To put it generally, the practice of magic for the control of nature will be found on the whole to increase with the variability and to decrease with the uniformity of nature throughout the year. Hence the increase will tend to become more and more conspicuous as we recede from the equator, where the annual changes of natural conditions are much less marked than elsewhere. This general rule is no doubt subject to many exceptions which depend on local varieties of climate. . . . But, on the whole, this department of magic, if not checked by civilisation or other causes, would naturally attain its highest vogue in the temperate and polar zones rather than in the equatorial regions ; while, on the other hand, the branch of magical art which deals directly with mankind, aiming for example at the cure or infliction of disease, tends for obvious reasons to be diffused equally over the globe without distinction of latitude or climate " (*Totemism and Exogamy,* i. 170). The reason why the latter branch of magic tends to be equally prevalent in all parts of the world is, of course, that in all parts of the world human nature is equally unstable, seemingly irregular, and incalculable by comparison with the stability, regularity, and uniformity of nature.

[1] I have not found the passage of Captain Parry which Hegel here quotes, whether from the English original or from a German translation. I should doubt whether the gallant English explorer would have spoken of an " empirical mode of existence," which appears to me to savour rather of the professor's lecture-room than of the captain's quarter-deck.

another it is higher than a condition of dependence upon nature and fear of it. . . .

"Such, then, is the very first form of religion, which cannot indeed as yet be properly called religion. To religion essentially pertains the moment of objectivity, and this means that spiritual power shows itself as a mode of the Universal relatively to self-consciousness, for the individual, for the particular empirical consciousness. This objectivity is an essential characteristic, on which all depends. Not until it is present does religion begin, does a God exist, and even in the lowest condition there is at least a beginning of it. The mountain, the river, is not in its character as this particular mass of earth, as this particular water, the Divine, but as a mode of the existence of the Divine, of an essential, universal Being. But we do not yet find this in magic as such. It is the individual consciousness as this particular consciousness, and consequently the very negation of the Universal, which is what has the power here; not a god in the magician, but the magician himself is the conjurer and conqueror of nature. . . . Out of magic the religion of magic is developed."[1]

[1] G. W. F. Hegel, *Lectures on the Philosophy of Religion*, translated by the Rev. E. B. Spiers, B.D., and J. Burdon Sanderson, i. (London, 1895) pp. 290-298. Further, Hegel observes (p. 300) that "magic has existed among all peoples and at every period."

END OF VOL. I

Printed by R. & R. CLARK, LIMITED, *Edinburgh.*

Works by Sir J. G. FRAZER, D.C.L., LL.D.

THE GOLDEN BOUGH

A STUDY IN MAGIC AND RELIGION

Third Edition, revised and enlarged. 8vo.

Part I. The Magic Art and the Evolution of Kings. 4th Impression. Two volumes. 20s. net.

   II. Taboo and the Perils of the Soul. 3rd Impression. One volume. 10s. net.

  III. The Dying God. 3rd Impression. One volume. 10s. net.

  IV. Adonis, Attis, Osiris. 3rd Impression. Two volumes. 20s. net.

   V. Spirits of the Corn and of the Wild. 2nd Impression. Two volumes. 20s. net.

  VI. The Scapegoat. One volume. 10s. net.

 VII. Balder the Beautiful: The Fire-Festivals of Europe and the Doctrine of the External Soul. 2nd Impression. Two volumes. 20s. net.

Vol. XII. Bibliography and General Index. 20s. net.

TIMES.—"The verdict of posterity will probably be that *The Golden Bough* has influenced the attitude of the human mind towards supernatural beliefs and symbolical rituals more profoundly than any other books published in the nineteenth century except those of Darwin and Herbert Spencer."

TOTEMISM AND EXOGAMY. A Treatise on Certain Early Forms of Superstition and Society. With Maps. Four vols. 8vo. 50s. net.

Mr. A. E. Crawley in *NATURE.*—"That portion of the book which is concerned with totemism (if we may express our own belief at the risk of offending Prof. Frazer's characteristic modesty) is actually 'The Complete History of Totemism, its Practice and its Theory, its Origin and its End.' . . . Nearly two thousand pages are occupied with an ethnographical survey of totemism, an invaluable compilation. The maps, including that of the distribution of totemic peoples, are a new and useful feature."

LECTURES ON THE EARLY HISTORY OF THE KINGSHIP. 8vo. 8s. 6d. net.

ATHENÆUM.—"It is the effect of a good book not only to teach, but also to stimulate and to suggest, and we think this the best and highest quality, and one that will recommend these lectures to all intelligent readers, as well as to the learned."

PSYCHE'S TASK. A Discourse concerning the Influence of Superstition on the Growth of Institutions. Second Edition, revised and enlarged. To which is added "The Scope of Social Anthropology." 8vo. 5s. net.

OUTLOOK.—"Whether we disagree or agree with Dr. Frazer's general conclusions, he has provided us with a veritable storehouse of correlated facts, for which, and for the learning that has gone to their collection, and for the intellectual brilliance that has gone to their arrangement, we can never be sufficiently grateful."

MACMILLAN AND CO., Ltd., LONDON.

I

Works by Sir J. G. FRAZER, D.C.L., LL.D.

THE BELIEF IN IMMORTALITY AND THE WORSHIP OF THE DEAD. Vol. I. The Belief among the Aborigines of Australia, the Torres Straits Islands, New Guinea, and Melanesia. The Gifford Lectures, St. Andrews, 1911–1912. 8vo. 10s. net.

MR. EDWARD CLODD in the *DAILY CHRONICLE.*—"'If a man die, shall he live again?' is a question asked chiliads before Job put it, and the generations of mankind repeat it. In this profoundly interesting volume, Professor Frazer, out of the treasury of his knowledge, and with consummate art of attractive presentment, gives the answers devised by the Lower Races."

FOLK-LORE OF THE OLD TESTAMENT. 8vo.
[*In Preparation.*

PAUSANIAS'S DESCRIPTION OF GREECE. Translated with a Commentary, Illustrations, and Maps. Second Edition. Six vols. 8vo. 126s. net.

ATHENÆUM.—"All these writings in many languages Mr. Frazer has read and digested with extraordinary care, so that his book will be for years *the* book of reference on such matters, not only in England, but in France and Germany. It is a perfect thesaurus of Greek topography, archæology, and art."

STUDIES IN GREEK SCENERY, LEGEND AND HISTORY. Selected from his Commentary on Pausanias by Sir J. G. FRAZER. Globe 8vo. 5s. net.
[*Eversley Series.*

GUARDIAN.—"Here we have material which every one who has visited Greece, or purposes to visit it, most certainly should read and enjoy. . . . We cannot imagine a more excellent book for the educated visitor to Greece."

LETTERS OF WILLIAM COWPER. Chosen and Edited, with a Memoir and a few Notes, by Sir J. G. FRAZER. Two vols. Globe 8vo. 10s. net. [*Eversley Series.*

MR. CLEMENT SHORTER in the *DAILY CHRONICLE.*—"The introductory Memoir, of some eighty pages in length, is a valuable addition to the many appraisements of Cowper that these later years have seen. . . . Dr. Frazer has given us two volumes that are an unqualified joy."

ESSAYS OF JOSEPH ADDISON. Chosen and Edited, with a Preface and a few Notes, by Sir J. G. FRAZER. Two vols. Globe 8vo. 10s. net. [*Eversley Series.*

MACMILLAN AND CO., LTD., LONDON.

2